BENJAMIN DISRAELI LETTERS: 1815-1834

BENJAMIN DISRAELI

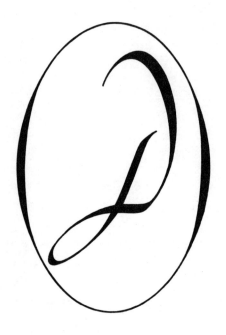

LETTERS: 1815–1834

Edited by

J.A.W. GUNN

JOHN MATTHEWS
Senior Editor

DONALD M. SCHURMAN

M.G. WIEBE
Associate Editor

University of Toronto Press Toronto, Buffalo, London

Toronto Buffalo London
Printed in Canada

ISBN 0-8020-5523-0

Canadian Cataloguing in Publication Data

Disraeli, Benjamin, 1804-1881.
Benjamin Disraeli letters

Contents: [v. 1] 1815-1834.
ISBN 0-8020-5523-0 (v. 1)

1. Disraeli, Benjamin, 1804-1881. 2. Prime ministers – Great Britain – Correspondence. 3. Great Britain – Politics and government – 1837-1901. I. Gunn, J. A. W. (John Alexander Wilson), 1937- II. Title.

DA564.B3A4 1982 941.081 0924 C82-094169-7

CONTENTS

MAPS AND ILLUSTRATIONS

ACKNOWLEDGEMENTS

We acknowledge with gratitude the gracious permission of Her Majesty the Queen for access to the correspondence between Disraeli and Queen Victoria held in the Royal Archives at Windsor.

The Edition has been made possible by generous funding to the Disraeli Project from the Canada Council and from its successor the Social Sciences and Humanities Research Council of Canada. This book has been published with the help of grants from the Canadian Federation for the Humanities, using funds provided by the Social Sciences and Humanities Research Council of Canada, and from the Publications Fund of the University of Toronto Press.

We are grateful for copyright permission to publish all previously unpublished Disraeli material. This permission was granted by the Executors of the Trustees of the Beaconsfield Trust, and by the National Trust.

We wish to express our gratitude to the members of:

Aubrey Noakes, London; James Ogden, Aberystwyth; Robert O'Kell, Winnipeg; David Painting, Swansea; Anthony Riley, Kingston; Michael Selzer, New York City; Edgar Wright, Sudbury, Ontario.

QUEEN'S UNIVERSITY

Principal R.L. Watts, John Beal, C.M.D. Crowder, Peter Dorn, Lin Good, Morris Love, Anne MacDermaid, William Morley, Duncan Sinclair, Ian Wilson, M.H. Yeates.

THE DISRAELI PROJECT

Belinda Beaton, Wendy Burton, Nils Claussen, Jennifer Chance, Anne Cronk, Musetta Dee, James Hamilton, Lynn Haver, William Hayes, Ellen Henderson, Alison Irons, Ben Lowe, Robert Mackinnon, Margaret Marshall, R.L. McIntosh, Jane Graves Nelson, Cameron Pulsifer, Rowena Reed, Robert Stevens, Robert W. Stewart, Bette Withnell.

The collection and editing of the letters has been made possible only by the help of many institutions and many individuals. (In the following list 'CRO' is used to designate a County Record Office or its equivalent.)

WE RECORD OUR GRATITUDE TO:

The Duke of Abercorn, Co Tyrone; Lord Aberdare, London; G. Adamson, Lake Forest, Illinois; American Jewish Archives, Cincinnati: Stanley Chyet, Fannie Zelcer; American Philosophical Society Library: Carl Miller; Lord Ancaster, Lincs; Archives Nationales, Paris: Mde D'Huart; The Duke of Argyll, Inverary; University of Arizona, Tucson: Louis Hieb; Peter Ashby, Oxford; Auckland Public Library: P. M. French; University of Auckland: G.J. Tee; Badische Landesbibliothek, Karlsruhe: Dr Werner Schulz; Mrs Robin Bagot, Kendal, Cumbria; Charles H. Ball, Fairview Park, Ohio; Baring Brothers, London: Major T.L. Ingram; Lord Bath, Longleat: Miss B.M. Austin; Countess Beauchamp, Malvern, Worcs; D.R. Bentham, Loughborough; Berkshire CRO, Reading: Miss A. Green; University of Birmingham Library: B.S. Benedikz; Birmingham Reference Library: W.A. Taylor; Bismarck Archiv, Hamburg; Julius Bisno, Los Angeles, California; Andrew Block, London; Kenneth Blackwell, McMaster University Archives, Hamilton, Ontario; the late Richard Blackwell, Oxford; Bodleian Library, Oxford: C.G. Harris, D.S. Porter, P.J. Bull; N.M. Bolingbroke-Kent, London; Richard Booth, Hay-on-Wye; Lord Bradford, Weston Park, Salop; Thom Braun, London; Brigham Young University, Utah: Scott Duval; V.J. Bristow, Ringwood, Hants; British Library: Dr D.P. Waley, A.N. Schofield, R.A. Smith, P.E. Allen; Princesse Joseph de Broglie, Paris; Lord Brooke, Warwick Castle: P.A.L. Pepys; Nicholas Browne, London; Princesse de Bourbon Palma, Paris; Bucks CRO, Aylesbury: E.F. Davis, H.A. Hanley; Miss Elizabeth Burton, Witney, Oxon; Lady Bury, Venice; David Butler, Nuffield College, Oxford; California State Library, Sutro Library: Richard Dillon; University of

California, Los Angeles: Anne Caiger; Cambridge University: Trinity College – Philip Gaskell, Pat Bradford. Corpus Christi College – R.I. Page. Churchill College – A.D. Childs; Lord Carrington, London; Brig P.B. Cavendish, Brussels; P.H. Cazenove, London; Mrs Maurice Cazenove, London; R. Cecil, Hambledon, Hants; Prof A. Chapeau, Angers, France; Calderdale Central Library, Halifax, Yorks: Alan Betteridge; Gilian Lady Chelmsford, Godalming, Surrey; Chester City Record Office: Miss A.M. Kennett; Chevening Estate Office, Maidstone: P.G. Burton; Chicago Public Library: Thomas A. Orlando; Hon David Lytton Cobbold, Knebworth; Columbia University Library, New York; Msgr le comte de Paris, Paris; Cornell University Library, Ithaca, New York: Donald D. Eddy, Mrs Joan Winterkorn; Cornwall CRO, Truro: Mr Hull; Cumbria CRO, Carlisle: B.A. Jones; Dartmouth College Library, Hanover: Kenneth C. Cramer; Sir Francis Dashwood, West Wycombe, Bucks; Lord Derby, Knowsley: Denis Lyonson; Derrydown Corporation, Cherry Hill, New Jersey; Devon CRO, Exeter: P.A. Kennedy; Charles du Cane, Glenealy, Co Wicklow; The Duke of Devonshire, Chatsworth: T.S. Wragg; Dr J.R. and Hon Mrs Dinwiddy, Clanricarde; Lady Dufferin and Ava, London; Duke University Library: B.E. Powell; Dean Leslie Dunlap, University of Iowa; Durham CRO: W.A.L. Seaman; Durham University: J.M. Fewster; Mr and Mrs A.C. Eastgate, London; the late Maurice Edelman and Mrs Tilli Edelman, Hughenden and London; Edinburgh University: Marjorie Robertson; Lord Egremont, Petworth; Lord Eliot, Porteliot, Cornwall; Lord Ely, Port Hope, Ontario; Eton College: Michael C. Meredith; Francis Edwards, London: Mr Russell, Charles Harris; Martin Elliott, Poffley End, Oxon; Lord Exmouth, Canonteign House; Lady Fairfax-Lucy, Warwick; G.R. Fancourt, Felpham, Sussex; Miss M. St J. Fancourt, Tunbridge Wells; Capt St John Fancourt, Sway, Hants; T.L. Fancourt, Timaru, New Zealand; Fitzwilliam Museum, Cambridge: Miss Phyllis M. Giles, P. Woudhuysen; Sybilla Flower, London; Folger Shakespeare Library, Washington DC: Philip A. Knachel, Lilly S. Lievsay; Fondation Saint-Louis, Paris: Mlle Francoise Garcin; Father Christopher Fullerton, London; Norman Gash, St Andrew's University; Ken Gibson, Farnham Royal, Bucks; Glamorgan CRO, Cardiff: Mrs P. Moore; John F. Glaser, Ripon College, Wisconsin; University of Glasgow: Anne Ross; Glasgow District County Libraries: W.A.G. Alison, Miss Wright; Gloucestershire CRO: Brian S. Smith; Bishop E.A. Gowing, Auckland, New Zealand; Lady Gretton, Oxford; C.P. Grogan, West Palm Beach, Florida; Leslie Guttridge-White, Pett, East Sussex; Lord Halifax, Garrowby, Yorks; Lord Hambleden, London: Hon David Smith, Mrs Ewins; H. Hammond, Kenilworth, Cape, S. Africa; Hampshire CRO, Winchester: Miss M.E. Cash; Lord Hampton, Holt, Worcs; Lord Harcourt, Oxon; Lord Hardwicke, London; Mrs Catherine Hare, Middle Claydon, Bucks; Lord Harrowby, Sandon Hall, Staffs; Sir Derek Hart-Dyke, Hamilton, Ontario; Jack Harte, County Rush, Ireland; Harvard University: Houghton Library – Rodney G. Dennis. Baker Library – Kenneth E. Carpenter; Hon Mrs Hastings, Moffat, Scotland; R. Hatchwell, Chippenham, Wilts; Haverford College: Edwin B.

Bronner; Hereford and Worcs CRO, Worcester: Miss M. Henderson; Lord Hertford, Alcester; High Wycombe Central Library: I.G. Sparks; Denis Hill-Wood, Hartley-Wintney, Hants; Richard Hobbs, c/o Corpus Christi College, Cambridge; Mrs E. Holyoake, Newton Abbot, Devon; Hounslow District Library, Middlesex: Andrea Cameron; Herts CRO: Peter Walne; House of Lords Record Office: H.S. Cobb; Hove Central Library, Sussex: Jack Dove; G.E. Ward Hunt, Wadenhoe, Northants; Huntington Library, California: Anne Caiger, Mary L. Robertson; Hunts CRO: P.J. Locke; Mrs Donald Hyde, Princeton, New Jersey; Lord Hylton, Bath; Lord Iliffe, Basildon; University of Illinois, Urbana-Champaign: Mrs Mary Ceibert; India Office Records, London: Martin Moir; Indiana University, Bloomington: Sandra Taylor; Maj Gen Sir Joslan Ingilby, Ripley Castle, Harrowgate; Inverclyde District Council Library, Greenock, Renfrew: A.J.J. McNeill; Iowa State Historical Department, Des Moines: Phyllis E. McLaughlin; Iowa University Libraries: Frank Paluka; National Library of Ireland, Dublin: Alfred MacLochlainn; Dr Emerson Jacob, Middletown, Pennsylvania; Miss Jean Jamieson, Toronto; The Jenkins Co, Austin, Texas; Jewish Museum, London: Phineas L. May; Jewish National Library, Jerusalem: Dr M. Nadav; Estate of Mrs E. Johnson, Bedford; E. Stanley Jones, Letchworth, Herts; Kent CRO, Maidstone: Felix Hull; Mr and Mrs Simon Kenyon-Slaney, Salop; Prof F.H.H. King, Hong Kong; Knox College, Galesburg, Illinois: Mrs Jacqueline K. Haring; Brian Lake, Jarndyce Books, London; Lambeth Palace Library, London: E.G.W. Bill; Brian Lambie, Curator, Gladstone Court Museum, Biggar, Lanark, Scotland; Lambton Estate Office, Chester-le-Street: Lord Lambton, Miss Hester Borron; Lancs CRO, Preston: R. Sharpe France, J. Keith Bishop; Lord Lanesborough, Leics; Lord Lansdowne, Bowood House: Lord Shelburne, J.A. Chamberlain; Leeds City Libraries: J.M. Collinson; Leics CRO, Leicester: Dr Leslie Parker; Leo Baeck Institute, New York: Dr Sybil Milton; Ed Levy, Palm Beach, Florida; Library of Congress, Washington DC: John C. Broderick; Lincs CRO, Lincoln: C. M. Lloyd; Lincs History and Tennyson Collection, Lincoln: Lawrence Elvin; Liverpool City Record Office: Janet Smith; Brig A. Llewellyn-Palmer, c/o Bodleian Library, Oxford; University College, London: Mrs J. Percival; Greater London Record Office: Miss E.D. Mercer; Lord Londonderry, Wynyard Park; Longman's Group: R.M. Cooper; Lord Lonsdale, Cumbria; Loras College, Dubuque, Iowa; Lord Loudoun, Hastings, Sussex; Lord Lytton, London; Montagu Lowry-Corry, Hants; Loyola University of Chicago; Sheila Macpherson, Kendal, Cumbria; Mr and Mrs F. McArdell, Hughenden Manor, High Wycombe, Bucks; Barbara S. McCrimmon, Tallahassee, Florida; McGill University, Montreal: Gerald French; Norris McWhirter, Enfield, Middlesex; Olive Madden, Oxford; John Maggs, London; Maine Historical Society, Portland: Thomas L. Gaffney; S. Maitland-Lewis, London; Lord Malmesbury, Hants; John Rylands University Library of Manchester: Dr F. Taylor; Manchester Public Libraries: Jean M. Ayton; Maples, Teesdale and Co, London: A. Taylor; Prof Peter Marsh, Syracuse, New York; Hon Mrs G.G. Martin, Crichel, Dorset; Massachusetts Historical Society: Dr Stephen T. Riley, Malcolm

Freibert; University of Michigan, Ann Arbor: John C. Dann, William L. Clements; Ministère des Affaires Étrangères, Paris: M. Dethan; Mitchell Library, Sydney, Australia: Jean Dyce; George Montague, Cannes, France; Morristown National Historical Park: Susan Kopczynski; Harold Mortlake, London; John Murray, London; W. Myers (Autographs) Ltd, London; National Maritime Museum, London; National Register of Archives, London: R.J. Olney; National Trust, London: St John Gore; New Jersey Historical Society: D.C. Skemer; The Duke of Newcastle, London; Newcastle-upon-Tyne Archives: W.A.L. Seaman; New York Public Library: Paul R. Rugen, John D. Stinson, Lola Szladits; State University of New York at Buffalo: K.C. Gay; New Zealand National Archives, Wellington: Sharon Dell; Duc de Noailles, Paris; Lord Northampton, Castle Ashby; Northants CRO, Northampton: P.I. King; Lord Northbrook, Winchester; The Duke of Northumberland, Alnwick Castle: D.P. Graham; Norton, Rose, Botterell and Roche, London; George A. Dunn (for the Executors of the Trustees of the Beaconsfield Trust); Nottingham City Archives: Mrs F.M. Wilkins-Jones; University of Nottingham Library: Mrs M.A. Welsh; Northern Ireland Public Record Office, Belfast: B. Trainor, G.J. Slater, A.T. Harrison; Kevin B. Nowlan, National University of Ireland, Dublin; A.W. Olmsted, Simsbury, Connecticut; Mrs M. Osers, Reading; Oxford University: Christ Church – Dr J.F.A. Mason. Balliol College – E.V. Quinn; Dr Leslie Parker, Leicester; A.W.H. Pearsall, National Maritime Museum, Greenwich; Sir William Pennington-Ramsden, Muncaster Castle, Cumbria; Pennsylvania State University Library; Historical Society of Pennsylvania, Philadelphia: James E. Mooney, G. Christopher; Carl H. Pforzheimer Library, New York: Mihai H. Handrea; Pierpoint Morgan Library: Herbert Cahoon; Henry Pownall, London; Lord Powis, Powis Castle; Primrose League, London; Princeton University: Alex D Wainwright; Public Record Office, London: J. R. Ede; Quaritch, London: Mr Hostwick; Ray Rawlins, Isle of Man; Prof Gordon N. Ray, Guggenheim Foundation, New York; University of Reading: J.A. Edwards; Lord Redesdale, Gloucs; The Duke of Richmond and Gordon, Goodwood; Lord Ridley, Northumberland; J. Roberts, Philadelphia, Pennsylvania; Charles E. Robinson, University of Delaware; University of Rochester: Phyllis Andrews; Capt Lord Roden, Co Down; Dr M.A.T. Rogers, Ramsden, Oxon; Mrs. T.D. Room, Launceston, Tasmania; Hinda Rose, London; Sir Philip Rose, Great Missenden, Bucks; Eva Lady Rosebery, Bedfordshire; L. Rosenberger, Chicago; Hon Jacob Rothschild, London; Rev Dr Geoffrey Rowell, Keble College, Oxford; The Royal Archives, Windsor Castle: Sir Robin Mackworth-Young, Mrs Jane Langton; Royal Botanic Gardens Library, Kew: V.T. Parry; Royal Geographic Society, London: Mr Cummings; The Duke of Rutland, Belvoir Castle: L.A. Parker; Hon Mrs E. Waller, London; Lord St Aldwin, Cirencester; Salford City Council: M.W. Devereux; Lord Salisbury, Hatfield House; Salop CRO, Shrewsbury: Mary C. Hill; Mrs Basil Samuel, Alresford, Hants; Lord Scarborough, Rotherham, Yorks; National Library of Scotland: Alan S. Bell; National Register of Archives (Scotland): J.K. Bates, D.M. Hunter, Miss M.D.

Young; Shakespeare Birthplace Trust, Stratford: Dr Levi Fox; Sheffield Central Library: John Babbington; Paul Smith, University of Southampton; Somerset CRO, Taunton: Ivor P. Hollis; Sotheby's, London: Felix Prior; Southend-on-Sea Central Museum: L. Helliwell; Mr and Mrs Harry Spiro, New York; Staffs CRO, Stafford: F.B. Stitt; The Governors of Stowe School, Bucks; Donald Sultana, Edinburgh; Lady Sutherland, Brora Castle; National Archives of Sweden, Stockholm: Folke Ludwigs; University of Syracuse Library: Carolyn A. Davis; Suffolk CRO, Ipswich: W.R. Serjeant; State Library of Tasmania, Launceston: P.F.J. Leonard; Michael Tebbutt, Salop; Lt Col Oliver Thynne, Berks; Trinity College, Dublin: R.B. McDowell; *The Times* Newspapers Ltd, London: Gordon Phillips; Travellers' Club, London: R.A. Williams; University of Texas, Austin: Dr David Farmer, Ellen S. Dunlap, Prof Clarence L. Cline; U.S. Information Service, Ottawa: Miss F. Swytink; William E. Uttall, Palm Beach, Florida; Sir Harry Verney, Sir Ralph Verney, Middle Claydon, Bucks: H.R.H. Cox; Vernon and Sons, High Wycombe; Victoria and Albert Museum, London: George W. Nash, A.P. Burton; Nicole Villa, Paris; National Library of Wales, Aberystwyth: K. Monica Davies; Comte Walewski, Paris; B.D.J. Walsh, London; Mrs R. Walters, Hove, Sussex; Walthamstow Central Library: J. Howes; Mrs Edith Warrilow, Willowdale, Ontario; Warwicks CRO: M.W. Farr; The Duke of Wellington: Apsley House – R.J. Olney. Stratfield Saye House – Joan Wilson; Wesleyan University, Middletown, Connecticut; Westminster Abbey Muniments Room: Howard M. Nixon; West Sussex CRO, Chichester: Mrs Patricia Gill, Mr McCann; Lord Wharncliffe, Wortley Hall; Robin Whitworth, Oxford; Wigan Record Office: G.A. Knight; Sir John Wiggin, Warwickshire; John Wilson, Witney, Oxon; Winchester College: P.J. Gwyn; Mr and Mrs Philip Wroughton, Woolley House, Wantage; Yale University: Kenneth Nesheim; Simon Young, London; Zeitlin and ver Brugge, Los Angeles, California.

INTRODUCTION

Collection of the Letters

Work began on the present edition of Disraeli's letters in 1972. For the most part the locations of those known to have survived were listed, and the task of editing them appeared to be formidable but not overwhelming. It was hoped that perhaps several new collections might be located, and that the serious deficiencies of Ralph Disraeli's editions could be corrected by finding some of the originals on which he had drawn.

For a long time scholars have been pointing out the value of an accurate and complete edition of Disraeli's letters. As early as 1882, the year after Disraeli's death, Sir Philip Rose wrote to Lord Rowton: 'If we should be so fortunate as to discover Lord B's letters to his family in reply to theirs, which no doubt were preserved, a work of the rarest interest can be compiled, which will exhibit the inner life of our friend, to the world, in a light of which even his most devoted friends can have no notion.' Memorandum of 1 Sept 1882; Rose Papers, H Box 308. Rose was speaking more accurately than he knew, and in ways other perhaps than he intended; but all subsequent biographers have commented on the indispensability of Disraeli's letters as primary sources for all facets of his complex life and personality, and have regretted the absence of a complete collection.

In 1967 Lord Blake had stressed this need in the preface (xxi) to his *Disraeli*: 'All subsequent writers about Disraeli must acknowledge their debt to Monypenny and Buckle. Perhaps one day some wealthy foundation will finance a complete edition of the correspondence of the best letter-writer among all English statesmen. Till that day the official biography remains the nearest equivalent.' Later in his biography (418) Lord Blake pays a further tribute to the special quality of the letters and to their value, both to historians and to literary scholars: 'Disraeli's letters give a picture of his whole way of life, and, as with his novels, indeed with everything he wrote, there is a sparkle, movement, vivacity which never fail to entrance. His prose when not rococo and ornate – and in his letters it seldom is – has the swift quality of sunshine seen through moving leaves or on tumbling waters. The crisp freshness is there even when he is describing events of a character anything but sunny.'

We believe that the collected edition will allow this special quality to be seen more clearly than has before been possible. With each of his correspondents Disraeli projected for himself a special role – always different from any other – which developed and changed as his own life did. On reading these letters together in chronological order for the first time one becomes aware of the complexity of a personality in which the total is greater than and different from the sum of the parts.

Collecting began, as one would expect, with the known locations. Thanks to the earlier initiative of Professor Peter Marsh of the University of Syracuse, the Hughenden Archives had been completely microfilmed, and it was possible to examine this very large collection with a thoroughness which would not have been achieved even by protracted attendance at Hughenden Manor. Visits to other collections began to yield unexpected results. One of the earliest was to Weston Park in Shropshire, where Lord Bradford was generous enough to permit free access to his archives. Disraeli's letters to Selina, Lady Bradford, and to her sister, Anne, Lady Chesterfield, give what has rightly been held to be the most comprehensive and detailed available portrait of his preoccupations during his second ministry between 1874 and 1880. Buckle printed 450 of them in the last two volumes of the biography. But it soon became obvious that Buckle had not been shown the complete collection and that he had not chosen to use all those he was shown. Even Lord Zetland's 1929 edition, though containing many more letters, was not complete.

The explanation is obvious enough, and it was to be repeated over and over again with all the major listed collections. Disraeli was uninhibited in his private correspondence; he said exactly what he thought about everybody, and supported his character assessments with a flood of anecdote filled with graphic detail. In the early part of this century many of his subjects were still alive, and would have been extremely upset, not to say litigious, had such letters then been published. After another sixty years, however, attitudes have changed. No obstacles have been raised, either by the descendants of those of whom Disraeli wrote, or by those owners of the letters we have so far located.

In most cases, hitherto unknown collections were found by tracing the descendants of Disraeli's known correspondents. In the Hughenden papers alone about fifty people who wrote to Disraeli are classed as major correspondents, and there are over eleven hundred in the list of general correspondents. The descendants of the peers were the first to be approached, as they were comparatively easy to find. The letters from the others on the two lists were combed for clues, and a number of the descendants of their writers were also located. Many of these people, when found, did not know that they possessed the Disraeli letters that were indeed among their papers, and some of the searches, jointly conducted, led to discoveries made with equal excitement for both owner and editor.

Belvoir Castle, thanks to the courtesy of the Duke of Rutland and his archivist, Dr Leslie Parker, proved to be a rich source, particularly for the 1840s and the Young England movement, but there were also some letters from the 1830s. The Dukes of Abercorn, Argyll, Newcastle, and Richmond and Gordon all had holdings of which initially they were not precisely aware

– and which testify how thoroughly Disraeli had made up for his father's comment after the publication of *The Young Duke* in 1831: 'What does Ben know of dukes?'

The letters to William Pyne, the man who more than any other kept Disraeli out of debtors' prison in the 1830s, turned up, not then catalogued, in the Fitzwilliam Museum in Cambridge. The Bodleian, in addition to its known holdings, had the private deposit collections of Lord Carrington and Lord Harcourt. We suspect that there are other such collections containing Disraeli letters which we have not unearthed, and which, being uncatalogued, we will know nothing about unless we are fortunate enough to discover their owners.

Lord Esher reported in 1905 that Disraeli's personal correspondence with Queen Victoria had been destroyed on the order of Edward VII. As more and more of the correspondence from the 1870s came to light, however, the more uncharacteristic such an action on the King's part appeared to be. When he was Prince of Wales, his relations with Disraeli were extremely warm, and on a number of occasions Disraelian diplomacy was exercised successfully with the Queen on the Prince's behalf. Through the good offices of the Royal Archivist, Sir Robin Mackworth-Young, and by gracious permission of Her Majesty the Queen, a considerable collection was assembled of both sides of the correspondence, the vast majority of which has not been published. This bears all the marks of a 'personal correspondence', and, whether or not other letters were destroyed over seventy-five years ago, enough remain to justify the claim that a personal correspondence has indeed survived.

It is a commonplace to say that Disraeli's letters to women always have a special quality, and that he needed a female correspondent for his confidant. We have now his letters to his sister Sarah, to his wife Mary Anne, to Lady Londonderry, Mrs Brydges-Willyams, Hannah Rothschild, Lady Blessington, the Sheridan sisters, Lady John Manners, Lady Bradford, Lady Chesterfield, the Queen and dozens of others. Disraeli's letters to women managed to achieve a tone of almost instant and conspiratorial intimacy. We have encountered cases where Disraeli had written to female correspondents who, in each instance, had cherished the letters and preserved them carefully. Following their deaths, the members of their families had found the letters and, disturbed by the implications of the familiarity of tone, had destroyed them. In none of these cases had Disraeli and his correspondent even met!

As all editors of collected letters have surely found, there is a wealth of anecdote which accumulates as the gathering goes on. Collections alleged to have been destroyed emerge unexpectedly in strange places; the vagaries of long-forgotten family conflicts determine why one branch should be the keepers of the ancestral records rather than another. On more than one occasion enquiries made quite by chance, where there were no known Disraeli associations, proved to be fruitful. Such randomness can lead an editor into a state of melancholy if he broods upon it. How many more caches are there? Should he knock on every third door, exhorting the occupants to bring out their Disraeli letters?

We have sent enquiries to all the county record offices and major public libraries in Britain, and have visited most of them. We have written to all the major and to a considerable portion of the minor scholarly libraries in North America, and have visited many of them. We have found letters in France and Germany, Israel and Japan, Australia and New Zealand. We have combed the sales catalogues of dealers from around the world from the mid-nineteenth century to the present. These have provided evidence of the existence of letters which, in some cases, we have gone on to find. In others we have used the catalogues to give the status of letters to extracts whose significance appears to warrant it.

We are very conscious of our failures. There are still so many gaps we had hoped to fill. We have not found Disraeli's letters to Lord Chandos, or to Lord George Bentinck. We had not really expected to find those to Henrietta Sykes, but our hope is not quite extinguished.

As most editors do, we have advertised in *The Times*, *TLS*, *The Daily Telegraph*, and in other British newspapers and periodicals. The results for us have been disappointing. Fewer than twenty letters were unearthed by this means. Far more fruitful have been the efforts of Mr and Mrs F. McArdell, the curators of Hughenden Manor, who seem to have an unerring instinct for possible letter owners among the visitors to the house, and who have ambushed them very successfully on our behalf. The efforts of Barbara North, formerly of the National Trust office at Hughenden, have also been invaluable in keeping us informed about those who made enquiries about the archives when they were kept there before being moved to the Bodleian in 1978.

Collection and processing continue to be parallel activities. New letters keep turning up which throw light on formerly obscure passages of others. The identification of the novel which Disraeli and his sister published under pseudonyms in 1834 came at a late stage in the processing of the 1833-4 letters and made necessary substantial alteration to many of the annotations. We intend to publish a supplementary volume at the end of the edition, containing all the letters which have emerged after the appropriate chronological volume has been published. In the meantime, the hunt goes on.

Letters: 1815-1837

The private letters of a statesman are always inviting material for historians. When the statesman happens as well to have claims to literary fame, his correspondence assumes a double significance. Benjamin Disraeli (1804-1881) belonged to an age that gave pride of place to the written word as an instrument of both business and pleasure. More than even his distinguished contemporaries, Disraeli brought to the epistolary art both the technique of a professional man of letters and a sense of destiny. Evidence of the first abounds in letters demonstrating a fine eye for detail and, let it be said, a capacity for the self-dramatization and wild literary conceits that mark his novels and tales. In fact, some of the finer descriptive passages in early letters to his family also appear verbatim in novels such as *Contarini Fleming*, nor is it always certain which version was written first. As to the many premonitions of future greatness, they are epitomized in his advice of 1830 to Benjamin Austen that it would be profitable to preserve his letters for posterity. Of course, even then the young Disraeli was not perfectly obscure, though he was known primarily as the author of *Vivian Grey*.

Posterity complied, with the result that the years of Disraeli's early manhood are relatively well documented. Few schoolboy anecdotes swell the record, but ample compensation comes in the next few years, when the young Disraeli invaded the world of affairs, and not merely as a spectator. Though neither prince nor prodigy, he nevertheless had begun to participate in major events by the age of twenty. He thus had experiences worth preserving here on their own account, by no means only for the insight that they give into his future development. There is but one letter of the 'dearest mama' genre; all others find him already launched, however uncertainly, into adult relations in literature and business. Because he wrote well and because a sort of eminence came early, the number of surviving documents compares favourably with those for, say, John Wilson Croker, whose papers yield no information about their important subject until he was in his thirtieth year. When, however, one considers the Dickens correspondence, preserved in some profusion from 1835, when the writer was twenty-three, the lack of information about Disraeli in the late 1820s is annoying, for in this empty period came his serious illness – now sometimes diagnosed after the fact as the unromantic malady of atrophic rhinitis – and other events about which we know all too little.

In total, the Disraeli correspondence is immense. As of early 1980, there are more than 10,000 letters entirely in his hand, excluding government papers, letters dictated to secretaries and documents that bear only his signature. This total far exceeds that for most major figures whose collected correspondence has already appeared, though it is not quite as large as is the surviving Dickens correspondence of over 13,000 letters. There are, to be sure, such fabled treasures as that suggested in Charles Dodgson's letter-book where numbers render any complete edition unlikely, and there is Besterman's great feat of assembling 20,000 Voltaire letters. Nevertheless, in the company of public men, Disraeli stands out even in terms of the volume of his output. Burke, Macaulay and J.S. Mill, who have been well served by modern scholarly editions of their letters, are not comparable in extent. For Russell, Peel, Melbourne and Gladstone there is no firm count, but published editions suggest, at least for the first three, a comparatively thin body of material.

As he had predicted, Disraeli's letters became objects of value in his lifetime; indeed, the earliest recorded sale dates from 1866. In 1878, the great Parisian autograph dealer Etienne Charavay, using a scale that ran from 'commun' through nine further gradations of increasing rarity, rated a Disraeli letter as R4. In the nineties, S.J. Davey, the London dealer, called Disraeli 'one of the rarest of modern names', and cited an instance of £100 being asked for a one-page letter signed 'Beaconsfield'. One cause of this rarity was the Disraeli family's retention of a huge store of manuscript materials. Unhappily for the editors, a process of selling off letters began in 1901. Over the next fifteen years the Hughenden archives were divested of at least 300 letters written to the family. Such items became a drug on the market, as noted in 1910 by the discerning collector A.M. Broadley: 'How Lord Beaconsfield's life is ever to be written with any hope of completeness, I cannot imagine. Hundreds of his letters have been sold since his death, and a specimen of average interest can now be obtained for 20s or less.'

Undeterred by Broadley's concern, Monypenny published the first volume of the monumental biography in that same year. But often he depended for his texts of letters upon Ralph Disraeli's several compilations of his brother's correspondence. Since the Hughenden papers were then, for the most part, unorganized and uncatalogued, it must have been difficult to know if there still existed any alternative to the published texts.

Doubtless unavoidable, Monypenny's decision was a costly one. As Broadley, himself the owner of some originals, pointed out, Ralph's work failed to rise above the undemanding conventions of other Victorian editions. That is, there had been no effort to respect the integrity of individual letters as discrete documents: not infrequently a number were conflated into a single and heavily edited narrative and then assigned a date that belonged, at best, to one of them only. This editorial insensitivity was least pronounced in the case of the *Home Letters*, consisting largely of detailed description of identifiable places. However, many letters that did not so depend for their meaning on association with a specific time and place were ruthlessly reshaped. Indeed, it is not always clear what purpose was served by the process, for it was not just inaccuracies or indiscretions that suffered. At times the editor seems to have sought to substitute his own judgement for that of the writer. Over the years, a certain number of items were reclaimed from the market, perhaps by Major Coningsby Disraeli, Ralph's son. But not until the cataloguing of the Hughenden papers in the 1960s could one finally declare that Broadley's alarm of fifty years before had been well founded.

Some 40 libraries or private collections have provided the texts of letters for the first two volumes. There are many more sources for the later years, when Disraeli's correspondence increased. Of current sources, by far the major contributor has been the Hughenden collection, with close to one-third of the total. Of the 697 letters to the end of 1837, only 90 lack originals; these have had to be taken from published sources – newspapers, books, auction or sales catalogues. This proportion of original documents, or photocopies of them, largely removes the limitations under which Monypenny and Buckle laboured. With our acquisition in 1976 of the original manuscripts of the *Home Letters*, the spell of Ralph Disraeli's sanctified errors has further been lifted and more of his versions can now be compared with the originals.

Given the whimsical character of nineteenth-century editing, it is not unusual for a much-needed modern edition to consist, as in the case of Byron's letters, largely of previously published items. Removing the confusions created by unexacting editing may be quite as valuable a task as the discovery of new documents. But most of Disraeli's correspondence escaped the ravages of his editor, for Ralph's efforts concentrated upon the early letters. Even for letters written before 1838, some 40 per cent – 283 in all – now appear for the first time, at least as far as can be ascertained. Apart from Ralph's volumes, and those of Monypenny and Buckle who so heavily relied upon him, the chief works that have printed at least fragments of a substantial number of letters are Smiles's life of John Murray and Professor Jerman's *The Young Disraeli*. But there are, of course, many sources that quote small portions of text. Perhaps the oddest case is one published account of a private collection of Disraeli letters in which some passages are quoted, not from the original documents, but from Ralph Disraeli's unauthentic version. Truth does not always fare well even in free and open encounter.

In order to understand a correspondence, one usually wishes to be able to consult both sides. Letters written to Disraeli are to be found in great numbers in the Hughenden papers for, unlike some public figures, he preserved such materials with care. Understandably, some items are missing, either because they seemed to be of no consequence, invitations, for example, or because their contents were potentially embarrassing. Clearly, Disraeli received far more dunning letters than he preserved; their disquieting contents would provide no incentive to treasure them. Some quite intimate letters from married women have survived, and Sara Austen, who played a large role in the writing of *Vivian Grey*, actually wrote some of hers in a cipher, though the contents were not very compromising. Lady Sykes, Disraeli's mistress in the period 1833-6, was capable of a memorable candour, but was more given to expressing sentiment than to explaining circumstances. When one considers the travels of Disraeli's youth and the fact that after 1829 he spent much of his time living at various addresses in London – not to mention the temptation of an open fire as a method of tidying – the survival of so much correspondence is remarkable.

No attempt has been made, as in some editions, to print the texts of letters addressed to Disraeli, though often they are quoted in the notes. Especially prominent are the letters from Sarah Disraeli, almost all of which remain preserved in the Hughenden papers, as did Disraeli's to her until the unfortunate sales before the First World War. For several decades, Disraeli and his sister exchanged letters with great frequency. Over one-third of the pre-1838 letters are addressed to Sarah, though this portion does not entirely coincide with the one-third drawn from Hughenden. The letters from her – a stream of family news, local gossip, acid comment on personalities and queries about London life – provide the background which enables us to understand the details of his existence. Because of the odd way in which she submerged her life in his, his life gains an unusual focus. Without her letters, we would too often be confronted with answers for which there were no previous questions.

Owing to the centrality of this prolonged and intimate correspondence, the editors might well have contemplated devoting whole volumes to it alone. The Horace Walpole letters and some early editions of Goethe's letters are so organized. But such an approach, however effective for purposes of focusing the themes of a thinker, poet or connoisseur, would not have served to illuminate either the thoughts or the career of this ambitious young man in the London of the Reform Bill. Inasmuch as the letters to Sarah supply the axis round which we must reconstruct this period in Disraeli's life, their supreme value lies precisely in the light that they cast upon those other documents that form the remainder of the record. The chronological arrangement of letters that are very different in tone or substance enhances the value of each. One can then employ letters, not only to illustrate character or to enshrine fine phrases, but to map a life in systematic fashion. The same consideration justifies the inclusion of all Disraeli's letters, for the very density of the correspondence contributes to our understanding. Indeed, it is precisely those brief messages – announcing, for instance, his presence at a specific place on a given date – that allow for further inferences about his activity. What seems meaningless in isolation becomes significant when placed in context.

Sometimes, of course, the juxtaposition of letters, never intended to be read together, does nothing to enhance Disraeli's reputation. One can tell one publisher, but not more than one, that he has first refusal of a manuscript; only one creditor at a time can be assured that he commands the highest priority.

Disraeli kept a diary only very irregularly; for the most part his activities were chronicled in letters home, chiefly to Sarah. These letters do immeasurable service if only because they constitute the line of continuity against which one may place his relations with other people. The seemingly prosaic task of dating an undated document may be the key to its meaning. Sarah was more punctilious than her brother in dating her letters, so that many chains of reasoning about the events referred to in some other letter begin with the bedrock supplied by comments either from Sarah or to her. In the absence of such a sustained record we would lack those landmarks that make it easy to place Disraeli within his several spheres of activity.

The world, and not Sarah, was the target of his ambition. To her, perhaps to her alone, he confided his hopes, interspersed with breathless accounts of occasions, social, literary or political, in which she was invited to share vicariously. Of his current writings he wrote to publishers; of his political designs – throughout most of the early period they were unrealized – he wrote to senior politicians. Both spheres might warrant mention in letters to a particularly favoured, and impatient, creditor such as Benjamin Austen. But to 'Sa' he wrote of both all the time, noting not just overt activity, but the meaning of his experiences. Even his love affairs leave their traces. One early courtship figures in accounts to Sarah, accompanied by firm instructions not to allow anyone else to intercept the letters. His affair with Lady Sykes was another matter, but here the very silences about his whereabouts sufficiently mark the period. The same delicacy spared Sarah most of the details of his debts, a topic that dominates a number of relations – those with Austen, Pyne and Culverwell.

There may well be major figures whose letters provide no perspective comparable to that afforded by the 'Sarah' correspondence, but all editors must hope for those shafts of light that invest their subject and his business with meaning. Some personalities stand in more need of candid testimony about their motives than do others. An irrepressible soul such as George Meredith expressed strong feelings in many letters to different people. The more austere Macaulay, by contrast, is sufficiently revealed in his private thoughts about public business largely through letters to his friend Thomas Flower Ellis. Without the presence of Sarah, Disraeli would seem one-dimensional, the home of a restless ambition that left no peace for honest self-scrutiny. Not, of course, that he was, in general, an understated person; far from it. However, neither the hyperbolic enthusiasms nor the bouts of self-pity apparent in his other relations were as expressive as his less mannered but more informative revelations to Sarah. During the greater part of his life, Disraeli appears to have required the solace of a confidant. For a long time – even after his marriage, though in reduced measure – this was Sarah. Peeresses and even a queen were later to take up part of that role.

What, in fact, do Disraeli's letters tell us that we might wish to know? For one thing, they provide a remarkably detailed account of life in the upper reaches of English society, viewed from below. Long before he came to dominate his era, Disraeli had become adept at portraying it, sometimes in exquisite detail. Few other members of the middle class managed to penetrate aristocratic society with comparable success, and fewer still brought with them the literary skill to tell what they saw there. Observations on the conversation of the town and the personnel of dinner parties are conspicuous in Disraeli's letters to those people, particularly Sarah, who were removed from the excitement. The letters, whether to amuse ladies or invite the interest of a publisher or the patience of a creditor, have above all an air of busyness. But only the most narrowly instrumental messages are confined to a single topic. Even the creditors heard of the debtor's moods and these are sometimes conveyed in telling ways. Who could not respond to the message that Disraeli, amid all his afflictions, was 'savagely gay'?

Carlyle, even as a young man, lectured his readers; Disraeli's attention to most topics was too fleeting to sustain any comparable *gravitas*. Where the letters are richest in information – as in those to Sarah – he is least artful, because least on display. Writing to others, he is apt to be extravagant in sentiment, even at the expense of content. Applied to the simple acceptance or refusal of an invitation, this artfulness has the effect of making the document more memorable than its ostensible message would suggest. That, presumably, is why such letters have survived, to be described in auction catalogues as 'charming'.

Some of the least memorable effusions were directed to Mary Anne Lewis, his future wife. Devoid of the information and opinion which he communicated to Sarah, these exercises in gallantry too often seem contrived rather than clever. In his flirtatious correspondence with the ladies of the Sheridan family Disraeli is shown to better advantage, for the letters are largely self-mocking *jeux d'esprit*.

Disraeli's earliest claim to attention was literary, and his pursuits before his election to Parliament were those of a man of letters. But the correspondence says comparatively little of his inspiration for his novels, though it does document the speed and concentration of his composition. Only for the political writings can we learn much of his sources – a mixture of private information, careful reading of the press, and history books. One of Disraeli's objects in writing had been to acquire both the name and the money to sustain a parliamentary career. By 1834, his involvement in literature came, more and more, to look like a stepping stone to Westminster. *The Revolutionary Epick* of that year was a source of pride to its author and the letters include ample detail on the process of composition, but the poem itself was neither a critical nor a commercial success. The editing of the letters has added several items to the canon of Disraeli's works, most notably in the discovery of his joint authorship, with Sarah, of *Hartlebury*, a novel of 1834. The book will never rank as great literature, but it attests to the extent of Disraeli's commitment at that time to a fusion of Tory and Radical principles. Two more novels preceded his election in 1837, but his concentration had then been primarily upon political affairs for several years.

The most important issue to which these letters speak is, thus, the course of Disraeli's political ambitions. In thc first biography of Disraeli, published in 1852, the grand question was already that of his alleged opportunism and want of principle. In this century Disraeli has been the subject of two of the major biographies in the language, but still uncertainty about his political aims persists. The letters will not serve to dispel all doubts, but they may render the problem more manageable. His political opinions appear to be instinctively Tory. In planning the Canningite newspaper of 1825 he talks of private gain and of British grandeur, but not of reform. When he regrets the outcome of the battle of Navarino or proclaims his intention of assisting the Porte in subduing rebellious subjects, no glimmer of political radicalism mars his orthodoxy.

On his return to England in 1831, Disraeli fell in with one Moritz von Haber, and through him was drawn into a scheme to thwart the Whig government's foreign policy by defeating it on the Reform Bill. The background to the writing of *Gallomania* – the instrument intended to dish this set of Whigs – has been a neglected chapter in Disraeli's early history, and the book remains among the least known of his writings. As letters from the spring of 1832 indicate, he was more anti-Whig than hostile to reform, but already he had to steer uneasily among the contrary demands of potential supporters. Thus we find his friend Mrs Bolton cautioning him to appear more dedicated to the cause of defeating the Whig bill, lest he alienate that alliance of reactionary Europeans and Tory ultras whose hopes lay with the *Gallomania*. Not much later, Edward Bulwer, his sponsor in Radical circles, anxiously sought reassurance that Disraeli was indeed committed to reform. Sarah, meanwhile, wrote to him about his plan to convert the Radicals of Wycombe to Toryism – an ambition never so described in Disraeli's letters to her.

If any setting could sustain Disraeli's self-proclaimed Radical proclivities, it was Wycombe, long a close borough in the Whig interest, and still, after passage of the Reform Bill, responsive to the wants of Lord Carrington. This nobleman was actually a Tory, but his son was a Whig member, and his wants did not include Disraeli. The fact that Disraeli failed to displace the Whigs and that one of the members after 1832 was Charles Grey, son of the prime minister, lent substance to Disraeli's rhetoric about freeing his home constituency from thraldom. These circumstances also helped to nourish his romantic attachment to the language of eighteenth-century Toryism – the creed of Bolingbroke and Wyndham. Again in 1834-5 Disraeli fought an election at Wycombe with support from Tories and Radicals, and again circumstances lent some credibility to his stand. Though no national coalescing of these elements was pending, conditions certainly favoured some realignment of parties, and talk about coalition government was heard. Even allowing for the unsettled times, however, the political letters vividly amplify Charles Greville's famous observation that Disraeli seemed to be 'a mighty impartial personage'. Within the space of a few days we find him impartially bestowing his attentions upon both Lord Durham, a decidedly radical Whig, and the Duke of Wellington. In both cases he sought a patron who might get him into Parliament. Some of Disraeli's pronouncements to Durham have a particularly disingenuous flavour, which can best be excused by noting the deep divisions that then afflicted the Tories.

From the spring of 1834, Disraeli's political fortunes had begun to improve; he had met Lord Lyndhurst and this influential patron was to place him firmly in the Tory camp. Still, the road to Parliament was not yet clear, for he continued to be haunted by troubles from his past. For such a young man, he had already compiled a lengthy public record – the reward, or the price, of his youthful endeavours. This proved to be a mixed blessing for one who aspired to a profession that valued consistency. Beset by charges of opportunism in his Taunton campaign of 1835, Disraeli had still to learn the truth of his later dictum that one should 'never explain'. His longest letters presented here are those to Edwards Beadon in justification of past conduct, and these have not previously figured in scholarly accounts of Disraeli's career.

Debts, contracted as long as ten years before, also continued to plague him, as they would in years to come. He was thus tempted by a variety of money-making schemes, some of which again brought him into contact with the mysterious Baron Haber. Introduced first as an agent of the exiled Charles X, Haber reappeared as a fund-raiser for the Spanish Carlists. This episode, which implicated Disraeli in some dubious financial engagements on behalf of a power against which the British had dispatched a force of mercenaries, has largely escaped previous attention. Neither has it been clear until now how close Disraeli came to permanent ruin at the hands of his creditors in the spring of 1837. Debtors' prison beckoned, and had that fate materialized there is doubt whether he would ever have been eligible, either in law or in reputation, for a parliamentary career. New findings about Disraeli's finances have come from the correspondence, recently discovered, with Richard Culverwell, and especially from letters to William Pyne which were available to Lord Blake only in the form of Monypenny's notes.

Disraeli's eventual election for Maidstone in the summer of 1837 marks the emergence of a formal public role after twelve years of intermittent activity on the fringes of power. When he was no more than twenty, he had negotiated with famous men and had been party to major financial speculations. The fact that these ventures all failed did nothing to rid Disraeli of a taste for high finance and high politics, preferably combined. On his travels in the Ottoman Empire, he was impressed by meetings with the exotic officialdom of the region. Back in England, his desire to be at the centre of events continued unabated. At first, he appears as a too-credulous young man, given to spreading abroad the misconceptions of émigré Carlists. Surprisingly, though, Disraeli was not a simple outsider, for he was advantageously placed to touch great events, if not always to see them clearly. Letters dating from the writing of *Gallomania* present him as convinced that he was privy to astounding secrets and poised to alter the balance of Europe. One must make allowances for his native hyperbole, but the fact remains that important men, British and foreign, took an interest in the writing of *Gallomania*. At the same time, however, he failed to identify the editor of *The Times* correctly. No mere parvenu, and certainly not without influential friends, his resources of all kinds nevertheless remained thin.

As his company, through 1833-4, grew more aristocratic, the quality of his information improved. But at least until his election to Parliament he lived on the most alluring rumour of the day. The Whig cabinet in disarray and his own triumph assured! How often Sarah and others must have read those premature tidings. The world could never somehow keep pace with his overheated imagination. This mood was not confined to politics; there were publishers who learned, more than once, of his writing the greatest book in the world. The bizarre habit of announcing the deaths of old ladies – who then remained stubbornly alive – was another measure of Disraeli's impetuosity. This quality was most significant, however, in his stormy rise to political eminence. A quarrel, such as that with Daniel O'Connell, probably did Disraeli as much harm as good, and it is implausible to suppose that it was a calculated bid for popularity. Because he set out early and was a long time in attaining his goals, one is sometimes tempted to laud his patience; wise saws of his old age support that impression. But the record suggests energy and endurance rather than patience. Disraeli was very much in a hurry and was thus apt to pursue new avenues to success before he had formally disavowed the old. This is enough to account for the common suspicion that he was not fastidious about his means of rising.

The first two volumes of the Collected Letters bring Disraeli only to the threshold of the Victorian era and to the onset of his career as a politician.

By late 1837 he had failed in his maiden speech, but all major successes lay in the future.

It would be premature for the editors to advertise here the treasures laid up for further volumes. More documents will yet be unearthed and the meaning of many already in our possession must still be pondered. For these reasons, it is impossible to present here, at the beginning of the first volumes, a cogent and accurate overview of the entire collection. Our object, therefore, is not to present a 'general' introduction for, as all writers and editors know, that is only useful when one has finished one's task and the whole picture is clear. Nor do we wish to write a potted biography. Rather we shall present a new introduction to each block of the letters. Each of these, building upon its predecessors, will, we are confident, assist in focusing scholarly reassessment of Disraeli's significance to his age. Undoubtedly the events of later years which require explanation involve larger issues than those covered to date. The bulk of those sets of correspondence which biographers of Disraeli have lacked are now available to us. Most of them relate to the period of Disraeli's eminence and so will form the content of our future labours.

A Note on Annotation

The best teller of this complex story is Disraeli himself, and we have made an effort to leave the telling to him. Notes there must be, however, for the letters teem with proper names and studied allusions. There are no earlier editions of the letters with adequate annotation, although some scholarly articles, based on small bodies of material, do give useful data, and the published correspondence to Lady Blessington, from the Morrison Collection, is annotated.

When an editor does not initially know what a phrase or an allusion means, then he has grasped the point of annotation. Assuming that what the editors have readily understood the informed reader might already know, we have concentrated upon those issues which at first gave us difficulty. At the same time, we have tried to bear in mind that the reader interested mainly in Disraeli's human qualities may need further guidance, and we trust that the more knowledgeable may forgive it. All people about whom we could learn anything are identified, with emphasis upon clarifying the context in which the name arises and its owner's relation to Disraeli. The place in history of Melbourne or Peel has no need of our services save in relation to matters in which Disraeli took an interest.

There is a biographical note for each person, normally placed where he or she is first mentioned. The main notes for individuals are marked in the index by boldface type. We have suppressed the temptation to provide a biographical section devoted to the names that appear very frequently; there seemed to be just too many of them. Family connections were the essence of individual identity for upper-class individuals of the period, especially the women. This circumstance accounts for the wealth of genealogical detail in the notes; without it, readers might remain unaware, for example, of the ties which united the members of various social gatherings or the personnel of the government of Malta during Disraeli's visit. Indeed, the general structure of British public life then remained very much a matter of social status symbolized by names. In addition to the information on individuals, social customs, quotations and expressions peculiar to other times and places have been noticed.

Where we have been unable either to identify persons who are mentioned only incidentally or to explain fleeting references, we have decided that saying nothing was sufficiently eloquent. Admittedly, this policy – in conjunction with our desire to avoid labouring the obvious – seems to run the danger of that schoolboy excuse for silence, that some considerations are too familiar to warrant attention and the rest too obscure to allow it. But no part of editing is more a matter of judgement than annotation, and we have, in fact, attempted to resolve those points which seem important to the understanding of any substantial passage. Nor have we averted our gaze from difficulties arising from uncertain dating of letters or from other gaps in the evidence. Explanations inserted in editorial comments serve as bridges between the letters. There are certain to be places where we have said too much for some tastes, too little for the needs of others. The readers who can elucidate what we could not will be particularly cherished.

EDITORIAL PRINCIPLES AND CONVENTIONS

The governing principle of the edition is the presentation of an accurate text; editorial intervention has been kept to the minimum consistent with this aim, and with that of assisting ease of reading and clarification of meaning. The letters are presented in chronological order; each is introduced by a letter number of large type in the outside margin. Each letter consists of three parts: (a) the headnote. This presents all relevant information about the letter as a physical object; (b) the text; (c) the annotations.

Headnote

ADDRESSEE

The name of Disraeli's correspondent is given in the shortest form consistent with clear identification.

DATE

The four elements – the name of day, number of day, month, year – are shown in that order. Square brackets enclose elements not included by Disraeli in his letter. For example, the expression 'Saturday 15 [July 1833]' indicates that Disraeli has written 'Sat. 15' and that the remaining information has been obtained from the postmark, or from references in the text to known external events or to other firmly dated letters.

Any doubtful element in the date is followed by a question mark. The expression '[Saturday 15? July 1833]' indicates confidence in the month and year, but doubt about the day. Where there is doubt about any part of the date, or where a letter has been definitely assigned to a date other than the one given in previously published sources, a dating note in the Editorial Comment explains the basis on which the assignment has been made.

When all elements of a date are doubtful, the question mark appears at the end, as in the expression '[July 1833?]'. In such cases the hypotheses which would suggest a month and year are presented in the Editorial Comment. Such a letter would appear within the chronological order at the end of the month or year to which it has been assigned.

The place from which the letter is written (eg 35 Duke Street, Bradenham) appears without square brackets only when Disraeli has written this information formally in the text of his letter. The location is given in square brackets without a question mark when it is certain because the context of the letter makes it obvious; or because the postmark is clear; or because the letter is one of a close sequence of letters written from a known location.

Where the probability is strong, but some doubt remains, the location is shown in square brackets with a question mark.

Where there are no data to support a hypothesis, no location is given.

LOCATION OF ORIGINAL AND REFERENCE NUMBER

The location of the original manuscript and its archival reference number, if any, are given. The names of the major MS collections are given in the short form noted in the List of Abbreviations. For example, H A/I/B/34 indicates MS in the Hughenden papers, at the Bodleian Library, Oxford, which has been classified within that collection as A/I/B/34.

PRINTED SOURCE

Where the original MS has not been located, a transcription from a printed source is indicated by a reference to the publication from which it has been obtained. The editors cannot, of course, vouch for the accuracy of the text in such cases. Experience has shown that it must be treated with caution, particularly if it is taken from material edited by Ralph Disraeli.

COVER

For the early period, covers are usually integral with the MS of the letter. A vertical solidus in the transcription indicates a change in line.

POSTMARKS

The shape is described and then each element is transcribed in order, moving from the top to the bottom, each new line being indicated by a vertical solidus. Pictorial examples of the types of postmarks in use during this period are given in a separate section of this introduction. Beside each is the way in which it would be described in the headnote.

PUBLICATION HISTORY

We do not attempt to list all the works in which a letter may have been previously published. We have tried to show first publication, and in some cases subsequent reprinting in, for example, Monypenny and Buckle, or Blake. If there is no entry here, we are not aware of earlier publication.

This includes notes on the dating and on the special problems of the physical state of the MS. Where necessary, bridging notes to introduce blocks of letters, and general comments appropriate to explain circumstances in Disraeli's life, are also provided. Additions in other hands have only been transcribed when they bear upon transmission, receipt, or content. We have not corrected Disraeli's spelling and syntax and did not wish to scatter '[*sic*]' throughout the text, so we have added a subheading in the Editorial Comment – *Sic*: followed by a list of words with abnormal spelling, and variant phrases – intended to reassure the reader that these are not typographical errors on our part. See also below, under Spelling. Errors with apostrophes are so frequent that these have not been included in the *Sic* list. Equally, where Disraeli has omitted French accents these have not been listed; however, accents that are present and incorrect have been noted.

Text

CORRECTION

There has been no silent correction of spelling or grammar.

INTERPOLATIONS

We have not indicated interpolations between lines; they are incorporated in the text as they occur.

ERASURES

We have not indicated Disraeli's own corrections except in those rare cases when the rejected word indicates some significant development in the thought expressed.

SQUARE BRACKETS

We have used square brackets in the text to indicate editorial additions, notably:

i To expand abbreviations which may be ambiguous or obscure.

ii To complete words or phrases in the interest of swift comprehension by the reader; for example, when Disraeli writes 'Xexamination' this has been rendered 'X[cross]examination'. Rarely, punctuation has also been added in square brackets in the interests of comprehensibility.

iii To complete words, parts of words, or phrases which are obscure or missing as a result of damage to the MS. These are rendered in italics inside square brackets. The nature of the damage is reported in the Editorial Comment section of the headnote, and reported again in the text only in those few cases where large sections of a MS page are missing, and where, therefore, there is an abrupt break, for example: [*lower half of third page missing*] or [*page of MS missing?*] or [*MS incomplete*].

CATCHWORDS

Disraeli very often uses catchwords, and they have been a great help not only in confirming the proper internal sequence of pages within a letter, but in enabling us in some cases to restore the original integrity of letters where, in some collections, a number of them have been unwittingly collated with pages mismatched. However, the duplication of catchwords in a printed text is annoying to the reader, and we have therefore silently dropped the repetition. However, where one form of the catchword is abbreviated and the other is given in full we have given the fuller version.

VERTICAL SOLIDUS

The vertical solidus, when used in the body of a letter, indicates page divisions in the manuscript; when used in the headnote, or in the upper right-hand superscription of the text, it indicates line divisions. The solidus is also used at the ends of letters to show the point at which Disraeli, adding a running postscript (as he often does), begins to write on the margin of a different page. That is why the solidus appears much more frequently at the ends of letters. The exact geography of the postscripts has been noted only where there is a special reason to do so.

ABBREVIATIONS

Abbreviations have been left in their original form where there is no ambiguity in the context: M.P., St. (for Street), Xmas, Co. (for Company), Ld. (for Lord). Where there is ambiguity they have been expanded in square brackets. Disraeli abbreviates 'could' both as cd and cod, and 'should' as shd and shod, the final d sometimes in superscript and sometimes not. The first form, cd and shd, presents no interruption to the reader, and has been left as written, but the second, when transcribed, is often ambiguous, and this form has been expanded to co[ul]d and sho[ul]d. The superscripts have been lowered.

Where Disraeli, throughout a letter, refers to someone by an initial, the name is expanded the first time it appears in each letter, eg L[yndhurst], but is left as L. on subsequent occasions. Sets of initials frequently used, ie BEL, ELB, LEL, are identified early in the sequence, but not thereafter.

AMPERSAND

Disraeli's usage varies widely from the extremes of clearly written 'and', clear ampersands, and every variety of wriggle in between. All these have been transcribed as 'and'.

ADDRESSEE

Disraeli sometimes writes the name and address of the person to whom the letter is written on the lower left of the first page, and sometimes at the end of the last page. These have all been placed at the upper left at the beginning of the transcription of the text.

LOCATION

Where present in Disraeli's text, the place from which a letter was written, and the date, have been standardized in format on one line at the upper right of the letter, with the line division of the original indicated by a vertical solidus.

SIGNATURE

Letters signed D, D., B.D., B D have been standardized as D and BD without periods. Fuller forms of signature have been transcribed as written.

[?]

A question mark in square brackets immediately follows any reading about which some doubt remains.

[. . .]

Three dots within square brackets indicate an illegible word, or a gap in the MS. The nature of the difficulty normally will have been indicated in the Editorial Comment section of the headnote.

PRINTED SOURCES

On some occasions letters which we have had to transcribe from printed sources contain obvious errors in transcription. Misreadings of proper names, notably in sales catalogues, are quite common. We have transcribed the text as it was printed, but we have placed, in square brackets, immediately following the word or phrase we think has been misread, the reading which we believe to be correct.

HANDWRITING

The clarity of Disraeli's handwriting varies enormously, depending upon the identity of his correspondent and the speed with which he was writing. A formal and careful letter to the Duke of Wellington is one thing; a note dashed to his sister quite another. Perhaps the largest single problem has been posed by isolated words in letters which are otherwise quite clear, and which do not suffer from the obscurities of speed and excessive abbreviation: suddenly one encounters a word which seems quite straightforward in its calligraphy but which makes no sense. There are still a few of these left, and they are followed in the text by [?]. There are many minor variations between our text and previously published versions of the same letter. Unless our reading alters the significance of the letter, we have not listed these variations in the headnote. To save postage, Disraeli, particularly in his letters from abroad, cultivated a very small hand, an expedient which poses its own problems, aggravated by pen and ink of poor quality, and porous paper, used on both sides, which permitted the ink to seep from one page to the other. See, for example, the illustration on page 158.

PUNCTUATION

Disraeli's sense of punctuation is, at best, spasmodic. When we have corrected it we have enclosed our addition in square brackets. There is one exception. Disraeli was much given to ending his sentences with a dash instead of a full stop: where the dash is clearly intended to be a full stop, and is followed by a capitalized word beginning a new sentence, we have silently inserted the full stop.

ACCENTS

Disraeli's enthusiasm for foreign words and phrases outran his knowledge of them. His accents are nearly always wrong, and his spelling of foreign place names is highly original, often presenting differing versions within the one letter. We have left them as he wrote them, adding them to the *Sic* list where appropriate.

SPELLING

We have left Disraeli's spelling as it is. Some spellings, uncommon even in his own time, he consistently uses for years, i.e. 'agreable', 'develope', others for a lifetime – champagne is always 'champaigne'. Particularly for proper names, the early spelling is likely to be phonetic, later rectified when he comes to know the correct spelling.

Annotations

SOURCES

Sources cited in the annotations are given in full where the source is used no more than twice in any volume, and otherwise given in the short forms shown in the list of abbreviations. Standard, readily available reference works such as dictionaries are not, of course, cited.

MAIN NOTES

The principal annotation about a person or a topic normally occurs at the first reference made by Disraeli, and is noted in boldface type in the index. Where the main note has already been given in an earlier volume, the index will provide its location.

We do not give annotations to annotations or to headnotes.

INDEX

Each volume has its own index. Indexes in volumes after the first will show all references in the current volume and, if the first and principal annotation has already been given in an earlier volume, a cross-reference will be included in boldface type, giving volume and letter number.

The following are some of the most commonly used postmarks in the 1815-37 period, together with the forms used to describe them in the headnotes:

In circle:
P | FE-3 | 1832

In double circle:
E | 7 OC 7 | 1811

In double circle:
JY | E29 [central number in small circle] | 1826

In Maltese cross:
V.S | VJU15S | 1831

[Foreign Post Office]
In dotted circle:
FPO | FE.2 | 1819

In packet:
T.P | Bge St Lambh.

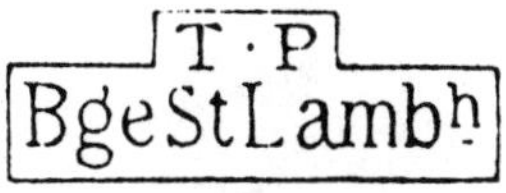

In oval: 7.NIGHT.7
AP.29 | 1834

xxxiv In crowned double circle: FREE | 17JU17 | 1825 | O

In circular form: ROCHFORD

In circular form: CHELTENHAM | [enclosing]: DE23 | 1836

In rectangle: No. 1

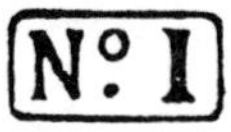

HONITON | Penny Post

DISRAELI CHRONOLOGY 1804-1834

The following is a brief chronology of Benjamin Disraeli's early life. It outlines the chief phases of his development and his changing preoccupations, particularly as these are reflected in his letters. A few parallel public events of importance are noted when they have impact on Disraeli's course. His principal places of residence are also noted to supplement the outline of his life, but no attempt is made to trace his day-by-day movements.

DATE	RESIDENCE	EVENTS
1804		
21 Dec	6 King's Road, Bedford Row	Benjamin Disraeli born, the first son of Isaac and Maria D'Israeli
1808-16		Early education at Miss Roper's school, Islington, and at the Rev John Potticary's school, Blackheath
1817	6 Bloomsbury Square	
31 July		Baptized into the Church of England
1817-20		Attends the Rev Eli Cogan's school, Higham Hall, at Walthamstow
1820-1		Self-education at home
1821		
10 Nov		Articled to the firm of Swain, Stevens *et al*, solicitors
1822		
13 Dec		Adopts 'Disraeli' as spelling of surname
1823		
July-Aug		Vacationing with family at Windsor

DATE	RESIDENCE	EVENTS
1824		
July-Sept		Tour of the Low Countries and Rhine with father and Meredith
Oct		Abandons Law Clerkship
1825		Speculates in Stock Exchange and loses heavily during year
Mar-June		Publishes promotional tracts on Mexican Mining ventures
Sept		Completes editing of and publishes anonymously *The Life of John Paul Jones* Meets Sir Walter Scott
Autumn		Associated with John Murray in launching *The Representative*, a short-lived daily newspaper
21 Dec		Twenty-first birthday
1826		
22 Apr		*Vivian Grey* Part I published anonymously
May		Quarrels with Murray; health breaks
8 Aug-15 Oct		Tours Italy with Sara and Benjamin Austen
1827		Poor health and mental depression persist throughout the year
23 Feb		*Vivian Grey* Part II published anonymously
30 April		Name entered at Lincoln's Inn as a prospective barrister
Aug		Vacationing at Fyfield, Essex; taken seriously ill
1828		
Jan		Staying at Mayfield Hall, Hastings
3 June		*Captain Popanilla* published
Aug		Vacationing at Lyme Regis
1829		
Spring		Contributes articles to the *Court Journal*
July	Bradenham	D'Israeli family moves permanently to Bradenham House near High Wycombe, Bucks

DATE	RESIDENCE	EVENTS
Nov	Union Hotel	
Dec	Bradenham	
1830		
Winter		Physical and mental debility is compounded by financial pressures
Spring		Begins composition of *The Young Duke* and *Alroy*
April	Union Hotel	Forms close friendship with Edward Lytton Bulwer
28 May	Travelling	Embarks on extended tour of Spain and the Middle East with William Meredith, his sister's fiancé. Sends 'home letters'
1831		
April		*The Young Duke* published
19 July		Sudden death of Meredith at Cairo ends eastern tour
23 Oct		Arrives back in England
Nov	Union Hotel	
12 Nov		Meets Baron Haber
25 Nov	15 Pall Mall East	Withdraws from Lincoln's Inn
Dec	Bradenham	
1832		
Jan		Begins political campaigning at High Wycombe
Feb	35 Duke Street, St James's	Active in fashionable London society
16 April		*Gallomania* published
15 May		*Contarini Fleming* published
7 June		Reform Act passes
26 June	Bradenham	Stands unsuccessfully in Wycombe by-election as a 'high Radical'
Summer	35 Duke Street	
12 Dec	Bradenham	Suffers a second electoral defeat at Wycombe in general election Stands briefly as a candidate for Bucks county, aligned with the Tory Marquess of Chandos

DATE	RESIDENCE	EVENTS
1833		
Feb	35 Duke Street	'Ixion in Heaven' appears in *The New Monthly Magazine*
5 Mar		*Alroy* published
Mar-Apr		Stands as an independent Radical candidate at Marylebone; withdraws before poll and explains his politics in the pamphlet *"What is He?"*
Summer		Meets Henrietta Sykes
Aug-Oct	Bradenham	
Nov	The Grange, Southend	Visiting Sir Francis and Lady Sykes
Dec	Bradenham	
1834		
Jan-Feb	The Grange, Southend	Engaged in composition of the *Revolutionary Epick*
15 Mar	Bradenham	Part I of the *Revolutionary Epick* published *A Year at Hartlebury or the Election*, a novel written jointly with Sarah Disraeli, published
May	31a Park Street	Resumes political activity; makes acquaintance of Daniel O'Connell
16 June		Publication of *The Revolutionary Epick*, Parts II and III Meets Lord Durham
Summer		Active in social circle of Lady Blessington and Count D'Orsay 'The Infernal Marriage' appears in *The New Monthly Magazine*
Aug-Sept		Gains friendship and patronage of Lord Lyndhurst
Oct	Bradenham	Acts as Lyndhurst's intermediary with the Marquess of Chandos
15 Nov	31a Park Street	Fall of the Melbourne government
Dec	Bradenham	Independent candidate for High Wycombe in the general election Publishes electoral address as a pamphlet, *The Crisis Examined*

ABBREVIATIONS IN VOLUME ONE

app	Appendix
APSY	Wellington Museum, Apsley House, London
AR	*The Annual Register* (followed by year of edition)
Army List	*A List of the Officers of the Army and Royal Marines on Full, Retired and Half-Pay*; after 1839: *The New Annual Army List* compiled by H.G. Hart (followed by year of edition)
Ashford	L.J. Ashford *The History of the Borough of High Wycombe* (1962)
BEA	Belvoir Castle, Lincolnshire
BECK	Beckford Collection, B.H. Blackwell Ltd, Oxford
Beeton	*Benjamin Disraeli, Earl of Beaconsfield. A Biography* S.O. Beeton, nd [1877] [attributed to T.P. O'Connor]
BEL	Benjamin Ephraim Lindo
BENT	D.R. Bentham, Loughborough, Leicestershire
BG	*The Bucks Gazette*, Aylesbury, Buckinghamshire
BH	*The Bucks Herald*, Aylesbury, Buckinghamshire
BL	The British Library, London
Blake	Robert Blake *Disraeli* (1966)
BLG	John Burke *A Genealogical and Heraldic Dictionary of the Landed Gentry of Great Britain and Ireland* (var. ed.)
Boase	Frederick Boase *Modern English Biography* (1892 repr 1965)
BODL	Bodleian Library, Oxford
Boyle's	*Boyle's Fashionable Court and Country Guide* (followed by year of edition)
BP	*Burke's Peerage and Baronetage*
BRST	Henry Bristow Ltd, Ringwood, Hampshire
CARR	Carrington Collection, Department of Western Manuscripts, Bodleian Library, Oxford
CJ	*The Court Journal*
CM	*The Court Magazine*

Colvin	H.M. Colvin *A Biographical Dictionary of English Architects, 1660-1840* (Cambridge, Massachusetts 1954)
D	Benjamin Disraeli (1804-1881)
DNB	Sir Leslie Stephen and Sir Sidney Lee eds *The Dictionary of National Biography* (1917 repr 1973)
ec	Editorial comment section of the headnote
EGT	A.C. Eastgate, Wimbledon
EJM	ex-Jewish Museum, Woburn House, London. The Museum began to sell its collection of Disraeli letters through Sotheby's in 1974. Much of this material was purchased by Francis Edwards, Marylebone, London and, where EJM is cited, the document was, at the time of collection, in the possession of that firm.
ELB	Edward Lytton Bulwer
ER	*The English Registry* (followed by year of edition)
FE	Francis Edwards, London
FITZ	Fitzwilliam Museum, Cambridge
Foster	J. Foster *Alumni Oxonienses* (1887, 1888)
Gash *Peel*	Norman Gash *Sir Robert Peel: the Life of Sir Robert Peel after 1830* (1972)
Gash *Politics*	Norman Gash *Politics in the Age of Peel* (1952)
Globe	*The Globe and Traveller*
GM	*The Gentleman's Magazine*
Greville	Lytton Strachey and Roger Fulford eds *The Greville Memoirs, 1814-60* (1938)
H	The Hughenden papers, Bodleian Library, Oxford
Hansard	*Hansard's Parliamentary Debates*
HARV	Harvard University, Cambridge, Massachusetts
Haydon	Benjamin Robert Haydon *Diary* ed Willard Bissel Pope (Cambridge 1960-3)
HCR	Hertfordshire County Record Office, Hertford
HL	Ralph Disraeli ed *Home Letters Written by the Late Earl of Beaconsfield in 1830 and 1831* (1885)
HM	Hughenden Museum, Hughenden Manor, High Wycombe, Buckinghamshire
HUNT	Huntington Library, San Marino, California
IDL	Inverclyde District Libraries, Greenock, Renfrewshire
ILLU	University of Illinois, Urbana-Champaign, Illinois
Isaac	Isaac D'Israeli
Jerman	B.R. Jerman *The Young Disraeli* (Princeton, New Jersey 1960)

JNL	Jewish National and University Library, Jerusalem
JW	John Wilson, Witney, Oxfordshire
KCMG	Knight Commander of the Order of St Michael and St George
Kitson Clark	George Kitson Clark *Peel and the Conservative Party: A Study in Party Politics, 1832-41* (1964)
LAMB	Lambton Estate Office, Durham
Law List	*Clarke's New Law List* compiled by S. Hill and later by T. Cockell (followed by year of edition)
Layard	Sir Austen Henry Layard 'The Early Life of Lord Beaconsfield' *Quarterly Review* Vol 168 (1889) 1-42
LBCS	Ralph Disraeli ed *Lord Beaconsfield's Correspondence with his Sister, 1832-1852* (1886)
LBL	Ralph Disraeli ed *Lord Beaconsfield's Letters, 1830-52* (1887)
LC	Library of Congress, Washington, DC
LGW	Leslie Guttridge-White, Pett, East Sussex
LLD	Doctor of Laws
LPOD	*Post Office London Directory* (followed by year of edition)
Madden	Richard Robert Madden *The Life and Correspondence of the Countess of Blessington* (New York 1855)
M&B	William Flavelle Monypenny and George Earle Buckle *The Life of Benjamin Disraeli, Earl of Beaconsfield* (1910-20) 6 vols
MC	*The Morning Chronicle*
Melville	Lewis Melville *The Life and Letters of William Beckford* (1910)
Meynell	Wilfred Meynell *Benjamin Disraeli: An Unconventional Biography* (1903)
MHS	Massachusetts Historical Society, Boston
MM	Murray Manuscripts, John Murray, London
MNHP	Morristown National Historical Park, Morristown, New Jersey
Morrison	*The Collection of Autograph Letters and Historical Documents formed by Alfred Morrison: The Blessington Papers* (1895)
MP	*The Morning Post*
MR	Murray *Representative* Manuscripts (These archives are divided into two groups: General - MM; papers concerned with the newspaper *The Representative* - MR)
Murray's *Northern*	John Murray *Handbook for the Continent: Being a Guide through Holland, Belgium, Prussia and Northern Germany* (1836)
Navy List	*An alphabetical List of the Flag Officers and other Commissioned Officers of His Majesty's Fleet*

Nickerson	Charles C. Nickerson 'Disraeli, Lockhart and Murray: An Episode in the History of the "Quarterly Review", *Victorian Studies* XV (March 1972) 279-306
NIPR	Public Record Office of Northern Ireland, Belfast
NLS	The National Library of Scotland, Edinburgh
NMM	*The New Monthly Magazine*
NMR	*The New Monthly Review*
NUC	*National Union Catalogue, pre-1956 imprints; a cumulative author list representing Library of Congress printed cards and titles reported by other libraries* (1968–)
NYPL	New York Public Library, New York (Berg MSS, Kohns MSS, Montague MSS)
O'Connor	T.P. O'Connor *Lord Beaconsfield: a Biography* (1879)
Ogden	James Ogden *Isaac D'Israeli* (1969)
Oliver	John Walter Oliver *The Life of William Beckford* (1932)
OSERS	Mary Osers, Sonning Common, Reading, Berkshire
PFRZ	The Carl H. Pforzheimer Library, New York
ph	Publication history section of the headnote
PRIM	Primrose League, London
PRIN	Princeton University, Princeton, New Jersey
PRO	Public Record Office, Chancery Lane, London
PS	Printed Source used when the original MS has not been located
QR	*The Quarterly Review*
QUA	Disraeli papers, Queen's University Archives, Kingston, Ontario
RAY	Collection of Professor Gordon N. Ray, New York
RD	Ralph Disraeli
RN	Royal Navy
Robson's *Directory*	*Robson's Commercial Directory of London and the Western Counties* (1840)
Robson's *Guide*	*Robson's British Court and Parliamentary Guide* (followed by year of edition)
Rogers	Samuel Rogers *The Italian Journal* ed J.R. Hale (1956)
Roth	Cecil Roth *Benjamin Disraeli, Earl of Beaconsfield* (New York 1952)
Sa	Sarah Disraeli
Sadleir *Bulwer*	Michael Sadleir *Bulwer: A Panorama* (1931)
Scott *Letters*	David Douglas ed *Familiar Letters of Sir Walter Scott* (Edinburgh 1894)

SHC	The Shakespeare Birthplace Trust, The Shakespeare Centre, Stratford-on-Avon
Smiles	Samuel Smiles *A Publisher and His Friends: Memoirs and Correspondence of the Late John Murray, with an Account of the Origin and Progress of the House, 1768-1843* (1891)
Stenton	Michael Stenton *Who's Who of British Members of Parliament: Volume I, 1832-85* (Hassocks 1976)
Stewart *Novels*	R.W. Stewart ed *Disraeli's Novels Reviewed, 1826-1968* (Metuchen, New Jersey 1975)
Stewart *Writings*	R.W. Stewart *Benjamin Disraeli: A list of writings by him, and writings about him, with notes* (Metuchen, New Jersey 1972). Citations are for item numbers.
STL	St Lawrence University, Canton, New York
Sultana	Donald Sultana *Benjamin Disraeli in Spain, Malta and Albania, 1830-32* (1976)
Swartz	Helen M. Swartz and Marvin Swartz eds *Disraeli's Reminiscences* (1975)
TCC	Trinity College, Cambridge
TEXU	University of Texas, Austin
UCLA	University of California, Los Angeles
UTT	Mr E. William Uttal, Palm Beach, Florida
Venn	John Venn and John Archibald Venn eds *Alumni Cantabrigienses* (1922-54)
WSRO	West Sussex Record Office, Chichester

CHRONOLOGICAL LIST OF LETTERS

1815-1834

NUMBER LOCATION OF ORIGINAL	DATE REFERENCE NUMBER	TO PLACE OF ORIGIN
1	[1815?]	MARIA D'ISRAELI
H	A/I/C/1	[Potticary's School, Blackheath?]
2	[Friday 2] January 1818	EDWARD JONES
BRST	1	Bloomsbury Square, [London]
3	[August 1820?]	[JOHN MURRAY]
MM	43	[Bloomsbury Square, London?]
4	[Friday] 13 December 1822	[DAWSON TURNER]
TCC	21	Bloomsbury Square, [London]
5	Tuesday [22 July 1823]	THOMAS FREDERICK MAPLES
H	A/II/B/2	[Windsor?]
6	[Tuesday] 12 August [1823]	THOMAS FREDERICK MAPLES
H	A/II/B/3	Windsor
7	[Tuesday] 25 May [1824?]	JOHN MURRAY
MR	2	Frederick's Place, [London]
8	[May 1824]	[JOHN MURRAY]
MR	1	[London]
9	[June 1824]	JOHN MURRAY
MR	3	Frederick's Place, [London]
10	[Thursday 29 July 1824]	SARAH DISRAELI
H	A/IV/B/5	[Bruges]
11	[Monday 2 August 1824]	SARAH DISRAELI
H	A/IV/B/6	[Antwerp]
12	[Friday 6 August 1824]	SARAH DISRAELI
H	A/IV/B/7	[Brussels]

NUMBER LOCATION OF ORIGINAL	DATE REFERENCE NUMBER	TO PLACE OF ORIGIN
13	[Saturday 14 August 1824]	SARAH DISRAELI
H	A/IV/B/8	[Cologne]
14	[Thursday 19 August 1824]	SARAH DISRAELI
H	A/IV/B/9	[Mainz]
15	[Monday 23 August 1824]	SARAH DISRAELI
H	A/IV/B/11	[Heidelberg]
16	Sunday [29 August 1824]	SARAH DISRAELI
H	A/IV/B/12	Coblenz
17	[October 1824?]	JOHN MURRAY
MM	40	Bloomsbury Square, [London]
18	[Monday 31 January 1825]	JOHN MURRAY
MM	21	[London]
19	[March 1825]	JOHN MURRAY
MM	29	[London]
20	[Friday 1 April? 1825]	[JOHN MURRAY]
MM	1	[London]
21	[April 1825?]	[ROBERT MESSER?]
H	R/II/B/9a, b, c	[London]
22	May 1825]	JOHN MURRAY
MR	5	[London]
23	Thursday [May 1825]	JOHN MURRAY
MR	6	[London]
24	Friday [5 August 1825]	ISAAC D'ISRAELI
H	A/I/C/2	[London]
25	[Thursday 18 August 1825]	THOMAS MULLETT EVANS
H	A/V/A/10	Hyde House, Amersham, Buckinghamshire
26	[Saturday 17 September 1825]	[JOHN MURRAY]
MR	8	Royal Hotel, Edinburgh
27	Sunday [18 September 1825]	[JOHN MURRAY]
MR	9	Royal Hotel, Edinburgh
28	Wednesday [21] September [1825]	[JOHN MURRAY]
MR	11	Chiefswood, [Melrose]

NUMBER LOCATION OF ORIGINAL	DATE REFERENCE NUMBER	TO PLACE OF ORIGIN
28A	Tuesday [27 September 1825]	GEORGE BOYD
QUA	418	Chiefswood, Melrose
29	[Friday 27? September 1825]	[JOHN MURRAY]
MR	14	Chiefswood, [Melrose]
30	[Thursday 20 October 1825?]	THOMAS CROFTON CROKER
MHS	Guild Library 1	[London]
31	[Tuesday] 25 October 1825	[Mr MAAS]
PS	32	[London]
32	Wednesday 26 October 1825	JOHN GIBSON LOCKHART
NLS	MS 931 no 118	[London]
33	[October 1825]	JOHN MURRAY
MR	17	[London]
34	[October 1825?]	[WILLIAM WRIGHT?]
QUA	141	[London]
35	Tuesday [1 November 1825]	JOHN GIBSON LOCKHART
NLS	MS 931 no 116	Whitehall Place, [London]
36	Saturday [12? November 1825]	JOHN GIBSON LOCKHART
NLS	MS 931 no 112	[London]
37	[Monday 21 November 1825]	JOHN GIBSON LOCKHART
NLS	MS 931 no 115	[London]
38	Tuesday [22 November 1825]	JOHN GIBSON LOCKHART
NLS	MS 931 no 117	[London]
39	[Wednesday] 23 November 1825	[JOHN MURRAY]
MR	25	Bloomsbury Square, [London]
40	Wednesday 23 November 1825	JOHN GIBSON LOCKHART
NLS	MS 931 no 119	[London]
41	[Thursday 24?] November 1825	JOHN GIBSON LOCKHART
NLS	MS 931 no 114	[London]

NUMBER LOCATION OF ORIGINAL	DATE REFERENCE NUMBER	TO PLACE OF ORIGIN
42	Friday 25 November 1825	JOHN GIBSON LOCKHART
NLS	MS 931 no 120	[London]
43	ay [28 November 1825?]	[ALFRED TURNER]
ILLU	xB B36561 Card 2	[London]
44	Monday [28 November 1825]	JOHN GIBSON LOCKHART
NLS	MS 931 no 113	[London]
45	Wednesday [30 November 1825?]	ALFRED TURNER
ILLU	xB B36561 Card 2	[Bloomsbury Square, London]
46	Thursday [1 December 1825]	[JOHN MURRAY]
MR	39	[London]
47	Saturday [3 December 1825]	ALFRED TURNER
ILLU	xB B36561 Card 2	[Bloomsbury Square, London]
48	Sunday 21 May 1826	[ANNE MURRAY]
MR	62	[Bloomsbury Square, London]
49	[July? 1826]	BENJAMIN AUSTEN
BL	ADD MS 45908 ff10-12	[London]
50	Wednesday 9 August 1826	ISAAC D'ISRAELI
H	A/IV/C/5	Paris
51	[Monday] 21 August 1826	ISAAC D'ISRAELI
H	A/IV/C/7	Geneva
52	[Saturday] 2 September 1826	ISAAC D'ISRAELI
H	A/IV/C/9	Milan
53	Wednesday 13 September 1826	ISAAC D'ISRAELI
H	A/IV/C/11	Venice
54	[Tuesday] 26 September 1826	ISAAC D'ISRAELI
H	A/IV/C/13	Florence
55	Friday] 29 September 1826	ISAAC D'ISRAELI
H	A/IV/C/14	Florence
56	Friday 29 September 1826	ISAAC D'ISRAELI
H	A/IV/C/15	Florence

NUMBER LOCATION OF ORIGINAL	DATE REFERENCE NUMBER	TO PLACE OF ORIGIN
57	[Tuesday] 10 October 1826	ISAAC D'ISRAELI
H	A/IV/C/16	Turin
58	Sunday 15 October 1826	SARAH DISRAELI
H	A/IV/C/18	Lyons
59	[Monday] 1 January 1827	FRANCIS DOUCE
BODL	MS Douce d26 f1	Bloomsbury Square, [London]
60	[Monday 5 March? 1827]	WILLIAM JERDAN
PS	24	[London?]
61	Monday 19 March 1827	JOHN MURRAY
MM	35	6 Bloomsbury Square, [London]
62	[April 1827?]	[ROBERT WARD]
PS	31	[London]
63	Saturday 14 [July] 1827	BENJAMIN AUSTEN
BL	ADD MS 45908 ff13-14	[London]
64	Thursday [3 January 1828]	THOMAS MULLETT EVANS
H	A/V/A/11	[Mayfield Hall?]
65	[Saturday] 8 March 1828	ROBERT FINCH
BODL	MS Finch d5 f132	6 Bloomsbury Square, [London]
66	[Monday] 10 March 1828	[SHARON TURNER]
RAY	1	Bloomsbury Square, [London]
67	[Wednesday] 19 March 1828	THOMAS JOSEPH PETTIGREW
PS	78	6 Bloomsbury Square, [London]
68	Tuesday 15 April 1828	FRANCIS DOUCE
BODL	MS Douce d25 ff53-4	Bloomsbury Square, [London]
69	[Thursday] 5 June 1828	EDWARD LAWFORD
BL	ADD MS 37502 ff38-9	Drapers' Hall, [London]
70	[December 1828?]	MR. DAVISON
BL	ADD MS 37232A f9	[London]
71	[Tuesday 12 May 1829?]	RICHARD BENTLEY
LC	Ac. 8033 [13]	[London]
72	[Monday] 23 November [1829]	BENJAMIN AUSTEN
BL	ADD MS 45908 ff15-16	Bradenham
73	Saturday [28 November 1829?]	BENJAMIN AUSTEN
BL	ADD MS 45908 ff88-9	[Union Hotel, London]

NUMBER LOCATION OF ORIGINAL	DATE REFERENCE NUMBER	TO PLACE OF ORIGIN
74	[Tuesday] 8 December 1829	BENJAMIN AUSTEN
BL	ADD MS 45908 ff17-18	Bradenham
75	[Sunday] 14 February 1830	CATHERINE GORE
TEXU	27	Bradenham
76	Sunday 14 February 1830	HENRY COLBURN
HARV	2	Bradenham
77	[Tuesday] 16 February 1830	BENJAMIN AUSTEN
BL	ADD MS 45908 f19	Bradenham
78	[Sunday] 7 March 1830	SARA AUSTEN
BL	ADD MS 45908 ff21-2	Bradenham
79	[March 1830]	BENJAMIN AUSTEN
BL	ADD MS 45908 ff23-4	[Bradenham]
80	[Monday] 5 April 1830	BENJAMIN AUSTEN
BL	ADD MS 45908 f25	[London]
81	[Tuesday] 13 April 1830	BENJAMIN AUSTEN
BL	ADD MS 45908 ff27-8	Bradenham
82	Sunday 9 May 1830	JOHN MURRAY
MM	22	Union Hotel, Cockspur Street, [London]
83	Sunday [9 May 1830]	[JOHN MURRAY]
MM	16	Union Hotel, [Cockspur Street, London]
84	[Sunday] 9 May 1830	THOMAS MULLETT EVANS
H	A/V/A/12	Union Hotel, Cockspur Street, London
85	[Wednesday] 12 May [1830]	THOMAS MULLETT EVANS
H	A/V/A/13	Union Hotel, [Cockspur Street, London]
86	[Thursday] 27 May 1830	JOHN MURRAY
MM	27	Bradenham
87	[Friday] 28 May 1830	[THOMAS JONES]
BL	ADD MS 59887 f1	[London]
88	[Friday 28? May 1830]	BENJAMIN AUSTEN
BL	ADD MS 45908 ff29-30	[London]
89	[Tuesday] 1 June 1830	SARAH DISRAELI
QUA	201	Royal Hotel, Falmouth, [Cornwall]

NUMBER LOCATION OF ORIGINAL	DATE REFERENCE NUMBER	TO PLACE OF ORIGIN
90	[Thursday] 1 July [1830]	ISAAC D'ISRAELI
QUA	202	Gibraltar
91	[Thursday] 1 July 1830	ISAAC D'ISRAELI
QUA	203	Gibraltar
92	[Wednesday] 14 July 1830	ISAAC D'ISRAELI
QUA	204	Cadiz
93	[Monday] 26 July 1830	ISAAC D'ISRAELI
QUA	205	Seville
94	[Sunday] 1 August 1830	MARIA D'ISRAELI
QUA	216	Granada
95	[Monday] 9 August 1830	SARAH DISRAELI
QUA	206	Gibraltar
96	[Friday] 20 August 1830	GEORGE BARROW
HM	1	Malta
97	[Wednesday] 25 August 1830	ISAAC D'ISRAELI
QUA	207	Malta
98	[Tuesday] 14 September 1830	BENJAMIN AUSTEN
BL	ADD MS 45908 ff31-2	Malta
99	[Friday 17?] September [1830]	[RALPH DISRAELI]
QUA	208	Malta
100	[Sunday] 10 October 1830	ISAAC D'ISRAELI
QUA	209	Corfu
101	[Monday] 25 October 1830	ISAAC D'ISRAELI
QUA	210	Prevesa, [Greece]
102	[Thursday] 18 November 1830	HENRY COLBURN
PRIN	Parrish Collection AM15767	[Nauplia, Greece]
103	[Thursday] 18 November [1830	BENJAMIN AUSTEN
BL	ADD MS 45908 ff33-4	[Nauplia, Greece]
104	[Tuesday] 30 November 1830	ISAAC D'ISRAELI
QUA	211	Athens and Constantinople
105	[Thursday 23? December 1830]	ISAAC D'ISRAELI
QUA	215	[Constantinople]

NUMBER LOCATION OF ORIGINAL	DATE REFERENCE NUMBER	TO PLACE OF ORIGIN
106	[Monday] 27 December 1830	BENJAMIN AUSTEN
BL	ADD MS 45908 ff35-6	Constantinople
107	[Monday] 27 December 1830	EDWARD LYTTON BULWER
HCR	D/EK/C5/1	Constantinople
108	[Sunday 9] January 1831	SARA AUSTEN
BL	ADD MS 45908 ff37-8	Constantinople
109	[Tuesday] 11 January 1831	ISAAC D'ISRAELI
QUA	212	Constantinople
110	[Sunday] 20 March 1831	SARAH DISRAELI
QUA	213	Alexandria
111	[Saturday] 28 May 1831	SARAH DISRAELI
QUA	214	[Cairo, Egypt]
112	[Wednesday] 20 July 1831	ISAAC D'ISRAELI
H	A/IV/E/30	Cairo
113	[Wednesday] 20 July 1831	GEORGIANA MEREDITH
FE	EJM 13	Cairo
114	[Wednesday 20 July 1831]	SARAH DISRAELI
H	A/I/B/1	[Cairo]
115	[Wednesday] 3 August 1831	BENJAMIN AUSTEN
BL	ADD MS 45908 ff39-40	Alexandria, [Egypt]
116	[Wednesday] 7 [September] 1831	ISAAC D'ISRAELI
EGT	1	Quarantine Station, Malta
117	Sunday 23 October 1831	ISAAC D'ISRAELI
H	A/IV/E/32	Falmouth
118	Monday [31 October 1831]	BENJAMIN AUSTEN
BL	ADD MS 45908 ff41-2	Union Hotel, [London]
119	[Thursday] 3 November 1831	GEORGIANA MEREDITH
FE	EJM 6-i	Bradenham
120	[Thursday] 3 November 1831	BENJAMIN AUSTEN
BL	ADD MS 45908 ff43-4	Bradenham

NUMBER LOCATION OF ORIGINAL	DATE REFERENCE NUMBER	TO PLACE OF ORIGIN
121	[Saturday] 5 November 1831	GEORGIANA MEREDITH
FE	EJM 6-ii	Bradenham
122	Friday 11 November [1831]	SARAH DISRAELI
H	A/I/B/2	15 Pall Mall East, [London]
123	Friday [11? November 1831]	SARA AUSTEN
BL	ADD MS 45908 ff48-9	[London]
124	Saturday [12 November 1831]	SARAH DISRAELI
H	A/I/B/3	15 Pall Mall East, [London]
125	Sunday [13 November 1831]	FRANCIS DOUCE
BODL	MS Douce d33 ff185-7	15 Pall Mall East, [London]
126	Monday 14 November 1831	SARAH DISRAELI
H	A/I/B/4	15 Pall Mall East, [London]
127	Tuesday 15 November [1831]	SARAH DISRAELI
H	A/I/B/5	[15] Pall Mall East, [London]
128	Thursday [17 November? 1831]	GEORGIANA MEREDITH
FE	EJM 6-v	[London?]
129	[Thursday] 17 November 1831	BENJAMIN AUSTEN
BL	ADD MS 45908 ff45-6	[London?]
130	[Wednesday] 21 December 1831	UNKNOWN
UTT	1	Bradenham
131	[Thursday] 29 December 1831	GEORGIANA MEREDITH
FE	EJM 6-iii	Bradenham
132	[Friday] 6 January 1832	BENJAMIN AUSTEN
BL	ADD MS 45908 ff50-1	Bradenham
133	[Thursday] 19 January [1832]	BENJAMIN AUSTEN
BL	ADD MS 45908 ff59-60	The Red Lion, High Wycombe
134	[Wednesday] 1 February 1832	ROBERT JOHN SMITH
CARR	1	Bradenham

NUMBER LOCATION OF ORIGINAL	DATE REFERENCE NUMBER	TO PLACE OF ORIGIN
135	[Friday] 10 February 1832	JOHN MURRAY
MM	19	Bradenham
136	[Friday] 10 February 1832	EVELYN MEREDITH
FE	EJM 7	Bradenham
137	Saturday [11 February 1832]	GEORGIANA MEREDITH
FE	EJM 6-iv	Bradenham
138	[Saturday 18 February 1832]	SARAH DISRAELI
H	A/I/B/6	35 Duke Street, St James's, [London]
139	[Saturday 18 February 1832]	JOHN MURRAY
MM	3	35 Duke Street, St James's, [London]
140	[Monday 20 February 1832]	SARAH DISRAELI
H	A/I/B/7	35 Duke Street, St James's, [London]
141	Wednesday [22 February 1832]	SARAH DISRAELI
H	A/I/B/8	35 Duke Street, St James's, [London]
142	Friday [24 February 1832]	SARAH DISRAELI
H	A/I/B/9	35 Duke Street, St James's, [London]
143	Sunday [26 February 1832?]	JOHN MURRAY
MM	8	35 Duke Street, St James's, [London]
144	Monday [27 February 1832]	SARAH DISRAELI
H	A/I/B/10	35 Duke Street, St James's, [London]
145	Thursday [1 March 1832]	JOHN MURRAY
MM	15	35 Duke Street, St James's, [London]
146	Thursday 1 March [1832]	SARAH DISRAELI
H	A/I/B/11	35 Duke Street, St James's, [London]
147	Friday [2? March 1832]	JOHN MURRAY
MM	9	35 Duke Street, St James's, [London]
148	Sunday [4 March 1832]	JOHN MURRAY
MM	34	[London]
149	[Monday 5 March 1832]	JOHN MURRAY
MM	12	35 Duke Street, St James's, [London]

NUMBER LOCATION OF ORIGINAL	DATE REFERENCE NUMBER	TO PLACE OF ORIGIN
150	[Monday] 5 March [1832]	SARAH DISRAELI
H	A/I/B/12	[35] Duke Street, [St James's, London]
151	[Wednesday 7 March 1832]	SARAH DISRAELI
H	A/I/B/13	[London]
152	Friday [9 March 1832]	SARAH DISRAELI
H	A/I/B/14	[London]
153	Friday [9 March 1832]	JOHN MURRAY JR
MM	28	[London]
154	[Saturday 10? March 1832]	[JOHN MURRAY]
MM	10	[London]
155	Monday [19 March? 1832]	BENJAMIN AUSTEN
BL	ADD MS 45908 ff52-4	[London]
156	Monday [19? March 1832]	[JOHN MURRAY]
MM	2	Bradenham
157	Friday [23? March 1832]	JOHN MURRAY
MM	11	[London]
158	Monday [26? March 1832]	[JOHN MURRAY]
MM	13	[London]
159	Monday [26 March 1832]	SARAH DISRAELI
H	A/I/B/28	[35 Duke Street, St James's, London]
160	[Wednesday 28 March 1832]	SARAH DISRAELI
H	A/I/B/16	Pay Office, [Whitehall, London]
161	Friday [30 March 1832]	[JOHN MURRAY]
MM	36	[35] Duke Street, [St James's, London]
162	[Friday 30 March 1832]	[JOHN MURRAY]
MM	37	[35 Duke Street, St James's, London]
163	[Friday 30? March 1832]	JOHN MURRAY
MM	14	[35 Duke Street, St James's, London]
164	Saturday [31 March 1832?]	JOHN MURRAY JR
MM	33	[London]
165	[Saturday 31 March 1832]	SARAH DISRAELI
H	A/I/B/15	[London]

NUMBER / LOCATION OF ORIGINAL	DATE / REFERENCE NUMBER	TO / PLACE OF ORIGIN
166	[Sunday 1 April? 1832]	[JOHN MURRAY]
MM	5	[London]
167	[Sunday 1 April? 1832]	[JOHN WILSON CROKER]
PS	79	[London]
168	Monday [2 April 1832]	JOHN MURRAY
MM	4	[35 Duke Street, St James's, London]
169	Monday 2 April 1832	SARAH DISRAELI
H	A/I/B/19	[London]
170	[Wednesday 4 April? 1832]	JOHN MURRAY JR
MM	44	[35 Duke Street, St James's, London]
171	Thursday [5?] April [1832]	[JOHN MURRAY]
MM	38	[35 Duke Street, St James's, London]
172	Friday [6? April 1832]	MARY ANNE LEWIS
H	A/I/A/1	[London]
173	[Saturday 7 April 1832]	SARAH DISRAELI
H	A/I/B/20	[London]
174	[Tuesday 10 April 1832]	SARAH DISRAELI
H	A/I/B/21	[35 Duke Street, St James's, London]
175	[Wednesday 11 April? 1832]	JOHN MURRAY JR
MM	41	[35 Duke Street, St James's, London]
176	[Thursday 12 April 1832]	JOHN MURRAY JR
MM	42	[35 Duke Street, St James's, London]
177	[Thursday] 12 April 1832	JOHN MURRAY JR
MM	32	[35 Duke Street, St James's, London]
178	Thursday [12 April 1832]	SARAH DISRAELI
H	A/I/B/22	[35 Duke Street, St James's, London]
179	Saturday 14 April [1832]	SARAH DISRAELI
H	A/I/B/23	[35 Duke Street, St James's, London]
180	[Monday 16? April 1832]	JOHN MURRAY JR
MM	30	[35 Duke Street, St James's, London]
181	[Monday 16? April 1832]	JOHN MURRAY JR
MM	6	[35 Duke Street, St James's, London]
182	Tuesday [17 April 1832]	SARAH DISRAELI
H	A/I/B/24	[35 Duke Street, St James's, London]
183	Friday [20 April 1832]	SARAH DISRAELI
H	A/I/B/25	[35 Duke Street, St James's, London]

NUMBER LOCATION OF ORIGINAL	DATE REFERENCE NUMBER	TO PLACE OF ORIGIN
184	Saturday [28 April? 1832]	SARA AUSTEN
BL	ADD MS 45908 ff148-9	Bradenham
185	Thursday [3? May 1832]	SARA AUSTEN
BL	ADD MS 45908 ff146-7	[35 Duke Street, St James's, London]
186	Sunday 6 May [1832]	JOHN MURRAY
MM	39	Bradenham
187	Wednesday [9 May 1832]	SARAH DISRAELI
H	A/I/B/26	[London]
188	Saturday [12 May 1832]	SARAH DISRAELI
H	A/I/B/27	[35] Duke Street, [St James's, London]
189	Tuesday [15 May 1832]	SARAH DISRAELI
H	A/I/B/29	[London]
190	[Friday] 18 May [1832]	SARAH DISRAELI
H	A/I/B/30	[35] Duke Street, St James's, [London]
191	Monday [21 May 1832]	SARAH DISRAELI
H	A/I/B/31	35 Duke Street, St James's, [London]
192	Thursday 24 May [1832]	SARAH DISRAELI
H	A/I/B/32	[London]
193	Saturday [26 May 1832]	SARAH DISRAELI
H	A/I/B/33	[London]
194	Monday [28 May 1832]	SARAH DISRAELI
H	A/I/B/44	[London]
195	Tuesday [29 May 1832]	SARAH DISRAELI
H	A/I/B/17	[35 Duke Street, St James's, London]
196	[Wednesday 30 May 1832]	SARAH DISRAELI
H	A/I/B/18	[35 Duke Street, St James's, London]
197	[Friday] 1 June [1832]	SARAH DISRAELI
H	A/I/B/34	[35] Duke Street, St James's, [London]
198	Saturday [2? June 1832]	BENJAMIN AUSTEN
BL	ADD MS 45908 ff55-6	[London]
199	[Monday] 4 June [1832]	JAMES GEORGE TATEM
OSER	1	Red Lion, Wycombe
200	Tuesday 5 June 1832	JOSEPH HUME
PS	30	Bradenham

NUMBER LOCATION OF ORIGINAL	DATE REFERENCE NUMBER	TO PLACE OF ORIGIN
201	Sunday [10 June 1832]	SARA AUSTEN
BL	ADD MS 45908 ff57-8	[Bradenham]
202	[Friday 22 June 1832]	[HENRY GWILLIM]
PS	47	Bradenham
203	[Wednesday] 27 June 1832	THE FREE AND INDEPENDENT ELECTORS OF WYCOMBE
H	B/I/A/16	Bradenham
204	[Thursday] 5 July [1832]	JOHN MURRAY
MM	31	[35] Duke Street, [St James's, London]
205	[Thursday 5 July 1832]	SARAH DISRAELI
H	A/I/B/35	[London]
206	Wednesday [18 July 1832]	SARAH DISRAELI
H	A/I/B/36	[London]
207	Saturday [21 July 1832]	SARAH DISRAELI
H	A/I/B/37	[London]
208	Friday [27 July 1832]	SARAH DISRAELI
H	A/I/B/38	[London]
209	Saturday [4 August 1832]	SARAH DISRAELI
H	A/I/B/40	[London]
210	Tuesday [7 August 1832]	SARAH DISRAELI
H	A/I/B/41	[35] Duke Street, [St James's, London]
211	Wednesday [8 August 1832]	SARAH DISRAELI
H	A/I/B/39	[London]
212	Friday [24 August 1832]	SARAH DISRAELI
H	A/I/B/42	[35] Duke Street, St James's, [London]
213	Friday [24 August? 1832]	SAMUEL CARTER HALL
NYPL	Montague 7	[35] Duke Street, St James's, [London]
214	Sunday [23 September? 1832]	SAMUEL CARTER HALL
JW	1	Bradenham
215	[Monday] 1 October 1832	THE INDEPENDENT ELECTORS OF THE BOROUGH OF CHEPPING WYCOMBE
PS	Times	Bradenham
216	[Saturday] 6 October [1832]	BENJAMIN AUSTEN
BL	ADD MS 45908 ff61-2	Bradenham

NUMBER LOCATION OF ORIGINAL	DATE REFERENCE NUMBER	TO PLACE OF ORIGIN
217	Wednesday 24 October [1832]	THOMAS MULLETT EVANS
H	A/V/A/14	Bradenham
218	Saturday [3? November 1832]	BENJAMIN AUSTEN
BL	ADD MS 45908 ff63-5	Bradenham
219	[Sunday] 11 November [1832]	THE EDITOR OF THE TIMES
PS	Times 2	Bradenham
220	Friday [23 November 1832?]	BENJAMIN AUSTEN
BL	ADD MS 45908 f173	[London]
221	[Wednesday] 12 December 1832	THE ELECTORS OF THE COUNTY OF BUCKS
H	B/I/A/23	Bradenham
222	[Thursday] 13 December [1832]	THE ELECTORS OF THE COUNTY OF BUCKS
PS	72	Aylesbury
223	[Monday] 17 December 1832	THE INDEPENDENT ELECTORS OF WYCOMBE
PS	48	Bradenham
224	[Saturday 22? December 1832]	[JOHN GIBSON LOCKHART]
H	B/XXI/L/243	[Bradenham?]
225	[Wednesday] 26 December [1832]	THE EDITOR OF THE TIMES
PS	Times 3	Bradenham
226	Sunday [30 December 1832?]	JOHN MURRAY
MM	7	[Bradenham?]
227	Tuesday [1? January 1833]	[JOHN GIBSON LOCKHART]
H	B/XXI/L/245	[Bradenham?]
228	Saturday [12 January 1833]	SARAH DISRAELI
H	A/I/B/45	[35] Duke Street, St James's, [London]
229	Friday [18 January 1833]	SARAH DISRAELI
FE	EJM 1	Bath

NUMBER LOCATION OF ORIGINAL	DATE REFERENCE NUMBER	TO PLACE OF ORIGIN
230	Thursday [24 January 1833]	[SARAH DISRAELI]
PS	35	Bath
231	Tuesday [29 January 1833]	SARAH DISRAELI
FITZ	Sarah 1	[London]
232	Thursday [31 January 1833]	SARAH DISRAELI
H	A/I/B/47	[London]
233	[Thursday 7 February 1833]	[SARAH DISRAELI]
PS	1	[London]
234	Thursday [14 February 1833]	SARAH DISRAELI
MNHP	1	[35] Duke Street, St James's, [London]
235	Saturday [16 February? 1833]	HELEN SELINA BLACKWOOD
NIPR	D1071B/E3/9B [2]	35 Duke Street, St James's, [London]
236	Wednesday [20 February? 1833]	CAROLINE HENRIETTA SHERIDAN
NIPR	MIC22R54:6	35 Duke Street, St James's, [London]
237	[Thursday 21 February? 1833]	[HELEN SELINA BLACKWOOD]
NIPR	D1071B/E3/9B/5	[London?]
238	[Friday 22 February 1833]	SARAH DISRAELI
PS	37	[London]
239	[Saturday] 23 February 1833	MACVEY NAPIER
BL	ADD MS 34616 ff45-6	35 Duke Street, St James's, [London]
240	Saturday [23 February? 1833]	[HELEN SELINA BLACKWOOD]
NIPR	D1071B/E3/9B:9	[London]
241	Monday [25 February? 1833]	BENJAMIN AUSTEN
BL	ADD MS 45908 ff66-7	[London]
242	[Saturday] 2 March [1833]	SARAH DISRAELI
FITZ	Sarah 2	[London]
243	Wednesday [6 March 1833]	SARAH DISRAELI
FITZ	Sarah 3	[London]

NUMBER LOCATION OF ORIGINAL	DATE REFERENCE NUMBER	TO PLACE OF ORIGIN
244	Thursday [7 March? 1833]	[HELEN SELINA BLACKWOOD]
NIPR	D1071B/E3/9B:13	[London]
245	[Thursday 7 March? 1833]	[HELEN SELINA BLACKWOOD]
NIPR	D1071B/E3/9B:14	[London]
246	Thursday [7 March? 1833]	CAROLINE HENRIETTA SHERIDAN
NIPR	D1071B/E3/9A:18	[London]
247	[Saturday 9 March? 1833]	[CAROLINE HENRIETTA SHERIDAN]
NIPR	D1071B/E3/9A:20	[London]
248	[Saturday] 9 March [1833]	THE ELECTORS OF THE BOROUGH OF MARYLEBONE
PS	Times 12	[London]
249	Sunday [10 March 1833]	[HELEN SELINA BLACKWOOD]
NIPR	D1071B/E3/9B:17	[London]
250	Tuesday 12 March [1833]	THE ELECTORS OF THE BOROUGH OF MARYLEBONE
PS	Times 13	[35] Duke Street, St James's, [London]
251	Thursday 14 March [1833]	SARAH DISRAELI
H	A/I/B/48	[London]
252	[Friday] 15 March 1833	MACVEY NAPIER
BL	ADD MS 34616 ff53-4	[London]
253	Saturday [16? March 1833]	SARA AUSTEN
BL	ADD MS 45908 ff68-9	[London]
254	Monday [18] March 1833	GEORGE HENRY DASHWOOD
H	B/I/A/39/1	35 Duke Street, St James's, [London]
255	Monday [18? March 1833]	[HELEN SELINA BLACKWOOD]
NIPR	D1071B/E3/9B:23	
256	Tuesday 19 March 1833	GEORGE HENRY DASHWOOD
H	B/I/A/39/3	35 Duke Street, St James's, [London]
257	[Tuesday 26 March 1833]	SARAH DISRAELI
PS	3	[London]
258	Thursday [28 March 1833]	SARAH DISRAELI
H	A/I/B/50	Albion Club, [London]

NUMBER LOCATION OF ORIGINAL	DATE REFERENCE NUMBER	TO PLACE OF ORIGIN
259	[March 1833?]	SARAH DISRAELI
PS	40	[London]
260	Thursday [4 April 1833]	SARAH DISRAELI
H	A/I/B/51	40 Brook Street, [London]
261	Saturday [6 April 1833]	SARAH DISRAELI
H	A/I/B/52	[London]
262	Monday [8 April 1833]	SARAH DISRAELI
H	A/I/B/54	[London]
263	[Tuesday] 9 April 1833	THE INDEPENDENT ELECTORS OF THE BOROUGH OF MARYLEBONE
FE	EJM 2	[London]
264	Sunday [14 April? 1833]	SARAH DISRAELI
H	A/I/B/53	[London]
265	Wednesday [17 April? 1833]	[HELEN SELINA BLACKWOOD]
NIPR	D1071B/E3/9B:27	35 Duke Street, St James's, [London]
266	[Sunday 21 April 1833?]	CHARLES MATHEWS
PS	56	[London?]
267	Tuesday [23 April 1833]	SARAH DISRAELI
H	A/I/B/55	Albion [Club, London]
268	Thursday [25 April 1833]	SARAH DISRAELI
H	A/I/B/56	Albion [Club, London]
269	Tuesday 30 April [1833]	SARAH DISRAELI
H	A/I/B/57	[London]
270	[April 1833]	SARAH DISRAELI
PS	38	[London]
271	Monday [13 May 1833]	SARAH DISRAELI
H	A/I/B/58	[London]
272	[Monday 13 May 1833]	HELEN SELINA BLACKWOOD
NIPR	D1071B/E3/9B:33	[London]
273	Wednesday [22 May 1833]	SARAH DISRAELI
TEXU	[25]	[London]
274	Wednesday [22 May 1833]	SARAH DISRAELI
H	A/I/B/49	[London]
275	Monday [3 June 1833]	SARAH DISRAELI
H	A/I/B/59	[London]
276	Wednesday [5 June 1833]	SARAH DISRAELI
H	A/I/B/60	[London]

NUMBER LOCATION OF ORIGINAL	DATE REFERENCE NUMBER	TO PLACE OF ORIGIN
277	Friday [7 June 1833]	SARAH DISRAELI
H	A/I/B/61	[London]
278	Monday [17 June 1833]	SARAH DISRAELI
H	A/I/B/62	[London]
279	[Wednesday 19 June 1833]	SARAH DISRAELI
H	A/I/B/63	Cocoa Tree [Club, London]
280	[Thursday 20 June 1833?]	MESSRS RIVINGTON
UCLA	D100 Box 42	35 Duke Street, St James's, [London]
281	Sunday [23 June 1833]	SARAH DISRAELI
H	A/I/B/64	[London]
282	Monday [24 June 1833]	BENJAMIN AUSTEN
BL	ADD MS 45908 ff70-2	35 Duke Street, St James's, [London]
283	Saturday [29 June 1833]	SARAH DISRAELI
H	A/I/B/65	[London]
284	Saturday [6 July 1833]	SARAH DISRAELI
H	A/I/B/66	[London]
285	[Saturday 20 July 1833?]	[SARAH DISRAELI]
PS	4	[London]
286	[Friday 26 July 1833]	SARAH DISRAELI
PS	39	[London]
287	Wednesday [7 August 1833]	SARAH DISRAELI
H	A/I/B/68	[London]
288	[Saturday 10 August 1833]	SARAH DISRAELI
H	A/I/B/67	[London]
289	[September? 1833]	[WYNDHAM LEWIS]
H	A/I/A/407	[London]
290	Tuesday [12 November 1833]	SARAH DISRAELI
H	A/I/B/69	[The Grange, Southend, Essex]
291	Friday [15 November 1833]	SARAH DISRAELI
H	A/I/B/70	The Grange, Southend, Essex
292	Wednesday [20 November 1833]	SARAH DISRAELI
H	A/I/B/43	Southend, [Essex]

NUMBER LOCATION OF ORIGINAL	DATE REFERENCE NUMBER	TO PLACE OF ORIGIN
293	Friday [22 November 1833]	SARAH DISRAELI
H	A/I/B/71	The Grange, Southend, Essex
294	[Monday 25? November 1833]	BENJAMIN AUSTEN
BL	ADD MS 45908 ff176-7	[London?]
295	Tuesday [26 November 1833]	SARAH DISRAELI
H	A/I/B/72	[London]
296	Saturday [30 November 1833]	BENJAMIN AUSTEN
BL	ADD MS 45908 ff73-5	Bradenham
297	Sunday [1 December 1833]	SARA AUSTEN
BL	ADD MS 45908 ff77-8	Bradenham
298	Tuesday [3 December 1833]	BENJAMIN AUSTEN
BL	ADD MS 45908 ff79-81	Bradenham
299	[Saturday] 7 December [1833]	BENJAMIN AUSTEN
BL	ADD MS 45908 ff84-5	Bradenham
300	[Tuesday 31? December 1833]	RICHARD BENTLEY
LC	Ac. 8033	[London]
301	Wednesday [1 January 1834?]	BENJAMIN AUSTEN
BL	ADD MS 45908 ff86-7	[London]
302	Sunday [5 January 1834]	SARAH DISRAELI
FITZ	Sarah 4	[Southend, Essex]
303	[Monday] 13 January [1834]	BENJAMIN AUSTEN and SARA AUSTEN
BL	ADD MS 45908 ff90-1	Southend, [Essex]
304	[Tuesday 14 January 1834]	SARAH DISRAELI
PS	59	[Southend?]
305	[Saturday] 25 January 1834	SARAH DISRAELI
PS	76	[The Grange, Southend, Essex]
306	Wednesday [29 January 1834]	SARAH DISRAELI
FITZ	Sarah 5	[Southend, Essex]

NUMBER LOCATION OF ORIGINAL	DATE REFERENCE NUMBER	TO PLACE OF ORIGIN
307	Thursday [13 February 1834]	SARAH DISRAELI
BEA	201	The Grange, [Southend, Essex]
308	[Monday 17? February 1834]	[SARAH DISRAELI]
PS	49	Southend, [Essex]
309	Friday [21 February 1834]	SARAH DISRAELI
H	A/I/B/46	[Southend, Essex]
310	Monday [24 February? 1834]	EDWARD MOXON
HUNT	HM20305-(34)	Osborns Hotel, Adelphi, London
311	[Monday 3 March 1834]	SARAH DISRAELI
PS	50	[Southend, Essex]
312	[Monday] 3 March 1834	THE DUKE OF WELLINGTON
APSY	1	[Southend, Essex]
313	Friday [7 March 1834]	SARAH DISRAELI
H	A/I/B/73	Harwich, [Essex]
314	Tuesday [11 March 1834]	SARAH DISRAELI
H	A/I/B/74	[Park Street, London]
315	[Sunday] 16 March 1834	ALBANY FONBLANQUE
PS	23	Bradenham
316	Sunday [23 March 1834]	BENJAMIN AUSTEN
BL	ADD MS 45908 ff94-5	Bradenham
317	Sunday [23 March 1834]	ALBANY FONBLANQUE
BENT	1	Bradenham
318	Wednesday [9 April 1834]	SARAH DISRAELI
HUNT	RB 32006 vol2 app99	[London]
319	Saturday [24 May? 1834]	BENJAMIN AUSTEN
BL	ADD MS 45908 ff96-7	[31a Park Street, Grosvenor Square, London]
320	[Monday 26 May 1834?]	BENJAMIN AUSTEN
BL	ADD MS 45908 f92	31a Park Street, Grosvenor Square, [London]
321	[Wednesday 28 May? 1834]	BENJAMIN AUSTEN
BL	ADD MS 45908 f93	[31a Park Street, Grosvenor Square, London]
321A	Wednesday [28 May? 1834]	SARA AUSTEN
STL	1	[31a Park Street, Grosvenor Square, London]

NUMBER / LOCATION OF ORIGINAL	DATE / REFERENCE NUMBER	TO / PLACE OF ORIGIN
322	Wednesday [28 May 1834]	SARAH DISRAELI
H	A/I/B/79	[31a Park Street, Grosvenor Square, London]
323	[Monday 2 June 1834]	SARAH DISRAELI
H	A/I/B/75	[London]
324	Wednesday [4 June 1834]	SARAH DISRAELI
H	A/I/B/76	[London]
325	Saturday [7 June 1834]	SARAH DISRAELI
H	A/I/B/77	[London]
326	Monday [9 June 1834]	SARAH DISRAELI
TEXU	[22]	[London]
327	[Friday 13 June? 1834]	WILLIAM BECKFORD
BECK	19	31a Park Street, [Grosvenor Square, London]
328	Saturday [14? June 1834]	LADY BLESSINGTON
PFRZ	Misc Ms. 900	31a Park Street, [Grosvenor Square, London]
329	Monday [16 June 1834]	SARAH DISRAELI
H	A/I/B/78	[London]
330	[Monday 16 June 1834?]	[WILLIAM BECKFORD?]
HARV	4	31a Park Street, Grosvenor Square, [London]
331	[Thursday 19 June 1834]	SARAH DISRAELI
BEA	202	[London]
332	[Monday 23 June 1834]	MARIA D'ISRAELI and SARAH DISRAELI
FITZ	Sarah 6	47 Gower Street, London
333	[June 1834?]	HENRY COLBURN
PS	52	[Bradenham?]
334	Wednesday [2 July? 1834]	LADY BLESSINGTON
PRIN	Parrish AM 19732	[London]
335	[Thursday 3 July 1834]	WILLIAM BECKFORD
BECK	3	[London]
336	Friday [4 July 1834]	SARAH DISRAELI
H	A/I/B/80	[London]
337	Monday [7 July 1834]	SARAH DISRAELI
BEA	203	[34 Grosvenor Street, London]

NUMBER LOCATION OF ORIGINAL	DATE REFERENCE NUMBER	TO PLACE OF ORIGIN
338	[Friday 11? July 1834]	[SARAH DISRAELI]
PS	5	[London]
339	[Wednesday 16 July 1834]	SARAH DISRAELI
FITZ	Sarah 7	[London]
340	Wednesday [23 July 1834]	SARAH DISRAELI
H	A/I/B/81	[London]
341	[Saturday 26? July 1834]	[SARAH DISRAELI]
PS	75	[London]
342	[Tuesday 29 July? 1834]	LADY BLESSINGTON
NYPL	Kohns 35	[London?]
343	[Friday] 1 August 1834	[SARAH DISRAELI]
PS	80	[London]
344	[Saturday 2 August? 1834]	LADY BLESSINGTON
PFRZ	Misc Ms. 913	[London?]
345	[Tuesday 5 August 1834]	LADY BLESSINGTON
PFRZ	Misc Ms. 890	Bradenham
346	Friday 15 August [1834]	LADY BLESSINGTON
PS	73	Bradenham
347	Tuesday [2 September? 1834]	LADY BLESSINGTON
PFRZ	Misc Ms. 895	Bradenham
348	Wednesday [3 September? 1834]	LADY BLESSINGTON
PFRZ	Misc Ms. 907	[Bradenham]
349	[Tuesday] 7 October [1834]	BENJAMIN AUSTEN
BL	ADD MS 45908 ff98-9	Bradenham
350	Friday [17 October 1834]	LADY BLESSINGTON
PFRZ	Misc Ms. 891	Bradenham
351	[Friday] 24 October 1834	BENJAMIN AUSTEN
BL	ADD MS 45908 ff100-1	Bradenham
352	[Tuesday 4 November? 1834]	[SARAH DISRAELI]
PS	6	[London]
353	Monday 17 November [1834]	LORD DURHAM
LAMB	1	[London?]

NUMBER / LOCATION OF ORIGINAL	DATE / REFERENCE NUMBER	TO / PLACE OF ORIGIN
354	Monday [24 November 1834]	SARAH DISRAELI
H	A/I/B/82	[London]
355	Saturday [29 November 1834]	SARAH DISRAELI
NYPL	Kohns 19	[London]
356	Thursday [4 December 1834]	[LORD LYNDHURST]
PRIM	1	31a Park Street, Grosvenor Square, [London]
357	Monday [8 December 1834]	SARAH DISRAELI
H	A/I/B/83	[London]
358	Thursday [11 December 1834]	SARAH DISRAELI
PRIN	Parrish AM 17270	[London]
359	Monday [22 December 1834]	MARIA D'ISRAELI
H	A/I/C/8	[London]
360	Tuesday [30? December 1834]	BENJAMIN AUSTEN
BL	ADD MS 45908 ff102-3	31a Park Street, Grosvenor Square, [London]
361	Tuesday [30? December 1834]	LORD DURHAM
LAMB	2	31a Park Street, Grosvenor Square, [London]

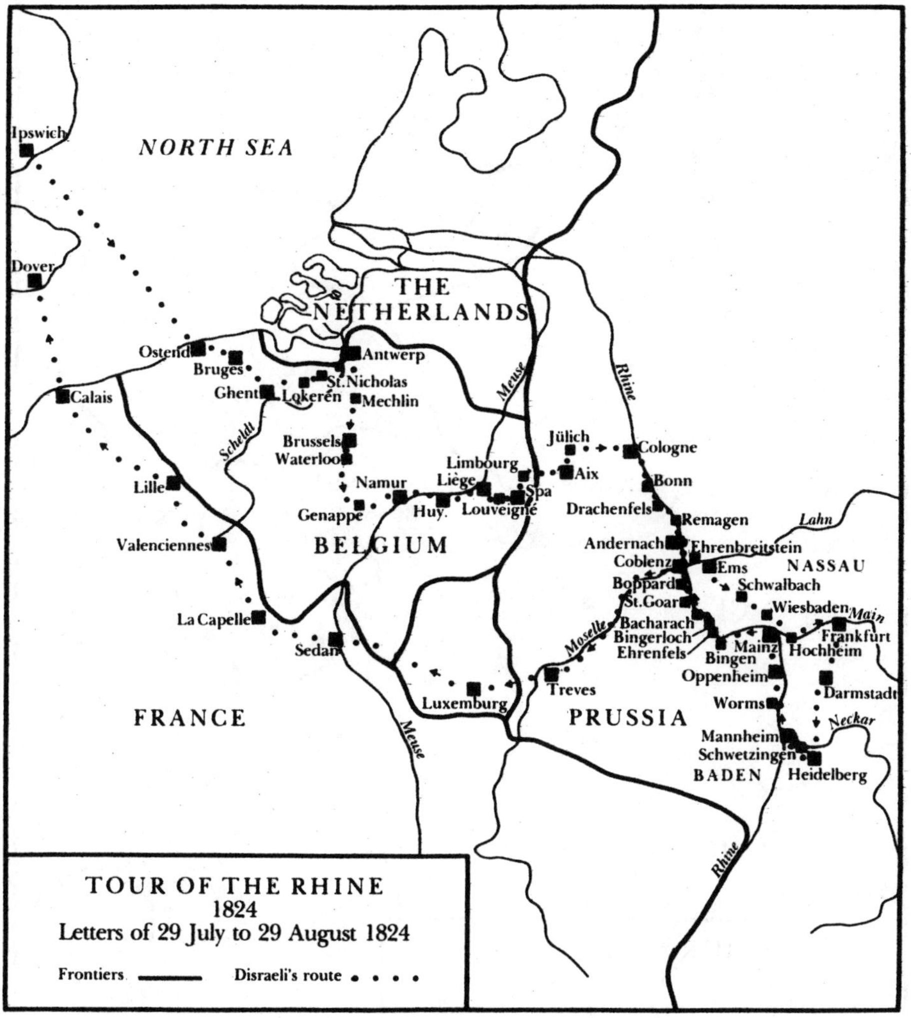

Journey to the Rhine, July-September 1824
Letters 10-16

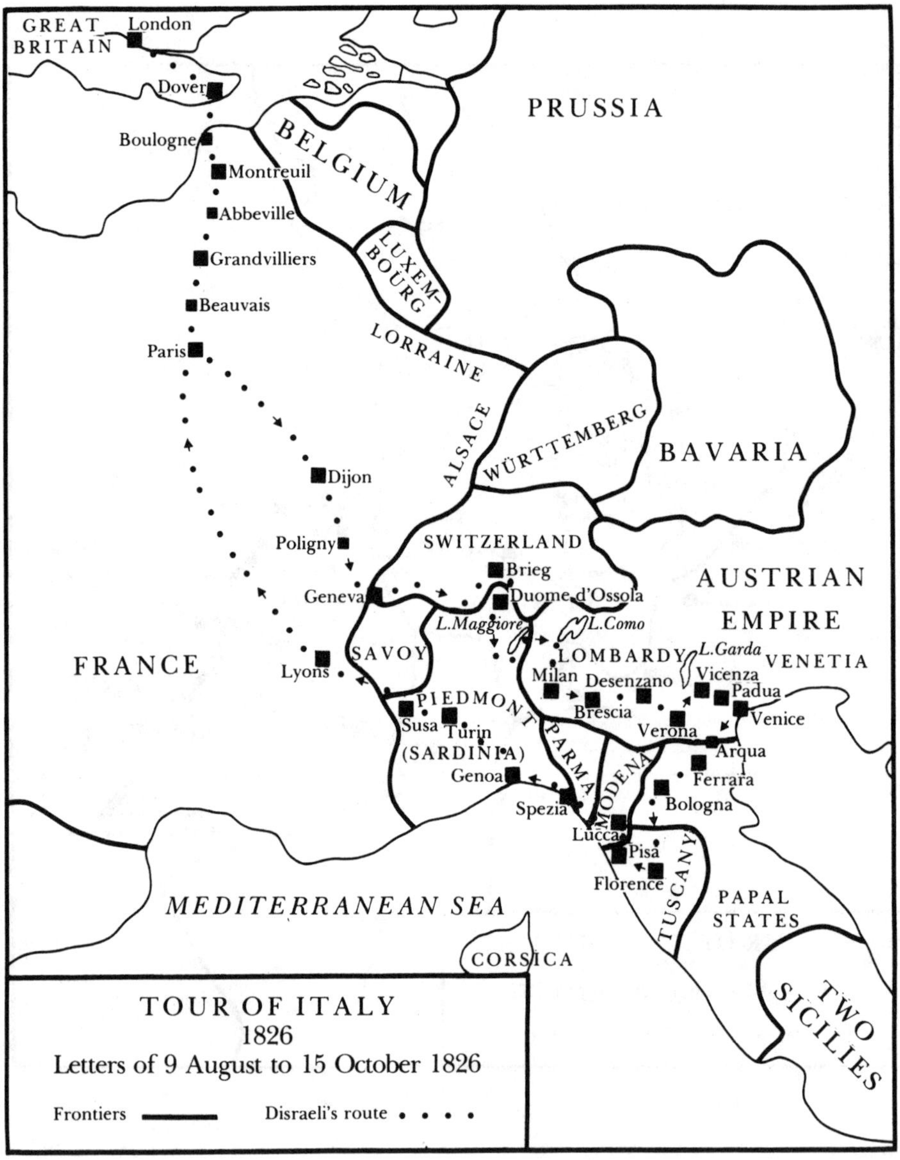

Journey to the Alps and Italy, August-October 1826
Letters 50-8

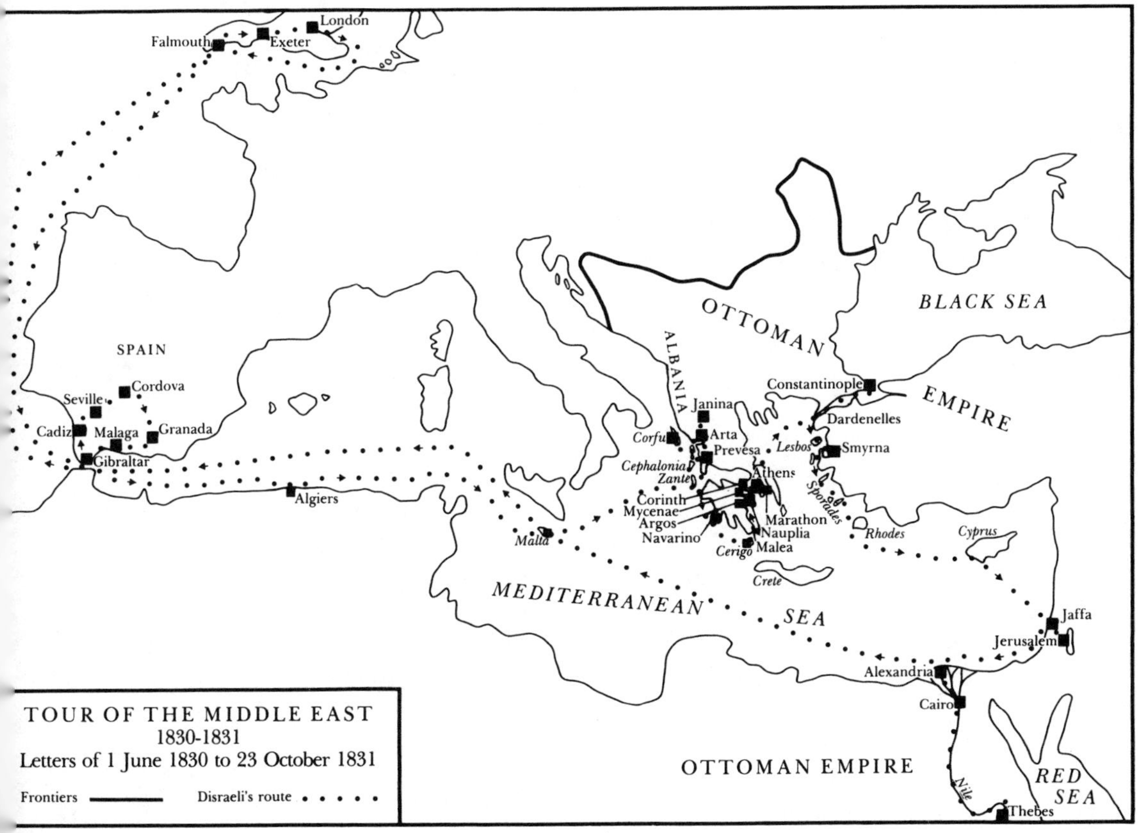

Journey to the Middle East, June 1830 to October 1831
Letters 89-117

BENJAMIN DISRAELI LETTERS: 1815-1834

TO MARIA D'ISRAELI [Potticary's School, Blackheath?, 1815?] 1

ORIGINAL: H A/I/C/1

PUBLICATION HISTORY: M&B I 21, undated

EDITORIAL COMMENT: As Monypenny observes (I 21), this letter owes its preservation to Isaac's use of the reverse for his own notes. Both the dating and the place of origin are purely conjectural.

The spelling of the name of the independent minister who conducted the Blackheath school which D attended has also been subject to variation. Monypenny (in the text and index of vol I) and Blake refer to Potticany, while Buckle (in the cumulative index in vol VI), Meynell and others speak of Potticary. There is a note from Isaac (H A/II/C/2) clearly written 'Potticary' and that is the spelling we have adopted. There is also uncertainty about the dates of D's attendance. Meynell (I 7) firmly states that he was there between 1813 and 1817. *Sic*: D Israeli.

Dear Maman,[1]
I have arrived safe
B D Israeli

TO EDWARD JONES Bloomsbury Square, [London], [Friday 2] January 1818 2

ORIGINAL: BRST 1

EDITORIAL COMMENT: A copy, endorsed: 'B Disraelis letter'. *Sic*: Albermale, Your's.

Bloomsbury Square | Jany 2nd | 1818

Dear Jones,[1]
Will you and your Brother and Sister favour me with your company at tea to-morrow evening. We trust that your Papa and Mamma will allow Fanny to come to us, it is quite a young party, we expect the little Miss Murrays[2] from Albermale Street. I hope you will have no objection to come among such young | people, but I am in hopes that you will have no dislike to come and see me and keep me company amongst them. We hope we shall be fortunate in finding you disengaged. Pray favour us early, 5 o'clock, and believe me, dear Jones
Your's truly
Benjamin D'Israeli
Pray request of your Mamma in all our names to allow Fanny to visit us tomorrow we are all so anxious to see her.

1 Maria D'Israeli (1775-1847), daughter of Naphtali Basevi (1738-1808), a London merchant, and Ricca Basevi, née Rieti (d 1798). She married Isaac D'Israeli in 1802. For D's often ambivalent attitude to his mother see Blake 15-16.

---

1 Edward Jones (1805-1892), admitted to Corpus Christi 18 November 1823; matriculated Michaelmas 1824; BA 1828, MA 1831. He was ordained deacon of Winchester in 1834, and appointed curate of Colmer, Hants, in 1834-5. From 1839 to 1880 he served as vicar of West Peckham, Kent. Venn part ii III. According to Meynell (I 2-3), Edward Jones was a schoolfellow of D's at Potticary's School, Blackheath, and was the son of the surgeon who attended at the birth of D's sister Sarah. Writing to *The Standard* (28 Apr 1887), he recalled his early acquaintance with D and indicated that they had still been in contact in the late 1830s.

2 Christina Jane (1811-1877) and Hester Anne (1813-1890), daughters of John Murray of 50 Albemarle Street.

3 TO [JOHN MURRAY] [Bloomsbury Square, London?, August 1820?]

ORIGINAL: MM 43

COVER: BD | J Murray Esq | Albemarle St.

PUBLICATION HISTORY: Smiles II 108, dated August 1822

EDITORIAL COMMENT: This letter is undated, although Smiles dates it as 'August 1822' and uses it as an example of Murray's confidence in D's abilities which was 'so firm that he consulted him as to the merits of a MS when D had scarcely reached his eighteenth year.' Yet this MS, Charles Edward Walker's play *Wallace*, was published in 1820 (by Oxberry) and presented on the stage at Covent Garden 14 November 1820 with Macready in the title role. Smiles II 107-8. In another hand at the head of the first page of the MS appears: 'MSS Rec | B. D'Israeli | in packet for | Aug 1820.' The sense of the letter would suggest Murray was indeed consulting D for his opinion on whether the play should be published, but before it had appeared either in print or on the stage. This would mean Murray's confidence was indeed extraordinary, for D would then not have reached his sixteenth birthday – an implication which perhaps Smiles could not accept.

Dear Sir,[1]

I ran my eye over 3 acts of Wallace, and as far as I could form an opinion I cannot conceive these acts to be as effective on the stage as you seemed to expect – however it is impossible to say what a very clever actor like Macready[2] may make | of some passages. Notwithstanding the many erasures the diction is still diffuse, and sometimes languishing, tho not inelegant. I cannot imagine it a powerful work as far as I have read – but indeed running over a part of a thing with people talking around is too unfair. I shall be anxious to hear how it succeeds.

Many thanks, dear | Sir, for sending it to me. Your note arrives. If on so slight a knowledge of the play I could venture to erase either of the words you set before me I fear it would be *yes* – but I feel cruel and wicked in saying so. I hope you got your dinner in comfort when you got rid of me and that gentle Pyramid.[3]

Yrs truly

BD

1 John Murray (1778-1843), the second of the famous publishing family of that name. He started *The Quarterly Review* in 1809, and upon moving to Albemarle Street in 1812 he became acquainted with Byron, whose works he published. He was a good friend of D's father, Isaac.

2 William Charles Macready (1793-1873), the well-known actor.

3 Smiles (II 108) identifies him as Giovanni Battista Belzoni (1778-1823), Italian explorer of Egyptian antiquities. He left England in 1812, arriving in Egypt in 1815, where he experimented for a time with hydraulic machines for raising the waters of the Nile. He removed the statue of Rameses II from Thebes and shipped it to England. He also explored and carried out excavations at the temples of Edfu and Abu Simbel, at the sepulchre of Seti I and at Karnak. Returning to England in 1819, he wrote his *Narrative of the Operations and Recent Discoveries within the Pyramids, Temples, Tombs and Excavations in Egypt and Nubia, etc.*. He died in 1823 in Benin on a journey to Timbuktu.

Likening him to a pyramid would have been a double allusion to Belzoni's large size and to his Egyptian interests.

TO [DAWSON TURNER] Bloomsbury Square, [London], [Friday] 13 December 1822 4

ORIGINAL: TCC 21
EDITORIAL COMMENT: Although the correspondent is not named, internal evidence makes the identification all but certain.

Bloomsbury Square | Decr. 13th: 1822

My dear Sir,[1]
I should not have troubled you with this letter, were it not uncertain, when my father[2] may write to Yarmouth, and I am quite ashamed of not having answered your kind message, before this time.

I regret, that business will utterly prevent me from accepting your Christmas invitation. I trust, that at another time, I may be more fortunate.

It will give me infinite pleasure, if I can in anyway be instrumental to the increase of your valuable collection of Autographs. The office[3] in which I am in, is not, I am afraid, as old as you may imagine it. It has existed about forty years, but does not possess any papers of a date more ancient than the commencement of the present century; for about 20 years ago, the firm little dreaming of Autographs and Autograph-collectors, had a general burning and I have no doubt but, that at this time, many invaluable treasures | were destroyed.

I have obtained permission however to examine the papers, which they do possess, and I shall be obliged to you therefore to transmit me the lists, which you mentioned.

I regret to give you so much trouble, when there seems so slight a chance of my obtaining anything, which you may value, but whatever may be the result, you will at least have the satisfaction of having had the collection examined.

My father sends his kindest remembrances, and desires me to say, that he is executing your commission.

Do not think me premature, if I offer you the Compliments of the Season, and believe me

1 Dawson Turner (1775-1858), of Yarmouth, botanist and antiquary, friend of Isaac, noted for his autograph collection of 40,000 letters.

2 Isaac D'Israeli (1766-1848), only child of Benjamin D'Israeli (1730-1816) and Sarah D'Israeli, née Shiprut de Gabay Villa Real (1743?-1825). See **32**n1. Isaac was a man of letters, noted for his miscellaneous erudition and for the purity of his style. His most popular work, *Curiosities of Literature*, appeared in 1791 and went through many editions. As an historian he was less eminent, for though he made extensive use of archives, his interpretations were sometimes deemed to be uncritical. Henry Morley *Of English Literature in the Reign of Victoria* (Leipzig 1881) 119-21.

On the D'Israeli ancestry, see Lucien Wolf 'The Disraeli Family' *Transactions of the Jewish Historical Society of England* V (1902-5) 202-18 and Roth ch 1. The only biography of Isaac is by Ogden.

3 The office of the firm of solicitors, Messrs Swain, Stevens, Maples, Pearse and Hunt of 6 Frederick's Place, Old Jewry. D was articled to one of the partners, William Stevens, on 10 November 1821. The indenture was signed by Stevens, Isaac D'Israeli and D. This is the last known occasion on which D signed his name with the apostrophe. H A/II/B/4. See also **10**n1.

my dear Sir
Yours very faithfully
B. *Disraeli*

I am afraid that I shall be able to procure nothing but the *Signatures* of lawyers.

5 TO THOMAS FREDERICK MAPLES [Windsor?], Tuesday [22 July 1823]

ORIGINAL: H A/II/B/2

COVER: July twenty second | 23 | T. F Maples Esqre | Fredericks Place | Old Jewry | *B Disraeli*

EDITORIAL COMMENT: A copy, sent by Frederick Maples, the recipient's son, to Lord Rowton in 1889.

Tuesday 1/2 pt. 7 oclock

T.F. Maples Esqre.

My dear Sir,[1]

I regret that I have not been able before this, to give you the information, which you desired, but I have been so unfortunate in my visits to Mr. Brown, the solicitor to Eton College, as always to find him and his clerk out.

I took the following description from a lease which I have just this moment seen and I trust it will fully answer your object.

"The provost of the Coll. Royal of the Blessed Mary of Eton near unto Windsor, in the Co. of Bucks Commonly called the Kings Coll. of our blessed Lady of Eton nigh or by Windsor in the sd. Co. of Bucks and the same College of the one part etc."

Excuse this brief epistle, but I am very | desirous of gaining this evenings post which goes off *immediately*.

I hope Mrs. Maples' health is better than it was when I left. It gives me pleasure to say that my mother is much better.

I am
My dear Sir
Yrs sincerely
B. Disraeli

6 TO THOMAS FREDERICK MAPLES Windsor, [Tuesday] 12 August [1823]

ORIGINAL: H A/II/B/3

COVER: August twelfth/23 | T.F. Maples Esqre | 52 Guilford Street, | London. | *B.D.*

PUBLICATION HISTORY: M&B I 41, dated 2 August 1823

EDITORIAL COMMENT: A copy, sent by Frederick Maples to Lord Rowton in 1889.

Windsor | Aug 12th.

T.F. Maples Esqr.

My dear Sir,

A letter which begins with Congratulations is generally a pleasant thing, and I therefore feel very grateful, for the opportunity of thus happily Commencing my epistle, to the young Stranger, who

1 Thomas Frederick Maples (d 1864), a solicitor and from 1806 a partner in the firm of Messrs Swain, Stevens, Maples, Pearse and Hunt.

Porrigens teneras manus
Matris e' gremio suae
Dulce rideat ad patrem
Semihiante labello[1]

But to leave Catullus and congratulations for a more matter of fact subject. As no particular time was settled for my return, and as you expressed a wish, that I would communicate to you upon it, I am under the necessity of intruding | upon you, surrounded of course by crowds of hurrying and eager friends who 'hail this new accession to the house of Montague' to ask the very uninteresting and business like question of, when you would wish me to return!

If you can find time to write me 1/2 a line upon this subject I shall feel much obliged.

Present my best Comp[limen]ts to Mrs. Maples.

With the wish that every day of your daughter's life may be as sunny as the present and that she may never know the miseries of a wet summer,

I remain
My dear Sir
Yours sincerely
B. Disraeli

TO JOHN MURRAY Frederick's Place, [London], [Tuesday] 25 May [1824?] 7

ORIGINAL: MR 2

PUBLICATION HISTORY: Smiles II 183-4, dated 25 May 1824

EDITORIAL COMMENT: The 3 in 1823 is overwritten with 4 in another hand. May 1824 is written above in yet another hand. *Dating*: by comparison with **8** and **9** which refer to 'Aylmer Papillon'.

Frederick's Place | May 25th. 1823

Jno. Murray, Esq.
etc.
My dear Sir,

The travels, to which I alluded this morning, would not bind up with Parry,[1] since a moderate duodecimo would contain the Adventures of a certain Mr. Aylmer Papillon in a terra incognita.

I certainly should never have mentioned them, had I been aware that you were so very much engaged, and I only allude to them once more, that | no confusion may arise from the half explanations which were given this morning.

1 The original reads: 'Torquatus volo parvulus | matris e gremio suae | porrigens teneras manus | dulce rideat ad patrem | semihiante labello.' (Catullus *Carmina* LXI 212-16). This may be translated: 'I would see a little Torquatus, stretching his baby hands from his mother's lap, smile a sweet smile at his father with lips half parted.' The original is a wedding poem, which concludes with the hope that a son will soon be born.

---

1 In 1824 John Murray published *Journal of a Second Voyage for the Discovery of a North-West Passage* by William Edward Parry (1790-1855), the arctic explorer. Behind D's facetious remark lies the practice, then common, of publishing several unrelated travel accounts as a single volume. The popular series of *New Voyages and Travels*, published by Sir Richard Phillips, was of this character.

You will oblige me by not mentioning this to anybody and
Believe me to be
my dear Sir
Your very faithful and obliged Ser[van]t
B Disraeli

8 TO [JOHN MURRAY] [London, May 1824]

ORIGINAL: MR 1
PUBLICATION HISTORY: Smiles II 182-3, dated May 1824
EDITORIAL COMMENT: Endorsements in another hand: 'May 1824', 'Aylmer Papillon A novel'. The last page of the MS is damaged.

My dear Sir,
Your very kind letter induces me to trouble you with this most trivial of trifles.

My plan has been in these few pages so to mix up any observations, which I had to make on the present state of society, with the bustle and hurry of a story, that my satire should never be protruded on my reader. If you will look at the last Chapter but one, entitled *Lady Modeley's*, you will see what I mean better than I can express it. The first pages of that chapter I have written in the same manner as I would a common | novel, but I have endeavoured to put in *action* at the *end* the present fashion of getting on in the world.

I write no humbug about candidly giving your opinion etc. etc. You must be aware, that you cannot do me a greater favor, than refusing to publish it, if you think *it won't do*, and who should be a better judge than yourself?

Believe me, ever to be,
my dear Sir,
Your most faithful and obliged
B. Disraeli |

The 2nd. and the last Chapters are unfortunately mislaid – but they have no particular connection with the story. They are both very short, the 1st. contains an adventure on the road and the last Mr. Papillon's banishment under the alien Act from a ministerial misconception of a metaphysical sonnet.[1]
Thursday morn –
Excuse want of seal – as we're doing a bit of summer today and there is not a fire in the house.

9 TO JOHN MURRAY Frederick's Place, [London], [June 1824]

ORIGINAL: MR 3
PUBLICATION HISTORY: Smiles II 184, dated June 1824
EDITORIAL COMMENT: Endorsement in another hand: 'June – 1824'.

1 'Aylmer Papillon' was a satirical novel which John Murray declined to publish. The tone and content of the two chapters which have survived (H E/V/A/1) – those described here as 'mislaid' – suggest that it foreshadowed D's satirical *Voyage of Captain Popanilla* (1828).

Frederick's Place — 10 | 9 — 29 Jul 1824

J. Murray Esq

My dear Sir,

Until I received your note this morning, I had flattered myself, that my indiscretion had been forgotten.

It is to me a matter of great regret, that, as appears by your letter, any more trouble should be given respecting this unfortunate MS., which will, most | probably, be considered too crude a production for the public, and which if it is even imagined to possess any interest, is certainly too late for this Season, and will be obsolete in the next.

I think therefore that the sooner it be put behind the fire, the better, and as you have some | small experience in burning MSS.,[1] you will be perhaps so kind as to consign it to the flames.[2]

Once more apologising for all the trouble I have given you

I remain

ever my dear Sir,

Yours very faithfully

B. Disraeli

TO SARAH DISRAELI — [Bruges, Thursday 29 July 1824] — **10**

ORIGINAL: H A/IV/B/5

COVER: [In Isaac's hand]: Mrs D'Israeli | ~~Bath Buildings~~ | 9 Bedford Row | Worthing | Sussex | en *Angleterre* | [At right angles]: L'Angleterre

POSTMARK: (1) In dotted circle: FPO | AU.2 | 1824 (2) In double circle: AU | G 2 [central number in small circle] | 1824 (3) BRUGGE

PUBLICATION HISTORY: M&B I 42-3, dated 29 July 1824, edited version

EDITORIAL COMMENT: All the letters from D written during the tour to the Rhineland (his first visit to the Continent) were included in letters from Isaac to his wife, the covers being addressed to her. The first page of the MS is torn. *Sic*: it's, paysanes, fleur du ble, Ysarn, gentleman, french, weasing.

My dear Sa![1]

I add a few lines not only out of my great affection for you, but also that you may not misconceive the meaning of the Governor's dubious paragraph respecting our triumph.[2] The truth is that we had a very stiff breeze and almost every individual was taken down stairs save ourselves, who bore [*it*] out in the most

1 This is an extraordinary taunt for a young man of nineteen to make to a publisher of Murray's standing. It refers, of course, to the burning of Byron's 'Memoirs', which had taken place at Murray's on 17 May 1824. For details of the complicated circumstances see *DNB* entry for Byron, and Smiles I ch 17.

2 Murray presumably took D at his word, and burned all he had of 'Aylmer Papillon'.

---

1 Sarah Disraeli (1802-1859), Isaac's eldest child. She never married, and served as D's faithful confidant. Her vicarious enjoyment of D's life in the world of affairs was nourished by his detailed letters over several decades. She followed D in dropping the apostrophe from the family surname, as did the other children. Both parents retained the old spelling.

2 Under the same cover Isaac wrote to his wife: 'The Voyage was certainly tedious ... and the young Voyagers exult that they sailed the waves in triumph – and were more sleepy than otherwise indisposed.' H A/IV/B/5.

manly and magnificent [*man*]ner, not even inclining to indisposition. [*We*] came in with a very fresh sea, the night [*w*]as most magnificent indeed I never witnessed [*a*] finer night. The Governor was most frisky on his landing and on the strength of mulled claret etc. was quite the lion of Ostend.[3] This latter place we found sufficiently disgusting, uninteresting for anything with the exception of it's fortifications and harbour. We left it at 8 o'clock same morning as we arrived, and proceeded to Bruges in diligence thro' a flat but richly wooded country full of chateaux long avenues and paysanes with wooden shoes and rich lace caps. Bruges is the City of cities. Nothing but Churches and grand maisons – not a hovel in it. The streets the handsomest and widest and the architecture the most varied and picturesque imaginable. Meredith[4] and myself perfectly well. I never knew the governor in such fine racy | spirits. I see the governor has hinted at the Hamiltonian adventure. Sir John is certainly rather a bore, but

upon my life

he has two daughters and a ladye wife – the first are regular prime girls, both fine women, the youngest devilish pretty, regularly unaffected, full of sketching and void of sentimentality.[5] He has introduced us with the greatest sangfroid and Meredith and myself intend to run away with them. We have put up at the same inn at Bruges, the fleur du ble, a capital one by the bye. Ysarn,[6] I take it, has given you a high character, inasmuch as your name was often graphically introduced and your opinion asked respecting patent pencils and crack camels hairs, gentleman who taught with india rubber and gentleman who teach sine etc. etc. etc. Meredith and myself talk french with a mixture of sublimity and sangfroid perfectly inimitable. We are off to Gand tomorrow by canal after having passed a long and luscious day at Bruges. I shall write to you from the for-

3 A pun on his father's role as social lion, and on the lion of Flanders, an heraldic device common throughout the region. Isaac D'Israeli rampant must have been a rare sight.

4 William George Meredith (1803?-1831), at this time Sarah Disraeli's unofficial fiancé. On his return home after this tour with D and Isaac, Meredith wrote an account entitled *A Tour of the Rhine* which was printed and privately circulated. Sir Philip Rose noted that 'a beautifully bound Copy is in the Library at Hughenden presented by Meredith to B.D.' H A/IV/B/3. *The Brasenose College Register, 1509-1909* (C.B. Heberden ed) I gives the following entry for Meredith: 'Meredith, William George, (London); Winchester. Com. Matr. arm. 22 Jan. 1821, aged 17; 3 Cl. and BA 1824; MA 1829; rem. 1831. Student Lincoln's Inn 1823.' During the 1820s Meredith was one of D's closest friends and they collaborated on a work entitled 'Rumpel Stilts Kin: a Dramatic Spectacle'. Written in 1823, it was first printed, for the Roxburghe Club, in 1952, with an introduction by Michael Sadleir. Meredith died at Cairo on 19 July 1831.

5 Sir John Hamilton (1755-1835), 1st Baronet, lieutenant general in the army, inspector general of the Portuguese army during the Peninsular War. He had four daughters: Emily Louisa, Harriette Georgiana, Arminta Ann and Eleanor Frances. *BP* (1829).

Harriette is mentioned by name in **14**, thus making the identification highly probable. Isaac in his portion of the letter said: 'We met on board Sir John and Lady Hamilton and two daughters.'

6 From the references here and in **14** 'Ysarn' would seem to have been a London spinster, and a mutual acquaintance of the D'Israelis and the Hamiltons (H A/I/B/469, 472). For some reason D and Sarah chose to employ her surname for Sarah wrote in 1831, 'Yzarn is paying us a visit ...' H A/IV/E/14. Probably the lady was Anne C. Yzarn, daughter of Peter Yzarn (d 1847), and sister of James B. Yzarn of the East India Company service. In 1851 she lived at Herne Hill, Brixton, aged fifty-seven. *East India Register and Directory* (1835, 1840); Population Returns 1851 Census, PRO.

mer place and as often as I can besides. Give my best love to ma mere and the dear young slave drivers. The governor presses me to finish and I therefore close this short letter.

My dear Sa
yours
B. Disraeli

The Governor's weasing has disappeared.

TO SARAH DISRAELI [Antwerp, Monday 2 August 1824] **11**

ORIGINAL: H A/IV/B/6

COVER: [In Isaac's hand]: Mrs D'Israeli | 9 Bath Buildings | Worthing | Sussex | *Angleterre* | [At right angles]: L'Angleterre

POSTMARK: (1) In dotted circle: FPO | AU.6 | 1824 (2) In double circle: AU | S6 [central number in small circle] | 1824 (3) ANTWERPEN

PUBLICATION HISTORY: M&B I 43-4, edited version dated 2 August 1824

EDITORIAL COMMENT: *Sic*: Sevigne, Matthews, flemish, Vandyke, it's, table d'hotes, entertainting, desert, francks, wusser.

My dear Sa,

We have been in Antwerp about 2 hours and 1/2, and the post goes off tomorrow morning. My father as usual emulous of saving postage, positively forbids our writing separate letters, and he has been, of course, the whole two hours and 1/2 writing his half page. I am myself extremely tired, and have not room, even if I had time, enough to write you a letter as long as I could desire, but I trust that by next post my father will sicken of his Sevigne fit, and resign the sheet in my favor.[1] We left Bruges excessively delighted on Friday morning in the barque. The vessel was very full. The Hamiltons etc. There was an Irishman among the passengers who would have made an inimitable hero for Matthews.[2] It was his debut on the continent, and with a most plentiful supply of ignorance and an utter want of taste, he was enthusiastically fond of paintings; for many years running, he had come up from Dublin on purpose to see the exhibition, and after a discourse with him on Rubens, the flemish School etc. on all which subjects he exhibited the most splendid enthusiasm, he coolly remarked that he should have enjoyed his journey much more had he not missed the Water Color Exhibition. I met him two or 3 times afterwards in different places, and his salutations were exceedingly rich; it was always "How do you do Sir, wonderful city this Sir wonderful! pray have you seen the crucifixion | by Vandyke,[3] wonderful picture Sir wonderful Sir." We arrived at Ghent after a pleasant passage of 6

1 D considered Isaac's contributions to be overelaborate when coupled with his insistence that, to save postage, they both use the same sheet of paper. The family was dedicated to the art of letter-writing and Sarah once wrote an essay, intended for publication, on Madame de Sévigné (1626-1696), who was the standard of excellence in such matters. H A/I/B/507 (19 Jan 1834).

2 Charles Mathews (1776-1835), the actor and comedian. D invariably spelled his name 'Matthews'.

3 Presumably the 'Carrying of the Cross' in St Paul's, Antwerp, by Sir Anthony Van Dyck (1599-1641).

hours on Friday at 3. I was agreeably surprised by the place which I had imagined would have been Bruges on a larger scale. It's character however is perfectly different. There seems a great deal of business going on, or at least the numerous canals and the river Scheldt, by which it is intersected, and which are tolerably well filled with shipping, give it that appearance. We of course visited Mr. Schamp's collection,[4] the University, Cathedral etc. and of course we always thought each thing more wonderful than another, were exceedingly delighted and tired ourselves to death. We left Ghent this morning after having attended high mass in [the] Cathedral. This service was sublime beyond conception and the music, one of Mozarts grandest masses was played by a full band! Our living has been tolerably good, the table d'hotes however as yet not very entertainting, but reasonable. We reached Antwerp this afternoon en voiture. We passed thro', among others, the very thriving towns of Lokeren and St. Nicholas. At the last place, we took it into our heads to dine, perfectly extemporaneous. We ordered of course something cold, not to be detained. The hostess however seemed peculiarly desirous to give us a specimen of her cookery, and there was a mysterious delay. Enter the waiter. A fricandeau the finest I ever tasted, perfectly admirable, a small and very delicate roast joint, veal chops dressed with a rich | sauce piquant, capital roast pigeons, a large dish of peas most wonderfully fine, cheese, desert, a salad preeminent even among the salads of Flanders which are unique for their delicate crispness and silvery whiteness, bread and beer ad. lib. served up in the neatest and purest manner imaginable, silver forks etc. cost only six francks, forming one of the finest specimens of exquisite and economic cookery I ever witnessed. We have had a good [dinner] of veal stewed with sorrel and not bad. The paper in this country is bad, the ink infamous and the pens wusser. Love to mere and all not forgetting Olivia and Belin[5] and

Dr Sa

your affec. Brother.

B. Disraeli

4 Schamp d'Aveschoot had a gallery in the rue des Champs. His remarkable collection, which included many Flemish masters, was dispersed at a sale in 1840. J. Emerson Tennent *Belgium* (1841) I 21.

5 D's cousin, Olivia Lindo (1800-1878) was one of four daughters of Ephraim Lindo (1763-1839), and of Maria D'Israeli's elder sister Sarah (née Basevi). In 1829 Olivia married Charles Trevor, then of 18 Norfolk Crescent, London. Olivia's sisters were Cecilia (1792-1877), Emily (1796-1864) and Louisa (1798-1872). 'Belin' was a short form for Benjamin Ephraim Lindo (1794?-1854), Olivia's brother, whom D often called BEL. Lindo family tree, printed by Ben Johnson and Co, York (1900), in the possession of the Queen's University Archives.

TO SARAH DISRAELI [Brussels, Friday 6 August 1824] **12**

ORIGINAL: H A/IV/B/7

COVER: [In Isaac's hand]: Mrs D'Israeli | 9 Bath Buildings | Worthing | Sussex | Angleterre | [At right angles]: L'Angleterre

POSTMARK: (1) In dotted circle: FPO | AU.9 | 1824 (2) In double circle: AU | Y9[central number in small circle] | 1824 (3) BRUSSEL | FRANCO

PUBLICATION HISTORY: M&B I 45-6, extracts dated 6 August 1824

EDITORIAL COMMENT: *Sic*: Brusselles, Anwers, Le Place, parisian, Mozelle, wusser, the too, loath, fattigue, flemish.

My dear Sa,

The sermones gubernatoriae are this time rather diminished. We have heard that a post has arrived from England this evening; there is therefore some little chance of a letter, if however we do not receive one we shall be off on Saturday morning. We were more delighted with Antwerp than with any place we have yet been at. We put up at the Grand Laboureur – unfortunately no table d'hote but capital private feeds – a vol au vent of pigeons admirable – our living for the last week has been the most luxurious possible and my mother must really reform her table before our return – at Brusselles we had a paté des grenouilles quite sublime. Anwers is a grand City. Le Grand Laboureur is the crack Hotel in the crack situation, Le Place de Mer. I have kept a journal[1] of dinners for myself and of doings in general for my father, so I shall leave the account of the churches cathedrals and cafés till we come home. We have had a perfect debauch of Rubens and Meredith and myself have destroyed the reputation of half the Cathedrals in Flanders by our mysterious hints of the spuriousness of their Sir Pauls.[2] | Monday was the birthday of a prince of Orange, and there was a grand review in the place – among them a regiment of Swiss. On Tuesday morning we set off for Brussels. We dined at Mechlin, and stayed between four and five hours there – dinner good and Cathedral magnificent – oysters as small as shrimps, but delicately sweet – hunted up an old Bookseller.[3] The entrance to Brussels is very striking – passing thro' a road bounded on both sides by magnificent chateaux and ornamented gardens. We arrived about 9 o clock and put up at the Hotel de Belle Vue, which is crammed full and sports a table d'hote of 40 persons. Brussels, at least the part in which we reside, the new town, is a perpetual Waterloo Place, a regular succession of grand places and Rue royales in a magnificent style of architecture.

The governor is particularly well. He has mounted a black stock, and this added to his former rather military appearance, very materially aided a very pleasant mistake which occurred some short time ago. Our affectionately slang appellation of Governor aided by the aforesaid military appearance has caused him to be lionized over a maison du force with regular major general honors.

1 D's journal is in the Hughenden papers (H A/III/B/11), and is discussed by C.L. Cline in 'The Unfinished Diary of Disraeli's Journey to Flanders and The Rhineland (1824)' *University of Texas Studies in English* XXIII (1943) 94-114.

2 During his period in England Peter Paul Rubens had been knighted by Charles I.

3 The name is either De Breyst or Verbeyst. Cline 'Unfinished Diary' 104.

We visited the Comedie last night; but the performances were meagre and the house ill attended. The King of Holland pays the actors and of course there is no theatrical spirit in Bruxelles. We pass the evenings very agreeably in cafés, where Meredith and myself play dominoes in a most magnificent manner and the governor, invents or discovers new ices, lectures on sorbettes and liqueurs and reads the Flanders papers which are a copy a week old of the parisian copies of the English. We then rush home to Selzer water and Mozelle, sugar and lemon, an invention of a waiter and my father, and which, to use our favorite national phrase, if it is equalled by any cup in Europe, is certainly not excelled. | You are told I see that the Andersons[4] are here. It is impossible to conceive anything half so vulgar as Miladi and her sister. They scarcely speak a word of grammar and are floored most horribly by the optative mood. Miss Young is however the wusser of the too. To any remark you make on the country, her invariable repartee is that for her part she thinks there is no place like Paris – this accompanied by a pleasant leer makes me utterly loath her. The wretch also is fond of domesticity "tho' she must confess that when one once gets abroad, one does not like to come home again, the first rummidge is the thing, after the first rummidge (rummage etc.) you get more used to fattigue every day." The Doctor is as amiably dozy and elaborately pleasant as ever.

My father thinks you may as well write to us at Mayence en Allemagne – as we shall probably pass twice thro', it seems the only place we can fix on for a letter. We are all extremely well and I hope that by this time you are settled at Worthing, that my mere has recovered, and that the Merediths have joined you. Meredith writes by this post to his famille. We have visited a great many private collections. Our banker at Brussels sports one and has very politely allowed us to visit it tomorrow morning. The flemish booksellers are horrid Dons, they are above a common shop; but coolly sport a whole house. Brussels is full of English. The Belle Vue crowded – an Irish officer rather grand – invited me to a pic nic party at Waterloo, also told me he thought an Irish gentleman was the completest gentleman in | the world when he chose, fancying his brogue did not detect him. We visit the fields of Waterloo not so much for the scenery but as Mrs. Young says, *for the idea.* I leave a space for tomorrow to say if post arrives. How are Ralph and James?[5]

Yours

B. DISRAELI

4 In his part of the same letter, Isaac referred to 'Dr. Anderson' and to the probability of seeing the family at Brighton. This was Dr Robert Anderson (d 1837), a physician of Dorset Gardens, Brighton. *The Stranger in Brighton and Baxter's New Brighton Directory* (Brighton 1822). His will, probated 18 July 1837, referred to his wife Frances and to her sister Dorothea Young. The latter's marital status is not clear, and apparently D also was uncertain, as he refers to her in this letter both as 'Miss' and as 'Mrs' Young.

5 D's younger brothers, Ralph (1809-1898) and James (1813-1868). Both attended Winchester. Clifford W. Holgate *Winchester Commoners, 1800-1835* (Salisbury 1893). Ralph eventually became deputy clerk of Parliament, and James (known as Jem), after many agricultural misadventures, became a commissioner of inland revenue.

TO SARAH DISRAELI [Cologne, Saturday 14 August 1824] 13

ORIGINAL: H A/IV/B/8

COVER: [In D's hand]: a Madame | [In Isaac's hand]: Madame D'Israeli | Bath Buildings | Worthing | Sussex | en Angleterre | [At right angles]: L'Angleterre

POSTMARK: (1) In dotted circle: FPO | AU 23 | 1824 (2) In double circle: AU | I 23 [central number in small circle] | 1824 (3) CÖLN | 14 AUG (4) FRANCO

PUBLICATION HISTORY: M&B I 47-8, extracts dated 14 August 1824

EDITORIAL COMMENT: The last page of the MS is torn. *Sic*: postmark: CÖLN, Vandykes, dutch, flemish, french, english, hamburg, Liegè, flanders.

Dear Sa,

We are in a city in which there are so many churches to lionize, that I am afraid we shall never get out of it. We arrived at Col[ogne] last night. I wrote to you last from Brussels. On Friday, the day on which the post left for England, we visited the Musee at Brussels, and in the evening we called on a person to whom we were recommended for prints etc. We found a large collection of paintings etc. and a most original possessor of them. He talked in a loud voice, and in a most swaggering manner of himself and his fortune. He informed us that he had been a Colonel of Cavalry; that he was the richest person in the world, and the possessor of the most rare curiosities. He opened a Cabinet full of jewels and cameos, exhibited a profusion of Vandykes and Rubens, paraded his wounds and dashed his bull neck into the Governors face to shew him a wound much in the manner of Mascarille.[1] My father was of course delighted and richly credulous. Vous etes un hero | was his constant exclamation. After spending two hours with him in which the Colonel was indefatigable in endeavouring to persuade the Gov. to buy a 30/- work my father left without purchasing, with such a man it was of course not requisite. On inquiring on our return, we of course found out that the hero was one of the richest quacks in Xdom, but extremely poor, and as for his military rank, un colonel du grand regiment des menteurs, as our host of the Belle Vue quaintly observed. On Saturday we left Brussels for Waterloo, lionized over the field of Battle and the adjoining country by Old Koster[2] himself a jolly antique. He harangued in a mixture of dutch, flemish, french and english very rich forming a kind of Belle Alliance lingo, most likely in complement to the place. The road to W. thro' the forest of Soignies. We dined at Genappe most admirably – by the bye we hired a carriage at Brussels. It is a complete travelling carriage left behind by a hamburg gentleman at the Bellevue, perhaps for his bill. We got to Namur by 11 o'clock at night. It is strongly fortified – at Genappe the country rises and the road for abt

1 The impudent valet who appears in three of Molière's comedies: 'L'Etourdi', 'Le Dépit amoureux' and 'Les Précieuses ridicules'.

2 A Flemish peasant who, having served as Napoleon's involuntary guide at the Battle of Waterloo, later made his living showing visitors around the field. The name Koster appears to be a Dutch version of Lacoste, the name by which the guide was usually known. Another variant that appears in travels is 'Da Costa'. Sir Walter Scott *Life of Napoleon Buonaparte* (Edinburgh 1827) III 246; Robert Southey *Journal of a Tour of the Netherlands* (1833) 213; J. Emerson Tennent *Belgium* (1841) II 146.

16 | **13**
14 Aug 1824

7 leagues is thro' a bold but highly cultivated country. We left Namur where there is little to see on Sunday afternoon. Our road lay thro' the valley of the Meuse and after proceeding for about 20 miles we arrived at Huy, a small village most romantically situated amidst lofty hills on the banks of the Meuse. The journey to Huy is a succession of scenery which I think the Rhine can scarcely equal. On Monday morning we continued our journey for about 20 miles, as far as Liegè; still thro' the | valley. The scenery if possible even more picturesque than before and the valley considerably wider. The day was, however unfavorable. Liege is a pretty City – part of it is built on the heights of the valley and in a view of the city there appears a succession of terraces to the level. It is the finest country in the world for fruit. We here first tasted stewed apricots as a vegetable and found them excellent. At Brussels every day we dined at the table d'hote[;] the company changed on the second day[–]a paté des grenouilles – english abounded and a vulgar but lucky prejudice against frogs – we had it all to ourselves. I eat myself blind. The beggars abound all thro' flanders – our charity is quite tired out. At seven in the morning on Tuesday we set off for Spa. We passed over a mountainous country and for miles continued to ascend. We left the valley of the Meuse on the right and passed thro' a most gorgeous country. We breakf[aste]d at Louvegne, a few houses surrounded by immense elevations – at a neat little cabaret, kept by ano[the]r old gent and a beautiful little daughter known 20 miles round as des braves gens. The day very fine. The road to Spa is a perfect debauch of gorgeous scenery. We arrived at the far famed watering place – pen and ink and particularly the miserable materiel with which I am scratching, can give you no idea of our rich adventures. You shall have an oral description of our expedition, rouge et noir, Mrs. Young and other diableries, when we meet. The Spa ware is perfectly contemptible. The water sparkling and pleasantly flavored – a kind of Champaigne au naturel. We rode on the Spa ponies to the distant springs. They are handsome little Galloways. The govr. was particularly equestrian. I have become a most exquisite billiard player – we showed off | to great advantage at the wells and Aix to which place we were off – on Wednesday. We were asleep when we entered the Prussian frontier and the Governor mistook the officer for an innkeeper and kindly informed him that he had taken refreshment at Limburg – the rest of this scene which was exquisite, when we meet. Aix is close and inelegant – the pictures we saw magnifique. We slept on Thursday at Juliers and had rich adventures at a Country inn and arrived at the Rhine last night. It is flowing in sight of our windows. Excuse false construction and vicious grammar as I have lost my english. Every thing has gone right [*ex*]cept hearing from you. I su[*ppos*]e you missed the English pos[*t*] We did not sufficiently calculate. As for our own journey if we find a letter at Mayence saying my dear mother is well, we may perhaps fav[*or y*]ou by not returning at all, as really you[*r m*]anners are so barbarous your dishes [*so d*]etestable that etc. Give my love to all. I trust my mother and yourself are well. I meant to have written to Ralph, but my father approves of concentrated postage. How is Jem, also the straw hats?

best comp[limen]ts to the M[eredith]s and O[livia].

Yours ever

B. Disraeli

TO SARAH DISRAELI [Mainz, Thursday 19 August 1824] 14

ORIGINAL: H A/IV/B/9

COVER: [In D's hand]: a Madame | [In Isaac's hand]: Madame D'Israeli | 9 Bedford Row | Worthing | Sussex | en Angleterre | [At right angles]: L'Angleterre

POSTMARK: (1) In dotted circle: FPO | [A]U.27 | 1824 (2) In double circle: AU | U 27 [central number in small circle] | 1824 (3) FRANCO | [others illegible]

PUBLICATION HISTORY: M&B I 49-50, extracts dated 19 August 1824

EDITORIAL COMMENT: *Dating*: there is no date or address on the letter, but the chronology of the itinerary confirms Monypenny's dating. *Sic*: your's, Mentz, Harriet, Ehrenbreitztin, Embs, those kind, restaurateur, pavillion, it's, proceeded, Wisbaden, Frankfort, Heidleburg, fleas, best, scools, worthing, all.

My dear Sa,

You have by this time received my letter from Brussels. We of course did not receive your's there. We arrived at Mentz yesterday morning and immediately rushed to the post office tho' we were all convinced of the utter impossibility of receiving a letter. To our great joy one was immediately handed us. It was very clever in you in writing to M. The non receipt of a letter was the only circumstance which threw a cloud over our enjoyment and to receive it so unexpectedly was quite delightful. My father recovered his spirits in an instant. I wrote to you from Cologne. We see so much and are so much in action that if I were to write at all en large I should not have proceeded much further than Ghent. The Hamiltons moreover are much too rich a family to discuss in a single letter which would not do justice to the doziest family in Xdom. We must therefore defer all details till our meeting. Respecting Ysarn they mentioned her much, and Harriet Hamilton[1] told me that she expected a letter from her I think at Antwerp. Since I last wrote from Cologne our adventures have been grand. So much was to be seen at Cologne that we hired a fiacre as we thought from our host determined to ride all over the City. To our great surprise a most elegant landaulet with the coachmen in military livery stopped at our gate. This we were informed was the fiacre and also nearly the only carriage in Cologne. We were almost stopped in our progress by the stares of the multitude who imagined we were Archdukes at least. We have always put up at the crack hotels which we find the most reasonable. We travel as I wrote you in a most elegant equipage and live perfectly en prince. | The governor allows us to debauch to the utmost and Hocheimer Johannisberg Rudelsheirnien Ashanhausen[2] and a thousand other varieties are unsealed and floored with equal rapidity. Yesterday we had Cabinets wein Rudel. On Sunday we left Col. early dined at Bonn where we stayed some short time – passed Drachenfels and the 7 mountains – Remagen and got on as far as Andernach where we slept. We reached Coblentz early next

1 A daughter of Sir John Hamilton. See 10n5.

2 Probably D's version of Rüdesheim and Assmannshausen.

morning – left it in the afternoon – visited Ehrenbreitztin for which our landlord got us a ticket[3] and lef[t] for the present the Rhine to proceed on our tour to the Baths of the Taunus Mountains. We entered the principality of Nassau and arrived at Embs at 5 o'clock. The scenery is of a nature baffling all description – the chief feature richly wooded mountains. The baths of Embs are now among the most fashionable of the continent. Spa and those kind of place are now out of date or visited merely by English. The establishment consists of a mansion which covers nearly an acre of ground and which was formerly a palace of Nassau. It contains upwards of 230 rooms besides 80 baths, which are similar to those at Aix. The lodgings are a concern of the prince and on each door the price of the bed etc. is affixed. Over this department a maitre d'hotel appointed by the Prince presides. The rest of the establishment is perfectly separate and is conducted by a restaurateur at his own risk. There is a Saloon of an immense length and magnificently furnished, at which there is a table d'hote every day at one, all other meals and refreshmts independent in different parts of the Saloon. Opposite to the Mansion are beautiful gardens running by the side of the river Lahn. The gardens are filled with arbors, a pavillion for band etc. There is also in them a large and elegant café billiard room redoubt etc. Underneath the palace in the | large cloisters and corridors are 3 or 4 large Bazaars in which all kinds of Bijouterie silks etc. etc. a perpetuity of Howard & James.[4] Such is a slight sketch of Embs, a most singular, indeed an unique spot. A watering place without shops and without houses; The very Castle of Indolence. Above all its situation is perhaps one of the most magical in the world. It is in a small valley surrounded by ranges of lofty but wooded mountains. The river Lahn winds thro' them and walks and gardens are on it's banks. Further on the heights and woods of Nassau studded with old grey ruins and without a sign of population. The visitors are perfectly in unison with the genius loci. Lounging and lackadaisical they bask on sunny banks or doze in acacia arbors. Some creep to the woods of Nassau, others are rowed down the river music perpetual. The ladies patronize superb Donkeys. There seems an utter void of all thought and energy and positively in this place even the billiard room and the gambling table are deserted. Above all no English. The Hamiltons, whom we met again, the only ones. After this account you will perhaps rejoice to hear that we left this fatal and delicious Paradise next day at 12 – a glorious morning – passed to and thro' Nassau[–]the country if possible increasing in loveliness – the road exceedingly mountainous – from one of the loftiest elevations we viewed the ruined castles of Stein and Nassau – crossed the lovely Lahn – journeyed over mountainous country at 1 1/2 mile an hour. The day turned to rain.

3 Ehrenbreitstein fortress occupied a formidable site 400 feet above the town which had been used as a strongpoint since Roman times. During the Napoleonic Wars the French had taken the fortress, but in 1801 they blew it up after evacuating it. In 1815, one of the terms of peace was the payment of 15 million francs from France to Prussia for the reconstruction of Ehrenbreitstein, a process which lasted from 1816 to 1826. Although still in progress at the time of D's visit, the work was already a notable tourist attraction, and tickets to inspect it were in short supply.

4 D meant Howell and James, silk merchants and jewellers in Regent Street.

Swallbach the second of the Taunus springs found the best hotel filled by the Hamiltons who had proceeded us – rose at six the next morning, before the Hamiltons as we found their four horses clearing the road – arrived at Wisbaden a regular dashing watering [place –]the 3rd. of the Taunus springs breakfasted and at 12 were walking in the streets of Mentz – we shall be off soon to Frankfort perhaps today – from which place Meredith will write. We are all excellently well. Have made many acquaintances – chiefly among the military – the governor being perpetually mistaken | for a general anglais. His black stock is grand and he has long left off powder. Pray remember me to the Merediths and Olivia. The promise of a letter will make us reach Heidleburg. We get on famously. Our last letters were directed to B[ath] Build[in]gs why have you changed. fleas I suppose, a very unpleasant smell, a cracked dish or some other housewives' care. best love to Mother – and the boys – tell Ralph lots of military music scools garrisons 6000 strong.

Ask at worthing if they know any thing of a Mr. Cockerill abroad – a great man in the vicinity of Aix etc. He has the grand house in every place etc. etc. all we can find out is that he is an iron man but whe[the]r old iron or mines can't say.[5]

Your affec Bro[ther]
B. Disraeli

TO SARAH DISRAELI [Heidelberg, Monday 23 August 1824] 15

ORIGINAL: H A/IV/B/11

COVER: [In D's hand?]: A Madame | [In Isaac's hand]: Madame D'Israeli | 9 Bedford Row | Worthing | Sussex | en *Angleterre* | [At right angles]: L'Angleterre

POSTMARK: (1) In double circle: SE | L 2[central number in small circle] | 1824 (2) In dotted circle: FPO | SE.2 | 1824 (3) In rectangle: BADE PAR | STRASBOURG (4) R.I HEIDELBERG

PUBLICATION HISTORY: M&B I 51-2, extracts dated 23 August 1824

EDITORIAL COMMENT: Isaac's letter is headed: 'Heidelburgh, Monday 23 1824 at Night.' There is no signature. *Sic*: Heidleburg, Mentz, Frankfort, english, Gatteau, Bonasoni's, Rembrants, Bethman, Franfort, Manheim, it's, Heidleberg, Beasley, Coblentz.

My dear Sa,

We arrived at Heidleburg, or as my father terms it Heligoland, this morning and received your letter. On Thursday the 19th. we left Mentz, crossed again the Rhine, reentered Nassau, and after proceeding thro' Hockheimer, arrived at Frankfort early. We remained in this city until Sunday morning and were very much amused. F. is a very populous, busy and dashing city. The Opera is one of the best in Germany. We went on Thursday night, Cherubini's Medea. The house crammed full. The boxes private, as in London, save two in the centre for strangers. | We were much amused. We lounged a great deal at Frankfort. Our banker was extremely civil, and gave us a ticket for the Casino, an institution similar to our crack London clubs, and not inferior to them in style or splendor.

5 John Cockerill (1790-1840) was an English-born engineer and industrialist, who, beginning in Belgium, had spread his enterprises over western Europe. Didot *Nouvelle biographie générale* (Paris 1856). The establishment at Aix-la-Chapelle is mentioned in Murray's *Northern* (7).

There we read all the english newspapers and billiardized.[1] Returning home we discovered at a confiseur's "Gatteau de Pouche," – something superb beyond conception, we committed an excess, and have talked of the ambrosia ever since. My father has bought some fine prints at F. – Alb[recht] Durers, Marc' Antonios,[2] Bonasoni's[3] and many Rembrants, very magnificent impressions and very reasonable. On Saturday we visited the collection of Mr. Bethman – in it Dannecker's grand Ariadne on the Lion[4] – which you remember described in Dodd[5] – in the evening we rushed to the Opera – The Zauberflote – here we met again Dr. Henderson, the author of the History of Wines.[6] We had met him before. The Gov. was introduced to him at the Athenaeum. He is travelling on a winebibbing tour, has been nearly in a state of gnostical intoxication the whole time. They are quite mad about him in Germany and the whole Rheingau, even to the ancient and sealed cellars of Johannisberg, are open to his beck. On Sunday, after visiting the Museum,[7] we left Franfort for Darmstadt, a lounging little city full of new and architectural streets. The Opera is celebrated throughout Europe and justly so. We attended it in the evening – Otello – the scenery is the most exquisite I ever met with. The discipline of the orchestra admirable. The grand Duke an immense amateur. The Royal box is a large pavilion of velvet and gold in the midst of the Theatre. The Duke himself, in grand military uniform, gave the word for the commencement of the Overture, standing up all the time, beating | time with one hand and watching the orchestra thro' an immense glass with the other.[8] We left Darmstadt this morning, a very fine day – travelled thro' a beautiful country at the foot of the Bergstrasse mountains, reached Heidelberg, which is beautifully situated on the Neckar, surrounded and partly built on lofty mountains. We called and delivered our letters to Mrs. Tobin, a cleverish, pleasant woman. She was very civil – pressed us very much to stay at Heidelberg, asked us to meet Lady Davy[9] and Lord Dudley,[10] who are

1 The Casino was described in Murray's *Northern* as one of the best clubs in Germany, to which visitors were admitted upon being introduced by a member. It subscribed to over a hundred different newspapers, including *Galignani's Messenger* and *The Times*.

2 Marcantonio Raimondi (c 1480-1534), Italian engraver.

3 Guilio Bonasone (1498?-1574?), Italian painter and engraver.

4 Philip Heinrich Bethmann (1811-1877) was head of a Frankfurt banking house. Greville v 104n. Bethmann's collection was apparently a well-known attraction of the district. Another traveller refers to his 'museum' with its statue of 'Ariadne on a Lion' by Johann Heinrich von Dannecker (1758-1841). Mrs Trollope *Belgium and Western Germany in 1833* (1834) I 246.

5 Thomas Dodd (1771-1850), auctioneer and printseller, and author of *The Connoisseur's Repertorium; or A Universal Historical Record of Painters, Engravers, Sculptors, and Architects, and of their Works* 6 vols (1825-31). D had perhaps seen Dannecker's 'Ariadne' in one of Dodd's earlier catalogues.

6 Alexander Henderson (1780-1863), physician, and author of *The History of Ancient and Modern Wines* (1824).

7 The Staedel Museum in Neu Mainzer Strasse, named after a private citizen who left his collection of paintings and engravings to the city. Murray's *Northern* 403.

8 According to Murray's *Northern* (425), Darmstadt had one of the finest operas in Germany. It also confirms D's account that the Grand Duke of Hesse-Darmstadt, Ludwig I (d 1830), conducted the orchestra on numerous occasions.

9 Probably Jane Davy née Kerr (1780-1855), who in 1812 married secondly Sir Humphry Davy (1778-1829), 1st Baronet, the chemist.

10 John William Ward (1781-1833), 4th Viscount Dudley and Ward, after 1827 1st Earl of Dudley, Tory MP for various constituencies between 1802 and 1823, foreign secretary 1827-8.

both at H. which we declined, as we set off tomorrow. We shall to Manheim. We think of returning home as it must be necessary, tho' we are all very inclined to reach Switzerland, and talked seriously this morning of going on to Baden, which is only 18 lea[gue]s distance. As however we visit the Rhine again in it's most interesting parts on our return, we shall give this up. We rise very early and travel chiefly in the early morning. We shall be back, I dare say, in a fortnight as there are no great cities to visit on our return. We have been only a month coming to Heidleberg and have done anything but hurry, spending in Brussels and Frankf[ur]t alone, upwards of a week. I hope you do not find Worthing *too* dull. I can't pay you the compliment of saying | your letters are very interesting. You row rather too much about Cabbage. I read of it about 3 months before I left England. You might have told us about Dibdin[11] tho' to be candid it is certainly an exquisite bore to repeat a whole epistle. Remember me to all – my best love to my mother. I wish the young heroes success in their sepulchral promenades.

We are here all quite well. Mr. Beasley I suppose has found Gretna Green too successful to give it up in a hurry.[12] I expect no more letters from you but shall enquire at Mannheim and Mentz and Coblentz before our excursion into Luxembourg. We are now in the Duchy of Baden – have been much disappointed in not seeing the Freischutz. It would have been a great treat to have seen it at Darmstadt.[13] Meredith is *too* [?] well.

your affectionate brother.

B. Disraeli

11 Thomas Frognall Dibdin (1776-1847), bibliographer and friend of Isaac D'Israeli. Dibdin's correspondence with Isaac, which is in the Hughenden papers, reveals a close relationship between the two men, which often included collaboration on various literary projects. Dibdin had frequently been subjected to critical attacks which questioned both the accuracy and the completeness of his work, and he, in turn, showed a propensity to complain that other people were anticipating his best ideas.

In April 1824, Dibdin had written to Isaac approving of two articles in *The Quarterly Review* but concluding 'One would think the sly Critic had peeped over my shoulders, and borrowed one idea, at least, from the pages of the L.C!' H G/I/306. D had no doubt read this when Isaac received it.

During D's absence abroad, on 9 August 1824, Dibdin published a work entitled *The Library Companion; or, The Young Man's Guide and The Old Man's Comfort, in the Choice of a Library.* Not unexpectedly, the critical reception given to the book was unfavourable. A parody soon appeared, entitled 'The Street Companion; or The Young Man's Guide and The Old Man's Comfort in the Choice of Shoes by Rev. Tom. Foggy Dribble (Pseud)'. *The London Magazine and Review* ns I (Jan 1825) 73-7.

'Cabbage' was a term widely used to mean plagiarism, but it is not known whether the reports which Sarah had been sending to D reflected Dibdin's customary complaints, or whether Isaac had been grumbling that Dibdin had been 'borrowing' from him.

12 Samuel Beazley (1786-1851) was a successful architect, specializing in theatres. He also wrote numerous comedies and farces – one of which, an operetta about the vagaries of the marriage laws, was called *Gretna Green.* It was first produced in 1822 and, although it seems not to have been running at the time of D's letter, D probably meant that Beazley had found that line of work an attractive alternative to his profession.

13 The Darmstadt Opera was particularly renowned for its performance of Weber's best-known work.

16 TO SARAH DISRAELI Coblenz, Sunday [29 August 1824]

ORIGINAL: H A/IV/B/12

COVER: [In D's hand?]: A Madame | [In Isaac's hand]: Madame D'Israeli | Bedford Row | Worthing | Sussex | en Angleterre | [At right angles]: L'Angleterre

POSTMARK: (1) In double circle: SE | S 6 [central number in small circle] | 1824 (2) In dotted circle: FPO | SE.6 | 1824 (3) COBLENZ | 29 AUG. (4) FRANCO

PUBLICATION HISTORY: M&B I 52-3, dated 29 August 1824

EDITORIAL COMMENT: This is the last letter from the tour which has been located. The itinerary for the remainder of the trip has usually been gleaned from *Vivian Grey* part I, book II ch 3, interpreting the description there as autobiographical. *Sic*: Coblentz, sour craut.

Coblentz. Sunday

My dear Sa,

My father will explain the reason of your being honored with this epistle. I wrote to you last from Heidelberg which pretty place we left on Wednesday last. We had the misfortune of having very rainy weather there, but the new moon has brought us at last the most beautiful weather that I ever remember. On Wednesday we walked over Schetzingen, large gardens full of temples waterworks and berceaus but rather stupid. We reached Mannheim a beautiful city – a fete on the birthday of the G[rand] Duke of Baden[1] – the Opera a very elegant house and very fully attended [,] Don Giovanni very bad. We met Dr. Henderson again in this city. From Mannheim we travelled thro' Worms, slept at Oppenheim and arrived again next morning at Mayence – on Friday. Yesterday having made necessary arrangements for the conveyance of our carriage we commenced our voyage down the Rhine. So much has been read and written about this descent that I will not bore you with descriptions of a country which you know almost as well as myself. I can only say that the most glowing descriptions do but imperfect justice to the magnificent scenery. It answered my highest expectations which after passing over the Bergstrasse and the Taunus is saying a great deal. We set off at 6 o'clock – stopped | at Bingen two hours for dinner, but the time not suiting us we had supplied ourselves with prog.[2] We therefore took a boat during these two hours and made an excursion to the ruined castle of Ehrenfels near Bingen and opposite the famous tower of Archbp. Hatto – passed thro' the Bingerlock, Bacharach, St. Goar, Boppart, near which last places the Rhine is as narrow and the banks as wild as in Switzerland. We landed in the evening again at Coblentz after passing thro' 60 miles of the most beautiful part of the river. Here we are digesting an excursion into Luxembourg. Our host at Coblentz is a most excellent fellow. My love to my mother and all. The weather continues most beautiful. Tell Ralph we had two military bands alternately playing while we dined at Mannheim. Jem I hope is prospering.

Yrs ever

B. Disraeli.

1 Ludwig Wilhelm Augustus (1763-1830).
2 Schoolboy slang for food.

We have met Lady Belmore[3] and suite two or three times. I wonder when they'll be tired of travelling. Our host at Coblentz has discovered since our last visit that the governor is a great author and has coolly informed him this morning he shall be obliged to him for his works.

Our dinners, if possible, improve. Game is rushing in, in all directions. Partridges abound. The Roebuck is superb beyond imagination. At Mannheim we had sour craut but this is not the season for it.

TO JOHN MURRAY Bloomsbury Square | [London], [October 1824?] **17**

ORIGINAL: MM 40

EDITORIAL COMMENT: In another hand: 'Octr – 1824 – | B. D'ISRAELI Esq'.

On returning from the Rhineland tour in September D persuaded his father to allow him to withdraw from his 'unprofitable studies' as articled clerk, and he did not return to the solicitors' office. Instead he was permitted to join his friend William Meredith in reading for the bar at Lincoln's Inn, where he was admitted 18 November 1824.

B[loomsbury] S[quare] *1 o'clock*

J. Murray Esq.

My dear Sir,

The accompanying table mat is from Treves. I wish that it were in my power to present you with a larger one, but unfortunately it is the largest that I could obtain. If | however it will serve for your domestic use, it will give me great pleasure.

Believe me
my dear Sir
Yr Ser[van]t
B. Disraeli

TO JOHN MURRAY [London, Monday 31 January 1825] **18**

ORIGINAL: MM 21

COVER: City 4 o'clock | John Murray Esqr. | Whitehall Place | [In another hand]: 1825 January | *D'Israeli B. Esq*

POSTMARK: (1) In double oval: 7. NIGHT 7 | JA. 31 | 1825 (2) In packet: T.P. | Lombard St

EDITORIAL COMMENT: *Sic*: Glynn, Columbian.

My dear Sir,

I recd. your draft only this morning. As I was particularly engaged at the time and as Glynn brought it,[1] I did not at the moment *in writing* acknowledge the receipt.

3 Lady Juliana Lowry-Corry (d 1861), second daughter of the 2nd Earl of Carrick. In 1800 she had married the 2nd Earl of Belmore.

1 Probably a member of the banking firm of Glyn, Mills, Halifax, Mills & Co, at 12 Birchin Lane. It is unlikely that Sir Richard Carr Glyn (1755-1838), 1st Baronet, a one-time lord mayor, would have delivered a bank draft in person, but he had several sons in the bank. H. Price *A Handbook of London Bankers* (1876) 57-8, 215; G.F. Russell Barker and Alan H. Stenning eds *The Records of Old Westminsters* (1928) I 375-6.

It was a holiday at the Stock Exchange today in consequence of the decapitation of Chas.I;[2] but many speculators attended on the Royal Exchange and consequently some little business was done among | the first men.

A seller of Anglo-Mexican[3] was not to be found.

I purchased your ten Columbian shares at 39. They rose afterwards; but to-morrow will be the day of action. I know the Contractors are buying and shall have my broker early on the Market. At the present the danger of speculating is turned into the difficulty of acting. |

I shall communicate immediately that anything decisive happens and in the meantime in great haste am

Ever yours
BD

---

19 TO JOHN MURRAY [London, March 1825]

ORIGINAL: MM 29

COVER: John Murray Esquire | Albemarle Street | 50, Piccadilly | [In another hand]: 1825 [hole in MS] March | D'Israli B. Esq

EDITORIAL COMMENT: *Dating*: from the reference to the publication of D's pamphlet. *Sic*: cover: D'Israli, pamplet, pamplets.

My dear Sir,

Mr. Powles[1] was not in town today, but Mr Hunt[2] informed me, that he had determined to interfere. I am requested to lose no time and documents have been sent me.

2 Although the tradition of thirtieth-of-January sermons had much declined, the date was still marked in other ways. When 30 January fell on a Sunday, the holiday was observed on the following day. *The Times* (1 Feb 1825).

3 The Anglo-Mexican Mining Association, born in the speculative mania of 1824, proved to be one of the more enduring enterprises of that sort. It was dissolved only in 1849. J.R. McCulloch *A Dictionary, Practical, Theoretical, and Historical, of Commerce and Commercial Navigation* 2nd ed (1834) 804, and subsequent eds; Christopher Richardson *Mr. John Diston Powles: or, the Antecedents, as a Promoter and Director of Foreign Mining Companies, of an Administrative Reformer* (1855) 12.

---

1 A key figure behind the mining stocks was John Diston Powles. Powles seems to have recovered from financial reverses suffered in the speculation of 1825 and remained prominent in the City for many years. His enterprises of the 1820s included the Anglo-Mexican Mining Association, of which he was a director, the Colombian Mining Association, and the complex business of negotiating a loan to the state of Gran Colombia. Henry English *A General Guide to Companies Formed for Working Foreign Mines* (1825) 4, 23; [English] *The Contractor Unmasked* (1823) 23. The closest approximation to a biography is Richardson's unfavourable account, already cited. Powles married three times and his fifth son, Louis Diston Powles (1842-1911), became a noted lawyer and judge. The elder Powles apparently died c 1865, but no will has been discovered. Pedigree of the Powles family, in the library of the Society of Genealogists, Harrington Gardens, London.

2 William Ogle Hunt (d 1860), of Swain, Stevens, Maples, Pearse and Hunt, solicitors to the Colombian Mining Company. *Law List* (1825), and Henry English *A Complete View of the Joint-Stock Companies Formed During the Years 1824 and 1825* (1827) 5.

Mr. Hunt's opinion of Sir W[illiam] A[dams][3] is the common one. I have been unable of course to ask Powles respecting him, but from what I see I imagine no encouragemt. is offered to him from the proprietors.

Respecting the public[ati]on of his pamplet I leave you to decide. It cannot interfere with mine[4] in any material way; but it will be for you to consider, whether it may not be most advisable for you to | interfere in the contest only to *decide* it, rather than commence the investigation of this important subject by a publication of partial research and *limited purpose*, which will do any thing but enlighten the public mind, and must necessarily invite controversy from every quarter.

All the pamplets of Sir W's which you have, have been before the Directors for many months. Hunt tells me that Powles said he had | folios of Adams which he had never read. This I think shows their opinion of him.

Ever yours

BD

TO [JOHN MURRAY] [London, Friday 1 April? 1825] 20

ORIGINAL: MM 1

EDITORIAL COMMENT: In another hand on the fourth page of the MS: 'Mines'. *Dating*: Parliament adjourned 31 March 1825. D would only inform Murray of this event immediately after it had taken place.

My dear Sir,

I balanced our accounts on Sunday evening and find myself worth 1009£ and crediting you £1650 exclusive of a fresh deposit which I paid upon your Anglo-Mexican.

My selling out was a most successful operation. By this means I had all the cash at my command awaiting the | expected opportunity. I think the Mining Companies have now passed thro' their ordeal. The Chancellor's judgment[1] was

3 Sir William Adams (1783-1827), oculist and surgeon, adopted his wife's name of Rawson on 9 March 1825. Under this name, he wrote *The Present Operation and Future Prospects of the Mexican Mine Association Analysed* (1825), puffing the mining stocks, especially United Mexican. His enthusiasm for various money-making schemes made him an object of some amusement. See the letter of July 1826 from John Rickman, one of the clerks at the table in the House of Commons, to Lord Colchester, in Charles, Lord Colchester ed *The Diary and Correspondence of Charles Abbot, Lord Colchester* (1861) III 443.

4 D's anonymous pamphlet, *An Inquiry into the Plans, Progress, and Policy of the American Mining Companies* (John Murray 1825). It appeared in March, and two more editions were printed. The prospect of a Spanish-American Eldorado created enormous interest, and the best publications of the day argued the merits of the various schemes. However, one reviewer's judgement on D's *Inquiry* was that 'Whoever wrote it is an ugly customer.' [William Maginn] 'The Quarterly Review and the American Mines' *Blackwood's Magazine* XVII (May 1825) 592-600 at 593.

---

1 On 29 March, John Scott (1751-1838), 1st Earl of Eldon, lord chancellor since 1807, rendered judgement in the case of *Kinder v Taylor and the Directors of the Real Del Monte Company*. He found in favour of the defendants and refused to grant an injunction, sought by Kinder, which would have forbidden the directors of the original mining company to transfer shares to a new company. *The Times* (30 Mar 1825); *The Law Journal* III (1825) 68ff; and Bishop Carleton Hunt *The Development of the Business Corporation in England, 1800-1867* (Cambridge, Massachusetts 1936) 38-41. The increased freedom thus given to unincorporated companies, specifically to the Real Del Monte directors, was obviously to D's advantage, as he held stock in the new company.

most satisfactory – it is evident that no legislative interference will be allowed, and that the administration are fully aware, that the prosperity of this country depends upon our patronage of America.

The Parliament has adjourned, and the Chancellor decided, at a fortunate | moment, the settling of the account at the Stock Exchange. The shares continue, necessarily from no business being done, in their depressed state, for a day or two, but I think this moment *is the crisis*, and that an immense and permanent rise is to be looked to.

I have therefore formed a partnership with you with proportionate interests according to the annexed | paper – the shares in which we are interested are in an iron case in my room with a paper of which the accompanying is a counterpart.[2] In case therefore of my death etc. everything will be straightforward. I hope that this partnership is but the forerunner of mutual brilliancy of fortune.

Ever yours,
BD

---

21 TO [ROBERT MESSER?] [London, April 1825?]

ORIGINAL: H R/II/B/9a, b, c

EDITORIAL COMMENT: This was a draft which was not sent, and this may account for a number of obscurities in meaning and style. There is no signature. *Dating*: D says that 'about seven months have now elapsed since my return to England'. He returned from the tour of the Rhineland with his father and William Meredith in September 1824. *Sic*: Columbia, it's, at at, breath.

---

2 The agreement reads:

Know all men hereby, that the shares in Companies and Associations formed for working the mines of America and all other shares certificates of shares papers and writings which are contained in this iron box are held by and belong to John Murray of Albemarle St. in the city of Westminster Esquire and Benjamin Disraeli of Lincoln's Inn in the County of Middlesex Esquire in partnership and that the interests of the sd. John Murray and Benjamin Disraeli in the said shares, certificates of shares papers and writings are as follows, videlicet. Two thirds of all interest which may exist in, all profit which may arise from and all liability which may be incurred by possessing the sd. shares certificates | papers and writings shall be vested in, accrue to and be incurred by sd. John Murray; And one third of the sd. interest with the same advantages and responsibilities shall be held by the sd. Benjamin Disraeli.

If any future shares and certificates of shares shall be purchased or obtained by the sd. partnership they shall be held upon the same terms as the foregoing. And in case any such are purchased or obtained or any of the first mentioned shares are sold by or otherwise parted with by the sd. John Murray and Benjamin Disraeli then a memorandum shall be added to these presents explaining the nature quantity and prime cost of such shares. Witness the hand of the said Benjamin Disraeli and John Murray.

Benjamin Disraeli
John Murray. [H R/II/B/2]

21 | 27 Apr 1825

My dear Sir,[1]

I am now engaged upon our business[2] and am preparing to put you in possession of the additional security which I mentioned. Before however this is executed I think it proper to place before you the whole state of my affairs, in order that you may rest perfectly satisfied as to your situation even independent of all security and that you may be enabled to form an opinion as to the expediency of auxiliary interference either as regards your rights or my convenience.

About seven months have now elapsed since my return to England, at which time I was not possessed of fifty guineas in the world, and arrived in London with the intention of resuming those unprofitable studies[3] in which I had already employed three years.

On settling again in the metropolis I was immediately struck by | the great revolution which was taking place in the financial relations of England and America and I was not astonished at the speedy recognition which ensued of Mexico and Columbia.[4] It immediately struck me that if fortunes ever were to be made this was the moment and I accordingly paid great attention to American affairs.

The consequence of the recognition was an attention to the Mexican mining Co[mpanie]s which had then been formed about a year and in which the public tho' utterly ignorant of the whole business immediately rushed to buy shares in. Those shares rose upwards of 100 p Ct. There was then no cause for any | rise whatever for no information of the progress of the Companies had been received and consequently the original holders who possessed their shares from the beginning took the opportunity of realising. An immense fall was the Consequence and the public enraged at the hopes which their own folly alone occasioned united in one furious attack upon the very Associations which had, but just before, been the object of so much attention.

The Lord Chancellor[5] was terrified at the tales of ruin which he daily heard and which were the offspring of Falsehood and Exaggeration. He determined however to use the evil and proposed a plan which | was very much like shooting a man to put him out of pain. A great panic took place – everything fell, even in their depreciated state and for some time it was supposed that the whole Commerce with America might be crushed.

1 Robert Messer was one of D's early creditors, the debt dating from 1824. From surviving financial statements (H A/V/A/1-9) it seems that Messer, the son of a stockbroker, bought mining stocks for D and others. By 1 February 1825, D and Thomas Mullett Evans, a clerk in the same solicitors' office as D, and his partner in mining speculations, owed Messer £2,061.8.8, and by 31 December 1826 the debt had increased to £2,833.10.11. Dunning letters written by Messer in 1828 and directed to Evans are in the Hughenden papers. H A/V/A/15-17. As late as 1849 the unfortunate Mr Messer was still attempting to obtain satisfaction from D for approximately £1,200 with accumulated interest at 5 per cent. H A/V/A/21-5.

2 A reference to the speculation on the stock exchange in which D was engaged, together with Thomas Mullett Evans, John Murray and John Diston Powles.

3 See **17**ec.

4 Canning's prompt recognition of the independence of the former Spanish colonies led to substantial British investment in Latin America.

5 Lord Eldon threatened the promoters of the Mexican Mining Co with the penalties of the 'Bubble Act' of 1720 (6 Geo I *c* 18). It was repealed later in 1825.

28 | **21**
Apr 1825

At this crisis I stepped forward and offered my services to a dismayed and despairing party. I proposed measures which as they were unanimously adopted, I have a right to suppose were prudently conceived and which no one can deny were vigorously ex[ecu]ted. A Committee of all the members of Parliament connected with the American Mining Companies was | formed, deputations waited on the ministers, and every means was taken to oppose the instant and urging evil. But the press which always follows the public was against us, and a cry of Bubble was raised which was echoed even in the houses of Parliament.

I immediately published the "Inquiry into the Plans, Progress and Policy of the American Mining Companies" – and rapid sales of numerous and large editions testify it's complete success. I was the first person who demonstrated the fallaciousness of the parallel which the Ld. Chancellor had formed bet[wee]n | the present time and the one which generated the S[outh] S[ea] Bubble – and finally after exertions during which for many nights I did not even sleep, the Ld. Chancellor was forced to give up his threatened interference.[6]

I published the 3rd. edit of my Inquiry and found myself in possession of shares in all the great mining Companies to the amount of many thousand pounds.

All the information which is now received from America passes thro' my hands. Since January we have received dispatches from Mexico alone above eight times. All these I have seen – moreover I have perused | secret reports which have not been seen even by many of the Directors themselves. I have read every book upon the subject and conversed with secret agents of the Companies in which I am interested and I have come to the conviction that the 100£ shares in the Mexican mining Companies will in a very few years be worth upwards of 1000£ apiece.

The public are now more violent against the mining Companies than ever – for this I care not, as long as their legislative interference | etc. is nought to me. They will be thunderstruck in a few months by the Companies which they believe do not possess any mines declaring large dividends and then the reaction will be terrific. All England will be buying in the same morning.

But to resume my narrative. After the publication of the third edit two things occurred to me. The one was a plan to get introduced to Canning[7] – the second of investing a considerable sum in a great colonial undertaking which had been maturing for the last three years and | [*page(s) missing in MS?*] For the last affair 4000 was immediately wanted to vest my shares with my feelings respecting them was madness. How I managed by the assistance of my uncle[8] and you is

6 D's publications in defence of the mining ventures resisted the parallel with the Bubble of 1720, and discouraged parliamentary inquiries into the affairs of the companies.

7 George Canning (1770-1827) had been foreign secretary in Liverpool's government since 1822 and, in opposition to Lord Eldon, favoured recognition of the former Spanish colonies. He was a friend of Sir Walter Scott and, though a Tory, supported a large number of progressive measures. He was prime minister for three months before his death in 1827.

8 Possibly George (formerly Joshua) Basevi Sr (1771-1851), brother of D's mother. He married Bathsheba Lindo. He has sometimes been confused with his son, George Basevi (1794-1845), the architect, who predeceased him. An unsuccessful involvement in D's speculations may be the reason for the later coolness of the Basevis to D.

well known to you. What I did to gain the first point was at that time also in p[ar]t related – and the Lawyers and Legislators[9] was in consequence dedicated.

But this last connection gave rise to a new occurrence and one from which I may obtain not only considerable profit, but which will also materially assist me in gaining the object of my highest ambition. The daily journal[10] must if properly managed soon become the leading newspaper, and I shall possess a considerable share of it. | My affairs at the present moment stand thus –

I possess a certain number of shares which are worth tho' at the lowest price they have yet sunk about 6000£ sterling, which I calculate at the end of this year will be worth 12000 – but 35 of which I calculate in the course of 5 years will be worth as many thousand.

I have 4000£ invested in a speculation which I expect will produce me in the course of 8 mon[th]s 1000 a year. And I [am] now getting everything ready for the introduction of a newspaper which will be supported and which will be contributed to by the greatest men in this kingdom and which will be under the immediate patronage of Mr Canning.

7 mon[th]s of unwearied exertion, and truly of harrowing care have produced this result, which when I contemplate I feel actually dizzy. It is | truly work for a life.

On the Mexican mines I rest my sheet anchor.

When I tell you that one single mine which everybody in this kingdom believes to be inundated and to be incapable of producing under five years at the least is, altho it has not been worked for 8 months – producing at the rate of £3000 *net profit* pr week and that at the end of the first year of working it, when everybody imagines that it is so much unproductive property it will give us a net profit at at the least of 150,000, when I tell you moreover that this mine contains veins of | immense and incalculable worth, which have only been discovered by our own surveyors and that it is their opinion that it alone may yield cent [100] pr Ct. for our money, when I tell you I have seen the weekly accounts of profit and loss and every paper and memorandum connected with it's management, when I tell you that all our agents are writing home to us to buy them additional, no matter *at what price*. Can you call me too sanguine?

Such is a slight sketch of the secrets of my life known only to you. I may consider my fortune as made, but I breath not an indication of it, till I am upon a rock.

9 *Lawyers and Legislators: or Notes on the American Mining Companies* (John Murray 1825). This, the second of D's anonymously published pamphlets, was dedicated to Canning. For the first see 19n4. A third such publication, *The Present State of Mexico* (John Murray 1825), was written in part by D.

10 *The Representative* was a proposed Tory daily newspaper intended to compete with *The Times*. The terms of its formation were decided in August. See 23n2. The paper ran from January to July 1826, and then went bankrupt.

22 TO JOHN MURRAY [London, May 1825]

ORIGINAL: MR 5

EDITORIAL COMMENT: In another hand: 'May 1825'.

J Murray Esq

My dear Sir,

I shall call in Albemarle St. tomorrow morning at half past ten o'clock. Do me the particular favor of seeing me at that time – as I wish to consult with you *on most important business* – no more drafts, so don't be alarmed.

Be easy about your mines – we were more behind the scenes than I even imagined – but Tace.[1]

Ever yours,

B. Disraeli

23 TO JOHN MURRAY [London], Thursday [May 1825]

ORIGINAL: MR 6

EDITORIAL COMMENT: Endorsements in other hands: on the first page of the MS '1825 – May'; on the fourth page '1825 – May B D'Israeli Esq'.

Thursday

Jno. Murray Esq

etc. etc.

My dear Sir,

I merely called yesterday to beg you not to trouble yourself with any thought of business.

Since I have seen you, the case has run thus.

I have seen Powles constantly who, if possible, grows warmer hourly, but who is perpetually asking me whether I think things are *definitively settled*.

I have told him, that there | was no visible, I might say, no invisible cause for the plan not being carried into effect, as all parties were equally desirous of executing it. And I explained that your illness was the only cause of your not having met him upon the subject.

He was perfectly satisfied and is now preparing a statement of what *he thinks | ought to be done, and what he can do*, which he will send me shortly, and which, I think, will be a very important document.

Thus stands the case. The only point that must not be neglected is the certainty that Ellis[1] etc. are aware of your progress, and are not contemplating any other plan.

1 Be silent.

1 Perhaps Charles Rose Ellis (1771-1845), created Baron Seaford July 1826. Ellis, MP for various constituencies 1793-1826, was the cousin of George Ellis, George Canning's intimate friend, and through him became acquainted with the famous statesman. Having inherited a large property in the West Indies, Charles Ellis had become the acknowledged head of the 'West Indian interest', a group that figured in the plans for *The Representative*. Canning had been a supporter of Murray's *Quarterly Review*, and George Ellis had been a contributor to it.

With the exception of this, of which, I suppose, you | have no doubt, there is no occasion for you to cast one thought *at present* upon the subject. The consideration of the subject may, therefore, be adjourned *sine die*, and if, I were you, I would give my mind some rest upo[n] all others.[2]

Ever yours

B. Disraeli

TO ISAAC D'ISRAELI [London], Friday [5 August 1825] 24

ORIGINAL: H A/I/C/2

COVER: I. Disraeli Esquire, | Robert Ward Esquire, | Hyde House, | near Amersham, | Bucks. | FRIDAY | [In Isaac's hand]: S. Turner memoires | Eng. Wisd. | see Roret. des anonymes in | le grand Vocabe. francais.

POSTMARK: (1) In double circle: AU | S 5[central number in small circle] | 1825

EDITORIAL COMMENT: In the past, Isaac had often rented houses in the country for the autumn season. He had, for example, rented one at Brighton in 1814, and one at Farnham Royal, Bucks, in 1818.

Isaac had come to know Robert Ward through Benjamin Austen, who was Ward's solicitor. See **49**n1. Austen arranged for Isaac to rent Ward's country residence, Hyde House near Amersham, for the 1825 season, and this letter shows that the D'Israelis left for their country holiday in late July or early August.

Ward's novel *Tremaine*, a successful pioneer of the 'silver-fork' *genre*, had just been published by Henry Colburn, the anonymity of the author being carefully preserved, even from the publisher, by the services of Austen and his wife Sara as intermediaries. During Isaac's tenancy of Hyde House, he became party to the secret, and Blake reports that 'Isaac read his landlord's novel in manuscript' (35).

D visited Hyde House, but remained based in Bloomsbury Square busy on the launching of *The Representative*. During his visits he came to know about the authorship of *Tremaine* and developed the seeds of the idea of writing what was to become *Vivian Grey* from the example it provided. However, Blake is right in pointing out the improbability of D's later claim (noted in M&B I 80) that he wrote *Vivian Grey* at Hyde House before his twenty-first birthday (21 Dec 1825). As these letters show, the autumn and early winter were packed with activity for D, and many of the events of this time became incorporated into the novel when it was written in 1826, when Sara Austen, in London, repeated and extended the pattern of arrangements she had helped to develop for the publication of *Tremaine*. She became D's go-between with Colburn to preserve the anonymity of the authorship of *Vivian Grey*, even to the extent of copying the manuscript in her own hand, and of negotiating the contract for publication.

The third page of the MS is torn. *Sic*: Smith, Parke's, inditer, course, domestics.

---

2 A memorandum of agreement between Murray, Powles and D was signed three months later:

London 3rd August 1825.

The undersigned parties agree to establish a Morning paper, the property in which is to be in the following proportions

viz Mr. Murray – one half
Mr. Powles – one quarter
Mr. Disraeli – one quarter

each party contributing to the expense capital and risk in those proportions.

The paper to be published by and be under the management of Mr. Murray.

John Murray
J D Powles
B Disraeli [MR 7]

32 | **24** Dear Father, Friday

5 Aug 1825 It has just occurred to me, that you might expect me tomorrow. I shall not be able to get down, but very probably will during the middle of next week.

A respectable and ancient gentlewoman called in B[loomsbury] S[quare] from whom it was learned, that my mother bore her journey but sadly. I trust that she has recovered, and that the rain has provided you with potatoes, and that you make your money out of Mr. Ward,[1] which desirable contingency it appeared unto me when you left London would | not occur.

I dined at Murrays on Thursday at a party which he gave to the former and present African expeditions[2] – there were an immense number of captain-voyageurs, and much talk about the savouriness of stewed lizard and rattlesnake ragouts. There were present Major Denham[3] – Captains Clapperton, Pearce, King and Smith[4] – Chinese Ellis[5] – a brother of Mungo Parke's[6] – Dr. Holland[7] etc. Wishaw, as the inditer of the biog[raphical] notice, which is prefixed to Parke's travels,[8] headed the table, and opposite him was Roger Wilbraham – white, sleek and smiling, like the Musk Ox on the | top of the stairs at the British Museum.[9] The party being well concocted went off well. Murray did his duty

1 Robert Ward (1765-1846), politician and novelist. A supporter of Pitt, he was MP for Cockermouth 1802-6, and for Haslemere 1807-23, and an under-secretary in the Foreign Office in 1805. After retiring from politics in 1823 he had turned to writing and produced *Tremaine; or the Man of Refinement* (1825) followed by *De Vere: or the Man of Independence* (1827). On 16 July 1828 he added the name Plumer. See also ec.

2 John Murray published many accounts of explorations, especially of Africa, and was secretary of the African Association.

3 Dixon Denham (1786-1828), explorer of the Sahara, was actually a lieutenant colonel at the time.

4 Hugh Clapperton (1788-1827), African explorer. Denham's and Clapperton's account of their travels was later published by Murray. Captain Robert Pearce, described as 'an excellent draughtsman', accompanied Clapperton to Africa and died there in December 1825. Clapperton *Journal of a Second Expedition into the Interior of Africa* (1829) ix, xiii; *GM* XCV part ii (Sept 1825) 265 and XCVI part ii (Nov 1826) 457. Philip Parker King (1793-1856), noted explorer and hydrographer, though he attained his captaincy only in 1830, is probably the man to whom D refers. 'Smith' is William Henry Smyth (1788-1865), African explorer promoted to captain in 1834; he retired as an admiral.

5 Henry Ellis (1777-1855), KCB 1848, not to be confused with his namesake, the principal librarian of the British Museum. He accompanied Earl Amherst to China and published an account of the event in 1817, entitled *Proceedings of Lord Amherst's Embassy to China*. Ellis later became ambassador to Persia.

6 Mungo Park (1771-1806), the African explorer, was one of fourteen children. Two of his brothers about whom something is known are Adam, who lived at Gravesend, and Archibald, of Madeira, a friend of Sir Walter Scott. Archibald was certainly alive at this time, for his son, Mungo Travers Park, was born in 1843. Foster III 1065.

7 Henry Holland (1788-1873) was a noted traveller. He graduated from Edinburgh in medicine in 1811, and in 1852 he became physician extraordinary to the Queen. He was created a baronet in 1853.

8 John Wishaw (1764?-1840) edited Mungo Park's travels, which John Murray published in 1815. An account of Murray's initial reluctance to publish is in Lady Seymour ed *The 'Pope' of Holland House: Selections from the Correspondence of John Wishaw and His Friends* (1906) 27.

9 Roger Wilbraham (1743?-1829), Whig MP for various constituencies 1784-96. Well known in literary circles, he was a student of Italian literature. As the musk-ox is no longer in its place, we are deprived of this slender clue to Wilbraham's nature. Gerrit Parmele Judd *Members of Parliament 1734-1832* (1955 repr Hamden, Connecticut 1972) 376; M.C.W. Wicks *The Italian Exiles in London, 1816-1848* (1937 repr Freeport, New York 1968) 21.

both as host and as a gentleman equally well, altho' one time in the evening he took off a course mourning ring and swore it was Belzoni's hair![10] I never heard of it till that day. Howr. it pr[*odu*]ced an effect – the company sympathised and passed the claret. I have no news on any subject – but perhaps may have when we meet. Tell the women, "Montague Stepney Browne, second son of Sir John Edmond Browne of Holles Street Dublin" is dead, in spite of his sister in law and eight carriages.[11]

If my grandmother[12] wants to | come down, remember I hold myself to my promise. I shall call on her before I see you. No letters have arrived, and I am told that the domestics incidents, such as grates, babyhouses etc! went off well.

Remember etc. to all and bel[iev]e
your affec Son,
BD

25

TO THOMAS MULLETT EVANS Hyde House, Amersham, Buckinghamshire, [Thursday 18 August 1825]

ORIGINAL: H A/V/A/10
COVER: T. M. *Evans* Esquire | Messrs. Swain and Co. | 6 Fredericks Place | *Old Jewry*
POSTMARK: (1) In double circle: C | 18AU18 | 1825. [The same postmark appears twice.]
EDITORIAL COMMENT: There is a draft version of this letter, with minor variations, in another section of the Hughenden papers (R/II/B/8).

---

at Robert Ward Esquire | Hyde House | nr. Amersham | Bucks

Dear Evans,

I arrived in town from Wimbledon on Monday night, and my time until 2 o'-clock the next day, was occupied in appointments without a second to spare. I was then obliged to leave town for a few | days on a visit where I am at present, and as I did not arrive till past post time, I have not been able to answer your note until this moment.

You put me in a very delicate situation. After every deliberation I cannot advise you to decline your country offer.[1] The reasons which induce | me to come to this conclusion, I need not give. They would not be agreeable to you and I assure you are not to me – for the detail of ill-success is seldom interesting.

10 Though news of Belzoni's death in 1823 took some time to reach England, it was certainly public knowledge by the summer of 1824 – a full year before the dinner. Thus Murray was telling his guests nothing new, except for the business of the mourning ring. For further details on the nineteenth-century use of hair jewellery, see John Morley *Death, Heaven and the Victorians* (1971) 66-7.

11 D was quoting *The Times* obituary of Montague Stepney Browne (b 1795), a barrister. The sister-in-law referred to was an heiress, Mary De Beauvoir Browne, who in 1825 had married his elder brother, John Edmond De Beauvoir Browne (1794-1869), after 1835 2nd Baronet.

12 Sarah D'Israeli.

---

1 Letters from Evans reveal that he shared with D the Londoner's impression that leaving town for Bristol constituted a 'country offer'. Evans was due to depart in January 1826, and later correspondence finds him a solicitor in the Bristol firm of Ball & Evans. H R/II/B/5,10; A/V/A/15.

I hope to have the pleasure of seeing you before you leave; but if not, I wish you every success in the anticipated connexion. If ever I can assist, be assured that you may command me with[ou]t reserve.

yours ever
BD

---

26 TO [JOHN MURRAY] Royal Hotel, Edinburgh, [Saturday 17 September 1825]

ORIGINAL: MR 8

PUBLICATION HISTORY: Smiles II 187-8, dated 21 September 1825; M&B I 63-4, extracts dated 17 September 1825

EDITORIAL COMMENT: In another hand on the first page of the MS: 'Sept 1825.' The conspiratorial note introduced here, and intensified in succeeding letters concerning *The Representative*, suggests that D thoroughly enjoyed transforming an ordinary business transaction into a cloak-and-dagger affair. *Dating*: by context and by comparison with **27**. *Sic*: Edinburg, neighbourood.

Royal Hotel – Edinburg –

My dear Sir,

I arrived in Edinburg yesterday night at 11 o'clock. I slept at Stamford, York and Newcastle, and by so doing felt quite fresh at the end of my journey.

I never preconceived a place better than Edinburg. It is exactly what I fancied it, and certainly is the most beautiful town in the world – you can scarcely call it a city – at least it has little of the roar of millions, and at this time is of course very empty.

I could not enter Scotland by the route you pointed out, and therefore was unable to ascertain the fact of the *Chevalier being at his castellum.*[1] I *should* have gone by Carlisle. I called on the gentleman[2] to whom Wright[3] gave me a letter this morning. He is at his country house. He will get a letter from | me this evening – you see therefore that I have lost little time.

I called at O[liver] and B[oyd]'s[4] this morning thinking that you might have written. You had not however. When you write to me, enclose to them – as they

1 Sir Walter Scott (1771-1832), the novelist and poet. In 1812 he had purchased a decaying farmhouse near Melrose with 100 acres of land. He had transformed it at great expense into 'Abbotsford', a large and sprawling Scottish baronial country house. The financial disaster which beset him was to occur the following year, in 1826.

2 John Gibson Lockhart (1794-1854), son-in-law and biographer of Sir Walter Scott. He began his literary career as a contributor to *Blackwood's Magazine*, gaining notoriety for his attacks on *The Edinburgh Review*, the so-called cockney school of poetry, S.T. Coleridge and Keats. In 1818 he met Sir Walter Scott and two years later married his daughter, Charlotte Sophia (1799-1837). Despite D's efforts to obtain his services, on 7 October 1825 Lockhart declined Murray's offer to become the editor of *The Representative*, but, at Murray's urging, did accept the editorship of *The Quarterly Review*, with specified services being made available to *The Representative*. See **42**n2. His *Memoirs of the Life of Sir Walter Scott* appeared in 1836-8. The standard modern biography is Marion Lochhead's *John Gibson Lockhart* (John Murray 1954).

3 William Wright, an attorney at 4 Cloak Lane, London, had given D a letter of introduction to Lockhart. See **28**.

4 Oliver & Boyd, Tweeddale House, 16 High Street, Edinburgh. Thomas Oliver (1776?-1853), a printer, formed a partnership with George Boyd (d 1843), a bookbinder, in 1807, and they soon became the largest wholesale booksellers in Scotland, being the agents for, among others, John Murray.

will forward wherever I may be, and my stay at an hotel is always uncertain. Mr. Boyd was most particularly civil. Their establishment is one of the completest I have ever seen. They are booksellers, bookbinders and printers all under the same roof – every thing but making paper. I intend to examine the whole minutely before I leave as it may be useful. I never thought of binding. Suppose you were to sew etc. your own publications?

I arrived at York in the midst of the Grand Festival.[5] It was late at night when I arrived, but the streets were crowded, and continued so for hours. I never witnessed a City in such an extreme bustle and so delightfully gay. It was | a perfect Carnival. I postponed my journey from five in the morning to eleven, and by so doing got an hour for the Minster, where I witnessed a scene which must have far surpassed by all accounts the celebrated commemoration in Westminster Abbey. York Minster baffles all conception. Westminster Abbey is a toy to it. I think it is impossible to conceive of what Gothic Architecture is susceptible until you see York. I speak with the Cathedrals of the Netherlands and the Rhine fresh in my memory.

I witnessed in York another splendid sight – the pouring in of all the nobility and | gentry of the neighbourood and neighbouring counties. The four-in-hands of the Yorkshire squires, the splendid rivalry in liveries and outriders, and the immense quantity of gorgeous equipages – numbers with four horses – formed a scene which you can only witness in the mighty and aristocratic county of York. It beat a Drawing Room hollow, as much as a Concert in York Minster does a concert in the Opera House. This delightful stay at York quite refreshed me, and I am not the | least fatigued by my journey.

As I have only been in Edinburg a few hours, of course I have little to say. I shall write immediately that any thing occurs. Kindest remembrances to Mrs. Murray and all.

Ever yrs

BD

I find Froissart a most entertaining companion – just the fellow for a travellers evening – and just the work too for it needs neither books of reference, nor accumulation of MS.

TO [JOHN MURRAY] Royal Hotel, Edinburgh, Sunday [18 September 1825] **27**

ORIGINAL: MR 9

PUBLICATION HISTORY: Smiles II 188-90, dated 22 September 1825; M&B I 64, extract dated 18 September 1825

EDITORIAL COMMENT: In another hand on the first page of the MS: 'Sept 1825'. There are also interpolations, in another hand, in the text: '(Sir W S)' following 'speak for itself'; '(ockhart)' following 'Mr L'; '(Canning)' following 'then unwell'; '(J M)' and '(Barrow?)' following 'African dinners'. *Sic*: Edinburg, Cheefswood.

---

5 The York Musical Festival was an annual week-long event, with musicians coming from all over Europe to perform. The proceeds went to charity, and, as D observed, the festival received widespread support. In 1825 it was held 10-17 September. *The Times* (13-18 Sept 1825).

36 | **27** Royal Hotel – Edinburg – | Sunday

18 Sep 1825 My dear Sir,

I sent a dispatch by Saturday night's post directed to Mr. Barrow.[1] You have doubtless received it safe. As I consider you are anxious to hear minutely the state of my operations I again send you a few lines.

I received this morning a very polite letter from L[ockhart]. He had just received that morning (Saturday) Wrights letter.[2] I enclose you copy of L's letter, as it will be interesting to you to see or judge what effect was produced on his mind by its perusal.[3] I have written to day to say that I will call at Cheefswood[4] on Tuesday. I intend to go to Melrose | tomorrow, but as I will not take the chance of meeting him the least tired I shall sleep at Melrose and call on the following morning. I shall of course accept his offer of staying there. I shall call again at B[oyd]'s before my departure tomorrow to see if there is any dispatch from you. You will judge whether in future it will be more expedient to send to B. or to Mr L's. The first one will prevent the franker suspecting the object of my visit – but on the other hand will make your letters come at least a day later. I shall give B. my direction to forward in case you send.

I shall continue to give you advices of all my movements. You will agree with me that I have at least not lost any time, but that all things have gone very well as yet.

There is of course no danger in our communications of anything unfairly

1 John Barrow (1764-1848), second secretary of the Admiralty 1804-6 and 1807-45. His travels in China and South Africa had made him an enthusiastic advocate of explorations, especially in the arctic, and he is credited with being the founder of the Royal Geographical Society. A friend of Murray, he was a frequent contributor of travel articles to *The Quarterly Review*. In 1835 he was made a baronet.

2 Probably the letter in which Wright informed Lockhart of D's forthcoming visit. NLS MS 924 105.

3 Using the new code set out later in this letter, the copy in D's hand religiously substituted '*M*' for Lockhart's name whenever it appeared:

Copy of *M's* letter

Dear Sir,

I am extremely sorry that you have had so much trouble in communicating with me, which moreover has arisen entirely from mistaken information as to the state of the Posts in this quarter.

On returning home today from a little distance I found the letter you allude to.

The character of the letter and of the business to which it refers entitle it to much consideration. As yet I have had no leisure nor means to form even an approximation | towards any opinion as to the proposal Mr W. mentions – far less to consult any friend. In a word I am perfectly in the dark as to everything else except that I am sure it will give Mrs. *M* and myself very great pleasure to see Mr. Disraeli under this roof, and that I shall take care to be at home from this time untill [*sic*] I either see or hear from him.

We are exactly 36 miles from Edinburg [*sic*] and even if you had no other objects in view I | flatter myself that this neighbourood [*sic*] has in Melrose and Abbotsford some attractions not unworthy of your notice.

I have the honor to be,

Yours with much esteem,

M [MR 10]

The other letters from Lockhart to D during this period have not been located.

4 Chiefswood, a part of Sir Walter Scott's estate to which Lockhart moved after marrying Scott's daughter in 1820.

transpiring – but from the | very delicate nature of names interested, it will be expedient to adopt some cloak.

The Chevalier will speak for itself –

M – from Melrose – for Mr. L.

X for a certain personage on whom we called one day – who lives a slight distance from town and who was then unwell.[5]

O For the political Puck.[6]

Mr. Chronometer will speak for itself, at least to all those who give African dinners.[7]

I think this necessary; and try to remember it.

I am quite delighted with Edinburg. Its beauties become every moment more apparent. The view from the Calton Hill finds me a frequent votary.

In the present state of affairs I suppose it will not be expedient to leave | the letter for Mrs. Bruce.[8] It will seem odd *p.p.c.*[9] at the same moment I bring a letter of introduction. If I return to Ed. I can avail myself of it. If the letter contains anything which would otherwise make Mrs. Murray wish it to be left, let me know.

Read my letters and *write to me.*

I revel in the various beauties of a Scotch breakfast – cold grouse and marmalade find me however constant.

Ever yrs

BD

TO [JOHN MURRAY] Chiefswood, [Melrose], Wednesday [21] September [1825] **28**

ORIGINAL: MR 11

PUBLICATION HISTORY: Smiles II 190-3, dated 25 September 1825; M&B I 64-6, edited version dated 21? September 1825

EDITORIAL COMMENT: On the second line of the MS '5' is written in another hand following the '2' of the date. *Dating*: in **27**, dated 18 September, D wrote that he would go to Chiefswood on Tuesday. *Sic*: Edinburg, cast, tory.

---

5 Smiles (II 187) identifies X as George Canning, then foreign secretary.

6 Possibly D himself.

7 Given John Barrow's association with the Admiralty, and the importance of the chronometer to navigation – it carried Greenwich time to sea – Barrow was probably the person so described. He has also been identified with another of D's code names (see **32**n12); however, that was in a letter to Lockhart, and it would have been entirely consistent for D to have kept this set of references for Murray alone, and to have developed other names for the same people when writing to others.

8 Smiles (I 71) mentions an Adam Bruce as solicitor to the Elliots, the family of Mrs John Murray.

9 'Pour prendre congé' – a formal leavetaking, which had been borrowed from diplomatic protocol for general social use. Cards marked 'p.p.c.' constituted notice of imminent departure.

21 Sep 1825

Chiefswood – Wednesday | Septr. | 2[1]

My dear Sir,

I arrived at Chiefswood yesterday. *M.* [Lockhart] had conceived that it was my father who was coming. He was led to believe this thro' Wright's letter.[1] In addition therefore to his natural reserve, there was of course an evident disappointment at seeing me. Everything looked as black as possible. I shall not detain you now by informing you of first particulars. I leave them for when we meet. Suffice it to say, that in a few hours we completely understood each other, and were upon the most intimate terms.

M. enters into our views with a facility and readiness which were capital. He thinks that nothing can be more magnificent or excellent, but two points immediately occurred –

1st. the difficulty of his leaving Edinburg with[ou]t | any ostensible purpose and 2ndly. the losing cast in society by so doing. He is fully aware, that he may end by making his situation as important as any in the empire, but the primary difficulty is insurmountable.

As regards his interest, I ment[ione]d that he sho[ul]d be guaranteed for three years 1000£ pr. ann. and should take an eighth of every paper which was established without risk his income ceasing on his so doing. These are much better terms than we had imagined we could have made. The 8th. is thought extremely handsome both by him and the Chev[alier] – but the income is not imagined to be too large. However I dropped that point as it should be arranged with you when we all meet.

The Chev. breakfasted here today | and afterwards we were all three closeted together. The Chev. entered into it excellently. He thought however that we could not depend upon Malcolm[,][2] Barrow etc. *keeping to it*, but this I do not fear. He of course has no idea of your influence or connections. With regard to the delicate point, I mentioned, *the Chev.* is willing to make any sacrifice in his personal comforts for Lockhart's advancement – but he feels that his son-in-law will "lose cast" by going to town without any thing ostensible. He agrees with me, that *M* cannot accept an official situation of any kind, as it would compromise his independence, but he thinks *parliamt for M indispensable*, and also very much to *our interest*. I dine at *Abb[otsford]* today | and we shall most probably again discuss matters.

Now these are the points which occur to me.

When *M* comes to town, it will be most important, that it should be distinctly

1 William Wright had sent two letters to Lockhart on 12 September (NLS MS 924 nos 105, 107). The former was a private letter apparently sent direct; the latter was the letter of introduction which D took with him, and which refers to D as 'Mr. D'Israeli, junr.' Murray had also written to Lockhart on 12 September referring to 'Mr. B. D'Israeli, son of my oldest friend'. Scott *Letters* II 355n. Thus there appears to have been no reason for Lockhart's bewilderment.

2 Perhaps Sir John Malcolm (1769-1833), East Indian administrator, author, governor of Bombay 1826-30, MP for Launceston 1831-2. John Murray published several of his works, including *The Political History of India from 1784 to 1823* (1826), *The Government of India* (1833), and *The Life of Robert, Lord Clive* (1836).

proved to him, that he *will* be supported by the great interests I have mentioned to him. He must see, that thro' Powles, all America and the Commercial Interest is at our beck – That Wilmot H[orton][3] etc. not as mere undersecretary, but as our private friend is most staunch – That the Church is firm – That the West India Interest will pledge themselves[–]that such men and in such situations | as Barrow etc. etc. are *distinctly in our power* – and finally that he is coming to London not to be an Editor of a Newspaper, but the Directeur General of an immense organ and at the head of a band of high bred gentlemen and important interests.

The Chev. and M, have unburthened themselves to me in a manner *the most confidential, that you can possibly conceive.* Of *M*'s capability, *perfect and complete capability*, there is no manner of doubt. Of his sound principle, and of his real | views in life I could in a moment satisfy you. Rest assured however, that you are dealing with a *perfect gentleman.* There has been no disguise to me of what *has been* done[4] – and the *Chev* had had a private conversation with me on the subject of a nature *the most satisfactory.*

With regard to other plans of ours, if we could get him up, we should find him | invaluable. I have a most singular and secret history on this subject when we meet.

Now on the grand point – Parliament. *M* cannot be a representative of a government boro'. It is impossible. He must be free as air. I am sure that if this could be arranged – all would be settled – but it is "*indispensable*", without you can suggest anything | else. M was two days in company with + this summer, as well as +'s and our friend – but nothing transpired of our views.[5] This is a most favorable time, to make a parliamentary arrangemt.

What do you think of making a confidant of Wilmot H. He is the kind of man, who would be right pleased by such conduct. There is no harm of Lockharts coming in for a tory Boro', because he is a Tory – but a ministerial Boro' is impossible to be managed.

If | this point could be arranged, I have no doubt, that I shall be able to organise, in the interest, with which I am now engaged, a most IMMENSE PARTY, and MOST SERVICEABLE ONE.

Be so kind as not to leave the vicinity of London, in case *M* and myself come

Robert John Wilmot Horton (1784-1841), knighted 1831, after 1834 3rd Baronet. At this time he was MP for Newcastle-under-Lyme and under-secretary for war and the colonies. Wilmot Horton and Colonel Doyle, acting as the representatives of Mrs Leigh and Lady Byron respectively, were implicated in the destruction of Byron's 'Memoirs', and hence Wilmot Horton would have been well known to Murray. Lord John Russell ed *Memoirs of Thomas Moore* (1853) IV 192; Smiles I 445.

This may be a reference to Lockhart's involvement, beginning in 1817, with *Blackwood's Magazine*. Lockhart's alleged responsibility for the *Chaldee MS.*, a blasphemous parody of the Scriptures, and other literary offences, had caused Murray to break off his partnership with William Blackwood. Although Murray appears to have overcome an antagonism to Lockhart dating from this period, some members of Murray's circle, such as Barrow, were less forgiving. See **37**&n2.

On their return from a trip to Ireland in the summer of 1825 Lockhart and Scott visited the Lake District, where they met Wordsworth, Southey, Canning and others.

up *suddenly* – but I pray you if you have any real desire to establish a mighty engine, to exert yourself at this present moment, and assist me | to *your very utmost.* Write as soon as possible to give me some idea of your movements and direct to me here – as I shall then be sure to obtain your communication.

The *Chev.* and all here have the highest idea of Wrights *nous* and think it most important, that he should be at the head of the legal department.

I write this dispatch in the most extreme haste.

Ever yrs

BD |

I have already written *twice*

28A TO GEORGE BOYD Chiefswood, Melrose, Tuesday [27 September 1825]

ORIGINAL: QUA 418

COVER: Messrs. Oliver and Boyd | High Street | Edinburgh | MR. BOYD

POSTMARK: (1) In circle: SEP | W 28 [central number in small circle] E | 1825 (2) In rectangle: MELROSE | 3 PA[ID] B

EDITORIAL COMMENT: In another hand on the flap: 'Letter | B. Disraeli | Chiefswood | 27 Sept recd 29th. 1825'. *Sic*: Edinburg.

Chiefswood – Melrose | Tuesday

Dear Sir,[1]

I have just received a parcel from you. From the contents of my letters I shall most probably return in a few days to England. I shall feel extremely obliged by your sending to me twenty pounds, as I fear I shall not be able again to | reach Edinburg.

Mr. Murray desires me to remember him to you and to say that the Quarterly will be published next Saturday, and that he has many important works in the press.

I regret exceedingly that it is not in my power personally to | acknowledge your attention and

I am,
dear Sir,
Truly yours,
B. Disraeli.

---

29 TO [JOHN MURRAY] Chiefswood, [Melrose], [Tuesday 27? September 1825]

ORIGINAL: MR 14

PUBLICATION HISTORY: Smiles II 194-5, dated September 1825

EDITORIAL COMMENT: In another hand: 'Sept 1825'. *Dating*: by comparison with **28A**. The last page of the MS is torn. *Sic*: Edinburg, Abbottsford.

Chiefswood

My dear Sir,

I am quite sure, that upon the business I am upon now, every line will be acceptable, and I therefore make no apology for this hurried dispatch. I have just

1 See **26**n4.

received a parcel from O[liver] and B[oyd]. I transmitted a letter from *M* [Lockhart] to Wright and which was for your mutual consideration, to you, via *Chronometer*, last Friday. I afterwards received a note from you dated *Chichester*, and fearing from that circumstance that some confusion would arise, I wrote a few lines to you at Mr Holland's.[1] I now find, that you will be in town on Monday; on which day I rather | imagine the said letter from *M* to Wright will arrive. I therefore trust that the suspected confusion will not arise.

I am very much obliged to you for your letters – but I am very sorry, that you have incurred any trouble, when it is most probable, that I shall not use them. The Abbotsford and Chiefswood families have placed me on such a friendly and familiar footing, that it is utterly impossible for me to leave them, while there exists any chance | of M's going to England. *M* has introduced me to most of the neighbouring gentry, and receives with a loud laugh any mention of my returning to Edinburg. I dined with Dr. Brewster[2] the other day. He has a pretty place nea[*r*] Melrose. It is impossible for m[*e*] to give you any written idea of the beauty and unique character of Abbottsford.

Adio.

BD

30

TO THOMAS CROFTON CROKER [London, Thursday 20 October 1825?]

ORIGINAL: MHS Guild Library 1

EDITORIAL COMMENT: On the evidence of Croker's note (see n2) to which this was the answer, D was seeking advice about a projected series of volumes on the English counties. The series seems never to have materialized.

My dear Croker,[1]

Absence from B[loomsbury] S[quare] has prevented me from answering your note[2] and has made me, I fear, very much inconvenience you. I shall not be able to gain Russell Place today, as I leave | town in half an hour.

Will you dine with [me] in B.S. on Monday at 1/2 past 6. and we will then discuss all points.

Yrs faithfully

B. Disraeli

1 The Rev William Woolams Holland, a minor canon of Chichester, was Murray's brother-in-law. *BLG* (1837).

2 David Brewster (1781-1868), physicist. Since 1802 he had edited the magazine known in 1825 as *The Edinburgh Journal of Science*. He was knighted in 1831.

---

1 Thomas Crofton Croker (1798-1854) was an Irish antiquary and author. He then lived at 13 Russell Place, Fitzroy Square.

2 H B/XXI/C/597 (19 Oct 1825).

31 TO [Mr MAAS] [London], [Tuesday] 25 October 1825

ORIGINAL: PS 32

PUBLICATION HISTORY: Smiles II 202-3, dated 25 October 1825; M&B I 69, undated extract

EDITORIAL COMMENT: Monypenny's notes contain only a brief extract from this text. *Sic*: Coblentz.

October 25th, 1825.

Dear Sir,[1]

Your hospitality, which I have twice enjoyed, convinces me that you will not consider this an intrusion. My friend, Mr. Murray, of Albemarle Street, London, the most eminent publisher that we have, is about to establish a daily journal of the first importance. With his great influence and connections, there is no doubt that he will succeed in his endeavour to make it the focus of the information of the whole world. Among other places at which he wishes to have correspondents is the Rhine, and he has applied to me for my advice upon this point. It has struck me that Coblentz is a very good situation for intelligence. Its proximity to the Rhine and the Moselle, its contiguity to the beautiful baths of the Taunus, and the innumerable travellers who pass through it, and spread everywhere the fame of your admirable hotel, all conduce to make it a place from which much interesting intelligence might be procured.

The most celebrated men in Europe have promised their assistance to Mr. Murray in his great project. I wish to know whether you can point out any one to him who will occasionally write him a letter from your city. Intelligence as to the company at Wiesbaden and Ems, and of the persons of eminence, particularly English, who pass through Coblentz, of the travellers down the Rhine, and such topics, are very interesting to us. You yourself would make a most admirable correspondent. The labour would be very light and very agreeable; and Mr. Murray would take care to acknowledge your kindness by various courtesies. If you object to say anything about politics you can omit mentioning the subject. I wish you would undertake it, as I am sure you would write most agreeable letters. Once a month would be sufficient, or rather write whenever you have anything that you think interesting. Will you be so kind as to write me in answer what you think of this proposal? The communication may be carried on in any language you please.

Last year when I was at Coblentz you were kind enough to show me a very pretty collection of ancient glass. Pray is it yet to be purchased? I think I know an English gentleman who would be happy to possess it. I hope this will not be the last letter which passes between us.

I am, dear Sir,

Yours most truly,

B. Disraeli

1 Murray's *Northern* (227) identifies Maas as the proprietor of the Trierche Hof in Coblenz. A copy of Murray's offer to Maas is in the *Representative* MSS (MR 29). Although this copy is not in D's hand, it appears that one of D's functions at *The Representative* was drafting letters for Murray to send under his (Murray's) name. For example, there is a draft in D's hand of a letter from Murray to Walter Henry Watts offering him a position (MR 21). There is also a draft in D's hand of a letter from Murray to Sir Walter Scott. MR 34.

TO JOHN GIBSON LOCKHART [London], Wednesday 26 October 1825 32

ORIGINAL: NLS MS 931 no 118

COVER: John Gibson Lockhart Esq, | etc. etc., etc., | Chiefswood, | Melrose, | N.B.

POSTMARK: (1) In double circle: OC | U 26[central number in small circle] | 1825 (2) In square: 1/2

PUBLICATION HISTORY: Scott *Letters* II 406-7, omitting the first paragraph, the paragraph about Moore, and the postscript; Nickerson 283-5

EDITORIAL COMMENT: *Sic*: Pashaw.

Oct 26. Wedy. | 25

Dear Lockhart,

I had intended to have sent you a packet today, or the next, but the death of my fathers mother,[1] an old Lady whom you might perhaps remember seeing at Hyde[2] has rather disorganised my operations. She was of so advanced an age, that we were all prepared for this event, and altho' we can look upon her sudden decease, only as a very fortunate release from suffering and infirmity, still you must be conscious, that even under these circumstances, death is somewhat affecting.

I have been engaged at the *magnum opus*[3] unceasingly since we parted, as well as Murray who is perfectly indefatigable. I have received six letters from different correspondents in the Levant and Morea who all appear very intelligent. I have written to them fully. Mr Briggs,[4] the great Alexandrian merchant and the agent in this country for the Pashaw of Ægypt,[5] has engaged to furnish us with information from that quarter. By his account Ægypt is now one of the most flourishing countries in the world, and his detail of the policy and conduct of the reigning Pashaw certainly prove him one of the most enlightened of modern rulers. Besides letters, Briggs receives by every ship a journal of the public occurrences of the Kingdom, and he has pledged himself to give us this regularly.

I have not yet engaged Maginn,[6] but I hope shortly to inform you of this business being arranged. |

1 Sarah D'Israeli, Isaac D'Israeli's mother, died, aged eighty-two, on 24 October 1825. M&B I 8. Her obituary in *The Times*, however, described her as being 'in her 84th year'. (28 Oct 1825). Roth (21-2) notes that 'we have her grandson's authority for believing that she ... regarded Judaism not as a religion but as a misfortune, and was ... buried in Willesden Church when she died.' In his old age, D described her to Rowton as 'a demon only equalled by Sarah Duchess of Marlborough, Frances Anne [Marchioness of Londonderry], and perhaps Catherine of Russia.' M&B I 7-8.

2 This is the first indication that, on one of his visits to London, Lockhart had been taken by D to meet the family at Hyde House.

3 *The Representative.*

4 Samuel Briggs, senior partner in the firm of Briggs & Thurburn, cottonbrokers. In 1803 Briggs had been named vice-consul at Alexandria; later he became British consul there. John Marlowe *Anglo-Egyptian Relations, 1800-1953* (1954) 60; Alfred C. Wood *A History of the Levant Company* (1935 repr 1964) 185, 197; *ER* (1810).

5 Mehemet (or Mohammed) Ali (1769-1849), founder of modern Egypt and viceroy.

6 William Maginn (1793-1842), LLD, poet, journalist and miscellaneous writer. After leaving Trinity College, Dublin, he was a journalist with *Blackwood's Magazine*, then with *The Literary Gazette*. Coming to London in 1823, he was enlisted by John Murray for *The Representative*. See **36**. He was sent to Paris as a foreign correspondent, but returned to edit the lighter side of the paper. He was involved in the establishment of *Fraser's Magazine* in 1830, and provided the text for the 'Gallery of Literary Characters', which featured drawings by Daniel Maclise.

I inform you, *au secret* of course, that Copleston is also engaged on the subject of Universities.[7] As in the present state of affairs there is every appearance of the opinions of the Church party upon this important subject being extremely varying, Mr Powles has written to the Bishop[8] to arrange that on his coming to town, a council consisting of two or three Churchmen and as many laics should be instituted, and that they should immediately take into consideration the whole affair and settle upon some system to be adopted and that their plan should be developed in our journal. That they should also invite Copleston to send in his ideas, and that you should, if in London, form one of the council and, if not, assist them by your advice. If this plan be adopted, I will immediately let you know. It seems rational[.]

I am vigorous in my researches after a *maison* for you and hope I shall succeed very shortly. Two or three are upon the *tapis*.

I observe today by the Times that Moore is about to reach Abbotsford with the intention of inducing the *Illustrissimus* to assist him in a projected Life of Ld. B[yron].[9] If this be true, pray beware, that Toad and Cupid[10] does not get any scent of the Volume you took down with you, and indeed I would advise you not to mention, in any manner, anything of Murray's Byronian | collection. From peculiar circumstances, I know ——'s affairs as well, I believe, as any one in Xdom. Beware of him! – his situation is such, that he *must* write – quartos and octavos can alone save him – and he goeth about like a hungry lion, seeking whom he can devour.[11]

Do me the favor of presenting my best compliments to Mrs. Lockhart and believe me, with great regard,

yours,

B. Disraeli

I say nothing of Guinea Hen[12] *au present*; but I will take care that any letters to a

7 Edward Copleston (1776-1849) was then provost of Oriel College, and author of pamphlets on various subjects, including defences of the universities as organized at that time. He later became bishop of Llandaff.

8 Shute Barrington (1734-1826), bishop of Durham 1791-1826. See also **36**n7.

9 Thomas Moore (1779-1852), Irish poet and close friend and biographer of Byron. Moore had met Byron in Venice in 1819, at which time Byron had made a gift to Moore of his 'Memoirs'. In 1821 Moore sold the 'Memoirs' to John Murray. See **9**n1. *The Times* of the day on which D wrote this letter recorded Moore's departure for Edinburgh to consult with Scott (the *Illustrissimus* of the text) about a planned biography of Byron.

10 In the context this can only be Moore. Nickerson (285) suggests that Moore's small size and his recent publication of *The Loves of the Angels* (1823) account for the double familiarity.

11 In May 1824, on the burning of the MSS of Byron's 'Memoirs' (see **9**n1), Moore repaid Murray the 2,000 guineas, with interest, which he had received to edit the work. But to do this he had to borrow the money from the publisher Longmans. It was to pay off this debt to Longmans that Moore agreed to write a life of Byron for Murray. D suggests that these circumstances had made Moore avid in the search for literary topics from which he might make money.

12 Nickerson suggests John Barrow. See also **27**n7. This letter illustrates D's habit of developing different sets of code names for the same people, depending on his correspondent. Here, Sir Walter Scott is not 'The Chevalier' as he is in letters to Murray, but 'Illustrissimus'. In the same way, Barrow – 'Mr Chronometer' to Murray – is 'Guinea Hen' to Lockhart.

certain gentleman[13] shall arrive only thro' me. My relations however in that quarter are (on my honour) in nowise different from what they were, when we parted.

TO JOHN MURRAY [London, October 1825] 33

ORIGINAL: MR 17

PUBLICATION HISTORY: Smiles II 201, edited version dated October 1825

EDITORIAL COMMENT: In another hand on the first page of the MS: 'Octr 1825'; and on the fourth: '1825. Octr. | B. D ISRAELI ESQ'. The context makes it clear D is writing from London. His return from 'the city' probably refers to Hurst's office in Cheapside, rather than to a departure from the capital.

1/2 pt. 1

Jno. Murray Esq
My dear Sir,
I have just returned from the city, and write you a hurried note.

When Basevi has arranged the terms, you should furnish Powles with the name of the Vendor's solicitor and Hurst[1] will then examine | the title and do the needful. No time should be lost in arranging this, as the examination of the title should take place, while the old fishman is moving.

Roworth[2] is to send all my proofs to | you. I have taken the liberty of having them sent to W[hitehall] P[lace][3] as I thought they would then be sure to meet your eye.

I send the map.

When we again meet, which I trust will be right speedily, | I hope to have a vigorous account of your movements – particularly as regards the foreign correspondence.

Yours ever
BD

I mention Hurst, as I think after what has passed it will be better; and he is more used to deeds of partnership and *agreements for services* etc. etc. than the Anglo Saxon.[4]

13 John Murray?

---

1 The context suggests a solicitor. The only London solicitor so named in this period was James Hurst of 26 Milk Street, Cheapside. *Law List* (1825). D appears to be referring to negotiations for offices for *The Representative*. According to Smiles (II 201), George Basevi was engaged to plan offices and to secure printing premises. Although, as Smiles records, 'a large house was eventually taken in Great George Street, Westminster, and duly fitted up as a printing office', when the paper appeared, the printer was Thomas Cape in Northumberland Court, Strand. The paper also had an address at 46 Fleet Street.

2 Charles Roworth, 38 Bell Yard, Temple Bar, printed *The Quarterly Review*. William B. Todd *A Directory of Printers ... 1800-1840* (1972) 166. The proofs and map were probably for a new edition of one of the mining pamphlets. **19**n4, **21**n9.

3 John Murray's London residence.

4 Probably Sharon Turner (1768-1847), solicitor and writer on Anglo-Saxon history, close friend of Isaac and D's godfather. Murray consulted Turner frequently on legal questions touching literary property. Turner also acted as the solicitor for *The Quarterly Review* during its formative years.

34 TO [WILLIAM WRIGHT?] [London, October 1825?]

ORIGINAL: QUA 141

EDITORIAL COMMENT: In another hand on reverse side: '1825 | *Benjamin Disraeli* | ~~J. Murray~~ | *London*'.

My dear Sir,[1]

Be so kind as to let Mr Murray know the moment that Mr Constable[2] arrives, as he wishes to have the pleasure of calling upon him.

Ever my dr Sir,

yrs

B. Disraeli.

1 The recipient appears to be William Wright, on the basis of the following letter from John Murray to Wright, dated October 1825 (Smiles II 247):

> My Dear Wright,
>
> Although I intend to do myself the pleasure of calling upon Mr. Constable at your house to-morrow immediately after church (for it is our charity sermon at Wimbledon, and I must attend), yet I should be most happy, if it were agreeable to you and to him, to favour us with your company at dinner at, I will say, five to-morrow. Mr. Constable is godfather to my son, who will be at home, and I am anxious to introduce him to Mr. C., who may not be long in town.

2 Archibald Constable (1774-1827), Scottish publisher of *The Edinburgh Review* and of Sir Walter Scott's poetry and novels. This is how D remembered his first meeting with Constable: 'As I came down to dinner, Sir Walter was walking up and down the hall with a very big, stout, florid man, apparently in earnest conversation. I was introduced to him before dinner as Mr Constable, the famous publisher of the Edinburgh Review and the Waverley novels, the authorship of them not then acknowledged, at least, not formally. It struck me, that I had never met before such an ostentatious man, or one whose conversation was so braggart. One would think that he had written the Waverley novels himself, and certainly that Abbotsford belonged to him.' H A/X/A/3, Swartz 9-10.

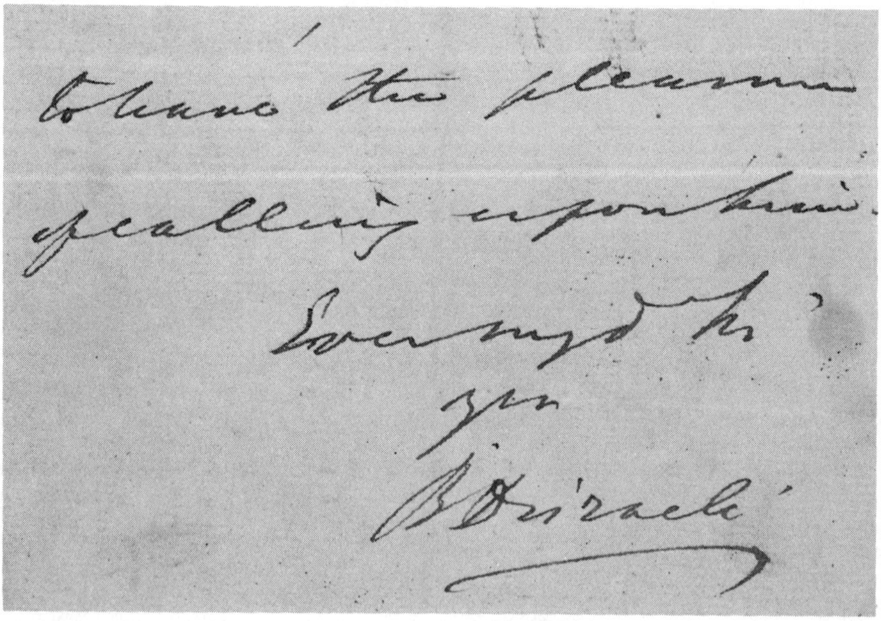
to have the pleasure
of calling upon him.
Ever my dr Sr,
yrs
B Disraeli

TO JOHN GIBSON LOCKHART 35

Whitehall Place, [London],
Tuesday [1 November 1825]

ORIGINAL: NLS MS 931 no 116

COVER: John Gibson Lockhart Esq | ~~Northumberland Street~~ | ~~Edinburgh~~ | [In another hand]: Chifswood | *Milrose Milrose*

POSTMARK: (1) In double circle: No | J 1[central number in small circle] | 1825 (2) In circle: NOV | W 3 E | 1825 (3) In circle: NOV | [illeg]4 E | [18]25 (4) Half circle over box: Q A Q | [1] | EDINBURGH | NOV 1825

PUBLICATION HISTORY: Nickerson 286-7

EDITORIAL COMMENT: *Sic*: Chifswood, Milrose.

There are calculations on the lower flap of the cover, presumably by Lockhart:

(1)	(2)		(3)
280	105		20)3605
21	21		180
280	105		
560	200		
5880	2105		
	1500		
	21)3605		
	130		
		21/160	
		1500	[*sic*]

Whitehall P. | Tuesday

Dear Lockhart,

I received your letter this morning. There is very great difficulty in getting houses in Westminster, everybody rushing to that quarter. I have seen however a great many houses in it. There are two, which appear to me to deserve attention. One is in Duke Street. It is a much superior house to the one we visited. It has a very pretty hall – an elegant little suite upstairs of two drawing rooms and boudoir – a handsome dining parlour, and a library – the last a very elegant, tho' not a very large room. There are two best bed rooms – one the size | of the drawing room and therefore very commodious and a dressingroom answering to the boudoir, and which is large enough for a room for Johnnie.[1] There are then three servants rooms – good – offices downstairs good – Kitchen admirable. All these rooms look on the park, to which there is an entrance. The rent of this house for a lease of nearly 21 years is only 105 pr. ann. but a premium of 1500£ is demanded as the house has been thoroughly repaired. I understand they will take 1000£ – but there requires 500£ I should think to be laid out in internal painting and decoration etc. Write me a line and tell me what you think of this? The situation, altho' not very agreeable to get at one way, is yet most genteel – many members of P[arliament] and people of grade residing there. This house also belongs to a clergyman,[2] who leaves on acc[oun]t of promotion.

There is a corner house in Whitehall | Place, also deserving attention – lease of 21 yrs. – no premium; might be got perhaps for £280 pr. ann – but requires

1 John Gibson Lockhart's son, John Hugh (b 1821), known as Hugh Littlejohn.

2 The Rev William J. Rodber (1791?-1843), secretary to the Society for Promoting the Building of Churches and Chapels. After 1826 he had a parish in Marylebone.

thoroughly painting etc. inside, the walls never having been touched since they were finished. The best drawing room and the dining room are bigger than Murrays, but this size would of course make furnishing more expensive. Send me your ideas on this also. I hope to have a letter from you by tomorrow's post, as you mention that you intend to write. I have been out all day after houses and only write this by twilight, that you may not be disappointed in receiving a letter. You must not therefore expect any news and must excuse the scrawl.

M[os]t f[aithfu]lly yrs

B. Disraeli

---

36 TO JOHN GIBSON LOCKHART [London], Saturday [12? November 1825]

ORIGINAL: NLS MS 931 no 112

PUBLICATION HISTORY: Scott *Letters* II 407-10, dated 'early in November'; Nickerson 287-90

EDITORIAL COMMENT: *Dating*: by Lockhart's letter to D of 3 November about obtaining a house in London, which crossed with D's to him on the same subject. *Sic*: Porsenna, Philpotts, Stuttgardt, Coblentz, Frankfort.

Saturday *night*

Dear Lockhart,

I should have written to you before this, but have waited with the expectation of receiving a letter from you as mentioned in your last. I hope you received mine directed to you at Edinburgh and dated somewhere, about the end of last month – the subject, your house.[1] I am the last person who could ever wish to make a bore of correspondence, nor have I the least desire that you should write to me a single letter, unless you have something to communicate, which may authorise the great trouble of your writing and my reading a letter; but I confess, *for Murray's sake*, I rather wished to have a line as to the feeling *now* existing at Abbotsford[2] on the grand plan. A communication of this kind infuses new life and energy into the Emperor.[3] It is perhaps foolish to mention this, but the truth is, Murray has long been accustomed to look up to authority, and the approbation of such a man as Scott is to him "meat drink and raiment."

Much | my dear Lockhart has happened since we parted – I think of importance[.] In the first place *Maginn is engaged*. I called upon the Dr. shortly after your departure. It is impossible for me to give you any adequate idea of our interesting interview. To present you with a few of the leading features, you must know, that M. speedily came to the point and told me, that 300 to 350£ pr. ann was the regular salary for the services we required, but that it would not suit his views to go for a less income than £500 pr. ann. "*but that he felt bound in honor and candor to tell us, that he did not conceive that our paper could afford or justify such an expenditure*". He then went on "*backing Barnes*[4] *against us*" ridiculing the

1 See **35**.

2 D was not only drafting letters for Murray to write to Scott, but also trying to stimulate encouraging responses from Scott to Murray, who remained worried by the opposition to Lockhart's appointment to *The Quarterly Review*. See also **39**n2.

3 Murray, whom Sir Walter Scott called the 'Emperor of the West'.

4 Thomas Barnes (1785-1841) was editor of *The Times* 1817-41.

attempt generally, swearing there was only one way to conduct a newspaper, | that a newspaper *was* a newspaper and other of these sage truisms. He "ventured to predict that with all our system in six months time we should be doing the same thing as the Old Times." – That he was "*the most experienced man as regards newspapers in London,*" that he knew what the system was capable of etc. etc. etc.

As I did conceive him to be decently honorable, and as I felt the importance of arguing the question with a man, who might fairly be considered as a very prosopopeia of the Public Press, I thought the experiment might be hazarded of giving him a slight and indefinite sketch of our intentions. | This I did with great caution and mentioning no names. To give you an idea of the effect which I produced is utterly impossible. The Dr. started from his chair like Giovanni in the Banquet scene, and seemed as astounded, as *attonitus*, as Porsenna when Scævola missed him.[5] A new world seemed opened to him, and this sneering scribe, this man of most experience, who had so smiled at our first mentioning of the business ended by saying, that as to the success of the affair, doubt could not exist and that a year could not elapse without our being the very first paper going.[6] Upon my faith Lockhart, I consider this a most important interview – because | really after all, it is becoming acquainted, as it were, with the private opinion of Barnes etc. In brief the Dr. goes to Paris, and Murray acquits him (this *au secret*) of his little engagement. He sets off some time in December, that he may have six weeks clear in Paris before we commence on operations – but his salary commences *from this time* and he is to assist us by his general advice and exertions until he goes off. Have I managed this well?

It has come to our knowledge that the Bp. of Durham, spirited on by his able council in the North (Philpotts Townsend & Co)[7] | is contemplating some move in the press. We intend to write to them informing them of our plans and requesting their cooperation.

I am most unceasingly employed about this business. The following is a sketch of our correspondence *at present established.*

5 Assuredly, these are two vivid images to indicate extreme astonishment: one is of the protagonist of Mozart's *Don Giovanni*, who rightly sees his own doom as his victim's statue comes to life (act II sc V), and the other is of Lars Porsena, King of the Tuscans, who besieged Rome in 509BC. During the siege, Gaius Mucius (later 'Scævola'-the 'left-handed') attempted to kill him, but was taken prisoner. Threatened by Lars Porsena with torture and death, Mucius thrust his right hand into a flame and held it there until it was consumed. The king was so thunder-struck (*attonitus*) by such courage that he made peace and withdrew. Livy II 12.

6 Ironically, just as D was confidently predicting its eclipse by *The Representative*, *The Times*, under Barnes, was beginning its great period of pre-eminence. Barnes himself was to become D's tutor in the journalism of political polemics. The reference to the 'Old Times' recognizes the existence of *The New Times*. Edited until 1826 by John Stoddart, better known as 'Dr Slop', it challenged the Thunderer in the period 1818-28. W.D. Bowen *The Story of 'The Times'* (1931) 105-6.

7 Henry Phillpotts (1778-1869), later bishop of Exeter, and George Townsend (1788-1857) were both at this time chaplains to Shute Barrington, bishop of Durham. All three were Tory opponents of Catholic Emancipation, which was then becoming an issue. In April 1825 Phillpotts began his controversy on this subject with Charles Butler in a series of fifteen letters, attacking Butler's *Book of the Roman Catholic Church*. Townsend contributed to the debate by publishing, also in 1825, *The Accusations of History against the Church of Rome*.

S.A.	N.A.
All South America –	All the North American Newspapers and private intelligence from a family of distinction at Washington by every packet. Mexico.

All the Morea –
All the Baltic
All the Levant
Smyrna
Constantinople
Greece.
} making about 27 correspondents.

Paris – a general agent.

Florence –
Rome –
} correspondents |

Netherlands – Two correspondents – both men of intelligence. Germany – Vienna – Berlin – Munich – Dresden – Stuttgardt –

Weimar – Coblentz Frankfort Hamburg and Treves.[8] I have been very much assisted in this grand *coup* of Germany by Mrs. Wm. Elliott,[9] who when devoid of humbug is very clever. All the letters which we have written to these places are not answered, but we do not anticipate the *slightest* doubt of their success. I have heard this day of a most admirable man at *St Petersburg* – In addition to these we must put down – The West Indies – Teneriffe I have no doubt, that in a few days I shall get a most excellent correspondent at Cadiz – but I have not | yet succeeded in Madrid which is most important. We have established also at Liverpool, Glasgow, Manchester, Birmingham etc. etc. – actually established. I see no visible obstacle to our beginning the 1st. day of February for our mechanical part, such as reporters, printers building etc. goes on as well as the other.

Pray present my kindest Complimts. to Mrs. Lockhart and remember me to John.

Yours ever faithfully

BD

I should think it most desirable for you to write a *serious* letter to Maginn.

8 The Murray *Representative* MSS (26-31) contain copies of letters to an R. Duckworth at Gibraltar, Joseph J. Saunders at Genoa, a Dr Julius at Hamburg, an Auguste Clavareau at Limburg, a Mr Henry Bynner at Trieste and Mr Maas at Coblenz. Six letters from Bynner to John Murray are in the Hughenden papers. H E/V/B/1a-f.

9 Monypenny (I 70n) identifies her as a woman of German birth who married Murray's brother-in-law.

TO JOHN GIBSON LOCKHART [London, Monday 21 November 1825] 37

ORIGINAL: NLS MS 931 no 115
COVER: J.G. Lockhart Esq: | Chiefswood | Melrose | *N.B.*
POSTMARK: (1) In double circle: NO | J21 [central number in small circle] | 1825 (2) In square: 1/2
PUBLICATION HISTORY: Scott *Letters* II 410; Nickerson 295-6
EDITORIAL COMMENT: *Sic*: *meleed.*

1/2 pt 5 o'clock.

My dear Lockhart,

I have arrived after a most fatiguing journey. I went immediately to the Emperor and my reception was most unfavorable. I would use a harsher word if I remembered one. He has spoken to Coleridge[1] and nothing could go off better – it is perfectly settled. But as to my unhappy mission – He swears that he understood, I undertook to go to Sir W[alter Scott] *au secret* and not to you, that I have ruined and *meleed* everything etc. – That he only wanted Sir W. to write a few letters in consequence of the spirit evinced against you etc. etc. I was too ill to answer him and I trust to the course of events to settle all things. | He swears also that I ought not to have mentioned Barrow's name etc. All these things, I need not tell you, appear to me very extraordinary, as I am not aware of having violated any confidence or instructions whatever. Stewart Rose has made a miserable business of it – instead of calling on Murray, he wrote to Barrow, and the latter has called on Murray in great ire.[2]

I hope all things will turn out well. Murray writes by tomorrow's post to Sir. W. Scott, and has extracted a promise from me | that I would not write by this to you. Consider therefore that this violation of my word is the consequence of my sincere friendship for you, and mention it not to the winds. I will write by tomorrow's post fully and positively.

Yrs. Ever

BD

You will not of course come to town upon this letter. I only write that you may be prepared.

1 John Taylor Coleridge (1790-1876), nephew of the poet, acted as editor of *The Quarterly Review* for three or four months during the interregnum between the retirement of William Gifford and the appointment of Lockhart.

2 William Stewart Rose (1775-1843) was a poet and translator, and reading clerk of the House of Lords 1800-24. As a close friend of Murray and Sir Walter Scott (who fitted up rooms for him at Abbotsford), Rose would presumably have known Lockhart, whose appointment as editor of *The Quarterly Review* Barrow opposed. Rose may not have known of Barrow's views when he wrote to him. Any favourable reference to Lockhart could have angered Barrow, sending him in protest to Murray.

38 TO JOHN GIBSON LOCKHART [London], Tuesday [22 November 1825]

ORIGINAL: NLS MS 931 no 117
COVER: Nov. 22. Tuesday. | John Gibson Lockhart Esq | Chiefswood | Melrose | *N.B.* | BD
POSTMARK: (1) In double circle: NO | N 22 [central number in small circle] | 1825
PUBLICATION HISTORY: Scott *Letters* II 411, omitting last two paragraphs; Nickerson 296-7
EDITORIAL COMMENT: 'Monday' is written in the superscription and then deleted by D.

Tuesday. | 5 o'clock.

My dear Lockhart,

Forget the letter,[1] which in a moment of great agitation about your business, and utterly exhausted in mind and body I wrote you yesterday evening. I rose this morning, having previously sworn by the God of the Silver Bow to slay the mighty Python of Humbug whose vigorous and enormous folds were so fast and fatally encircling us. Thanks the God![2] I have succeeded! You will now come to London in *triumph.*

Yours ever

BD

Give | my best compliments to your Lady, and your visitors, with whom I regret my too short acquaintance.

Murray is desirous of writing you as to all that has happened. I could not refrain giving you the gratifying result, but consider this letter as *perfectly confidential.*

As I am writing foreign letters | I have scribbled by mistake on foreign letter paper, which I trust you will decypher.

Thanks for yr. kind letter. I am quite well.

39 TO [JOHN MURRAY] Bloomsbury Square, [London], [Wednesday] 23 November 1825

ORIGINAL: MR 25
PUBLICATION HISTORY: Smiles II 205, dated 23 November 1825
EDITORIAL COMMENT: In another hand on the first page of the MS: 'Novr 23 1825'.

23 Novr. 1825 | Bloomsbury Sqr

My dear Sir,

Leave a note for Mr. Watts,[1] and request him to come on to Bloomsbury Square where you will meet him to execute. I want to see you *immediately*. A letter of

1 See **37**.

2 Apollo, who with an arrow slew the Python which infested the caves of Parnassus. The Apollo Belvedere in the Vatican represents him in the moment of victory, and Byron's description of the statue may well have been the inspiration for the tone of D's use of the image here. *Childe Harold* IV 161.

1 Walter Henry Watts (1776-1842), parliamentary reporter for *The Morning Chronicle* 1813-40. He was also editor of *The Annual Biography and Obituary* 1817-31. See MR 21 from John Murray to Watts (in D's hand), dated 3 November 1825, in which Murray offered Watts £350 per annum for his 'services as a parliamentary Reporter and general advice in the business.' Watts politely declined the next day (MR 22).

Lockharts of the *first importance* which will throw some light upon the | machinations of the junta of official scamps[2] who have too long enslaved you.

Yrs affectionately

BD

40

TO JOHN GIBSON LOCKHART [London], Wednesday 23 November 1825

ORIGINAL: NLS MS 931 no 119

COVER: John Gibson Lockhart Esquire | Chiefswood | Melrose | *N.B.*

POSTMARK: (1) In double circle: NO | Q 23 [central number in small circle] | 1825

PUBLICATION HISTORY: Scott *Letters* II 411-12; Nickerson 297-9

EDITORIAL COMMENT: *Sic*: less.

November 23 – 1825 – | Wednesday.

My dear Lockhart,

Ecce iterum Crispinus![1] I think I have kept my word and am pestering you with communications right sufficient. I am quite alarmed for the postmasters bill, which by the bye will not be the less light for the, by no means slender, sums incurred by my own postage during my two visits, and which I am ashamed to say your fascinating conversation prevented me from daily remembering and reimbursing.

The Emperor is writing you a long and full letter, but his morning has been so broken into, that he has desired me again to write, less you might imagine that all was not right.

I feel that a day should not pass without your having a somewhat more definite idea of what has passed than my last communication afforded. I confess it is a very difficult subject to handle in a sheet of paper. You must know that I called on Tuesday morning at Murrays and finding that he was in a more temperate humor I determined to bring matters to a crisis. What I said in our three hours uninterrupted conversation it is difficult to detail. My communications were the results of what I had seen, of what I had felt, since we had become acquainted. I detailed my sentiments as to your character – my experience of your disposition – my knowledge of your views in life. The result you are acquainted with. Do not think Murrays conduct in this last affair wavering and inconsistent. His situation | has been very trying. You and he have never rightly understood

2 Murray had a circle of advisers, all of whom were in official positions. The most influential of these were John Barrow and John Wilson Croker, both at the Admiralty. These men had both been long associated with *The Quarterly Review*, and they complained loudly at Murray's intention to appoint Lockhart to any editorial position on that journal. Their friendship had earned for Murray the position of publisher to the Admiralty. William Stewart Rose had also been associated with this group. George Paston [Emily Morse Symonds] *At John Murray's: Records of a Literary Circle, 1843-1892* (1932) 18-19. Andrew Lang *Life and Letters of J.G. Lockhart* (1897) I 369-71. See also **41**.

---

1 'Behold again Crispinus', or, more colloquially, 'Here's Crispinus again.' Juvenal *Satires* IV 1. Crispinus is portrayed in the poem as the debauched intimate of the Emperor Domitian, the last of the Flavian emperors. Thus D may be jokingly referring to his position of intimacy with the 'Emperor' Murray.

each other. When such connections were about to be formed between two men, they should have become acquainted not by the stimulus of wine. There should have been some interchange of sentiment and feeling. The fault I know was not yours – the result however was bad. All men have their sober moments and Murray in his is a man of pure and honorable – I might say, elevated sentiments. He wanted only to understand you. He wanted only to be told, what has now made him esteem the happiest incident in his life his connection with Mr. Lockhart.

I am speaking soberly and seriously. The trash which has been too long bandied about, as to your character, you[r] feelings, your society,[2] can only be effectively repelled by your conduct as really known – by an acquaintance with yourself "*in spirit and in truth.*"[3]

The Baronets letter has opportunely assisted me. When I say, it was worthy of him, I say sufficient.[4]

When you come to London you will be introduced on the best understood terms not only to all the regular supporters of the Q[uarterly] R[eview] but to Coleridge himself, who will feel honored by your acquaintance and will be most happy to assist you in the mechanical detail.

As to your coming to London it cannot be too speedy. I expect in less than 8 and 40 hours | to have arranged everything about your house. Many are offered and all suitable. The other affairs are prancing on in such prosperity, that a strong desire is expressed by all parties to commence operations sooner. The Emperor will write howr. When you come to town, it will be advisable for us to have some *private* conversation before you see him, as I think it proper for both of you that you should be put in possession of what has passed without obliging him to detail.

My compliments to all. And my best respects to Sir W[alter Scott] when you write.

I shall not add to the unpleasant sensations which you may have already experienced by presuming to offer you advice from a young gentleman aged – twenty. I may however my dear Lockhart indulge in the hope, that your destiny may be crossed no more, and that no indiscretion may prevent your splendid talents from having their full and fair play. If so, the result will be as honorable to yourself as it will be gratifying to your

very attached friend

B. Disraeli

2 A scarcely tactful reference to the rumours about Lockhart's earlier journalistic career with *Blackwood's Magazine*.

3 John 4:24.

4 When Scott heard rumours that Lockhart's nomination as editor of *The Quarterly Review* was running into trouble, he wrote a long letter to Murray in Lockhart's defence. The letter – dated 17 November 1825 – is quoted in full in Smiles (II 220-4).

TO JOHN GIBSON LOCKHART [London], [Thursday 24?] November 1825 41

ORIGINAL: NLS MS 931 no 114
COVER: Genl. pt. | John Gibson Lockhart Esquire, | Chiefswood, | Melrose, | N.B.
POSTMARK: (1) In double circle: NO | [illegible] | 1825
PUBLICATION HISTORY: Scott *Letters* II 413-14; Nickerson 299-301
EDITORIAL COMMENT: *Dating*: by context. The last page of the MS is torn.

J.G. Lockhart Esq
Chiefswood
My dear Lockhart,

I received your letter of Monday enclosing one for me this morning. I immediately put yours in an envelope and forwarded it to Murray without comment. He has this moment left me, having called in consequence. He tells me that he wrote to you last night – I did the same and have troubled you with epistles every day since I left Chiefswood. I hope you have received them all.

I have often complained to you of Murray's inconsistency, vacillation and indecision. I have done more, I have complained of them to himself. I regret it. Had I had any conception of the utter worthlessness of the intriguing, selfish and narrowminded officials by whom he has been so long surrounded, I certainly would have restrained my sentiments, and have pitied the noble and generous minded being who was subjected to such disgusting thraldom. When I tell you, that in the whole of this business Murray does really appear to have behaved in a manner more correct and more conscientious than I did previously consider human nature to be capable of, I feel that there is no person in the world to whom it can give such pleasure as yourself. It is impossible in a letter to give you any idea of the agitating and curious scenes which have taken place during these last days. The scales however have at length fallen from our friends eyes, and the walls of the Admiralty[1] have resounded to his firm and bold but gentlemanly tones. He is now in no state of excitement to which any reaction can ensue. His mind has undergone a revolution which | it has taken ten years to bring about, and which, I honestly confess, I did conceive could never have occurred. You would not know him for the same man. Thank God I did not postpone my departure to town one other second!

On the whole my good and excellent Lockhart I do most sincerely rejoice that our affairs have taken this turn. Some ill blood may for a moment have existed, some intemperate expressions may have perhaps on both sides been uttered, but after all without these mental purges where should we have been? Half confidence and hollow friendship, and wavering councils, are of all things the most terrible, and I cannot see, that if this affair had not happened, you could have come to London without these being your welcomers. I am most obliged to you for the frank and straightforward manner in which you have delivered yourself in this days letter. Honor me with your perfect confidence always, and I hope you will have no cause to repent.

1 See **39**n2.

We are most nervously anxious to see you in London. Affairs assume a most important aspect. I need not say what place you hold now really in Murrays confidence. He says without any violent protestations and with a coolness which I never remember to have witnessed in him, that he listens to no more *opinions* on these affairs and that while he has cash in his pocket and blood in his veins he stands by John Gibson Lockhart, even unto the death. You knew my former | opinion of the Emperor – you know I have had some little experience with him and you have sometimes expressed your opinion that I was not utterly ignorant of this world's ways. Now I deliberately and solemnly declare that I have as much confidence in the permanency of Murrays present disposition as I have in your honor.

But to your coming to town – Murray is most anxious to know whether you and Mrs. Lockhart, her maid and your Son and his peculiar suite will not come up immediately to Whitehall Place. Everything is already prep[*ared*] for your presence, *actually* prepared and allow me to hope that you will come. Before that time I very probably shall have a house for you but it appears to me by no means undesirable that Mrs. Lockhart should not be bored by novel domesticities immediately on her arrival. I do most sincerely hope therefore that you will comply with the imperial request.

There is one thing which I again mention. It is *absolutely necessary*, that you and I should have a conversation before you see Murray. I have no objection to his knowing it, but mind me, it is absolutely necessary.

Yours ever

B. Disraeli

It is in vain to give you any details. I keep them, till we meet.

---

42 TO JOHN GIBSON LOCKHART [London], Friday 25 November 1825

ORIGINAL: NLS MS 931 no 120

COVER: John Gibson Lockhart Esq: | Chiefswood | Melrose | N.B.

POSTMARK: (1) In double circle: NO | C 25 [central number in small circle] | 1825

PUBLICATION HISTORY: Scott *Letters* II 419, omitting the last two paragraphs of the postscript. Nickerson 301-3

EDITORIAL COMMENT: *Sic*: seee.

Friday. Nov. 25 | 1825

My dear Lockhart,

I have just received yr. lre [letter] of Tuesday evening. God grant your communic[ati]on with *my father in law*[1] may lead to no ill consequences. You are perhaps by this time convinced that you have been on a wrong scent. As for Murray, he has done more in eight and forty hours than if he had been sweating at the business as many weeks – and actually the *Prince of Pluck and Count of Confidence* must now be added to his numerous titles. I shall not show however

1 This is apparently a private reference rather than a code; for it seems that Lockhart had been 'chaffing him about his attentions to one of the Miss Murrays'. George Paston *At John Murray's: Records of a Literary Circle, 1843-1892* (1932) 19n.

to him the letter I received from you today, because I think when all goes right, I may as well be silent.

I much regret to say that I have been unable to arrange the business of yr. house as I had hoped. The prices are so enormous and the season has commenced so early that I do not feel justified in closing with anything. Basevi who has been so zealously kind in this business (for it is not etiquette for an architect to interfere in these matters) has counselled me today to advise you to come up and settle for yourself.

In the mean time our affairs | are *momentarily* growing more important. You are wanted every second of the day. For heavens sake then close with the imperial offer[2] and come to town IMMEDIATELY. This, this indeed is most, most important for us both. Pray come.

As to other matters – my father sends you his Compliments and says if you think an article on Charles 1st. worthy your attention, he will *pledge himself* that you shall have it for your first number.[3] As he has of late years cut the Q[uarterly] R[eview] he begs it to be understood that he now resumes his labors merely because *you* are its Conductor and that if at any time *circumstances may arise from which you may deem it desirable for your interests that this fact be known*, you are perfectly at liberty to say so.

I have had a view of the gubernatorial article and I must say, altho' I hope I am the last fellow in the world who has a foolish penchant for parental effusions, that for | exquisite philosophy, beautiful feeling, intense interest and profound research, it was never equalled.

Your fear that Murray may be endangered by a conference with Croker[4] makes me smile. Perhaps you smile too at my remark, but my dear fellow, as the showman says, "you will see what you will seee" –

in the greatest haste

BD

I have just received a letter from Powles and shall dine with him today. I must again impress upon you the mighty importance of your presence in London. May the next post bring news of your movement southward.

2 Murray (the 'Emperor') had offered to Lockhart the editorship of either *The Quarterly Review* or *The Representative*. There were two separate agreements: one for Lockhart's editorship of the *Quarterly*, and one specifying his obligations to *The Representative*. The terms of the agreement between Lockhart and Murray concerning *The Representative*, signed on 20 October 1825, were that Lockhart was to be paid £1,500 per annum for the years 1826, 1827 and 1828. Lockhart also agreed to write articles 'consistent with his rank in life'. At any time during the period of the agreement Lockhart had the option of exchanging his salary for one-eighth share of the newspaper for fourteen years, without advancing any capital of his own. Any losses were to be 'wholly borne' by Murray. The witnesses to the agreement were William Wright and D. MR unnumbered.

3 Either Lockhart did not take up the offer or Isaac withdrew it, for no article on Charles I appeared in *The Quarterly Review*. Isaac, who had contributed at least five articles to the review between 1809 and 1820 (Ogden 214-15), was at this time at work on his five-volume study of Charles I for Colburn, the first two volumes of which appeared in 1828. Colburn published volumes III and IV in 1830 and V in 1831.

4 John Wilson Croker (1780-1857), man of letters, Tory MP 1807-32 for various constituencies.

Complimts. to Mrs L., etc. | I have written every day since I left Chiefswood. I mention this lest any sho[ul]d have miscarried.

I have got a title.[5]

---

43 TO [ALFRED TURNER] [London], Monday [28 November 1825?]

ORIGINAL: ILLU xB B365b1 Card 2

COVER: Alfred Turner Esqre | 32 Red Lion Square | *B.D.*

EDITORIAL COMMENT: A copy: the MS is in Sarah's hand. *Dating*: by comparison with **47**, dated 3 December 1825. The present letter was probably written on the preceding Monday.

Monday Morning

My dear Sir,[1]

I am most unexpectedly called out by pressing business, which I am sorry must prevent my receiving you this morning. Will you have the goodness to prepare 2 agreements for general services, similar to the one with Mr. Derbishire for

Mr. Edward Byrne[2]
2 Lyons Inn
and Mr. Charles Roger Dodd[3]
17 Penlington Place Lambeth

the first for 5 G[uinea]s a week | from the 1st. of January, the 2nd. 5 G[uinea]s pr. week from the commencement of the Paper. Have you any News of the Abstract?

Dr. Sir
faithfully Yours
B. Disraeli

At this time he represented Bodmin. He was first secretary to the Admiralty from 1809 to 1830.

5 Probably the title for the, as yet unnamed, prospective newspaper. Writing to Murray from 25 Pall Mall on 21 December 1825, Lockhart said 'I am delighted and what is more satisfied with Disraeli's title

The Representative

If Mr Powles does not produce some thundering objection Let this be fixed in God's name.' MR 35.

---

1 Alfred Turner (d 1864), eldest son and law partner of Sharon Turner.

2 One journalist named Derbishire worked for *The Morning Chronicle*, became editor of *The Sunday Times* in 1835, and then returned to *The Morning Chronicle* as Spanish correspondent. At one time he also edited *The Courier*. [James Grant] *The Great Metropolis* 2nd ed (1837) II 145. Edward Byrne was perhaps related to the family who were proprietors of *The Morning Post*. Nicholas Byrne (d 1833) was succeeded as editor-proprietor by his eldest son, William Pitt Byrne. Harold Herd *Seven Editors* (1955) 40-56.

3 Charles Roger Phipps Dodd (1793-1855), a *Times* reporter, best remembered as editor of *Dod's Parliamentary Companion*. After 1847 he dropped the final letter from the spelling of his surname.

TO JOHN GIBSON LOCKHART [London], Monday [28 November 1825] 44

ORIGINAL: NLS MS 931 no 113
COVER: John Gibson Lockhart Esqr. | Chiefswood | Melrose | N.B.
POSTMARK: (1) In double circle: NO | F 28 [central number in small circle] | 1825 (2) In square: 1/2
PUBLICATION HISTORY: Scott *Letters* II 417-18, omitting the first paragraph; Nickerson 303-4
EDITORIAL COMMENT: *Sic*: whig.

Monday 1/2 pt 4

My dear Lockhart,
As my letter about yr. house[1] may give you a great deal of uneasiness, I just write to say, that I have this afternoon recd. a communication from Trollope,[2] the West[minste]r house agent, that the house of the Revd. Rodber[3] in Duke St which we looked over tog[ethe]r is to let for the season or year. Rodber has sold the lease to the present lessor who wishes to go to the Continent for a yr. before he takes up his residence in Duke St. and wishes to let it for this year furnished. Altho' the house is not at all desirable as a permanent residence, yet taking into consideration the unparalleled difficulty of getting houses at all and also the contiguousness of the prem[is]es in question to Murray[4] (a most important consideration for the first year of our labors) I have thought proper to require the terms etc. from Trollope without loss of time, and shall then, if they suit, conclude the bargain.

I have received your letter, and I believe have attended to everything necessary. I should not | of course have pressed yr. immediate coming to town had I been aware of the circ[umstance]s you mention. The sooner you arrive after, the better. Indeed the experience of every moment makes me the more urgent for your presence.

As to the paper, everything goes on swimmingly. The terrific agitation in which the City and the whole commercial interest has been thrown during the last three weeks may have prevented Powles from writing to you, but I know that he is attending to the points you mention.[5]

As to the review – Coleridge, if possible, is more friendly. I mentioned I believe to you about my father. I have called at Wrights three or four times and have kept him up to the sticking point. The Chancery Comm[issi]oners publish their report at the commencement of this year and it is therefore very important that you should have a first rate article on the subject. Means might be taken to get a previous view of the report, and place it at the head of the article.[6] I have

1 See **42**.
2 G. Trollope, house agent at 15 Parliament Street, London.
3 See **35**n2.
4 Duke Street is two blocks west of Albemarle Street, where John Murray's offices were located.
5 This may be a reference to the fluctuations in trading in Colombian bonds, which rose from 58 3/4 on 17 November 1825 to a high of 65 on 23 November, before falling off to 63 on the 25th. There was generally heavy trading in South American stocks and bonds during this period. *The Times* (18-26 Nov 1825). John Diston Powles would obviously have been preoccupied with the South American market.
6 Presumably a review by John Taylor Coleridge of the report on the Court of Chancery planned for a future issue of *The Representative*. No review appeared in *The Representative* – but there was a comment on the report in the fourth issue (28 Jan 1826).

attended to this. Palgrave[7] came to town last week and called on Murray yesterday in consequence of the Q[uarterly] R[eview] reports. He was delighted at hearing you were to be Editor, and enquired whether his assistance would in future [be] acceptable.[8] He was of course not a little pleased when he found that his services had been already desired. |

Merivale[9] (a gentlemanly whig) called immediately after to congratulate M. on the *coup* he had made in bringing you up to London etc. etc. great unknown etc. etc. such a father in law etc. etc. etc. In short all goes right and you have only to come to London to take advantage of affairs – and indeed as the Marchioness of Hastings[10] says, in the letter which Mrs. Lawrence Lockhart[11] wo[ul]d not let me bring to town "who the devil ever heard anything against you" which consid[erin]g all we know, was rather an odd observ[atio]n.

in gt haste

BD

Chenevix[12] will be in London as soon as yourself. I have had immense trouble about the Burke and am flattered today with the prospect of success.[13]

I have heard nothing from Maginn and am most anxious to see him.

I send you "the Age".[14] Is it credible, that it has come to this!!!!

As a result of criticism of the slow and expensive procedures of the Court of Chancery, a commission had been set up in 1824 to investigate. The report, dated 2 March 1826, contained 187 recommendations for reform. Lockhart seems to have followed D's advice to give prominence to the report, for *The Quarterly Review* devoted two articles to it: XXXIV (Sept 1826) 540-79; XXXVIII (July 1828) 241-97.

7 Francis Palgrave (1788-1861), barrister, author and deputy keeper of the records 1838-61. He was knighted in 1832.

8 *The Times* of 17 November 1825 carried a report that Lockhart had been appointed editor of *The Quarterly Review*.

9 John Herman Merivale (1779-1844), scholar and minor poet. He sat on the above-mentioned Chancery Commission, and concurred with its recommendations. He later wrote *A Letter to William Courtenay, Esq., on the Subject of the Chancery Commission* (1827).

10 Lady Flora Muir Rawdon (1780-1840), Countess of Loudoun in her own right, only daughter of the 5th Earl of Loudoun, had married in 1804 Francis Rawdon, 2nd Earl of Moira and 1st Marquess of Hastings.

11 John Gibson Lockhart's sister-in-law. The Rev Lawrence Lockhart was the minister of the parish of Inchinnan, Renfrewshire, Scotland.

12 Richard Chenevix (1774-1830), Irish-born chemist, mineralogist, dramatist and poet, and an occasional contributor to the *The Edinburgh Review* and *The Quarterly Review*. He is best known for his *Essay upon National Character*, published posthumously in 1830.

13 Possibly D had been charged with the task of obtaining a suitable reviewer for James Prior's *Memoir of the Life and Character of the Right Hon. Edmund Burke*. It was eventually reviewed by Lord Wellesley in *The Quarterly Review* for September 1826.

14 *The Age* (1825-43) was a scurrilous and libellous weekly, edited by Charles Molloy Westmacott (1787?-1868). Michael Sadleir gives a sketch of its history in *Bulwer* 340-5. Nickerson suggests that the copy which D had enclosed for Lockhart might have been the number for 27 November, which contained a ferocious attack upon Joseph Hume, the Radical MP, and Leonard Horner, both of whom had just delivered speeches in Edinburgh. But the previous week's number had included a short item in which Sir Walter Scott was quoted as attributing his good relations with Tom Moore to Moore's being a Jacobin and Scott's being a Jacobite. *The Age* nos 28, 29 (20, 27 Nov 1825).

TO ALFRED TURNER [Bloomsbury Square, London], Wednesday [30 November 1825?] 45

ORIGINAL: ILLU xB B365b1 Card 2
COVER: Alfred Turner Esqre | Red Lion Square | If not within Mr Disraeli would feel obliged by Mr. Wm. Turner stepping on to Bloomsy Sq.
EDITORIAL COMMENT: *Dating*: by comparison with **46** and **47**.

Wedny. | Alfred Turner Esq

My dear Sir,
I shall be at home the whole morning and would feel obliged by your calling on me if not inconvenient to you.
Yrs. faithfullly,
B. Disraeli

TO [JOHN MURRAY] [London], Thursday [1 December 1825] 46

ORIGINAL: MR 39
PUBLICATION HISTORY: Smiles II 205-6, extract dated December 1825
EDITORIAL COMMENT: In another hand on the first page of the MS: 'Jany 1826'. *Dating*: as Lockhart left for London on 5 December, the last sentence identifies this Thursday as 1 December. *Sic*: inclose, Windyer, Wyndier.

Thursday.

My dear Sir,
I inclose two letters which I received yesterday from Mr Powles (Nos. 1 and 2). Do me the favor to read them both.

The sensation about the paper is very great. A meeting of the proprietors of the New Times was held yesterday, in order to conciliate the Reporters whom they have universally offended. I have received two letters from Watts and in consequence have engaged Mr. Hall[1] and a Mr. Windyer Senr[2] – both of whom

1 Samuel Carter Hall (1800-1889), author and editor. In the early 1820s he had been acting as parliamentary reporter in the House of Lords, and writing reviews and criticisms of art for *The British Press*. In 1823 he had edited the short-lived *Literary Observer*; during 1825 he contributed to *The New Times*, and in 1826 he began the annual called *The Amulet*. His later journalistic career included an association with *The New Monthly Magazine*, of which he was briefly editor. On 28 April 1880 D granted him a civil-list pension of £150 a year 'for his long and valuable services to literature and art'.

In his *Retrospect of a Long Life* (New York 1883) 72-3, Hall gives a brief account of his connection with *The Representative*. 'I was appointed one of its corps of parliamentary reporters. Rarely had a publication been launched into the world of literature with such "great expectations". It was believed that the supply of money was inexhaustible; and it was known that the best literary aid of the day was at the command of the proprietor. There had been time for ample preparation; new type and fine paper were among the accessories ... The day preceding the issue of the first number, Mr. Murray might have obtained a very large sum for a share of the copyright, of which he was the sole proprietor; the day after that issue the copyright was worth comparatively nothing.'

The identity of the editor of *The Representative* is still a mystery. Hall comments: 'Editor there was literally none from the beginning to the end'. However, further remarks suggest that someone *was* entrusted with the function of editor though he performed his duties very badly and seems to have remained unknown to the staff! Smiles observes: 'Failing Lockhart, an editor, named Tyndale, had been appointed on short notice, though he was an obscure and

we shall find most excellent reporters and men of business. The latter has been on the Times.

Mr. Hall and Mr. Windyer will call on me tomorrow also for their agreements, and I shall give each of them a note to you to have the agreements executed.

I should not have troubled you with this had it been in my power to have reached you today. Pray favor me with a note, informg | me whether Hall and Wyndier shall call in Whitehall Place or Alb[emarle] St. and what hour may suit your convenience.

It is no use to write to Lockhart *after* today.

Yrs ever

BD

---

47 TO ALFRED TURNER

[Bloomsbury Square, London], Saturday [3 December 1825]

ORIGINAL: ILLU xB B365b1 Card 2

COVER: Alfred Turner Esq | Red Lion Sq: | [In another hand on the back]: B. Disreali | Bloomsbury | Square | 1825 | [inverted]: B. Disreali

EDITORIAL COMMENT: *Dating*: by comparison with **46**. The last page of the MS is torn. *Sic* cover: Disreali.

Saturday

My dear Sir,

There is another gentleman whose name today bears a very different aspect to what it did yesterday – for *Wyndier* lege *Windeyer*. It will perhaps be necessary to have fresh agreements in consequence of this error in your instructions. If | so, be kind enough to send up Mr. Windeyers agreements to Albemarle St. when finished and inform him at what hour he may call to execute the same. I have given him a letter to Murray for this purpose.

Do not let this however interfere with our previous arrangements as to *Hall* | and Derbishire and send me on their agreements to look at, before they are forwarded to Albemarle St.

Dr. Maginn's agreement appears to me to be very good – the Doctor has arrived. I will send you the agreemt. in the course of the morning and you can let me have the engrossmts. on [*Mon*]day.

Yrs fa[*ithfully*]

D

uninfluential person. He soon disappeared in favour of others, who were no better.' Smiles also quotes an anecdote from Hall, that John Murray called back a friend whom he had just seen off in a cab. Responding to his friend's alarmed enquiry of what it was he wanted, Murray replied, 'I want an editor! I want an editor!' Smiles concludes, 'This was his constant cry; but a cry which was never satisfied.' Smiles II 210. Hall also remarks, 'That Mr. D'Israeli never was the editor, I am certain.'

2 Charles Windeyer (1780-1855), journalist. A law reporter for *The Law Chronicle* and also connected with *The Times*, he is remembered as the first recognized reporter of the debates in the House of Lords. In 1828 he emigrated to Australia, where he became a magistrate. D's uncertainty about his name made a new contract necessary when he discovered the correct spelling. See **47**.

TO [ANNE MURRAY] [Bloomsbury Square, London], Sunday 21 May 1826 **48**

ORIGINAL: MR 62

PUBLICATION HISTORY: Blake 45, extract dated 21 May 1826

EDITORIAL COMMENT: There is a gap in the correspondence of over five months. *The Representative* had begun in January and it was quickly evident that the bright hopes of its founders would not be realized. The paper would limp on for another six weeks after this letter, but it was clear that Murray would be left with a considerable financial loss.

D must have spent most of the time writing, at great speed, the first part of *Vivian Grey*, which had been published anonymously by Colburn a month before this letter, on 22 April. See also **24**ec, and **60**n2. Although the identity of the author had been a well-kept secret, and speculation had contributed to the novel's initial success, Murray became aware of D's authorship and was greatly offended by the book, believing that one of its characters, the Marquis of Carabas, was a thinly disguised parody of himself. To Murray it seemed that not only had D rushed him into a disastrous financial loss (it amounted to £26,000), but he had then withdrawn, when failure was apparent, to write a book which made fun of him for doing what D had urged him to do. It was too much, and a severe strain was placed on the relations between Murray and the D'Israeli family. For a full account see M&B I 74-8, Blake 44-8. *Sic*: have altogether have, has spoke.

Sunday morning 8 o'clock | May 21st. 1826

Dear Madam,[1]

I request your particular attention to this letter, which I do assure you is written purely out of respect and regard for you and your family. These feelings have hitherto prevented me from noticing in any manner Mr. Murray's conduct towards me – they prevent me at this moment from applying any epithet to his conduct characteristic of my opinion of its nature – and they would have altogether have prevented me from noticing it at all, as long as the knowledge of it was confined to a few private and mutual friends. But Mr. Murray has overstepped the bounds, which the remembrance of former friendship, has too indulgently conceded him, and he has spoke and is now speaking of me to the world generally in terms which to me are as inexplicable, as they appear to be outrageous.

Under these circumstances, one course is apparently only left to me, and that is of the most decided and deplorable nature, but before I have recourse to it I wish, for the sake of all interested, to | give you every opportunity of rendering it unnecessary.[2] I earnestly beg of you to allow no misconceived opinions of self dignity – no preconceived opinions of my character, to prevent you from acting in this business temperately, wisely, and *promptly*. Promptitude is absolutely necessary. I only heard last night of your communication to Mr. and Mrs. Spence[3] – and I already feel that I am perhaps wrong in losing another four and twenty hours.

1 Anne Murray (d 20 Oct 1845), daughter of Charles Elliot; she had married John Murray on 6 March 1807. Smiles I 67, 73.

2 Monypenny interpreted this as a 'menace of legal action' (M&B I 75), but Blake thinks it more likely D was hinting at the possibility of a challenge. Blake 45.

3 Probably George Spence and his wife Anne, née Kelsall, whom he had married in 1819.

I have not mentioned to the family, that I have written this letter, but I shall do so when we meet this morning. If you think that any communication between yourself and my mother[4] can produce any beneficial effect, I am sure she will not be hindered by the remembrance of what is past from immediately meeting you. I hope that the bearer of this may return with an answer.

I am, dear Madam,
your very obedt Ser[van]t,
B. Disraeli

---

49 TO BENJAMIN AUSTEN [London, July? 1826]

ORIGINAL: BL ADD MS 45908 ff10-12

COVER: Benjn. Austen Esq | Holborn Ct | 11 Grays Inn Ct.

PUBLICATION HISTORY: [Sir Austen Henry Layard] 'The Early Life of Lord Beaconsfield' *QR* 168 (Jan 1889) 1-42 at 12, undated extract; M&B I 94-5, dated July? 1826; Jerman 74-5, dated June 1826

EDITORIAL COMMENT: The Austens and the D'Israelis apparently came to know each other in early 1825, when Sara Austen approached Isaac to write a review of *Tremaine* for *The Quarterly Review*. See **24**ec. The Austen residence in Guildford Street was close to Bloomsbury Square, and after the period at Hyde House, the families became more intimate. No letters have been located from D to Sara Aus-

---

4 Maria D'Israeli wrote to John Murray on the same day:

Bloomsbury Sq 21 May 1826

Dear Sir,

Having learnt that my Son has written to Mrs Murray this morning I am now doing what had I pleased myself I should have done sometime since which is to write to you, to request an explanation of your conduct which the kindness and pliability of Mr. D'Israeli's character never could obtain, for while you were expressing great friendship, we were constantly hearing of the great losses Mr. Murray had sustained through the mismanagement and bad conduct of my Son. Surely Sir, were this story truely [*sic*] told it would not be believed that the experienced publisher of Albemarle Street could be deceived by the plans of a boy of twenty whom you had known from his cradle and whose resources you must have as well known as his Father and had you condescended to consult that Father the folly might not have been committed. |

You then Sir perhaps would have found tho' a *clever boy* he was no "prodigy" and I must say I believe that the failure of the Representative lay much more with the proprietor and his Editor than it ever did with my Son – but I feel your disappointment and can forgive your irritability, yet I must resent your late attack on Benjamin. What can you mean by saying as an excuse for not meeting D'Israeli and myself at the house of Mr Spence that our son *had divulged and made public your Secrets* this surely you must know is not truth – and can you as the father of a family think yourself justified in hurting the character and future prospects of a young Man to whose Father you subscribe yourself his faithful friend and to whose Mother her most obliged.

I now must beg an explanation of this Enigma. I have allways [*sic*] carefully abstained from speaking on this subject | or attaching any reason for your strange conduct at Mrs Hardwick's, but this cannot last for I must not suffer Ben to lay [*sic*] any longer under an odium which can be explained away by the truth being told.

I really cannot beleive [*sic*] John Murray who has so often professed such strong friendship for D'Israeli should be now going about blasting the character of that Friends Son because he had formed in his versatile imagination *a perfect being* and expected impossibilities and found him on trial a *mere mortal* and a very very young Man.

I fear I have made this letter too long and that you will destroy it instead of reading it pray for old friendship do not do that but give me the explanation I so ardently require.

And believe me ever your
Sincere well wisher
Maria D'Israeli [MR 61]

ten during the time she was helping him to prepare *Vivian Grey*, but there are a number from her to D in the Hughenden papers. Most of them are friendly but formal, except one (H A/IV/D/2) which breaks half-way through into a cipher. The passionate tone, allied with the existence of a mutually understood private cipher, presumably for just such messages, suggests a development of D's penchant for codes, and the existence of an elaborate flirtation, if nothing more. Blake (36) believes Sara Austen was 'at least half in love' with D. Jerman gives the most detailed account of the relations between D and the Austens. See also **60**n3. *Dating*: the Austens had invited D to accompany them on their tour to Italy. Layard stated that this letter was written immediately before the tour, which began in early August. *Sic*: danse, headache.

Dear Austen,[1]

Having met many women who were *too* beautiful at the last nights danse, I slept off the memory of their loveliness by an extra three hours of oblivion, and was therefore unable to answer your note immediately; which however I am now doing surrounded by a much better breakfast than graced yr. board this morning.

A devil, tho' an ugly name, is certainly the wisest style of dejeuner – an innocent | egg perhaps the silliest – why I say *innocent* I know not – for certainly if a devilled Turkey's leg is the real "limb of Satan", the other article may not inaptly be considered the "yoke of sin." According to yr. advice, I have "perused your note with attention, and considered your offer with care;" and as the man says who is going to be hired "I think the situation will suit." It ill befits any man to | dilate upon his own excellence, but I may perhaps be allowed to observe that my various, not to say, innumerable accomplishments are not altogr. unknown to you – and as for my moral capacities, why I can have a good character from my last place, which I left on account of the disappearance of the silver spoons; I defy also anyone to declare that I am not sober and honest, ex[cep]t when I am entrusted with the key of the wine cellar, when I must candidly confess I have an ugly habit of stealing the | Claret, getting drunk, and kissing the maids. Nevertheless I've no doubt but that we shall agree very well. You certainly could not come to any person better fitted for ordering a dinner, and as to casting up accounts – if there's anything in the world which I excel in, thats the very one. And as I've got the habit of never attending to the shillings and pence because they make my headache, I generally detect the aubergiste in a super-charge. | I send this to Grays Inn – on account of your writing. Dont work too much, or it'll make you bilious. After all, a cold eel pie is as good a thing for breakfast as I know. I can't say but what it 'tayn't.

BD

1 Benjamin Austen (1789-1861) was a solicitor in partnership with C.W. Hobson at 4 Raymond Buildings, Gray's Inn. He was the uncle of Austen Henry Layard (1817-1894), who was to become the famous archaeologist, Austen's sister, Marianne (b 1789), having married Henry Peter John Layard (1783-1834), son of the dean of Bristol. Austen's father acted as banker to the Duke of Suffolk's wife, who was known as the Countess d'Este. *LPOD* (1832); Jerman 46.

According to A.H. Layard (9), Austen's wife, Sara (1796-1888), was 'the daughter of a gentleman of the name of Rickett, who resided in Oundle, Northamptonshire. He was descended from a good old English family, and was a man of literary and scientific tastes.' In a footnote Jerman (46) adds that the parish of Oundle 'has no record of her birth or marriage. One of her brothers, however, resided for a time at Cotterstock, a village nearby. It would seem that the elder Ricketts were dead by the time Sara Rickett became Mrs Austen.'

Benjamin Austen (1828)
by Daniel Maclise

Sara Austen (1828)
by Daniel Maclise

TO ISAAC D'ISRAELI Paris, Wednesday 9 August 1826 50

ORIGINAL: H A/IV/C/5

COVER: I. D'Israeli Esquire, | Post Office, | Dover, | Angleterre.

POSTMARK: (1) In dotted circle: FPO | AU. 14 | 1826 (2) In double circle: AU | Q 14 [central number in small circle] | 1826 (3) In octagon: 68 | P.P. | E (4) PORT-PAYE

PUBLICATION HISTORY: M&B I 95-6, extracts dated 9 August 1826

EDITORIAL COMMENT: *Sic*: Brittania, accomodation, stopt, *westend*, staid, french, Thuillerics, Elysseès.

Paris. August 9. Wednesday 1826.

My dear Father,

You received doubtless a letter written by Mrs. Austen on board the packet and sent on our arrival at Boulogne by the Captain of our packet, the Brittania, to you. She would have written to Sarah this post but I opposed the arrangemt. which had been made bet[wee]n them for Mrs. A's sharing my sheet of paper, and she therefore will write by another opportunity. In the first place I am quite well and have never experienced such good health for the last three years. The lightness of the air and the cuisine have effected that revolution in my digestion which I have so long wished – the process being now like lightning. Mrs. Austen on the whole has been very well indeed but I am sorry to say that Austen has not altho' he has now recovered. I am unquestionably the best of the party, for I not only am as well as I was in England, but ten thousand times better. Our journey to Paris was much pleasanter than I expected – we slept the first night at Montreuil, at the Hot[el] de L'Europe – the inn you mentioned. It was full of English, but the accomodation is as delightful as ever. Being overtaken by a storm in the next days journey we stopped short at Grandvilliers instead of reaching Beauvais passing in our way thro' Abbeville where we stopt 2 hours. The next day passing thro' Beauvais where we stopped a couple of hours to see the old Cathedral, painted glass, tapestry etc. we reached Paris, Sunday afternoon and are now at the Hotel de Terrace, Rue de Rivoli, the best situation here, having obtained these apartments in a manner which wo[ul]d make an excellent chapter in Gil Blas[1] and beat the adventure of the *Hotel Garni* hollow – but I must keep this and all *scenes* for oral communication. "Paris | is delightful." I never was so much struck with anything in the whole course of my life. I expected another London – but there are no points of resemblance. I did not expect in so short a distance to have met such a contrariety of manners and life. Our entrance was most favorable – the weather being intensely hot and the whole population being *sub dio*. It was like what we read of Naples. The whole world was out, sitting on chairs, dancing etc. etc. Certainly the Quais and the Boulevards are two most miraculous features in this City. You must also bear in mind that since you were here a much more extensive architectural revolution has taken place in this capital than there has even in our own. The magnificent

1 Obviously the picaresque character of Gil Blas appealed to D, as he often referred to it.

terraces, palaces, and streets which have been erected within these *seven years* would astonish you. They have one great advantage over our Regent St. which strikes me more forcibly every day – *elevation*. This gives an air of magnificence and grandeur which we do not attain – all our new houses are so low. At the same time Paris is not to be compared in any way to London. Paris is the beau ideal of a magnificent City – but it might have been fancied without having been *seen*. On the contrary London is a wonder, a mystery, which never could be *preconceived*, and which never can be exhausted, whereas, I imagine, Paris can. On Monday we took a drive thro' all the *westend* of this City, and in the evening drove about the Boulevards which literally were Double lined with multitudes on chairs[;] we then went to Tortonis – yesterday I lionized the old City, and the Quais – Notre Dame etc. I was very much struck by the resemblance of the old Town of Edinburgh to the ancient parts of Paris – indeed at some times the resemblance was perfect. I am going to the Louvre this morning and to the Opera this evening for we do not leave Paris until Friday, on account of the great time and difficulty which we experience and is requisite for the arrangement of our passports. For this delay I confess I am not sorry. It will make no difference in our arrangements, as we intended to have staid at Paris on our way back, but it does make a difference in our post days with you. Be so good as to put all our days on *four days*. |

I have not yet kept any journal but, of course, shall.[2] My fellow travellers will however make up for all my negligence. Austen's journal commencing at Guildford St. with the incidents of wheel greasing and vail giving not forgotten, and Mrs. A having already filled her quarto, altho' having more modestly commenced only at Dover. By having shafts put on our carriage at Boulogne we only pay for the horses we use – vizt. three. Ano[the]r English party of the same number travelling in a similar carriage have the pleasure of paying for four from their obstinacy in not having their pole taken off, or their cockneyism in not liking to destroy the effect of their London equipage. I saw a french wedding in the Church of St Roque, which is a very curious ceremony, and I will tell you more about it when we meet. Do you remember seeing in the paper the day we left Dover the marriage of a cidevant member of your book society – Mr. Hundleby.[3] We met him at Montreuil enjoying "the Continent" with an ugly wife, an uglier bridesmaid, and a more hideous mother in law or aunt. The Quai Voltaire is delicious. You cannot conceive the convenience of our carriage. No botheration every night of unpacking, no fevers in the morning with cording and strapping. Really this conduces greatly to our health and pleasure. I rejoice daily that we did not take an open travelling carriage. The Thuilleries gardens are very beautiful, and form with the Place Louis 15 and the Champs Elysseès etc. a much more extensive place than I had conceived. The equipages here are much improved since you were here. There are a great number of English Carriages harness etc. and still more of English horses, but yet nothing

2 The journal is in the Hughenden papers, H A/III/C.

3 *The Times* of 3 August 1826 announced the marriage of Mr Hundleby, of Freeman's Court, to Emily Curtis.

to be compared in sumptuousness or number of equipages with London. We shall write from Geneva, both Mrs. Austen and myself – but not before as we shall spend the whole of the seven following days to Thursday (tomorrow) in travelling. I have to finish my letter abruptly, for if it does not go immediately it will be delayed two days. I hope my mother is better, – that you all are well. Ralph of course has joined you, and Jem I trust is *sloshy* as ever. Give my best love to all. | I hope to find a letter from Sa. at Geneva. Remember me to Olivia. God bless you

Yrs mst affectly

B. Disraeli.

51

TO ISAAC D'ISRAELI — Geneva, [Monday] 21 August 1826

ORIGINAL: H A/IV/C/7

COVER: I. D'Israeli Esqre. | Post Office | Dover, | England. | [At right angles]: *Angleterre*

POSTMARK: (1) In dotted circle: F.P.O. | AU.2[8] | 1826 (2) In double circle: AU | A 28 [central number in small circle] | 1826 (3) In rectangle: SUISSE | PAR | FERNEY

PUBLICATION HISTORY: M&B I 96-8, dated 21 August 1826, with omissions

EDITORIAL COMMENT: *Sic*: ultra marine, blanchesseuse, gen d'arme, accomodation.

Geneva. August 21. 1826

My dear Father,

Mrs. Austen wrote from Dijon to Sarah and her letter was, I hope, duly received. You doubtless received mine from Paris in which I mentioned hers from Boulogne. We stayed at Dijon one day in consequence of the indisposition of Mrs. Austen, which however was fortunately of slight duration, tho' women's illness when travelling is always alarming. Dijon I liked very much. It is a flourishing busy and lively town the capital of Burgundy, thro' which most splendid province we have travelled for many days. At Dijon provisions abound and the wines are of the most magnificent description – the commonest *vin ordinaire* being the most delightful that I ever drank. After quitting Dijon two more days travelling thro' Burg[un]dy brought us to Poligny at the foot of the Jura Alps. We commenced their ascent at five o'clock on the morning of the 17th and took two days in getting to this city where we arrived on Friday last. I shall not attempt to describe any of the scenery thro' which I have passed, or in which I am living: but I do not refrain from so doing because you may find descriptions in 500 printed volumes: the truth is, it is *impossible* to *describe* them, and nevertheless much more difficult to *imagine* them. I have never yet preconceived a scene which has not in reality turned out utterly different. The Jura Alps are a fine preparation for the high Alps. At the termination of the Jura ridge which bounds one side of the plain of Geneva did I on Friday morning witness the most magnificent sight in the world – the whole range of the High Alps with Mont Blanc in the centre *without a cloud* – the effect was so miraculous that for a long time I did not perceive the lovely scene under me the plain and city and lake of Geneva – the latter of ultra marine blue. Such a view of the Alps has been seen by few persons in this country and was occasioned by the unparalleled dryness and heat of the season which as we are daily informed by travellers exceeds by much the heat now experienced on the o[the]r side of the Alps –

in Italy. The heat does not however affect me the least. I have not had a days, nay an hours illness, since I left England. To understand the beauty and rareness of the view of the Alps which I have mentioned, you must know that on *cloudless* days here, the peaks of the High Alps are always covered with clouds: you can now conceive the extreme rareness of this sight. Geneva is a dingy and uninteresting City. We are not however at this City, but at Secheron, an establishment of a very curious nature about half a mile off and on the banks of the lake. Secheron is a Chateau of the first magnitude with gardens and terraces to the lake's margin and everything that you can conceive luxurious and splendid fitted up on speculation as an hotel. Everything is made and provided within the walls of the place. There is a baker in the house, a blanchesseuse, a coachmaker etc. etc. – but as all Travellers and especially the English are extremely anxious to obtain rooms here, nothing is of course more difficult. | A friend, the celebrated Mr. Capes,[1] respecting whom I have already written a comedy for the Haymarket (Bob Capes: Mr. Liston)[2] and who was travelling with a start of three days over us promised to act as our courier. "He was sure to have rooms, if anybody could – never was such a fellow as he for getting rooms – been to Switzerland three times, known by everybody on the road tho' he couldn't speak a word of French" etc. etc. The joke was our courier was turned away and by the merest fortune in the world a couple of rooms at the top of the house were vacant – twenty carriages were turned away in the course of the afternoon, and not one person has quitted since we have been here. Here are a great number of English and French nobility among the former the Marquess of Bath[3] and family. I take a row on the lake every night with Maurice, Lord Byron's celebrated boatman. Maurice is very handsome and very vain, but he has been made so by the English of whom he is the regular pet. He talks of nothing but Lord Byron particularly if you show the least interest in the subject. He told me that in the night of the famous storm described in the 3rd. Canto C[hilde] H[arold] had they been out five minutes more the boat must have been wrecked. He told Lord Byron at first of the danger of such a night voyage, and the only answer which B. made was stripping quite naked and folding round him a great robe de chambre – so that in case of wreck he was ready prepared to swim immediately. Ld. B. he assures me was out all night with[ou]t even stockings, and up most of the night to his knees in water. I asked him if he spoke. He said that he seldom conversed with him or any one at any time, but that this night he Maurice was so employed in managing the boat and sail etc.

1 Mrs Austen told essentially the same story to Isaac, in a letter of 5 August (H A/IV/C/4). There she reported having met Capes on the Channel crossing, and she noted that he was known professionally to her husband. Her letter bears a note, in another hand, suggesting a connection with the firm of Capes & Stuart, solicitors, of 48 Bedford Row. D's friend was perhaps a son of George Capes, the senior partner.

2 John Liston (1776?-1846), well-known comic actor. Liston was noted both for an impressive gravity of manner and for his remarkable ugliness. Arthur H. Engelbach *Anecdotes of the Theatre* (1914) 90, 179. It is not clear which trait best fitted him to portray Mr Capes.

3 Thomas Thynne (1765-1837), 2nd Marquess of Bath.

that conversation would have been quite impossible. One day Byron sent for him and sitting down in the boat, he put a pistol on each side (which was his invariable practice) and then gave him 300 Napoleons ordering him to row to Chillon. He then had two torches lighted in the dungeon and wrote for two hours and a half. On coming out the gen d'arme who guarded the castle humbly asked for quelque chose à boire. "Give him a Napoleon" said his Lordship. "De trop milor" said Maurice, who being but recently installed in his stewardship was somewhat mindful of his masters interest. "Do you know who I am" rejoined the master, "Give it him and tell him that the donor is Lord Byron!" This wonderful piece of information must have produced a great effect on the poor miserable tippling gen d'arme. But in the slightest things was Byron by Maurice's account, | most ludicrously ostentatious. He gave him one day five napoleons for a swimming race across the lake. At the sight of the Clubfoot Maurice thought he was sure to win, but his Lordship gained by five minutes. Byron he says was not a quick swimmer but he was never exhausted, by which means he generally won when the distance was great. One morning Maurice called for him very early to swim. Byron brought to the boat his breakfast consisting of cold duck etc. and three or four bottles of wine. He scarcely eat anything but drank all the wine, and then amused himself, while they were sailing to the appointed place, by throwing the provisions gradually into the water. Upon this honest Maurice gently hinted that he had not himself breakfasted, and that he should swim much better if he had some portion of his Lords[hi]p's superfluity. "Friend Maurice" sd. B "it ill becomes true Christians to think of themselves, I shall give you none – you see I eat no breakfast myself do you also refrain – for the sake of the fishes." He then continued his donations to the fishes (which here are beautiful) and wo[ul]d not bestow a single crumb on his companion. "This was all very well" says Maurice "but his Lords[hi]p forgot one little circumstance. He had no appetite – I had." He says that he never saw a man eat so little as B. in all his life, but that he wo[ul]d drink three or four bottles of the richest wines for his breakfast. I shall perhaps remember more when we meet. I have been on the lake at all hours, and seen Mt. Blanc by all lights – twice by sunset when the whole mighty mountain is quite rosy. The effect is beyond all description. The living at Secheron is most excellent – we much wanted it, except at Dijon I have scarcely had anything to eat since I left Paris. In the Juras we were literally with[ou]t a meal. The honey of the Alps – wild strawberries, butter cheese and eggs are all very well in romance and certainly are not to be despised as collaterals, but with us they were principals for successive days. Travellers require nourishing food. In the Juras we could not even get a bottle of common wine – and the bread was black and not only sour but acid. I have been at Ferney, but have not room at present to give you an account of the | place which is very different from what you wo[ul]d imagine. I leave this place tomorrow, for the wildest parts of the High Alps which we are to traverse on mules and by tracks little known. By these means we shall monopolise the little accomodation which does exist. We stand no chance of getting any on the common road from the crowds of English which are scouring it. We have made this alteration in our route by the advice of a Swiss Gentleman of Austen's acquaintance, and he informs us that the scenery is much more magnificent. It will be out of my power to write before I reach Milan as I shall not be stationary after tomorrow for a single hour until I arrive there. Mrs A. will also write to Sa from Milan. I hope to find letters from England there, and shall enquire at the post at Geneva to day tho' I do not expect any. Mrs. A. is very well, and sports French with even greater rapidity than she does English. | I hope to God my mother is better. Love to all. Tell Jem and Ralph I'd give anything for an election.

Yr m[os]t affec Son
B. Disraeli.

52

TO ISAAC D'ISRAELI — Milan, [Saturday] 2 September 1826

ORIGINAL: H A/IV/C/9

COVER: Milan Septr. 2 | I. D'Israeli Esqre | Post Office | *Dover* | *Inghilterra* | [At right angles]: *Angleterre*

POSTMARK: (1) In dotted circle: FPO | SE-14 | 1826 (2) In double circle: SE | V 14[central number in small circle] | 1826 (3) In rectangle: MILANO (4) In small rectangle: L.[E?]

PUBLICATION HISTORY: M&B I 99-102, dated 2 September 1826, with omissions

EDITORIAL COMMENT: *Sic*: Austin, protegè, french, laid, cloke, staid, vallies, cupola'd, uninclosed, the the, entreè, passed, Bennett, last supper, Ciceronis, countreymen.

Milan. September 2. 1826.

My dear father,

We arrived here on Thursday last and were much disappointed at not finding any letters from England. We have reason however now to believe that two letters intended for us have been sent to another Mr. Austin – the Queen's protegè Billy Austen[1] who lives on the lake of Como. We have taken measures to obtain them and most probably will obtain them tomorrow or Sunday but as the Post for England leaves this City to day I am under the necessity of writing to you with[ou]t having previously received your letters. I shall write again immediately that I receive them. I am most anxious to hear after my mother and shall be sadly annoyed if we do not obtain our letters before we leave Milan. I wrote to you last from Geneva and had written previously from Paris. Mrs A. having written from Dijon and Boulogne. She also writes this post to Sarah. I mentioned that I had been to Ferney in my last letter. The usual print of this chateau and partic[ular]ly the one in Duppa's book[2] is faithful – but I was greatly surprised to find it the inhabited seat of a french nobleman and his family – the Count de Bude.[3] Only two rooms are shown – left furnished as in Voltaire's time. The rest of the house which is very large is inhabited and cannot be seen. The grounds are large and excellently kept up in the English fashion; wild and woody. In short Ferney instead of being as I had imagined a dingy unfurnished

1 Queen Caroline's ward, alleged by some to be her son.

2 Richard Duppa (1770-1831) *Miscellaneous Observations and Opinions on the Continent* (1825) facing page 76.

3 A later source leaves both name and title in some doubt, while confirming the general sense of D's comment. See Murray's *Handbook for Switzerland* (1838) 140, in which Ferney is said to belong 'to the family of M. Bude de Boissey'.

ancient mansion is a complete fashionable show place, the Dropmore[4] of Geneva. There is one beautiful berceau called the walk of Voltaire but I should have thought that the trees of w[hi]ch it is composed were too juvenile for his time. Of the situation of Ferney I had no previous idea, and can give you no present description. It is sublime – placed between two of the most splendid ranges of Alps in the world, with eternal snows and a gigantic lake, and forests of pines, it should have inspired a more Homeric epic than the Henriade, and chastened a more libidinous effusion than the Pucelle.[5]

I had my heart's content before I left Geneva – the night before. My friend Maurice sent for me after a very cloudy Day to say that there was every prospect of a fine storm upon the lake. As it was just after dinner and Austen was with me I was obliged to take a companion, but as we had discussed a considerable quantity of Burgundy I was soon freed from his presence for he laid down in the boat on my cloke and ere half an hour was passed was fast asleep, never disturbing us save with an occasional request to participate in our brandy bottle. As for myself I was | soon sobered, not by sleep but by the scene. It was sublime – lightning almost continuous – and sometimes in four places – but as the evening advanced the lake became quite calm and we never had a drop of rain. I would willingly have staid out all night but we were to leave the next morning at five and nothing was packed up. We left Secheron next morning much pleased with the environs of Geneva and travelling by the south side of the lake entered Savoy. I am wearied of avowing my inability of description. I passed thro' and by Thonon, Lausanne, La Meillerie, St Gingough, Vevau [Vevey], Clareno, Chillon. Imagine the rest. The morning had been rather misty but cleared up bright, but the early showers occasioned some beautiful prismatic effects which I shall never forget. After the lake, we entered the valley of the Rhone and approached the High Alps. The scenery was really painfully sublime. We gazed till our eyes ached and yet dared not withdraw them from the passing wonders. Astounded by the scenery we passed four or five days much longer than we had intended among the Alps but these wonderful Swiss valleys are only the wonders of a moment, more monotonous places to live in cannot be conceived – no walks or rides – on one side the road you have come – on the other the one you are to pursue – I suffered from the closeness of the air and the goitres and the cretins are horror itself. We travelled all thro' the valley of the Rhone which is 100 miles long. I have seen all varieties of Alpine scenery and viewed all varieties of Alpine destruction. Surely the ravages of volcanos cannot be so terrific as those of the avalanche. I endeavoured to see all species of destruction of this genus, and tho' I have visited the village in ruins, and the former fields of wheat, the fields of last summer more barren and as stony as the shingles I think I prefer one scene to all others. I was taken by a peasant to a place a small plain where the peak of an Alp had fallen down this spring. Viewed from the plain, the brother peak looked about two yards wide, yet the fragments of the one

Dropmore House in Buckinghamshire. It was built for Lord Grenville shortly after 1792.

La Henriade (1723), a poem exalting Henri IV, and *La Pucelle d'Orléans* (1755), a mock epic, both by Voltaire.

which had fallen and which was not | even as large had filled some acres with stones larger than elephants! The passage of the Simplon is the grand crown[in]g scene to all these horrors. We staid one day at Brigg where the passage commences on account of the stormy weather, but as it did not abate we set off the next day. Nothing could be more awful than the first part of our passage – the sublimity of the scenery was increased by the partial mists and the gusts of rain. Nothing is more terrific than the near roar of a Cataract which is covered by a mist. It is horrible. When we arrived at the summit of the road, the weather cleared and we found ourselves surrounded by perpetual snow. The scenery here and for a mile or two before was perfect desolation – cataracts coursing down crumbled avalanches whose horrible surface was only varied by the presence of one or two blasted firs. Here in this dreary and desolate scene burst forth a small streak of blue sky, the harbinger of the Italian heaven. During our whole descent down the Italian side which is by far the most splendid we enjoyed the sun. We were for a long time however very cold. I never shall forget the descent – waterfalls are innumerable from the hell of waters to streams finer than gauze – roads cut thro' solid rock archways and called *grottos* – galleries over precipices whose terminations are invisible – passes in which the descended avalanches of snow are viewed even after their fall with horror – bridges which always span a roaring and rushing torrent – narrow vallies backed with eternal snow peeping over the nearer and blacker background, all combine to produce a succession of scenes which contrasted with the beautiful roads and elegant bridges – the best signs of civilization – cannot surely be paralleled. The contrast on descending into Italy is wonderfully striking. The mountains still continue but their height is very moderated – they are covered with vines and glitter with white villages, churches and villas. Duomo d'Ossola is beautifully situated in a large and lovely valley of Piedmont. After sleeping here we continued our journey thro' the valley of Mt. Rose, so called because an enormous Alp only a few feet lower than Mt Blanc is seen in | great perfection from this valley. We proceeded to Baveno thro' Fariolo, both on the Lago Maggiore. Here we quitted the high route as we had determined to visit the Italian lakes previously to reaching Milan. We visited the Borromean Islands – Isola Bella rises from the bosom of the lake like a fairy palace. It is the most expensive of toys and the most fantastic – most enjoyed by those to whom it does not belong for they see it but once, and the second time, in spite of its magnificent palace and its ten terraces and its beautiful prospects and its statues, grottoes tropical vegetation and oriental birds it must appear a prison. After quitting Isola Bella we continued on the lake until we reached Arona which is situated on the other side and which is the frontier town of Lombardy. From Arona we travelled on to Varese where we slept. Nothing could be more wonderful than our journey, nothing more striking than an entrance into Italy from the wildest parts of Switzerland. Our ride from Arona commanded my uninterrupted gaze altho' for weeks the business of my life has been only to admire nature – but the scenery is so different – so exceedingly beautiful – so inconceivably lovely – the purple mountains – the glittering lakes – the cupola'd convents, the many windowed villas crowning luxuriant wooded hills – the undulation of shore – the projecting headland – the receding bay – the roadside uninclosed – yet bounded with walnut and vine and fig and acacia and almond trees bending down under the load of their fruit – the wonderful effect of light and shade – the trunks of every tree looking black as ebony and their thicker foliage from the excessive light – looking quite thin and transparent in the sunshine – the | thousand villages – each with a church with a tall thin tower – the large melons trailing over walls and above all the extended prospect are so striking after the gloom of Alpine passes, are so different in their sunny light from the reflected, unearthly glitter of eternal snows that we are constrained to feel that in speaking of Italy Romance has omitted for once to exaggerate. But you must remember that we are in the most beautiful part of northern Italy and that I have not yet entered the plains of Lombardy. I say the most beautiful part, for I have just quitted the Lago Maggiore and I am about to introduce you to the Lake of Como. It is a much smaller lake than Maggiore and yet quite different – wooded mountains green with vineyards and descending immediately into the water with[ou]t any shore to the lake. It is literally covered with glittering palaces. It is difficult to make you understand the difference between these two magical lakes but Maggiore with the exception of Isola Bella is of a severer kind of beauty, less art is evident, as indeed much less art is put in action – in short they are both lakes – both perfectly beautiful – and both quite different from each other – that is to say – Lago Maggiore is a precious stone and the Lake of Como is a gem – perhaps you now understand me a little better. We were on the lake six or seven hours. We visited the Villa Pliniana – so called not because it was the residence of a Pliny but because of a celebrated intermittent spring the curiosity of which supplied a chapter to the naturalist and a letter to the nephew.[6] I also saw the Villa d'Este – the residence of the late Queen – the apartments are left in exactly the same state as in her life time – there is the theatre in which she acted Colombine and the celebrated statues of Adam and Eve covered with the yet more celebrated fig leaves. It is a villa of the first grade – and splendidly adorned, | but the ornaments are with[ou]t an exception so universally indelicate that it was painful to view them in the presence of a Lady and only the drawingrooms and saloons are exhibited for the the upper apartments are of a nature beyond all imagin[ati]on. We were refused admittance – and I have heard from unquestionable authority that large sums have not bought an entreè. We were of course not informed at the time of the reason of the refusal. Here if they possessed any interest might you obtain thousands of stories of her late Majesty – but the time is passed thank God for

Pliny the Elder devoted a chapter of his natural history to 'Mirabilia fontium et fluminium' – 'Remarkable properties of springs and rivers' – in which he said: 'In Comensi iuxta Larium lacum fons largus horis singulis semper intumescit ac vesidit.' 'In the district by the Lakes of Como a copious spring always swells up and sinks back again every hour.' *Naturalis Historia* II cvi 232. Pliny the Younger wrote a letter to Licinius Sura describing the spring, and asking for a probable explanation of its curious behaviour. *Letters* IV xxx i-ii.

them. Our riots in her favor are the laughing stock of Italy.[7] More when we meet. The banks of the Lake of Como are covered with the villas of the Milanese nobility, who are the wealthiest in Italy. Here also resides Mr. Grey Bennett with his Lady[8] and children. An elegant little villa with gardens grapery etc. may be here had for two to three napoleons a week – a palace for about seven – many of the English nobility passed a couple of months last summer on this lake. With respect to the villa of Paulus Jovius, there is a grand palace called Balbiano where he is said to have lived – but the family of Giovio now reside in the town of Como. I believe they are noble which is not a despicable distinction here – more of this also when we meet.

Dr. Ciceri[9] to whom Forbes[10] gave me a letter is of the greatest use to us at Milan. He is a very singular character and of great importance in this City. We find him extremely courteous, and thro' him see everything here to great advantage. I was yesterday at the refectory of Santa Maria dell'Grazie to see the last supper. It is in a much better state than I had imagined. The engraving of Morghen[11] is very unlike – I do not think that the expression of any of the countenances is correct. Morghen is himself no judge of painting and a great miser and engraved from a miserable and inaccurate | copy by an artist of the lowest character. Instead of being admired by the cognoscenti in Italy as in England they are extremely desirous of having this wonderful production again engraved from a copy by a good artist and Sir Thomas Lawrence[12] has promised Ciceri to send one over and get it engraved in England. The pride of Ciceri is to be considered an Englishman. He lives among the English nobility who travel thro' and reside here and is their factotum on every subject. He lodges in a palace, and dines every day on a beef steak. He is known to everybody in Italy and manages the business of all Milan. He is a sort of an intellectual Paul Pry[13] – the best of Ciceronis of course and with a little management the most courteous of men, but he is a little surly at first because he conceives that that is keeping up

7 The Villa d'Este had been bought in 1816 by Queen Caroline, then Princess of Wales, for £7,500, and named by her after the family from which she was descended. She spent an additional £30,000 on improvements and furnishings, and, according to evidence presented in 1820 at her trial for adultery, the villa was notorious throughout northern Italy as the site of numerous orgies. Christopher Hibbert *George IV, Regent and King, 1811-30* (1975) 135, 138, 141, 153. For two days following Caroline's return to England in June 1820 crowds demonstrated around the house where she was staying. One observer reported 'she showed herself to a wildly excited mob that streamed through the streets all night with torches, making passers-by shout "Long Live the Queen!", and roaring their support of "Queen Caroline and her son, King Austin".' Peter Quennell ed *The Private Letters of Princess Lieven to Prince Metternich, 1820-26* (1948) 30.

8 Henry Grey Bennet (1777-1836), second son of the 4th Earl of Tankerville, married Gertrude Frances (d 1841), eldest daughter of Lord William Russell, in 1816. Greville I 71n.

9 Lady Murray's report of a visit to Milan in 1835 refers to a Venus by the Venetian Schiavone 'bequeathed by Doctor Ciceri to Signor Fidanza'. *A Journal of a Tour in Italy* [1836?] I 192.

10 Probably Charles Fergusson Forbes (1779-1852), one-time army surgeon who had served extensively in the Mediterranean area, and who became a prominent London doctor specializing in diseases of the eye. He was knighted in 1844.

11 Raffaello Sanzio Morghen (1758-1833), Italian engraver. He had engraved Leonardo da Vinci's 'Last Supper' for the Grand Duke of Florence.

12 Sir Thomas Lawrence (1769-1830). He had succeeded Benjamin West as president of the Royal Academy in 1820.

13 The idle, meddling hero of Thomas Poole's comedy *Paul Pry* (1825).

the English character. However our acquaintance with him is extremely fortunate and I dare say will influence the pleasure of the rest of our tour. It was thro' him that we have a chance of obtain[in]g our lost letters for he drops in at the post every morning to enquire what letters there are for English – and is applied to by all parties when ever anything is in dispute about that wonderful nation. We have had delightful weather ever since we left England, and I have not had a moments illness. I long for a letter and hope to God I shall obtain it to morrow. My mother I am very anxious about. I have not seen English papers till I got here when Ciceri lent us a pile of Galignanis which are not allowed here, but which of course he obtains.[14] Things look gloomy enough in England. Colonel Wardle[15] among other people is living in this city. My fellow travellers are very kind and very accommodating. Austen is particularly learned in coins and postillions and exchange. | We have met lots of people whom the Austens know and these occasional rencontres are very agreeable. I meant to have written a whole letter about La Scala and the ballet here which ranks almost with Tragedy but my long letter is full. I shall write from here again when I have received yours, or from Venice where I shall be on Thursday. We travel slowly which is delightful. Could you but see a few of our countreymen – how much they do and how little they enjoy and understand – the excitement of idiotism I never witnessed before and it is very ludicrous – but I must introduce you to characters orally.

God bless you all
Your affec Son
B. Disraeli

TO ISAAC D'ISRAELI — Venice, Wednesday 13 September 1826 — **53**

ORIGINAL: H A/IV/C/11
COVER: I. D'Israeli Esqre | Post Office | *Dover* | *Inghilterra* | [At right angles]: *Angleterre*
POSTMARK: (1) In dotted circle: FPO | SE.25 | 1826 (2) In double circle: S[E] | W 25[central number in small circle] | [1826] (3) Venezia (4) L.I.
PUBLICATION HISTORY: M&B I 102-3, 103-4, extracts dated 1826.

Venice Wednesday Sept. 13th. 1826

My dear Father,
We have not been able yet to obtain our missing letters but have a chance at Florence where we shall be on Sunday. I wrote you a double letter from Milan which I trust you duly received. The day after I wrote, I went to the famous Ambrosian Library. The collection is not large 35000 printed books: but it is

14 *Galignani's Messenger*, a daily newspaper, in English, was published in Paris between 1814 and 1895. From 1830 there were morning and evening editions, and it catered to the interests of the English traveller abroad. Strict licensing regulations prohibited its circulation at this time in Lombardy, or anywhere else in the Austrian Empire.

15 Lt Col Gwyllym Lloyd Wardle (1762?-1833), soldier and politician. In 1809 he had raised in the Commons a scandal about the sale of commissions by Mary Anne Clarke, mistress of the Duke of York, and had forced the Duke's resignation as commander in chief. Wardle later fled to the Continent to escape his creditors, and died in Florence.

very rich in MSS. Of course I saw the Petrarch Virgil[1] and all the lions and much more thro' the kindness of Ciceri. This library was founded by a Cardinal Borromeo, the great family at Milan. The present members are the trustees. Herein a small collection of paintings: I saw the original sketch of the school of Athens – Raphaels own face omitted. Milan may be thoroughly seen as far as churches and pictures in the course of two days. I do not however regret my longer stay there. It is a city not particularly distinguished by architectural beauty. The streets are in general narrow and the houses lofty but the union of these two defects ensure constant shade, and are a mode of building peculiarly adapted to sunny climates. The churches are not very numerous, and with the exception of the interior of St. Vittorio are not to be noticed in an architectural point of view. The Cathedral of White marble stands alone with[ou]t a rival, but whether rivalry is desirable, is dubious. Forsyths pungent criticism is just. Read it.[2] The ramparts round Milan are most noble. They extend seven miles. On each side rows of trees and a capital road. The Corso is a fine street; broad and long. This with a part of the ramparts form "the Corso" which is hardly inferior at the sacred hour in quantity of equipages to our Hyde Park, and that is saying very much. Certainly the quantity is out of all ratio with the population of this City, and can only be accounted for by the temper of the Italians who sacrifice every thing for a box at the Opera, and a carriage on the Corso. The Corso however is one of the most striking sights on the Continent. The equipages are certainly not to be compared to ours, but still they are very good. The liveries are very picturesque. All are allowed chasseurs, which are here no diplomatic distinction – great rivalries in the dress of these picturesque attendants consequently take place and servants in eastern costume are sometimes observable. The Milanese are the wealthiest of the Italians. Among the nobles 20,000 pr. ann. is not unknown and its moiety is not uncommon – 6 to 4000 common. The Borromeos whose estates are encumbered have still 14000 pr. ann. but what is the best evidence of the prosperity of this population is the[3] | existence of a wealthy class of gentry not noble – 2 to 3000 pr. ann. is very common – with all this Milan is cheap – for these fortunes are not the mushroom productions of national debts and government contracts, but of real property – of hereditary estates with regard to the nobles and of purchased church lands as to the others. Not a monastery exists in Lombardy. Count Ciconia[4] is the leader of the ton at Milan. He is a dandy of genius – worthy of Brummell. He is about 45 – dresses very plainly – has been frequently in England and pays constant trips there to

1 The Biblioteca Ambrosiana, built by Lelio Buzzi in 1607-9, contains Petrarch's copy of Virgil.

2 Joseph Forsyth (1763-1815) first published in 1813 *Remarks on Antiquities, Arts, and Letters, during an Excursion in Italy in the Years 1802 and 1803*. In the first edition he had said nothing of the architecture of Milan, but by the third edition, of 1824, he had included a section on that city. Commenting on the cathedral, he described it as 'wonderfully contrived to bury millions of money in ornaments which are never seen. Whole quarries of marble have been manufactured here into statues ... and high sculpture has been squandered on objects which vanish individually in the mass.' 3rd ed (1824) II 134.

3 The final ten words on this page of the MS are repeated on the next.

4 D's spelling is suspect here. The Count's family was probably that described as 'Cicogna di Milano' in G.B. di Crollalanza *Dizionario storico-blasonico delle famiglie nobili e notabili italiane* (Pisa 1886) I.

study. He is young in figure but his face is long and old – a bachelor with a loud shrill voice. He is curious in horses – drives four in hand in perfect style – and was attended always by English grooms till their idleness forced him to give them up. They will not do for Italy. Ciconia is as rapid in the change of his style and dress as in his conceptions[.] White hats are at Milan the rage – which Ciconia introduced. He appeared the last day on the Corso in a black one. This forms the subject of the afternoons conversation at all the Cafés and circles. The dandies here are numerous and splendid – Italians – Austrians – Hungarians – mustaches of all colours and descriptions. Here is no regular season. The Milanese with a beautiful country and splendid villas are not fond of a rural life and never leave the City, till October when the rains generally commence. Ciconia, I sho[ul]d not omit to say, is considered a shrewd hand at a bargain and a most excellent manager, mak[in]g a great figure on a small income – 2500 pr. ann. He is of a very good family. Provisions at Milan and throughout all Lombardy are excellent. The bread is peculiarly white. The wine is to be had for nothing, but not brilliant, tho' sound. The mode of their cultivation is beautiful in appearance. Elegance must be studied in an Italian vineyard. We left Milan, and sleeping at Brescia, a flourishing city full of life and business, we proceeded next day to Dezenzano – where we breakfasted on delicious trout and aronas on the banks of the Lago de Guarda and opposite to the villa of Catullus. This Lake is much vaunted for its beauty but I prefer the Maggiore, which it resembles. From Dezenzano to Verona thro' a rich country bounded on one side by the moderate but beautiful elevations of the Trentine Alps. Verona is one of the most agreeable cities I ever saw. | It is interesting for its ancient fortunes and convenient from its present prosperity – rare union! It is a large city – I sho[ul]d have thought too large for its population (45000) but the streets are always bustling. They are also very wide and the houses are extremely handsome. I do not remember a narrow alley looking place in all Verona. This city is full of pictures which have never been painted. Every step excites emotion and gives rise to unaffected reflection. In the course of a short stroll, you may pass by a Roman amphitheatre – still used – then the castle of some petty prince of the middle ages – and while you are contrasting the sublime elevation of antiquity with the heterogeneous palace of a Scaliger[5] your eyes light on a gate of oriental appearance and fantastic ornament erected by the Venetians when they were the conquerors of the most fertile district of northern Italy. Memorials of this wonderful people are constantly before you. In the marketplace rises a lofty pillar which evidently once bore some sculptured burden. Ask – it was the winged Lion of St. Mark. Stand in the Piazza dei Signori at Verona. There is the palace of the council by Sansovino – on another side is a Saracenic palace once an office of Venetian administration – three or four perspectives are afforded by various arches which open into streets or other piazzas, and a magnificent tower rises from a corner. The illusion is perfect – the eye rests with pain on the passing citizens in their modern costumes – you look for black vel-

5 The Scaligeri were a leading Veronese family of the thirteenth and fourteenth centuries under whose rule Verona rose to a position of political and artistic prominence.

vets and gold chains – white feathers and red stockings. It is odd to write a letter from Venice and not mention it – it is still more singular to write about the picturesque appearance of a single square at Verona when I am sitting in sight of St. Marks and the ducal palace of Venice, but I have been in this city five days and have not yet been able to write one single line about it – besides you wish to have an idea of all that I see and between Verona of which I have not said half enough and Venice there is much to mention – Vicenza for instance – full of Palladio. I leave for Ferrara in half an hour – but did not like to go with[ou]t writing to you. I shall endeavour to write again | before I reach Florence – perhaps from Bologna. I am quite well – no contretemps. I can only hope that you are all as I am and I pant for a letter at Florence[.]

God bless you all

Yr. affec Son

B. Disraeli

---

54 TO ISAAC D'ISRAELI — Florence, [Tuesday] 26 September 1826

ORIGINAL: H A/IV/C/13

COVER: I. D'Israeli Esqre | Lawn House | Marine Parade | *Dover* | *Inghilterra* | [At right angles]: Angleterre

POSTMARK: (1) In dotted circle: FPO | OC-9 | 1826 (2) In double circle: O[C] | C 9[central number in small circle] | 1826 (3) FIRENZE (4) In small rectangle: I.T.

PUBLICATION HISTORY: M&B I 104, extract dated 1826

EDITORIAL COMMENT: *Sic*: Francescan, roman, the that, Theatro Olympico, Pallaces.

Florence September 26th. 1826

My dear Father,

We arrived at this city last Sunday week and have here received Sarahs letter addressed to me at Florence and your letter to Mrs. Austen which we missed at Milan. Mrs. A. has written to my mother from this and since I've been in Italy I have written double letter from Milan and single from Venice: all, I trust, duly received. Your letters have given us a great deal of pleasure and you continue I hope to like Dover and enjoy health.

When I was at Verona, at which place, I believe, my last letter ceased, I visited the tomb of Julia.[1] It is a sarcophagus of Verona marble with a cavity for the head, a socket for a candle and two holes for the admission of air – the date 1303, the supposed year of her death – the family names were as you probably know, Capello and Montecchio. The tomb is in an old Francescan convent and the story is highly popular at Verona, a great part of the sarcop[hagus] having been broken away by the Italians for snuff boxes, but this is at present and has been for some years perfectly prohibited. Whether this be the real tomb of one, who was, undoubtedly, a real heroine, of course I cannot decide. I wo[ul]d not

1 A fourteenth-century tomb, alleged to be that of Juliet of the house of Capulet, located in a cloister off the Via del Pontiere. Juliet, in Italian, is usually rendered as 'Giulietta', but 'Giulia' is not unknown and appears sometimes in the title *Romeo e Giulia*. Thus D has recorded the Italian pronunciation, but failed to capture the spelling.

however hazard a doubt to the old woman who shewed it, and who prattled about the "good father Lorenzo" with credulous naiveté. I saw only two Paul Veroneses[2] at Verona and neither of them remarkable pictures – but I have seen thousands of this wonderful master since at Venice where among a crowd of genius he was still most remarkable. Here, roman antiquity, as you well know, abounds: the amphitheatre of course is the most interesting remnant. Its interior is perfect, having been restored – and is indeed still used – a wooden theatre having been erected in its centre, and a certain part of the amphitheatre seats being railed in to serve as boxes. With one exception, one small bit, the elevation of this great work is demolished, the surrounding wall which you see represented in engravings being but the inner wall of the porticos, and much lower than the original exterior. The Veronese nobility are not so wealthy as the Milanese: among other palaces I remarked the that of the Marquess Maffei the lineal descendant of the noble illustrator of Verona.[3] The present nobleman has a fine collection of antique gems. | From Verona thro' a beautiful country, where the vine is married to the mulberry we travelled to Vicenza. The famous Palladian palaces are in decay. They are built of brick, sometimes plastered, occasionally *whitewashed* – the red material is constantly appearing and vies in hideous color with the ever offensive roof. It is a miserable thing that a man worthy of Athens or Rome should have worked with such materials. In the whole course of my travelling nothing has struck me as more false than the perpetual lament in England of the want of marble and the as constant envy of our more fortunate neighbours the Italians. The truth is that a marble structure or even a stone building is infinitely more rare in Italy than in England. All is brick and plaster and as I sd. before, occasionally *whitewash*. The only difference between England and Italy is that our poor material is not offensive because it is kept neat and clean. There is not a street in Italy as to houses which is equal in cleanliness to Regent St. and no palace which looks half as white or as imposing as the County fire office[4] or buildings of that calibre – all the smoke of all the machinery of Birmingham and Manchester united will not do as much mischief to a building as the indolence of man, and sunny skies are of little use where the beings they shine on are contented with the dirt of a hovel provided it be bestowed in a palace. In Italy cobwebs must be accompanied with cornices and stinks must be endured in saloons. Abstract filth is alone odious. Forsyth, who however is not seldom a blunderer, has said of Palladio all that need be said by any man, and more than has been sd. by any man – "Reproducing ancient beauty in combinations unknown to the ancients themselves," is the whole secret and is keenly expressed. I prefer the gates of Palladio to his palaces, p[er]haps

2 Paolo Caliari Veronese (c 1528-1588).

3 The Palazzo Maffei (1668), located near the Corso Anastasia, was once the palace of Francesco Scipione, Marchese di Maffei (1675-1755), Italian dramatist, archeologist and illustrator. *Verona illustrata* (1731-2) was one of his best-known works.

4 Designed by the architect Robert Abraham, the Fire Office had been erected at 50 Regent Street in 1819. With its Corinthian columns and statue of Britannia, the building was a showpiece of the time, but some experts proclaimed it an inferior copy of Old Somerset House by Inigo Jones. W.H. Leeds *Illustrations of the Public Buildings of London* (1838) II 157-60.

because they are of stone. Of these that of the Campo Marzo is the most noble and that leading to the celebrated Church of the Madonna the most novel. This last one is a gate which opens on two hundred steps leading to a celebrated temple of the virgin. The pilgrims toiling up this magnificent ascent viewed thro' the Palladian portal formed a picture worthy of Piranesi.[5] The famous Theatro Olympico[6] is now finishing and when finished will be of no use. It will be a wonderful thing however to visit in this | age a perfect roman theatre, perfect even as to the scenes. Gazing on this building I know not by what I was most affected – with admiration of the art which had created it – or by the ideal presence of antiquity. Matter however is more powerful than mind, and the deepest abstraction is of trifling duration. Here you are soon engaged in the sole admiration of a specimen of perfect Roman architecture. How exquisite are the proportions! how subdued are the component parts! how harmonious is the mighty whole! Gazing in the Theatro Olympico we forget the gothic fretwork! Who can hesitate to admit architecture in the graceful catalogue of the fine arts – an art which alike enchants the eye, subdues the passions, and elevates the soul. Besides many public buildings Vicenza is full of Pallaces by her great architect. Of these, the most elegant is the Chiericate: the most gorgeous the Barbarono;[7] the most simple the Franchescine. I mention these names that if there be any illustrated works of Palladio it may be in your power to turn to the plates. I saw also the villa of the Marquess Capra, the model of Chiswick.[8] It is in a miserably dilapidated state, but its red-tiled roof will never please the curious. The proportions are exquisite – and the interior is beautiful – but why Forsyth sho[ul]d conceive such a style of building suited to our windy climate passes my understanding. The views from this palace are beautiful. Here is a house shown as that of Palladio himself. It is an elegant building but the tradition is a fable. Vicenza tho' full of palaces, is not an elegant town.

On the 7th. Inst. we were at Padua from many causes a gloomy and decayed city. It is so large that its streets seem depopulated tho' its still remaining population exceeds 40,000, and its houses are built with porticos of unequal size and of universally inelegant appearance. The town hall here is the most ancient, the largest and the most ugly room in Xdom. In it are some antiquities, Egyptian, presented by Belzoni, one of the numerous eminent men whom Padua has Produced. His grateful city has struck a medal to his memory, and are about to raise a marble medallion of his head in the Library. Here is a public place or garden surrounded by statues of all the eminent men whom Padua has produced – well executed. The effect wo[ul]d be agreeable in any city except Padua, but here everything is sombre. Mrs. Austen's letter to my mother did not go yesterday as we expected – you will therefore receive this at the same time but I

5 Giovanni Battista Piranesi (1720-1778), etcher and architect.

6 The Teatro Olimpico, located in the Corso Palladio, was Palladio's last work.

7 The Palazzo Chiericate (1550-7) and the Palazzo Porto Barbaran (1570), in the Contra Porti, both by Palladio.

8 The Rontonda Capra, begun by Palladio in 1551 and finished by Scamozzi in 1606, had provided the model for Chiswick House, a Palladian mansion west of London, designed and built by Lord Burlington early in the eighteenth century.

shall nevertheless write to you again by next post. | It is odd to write from this beautiful and wonderful City and not mention it, but I imagine that you will be more pleased by the plan which I have adopted of giving you a short account of every place we pass thro', than with a more hurried communication which wo[ul]d carry me on much further. Nothing can go on more pleasantly than we do, and I trust more profitably. I am sure there is no excuse for any reflecting man who does not come home from Italy and Switzerland with a mind more matured and a taste more correct. I shall for many reasons consider my coming as one of the luckiest incidents of my life. I am *quite* well in health. God bless you all. Stephen Weston[9] is at Naples (I believe now)[.] He left Venice a few weeks before us for that City.

Your most affec Son
B. Disraeli

TO ISAAC D'ISRAELI — Florence, [Friday] 29 September 1826 — 55

ORIGINAL: H A/IV/C/14

COVER: I. D'Israeli Esqre | Lawn House | Marine Parade | *Dover* – | *Inghilterra* | [At right angles]: *Angleterre*

POSTMARK: (1) In dotted circle: FPO | OC-12 | [1826] (2) In double circle: [illegible] (3) FIRENZE (4) In small rectangle: I.T (5) Toscana

PUBLICATION HISTORY: M&B I 104-5, 105, extracts dated 1826

EDITORIAL COMMENT: *Sic*: féte, Lagune, moonlights, lazulli, last supper, latter.

Florence Septr. 29th. 1826

My dear Father,

I wrote to you two days ago from this city and the same post also carried a letter from Mrs. Austen to my mother. We are all quite well, but regret that we have not received another letter from Dover at this place. I hope however that this pleasure is only postponed till Genoa. My last letter carried you to the borders of the great Lagune of Venice. The first thing which struck me on arriving at that wonderful city was its extreme distance from the Continent. It is nearly five miles from the land of Italy and has the appearance at a distance of a large island. I entered Venice with a magnificent setting sun on a grand féte day.[1] As we glided in a gondola up the great Lagune we passed St. Marks, the Campanile, the Palace of the Doges, the Bridge of Sighs, the Prison before we reached our Hotel – once the proud residence of the Bernardinis[2] a family which has given more than one doge to the old Republic – the floors of our rooms were of marble – the hangings of satin – the ceilings painted by Tintoretto and his scholars, full of Turkish Triumphs and trophies – the chairs of Satin and the gild[in]g tho' of two hundred years duration as brightly burnished as the new

9 Stephen Weston (1747-1830), traveller, antiquarian and translator; author of *Viaggiana: Remarks on the Buildings, etc, of Rome* (1776).

---

1 The day on which D arrived in Venice, 8 September, was celebrated as the birthday of the Virgin Mary.

2 A prominent Venetian family of the fifteenth century. On the MS, in another hand, following 'Hotel': 'Dameli's'.

84 | **55** mosaic invention. After a hasty dinner we rushed to the mighty place of St.
29 Sep 1826 Mark. It was crowded – two Greek and one Turkish ship[s] of war were from accidental circumstances in port, and their crews mingled with the other spectators – the Greeks are most magnificent men with high foreheads and higher caps and elevated eye brows: then there was the Austrian military band and the bearded jew with his black velvet cap was not wanting – three gorgeous flags waved on the mighty staffs which are opposite the church in all the old drawings and which once bore the Standards of Candia, Crete and the Morea – tired with travelling, we left the gay scene crowded – but the moon was so bright that a juggler was conjuring in a circle under our window, and an itinerant Italian opera performing by our bridge. Serenades were constant during the whole night – indeed music is never silent in Venice. I wish I co[ul]d give you an idea of the moonlights there, but that is impossible. Venice by moonlight is an enchanted city – the effect of the floods of silver light upon the moresco architecture – the perfect absence of all harsh sounds of carts and carriages – the never | ceasing music on the waters produce an effect on the mind which cannot be experienced I am sure in any other city in the world. Altho' succeeding days at Venice were not so gay and animated as our first I must however say that I did not perceive those evident signs of decay which all so much talk of – the "marble halls" seem in very good repair, and stand very little chance of falling in the water – the canals are quite full and mud is never visible and no city in the world was more free from nauseous smells and similar nuisances. The view of Venice in Hakewill[3] is the Grand Canal on which most of the palaces of the High nobility are situate – sailing down this broad Stream the palaces of Foscari – Grimani, Barberigo,[4] and other names which make the coldest heart thrill rise rapidly before you – the end of it empties itself in the Great Lagune, on the banks of which are situate the buildings of St. Mark etc. The Rialto, you know, spans the Great canal. The palace of the Doges is still kept up for public offices, library etc. Its walls are painted by the greatest masters of the miraculous Venetian school and its roof is gilt and adorned in a manner which leaves far behind all the magnificence of all the palaces in the world. In every room you are reminded of the glory and the triumphs of the Republic, the door of one chamber once closed upon the mosque of St. Sophia – the pillars of another graced a temple in the Morea – and even Solomons temple is not forgotten, and two pillars of fantastic architecture were carved from large columns of granite which were brought in triumph by a noble Venetian from the ruins of Jerusalem. St. Mark's Church is a pile of precious stones – the walls are of all kinds of the rarest marbles and even of jasper, lapis lazulli and the richest porphyry and oriental agates – the interior is cased with mosaics of gold and in the front figure five hundred pillars of all kinds of architecture and colors – some of which | are of verd antique. The four brazen horses amble, not *prance* as some have described, on the front, and five cupolas – hooded cupolas, crown this

3 James Hakewill (1778-1843) *A Picturesque Tour of Italy* (1820) scene XII plate 2.

4 All three were powerful Venetian families, members of which were doges of Venice in the fifteenth and sixteenth centuries.

Christian mosque. It is impossible however to give any written description of Venice at least in a letter: with the aid of prints however I can manage to make you form a good idea, which some winter evening I will. It is vain to write anything here of the pictures – the churches – the palaces with which this city abounds. According to the common opinion I saw all that ought to be seen – but I never felt less inclined to quit a place than I did Venice. It is in these spots that I wish to stay, for it is in such places that the mind receives that degree of wholesome excitation which is one of the great benefits of travel, I mean an excitation which quickens the feelings and the fancy, and which enables the mind to arrive at results with greater facility and rapidity than we do at home, and in our studies. We were five days at Venice – arriving on Friday and leaving on following Wednesday. I must not forget to mention our delightful drive from Padua to that City by the banks of the Brenta, which really is lined with villas and palaces. From Venice we journeyed to Ferrara in two days, part of one of which we spent in visiting Arqua, a soft quiet hamlet in the bosom of green hills – but turn to Childe Harold, the poetry and the prose note will save me a description of one of the sweetest spots in Italy. I saw the famous cat and read the epitaph. Isn't there a controversy about this cat? How co[ul]d it arise?[5] Ferrara is a most interesting city. Here in a rich and admirably arranged library I saw the MSS. of Ariosto, Tasso and Guarini[6] and the tomb of the former. We of course visited the cell of Tasso – the door posts of this gloomy dungeon are covered with the names of its visitors – here scratched with a great nail on the brick wall I saw sprawled Byron – Sam Rogers printed | in pencil in a neat bankers hand was immediately underneath.[7] I am forced to close this letter much sooner than I had intended, but I am suffering so severely this day from the Sirocco, that I can scarcely guide my pen. I fear you will find this very incorrectly written, but in the evening I shall make ano[the]r attempt to write to you. To make sure however of your receiving one letter I shall send this to the post to night. Mr. Saunders,[8] whom I have just seen, has mentioned to me where he thinks I can get a fine set of Morghen's poets.[9] If the price be reasonable, I shall purchase them for you. He also advises me to purchase the retouched last supper which is superior to all the latter original impressions etc. etc. as he thinks that it will rise in value as the only memorial of a work which becomes every day more interesting from its perishing nature. God bless you all. I can scarcely guide my pen.

BD

5 Byron describes the scene in *Childe Harold* IV 30-2, and in notes to Canto IV. Petrarch's cat, dried, was kept in a glass case over the door of his house in Arquà where Petrarch died in 1374. The Italian inscription declares the cat to have been 'second only to Laura'. Rogers 181.

6 The Dukes of Ferrara had been the patrons of Ludovico Ariosto (1474-1553) and Torquato Tasso (1544-1595). Guarini is presumably Giovanni Battista Guarini (1537?-1612).

7 Samuel Rogers (1763-1855), banker, poet and friend of Isaac D'Israeli and Byron. He visited Tasso's tomb in Ferrara on 25 October 1814. Rogers 180.

8 Joseph Saunders.

9 Raffaello Sanzio Morghen had engraved portraits of Dante, Petrarch, Ariosto, Tasso and other Italian poets and celebrities.

56 TO ISAAC D'ISRAELI Florence, Friday 29 September 1826

ORIGINAL: H A/IV/C/15

COVER: I. D'Israeli, Esqre. | Lawn House | Marine Parade | *Dover* | *Inghilterra* | [At right angles]: *Angleterre*

POSTMARK: (1) In dotted circle: FPO | OC-12 | 1826 (2) In double circle: [OC] | 12[central number in small circle] | 1826 (3) FIRENZE (4) Toscana (5) in small rectangle: [I.]T.

PUBLICATION HISTORY: M&B I 107-8, extracts dated 29 September 1826

EDITORIAL COMMENT: *Sic*: 7,0000, Carracis, Albano, Appennines, Bertolini, florentine, Medicis, countreymen, last supper, Vandyke, Wilna, Bartolomeo, flemish, french, Rembrants, *prix fixé*.

Florence. Friday Eveng. Septr. 29. 1826.

My dear father,

I have written you a letter to day by this same post w[hi]ch doubtless you will receive by the same delivery as the present. Ferrara which I last mentioned is the first city in the papal dominions and in the Cathedral I saw for the first time the Cardinals throne. In this city and in this city only I saw the Regular *Ghetto*, a tolerably long street enclosed with red wooden gates and holding about 3000 Jews.[1] In our way to this city we crossed among other rivers the celebrated Po which is much wider than the average breadth of the Thames. From Ferrara we proceeded to Bologna, a city containing 7,0000 inhabitants – full of handsome churches magnificent palaces and fine streets, free, flourishing and with an increasing population. The university is here celebrated and some of the most eminent scholars of Italy live in this town. One of the Professors is Mezzofanti[2] – upon whom I called, but whom I unfortunately co[ul]d not see. One of the great advantages of travelling in Italy is the ability of visiting the great galleries which are formed in those cities which were formerly the chief abodes of the arts and the opportunity thereon consequent of forming from the number of specimens of the masters seen a comprehensive opinion of their peculiarities and merits. Venice revealed to me the Venetian school – Titian, Giorgione, Tintoretto, Paul Veronese, Palma[3] etc. etc. Bologna in its public Gallery introduced me to perhaps a still more illustrious band – taken altogether the finest school in Italy – the three Carracis and their four wonderful scholars – Domenichino, Guido[,] Albano, Guercino.[4] The latter, perhaps the most wonderful, and who from his miraculous and enchanting use of Chiaroscuro was called the *magician of art* is a native of a little town a few miles from Bologna – *Cento*, which perhaps

1 The Ghetto in Ferrara, established in 1624, was partially demolished in 1797, but re-established in 1826. It was completely torn down in 1859. *Encyclopaedia Judaica* (Jerusalem 1971).

2 Guiseppe Caspar Mezzofanti (1774-1849), professor of Arabic at Bologna.

3 Probably Jacomo Palma (c 1480-1528), called 'Palma Vecchio' to distinguish him from his grand-nephew, Palma Giovane, who was also a painter.

4 The Caraccis were a Bolognese family of painters in the early seventeenth century, whose most famous students were: Domenico Zampieri (or Sampieri), known as Domenichino (1581-1641); Guido Reni (1575-1642); Francesco Albani (1578-1660), a Bolognese painter of idyllic landscapes which were very popular in England in the late eighteenth century; and Gian-Francesco Barbieri (1591-1666), called Guercino, 'the squinter'.

you remember.[5] I left Bologna on the second day with regret and bid farewell to the north of Italy. My visit | to the south did not extend far. I only just crossed the Apennines, but my passage led me to one of the most delightful cities in the world, fair Florence. The passage of the Appennines took us two days. After the Alps all mountain scenery must be tame. The Apennines however are soft and green, and you sink down from their moderate elevations into the magnificent Val d'Arno with a mind tho' untired by Alpine magnificence, yet soothed and delighted. Florence only contains 70,000 inhabitants but its surround[in]g hills are covered with villas and convents and villages – yet Florence with its small population has so much amusement – possesses so many sources of occupation – so many resources for the employmt. of time – is so gay bustling and various that I declare after a fortnights stay here, it is almost as difficult for me to find my way about here and to walk the length of a street with[ou]t being delighted with a new object, as it is for a foreigner in London. On the contrary, I exhausted the topography of Milan and o[the]r capitals in two days, even Paris in four, and after the first four and twenty hours, ceased to wonder. The florentine school of painters is of course seen to advantage in the great Gallery here – but this great Gallery together with the accompanying private collection of the Grand Duke[6] in the Pitti Palace – the most wonderful collection in the world – afford you specimens of the artists of all countries and some of the most magnificent of most. Among these are many of the finest works of Raphael and o[the]r painters of the Roman school – so that I have now a very tolerable idea of the comparative styles and | merits of the four great Italian schools. I gazed upon the Venus de Medicis with[ou]t prejudice and left it with veneration – but I will not tire you with the tattle of the marble mart. There are some clever artists and sculptors at Florence. Among the latter since the death of Canova[7] Bertolini is reckoned the most eminent in Italy.[8] He is a man of genius. I had the honor of a very long conversation with him – of course upon his art. He is a friend of Chantrey[9] but the God of his Idolatry and indeed of all the Italians is Flaxman.[10] Bertolini sd. that he considered that Flaxman had revived the taste of Europe – that he was a classic and that he thought that a young man might study his works with as much advantage as the treasures of the Vatican or the Tribune. He asked me to explain the reason of the indifference of the English to this great man and expressed his surprise at finding him almost unknown to the great number of our travelling countreymen and little esteemed even by our

5 Cento was the place from which D's grandfather, Benjamin D'Israeli, came to England in 1748.
6 Leopold II (1797-1870) was Grand Duke of Tuscany from 1824 until 1859, when he abdicated.
7 Antonio Canova (1757-1822), whose influence dominated English art and most European sculpture from the end of the eighteenth century through the Victorian period.
8 Presumably Lorenzo Bartolini (1777-1850), Florentine sculptor who made a bust of Byron. One traveller of the time had only praise for Bartolini's artistry. J.D. Sinclair *An Autumn in Italy* (Edinburgh 1829) 129. But Henry Matthews, noting that the sculptor was all the rage among the English, was less impressed. He added that 'you will find all your acquaintance drawn up in fearful array, in hard marble; some at full length!' *The Diary of an Invalid* 2nd ed (1820) 59.
9 Francis Legatt Chantrey (1781-1841) was at this time the best-known sculptor of portrait busts in England. He was knighted in 1835.
10 John Flaxman (1755-1826), English sculptor and engraver who had studied in Rome 1787-94.

great artists. He mentioned Wilkies[11] opinion of Flaxman with his eyes up to the sky. It seems the English Teniers[12] is no great admirer of one whom Bertolini says is the greatest poet that ever lived, tho' he never wrote a verse. The studios of all these men are open to all Travellers and form the most agreeable and instructive lounges. I've been to Morghens but am sorry to say that I did not see him. He has quite gone to the dogs here and has just given up his art. I have not been able to pick up anything for you worth the trouble of carrying to England. All Morghen's | works are touched and retouched – I see nothing choice. The plate of the last supper has just been retouched by one of his scholars and well done. I have a mind to bring it to England for you – but the price frightens me. Between 4 and 5 gu[ine]as for a retouched, very retouched plate! In one of my speculations I have been disappointed. In the Pitti palace there is a most beautiful portrait of Charles 1st. by Vandyke – the most pleasing and noble likeness that I have ever seen. It is a picture highly esteemed. I engaged a miniature painter here (a class of artists much esteemed at Florence) to make me an exquisite copy of this picture with which I intended to surprise you. After a weeks work he has brought it today but has missed the likeness! and yet he was the court painter, Signor Carloni.[13] I have refused to take the work and am embroiled in a row – but in this country firmness is alone necessary and the Italians let you do what you like, so I've no fear as to the result – my mortification and disappointment howr. are extreme. We have some agreeable acquaintance here. Among these a very extraordinary man of the name of Saunders. He is a descendant of one of those Scotch families who used so often to emigrate on speculation to Russia. He was the intimate friend of the late Emperor Alex[ande]r,[14] and is highly esteemed by the present Emperor, and is one of those who chiefly assisted the deceased monarch in his plans for ameliorat[in]g the condition of the Russians and encouraging the taste for the | fine arts in Russia. He is now residing in Italy for his health which he has injured by over study, having just completed or being near the completion of a work which has now employed twenty years of his life – "A philosophical History of the Fine Arts." He is still attached to the court of Russia, is an aulic Councillor etc. He is a deep student, full of philosophy – first principles – and the study of the beautiful – but eloquent and profound.[15] Tho' of a very close temper he was so delighted to get hold of some one who had a literary turn, that we have become tolerably intimate, and I occasionally visit him at his country villa, which by the bye is the

11 David Wilkie (1785-1841), the Scottish painter, was knighted in 1836.

12 D probably makes this comparison because Wilkie, like the Flemish painter David Teniers the Younger (1610-1690), painted scenes of peasant life.

13 Probably Carlo Carloni, painter and engraver.

14 Czar Alexander I (1777-1825).

15 The Chevalier Joseph Saunders may well, as D said, have been the son of a Scot transplanted to Russia, though his father, John Saunders, apparently died in London in 1822. As of 1833, Saunders had not yet published his 'History' and, though it remained on his mind, it probably never appeared. His children established themselves in eastern Europe and by 1843 he had taken up residence in Poland. The Archives of Queen's University contain 36 letters that Saunders wrote from various European locations to Sara Austen. Several of these record his dismay at D's political ambitions.

villa Vespucci rented by him of a noble family of that name, the lineal descendants of the famous Americus.[16] Among other things he persuaded the Emperor of Russia to found at the University of Wilna[17] a chair for the Professorship of the fine arts – a thing hitherto unknown in Europe – here he read the first course of lectures himself – and is still a honorary Professor – altogether a very singular man whom a letter will give you no idea of. Among his other pursuits he occasionally amuses himself with engraving in which art you will be surprised to hear that he even excels Morghen. Such however is the fact, tho' he had of course no regular instruction in the art. The portrait of his great friend Canova and a few other things have made a great noise in Italy, and he is well known among the cognoscenti. He is now engraving the most valuable picture in Italy – the masterpiece of Fra Bartolomeo[18] – in the line manner, much larger than the Doctors of the | Church.

Florence is not only one of the most delightful cities to live in, but is also the cheapest in Europe. Here cheapness *real* cheapness is to be found – for here luxuries are cheap. An English family of the highest respectability may live in Florence with every convenience and keep a handsome carriage horses liveries etc. for five hundred a year. I speak here of an average sized family, as ours. On this income you might enter into the best society, and the best society here is excellent. You may live in a palace built by Michael Angelo – keep a villa two miles from the city in a most beautiful situation with vineyards fruit and pleasure gardens etc. etc. keep *two* carriages have your opera box and live in every way as the first florentine nobility – go to court – have your own night for receiving company etc. etc. on less than a thousand a year, and this with no miserable managing, but with the enjoyment of every comfort and luxury. Provisions are here better than at Paris. Meat averages from 2d to 2 1/2d pr. lb and is excellent, bread is proportionately cheap and your own vineyard wo[ul]d supply you with the most delicious wine at something near a halfpenny a bottle – fruit costs nothing – a turkey, a fat, sweet, bird, ninepence, etc. etc. An open and shut carriage – equipages which wo[ul]d not be considered improper even in Hyde Park – indeed of the most fashionable appearance – horses and coachman's keep, livery included will not cost here more than £70 pr. ann.

Unless you come to Italy, you can have no idea of what art really is. In fact the *names* of Italian | painters are alone known to us in England. In flemish and french pictures we beat the Italians out of the field – there are no Rembrants and no Claudes[19] like those of our Kings[20] and Angersteins[21] – but what sur-

16 Amerigo Vespucci (1451-1512).
17 The University of Vilna (Wilno) was founded in 1803 by Czar Alexander I.
18 Fra Baccio Della Porta Bartolommeo (1472?-1517), Italian painter of the Florentine school. The 'masterpiece' could be any one of the major works, including the 'Vision of St Bernard', 'The Salvator Mundi', the 'Pietà', 'St Mark', 'St Sebastian', all then to be found in Florence.
19 Claude Gellée (1600-1682), called Le Lorrain and known in England as Claude Lorraine, French landscape painter.
20 Richard King (d Apr 1829), collector who left his paintings and library to his son, Richard John King (1818-1879), a noted antiquary.
21 John Julius Angerstein (1735-1823), London merchant and patron of the arts. His collection of

prises you most is the quantity – the shoals of undoubted originals by the first masters which are in the possession of private individuals in this country to which collections like Ld. Grosvenors[22] etc. are absolutely ridiculous. I have seen enough in Italy to know that we are not setting about the right way in England to form a national Gallery. The Marquess Gerini[23] a Florentine nobleman of ancient family died the other day in debt – leav[in]g no property behind him but a magnificent collection of pictures. These were immediately seized by the police for his hungry creditors, and sold under the immediate direction of the government. Large prices co[ul]d not be expected in Italy, and as the great point was to satisfy his creditors a summary process was adopted. The police fixed prices to each picture and opened sale rooms in his palace. The finest pictures were sold for a song. Why had not the national Gallery an agent on the spot. What is Ld. Burghersh pd. for? I am sure he has little enough to do here.[24] But see the result! I myself know of one celebrated picture by Salvator Rosa which was bought at this Gerini palace for 80£, and which has been shipped off to England for our national Gallery on speculation, *prix fixé* £1000![25] We leave Florence on Monday morning and shall be at Genoa on Thursday or Friday, going thro' Pisa and by the shores of the Mediterranean. I expect to be at Dover on the 24th. of next month or very near it. No expedition of equal duration with our own co[ul]d possibly have been more successful. I shall travel so rapidly home after crossing Mont Cenis, that it is probable I shall not be able to write to you again before I reach Paris – but I will endeavour to do so at Genoa. I long to see you all – and wo[ul]d wish that this letter was more full of matter – I have still plenty in store – but the weather overcomes me. Can I however complain, when I have not | yet had one single Day's real indisposition. Let Meredith know, if any communication is going on between the families, that I have written to him from this place. I am glad to hear that Ralph conducted himself this vacation with such sense and propriety, and I hope that he will be well disposed to enter on his new studies with spirit and firmness. God bless you – my Mother I pray Heaven continues better – Love to her and Sarah. I shall endeavour to write from Genoa.

Yours most affect[ionatel]y
B. Disraeli

paintings was purchased by the British government on his death, and formed the nucleus of a National Collection, which was opened to the public in 1824, and from which was developed the collection of the National Gallery that was founded in 1838.

22 Robert Grosvenor (1767-1845), 2nd Earl Grosvenor and 1st Marquess of Westminster, who greatly enlarged the famous Grosvenor collection of pictures.

23 Rogers writes of a visit to the Palazzo Gerini, adding that although there were many pictures none was eminent.

24 John Fane (1784-1859), Baron Burghersh, after 1841 11th Earl of Westmorland, was at this time British envoy extraordinary to Tuscany, Parma, Modena and Lucca, and living in Florence. D seems to suggest that one of his additional functions should be to act as a scout for the acquisition of Italian paintings for the newly opened National Collection in London.

25 There are several paintings by Salvator Rosa (1615-1673) in the National Gallery, but none seems to have been bought at the time of the Gerini sale. A private purchaser no doubt acquired the work mentioned here. Phillips, the auctioneer, advertised paintings from the Gerini collection, including some by Rosa, for a London sale in 1830. *The Times* (21 Apr 1830).

TO ISAAC D'ISRAELI Turin, [Tuesday] 10 October 1826 **57**

ORIGINAL: H A/IV/C/16

COVER: [Probably not in D's hand]: I. D'Israeli Esqre. | ~~Lawn House~~ | ~~Marine Parade~~ | No 6 Bloomsbury Square | ~~Dover.~~ | *London* | *Angleterre*

POSTMARK: (1) In dotted circle: FPO | OC.19 | 1826 (2) In circle: + | 23OC23 | 1826 (3) In double circle: OC | H 19[central number in small circle] | 1826 (4) TORINO

PUBLICATION HISTORY: M&B I 109-10, extracts dated 10 October 1826

EDITORIAL COMMENT: Few of the letters sent by members of the family to D on his trips abroad have been located; it seems probable that he did not keep them. One has no way of knowing, therefore, 'the mournful contents' of Sarah's letter. *Sic*: valet de places, *arabisques*, streamy, Ratcliffe, misanthrophy.

October 10: 1826. Turin

My dear father,

As our movements are now very rapid, and as I do not like to leave letters behind to be put in the post by corrupt valet de places I cannot communicate to you very often or at very great length and am obliged to seize any spare ten minutes that present themselves. I found your letter at Genoa and very much grieve at the mournful contents of Sarah's. You say nothing in it of your movements; whether I may expect the pleasure of meeting you at Dover etc? the letter at Lyons will I trust be satisfactory on this head and will I hope also be addressed to Mrs. Austen who complains sadly of the manner in which Sa has kept her promise of corresponding.

We travelled from delightful Florence thro' the luxuriant Val d'Arno to Pisa where the Cathedral and its more wonderful Baptistery – the leaning Tower and the Campo Santo rivetted our attention. These four interesting objects, all of Marble, are situated together. Forsyth's description of the Campo Santo is very masterly, and I recommend you to read it.[1] It is one of the most nervous descriptions in the language, but not quite just, for in the *arabisques* of the Campo Santo, which Forsyth perhaps overlooked, may be found the originals of some of Raphaels sweetest conceptions. The country from Pisa to Lucca and indeed the whole of that little state is most lovely. Lucca, small as it is, is in the most flourishing condition. The inhabitants are the most industrious of

1 In his description of the art to be found in the Campo Santo, Forsyth said: 'Here the immensity of surface to be covered forbade all study of perfection, and only required facility and expedition. The first pictures show us what the artist was when separated from the workman. They betray a thin, timid, ill-fed pencil; they present corpses rather than men, sticks rather than trees, inflexible forms, flat surfaces, long extremities, raw tints, any thing but nature. As you follow the chronology of the wall, you catch perspective entering into the pictures, deepening the back-ground, and then adjusting the groups to the plans. You see the human figure first straight, or rather stretched; then foreshortened, then enlarged: rounded, salient, free, various, expressive. Throughout this sacred ground, painting preserves the austerity of the Tuscan school: she rises sometimes to its energy and movement, she is no where sparing of figures, and has produced much of the singular, the terrible, the impressive; – but nothing that is truly excellent.' Joseph Forsyth *Remarks on Antiquities, Arts, and Letters during an Excursion in Italy* 2nd ed (Geneva 1820) 16-17.

southern Italy. Sated as we were with scenery and desirous almost to avoid any mention of the subject, yet we have yet scarcely ceased to talk in wonder and admiration of the shores of the Mediterranean. The journey from Spezzia to Genoa baffles all idea. The glittering shores of Naples are perhaps in their kind unrivalled, but taken as a whole there seems but one opinion in Italy, that the route I before mentioned embraces the most enchanting part of Italy. For two days we wandered among the most exquisite and the wildest parts of the Apennines – not the Apennines that we had before been used to – but the Apennines of romance and Mrs Ratcliffe[2] – with streamy blue distances and unfathomable woody dells, and ruined castles, and constant views of the blue Mediterranean, and its thousand bays. On the third day we descended nearly to its shore, but | what a shore! It required no stretch of the imagination to fancy ourselves in Asia and under an oriental sky, for aloes, huge, everlasting, aloes here grow on the shingles, and groves of olive trees, dates and figs, and clusters of eastern trees abound upon the green mountains, which descend into the sea, and whose only artificial ornaments are towns of colored marble, and amphitheatres of Palaces. The shore as I sd. before, is broken into innumerable bays, which vie with each other for superiority, until they all yield to their Queen – the gorgeous bay of Genoa on whose mountain banks rises in a crescent Genoa la Superba a crowd of palaces, villas, and convents – but I am writing of that which should be seen – however the scenery of the Mediterranean wo[ul]d alone repay me for twice ten thousand the fatigues I have suffered. Two days travelling, during one of which we again crossed the great chain of the Apennines and entered Northern Italy, have brought us to Turin. The mighty chain of the High Alps covered with snow now meets our eyes and tomorrow we shall cross Mont Cenis. Turin is a city, of uniform magnificence – a Mannheim on a large scale. After Cenis we shall travel through the South of France to Lyons and from thence to Paris. I expect to be on the 24th. at Dover. Thus end my travels. I trust I have not travelled in vain. As to the general utility of travelling I have more to say than I can say now. As to the particular point of my own travelling – Nature and Art have been tolerably well revealed to me. The Alps, the Apennines and two seas have pretty well done for the first, and tho' I may see more cities I cannot see more varieties of European nature. Five capitals and twelve great cities, innumerable remains of antiquity and the choicest specimens of modern art have told | me what man has done and is doing. I feel now that it is not prejudice, when I declare that England with all her imperfections is worth all the world together, and I hope it is not misanthrophy when I feel that I love lakes and mountains better than courts and cities, and trees better than men. That is to say men in general. Yours I must always be most affectionately. In a fortnight I shall have the inexpressible happiness of joining you. Jem's debut gives me great pleasure. You say nothing of my mother which alarms me. I must run to gain the post.

B. Disraeli

2 Ann Radcliffe (1764-1823), the Gothic novelist, several of whose novels are set in Italy.

With respect to the Basevis, we intend to be in Paris only one day. I shall of course do all that is possible to find them, but with no direction you can form an idea how difficult it is to find in twelve hours a person in London or Paris – perhaps the Lyons letter will give me some clue. |

You have received doubtless all my Italian lres [letters] – from Milan, Venice, Florence (2).

TO SARAH DISRAELI Lyons, Sunday 15 October 1826

58

ORIGINAL: H A/IV/C/18

COVER: [In another hand]: Miss D'Israeli | 6 Bloomsbury Square | *London* | *Angleterre* | [inverted at top]: If not in Bloomsbury Square, to be forwarded to Dover.

POSTMARK: (1) In dotted circle: FPO | OC. 23 | 1826

PUBLICATION HISTORY: M&B I 110-11, dated 15 October 1826

EDITORIAL COMMENT: *Sic*: contretemp, Everything things, Lisle, inertion, Vandyke.

Lyons. October 15th. 1826. Sunday

Dearest Sa,

We arrived at this city last night, and shall leave it tomorrow morning. The post brings us a number of letters, two from you, at least from Dover. Mrs. Austen desires me to tell you that nothing but the receipt of a letter of rather an agitating nature from a branch of her family wo[ul]d have prevented her answering yours here – she will write to you with[ou]t fail from Paris. The post also brings a letter from Layards[1] saying they are settled at Moulins and a letter from Grays Inn informing Austen that all is well and not to hurry himself for a day or two. I shall therefore now certainly be able to see the James Basevis[2] as our arrival in England will be postponed for a couple of days. I am glad that this arrangement will give me an opportunity of gratifying my mother; otherwise I sho[ul]d grieve at the postponement, as I wish very much to be with you. Our course to Paris will be somewhat altered to give us the opportunity of seeing the Layards – this I do not regret as I shall now return back by the banks of the Loire.

Nothing can have been more prosperous than our whole journey. Not a single contretemp and my compagnons de voyage uniformly agreeable. Everything things that I wished has been realized, and more than I wished granted. I have got all the kind of knowledge that I desired, and much more, but that much more I am convinced was equally necessary. To discover new wants and find them instantly gratified – or rather to discover unexpected necessities anticipated, is the most pleasing of all things. From Turin we travelled to Susa and crossed Mont Cenis, which considering the mountain pass merely is | not to be compared to the Simplon. It is vast without being sublime – and dreary with[ou]t any of the grand effects of desolation. Some points however are won-

1 Henry Peter John Layard, Austen's brother-in-law, and his family.

2 James Basevi (1784-1861), Maria D'Israeli's brother, married Charlotte Elizabeth Robinson of Bath; they had no issue. *GM* LXXXI part i (June 1811) 671; Basevi family tree in Jewish Museum, London.

derful – a small lake at the top of the range in the midst of eternal snow, a small blue lake with banks of white marble attracted my attentive admiration. It is about half a mile from the road and I walked there while our trout were cooking. Cenis however leads to Savoy which I prefer to Switzerland. The valley of the Ar[n]o is even finer than the valley of the Rhone – it is as sublime, and yet not gloomy – the lofty mountains are covered with firs, and tipped with the snows of centuries – brilliant cascades falling from elevations of 2 to 300 feet contrasted with the variety of autumnal tints, and banished monotony without disturbing reflection. From Savoy we entered France thro' the road of the Echelles – roads cut thro' rocks, and grottoes hollowed thro' mountains, whose peaks are hid in the clouds.

Lyons is a fine city – like Lisle full of regular, modern and uninteresting architecture, but finely situated.

I suppose I shall be in London 27th. or 28th. of this month. Jem's fortune has made me very happy. I am glad that I at last get some account of my mother – my best love to her: we meet soon. My father says that he has been very idle and I fear from his tone that I am to believe him. I have been just the reverse, but I wo[ul]d throw all my papers into the Channel only to hear that he had written fifty pages. This continued inertion makes me sad, but I have hopes that if we get on with[ou]t fresh vexations for six months | more, that his spirits may be raised. I had a great row about the portrait of Charles 1st. but was quite successful. The consequence is that I have got a new miniature in which the likeness is exactly hit and at a cheaper rate. Talking of Charles 1st. there is a most extraordinary likeness of him in the collection of the Royal Palace of Turin – a full length, young, not above 25, full in the face with[ou]t a wrinkle or a marked care – stand[in]g in the court of a magnificent palace, which does not bear the look of pictorial architecture. The picture is by Vandyke; at least they say so, and is highly valued. It is the most interesting I have ever seen, but I do not think by Sir Anthony. As I have kept no journal,[3] be kind enough to preserve those letters w[hi]ch you have not burnt.

With best love to all
most affectionately yours
BD

Of course you will not be surprised at this short letter – as had Mrs. A written, you wo[ul]d not have received it – it appears, altho' my father does not mention it, that you have received my lres [letters] up to Venice, (that city inclusive). There are due then if I remember right *two* from Florence – one, a *double* letter – and one letter from Turin – this epistle completes my travels. I wish they were better written, but I have of course often been pressed for time – the matter howr. has been considered – if the style has not.

T.O. |

I wrote to Meredith from Florence.

3 But he did. See **50**n2.

TO FRANCIS DOUCE Bloomsbury Square, [London], [Monday] 1 January 1827 59

ORIGINAL: BODL MS Douce d26 f1

EDITORIAL COMMENT: D returned from his tour in late October 1826. Despite poor health, which was now to beset him for the next three years, D was busy writing part II of *Vivian Grey*, which was considerably longer than part I, and which was to be published in less than two months from this date. As Blake points out (54), he was intermittent in his studies at Lincoln's Inn and had no clear plan for a career. See **66**ec.

Bloomsbury Sq. Jany. 1. 1827.

Fras: Douce Esqr.[1]

My dear Sir,

Since my return to England I have been so severely and constantly indisposed, that I have had very few opportunities of calling on my friends, among whom I trust I may number a gentleman so entitled to my regard and respect as yourself.

The accompanying figure attracted my notice in an old collection at Venice. You will immediately recognise it as one of those quaint and agreeable personages with whom your interesting researches have made us so intimately acquainted. It very probably is not entitled to a moment of your attention, but if it be ever so valueless –, it will at least prove, that even on the shores of the Adriatic I did not forget yr various kindnesses.

I | am led to believe that the accompanying medal may be more worthy of your acceptance. It was given me by a noble Venetian and as you will instantly perceive is an old ducal Coronation medal. The execution is very bold; and according to him among the ducal series, singular.

Allow me to wish you
– multos et felices annos –
I am my dear Sir,
with great truth,
Your very faithfl Ser[van]t,
Ben. Disraeli.

TO WILLIAM JERDAN [London?, Monday 5 March? 1827] 60

ORIGINAL: PS 24

PUBLICATION HISTORY: William Jerdan *Autobiography* (1853) IV 78-9, dated [1827]

EDITORIAL COMMENT: *Dating*: the date assigned is conjectural, but the reference to the 'former' as opposed to the 'present' volumes makes it clear that Colburn had referred Jerdan to D for the purpose of compiling a key to the characters for all five volumes of *Vivian Grey*, part II in 3 volumes having been published on 23 February 1827. See also n2.

1 Francis Douce (1757-1834), collector of antiquarian books and objets d'art, was a close friend of Isaac D'Israeli.

5 Mar 1827

(PRIVATE)

[Sir,][1]

I am very much surprised at Mr. Colburn's[2] request. How my knowledge of the characters in *Vivian Grey* can be necessary to, or, indeed, in the slightest degree assist any one in understanding the work, is to me a most inexplicable mystery. Let it be taken for granted that the characters are purely ideal, and the whole affair is settled. If any collateral information be required, in order to understand the work, either *Vivian Grey* is unworthy to be read, or, which is, of course, an impossible conclusion, the reader is not sagacious enough to penetrate its meaning.

Of course, I have no intention of denying that these volumes are, in a very great degree, founded on my own observation and experience. Possibly, in some instances, I may have very accurately depicted existing characters. But *Vivian Grey* is not given to the public as a gallery of portraits, nor have I any wish that it should be considered as such. It will give me great pleasure if the public recognise it as a faithful picture of human nature in general. Whether it be anything further, rests with the author, and should only interest him. I cannot prevent surmises; but I shall always take care that from me they shall receive neither denial nor confirmation.

In part of the former volumes, a number of names and characters were introduced which were evident portraits or caricatures. I can understand any reader of those pages being naturally desirous to comprehend their full meaning, and seeking auxiliary means to procure the desired knowledge; but to comprehend the full meaning of the present volumes, the public has only to read them; and if there be anything obscure or unsatisfactory, it is the author's fault – he is a blunderer. All the notes and keys in the kingdom will not make him more intelligible.

The Author of *V.G.*[3]

1 William Jerdan (1782-1869), journalist. In 1817 he became editor of *The Literary Gazette*. See n2. Between 1830 and 1834 he brought out annually an illustrated volume of memoirs of contemporary celebrities, entitled *National Portrait Gallery of the Nineteenth Century*.

Jerdan introduced this letter in his *Autobiography* (78) by saying: 'as the matter of the identification of Mr. Disraeli's dramatis personae continues to excite so much public notice, I cannot do better, little though it be, than copy his own letter on the subject at the time, when a sly attempt was made to worm the secret out of him, and get a key to the characters. But the modern Samson was not to be taken in.'

2 Henry Colburn (d 1855) was publisher of *The New Monthly Magazine, The Literary Gazette, The Court Journal*, and of many of D's novels including *Vivian Grey*. Colburn was held in little awe by his authors, and on occasion D was condescending to him. See **333**. However, D seems to have admired Mrs Colburn. Richard Renton *John Forster and his Friendships* (1912) 237.

3 *Vivian Grey* (part I, in two volumes), D's first novel, had been published anonymously by Colburn on 22 April 1826. See also **24**ec, **48**ec and **49**ec. Sara Austen's letters to D reveal that D was at work on *Vivian Grey* from late February to about the third week of March 1826; just how much of the novel was written before that time is difficult to determine. In a letter dated 25 February 1826 Sara Austen informed D: 'I am *quite delighted* with it [*Vivian Grey*], *and enter into the spirit of the book entirely*. I have now gone through it twice – and the more I read the better I am pleased.' She asked him to send her the rest of the MS 'as soon as possible', offered him a standing invitation to visit her '*whenever you like to come – at all hours*'. H A/IV/D/4. Subsequent letters re-

TO JOHN MURRAY 6 Bloomsbury Square, [London], Monday 19 March 1827 61

ORIGINAL: MM 35

COVER: John Murray Esq | Albemarle St. | [In another hand]: 1827 March 19*th* | D'Israeli B –

PUBLICATION HISTORY: Smiles II 254-5, dated 19 March 1827

EDITORIAL COMMENT: Three weeks earlier, on 23 February 1827, *Vivian Grey* part II had been published, and Colburn had paid D £500. It is worth noting that in this, the first direct contact with Murray since the rupture of a year earlier, D used a large proportion of his newly acquired funds to make, in lordly fashion, a gesture of repayment of at least one part of his debt, incurred when he was under twenty-one, and thus not legally enforceable. *Sic*: inclose, inclosing.

6 Bloomsbury Square | Monday March 19th 1827

John Murray Esq
50 Albemarle St.
Sir,

I beg to inclose you the sum of one hundred and forty pounds, which I believe to be the amount due to you for certain pamphlets, published respecting the American Mining Companies, as stated in accounts sent in some time since. I have never been able to obtain a settlement of those accounts from the parties originally responsible, and it has hitherto been quite out of my power to exempt myself from the liability, which, I have ever been conscious, on their incompetency, resulted from the peculiar circumstances of the case to myself.

In now inclosing you what I consider to be the amount, I beg also to state, that I have fixed upon it from memory, having been unsuccessful in my endeavours to obtain even a return of | the accounts from the original parties, and being unwilling to trouble you again for a second set of accounts, which had been so long and so improperly kept unsettled. In the event therefore of there being any mistake, I will be obliged by your clerk instantly informing me of it, and it will be as instantly rectified – and I will also thank you to inclose me a receipt – in order to substantiate my claims and enforce my demand against the parties originally responsible.

veal her urging D to tell Isaac of their plans, and show her supervising the work through the printers. In particular she was most anxious that complete anonymity be preserved: 'Cannot you', she asked, 'get Mr. D.I. [Isaac] to correct in pencil and I will alter it – light lead would easily rub out. *You must not risk anything with C[olburn].*' H A/IV/D/14.

Partly as a consequence of Colburn's puffing of the novel, speculation was widespread about its authorship – Croker, Theodore Hook, Lockhart and Maginn were some of the names mentioned. William Jerdan appears to have been one of the first to suspect that D was the author; in a letter to D, Sara Austen retailed a rumour reported to her by Ward that D was the author of *Vivian Grey*, and that Ward had 'traced the report *clearly to Jerdan*.' H A/IV/D/11. See also Jerman 56-70.

Several keys to the characters were published, the first in *The Star Chamber* on 24 May 1826. *Vivian Grey* part II (in three further volumes) was published by Colburn on 23 February 1827, and the key referred to in this letter may be the one by William Marsh, published in 1827 and, according to Jerman (60n), 'certainly prepared by someone in Colburn's employ to puff the entire five volumes of *Vivian Grey*.' The publisher boasted that the key was in its tenth edition and this claim was solemnly reproduced in an edition published in Philadelphia. Copies of earlier editions have not been found, raising the suspicion that the key was also being puffed. For an account of critical opinion on the novel see R.W. Stewart 'The Publication and Reception of Disraeli's *Vivian Grey*' *QR* CCXCVIII (Oct 1960) 409-17; and Stewart *Novels* 113-30.

I have to express my sense of your courtesy in this business and
I am Sir
Yours etc.
Benjamin Disraeli

62

TO [ROBERT WARD] [London, April 1827?]

ORIGINAL: PS 31

PUBLICATION HISTORY: E. Phipps *Life of Plumer Ward* II 164-6, undated

EDITORIAL COMMENT: *Dating*: by comparison with Ward's letter to D of 17 April 1827 (H B/XXI/W/120) in which he thanked D for his 'kind view of De Vere'. *Sic*: Raffaelle.

[Sir,][1]

Yours is a work as improving as delightful – one which must always be remembered with profit, as it must ever be recurred to with pleasure. The vein of unaffected philosophy, practical wisdom, and ennobling morality which pervades it, will render it an object of study, or a source of interest, when incidents however artfully contrived, and characters however skilfully delineated, must, from our previous acquaintance with them, cease to engage our attention, and excite our sympathies. I have read this morning, for the twentieth time, De Vere's first interview with Sir W. Flowerdale, and probably may read it every year of my life with unabated pleasure, since every year of my existence must afford a fresh commentary upon such views of human life. It is, indeed, admirable. The Man of Content and the Man of Imagination are a couple of cabinet pictures; the last is my favourite, and is highly coloured. 'Tis in truth richly fanciful. These episodes, too, are in the right vein, since they develop the philosophy of the work. Indeed, without them, the moral plot would be deficient. Clayton is excellently conceived, and admirably sustained. His sensibility was a grand hit. This character is, if I mistake not, original in literature, though not in human life. I, for one, have met with Clayton. Lord Mowbray's death is actually sublime, and his daughter becomes every page more delightful; but she will not supersede, in my most agreeable associations, the inimitable Georgina, whom I shall always uphold, as not only the most delightful heroine, but the most engaging woman, to whom I ever had the honour of being introduced. But if I descant upon every character, I shall trespass most unwarrantably upon your patience, and therefore I say nothing of the sagacious Herbert, the classic Wentworth, the arrogant Cleveland, and the timid Oldcastle, nor of the dignified Lady Eleanor, nor of the delightful Lady Clanellan. Cleveland's love for Constance is finely discriminated, and Oldcastle's interview with De Vere on the embassy is beyond praise. Such passages, however, as this last are caviare to the general; nevertheless, time and the *cognoscenti* will discover them. I mention no faults, which may surprise you; for what critic ever bored an author with so long a letter, without hinting at a few blemishes, merely to prove that his previous praises were sincere. Candidly, and upon my honour, I see none. When a man has himself a little acquaintance with the art of writing, he begins to grow a very

1 Ward's novel *De Vere: or the Man of Independence* had recently been published.

temperate critic. He then discovers that, because an author has a peculiar way of conceiving his subject, it does not follow that that peculiar mode is a faulty one; but, on the contrary, that it is the author's style, a style or manner by which he is distinguished from other artists, and that unless he commit what the critic may consider faults, he never will produce what all agree to be beauties. All works are not to be written on the same principles, nor do I quarrel with the Flora of Titian, because her countenance is not that of the Madonna of Raffaelle. Yet some men do; but, after all, there are some men who set the sundial by their own watches.

One thing has peculiarly delighted me in 'De Vere,' and that is, that a writer who has proved himself conversant above all others of the age with the fascinations of courts and senates, should on all occasions, and in a manner so preeminently beautiful, have evinced his deep study and fervent adoration of Nature.

[D]

63

TO BENJAMIN AUSTEN — [London], Saturday 14 [July] 1827

ORIGINAL: BL ADD MS 45908 ff13-14

COVER: Benjamin Austen Esquire | Ramsgate.

PUBLICATION HISTORY: Layard 14-15, dated 14 June 1827, in part; M&B I 116-17 extracts dated 14 June 1827; Jerman 85-7, dated 14 June 1827

EDITORIAL COMMENT: *Dating*: not only was 14 June a Thursday in 1827, but Lord de Tabley's pictures were not sold until Saturday 7 July 1827. D therefore must have written 'June' instead of the correct 'July'. *Sic*: Wisbaden, insure, Fusileers, altogether, Taylor.

Saturday one o'clock | 14th. June 1827.

My dear Austen,

It has given me great pleasure to find that the accounts from you this morning continue favorable, and that you have arranged for a further enjoyment of your native air – the atmosphere of Ramsgate, that glory of Kent and first of watering places, and worthy rival of Ems and Wisbaden. As, however, you have postponed your return I cannot refrain from writing to you, if it be only to inform you of my existence and that I continue just "as ill" as ever. Little else have I to tell you, being in the situation of those youthful jackanapes at school – who write home to their parents every week to tell them that they have nothing to say. Your good lady I am aware sends you daily bulletins and I am quite sure that nothing certain or contingent in this odd world can possibly escape the comprehensive circuit of her lively pen. This fine morning witnessed the departure of my mother and Jem to Fern-Acres[1] to insure the return of our long lost and muchly deplored sister. The weather favors them as it has done you. I wanted to persuade Mrs Austen to join them, imagining that it might be some little relaxation in the midst of her anxieties and most various occupations, but she pleaded your letters to be pondered over and to be answered and I co[ul]d say no more.

Fern Acres, near Fulmer in Buckinghamshire, was the home of the Rev Henry James Slingsby (1786?-1844), later rector of Stour Provost, Dorsetshire. *GM* XCVI part ii (July 1826) 93; Venn part ii, V; *AR* (1844) app 236.

The | affair of Slingsbys on Thursday was very gay – at least I hear so – I did not attend. Lots of syllabubs, officers and stars, tho' these last were merely celestial. The Moon disappointed them by rising at midnight and then holding her silver state on the wrong side of the mansion. They should have fixed their day a little earlier. This unfortunate circumstance was a death blow to much intended sentiment, and two or three officers of Fusileers who had got up something about "Queen of the silver bow" and "resplendent lamp of night" were unable to quote, and left their sonnets in their pockets.

The result of Lord de Tabley's pictures very unexpected and very unsatisfactory. It turns out that the whole of this vaunted collection never cost above £5000 and have sold for about £7000.[2] Considering that his Lordship has had the picking of the English school – that he got the finest Gainsboroughs for a price lower than you wo[ul]d now give Glover,[3] I cannot but think that the affair has turned out as badly for the British School as it well co[ul]d. How[ev]er some fools congratulate themselves and talk of proof having at length been adduced in the most signal manner, that it is a wise and profitable thing to invest money in the works of British artists etc. etc. etc. Did you ever know such fools! I always thought so myself, till the very event which gives rise to their present crowing and congratulations. |

As I understand you are in want of a book, I send you the most amusing in any language – for such I do not hesitate to style the Memoirs of Benvenuto Cellini.[4] It is many years since I read it and I was then enchanted. I sh[oul]d have been entranced with rapture had I then been in Italy. The whole scene lies at Rome, FLORENCE (especially) Milan – Padua – Paris, Fontainbleau, Lyons etc. You will read it with great delight and sympathise with all his scrapes. The part that will least please you will not be his interesting history of his Perseus – his beautiful Perseus which you well remember in the more beautiful Palazzo Vecchio at Firenze.[5]

My father says he has much to talk about. I shall be very happy when we are altogether once more and at Fyfield. You of course know that Dorrien has given us the house a week sooner.[6] Pray come to town as soon as you feel a little resuscitated, as I am sure you will be much better with all of us. Jem is richer than

2 Part of the collection of John Fleming Leicester (1762-1827), 1st Baron de Tabley, was sold by auction at Christie's and fetched £7,466. *The Times* (27 June; 7, 9 July 1827).

3 In the MS the name appears to be 'Clover' although the initial letter is unlike either D's usual capital C or his capital G. It has been assumed from the context that he must have meant 'Glover'. John Glover (1767-1849) was a landscape painter who, between 1818 and 1823, exhibited seven pictures at the Royal Academy, four of which were Italian in subject.

4 Cellini's autobiography was translated into English in 1822 by William Roscoe. The 'beautiful Perseus' mentioned by D is Cellini's bronze, 'Perseus with the Head of Medusa'.

5 The Palazzo Vecchio was the seat of the government of the Florentine Republic, and afterwards became the town hall of Florence.

6 George Dorrien (1767-1835), of the banking house of Dorrien, Magens & Co, was governor of the Bank of England 1818-35. He was the owner of Fyfield House, Essex, additions to which had been designed by the architect John Papworth in 1815-17. W. Marston Acres *The Bank of England from Within, 1694-1900* (1931) II 623; Colvin 440. The D'Israelis rented Fyfield for the 1827 autumn season, as they had rented Hyde House in 1825, and Lawn House, Dover, in 1826.

ever and struts about town in a kind of cloth shooting jacket made by the celebrated Hyde of Winchester – almost as celebrated as a Taylor as Dr. Chard is as a musician.[7] In this quaint costume, with the additional assistance of a sporting handkerchief he looks very much like one of those elegant, half blackguard, half gentleman | speculators in horseflesh, who crowd Winchester market and dine at the "good ordinary at two o'clock – " for which great grub, if you remember, the bell rang loud and long as we crossed from the Cathedral.

All here send their kindest and most sympathetic regards. Add to these those of your

sincere friend

BD

Ralph's adventures at the Inn were quite Gilblasish. He arrived there about two o'clock and told them to awaken him for the earliest coach. This they did in the course of about two hours. He jumped out of bed with his eyes still shut and did not find out till he arrived in town, that he had mounted one of the night coaches at about 4 o'clock – and so he was in excellent office time!

64

TO THOMAS MULLETT EVANS [Mayfield Hall?], Thursday [3 January 1828]

ORIGINAL: H A/V/A/11

COVER: pr 2y. post 8 o'clock Friday morng. | Thomas Evans Esquire | at Vines Esqre | 10 Size Lane | Bucklersbury | City

POSTMARK: (1) In oval: 2A. NOON. 2 | 4-JA | x 1828 x (2) [illegible] – nd St.

EDITORIAL COMMENT: *Sic*: dye.

Thursday night

My dear Evans,

I am very much obliged to [you] for your note. Need I say I wish you success in your morrow's negotiation. In case the contingency you mention arise I think on reflection that you had better direct to me at Bloomsbury Sq. and that the letter should be forwarded – because I may possibly move from Mayfield Hall to Hastings, in which case my family will be apprised of it.

On further reflection I | think you had better direct to me at Hastings where Day's brother and his family are at present residing.

Direct to me

at Day's Esq.

Hastings.

I mention this because all Meredith's letters go so, and I know that Richard Day

7 George William Chard (1765?-1849) was organist of Winchester Cathedral 1802-49. Hyde's fame has proved more fragile.

at Mayfield[1] gets his a day's earlier by it in the regular course of delivery. I shall therefore certainly expect you to direct to Hastings in case you find it necessary to communicate.

I expect certainly to be in town by Monday week at the latest. It may however be | Tuesday. That will positively be the latest. I trust that all will go well. At any rate whatever happen, keep yourself cool, and whatever you resolve on, resolve on with temperance.

God bless you

BD

I have written this in a tremendous hurry and in a horrible noise. I am afraid you will find it horribly confused. I can only recapitulate – *direct to me at Hastings*, and BE NOT RASH. All is on the dye – throw it with caution.[2]

65

TO ROBERT FINCH 6 Bloomsbury Square, [London], [Saturday] 8 March 1828

ORIGINAL: BODL MS Finch d5 f132.

6 Bloomsbury Square | March 8th. 1828

Revd. R. Finch[1]
etc. etc. etc.
My dear Sir,

My father regrets extremely, that he missed the opportunity of being introduced to you yesterday – which would have given him great pleasure. He desires me | to request the honor of your company at dinner on Saturday next the 15th. I trust the accompanying card may find you disengaged.

I am,
my dear Sir,
Very truly yours,
Benjn. DISRAELI.

66

TO SHARON TURNER Bloomsbury Square, [London], [Monday] 10 March 1828

ORIGINAL: RAY 1

COVER: Sharon Turner Esq | etc. etc. etc. | Red Lion Square | [Endorsement in another hand]: B Disraeli | 10th. March 1828

PUBLICATION HISTORY: M&B I 116, dated March 1828, cites the second, third and fourth sentences of the fourth paragraph.

EDITORIAL COMMENT: This is one of the few sources of personal information from the period of D's

---

1 The Day family had lived at Mayfield, about twenty miles from Hastings, from at least the early decades of the eighteenth century. Foster I 357. William Day of Mayfield was one of the principal landholders of the district; and probably it is he who is mentioned in (vol II) **384**. By the time of the 1851 census the family no longer lived in Mayfield. Thomas Walker Horsfield *The History, Antiquities, and Topography of the County of Sussex* (Lewes 1835) 415.

By 1835 there was a Richard Day living at Bexhill, near Hastings. He married Jane Worge of Battle, and died in London in December 1845, aged 45. Horsfield 427; *BLG* (1846) II 1634-5; *GM* 25 (Jan 1846) 104.

2 D and Evans still owed £1,266.10.1 to Robert Messer, who was then pressing Evans for a meeting of the three of them. H A/V/A/15 (5 Jan 1828); H A/V/A/2.

---

1 Robert Finch (1783-1830), antiquary, whose collections of books and objets d'art are preserved in the Ashmolean Museum, Oxford. He spent most of the last sixteen years of his life abroad, and in the spring of 1828 he was making one of his rare visits to England. *GM* C part ii (Dec 1830) 567-8.

serious illness. D found in Sharon Turner, his godfather and a man thirty-six years older (see 33n4), a temporary confidant to whom he could express his sense of frustration. Near the end of his life he commented to Lady Derby on his 'miserable youth' when, he said, 'I was devoured by ambition I did not see any means of gratifying.' Meynell I 24.

Monypenny notes that, for much of the 1827-30 period, 'A mysterious disease held him in its grip and paralysed his energies.' In January 1829 Isaac wrote, 'My son's life within the last year and a half, with a very slight exception, has been a blank in his existence. His complaint is one of those perplexing cases which remain uncertain and obscure, till they are finally got rid of. Meanwhile patience and resignation must be his lot – two drugs in human life, bitter of digestion, in an ardent and excitable mind.' At the time, D's complaint was described as 'chronic inflammation of the membranes of the brain'; a phrase which seems to have been as much used to indicate medical uncertainty in the nineteenth century as 'virus infection' is in the twentieth. M&B I 115-16.

Bloomsbury Sq | March 10th 1828

My dear Sir,

I fear that you must consider me a very ungrateful or a very insensible personage, but I trust I am neither. I have taken up my pen various times with the intention of writing to you, but overwhelming indisposition has rendered it impossible, and I have delayed, until I co[ul]d do it with ease, that which, although a duty, I wished also to consider a pleasure.

I am | highly gratified by your remembrance of me. You are one of those men whose talents I have always admired, whose virtues I have ever respected, and whose friendship I have rather aspired to, than deserved.

It is with great regret, that I hear you still mention 'bodily infirmities'. How you succeed in struggling so successfully against the triple destinies of Law, Literature and Illness has often excited my admiration. | You have done great things, which, rest assured, will be heard of in after days, when this false and frivolous age will not perhaps be thought so wonderfully wise and virtuous as, in the plenitude of national conceit, it imagines itself. Indeed yourself, and my father, and Southey, commenced your careers at so early a period, that now without any of the decay or deadness of old age you are enjoying an established and classical | reputation, and to you, and them, the applause of the public must almost sound like the whisper of Posterity.

I am very much obliged to you for your kind wishes regarding myself. I am at present quite idle being at this moment slowly recovering from one of those tremendous disorganisations which happen to all men at some period of their lives, and which perhaps are equally necessary for | the formation both of the body and the constitution. Whether I shall ever do anything which may mark me out from the crowd I know not. I am one of those to whom moderate reputation can give no pleasure,[1] and who, in all probability, am incapable of achieving a great one. But how this may be I care not. I have ceased to be dazzled with the glittering bubbles which float on | the troubled ocean of existence. Whatever is granted I shall receive with composure, and that which is withholden I shall not regret.

Blake (54) remarks that scorn for a 'moderate reputation' is 'the quintessence of Disraeli, indeed the key to his character and career.'

Benjamin Disraeli (1828)
by Daniel Maclise

Sarah Disraeli (1828)
by Daniel Maclise

Oblige me by making my kindest remembrances to Mrs. Turner and your family. My severe illness has of late prevented me from seeing them as much as I could wish, but I can never forget my best and oldest friends.[2]

Believe me, my dear Sir,
with great respect and regard
yours
Benjamin Disraeli

67 TO THOMAS JOSEPH PETTIGREW

6 Bloomsbury Square, [London], [Wednesday] 19 March 1828

ORIGINAL: PS 78

PUBLICATION HISTORY: W.V. Daniell *Catalogue of Autograph Letters* (1906) item 341

EDITORIAL COMMENT: The letter is described in the catalogue as: 'A.L.s. 2pp. 8vo. 6, *Bloomsbury Sq., March 19th*, 1828, to T.J. Pettigrew.'

[Dear Sir][1]

I am so decided an invalid, that at present I am obliged to forego altogether the *deliciae* of society,

68 TO FRANCIS DOUCE

Bloomsbury Square, [London], Tuesday 15 April 1828

ORIGINAL: BODL MS Douce d25 ff53-4.

EDITORIAL COMMENT: *Sic*: de. Repub.

Bloomsbury Square Tuesday | April 15th. 1828

F. Douce Esq
etc. etc. etc.
My dear Sir,

I have taken the liberty of sending you the de. Repub[lica],[1] altho' you intimated, when I last had the pleasure of seeing you, that you had scarcely leisure to examine it.

The truth is, that I was unwilling to miss the opportunity, by my mother's going to Kensington,[2] of sending you the volume, which I have quite finished and

2 Many years later D credited Sharon Turner with having persuaded Isaac to have his children baptized as Christians in 1817. M&B I 23.

1 Thomas Joseph Pettigrew (1791-1865) was a well-known member of the London medical profession. He had been surgeon to the Royal Dispensary for Children, senior surgeon to Charing Cross Hospital and a founder of the Royal Philosophical Society. At this time, in addition to his other duties, he was surgeon to the Duke of Sussex and was compiling a catalogue of his library in Kensington Palace (*Bibliotheca Sussexiana* 1827-39). He practised in Savile Row 1835-54.

The complete letter, which has not been located, might indicate whether Pettigrew was treating D for his illness.

1 The rediscovery of the MS at the Vatican in 1820 had spurred a series of new editions of Cicero's *De re publica* during the twenties.

2 Although *DNB* states that Douce disposed of his Upper Gower Street house after 1823 and moved to Kensington Square, the D'Israeli family always addressed correspondence in these years to 15 Upper Gower Street, and Robson's *Guide* for 1833 lists him at that address.

which I trust you will keep as long as you like, as I shall in nowise be inconvenienced by the detention.

I found it impossible in any moderate bounds, by a written statement to give the faithful and accurate description of the MS., which I thought requisite, and I have therefore only written a few "notulae" which | may perhaps be of a little use in pointing out the most interesting s[ection]s of the "Prefatio".

I regret that I have not been able to procure you an impression of the plate, but I trust nevertheless that eventually I shall be able. In the mean time you must make shift with my poor specimen, in which, I fear, your practised eyes will find considerable deviations from the engraving.

I am, my dear Sir,

Your very faithful and obliged Servant

B. DISRAELI |

Again I beg to repeat that I hope you will not trouble yourself about returning the vol. Any time that I have the pleasure of calling upon you, I can take it.

69

TO EDWARD LAWFORD Drapers' Hall, [London], [Thursday] 5 June 1828

ORIGINAL: BL ADD MS 37502 ff38-9

EDITORIAL COMMENT: Two days before, on 3 June, Colburn had published D's *The Voyage of Captain Popanilla*, dedicated to Robert Ward. The book is a political satire on the Benthamites, in the mode of Swift and Voltaire. There was an American edition in 1828 and a new Colburn edition in 1829 with illustrations by Maclise. See also **71**n3. Endorsements on the last page in other hands: (1) '5 June 1828 | Mr. Disraeli | Law Institution' (2) In pencil: 'Mr. Disraeli seems to have called at Drapers Hall to solicit Mr Edward Lawford's influence on behalf of Mr. Basevi and not finding him at home, sat down and wrote the foregoing. I.M. Waterhouse[?].'

Drapers Hall | June 5th. 1828

Ed. Lawford Esqr[1]
etc. etc. etc.
Dear Sir,

I am about to take a very great liberty, which the invariable civility I have ever experienced from you may excuse, but will scarcely justify.

Your very influential name is to be found among the Members of the Committee of the Law Institution. My cousin, Mr George Basevi, of Saville Row is a candidate for the appointment of architect to that Society. Mr Basevi was a pupil of Mr. Soane[2] – he studied for some years both at Rome and Athens, and since his return to England, about ten | years back, he has been eminently successful in his profession, having been entrusted with much important business both public and private, and having at this moment confided to him the erection of Belgrave Square on Lord Grosvenor's estate,[3] an undertaking which, whether

1 Edward Lawford (1788?-1864) was solicitor to the East India Co in London, and for many years Clerk of the Drapers' Company. He died in Switzerland. Percival Boyd *Roll of the Drapers Company of London* (Croydon 1934) 113; *GM* 218 (May 1864) 674.

2 John Soane (1753-1837), architect and founder of the Soane Museum. In 1806 he had been named professor of architecture at the Royal Academy and he was knighted in 1831.

3 In 1826 Lord Grosvenor had obtained special powers from Parliament to lay out, in roads and squares, that part of his London estate now called Belgravia. George Basevi was one of the architects. Colvin 63.

we regard it in a pecuniary or a more refined view, may certainly be classed among the most important ever entrusted to a modern architect. I mention all this merely to prove that in venturing | to solicit your vote and influence for Mr. Basevi, I am not presuming to intrude upon your attention either an incompetent or an improper personage.

Had not he understood that a meeting of the Committee would take place to day – he could, and would have obtained an application to you calculated to carry more weight than my own – but time pressed – and I was *rash* – I trust that you will not say *impertinent*.

Mr. | George Meredith[4] is an old and particular friend of Mr. Basevi's – and I am sure will feel greatly interested in his success.[5]

Let me conclude this very hasty letter, by most sincerely apologising for the trouble I have given you, and by assuring you that I have the honor to subscribe myself,

with great respect,
Your most obedt humble
Ser[van]t
Bn. Disraeli

---

70 TO MR. DAVISON [London, December 1828?]

ORIGINAL: BL ADD MS 37232A f9

EDITORIAL COMMENT: *Dating*: the Bloomsbury reference places this before 1829, when the D'Israelis moved to Bradenham. The left margin of the MS has been trimmed.

---

6 o'clock

My dear Davison,[1]

I am very vexed that I missed you this morning. I arrived in town today – and am now living the *vie solitaire* in Bloomsbury.

Will you come and ameliorate a Bachelors torments by partaking of his goblet.

I am alone, as Ossian says, but luckily not | upon the hill of Storms.

Instead of that catch-col[*d*] situation, a good fire side will greet you.

Mind you come.

yours ever,
B. Disraeli

Excuse scrawl etc.

4 George Meredith of Nottingham Place and Berrington Court, Worcs, was the father of D's great friend William George Meredith. The elder Meredith (d 5 Dec 1831) was a member of the Drapers' Company from 1795 until his death. *A List of the Master and Wardens, Court of Assistants and Livery of the Worshipful Company of Drapers*, various years.

5 Basevi did not get the commission. The architect for the new Law Institution building in Chancery Lane was Lewis Vulliamy (1791-1871), who supervised both the construction in 1830-2 and the alterations in 1836. Colvin 643.

---

1 Probably a legal acquaintance; there were a number of London solicitors named Davison.

TO RICHARD BENTLEY [London, Tuesday 12 May 1829?] 71

ORIGINAL: LC Ac. 8033 [13]
COVER: May 12th. | Mr. Richard Bentley | Dorset Street | *Salisbury Square*
EDITORIAL COMMENT: *Dating*: by reference to the new edition of *Popanilla* (1829).

To
Mr. Richard Bentley[1]
Sir,
We are getting on with Mr. Meredith's work[2] in a most imbecile, unsatisfactory, and contemptible manner. The work ought to have been published a month ago. Exert your ancient | energies – maintain your character, and let the proofs follow each other like flashes of lightning.

I am, Sir,
Yours truly
Benjn Disraeli |

I have been expecting daily proof of the title page, dedication etc. of the New Edit. of Popanilla.[3] If these have not been forwarded to you, have the kindness to apply for them at Burlington St. and proceed with them immediately. Too much time has been lost.

TO BENJAMIN AUSTEN Bradenham, [Monday] 23 November [1829] 72

ORIGINAL: BL ADD MS 45908 ff15-16
PUBLICATION HISTORY: M&B I 121, extracts dated November 1829; Jerman 90-1, dated 28 November 1829
EDITORIAL COMMENT: Towards the end of 1829, despite the extravagance of his description of his health, D was attempting to persuade Isaac to set him up as a country gentleman with his own estate. As the family had just moved to Bradenham, at least partly for D's health, Isaac not unreasonably refused.

1 Richard Bentley (1794-1871) then operated, in partnership with his brother Samuel, a printing office in Dorset Street, Salisbury Square. The fact that Bentley was Henry Colburn's printer explains why, later in the letter, D instructed him to apply in Burlington Street, where Colburn's offices were located, for the proofs of *Popanilla*. Bentley and Colburn later became partners and, when the partnership was dissolved in 1832, Bentley continued to operate from Burlington Street. Frank Arthur Mumby *Publishing and Bookselling* (1930) 324.
2 William George Meredith *Memorials of Charles John, King of Sweden and Norway ... With a Discourse on the Political Character of Sweden* (Colburn 1829).
3 A new edition of D's *The Voyage of Captain Popanilla* appeared late in 1829. See **69**ec.

Puttick and Simpson catalogue (19 July 1877), item 120, lists a letter from D among a group probably to Charles Ollier, who was then a principal assistant to Colburn. The letter is described as 'A.L.s. 4pp. 8vo. and Address, *Tuesday night* [1828]'. If to Ollier, the letter (which has not been located), in asking for an interview with Colburn, probably refers to the publication of the first edition of *Popanilla* in June 1828: 'With regard to the printer, I should like to have an interview with his Satanic majesty before the appearance of any of his devils.'

Bradenham House[1] | Novr. 23.

28 Nov 1829 My dear Austen,

You are my sheet anchor and the most valuable of friends. Would I co[ul]d testify my gratitude in any other way than by being the source of perpetual trouble, but I may someday. Your information is quite satisfactory, and obtained with your usual tact and | acuteness.[2]

I am desperately ill – and shall be in town in a day or two, *incog.* of course, but I hope to get to your chambers, if nowhere else, and shake your honest hand.

Farewell

Disraeli |

Tell Madam I shall call upon her if possible, but I can only call, because I am necessarily betrayed by her, and in consequence "*the heathen rage most furiously.*"[3]

---

73 TO BENJAMIN AUSTEN

[Union Hotel, London]
Saturday [28 November 1829?]

ORIGINAL: BL ADD MS 45908 ff88-9

COVER: PRIVATE | *Benjamin Austen Esqr*

EDITORIAL COMMENT: *Dating*: from internal evidence; the tone and content suggest this to be a sequel to the preceding letter.

Saturday,

My dear fellow,

I found you, as I feared, out. You are also engaged to dinner today, but I shall perhaps see you in the evening when I intend to pay your good Lady a visit.

As, from fear of the Philistines, I cannot come and dine with you, you must

1 In the summer of 1829 the family moved from London to Bradenham House, a few miles from High Wycombe in Buckinghamshire. Concerned about both D and Maria, Isaac gave as his reason 'the precarious health of several members of my family'. The house, dating from the reign of Henry VIII, was remodelled in the eighteenth century to its present attractive guise of a Queen Anne manor house. As the house dominated the small village, and as the church and rectory were attached to the property, the occupant inevitably assumed the role of the local squire. There were 1,351 well-wooded acres on the slopes of the Chilterns, and a nominal gross rent-roll of £1,689 per annum.

Isaac did not purchase the property where he was to spend the remaining nineteen years of his life, but obtained a leasehold; indeed for thirty years (between 1824 and 1854) the title of the estate – property and advowson – was subject to litigation in the Court of Chancery. Among the privileges acquired by Isaac was that of presenting candidates for the living at Bradenham Church, and his status as a Jew does not appear to have deterred the Diocese of Oxford from confirming his right, nor does it seem to have inhibited Isaac from exercising it.

D retained a strong affection for Bradenham all his life and, as has been noted, his description of Hurstley in chapter 11 of *Endymion* (1880) is a recognizable and nostalgic portrait of his old home. Ogden 155-6; M&B I 120-1; Blake 54; James Joseph Sheahan *History and Topography of Buckinghamshire* (1862) 878, 881; *Return of Owners of Land in England and Wales* (1873).

2 This was in connection with D's plan to have Isaac purchase an estate for him at Stockton. See **74**.

3 'Why do the heathen so furiously rage together: and why do the people imagine a vain thing?' *Book of Common Prayer*. Sheriff's officers, sent by D's creditors, and ready to serve their writs, kept an eye on the residences of his known friends.

Bradenham Manor
from a water-colour by Mrs Partridge

come | and dine with me, when we can discourse *de omnibus rebus et quibusdam aliis.* What say you to Monday at 1/2 past 6? or if engaged Tuesday – but Monday I sho[ul]d rather prefer. I cannot refresh you with the | rich and red Tonnerre, yet the Union Lafitte is not despicable, and I most particularly hope you will favor me by trying it.

Yours ever

BD

---

74 TO BENJAMIN AUSTEN — Bradenham, [Tuesday] 8 December 1829

ORIGINAL: BL ADD MS 45908 ff17-18

COVER: PRIVATE | Benjamin Austen Esqre. | 4 Raymond Buildgs | Grays Inn | *London*

POSTMARK: (1) In circle: [Illegible] | 1829 (2) In small rectangle: No. 1 (3) HWYCOMBE | Penny Post

PUBLICATION HISTORY: Layard 16, dated December 1829, in part; M&B I 121-2, dated 8 December 1829, in part; Jerman 91-2, dated 8 December 1829, in part

EDITORIAL COMMENT: His scheme to be a landed country gentleman having been rejected, D turned to his second plan. For some time he had been working on the MS of *Alroy*, and he had become increasingly interested in Arab and Semitic culture. His appetite for foreign travel had been whetted by his two earlier tours, and he convinced himself that both his physical and mental health required an extensive grand tour of the Mediterranean and the Middle East. As this letter reveals, Isaac refused to finance the trip. D thereupon determined to raise the necessary funds himself, and at once put *Alroy* aside and began work on what was intended to be a pot-boiler, *The Young Duke*. He finished it by the end of March 1830 and, though it was not published until April 1831, Colburn offered £500 for it in post-dated bills. That, with a loan from Austen, was enough for him to carry out his plan.

Bradenham. Decr. 8. 1829

Benjn Austen Esqr

My dear Austen,

We received last night, via Canonbury,[1] very alarming accounts of Louisa.[2] She appears to have become much worse since I left London. We very much desire to know how she is. Sa wo[ul]d have written, had not I sd. that I was about to communicate to you.

I am sorry to say that Stockton is no go. The fact is, that great and general as is the agricultural distress, this county is suffering much worse even than its neighbours, and the Governor is fairly frightened. Here rents are never paid, farms are daily thrown up, and stock is given away. Under these circumstances it is impossible for me to persuade my father, that Mr Edward Boddington[3] is

1 The Lindo family lived at Canonbury. A letter of 25 February 1831 from Sarah recorded that the Lindos were moving from their house in that part of London. H A/IV/E/17.

2 Louisa Rickett, afterwards Mrs Charles Linton, Sara Austen's sister. See **79** and **81** for her brief engagement to D's cousin BEL.

3 Samuel Boddington was known to D but, in a family well supplied with published pedigrees, there is no mention of an Edward then living.

Jerman (90) says that the Stockton estate carried with it a seat in Parliament (with immunity from arrest for debt), which D saw as a way out of his financial problems. However, although there are many Stocktons, none has yet been identified with a rotten borough. The most likely candidate is Stockton in Warwickshire, a parish then owned by the Clapham family, ten miles southwest of Rugby. In Rugby there was an Edward Boddington who was a butcher, and it is conceivable, in view of the nature of D's comments, that he had been trying to convince Isaac of, for example, a firm contract with Boddington to purchase livestock regularly from the Stockton estate, but that Isaac had not been convinced. All this, however, is sheer conjecture. William West *The History, Topography and Directory of Warwickshire* (Birmingham 1830) 735, 752.

any other but one of those respectable individuals whose flesh is made of straw, and blood of moonshine. I have sd. all that I can venture – I cannot take the responsibility upon myself in | any further degree, particularly as I have more than once interfered in his affairs, and never with any particular success. Therefore I must give up all idea of an estate, which would have exactly suited me.

I am sorry to say that my other, and still more important plan, prospers as badly. I have partly broken it, and it was at once fairly knocked on the head in a calmer manner, than I sho[ul]d have expected from my somewhat rapid, but too indulgent Sire. Altogether, I am sufficiently dozy, but will not quite despair. A sanguine temper supports me still. There is yet *time*, and *that*, according to the great Frederick, is *everything*. The fact is I am

"spell-bound within the clustering Cyclades"[4]

and go I must, tho' I fear I must *hack* for it. A literary prostitute I have never yet been, | tho' born in an age of general prostitution, and tho' I have more than once been subject to temptations which might have been the *ruination* of a less virtuous young woman. My muse however is still a virgin, but the mystical flower, I fear, must soon be plucked. Colburn I suppose will be the bawd. Tempting Mother Colburn! However, as Frederick says, I have yet *time*, and I may be saved.[5] Keep this letter to yourself *without exception*, and indeed all I write to you. Tho' generally accused of uncommunicativeness, I like a gentle chat with a friend, provided it be strictly confidential, and he be a tried and trusty one, like yourself. Women are delightful creatures, particularly if they be pretty, which they always are, but then they *chatter* (they can't help it), and I have no ambition, in case my dearest project fails, to | be pointed out as the young gentleman, who *was* going to Constantinople. Let it be secret as the cave of the winds, and then, perhaps, a friendly breeze may yet bear me to Syria.

Farewell, mon ami,

BD

By the bye, I advise you to take care of my letters, for if I become half as famous as I intend to be, you may sell them for ten guineas a piece to the Keepsake for 1840 – that being the price, *on dit*, at which that delicate creature D[ouglas] K[innaird] furnishes a Byronic epistle to the Annuals.[6]

TO CATHERINE GORE Bradenham, [Sunday] 14 February 1830 75

ORIGINAL: TEXU 27

EDITORIAL COMMENT: Written during the period of D's concentrated work on the MS of *The Young Duke*, this letter reveals a dramatic rise in his morale. His self-mockery of his state of health is put to a literary purpose, and the whole tone of the letter represents an experiment in projection of a mannered role that is itself an extension of the novel he was then writing. The end of **76** to Colburn shows him in another role on the subject of Mrs. Gore's novel. As the letters of a month later reveal, however, this euphoria was coupled with equally extreme periods of depression. *Sic*: agreable.

---

4 Byron *The Corsair* III 62.

5 Presumably Frederick II, the Great (1712-1786), King of Prussia. Doubtless the occasion was one of his many playful assaults on churchmen. Zimmermann, De Catt and others record comparable comments.

6 Douglas Kinnaird (1788-1830), a friend of Byron, published in December 1829 some of Byron's letters in *The Keepsake* for 1830. Andrew Boyle *An Index to the Annuals* (Worcester 1967) 45.

114 | **75** Bradenham House | February 14. 1830 | Wycombe

14 Feb 1830 Mrs. Charles Gore[1]

I do not write for the C[ourt] J[ournal] for the same reason that I never shall see you – because I am dying. My only chance, and a very forlorn one, of not immediately quitting this life, is immediately quitting this country, almost a greater bore, and had your agreable volumes been published a month later, they wo[ul]d not have been my travelling companions.

I did not receive them until last night, which I mention, because I suspect from the direction they | have been roaming: my father now residing solely at Bradenham.

He is never in town, but when we again meet, I shall tell him that you recognise in him a literary godfather, and that he is answerable for all your sins. He will not be aghast at the responsibility, because he is gallant as well as grey, and you are a favorite.

What does Colburn mean by imagining that anything we write can be "a failure"? Does the villain rebel? I have no doubt that your book is as clever as everything you write must always be, but if ever you be d——d. (I use the word technically and *"don't mean to be coarse"*), it must be, because like Congreve, you have too much wit. |

I am sorry that you remember my boyish indiscretions[.] I had once hoped to atone for those terrible crudities, but this last delusion also vanishes. What is Life? Youth is a blunder, Manhood a Moral, and Old Age a Regret.[2]

As you have chosen to tear off my mask, permit me to say, if indeed I am not speaking of a thing forgotten, that in assuming the name and tone of Mivartinos, I wished to gain the C.J. the reputation of having a far more successful writer for its correspondent, than myself.[3] I thought that when he once had the reputation of fighting under our flag, he really would have struggled for some

1 Catherine Grace Frances Gore, née Moody (1799-1861), enormously prolific novelist and playwright, published over seventy works. Her novel *Manners of the Day* appeared in 1830, published by Colburn, and is certainly the book to which D refers. In 1823 she had married Capt Charles Arthur Gore (d 1846). Her will specified that her papers be burned; there has been no biography.

2 D will remember this epigram and build on it fourteen years later in *Coningsby* (book III, ch 1): 'Youth is a blunder; Manhood a struggle; old Age a regret.'

3 The pseudonym 'Mivartinos' was employed by D on a number of articles published in *The Court Journal*. See 'A Colloquy on the Progress and Prospects of the "Court Journal"' *CJ* no 4 (23 May 1829) 49-51, where Mivartinos is one of the characters; 'Second Edition! Terrible Non-Occurrence!! Flight of a Distinguished Individual!!!' *CJ* no 5 (30 May 1829) 65-7; 'The Trial of Mivartinos' *CJ* no 6 (6 June 1829) 82-93 and 'The Levee of Augustus Villeroy' *CJ* no 8 (20 June 1829) 114-18. Mivartinos was a name obviously derived from Mivart's Hotel, then a fashionable haunt for foreign visitors. Edward Bulwer lived at the hotel before his marriage, and he was convinced that the articles, whose author he had not identified, were written as parodies of his own style. Louisa Devey ed *Letters of the late Edward Bulwer, Lord Lytton, to his Wife* (New York 1889) 384-5.

laurels. It was in this vein, that | I ventured to address you those letters whose arrival you pardoned. I did not expect to be discovered or betrayed. They contain no genuine expression of my feelings, except inasmuch as they declare my admiration of your talents.

I will not re-iterate that admiration here; because praise from one so insignificant as myself, cannot be grateful to you, and as far as the public is concerned, I have no strength to wield a pen, which would willingly move in your favor.

Adieu! dear Madam. Wherever it may be my fate to linger, I shall not forget your courtesy, nor cease to hope, that your career may be as eminent as your merit.

Benjamin Disraeli

76

TO HENRY COLBURN Bradenham, Sunday 14 February 1830

ORIGINAL: HARV 2

COVER: *private* | Henry Colburn Esqre | Northumberland Place | Northumberland Street | New Road | London

POSTMARK: (1) In circle: [illegible] | 15.FE | 1830 (2) In rectangle: No. 1 (3) HWYCOMBE | Penny Post

EDITORIAL COMMENT: *The Young Duke* was planned for Colburn from the start. However, D still sought to interest Murray in the novel. See **82**, **83** and **86**.

Bradenham House. Sunday | Feb. 14. 1830.

PRIVATE

Dear Sir,

Forward the enclosed[1] and don't look pale about the postage, which I will religiously discharge when we meet. I have not forgotten you, tho' the preparations for my departure and another cause have prevented me lately sending you a contribution. In a word, being declared to be in a decline, which is all stuff, but really with positive Exile, probable Death, and possible Damnation hanging over me, I have been fool enough to be intent upon a novel – But such a novel! It will astound you, draw tears from Princesses, and grins from Printers devils: it will atone for all the stupid books you have been lately publishing, and allow me to die in a blaze. In a word to give you an idea of it. It is exactly the kind of work which you wo[ul]d write yourself, if you had time, and delightfully adapted to the most corrupt taste. This immortal work which will set all Europe afire and not be forgotten till at least 3 months has only one fault – it is not written.

Seriously however *a volume and 1/2* are finished, but as I must go off before the end of March, I am afraid it is impossible to let you have it, but perhaps I can finish it at Rome before I go off to Greece, and then you can have it for next Season. A pity because it is exactly suited to the present.[2] Write if you wish me to hatch this Phoenix – but any rate be SECRET AS THE GRAVE.

1 D's letter to Catherine Gore of the same date (**75**).

2 Monypenny reports a comment which D made to William Meredith concerning *The Young Duke* at 'the end of March 1830': 'It is a series of scenes every one of which would make the fortune of a fashionable novel: I am confident of its success, and that it will complete the corruption of the public taste.' M&B I 123. The original has not been located.

in haste
B. Disraeli

P.S. I have not yet read Mrs. C[atherine] G[ore]'s novel, which howr. I have. You are publishing a good deal of dull stuff. *Imitations of imitations.*[3]

---

77 TO BENJAMIN AUSTEN — Bradenham, [Tuesday] 16 February 1830

ORIGINAL: BL ADD MS 45908 f19

COVER: Benjamin Austen Esqr. | 4 Raymond Blgs | Grays Inn | London | PRIVATE.

POSTMARK: (1) In double circle: F | 17FE17 | 1830 (2) In small rectangle: No. 1 (3) HWYCOMBE | Penny Post

PUBLICATION HISTORY: Jerman 93, extract dated 16 February 1830.

Bradenham House | Febr 16 1830.

Benj Austen Esq

My dear Austen,

I am not squeamish about putting friendship to the test, as you know better than any other man, you to whom I [am] indebted for so much good service, but there is a line of demarcation beyond which I cannot even pass, and I should pass it, if I were to avail myself of your generous offer. When we meet, which I hope we shall soon, I shall speak to you in confidence as to my plans, which however are vague | and indefinite. In the mean time let me express my grateful sense of your unparalleled kindness; and pardon me if I add, that I think better of myself for having excited so warm a friendship in the heart of an honorable and excellent man.

I shall expect you and Lindo on Saturday, if fine. If however that day will not suit you, let me have a line, but otherwise do not give yourself the trouble of writing. With the hope of soon meeting Believe me as ever

Yours
BD

---

78 TO SARA AUSTEN — Bradenham, [Sunday] 7 March 1830

ORIGINAL: BL ADD MS 45908 ff21-2

PUBLICATION HISTORY: Layard 17, dated 7 March 1830, in part; M&B I 122-3, dated 7 March 1830, with omissions; Jerman 94, dated 7 March 1830.

Bradenham House | Mar. 7. 1830

Mrs. Austen

My dear Madame,

Your repeated kind messages require my personal acknowledgement, and deserve something better.

With regard to myself in a word, I cannot be worse.

With regard to London, it is of all places the one, in my present situation, least | suited to me. Solitude and silence do not make my existence easy, but they make it endurable.

My plans about leaving England are more unsettled than ever. I anticipate no

3 D used a very different tone in writing to the author.

benefit, from it, nor from anything else, but I am desirous of quitting England that I may lead even a more recluse life than I do at present, and emancipate myself from perpetual commiserations. |

When I was in town last I consulted secretly many eminent men. I received from them no consolation. Without any exception, they approved of Mr Bolton's[1] treatment, tho' they were not surprised that it produced no benefit.

I shall soon have the pleasure of seeing you, and, as I rejoice to hear, in confirmed health.

I grieve to | say my hair grows very badly, and I think more grey, which I can unfeignedly declare – occasions me more anguish than even the prospect of death.

Yours ever
BD

79

TO BENJAMIN AUSTEN [Bradenham, March 1830]

ORIGINAL: BL ADD MS 45908 ff23-4
PUBLICATION HISTORY: Jerman 102-3, dated March 1830.
EDITORIAL COMMENT: *Sic*: it, true.

My dear Austen,

"*Throw but a stone – the Giant dies*"[1] – so they say, but I do not find it, true, and altho' I rouse myself from my stupor to write a line, it is but a line, and costs me I assure you no slight effort. I am in fact half defunct – but enough of this.

All idea of the East, and indeed all idea of Travelling, *given up* – I fear without a | chance of revival – or rather I sho[ul]d not say *fear*, because if the opportunity offered, I doubt whether I have now the strength and spirit to avail myself of it. I have been daily declining ever since I saw you last.

"*The happy, happy, happy pair*"[2] of course engross all your thoughts. The notification of the event to be, occasioned me more pleasure, than | surprise. I know no individuals more likely to attain that happiness which all miss. You have well

1 George Buckley Bolton (d 1847) was a fashionable physician at 3 King Street, St James's. For anecdotes about him see the Rev J. Richardson *Recollections, Political, Literary, Dramatic and Miscellaneous ...* (1856) I 73-5. Bolton treated D for his unknown illness. D is alleged to have had an affair with Bolton's wife, Clarissa Marion, known as 'Clara' (d 1839), whose letters to D between 6 June and 19 November 1832 are in the Hughenden papers (H A/IV/G/1-14). In tone they are very like Sara Austen's of 1826. A covering note to these letters, written by Sir Philip Rose after D's death, asserts that the D'Israeli family looked upon Mrs Bolton as D's mistress (H A/XI/A/8), and that document is the basis for all subsequent speculation. It seems probable that D dropped Clara Bolton on meeting Henrietta Sykes in 1833, a defection which seems to have been bitterly resented by Clara. Although she promptly became the mistress of Sir Francis Sykes, Henrietta's husband, Henrietta's letters to D record Clara's efforts to have Sykes bar D from his house. H A/IV/H/2,88. See also Blake 75-7, 101-3.

'Fling but a stone, the giant dies, | Laugh and be well.' Matthew Green *The Spleen* 92-3.

'The lovely Thais by his side | Sate like a blooming Eastern bride | In flow'r of youth and beauty's pride. | Happy, happy, happy pair!' John Dryden 'Alexander's Feast'. D's effusion was occasioned by the engagement of Louisa Rickett, Sara Austen's sister, to D's cousin, Benjamin Lindo. By 13 April it had been broken off.

described his character, and I think none are better acquainted with her virtues than you and myself.

Madame I am glad to hear prospers. Remember me to her and all, and as I sho[ul]d be sorry that any | one I so much regard as yourself, sho[ul]d imagine he were neglected by me, do me the favor in future to consider me your *deceased*, tho' sincere,

friend

Benj. Disraeli

1000 thanks for your proffered hospitality, but I have no intention of coming to Babylon.

80

TO BENJAMIN AUSTEN [London], [Monday] 5 April 1830

ORIGINAL: BL ADD MS 45908 f25
COVER: Benjamin Austen Esqr.

April 5. 1830

Benjn. Austen Esqr
Grays Inn
My dear Austen,

I have received your cheque for fifty pounds, for which I am your debtor. Receive my thanks and believe me

ever yours

B. Disraeli

81

TO BENJAMIN AUSTEN Bradenham, [Tuesday] 13 April 1830

ORIGINAL: BL ADD MS 45908 ff27-8
PUBLICATION HISTORY: Jerman 105-6, dated 13 April 1830.
EDITORIAL COMMENT: *Sic*: Msslle.

Bradenham House | April 13th. 1830

My dear Austen,

Whatever might have been my opinion of Louisas conduct,[1] depend upon it, if it had been unfavorable, I sho[ul]d not have expressed it to you. The truth is she conducted herself as eleven young ladies wo[ul]d out of twelve, and probably the twelfth wo[ul]d not have deported herself with such propriety. What I meant to express to you was, that he | had not availed himself of the advantages of his situation, and that, in expressing his belief, that improper influence was exercised over her, he only proves that he had not succeeded in securing her affections, which shows a great want of *gumption*.

Excuse me for not looking at the letters, and for not discoursing anymore on this disagreeable subject. We have got through it better than | I anticipated, and I hope the feelings between the families will not now change.

I have got into a confounded scrape about the invitations. Get me through it.

1 The engagement between Louisa Rickett and Benjamin Lindo was broken off. Jerman 104.

The truth is, between cupping and your unexpected and nervous interview, my head was turned. I have passed the last week, nearly in a *trance* from the digitalis. I sleep literally sixteen out of the | twenty four hours, and am quite dozy now.

Remember me to Madame and Msslle and believe me

Yours ever

BD

TO JOHN MURRAY — Union Hotel, Cockspur Street, [London], Sunday 9 May 1830 — 82

ORIGINAL: MM 22

EDITORIAL COMMENT: In another hand on the last page: '1830 May 9 | D'Israeli Benjn. Esq | and copy of Mr Murray's | answer on May 10'.

Union Hotel. Cockspur Street | Sunday. May 9. 1830

Mr. Benjamin Disraeli wishes to see Mr. Murray. Mr. Disraeli will attend any appointment in Albemarle Street, which Mr. Murray may have the kindness to make.[1]

TO [JOHN MURRAY] — Union Hotel, [Cockspur Street, London], Sunday [9 May 1830] — 83

ORIGINAL: MM 16

PUBLICATION HISTORY: Smiles II 332-3, dated 1830, omitting the first paragraph

EDITORIAL COMMENT: In another hand: '1830 (no date) | D'Israeli, Benjn Esq'. *Dating*: it may be difficult to reconcile the cool third-person style of the letter immediately preceding this, and Murray's equally cool reply, with the assumption that this is the second letter which D wrote to Murray on Sunday 9 May 1830. The dating is justified by D's comments that he had 'just' received Murray's note and that he was replying 'to it with speed', and by the statement in Murray's note that Mitchell had left town. As publication of *The Young Duke* would provide him with the potential income to pay back Austen's loan, D was anxious to have the arrangements made before he left on his tour of the Middle East, and he could well have decided to swallow his pride to that end. *Sic*: overated.

Union Hotel. | Sunday Afternoon

Sir

I have just had the honor of receiving your note: if I reply to it with speed, do not suppose that I answer it without deliberation.

The object of my interview with you is *purely literary*. It has always been my

1 Copies of Murray's answers to this letter and to D's reply (**83**) are preserved on the same sheet of paper in the Murray Archives. The first, dated Sunday 9 May, is in Murray's own hand, and the second, dated 10 May, is in the hand of Murray's clerk. See **83**n3. Murray's first reply was:

> Mr. Murray will receive any communication which Mr. Benjn Disraeli may have occasion to make either by Letter or through the kindness of their mutual friends. Mr. Mitchell has unexpectedly left town.
> By Mr. Geo. Basevi Jnr.
> Benj. Lindo
> Albemarle St.
> May 9 1830. [MM 23]

The two lines referring to D's cousins were intended, in the draft, to be a substitute phrase for 'through the kindness of their mutual friends'.

Edward Lytton Bulwer
by Daniel Maclise

wish, that if ever it were my fate to write anything calculated to arrest public attention, that you sho[ul]d be the organ of introducing it to public notice. A letter I received this morning from my elected critic[1] was the reason of my addressing myself to you. |

I am sorry that Mr. Mitchell[2] is out of town, because he is a person in whom you rightly have confidence; but from some observations he made to me the other day, it is perhaps not to be regretted that he does not interfere in this business. As he has overated some juvenile indiscretions of mine I fear he is too friendly a critic.

I am thus explicit, because I think that candor, for all reasons, is highly desirable. If you feel any inclination to pursue this affair, act as you like; and fix upon any critic | you please. I have no objection to Mr. Lockhart, who is certainly an able one, and is, I believe, influenced by no undue partiality towards me.

At all events, this is an affair of no great importance, and whatever may be your determination, it will not change the feelings which influenced, on my part, this application.

I have the honor,
to be, Sir,
Your obedt Serv[an]t
Benj. Disraeli T.O. |

I think it proper to observe, that I cannot crudely deliver my MS. to anyone. I must have the honor of seeing you, or your critic.

I shall keep this negotiation open for a couple of days, that is, I shall wait for your answer till Tuesday morning, although, from particular circumstances, Time is important to me.[3]

1 The critic was Edward George Earle Lytton Bulwer (1803-1873), novelist and politician, who later changed his surname to Bulwer-Lytton, and became in 1866 1st Baron Lytton. D's friendship with him, which began in 1829, was not free from a measure of rivalry. Few of D's early letters to him survive in the Lytton papers, but Bulwer's side of the correspondence is in the Hughenden papers. D had asked Bulwer for his opinion of *The Young Duke* before he approached Murray. For Bulwer's role as critic see **86**&n2.

There is only one surviving dated letter from Bulwer between 14 April 1830, which is obviously too early, and October 1831. However, an undated letter (H B/XX/Ly/6) refers to the probability of his having copies of *Paul Clifford* by the next day. Bulwer's novel was published on or about 15 May 1830. Though there seems to be no Bulwer letter that exactly corresponds to D's description of a letter of 'this morning', one may assume that D took some liberty with inconsequential facts in explaining himself to Murray.

2 Probably Thomas 'Aristophanes' Mitchell (1783-1845), best known for his critical writings in *The Quarterly Review*. Though primarily a classical scholar, he had been a friend of Byron and moved in literary circles.

3 D's appeal had no success. The copy of Murray's reply, written in his clerk's hand, reads:

Mr. Murray is obliged to decline at present any personal interview, but if Mr. Benjn. D'Israeli is disposed to confide his MS to Mr. Murray as a man of business, Mr. D'Israeli is assured that it will be entertained in every respect with the strictest honour and impartiality.
Albemarle St.,
May 10th, 1830. [MM 23]

At this point D gave up his hopes that Murray would publish *The Young Duke*, but, in his letter to Murray of 27 May 1830, kept the door open for other MSS which he hoped to submit in the future.

84 TO THOMAS MULLETT EVANS Union Hotel, Cockspur Street, London, [Sunday] 9 May 1830

ORIGINAL: H A/V/A/12

COVER: PRIVATE AND PAID | Thomas Mullett Evans Esqre. | Solicitor | *Bristol.*

POSTMARK: (1) In Maltese cross: C.H/ [illegible] | 1830 [illegible]

PUBLICATION HISTORY: A.C. Ewald 'Two Letters from Disraeli to T.M. Evans' *The Athenaeum* no 2,845 (6 May 1882) 568-9.

Union Hotel Cockspur St. London | May 9. 1830

PRIVATE AND CONFIDENTIAL

My dear Evans,

We have been too long silent. It has been my fault, but if you co[ul]d form the slightest idea of the severe visitation under which I have been long, and am still, suffering, I am confident you wo[ul]d not only accept my excuses, but sympathise with their cause. For the last three years – I will not talk of enjoyment – Life has not afforded me a moments ease; and after having lived in perfect solitude for nearly eighteen months, I am about to be shipped off for the last resource of a warmer climate.[1]

To leave England at all, particularly in the state in which I am, is to me most distressing; to leave it without finally arranging my distracted affairs,[2] costs me a pang, which is indeed bitter. But I can assure you at this moment, when so many harrowing interests solicit the attention of my weakened mind, there is no subject on which I oftener think, than our past relations, and no person, who more constantly occurs to me, than yourself.

I | assure you, dear Evans, that it wo[ul]d be very difficult to find one, who is really more interested in the welfare of another, than I am in yours, and although you may perhaps doubt the sincerity of this declaration, I nevertheless make it. It wo[ul]d be a great consolation for me, if before my departure I co[ul]d hear from yourself, that you were prospering in the world, a great satisfaction if you wo[ul]d communicate to me with the candor, which I wish to be the characteristic of our letters.

Altho' I have not been fortunate enough in finally arranging my affairs, I

1 D and George Meredith left London in late May 1830 for their tour of the Mediterranean and Middle East.

2 Many of D's debts were still outstanding from his stock-exchange speculations in 1825. In a letter of 1849, Robert Messer wrote that since January 1831 D had continued to owe him '*£1500 odd*'. H A/V/A/20. See **21**n1 and **25**.

flatter myself I have succeeded in making some temporary dispositions. Nothing of importance has been done with *M.*,[3] but he is inclined to wait till my return if possible, and if he cannot, to be silent. I feel less for him, than for others, because I now see too well what was the cause of all our errors, and curse the hour, he practised, as he thought so cunningly, upon our inexperienced youth. But this only to yourself, for he is after all an object of pity, and I wo[ul]d to God, that I co[ul]d do something for him more than I am bound to do.

To yourself, who, most unintentionally – on my part, have suffered from my madness – It is for you I feel, indeed keenly, you, whose | generous and manly soul I have ever honored and credit me, have ever done justice to. All I can say is, that the first step I take, when the power is mine, shall be in your favor, and that sooner, or later, the power will be mine, and that, some day or other, we may look back to these early adventures, rather as matter of philosophical speculation, than individual sorrow, I confidently believe.

For there is something within me, which in spite of all the dicta of the faculty, and in the face of the prostrate state in which I lie, that whispers to me I shall yet weather this fearful storm, and that a more prosperous career may yet open to me.

My father has quitted London, and now resides at *Bradenham House, nr. Wycombe, Bucks* – a place, where I hope some day to see you, tho' at present I am only the inmate of an unsocial hotel, and preparing for my embarkation in the course of this current month. Anything addressed to me at the Union will reach one, who will always consider himself,

Your sincere friend.

BD

Write as soon as possible.

85

TO THOMAS MULLETT EVANS Union Hotel, [Cockspur Street, London], [Wednesday] 12 May [1830]

ORIGINAL: H A/V/A/13
COVER: Thomas Mullett Evans Esq | Solicitor | *Bristol* | private and paid
POSTMARK: (1) In Maltese cross: PAID | 12 MY 30 | CX.

Union. | May 12.

My dear Evans,

I shall be in town only for a few days, and in all probability shall leave it Monday or Tuesday; at the farthest: yet I much desire to meet. Even if you had the goodness to come, my time is of course greatly engrossed, and it might chance, that we sho[ul]d not see enough of each other.

Another plan occurs to me. I must be at Falmouth by the 30 or 31st. of the month, and after a week or so at | Bradenham, shall proceed there by easy journeys. Could not I come *round* by Bristol. I am not much of an English topographer, but this seems feasible. With your business like brain, you will arrange [it]

3 Messer, presumably.

in a moment. I cannot travel by night – but can do 100 miles a day. Let me have a line with a route[.]

Yrs ever

BD

86 TO JOHN MURRAY Bradenham, [Thursday] 27 May 1830

ORIGINAL: MM 27

COVER: private | John Murray Esqr | Albemarle Street | 50 | [In another hand on back]: 1830 May 27. | D'Israeli Benjn. Esq | and copy of Mr | Murrays answer on | May 29

POSTMARK: (1) In oval: 2.A.NOON.2 | 28.MY | x1830x (2) In packet: [illegible]

PUBLICATION HISTORY: Smiles II 333-4, dated 27 May 1830

EDITORIAL COMMENT: In another hand on the last page: '1830 May 27 | D'Israeli Benjn. Esq | and copy of Mr Murrays | answer on May 29'.

Bradenham House, Bucks | May 27, 1830

John Murray Esq.

Sir,

I am unwilling to leave England, which I do on Saturday, without noticing your last communication,[1] because I should regret very much, if you were to misconceive the motives which actuated me in not complying with the suggestion therein contained. I can assure you I have perfect confidence both in your "honor" and your "impartiality", for the first I have never doubted, and the second it is your interest to exercise.

The | truth is my friend and myself differed in the estimate of the MS.[2] alluded to, and while I felt justified, from his opinion, in submitting it to your judgment, I felt it due to my own, to explain verbally the contending views of the case, for reasons which must be obvious.

As you forced me to decide, I decided as I thought most prudently. The work is one which I dare say, wo[ul]d neither disgrace you to publish, nor me to write, but it is not the kind of production, which should recommence our connection, or be | introduced to the world by the publisher of Byron and Anastasius.[3]

I am now about to leave England for an indefinite, perhaps for a long period. When I return, if I do return, I trust it will be in my power for the *third time* to endeavour that you should be the means of submitting my work to the public. For this I shall be ever ready to make great sacrifices, and let me then hope that | when I next offer my volumes to your examination, like the Sibylline books,

1 See **83**n3.

2 The MS of *The Young Duke*, which D had referred to Edward Lytton Bulwer. In a letter to D dated 10 April 1830 Bulwer offered the following criticism of the novel: 'You do not seem to me to have done justice to your own powers when you are so indulgent to flippancies ... At all events if you do not think twice and act a little on this point I fear you are likely to be attacked and vituperized to a degree which fame can scarcely recompense. Recollect that you have written a book [*Vivian Grey*] of wonderful promise – but which got you enemies. You have therefore to meet in this a very severe ordeal both of expectation and malice.' H B/XX/Ly/4.

3 *Anastasius* (1819), a very popular picaresque novel by Thomas Hope (1770?-1831).

their inspiration may at length be recognised.[4]

I am, Sir,

Your obed Ser[van]t

B. Disraeli

87

TO [THOMAS JONES] [London], [Friday] 28 May 1830

ORIGINAL: BL ADD MS 59887 f1

COVER: 28th May 1830. Mr. Disraeli's Acknowledgement of Debt due to Mr. Jones.

May. 28.th. 1830

I hereby declare that I am indebted to my friend Thomas Jones Esqre[1] in the sum of three thousand pounds for money advanced for my use – and that there is interest in arrear on the sd. sum to the amount of one hundred and seventy five pounds, and in case the property which I may leave behind me will not meet this engagement, I | request my dear father to make good the same, feeling confident that my friend Thos. Jones will consult my father's convenience in such repayment

B. Disraeli

88

TO BENJAMIN AUSTEN [London, Friday 28? May 1830]

ORIGINAL: BL ADD MS 45908 ff29-30

COVER: IMMEDIATE AND PRIVATE | Benjamin Austen Esq | Raymond Blgs | Grays Inn

PUBLICATION HISTORY: Jerman 106-7, dated late May 1830

EDITORIAL COMMENT: *Sic*: wherabouts.

My dear Austen,

A thousand thanks for all your kindness. I have just arrived, and write this in case I may not be so fortunate as to find you. I enclose the £8.7.6. and shall advise you when I draw, not only for your convenience,[1] but for the gratification of informing my friends of my wherabouts.

We may yet meet at Naples. In the meantime, my dear fellow, rest assured;

4 Murray replied:

Albemarle St
May 29th 1830.

Mr. Murray acknowledges the receipt of Mr. Benjamin Disraelis polite letter of the 27th.

Mr. Murray will be ready, at all times, to receive any MS which Mr. B. Disraeli may think proper to confide to him. Mr M hopes, that the result of Mr. Disraelis Travels will be the compleat restoration of his health, with the gratification of his expectations.

D did not receive Murray's letter until his arrival at Malta. For his reaction to it see **97**n2.

---

1 Thomas Jones, father of Edward (see **2**), appears to have practised as a surgeon-accoucheur until the late 1830s. There are entries in London directories for Thomas Jones both at 51 Strand and at 23 Princes Street, Cavendish Square, and both entries cease at much the same time – 1838-9. As the name was not a rare one, it is uncertain whether the entries refer to one person or two.

D's relations with Jones date from 1825 (H R/II/B/4) and Jones's financial claims remained unsatisfied in 1840. An undated document of ten pages, auctioned as recently as 1977, apparently spells out the nature of D's obligation. Another letter, recorded in sales catalogues, suggests that D and Jones were still corresponding as late as 1854.

---

1 It was Austen who made D's journey to the Middle East possible. He had given D a letter of credit for £500.

that nothing but your conduct will ever influence mine towards you, and therefore I think ourselves pretty safe. I | shall endeavour not to abuse your good offers. Remember me most kindly to my kind friend Madame, and to Louisa who I trust continues convalescent. I can't say much for my confounded head; which has retrograded with the weather, but continued heat may yet cure me. In the mean time I will be sanguine, for if I despair, all is over. |

Farewell my dear friend. All prosperity attend you and yours. Believe me, I shall ever take a warm interest in your welfare.

B. Disraeli.

89 TO SARAH DISRAELI

Royal Hotel, Falmouth, [Cornwall], [Tuesday] 1 June 1830

ORIGINAL: QUA 201
COVER: Miss Disraeli | Bradenham House | Bucks. | [In another hand]: H. Wickham
POSTMARK: (1) FALMOUTH in circular form, enclosing: JU 1 | 1830 (2) In circle: E | 3 JU 3 | 1830
PUBLICATION HISTORY: HL 1-5, dated 1 June 1830, with postscript omitted
EDITORIAL COMMENT: *Sic*: cover: H. Wickham, Avala, Frankfort.

Royal Hotel Falmouth June 1. | 1830

My dear Sa,

We arrived here this morning at four o'clock instead of Sunday evening, having had a very rough passage indeed, the wind ahead the whole time. I was not only not sick, but did not even feel a qualm. Meredith also pretty well, but he can not match me as a sailor. So far, so good: but for the rest the steam packet is a beastly conveyance, and the total absence of all comfort, decency, and refinement is trying. We made acquaintance in the packet with a Spanish Officer, Colonel Avala,[1] who is going to Cadiz, a very knowing fellow, exceedingly polished and Parisian, having long resided in France. We were introduced to him by the Captain as interpreters, being the only men on board supposed to know French. Consequently a certain degree of intimacy took place, and as he repaired to the same hotel, we mess | together. We cannot make out what he is, as tho' excessively complaisant, he is very close. We suppose something political, but none of your Sherry Merchants, as his costume is remarkable, his conversation very refined, and moreover beaucoup d'argent. In the mean time, our French improves, and perhaps he may [be] of use to us in Spain.

Here at Falmouth, which by the bye is one of the most charming places I ever saw, (I mean the scenery around), I met a Mr Cornish who I believe is a medical man here and one of the Corporation.[2] He found me out, and introduced me to

1 Properly spelled 'Alava', the name is a common one in Spain. However, bearing in mind D's later comment that Alava had turned out to be a 'person of much distinction' (**91**), there may have been a connection between the Colonel and the famous Alava of the day. This was Don Miguel de Alava (1770-1843), Wellington's comrade in arms, who was in exile in England until 1833. The following year, he was appointed Spanish ambassador to the Court of St James's.

2 Mr James Cornish (b 1792) was certainly a burgess of the Corporation, but apparently not a physician. Susan E. Gay *Old Falmouth* (1903) 164-5; J. Philip *Panorama of Falmouth* (Falmouth 1827) 35.

the Casino or Club something like Frankfort, having in his library an American Edit: of V[ivian] G[rey] compressed in three volumes,[3] and full of admiration etc. But this is nothing. Would you believe it, – he has every one of my father's works except James and Charles,[4] which howr. he has read through the Book Society, interleaved and full of MS. notes and very literary ones. He has even the Bowles and Byron Controversy[5] all bound up with the review, and a MS. note to prove that Disraeli was | the author of the review from parallel passages from the Quarrels etc.[6] You never saw such a man. He literally knows my fathers works *by heart,* and thinks our revered sire the greatest man that ever lived. He says that Byron got all his literature from padre, and adduces instances which have even escaped us. You never met such an enthusiastic votary. I really wish my father co[ul]d send him a book. Unfortunately he has even the *last* edit: of the Lit[erary] Char[acter]:[7] he has three or four edits of the Curios[itie]s[8] and among them the first. I told him that when I wrote home, I sho[ul]d mention him. I have not even hinted at my father sending him anything, but really these ardent admirers of the united genius of the family sho[ul]d be encouraged. But I do not see that we co[ul]d do anything – Charles of course being out of the question to give, and James not being exactly the thing, even if practicable.[9] Meredith will write when we leave Falmouth which I think will be Friday. If I have anything more to say about Cornish, I will then let you know. |

I have of course nothing particular to say, but I thought you wo[ul]d like to hear, therefore I write tho' I fear you will all grumble at postage for such empty letters, but in time you will have fuller ones. We are very glad to have got rid of Louis Clement, and are in very fine condition indeed.

3 No three-volume edition of *Vivian Grey* published in the United States before 1830 has been located. However, a two-volume edition had been published in Philadelphia in 1827 by Carey, Lea and Carey.

4 *Inquiry into the Literary and Political Character of James I* (John Murray 1816), and *Commentaries on the Life and Reign of Charles the First, King of England* (5 vols 1826-31) published by Colburn (vols I-II) and Colburn and Bentley (vols III-V). It should be noted that Isaac was probably more affected by the 1826 rupture with Murray than D was. The vast majority of Isaac's works before that year had been published by Murray. After it, Isaac submitted nothing to Murray again for the rest of his life.

5 Isaac reviewed Edmond Malone's and Samuel Weller Singer's editions of Joseph Spence's *Anecdotes* (both published in 1820) together with William Bowles's 'The Invariable Principles of Poetry' (1819) in *The Quarterly Review* XXIII (July 1820) 400-34. He defended Alexander Pope's poetry and attacked Bowles's more romantic theories. When Bowles replied to the review, Byron produced a pamphlet on the subject, to which Bowles replied. J.J. van Rennes *Bowles, Byron and the Pope Controversy* (Amsterdam 1927); Ogden 91-4.

6 *Quarrels of Authors, or Some Memoirs for our Literary History* (1814).

7 *An essay on the Manner and Genius of the Literary Character* was first published in 1795, and the most recent edition, revised and enlarged, had been published in 1828.

8 The first series of *Curiosities of Literature, Consisting of Anecdotes, Characters, Sketches, and Dissertations Literary, Critical, and Historical* had begun to appear in 1791. By 1824 there had been seven editions and several reprintings.

9 *Charles I* was still in process of appearing and, as a five-volume work, would have been too expensive for D to expect Isaac to bestow on a chance acquaintance. *James I* was long out of print, and had had a mixed reception. Ogden 124.

Love, to all –
Your most affect. Brother
BD

P.S. We have, of course, heard nothing yet from Broadfoot,[10] and do not much care; We must buy bedding for the Mediterranean packets – a bore.

---

90 TO ISAAC D'ISRAELI — Gibraltar, [Thursday] 1 July [1830]

ORIGINAL: QUA 202

COVER: I. Disraeli Esqre. | Bradenham House | Wycomb. | Bucks. | England viâ *Madrid* | and *Paris*

POSTMARK: (1) In dotted circle: FPO | JY.20 | 1830 (2) In circle: W | JY.20 | 1830 (3) ESPAGNE PAR | ST.JEAN-DE-LUZ

PUBLICATION HISTORY: HL 6-13, dated 1 July 1830, omitting the last sentence, which in the original is written above the superscription as a postscript

EDITORIAL COMMENT: Despite his parents' retention of the old spelling of the family surname, from this point D's letters to them were addressed with the name in the revised form which he used himself. There is no signature. *Sic*: agreable, past, Easter melodrame, scull, Alemada, expence, Caravensara, Cacador.

Gibraltar. July. 1.

My dear father,

I write to you from a country where the hedges consist of aloes all in blossom, fourteen, sixteen, feet high. Conceive the contrast to our beloved and beechy Bucks. I say nothing of geraniums and myrtles, bowers of oranges, and woods of olives, tho' the occasional palm sho[ul]d not be forgotten for its great novelty and uncommon grace. We arrived here after a very brief and very agreable passage past in very agreable society. You have already heard of our detention at Falmouth for a week. As from the change of my plans, Gib. has become to me what I had intended Malta to have been, conceive the awkwardness of my situation, when the only person, to whom I had a letter, Colonel Falla,[1] is in England, but the introduction to Broadfoot has counteracted all inconvenience. He is here really a person of the first importance, and has treated us with the most marked consideration, so I co[ul]d not have been better off, if I had had letters to all the authorities. This rock is a wonderful place with a population infinitely diversified – Moors with costume radiant as a rainbow or an Easter melodrame,[2]

10 Alexander Broadfoot (d 1837), MD (1803) from Edinburgh, inspector general of health for the Ionian Islands, and assistant inspector of health at Gibraltar. Lt Col Harry A.L. Howell ed *Roll of Commissioned Officers in the Medical Service of the British Army* (Aberdeen 1917) 182. George Barrow had provided a letter of introduction to Broadfoot. See **96**.

---

1 Lt Col Daniel Falla (d 1851), then Town Major of Gibraltar.

2 Ralph Disraeli transcribes this as 'Eastern melodrama' (HL 7); however, the writing on the MS is very clear for the terminal letter of each word. There are two other instances when D uses 'Easter' in a similar sense (**108** and **109**), and in each case the writing is clear and there is no trace of a vestigal final 'n'.

'Melo-Drame', at the beginning of the nineteenth century, had few of the characteristics associated with later Victorian melodrama. It was made up largely of a series of spectacles, set in scenes of picturesque fantasy and accompanied by music, pantomime, ballet and elaborate costuming. Although the term 'Easter melodrame' does not appear to have survived as a category

Jews with gaberdines and scull caps, Genoese, Highlanders, and Spaniards, whose dress is as picturesque as that of the sons of Ivor. There are two public libraries, the Garrison Library, with more than 12,000 vols. and the Merchants with upwards of 1/2 that number. In the Garrison are all yr. works even the last edition of the Literary Character, in the Merchants, the greater part. Each possesses a copy of another book[3] sd. to be written by a member of our family, and which is looked upon at Gibraltar as one of the masterpieces of the 19th. Centy. You may feel their intellectual pulse from this. At first I apologised and talked of youthful blunders and all that, really being ashamed, but finding them to my astonishment sincere, and fearing they were stupid enough to adopt my last opinion I shifted my position just in time, looked very grand, and pass myself off for a child of the Sun, like the Spaniards in Peru.

We were presented by B. to the Governor, Sir George Don,[4] a Genl. and G.C.B. a very fine old gentleman, of the Windsor Terrace school, courtly | almost regal in his manner, paternal, almost officious in his temper – a sort of mixture of Lord St. Vincent[5] and the Prince de Ligne[6] – English in his general style, but highly polished and experienced in European Society. His palace, the Government House, is an old Convent and one of the most delightful residences I know, with a garden under the superintendance of Lady Don full of rare exotics with a beautiful Terrace over the sea, a berceau of vines, and other delicacies which wo[ul]d quite delight you. Besides this, Sir Geo. has a delightful Pavilion modestly called the Cottage at the extreme point of the Rock, and a villa at San Roque in Spain about 10 miles off. Thus by a constant change of residence, he counteracts the monotony of his situation. He possesses a large private fortune, all of which he here disburses, and has ornamented Gibraltar, as a lover does his mistress. The Alemada[7] here is superior to that at Cadiz, with banks of pink geraniums truly delicious. But Gibraltar is a limited theatre for his Excellency, and he has civilised Spain for twenty miles round, by making roads at his own expence, building bridges, and reforming posadas. He behaved to us with great kindness, asked us to dine and gave us a route himself for an excursion to the

used by historians of the theatre, they do record a growing tendency for dramatic presentations during Lent to be serious and morally improving in character. After Easter there was a resumption of performances of song, dance, spectacle and mime, and it may, therefore, be in this sense that D is using what would otherwise be a puzzling association of terms. Joseph Donohue *Theatre in the Age of Kean* (Oxford 1975) 106-7, 109.

At least one example of this *genre* of which D was aware was *Cherry and Fair Star; or, the Children of Cyprus*, described as 'the New, Grand, Asiatick, Melo-Dramatick Romance', probably by John Fawcett, produced by Charles Farley at the Theatre Royal, Covent Garden, on Easter Monday, 8 April 1822. D and Sarah chose the pseudonyms 'Cherry' and 'Fair Star' to conceal their authorship of their joint novel *A Year at Hartlebury, or The Election* when it was published in 1834. See **304**n1 ff.

3 *Vivian Grey.*

4 Gen Sir George Don (1754-1832), lieutenant governor of Gibraltar 1814-20 and 1825-31. Lieutenant governors performed all the duties for nominal absentee governors.

5 Adm John Jervis (1734-1823), 1st Earl St Vincent.

6 Charles Joseph, Prince de Ligne (1735-1814). He was made a lieutenant field marshal as a result of his service in the Austrian army in the Seven Years' War.

7 The Alameda Gardens, in the southern part of Gibraltar.

Sierra da Ronda, a savage mountain district abounding in the most beautiful scenery and bugs. We returned from this excursion, which took us a week yesterday, greatly gratified. The country in which we travelled is a land entirely of robbers and smugglers. They commit no personal violence, but lay you on the ground and clean out your pockets. If you have less than sixteen dollars, they shoot you; that is the tariff, and is a loss worth risking. I took care to have very little more – and no baggage which I co[ul]d not stow in the red bag which my mother remembers making for my pistols. We travelled on horseback, rising at four and stopping on account of the heat from ten till five in the evening and then proceeding for three more hours. There are a number | of little villages in this sierra entirely inhabited by robbers and smugglers, all of which boast a place called a posada. This is in fact a Caravensara. The same room holds the cattle, the kitchen, the family and boards and mats for travellers to sleep on – one or two have small rooms with beds for the chance of an officer from the garrison, and these were always clean – indeed nothing is more remarkable than the delicacy and the cleanliness of the lower orders in this country and the precautions which they universally take, by frequent white washing, to guard against vermin, but nothing can succeed against this generating Sun, and I have suffered severely, tho' not as much as I expected. These Posadas are, I say, mere Caravans[e]ras they afford no provisions, and you must cater as you proceed, and what is more, cook when you have catered, for that is a science not understood in Spain, or known only as an abomination. You will wonder how we managed to extract pleasure from a life, which afforded us hourly peril for our purses, and perhaps for our lives, which induced fatigue greater than I ever experienced, for here are no roads, and we were never less than eight hours a day on horseback, picking our way through a course which can only be compared to the steep bed of an exhausted cataract, and with so slight a prospect of obtaining for a reward either food or rest. I will tell you. The country was beautiful, the novelty of the life was great, and above all we had Brunet.[8] What a man! Born in Italy of French parents, he has visited as the Captain of a Privateer all the countries of the Mediterranean – Egypt, Turkey, Syria. Early in life as valet to Lord Hood,[9] he was in England and has even been at Guinea. After fourteen years cruising, he was taken by the Algerines, and was in various parts of Barbary for five or six years. At last he obtains his liberty and settles at Gibraltar, where he becomes Cacador[10] to the Governor, for he is, among his universal accomplishments, a celebrated shot. He can speak all languages but English of which he makes a sad affair – even | Latin, and he hints at a little Greek. He is fifty, but light as a butterfly, and gay as a bird: in person not unlike English at Lyme, if you can imagine so insipid a character with a vivacity that never flags, and a tongue that never rests. Brunet did every thing, remedied every inconvenience, and found an expedient for every difficulty. Never did I live so well as among these wild mountains of Andalusia, so exquisite is his

8 D had a penchant for vivid servants, as is pointed out by Sultana 66.
9 Adm Samuel Hood (1724-1816), 1st Baron and Viscount Hood.
10 Cazador, meaning 'hunter'.

cookery. Seriously he is an artist of the first magnitude, and used to amuse himself by giving us some very exquisite dish among these barbarians, for he affects a great contempt of the Spaniards, and an equal admiration, of the Moors. Whenever we complained, he shrugged his shoulders with a look of ineffable contempt, exclaiming "*Nous ne sommes pas in Barbarie!*" Recalling our associations with that word and country, it was superbly ludicrous.

Alas! my sheet has already disappeared, and I have said nothing. I will write you another letter by this post. |

Lady Don is ill; I have therefore not yet seen her.

TO ISAAC D'ISRAELI Gibraltar, [Thursday] 1 July 1830 **91**

ORIGINAL: QUA 203

COVER: I. Disraeli Esq | Bradenham House | Wycomb. Bucks. | England viâ *Madrid* | and *Paris*

POSTMARK: (1) In dotted circle: FPO | JY.20 | 1830 (2) In circle: W | JY.20 | 1830 (3) ESPAGNE PAR | ST. JEAN-DE-LUZ

PUBLICATION HISTORY: HL 14-21, dated 1 July 1830

EDITORIAL COMMENT: *Sic*: gennet, burthern, Gehoegans, avanture, publickly, expence.

Gibraltar. July. 1. 1830.

2

My dear father,

I have already written to you by this post, and altho' I do not think that I have sufficient intelligence to warrant me in sending you another letter, nevertheless by doing so, I err on the right side. To conclude the slight character which I gave you of Brunet in my last, let me tell you that he is at present making me a travelling suit of stuff, for he is a very good tailor. I heard only of one traveller among the Sierra da Ronda, and he was of course an Englishman. I made his acquaintance at Ronda, our ultimate point and a town on the other side of the mountains, a town with a garrison and some slight marks of civilisation. The traveller was Colonel Batty, sketching[1] – a gentlemanly person and very courteous: he wished me to join him to Granada. I never knew anyone sketch with such elegance, precision, and accuracy; long practice has made him unrivalled in this art, and far superior I sho[ul]d think to any professional artist. In the Sierra every man was armed. We returned through a country which reminded me of the Apennines; the rest was unlike anything I had seen and decidedly characteristic. There at Castellar we slept in the very haunt of the banditti, among the good fellows of Jose Maria, the Captain Rolando of this part,[2] and were not touched. In fact we were not promising prey – tho' picturesque enough in our appearance. Imagine M[eredith] and myself on two little Andalusian mountain horses with long tails and gennet necks, followed by a larger beast of burthern

1 Lt Col Robert Batty (d 1848), soldier and amateur draughtsman. He was the author of accounts of the Napoleonic Wars and of several popular travel books. He married the daughter of John Barrow.

2 Jose Maria el Tempranillo, famous Spanish bandit who lived in Andalusia in the early nineteenth century. Captain Rolando is the bandit chief introduced in book 1 ch 4 of Alain-René Lesage's *The Adventures of Gil Blas de Santillana* (1715-35).

with our baggage, and the inimitable Brunet, cocked upon its neck with a white hat and slippers, lively, shrivelled, and noisy as a pea dancing upon | tin: Our Spanish guide, tall and with a dress excessively brodé and covered with brilliant buttons walking by the side and occasionally adding to the burthern of our sumpter steed. The air of the mountains, the rising Sun, the rising appetite, the variety of picturesque persons and things we met, and the impending danger made a delightful life, and had it not been for the great enemy, I sho[ul]d have given myself up entirely to the magic of the life, but that spoiled all. It is not worse, sometimes I think it lighter about the head, but the palpitation about the heart greatly increases: otherwise my health is wonderful. Never have I been better, but what use is this, when the end of all existence is debarred me. I say no more upon this melancholy subject, by which I am ever, and infinitely depressed, and often most so, when the world least imagines it – but to complain is useless, and to endure almost impossible, but existence is certainly less irksome in the mild distraction of this various life. You and all I trust, are well and happy. Let me hear from you a great deal at Malta. I shall not be there, I dare say till the middle of August, so you can write by that packet and indeed you had better always direct your letters to me at Malta, and they shall be forwarded to me from that place, which is a fine central position.

Well to return. In spite of our frequent enquiries after the robbers, my being told "that is one of them" or that "Jose Maria was here two nights ago," or "is expected here to night," I was a little disappointed I confess to return quite safe, and really began to believe we had been half mystified. Judge then our feelings, when on | re-entering the hotel, the first sight that meets us and the first news that greets us, are two Englishmen just arrived from Cadiz, utterly rifled and stripped. They were attacked near a village at which we had been, not far from Gibraltar, by nine men in buckram.[3] The robbers did not even ask for their keys, but *cut* open their portmanteaus and sacks, literally ripped them open, divided their new Gehoegans[4] on the spot, took even their papers, and with barely clothes to cover them, dismissed them in the most courteous manner with two dollars for their journey. Quelle avanture! as Parry says.[5] They are now, poor devils inmates, of Griffiths Hotel Gibraltar, where they are about to be again plundered, if I may judge from my own experience, tho' not professionally.

Meredith maintains the high character he won in former days in Germany, and is a most admirable travelling companion. I have had more than one offer of that sort at this place, which allows me to pay him a compliment publickly etc.

Tell my mother, that as it is the fashion among the dandies of this place, that is the officers, for there are no others, not to wear waistcoats in the morning, her new studs come into fine play, and maintain my reputation of being a great

3 Although 'men in buckram' was established as a phrase connoting 'imaginary men' (from Falstaff's boasting about beating back imaginary attackers), it seems evident that D did not use the term in that sense here, nor later in **95**.

4 Shirts from Geoghegan & Co, 178 Regent Street. *LPOD* 1832; HL 18n.

5 Presumably Sir William Parry, the arctic explorer. This expression is not in keeping with the restrained tone of Parry's travel journals, but D's contacts with Murray may have shown him another side of the explorer.

judge of costume to the admiration and envy of many subalterns. I have also the fame of being the first who ever passed the Straits with two canes, a morning and an evening cane. I change my cane as the gun fires, and hope to carry them both on to Cairo. It is wonderful the effect these magical wands produce. I owe to them even more attentions than to being the supposed author of – what is it – I forget.

These straits by the bye – that is the passage for the last ten miles or so to Gib. between the two opposite | coasts of Africa and Europe with the Ocean for a river and the shores all mountains, is by far the sublimest thing I have yet seen. We are now preparing for another and longer trip into Spain. The part we intend to visit is the South of Spain, that celebrated Andalusia of which you have heard so much, comprising all the remains of the once famous kingdoms of the Moors. We propose returning to Cadiz to our friend Alava [,] who turned out to be a person of much distinction [,] ascending the Guadalquivir to Seville, there to Cordova, Granada, and Malaga. Look at the map and get W[ashington] I[rving]'s Chronicle.[6] I do not think much of it as a literary production, for the character he has assumed too much restrains him, tho' his humor sometimes breaks out, but you will find it most interesting, when you remember I am wandering among the scenes. When I beg *you* to write, I mean my beloved Sa, because I know you think it a bore, but do all as you like. To her and to my dearest mother a thousand kisses. Tell Ralph I have not forgotten my promise of an occasional letter, and my dear pistol-cleaner that he forgot to oil the locks which rusted in consequence. I thank the Gods daily I am freed of Louis Clement who wo[ul]d have been an expence and a bore. Tell Irving he has left a golden name in Spain. Few English visit Gibraltar. Tell Ld. Mahon,[7] enquiries made after his health. Adieu my beloved Sire.

Your most affec. Son

BD

Tell Irving, if you see him, I go to Mrs Stocker at Seville thro' Batty.

TO ISAAC D'ISRAELI — Cadiz, [Wednesday] 14 July 1830 — 92

ORIGINAL: QUA 204
COVER: I. Disraeli Esqr
PUBLICATION HISTORY: HL 22-9, dated 14 July 1830
EDITORIAL COMMENT: Ralph Disraeli's major conflations and excisions are the most striking reasons for the unreliability of his texts, but there is also a constant silent alteration of individual words and phrases. One example of his curious bowdlerizing is the substitution of 'fib' for 'lie' in the fourth sentence of this letter. *Sic*: agreable, aid-de camps, recherchеé, sulleness, Baron, Valdes.

---

6 *A Chronicle of the Conquest of Granada* (1829) by Washington Irving (1783-1859). The American poet and writer had come to Britain in 1815 and Isaac had met him at Murray's in 1817. They remained friends until Irving's return to the United States in 1832. Ogden 114-15.

7 Philip Henry Stanhope (1805-1875), Viscount Stanhope of Mahon, after 1855 5th Earl Stanhope. Later an eminent historian, Lord Mahon was elected Tory MP for Wootton Bassett in 1830-2, and for Hertford 1835-52.

14 Jul 1830

Cadiz. July 14. 1830

My dear father,

H.M.S. Messenger, in which I went out, is, I hear, expected at Cadiz to day on its return from Corfu, and therefore I send you this letter though I doubt whether anything justifies me writing except the circumstance of your so speedily receiving it. We passed a very pleasant week at Gibraltar after our return from Ronda. We dined with the Governor at his Cottage at Europa a most charming Pavilion – and met a most agreable party. Lady Don was well enough to dine with us, and did me the honor of informing me that I was the cause of the exertion, which though of course a lie, was nevertheless flattering. She is, tho' very old, without exception one of the most agreable personages that I ever met, excessively acute and piquante, with an aptitude of detecting character and a tact in assuming it, very remarkable. To listen to her, you wo[ul]d think you were charming away the hours with a blooming beauty in May Fair, and tho' excessively infirm, her eye is so brilliant and so full of moquerie, that you quite forget her wrinkles. Altogether the scene very much resembled a small German Court. There was His Excellency in uniform covered with orders exactly like the old G[rand] Duke of Darmstadt directing everything – his wife the clever Prussian Princess that shared his crown, the aid-de camps made excellent chamberlains – and the servants in number and formality quite equalled those of a Residenz. The repast was really elegant and rechercheé even for this curious age. Sir Geo. will yet head his table and yet carve, recommend a favorite dish and deluge you with his summer drink, half champaigne and half lemonade. After dinner Lady Don rode out with the very pretty wife of Colonel Considine,[1] and the men dispersed in various directions. It was the fate of Meredith and myself to be lionized to some cave or other with Sir Geo. What a scene and what a procession. First came two Grooms on two Barbs, then a carriage with four | horses, at the window at which H.E. sits, a walking footman, and then an outrider – all at a funereal pace. We were directed to meet our host at the cave, ten minutes walk. During this time Sir G. tries one of the Arabians, but at the gentlest walk, and the footman changes his position in consequence to his side; but it is windy, our valiant, but infirm, friend is afraid of being blown off, and when he reaches the point of destination, we find him again in the carriage. In spite of his infirmities, he will get out to lionize, but before he disembarks, he changes his foraging cap for a full Generals cock with a plume as big as the Otranto one,[2] and this because the hero will never be seen in public in undress, altho' we were in a solitary cave looking over the Ocean, and inhabited only by monkeys. The cave is shewn, and we all get into the carriage, because he is sure we are tired, the foraging cap is again assumed and we travel back to the cottage, Meredith, myself, the Governor, and the cocked hat, each in a seat. In the evening he has his rub-

1 Lt Col James Considine (d 1845) of the 53rd Regiment of Foot. Army List (1845) 161. No information about his wife has emerged; she is not mentioned in her husband's will.

2 An allusion to the sable plumes on the gigantic enchanted helmet in Horace Walpole's *The Castle of Otranto* (1764).

ber which he never misses, and is surprised I do not play "the only game for gentlemen, you sho[ul]d play, learn."[3] However I preferred the conversation of his agreable lady altho' the charms of Mrs. Considine were puzzling and I was very much like Hercules between etc. – you know the rest.[4]

I am sorry to say all my hair is coming off, just at the moment it had attained the highest perfection and was universally mistaken for a wig, so that I am obliged to let the women pull it, merely to satisfy their —— curiosity. Let me know what my mother thinks. There are no wigs here that I co[ul]d wear. Pomade and all that is quite a delusion. Somebody recommends me cocoa nut oil which I co[ul]d get here – but suppose it turns it grey, or blue or green! I made a very pleasant acquaintance at Gibraltar, Sir Charles Gordon, | a brother of Lord Aberdeen and Colonel of the Royal Highlanders.[5] He was absent during my first visit. He is not unlike his brother in appearance but the frigidity of the Gordons has expanded into urbanity, instead of subsiding into sulleness – in short a man with a warm heart tho' a cold manner, and exceedingly amusing with the reputation of being always silent – as contraries sometimes agree, we became excessively friendly. He asked me to dine with him, and to go to Ceuta on the African Coast, but I was engaged. I met him howr. at Sir Georges and also at Colonel Harding's[6] where I dined, and he called on me at Griffiths. He is going to Constantinople and expressed a wish that we might be travelling companions, but our plans do not agree. The Judge Advocate at Gibraltar is that Mr. Baron Field[7] who once wrote a book, and whom all the world took for a noble, but it turned out that Baron was to him what Thomas is to other men. He pounced upon me, said he had seen you at Murrays, first man of the day, and all that, and evidently expected to do an amazing bit of literature, but I found

3 Whist.

4 When Heracles was passing from boyhood to youth's estate, wherein the young, now becoming their own masters, show whether they will approach life by the path of virtue or the path of vice, he went out into a quiet place, and sat pondering which road to take. And there appeared two women of great stature making towards him. The one was fair to see and of high bearing; and her limbs were adorned with purity, her eyes with modesty; sober was her figure, and her robe was white.

The other was plump and soft, with high feeding. Her face was made up to heighten its natural white and pink, her figure to exaggerate her height. Open-eyed was she; and dressed so as to disclose all her charms. Now she eyed herself; anon looked whether any noticed her; and often stole a glance at her own shadow. Xenophon *Memorabilia* II i 21-2, trans E.C. Marchant (1923) 95.

Presumably Hercules chose virtue and we hear no more of Mrs Considine.

Sir Charles Gordon (1790-1835), brother of George Gordon, 4th Earl of Aberdeen; lieutenant colonel in the Black Watch (42nd Highlanders).

George Judd Harding (1788-1860), then a lieutenant colonel, later lieutenant general, governor of Guernsey 1855-9. He was knighted in 1860.

Barron Field (1786-1846), lawyer and miscellaneous writer. A close friend of Charles Lamb, he was a member of the literary circle that included Coleridge, Wordsworth, Hazlitt and Leigh Hunt. In 1819, during his appointment as judge of the Supreme Court of New South Wales (1817-24), he had had privately printed *The First Fruits of Australian Poetry*, a collection of poems, some whimsical some serious, which had greatly amused his literary friends. Field was chief justice of Gibraltar at the time of D's visit, and while D may have known of the book of verse, the work to which he refers is probably the better-known *An Analysis of Blackstone's 'Commentaries'* (1811).

him a bore and vulgar, a Storks without breeding,[8] consequently I gave him a lecture on canes, which made him stare and he has avoided me ever since. The truth is, he wished to saddle his brother[9] upon me for a compagnon de voyage, whom I discovered in the course of half an hour to be both deaf, dumb, and blind, but yet more endurable, than the noisy, obtrusive, jargonic judge, who is a true lawyer, ever illustrating the obvious, explaining the evident, and expatiating on the commonplace. We travelled here on horseback in two days, and passed on either side Medina Sidonia, and that Tarifa which Valdes took to our cost.[10] The English Consul here maintains a very elegant establishment, and has a very accomplished and amusing family. He prides himself on making all English "of distinction" dine with him every day – fortunately his cook is ill, for being French and a very good one I sho[ul]d have sunk under it. But Mrs. Brackenbury[11] "receives" every evening, and whenever one is at a loss, it is agreable to take refuge in a house which is literally a palace covered with pictures, where the daughters are all pretty, and sing boleros. I have met here Mr. Frank Hall | Standish,[12] once a celebrated dandy, and who wrote a life of Voltaire you remember. We have heard of the King's death, which is the destruction of my dress waistcoats.[13] I truly grieve. News arrived last night of the capture of Algiers,[14] but all this will reach you before my letter. My general health is excellent. I have never had a moments illness since I left home, not counting an occasional indigestion, but I mean no fever and so on. The great enemy I think is weaker, but the palpitation at the heart the reverse. I find wherever I go plenty of friends and nothing but attention. Pray let me hear from home. My love to all. I hope to find letters at Gibraltar when I return there, which will be a month, it may be. I like this horse travelling very much. On an average I am eight hours a day on horseback. The great thing is to avoid the Sun. We have had rain only one day since we have been out, and that was among the mountains, otherwise a cloudless sky, the | nights are delicious. I have literally heard nothing of England, since I left and long for letters.

8 Probably Henry Storks (1778-1866), at the time chief justice of the Isle of Ely. He appears to have had a persistent reputation as a monumental bore. See also (vol II) **373**n5.

9 John Francis Field, a clerk in the India Office.

10 Cayetano Valdez (1767-1835) was a Constitutionalist conspirator who led a successful attack on the fortress of Tarifa in August 1824. After a brief occupation the Constitutionalists were dislodged by Royalist and French troops. British opinion had been sympathetic to Valdez's cause; indeed the attack had been launched from Gibraltar. However, the failure of this invasion had been embarrassing to Britain, for it had strained relations with France without weakening the worrisome French influence in Spain. *MC* no 17,274 (28 Aug 1824).

11 John Macpherson Brackenbury (1778-1847), British consul for the province of Andalusia, was knighted in 1845. He married Sophia (d 1841), née Nicholson. Their family consisted of three sons and six daughters. John Macpherson, the second son, succeeded his father as consul in 1842. *BLG*; *GM* ns XVII (Mar 1842) 319.

12 Frank Hall Standish (1799-1840), art collector and author of *The Life of Voltaire* (1821).

13 For the short term, a period of mourning would have to be observed for George IV, who died 26 June 1830. For the long term, William IV's taste in waistcoats was considerably more subdued than his brother's had been. Whether D realized it or not, the flamboyance of the Regency was over.

14 A month previously French troops had landed at Algiers, thus taking the first step in founding an empire in North Africa.

Your most affec Son
BD

I have quite forgot to say a word about Cadiz, which is charming! brilliant beyond description. "Fair Florence" is a very dingy affair compared with it. The white houses and the green jalousies sparkle in the Sun. Figaro is in every street, and Rosina in every balcony.

TO ISAAC D'ISRAELI Seville, [Monday] 26 July 1830 93

ORIGINAL: QUA 205

COVER: FRANCE | I. Disraeli Esquire | Bradenham House | *WYCOMB*. Bucks | Inghilterra | ~~via Madrid et Paris~~ | [In another hand]: 2/7 | [on flap]: 16.1 | 15.9 | 2.12.10

POSTMARK: (1) In circle: D | JA.31 | 1831 (2) ESPAGNE PAR | ST.JEAN-DE-LUZ

PUBLICATION HISTORY: HL 30-7, dated 26 July 1830

EDITORIAL COMMENT: There is a small hole in the second page of the MS. The British postmark shows that this letter took over six months to arrive from Spain. There is no signature. *Sic*: Time, agreable, courier, au pied de lettre, Mashalla, chef d'oeuvres, tauridores, agreably.

Seville July 26. 1830

My dear father,

The Sevillians say that *Cadiz es toda facada*[1] by which they endeavour to conceal their envy at the superior beauty of a modern rival. The old proverb *Qui non a vista Seviglia non a vista maraviglia*[2] must have been founded on its reputation in the Time of the Moors for its exterior appearance and general effect are certainly not its most striking qualities. It is ancient and rambling but populous and wealthy. Its internal architecture is imposing. The houses are all built (at least the principal ones) round a quadrangle or *patio*. This is quite Moorish. There are two suites of apartments, and at this time of the year, the family reside in the lower and cooler one. The place is fearfully hot, hot enough even for me, but the heat certainly agrees with my constitution and even my head is better. The improvement however is very slight, and it will at the best be a long affair. If I co[ul]d get on as well as I have done this fortnight though, I sho[ul]d have hope. My general health is most remarkable. I do not suffer from any of the complaints of which my countrymen are the victims. Cadiz I left with regret, tho' there is little to interest except its artificial beauty. It is not unlike Venice in its situation, but there the resemblance ceases. Cadiz is without an association, not a church, a picture, or a palace. The family of the Consul is a most agreable one; you must not associate with this somewhat humble title a character at all in unison. Mr Brackenbury is great enough for an ambassador and lives well enough for one, but with some foibles, he is a very hospitable personage, and I owe many agreable hours to its exercise. You see what a Sevillian ecritoire is by this dispatch. I have already expended on it more time than I wo[ul]d have

1 'Cadiz is all a façade.'

2 'Chi non ha visto Seviglia non ha visto meravglia' – an Italian translation (with errors) of a Spanish saying – 'Quien no ha visto Sevilla no ha visto maravilla': 'He who has not seen Seville has missed a marvel.'

served for writing many letters, and am almost in a state of frenzy from the process of painting my ideas in this horrible scrawl. It is like writing with blacking, and with a skewer. Mr. Standish returned to Seville where he resides at present, and called on me the next day. We dined with him yesterday. | He is a most singular character – a spoiled child of fortune, who thinks himself, and who is perhaps now a sort of philosopher. But all these characters must be discussed over our fireside or on the Terrace. Fleuriz the Governor of Cadiz is a singular brute. When we meet I will tell you how I Pelhamised him.[3] All the English complain that when they are presented to him he bows and says nothing, uttering none of those courtly inanities which are expected on such occasions and for which crowned heads, and all sorts of Viceroys are celebrated. Brackenbury had been reading a review of the Commentaries in the courier in the morning, and full thereof, announced me to Fleuriz as the son of the greatest author in England.[4] The usual reception however only greeted me, but I being prepared for the savage, was by no means silent and made him stare for half an hour in a most extraordinary manner. He was sitting over some prints just arrived from England, a view of Algiers and the fashions for June. The question was whether the place was Algiers for it had no title. Just fresh from Gibraltar I ventured to inform his Excellency that it was, and that a group of gentlemen intended to represent Ralph and a couple of his friends, but displaying those extraordinary coats and countenances that Mr. Ackermann[5] offers monthly as an improvement upon Nature and Nugee,[6] were personages no less eminent than the Dey and his two principal Conseillers d'Etat. The dull Fleuriz took everything au pied de lettre and after due examination insinuated scepticism. Whereupon I offer renewed arguments to prove the dress to be Moorish. Fleuriz calls a Mademoiselle to translate the inscription, but the inscription only proves that they are "fashions for June"[,] at Algiers I add, appealing to everyone whether they had ever seen such beings in London. Six Miss Brackenburys | equally pretty, protest they have not. Fleuriz unable to comprehend badinage, gives a Mashalla[7] look of pious resignation and has bowed to the ground every night since that he has met me.

You will perhaps receive a couple of pounds of Seville snuff in the course of a month or so. It is very celebrated. The finest kind is a sort of light yellow. You will receive two sorts. Seville is full of Murillo, who appears to me the most original of artists. In London we think of him only as the painter of beggar boys, be-

3 The hero of Bulwer's fashionable novel *Pelham* (1828) consistently displayed a condescending manner. There were sterner ripostes in store for governors of Cadiz. Less than a year later, the successor of Fleuriz, one Oliveira, was assassinated. *The Times* (17 Mar 1831).

4 *The Courier* no 12,049 (6 July 1830) described Isaac's style as 'among the most correct and scholar-like' of all the popular authors. The reviewer added, cogently, that it was always difficult to know what was new in Isaac's history, since he never called attention to his departures from received opinion.

5 Rudolph Ackermann (1764-1834), fine-art publisher and bookseller. Among his many popular publications was the lavishly illustrated *Repository of Arts, Literature, Fashion, Manufactures etc*, which appeared in monthly parts, edited by Frederic Shoberl.

6 F.G. Nugee, tailor, 20 St James's Street. *LPOD* (1832).

7 Mashallah – an Arabic expression meaning 'what God wills (must come to pass).'

cause we happen to possess the only picture of the kind that he ever produced. No man has painted more, or oftener reached the ideal. He never fails. Where can his bad pictures be, I constantly ask. All here, and every house and church are full, are chef d'oeuvres.

I have seen more than one bull fight. The sight is magnificent. I form some idea of the public games of the ancients, and in the taste of the Spaniards for these entertainments can easily comprehend the Panem et Circenses. The effect however is marred by the wre[*tc*]hed hacks which they ride. So many horses are killed, that they can afford only the vilest. We are very comfortable here at an English boarding house kept by a widow, where Irving lived,[8] but go tomorrow. The costume of the tauridores or band of footmen who attend the picadores, or horsemen with pikes, is brilliant beyond anything I have ever seen. Mrs. Stalker, our hostess lent me Leucadio Doblado[9] which I read here with interest. The affecting story of the Nun who was allowed for a short time to see the world, is that of Blanco's own sister.[10] So a gentleman told me, who knows and has known the family for years. Blanco's brother is a very eminent merchant here in the house of Cahill, White, and Beck.[11] Old White was the greatest of bigots, and wished to make all his children priests and nuns. We came here up the Guadalquiv[ir], and tomorrow proceed by a diligence to Cordova. | This is a very stupid letter, but I was determined to write to you from Seville, and will whenever it is in my power. You sho[ul]d have received your last letter *free*. We have found here a most agreable friend in Mr. Williams[12] an English Merchant married to a Spanish Lady and considered the greatest connoisseur in paintings in Spain. He has nearly thirty of the finest Murillos. I had a letter to him from Brackenbury. It is astonishing with what kindness he behaves to us. His house is open to us at all times, and we pass our evenings most agreably sitting in his Patio turning over the original drawings of Murillo while his Spanish sister in law Dolores sings a bolero. It is the mode to call all the ladies here by their Christian name directly you are introduced. So much for Spanish etiquette. On the other hand, my tailor is offended if I do not ask him to take a chair, and always address him Signor. It is all banished to the lower classes. When he brought home [my] jacket he told me his whole fortune was at my command. God bless you all. I shall soon hear from you.

8 From 1826 to 1829 Washington Irving was a diplomatic attaché in Madrid and engaged in research for his *Life of Christopher Columbus* (1828). He returned to London in 1829 and was secretary to the United States legation until 1832.

9 Joseph Blanco White (1775-1841), Anglo-Spanish poet who published under the name of Don Leucadio Doblado. He left Spain for England, where his *Letters from Spain*, first published 1807, 2nd ed rev 1825, established a minor reputation for him.

10 White's bitterness at the bleak existence to which his sister was condemned is amply documented in his writings. His sister (died c 1821) was referred to as 'Maria Francisca'. *Letters from Spain* (1825) 22-31; John Hamilton Thom ed *The Life of the Rev. Joseph Blanco White, Written by Himself* (1845) I 120-5; III 343-5.

11 Blanco White's father, William, described by his son as oppressively pious, was born in Seville, and became a successful exporter of Spanish produce. His partner in this enterprise was an Irishman named Thomas Cahill, who was also the elder White's brother-in-law. Luke Beck, another Irishman, married into the Cahill family and joined Blanco White's younger brother, Ferdinand (b 1785), in the firm. Thom I 3-9; III 201, 315, 470.

12 *The English Registry* for 1834 lists Julian B. Williams as British consul in Seville.

94 TO MARIA D'ISRAELI Granada, [Sunday] 1 August 1830

ORIGINAL: QUA 216

COVER: Mrs. Disraeli | Bradenham House | Wycomb Bucks | Inghilterra. | viâ Madrid y Paris. | [At right angles]: Francia | [In another hand]: 2.8 | 0.10 | 3.6.

POSTMARK: (1) In dotted circle: FPO | AU.23 | 1830 (2) In circle: D | AU.23 | 1830 (3) ESPAGNE PAR | ST.JEAN-DE-LUZ (4) Under crown: GRANADA

PUBLICATION HISTORY: LBL 17-26, dated 1 August 1830, with omissions; M&B I 149-52, dated 1 August, with omissions

EDITORIAL COMMENT: This is the letter which D refers to elsewhere as being written on an 'elephantine' sheet. The paper is 21cm by 30cm, and there are four closely written pages. The greater part of the letter was inserted in *Contarini Fleming* part V chs 6 and 7. Indeed there is scarcely a sentence in those chapters not drawn from this letter. Part of the second sheet of the MS is torn. *Sic*: Grenada, agreable, envelope, Ossuna, aggravate, anyway, Each, I have rode, tomata, an usual, Tomata, Tomatas, AlHambra.

Grenada August. 1. 1830.

My dear Mother,

Altho you doubtless assist, as the French phrase it, at the reading of my dispatches you will I am sure be pleased to receive one direct from your absent son. It has just occurred to me that I have never yet mentioned the Spanish Ladies, and I do not think that I can address anything that I have to say upon this agreable subject to anyon[*e*] more suitable than yourself. You know that I am rather an admirer of the blonde, and to be perfectly candid, I will confess to you, that the only times which I have been so unfortunate as to be captivated, or captured, in this country were both by Englishwomen. But las Espagnolas are nevertheless very interesting personages. What we associate with the idea of female beauty is not common in this country. There are none of those seraphic countenances which strike you dumb or blind, but faces in abundance which will never pass without commanding a pleasing glance. Their charm consists in their sensibility. Each incident every person, every word, touches the fancy of a Spanish Lady and her features are constantly confuting the creed of Mahomed, and proving that she has a soul: but there is nothing quick, harsh, or forced about her. She is extremely unaffected and not at all French. Her eyes gleam rather than sparkle, she speaks with guileless vivacity but in sweet tones, and there is in all her carriage, particularly when she walks, a certain dignified grace, which never leaves her, and which is very remarkable. The general female dress in this country is of black silk called a *basquina*, and a black silk shawl with which they usually envelope their head called a *mantilla*. As they walk along in this costume in an evening, with their soft dark eyes dangerously conspicuous, you willingly believe in their universal beauty. They are remarkable for the beauty of their hair. Of this they are very proud, and indeed its luxuriance is only equalled by the attention which they lavish on its culture. I have seen a young girl of fourteen whose hair reached her feet and was as glossy as the curl of a Lady Caroline. All day long, even the lowest order, are brushing, curling and arranging it. A fruitwoman has her hair dressed with as much care as the Duchess of Ossuna.[1] At this time of the year they do not wear the mantilla generally over

1 By which D obviously meant 'any grand lady'. The then Duke of Osuna died unmarried. The dowager Duchess died in 1830. *Enciclopedia universal illustrada* (Barcelona nd).

the head, but show their combs which are of immense size. The fashion of these combs varies constantly, every two or three months. It is the part of the costume of which the Spanish female is most proud. The moment that a new comb appears, even the servant wench will have her old one melted down and thus with the cost of a dollar or two appear the next holiday in the newest style. These combs are worn at the back of the head. They are of tortoise shell: the very fashionable wear them of the white.[2] I sat next to a lady of high distinction at a bull fight at Seville. She was the daughter in law of the Captain General and the most beautiful Spaniard I have yet met. Her comb was white, and she wore a mantilla of blonde. I have no doubt extremely valuable for it was very dirty. The effect however was very charming. Her hair was glossy black, and her eyes like an antelopes, but all her other features deliciously soft, and she was further adorned which is rare in Spain with a rosy cheek, for here our heroines are rather sallow. But they counteract this defect by never appearing until twilight, which calls them from their bowers, fresh, though languid from the late siesta. To conclude, the only fault of the Spanish beauty is that she too soon indulges in the magnificence of en bon point. There are however many exceptions to this. At seventeen a Spanish beauty is poetical – tall, lithe and clear tho' sallow – but you have seen | Mercandotti.[3] As she advances, if she do not lose her shape, she resembles Juno rather than Venus. Majestic she ever is, and if her feet are less twinkling than in her first career, look on her hand and you'll forgive them all.[4]

There is a calm voluptuousness about the life here that wonderfully accords with my disposition so that if I were resident and had my intellect at command, I do not know any place where I could make it more productive. The imagination is ever at work, and beauty and grace are not scared away by those sounds and sights, those constant cares, and changing feelings which are the proud possession of our free land of eastern winds. You rise at eight, and sho[ul]d breakfast lightly, altho a table covered with all fruits renders that rather difficult to one who inherits with other qualities good and bad, that passion for the most delightful productions of Nature with which my beloved sire can sympathise. I only wish I had him here over a medley of grape and melon, gourd, and prickly pear. In the morning you never quit the house, and these are hours which

2 Tortoise shell is not, of course, 'melted down' as metals or modern plastics are. It may, however, be remoulded and reshaped by the careful application of the right degree of heat – too much, and the shell becomes very dark. The 'white' is thus a relative term – the very light tones testifying that the article had not been remodelled to fit the fashion, but was an 'original'.

3 Maria Mercandotti (b 1806?), Spanish dancer who made her English debut at the King's Theatre in the season 1822-3. Her career ended when she eloped with Edward 'Ball' Hughes, a friend of her protector, Lord Fife. Bernard Blackmantle [Charles Molloy Westmacott] *The English Spy* (1825) I 203, 284; C.E. Pearce *Mme Vestris and Her Times* (New York nd) 72-4; Parmenia Migel *The Ballerinas* (New York 1972) 109-10.

4 This variation on Pope's lines from *The Rape of the Lock* (II 17-18) is but one of numerous such attempts to adapt the language of the famous couplet: 'If to her share some female errors fall, | Look on her face, and you'll forget 'em all.'

Other wits of D's time had sometimes given a less positive turn to the lines – 'Look on her face, and you'll believe 'em all' being a popular alternative.

might be profitably employed under the inspiration of a climate which is itself poetry, for it sheds over everything a golden hue, which does not exist in the objects themselves illuminated. At present I indulge only in a calm reverie, for I find the least exertion of mind instantly aggravate all my symptoms, and even this letter is an exertion which you wo[ul]d hardly credit. But to exist, and to feel existence more tolerable, to observe, and to remember, to record a thought that suddenly starts up, or catch a new image which glances over the surface of my mind – this is still left me. But the moment that I attempt to meditate or combine, to ascertain a question that is doubtful or in anyway to call the greater powers of intellect into play, that moment I feel I am a lost man. The palpitation in my heart and head increases in violence, an indescribable feeling of idiocy comes over me, and for hours I am plunged in a state of the darkest despair. When the curse has subsided to its usual grade of horror, my sanguine temper calls me again to life and hope. My general health was never better and this allows me to endure, or rather to support, with more ease the life I am now pursuing. I do not for a moment give way to my real feelings except under a paroxysm. I am determined to prove to all that I am not suffering under hypochondria, and I court instead of shunning society. But I pursue this life only for a year; if at the end of that period I find no relief, I resign myself to my fate. Were I a catholic without the ties of love which alone reconcile me to my bitter existence, I wo[ul]d then enter a Convent, but as I am a member of a family to which I am devotedly attached, and a good Protestant, I shall return to them and to my country, but to a solitary room which I never leave. I see no one, and speak with no one. I am serious. Prepare yourself for this, but hope better things. If you ask me whether I am better, I answer *Yes*.[5] You know how much better I am on a sunny day in England – well I have had two months of sunny days infinitely warmer. I have during all this period enjoyed general health, of which I have no memory during my life. All the English I have met are ill and live upon a diet. I eat everything, and my appetite Each day increases. I have constantly rode eight hours a day on horseback. I travelled through three successive nights and saw the Sun set and rise without quitting my saddle, which few men can say, yet | have I never known fatigue. This is literally the fact. A feverish feeling of which all travellers complain I have not known for an instant. So extraordinary and so beneficial is the influence of this climate upon me, and so entirely does my frame sympathise with this expanding Sun. But is all this a subject of congratulation when the great evil does not proportionately, I sho[ul]d say does not at all amend. The great hope that with the improvement of my general health it wo[ul]d disappear seems vanishing. To what am I to cling? Enough of this: it is three o clock and nearly dinner; I doff my dressing gown and slippers, my only costume, and prepare my toilette. The Spanish cuisine is not much to my taste, for garlic and bad oil preponderate, but it has its points. Its soups are good. *The most agreable dish* in the world is an Olio. I will explain it to you, for my father would delight in it. There are two large dishes:

5 RD omits all this section, beginning from 'But to exist ... ', retaining only the phrase 'My general health was never better'.

one at each end of the table. The one at the top contains bouilli beef, boiled pork (fat) sausage, black pudding, all these not mixed together but in their separate portions. The other dish is a medley of vegetables and fruits, generally french beans, caravanseras, slices of melons and whole pears. Help each person to a portion of the meats and then to the medley – Mix them in your plate together and drown them in tomata sauce. There is no garlic and no grease of any kind. I have eaten this everyday. It is truly delightful. Of course you can fix upon those ingredients most at hand – I have described an usual Olio. The Tomata sauce here is very light, piquant, and pleasant. It is thin. We have it with us too thick and rich. The Spaniards eat the Tomata in all possible ways. I obtained the receipt for one dish, which infinitely pleased me, and with which I think my father would be charmed. It is very simple. Take four pounds of Tomatas, fry them very small; add four eggs, yoke and all. Mix [*them*] well. They sho[ul]d be served up very dry, and indeed on the whole lo[*oks*] like a Dry soup, but of a very pretty color. I need not tell the mistress [*of*] so experienced a cuisine as you, to add a small quantity of onion in frying the tomatas. By the bye, Adams,[6] I hope, is well. After dinner you take your Siesta. I generally sleep for two hours. I think this practice conducive to health. Old people however are apt to carry it to excess. By the time I have risen and arranged my toilette, it is time to steal out, and call upon any agreable family whose Tertullia[7] you may choose to honor, which you do after the first time uninvited, and with them you take your tea or chocolate. This is often alfresco. Under the piazza or colonnade of the patio. Here you while away the Time until it is cool enough for the Alameda or public walk. At Cadiz and even at Seville, up the Guadalquivir you are sure of a delightful breeze from the water. The sea breeze comes like a spirit. The effect is quite magical. As you are lolling in listless languor in the hot and perfumed air, an invisible guest comes dancing into the party and touches them all with an enchanted wand. All start, all smile. It has come – it is the Sea-breeze. There is much discussion whe[the]r it is as strong or whether weaker than the night before. The ladies furl their fans, and seize their mantillas, the cavaliers stretch their legs and give signs of life. All rise. I offer my arm to Dolores or Florentina (Is not this familiarity strange?) and in ten minutes, you | are on the Alameda – What a change! All is now life and liveliness. Such bowing, such kissing, such fluttering of fans, such gentle criticisms of gentle friends. But the fan is the most wonderful part of the whole scene. A Spanish lady with her fan might shame the tactics of a troop of horse. Now she unfurls it with the slow pomp and conscious elegance of a peacock, now she flutters it with all the languor of a listless beauty, now with all the liveliness of a vivacious one. Now, in the midst of a very Tornado, she closes it with a whirr which makes you start – Pop! In the midst of your confusion, Dolores taps you on your elbow; you turn round to listen and Florentina pokes you in your side. Magical instrument! You know that it speaks a particular language, and gallantry requires no other mode to express its most subtle conceits or its most unreasonable demands, than this

6 The D'Israeli family's cook.
7 Spanish term for an evening party.

delicate organ. But remember, while you read, that here, as in England, it is not confined alone to your delightful sex. I also have my fans, which makes my cane extremely jealous. If you think I have grown extraordinarily effeminate, learn that in this scorching clime, the soldier will not mount guard without one. Night wears on. We sit, we take a panal, which is as quick work as snapdragon, and far more elegant,[8] again we stroll. Midnight clears the public walk, but few Spanish families ret[*ire*] till two. A solitary bachelor like myself still wanders, or still lounges on a bench in the *warm* moonlight. (Caraccioli's story has been misunderstood. He alluded to the *heat*)[9] the last guitar dies away, and the Cathedral clock breaks up your reverie. You too seek your couch, and amid a sweet flow of loveliness and light, and music and fresh air, thus dies a day in Spain.

Adieu, my dearest mother. If possible I write to my father from this place. 1000 loves to all.

B Disraeli

Tell Emily[10] that I have not forgotten her, but have plucked for her Album a sprig from the Court of Myrtles in AlHambra, but as I travel on horseback, only with my saddlebags, I fear much it will lose its lustre, before it is secured in my writing case at Gibraltar.

---

95 TO SARAH DISRAELI — Gibraltar, [Monday] 9 August 1830

ORIGINAL: QUA 206

COVER: *By the Steam Packet.* | Miss Disraeli | Bradenham. House | Wycomb. Bucks | Inghilterra | ~~Viâ Madrid y Paris~~ | [At right angles]: ~~Francia~~

POSTMARK: (1) In circle: K | AU.25 | 1830 (2) In dotted circle: FPO | AU.25 | 1830 (3) In semi-circle: GIBRALTAR

PUBLICATION HISTORY: HL 38-47, dated 9 August 1830, with the omission of the sixth sentence before the signature

EDITORIAL COMMENT: *Sic*: Medittn, Grenada, Tomata, agreable, lay perdus, Cordove, leant, Englishman, are waken.

Gibraltar. August 9.

My dear Sa,

We arrived here yesterday tired to death but very well. The Meditt[erranea]n packet is expected hourly and I lose not a moment in writing to you which I do in compliment to your most welcome letter, which awaited me here, and which, tho' short enough, was most sweet. The very long one about all the things I want to know makes my mouth water. There is not the slightest doubt of its duly reaching me. I am surprised to find you complain of my writing seldom, as

8 Panal consisted of small pieces of honeycomb which were served in various ways as sweetmeats. Snapdragon was an English Christmas game in which raisins were extracted from a dish of burning brandy and eaten while still aflame.

9 Dominique, Marchese Caraccioli (1715-1789). In 1763 he became Neapolitan ambassador to the Court of St James's. Disliking the English and London and longing for the climate of Italy, he often complained that the English sun could not equal the moon of Naples. J.F. Michaud *Biographie universelle ancienne et moderne* rev ed (Paris 1854-65).

10 Emily Lindo, D's cousin.

I have really made every exertion to give you a fair account of all my doings. I sent two letters to my father from Gib. but as they went by the same post you may perhaps count them as one, but they were on separate sheets, one from Cadiz and one from Seville also to him and one on an Elephantine sheet from Grenada to my mother, all about Spanish Ladies and Tomata Sauce. I trust all these will duly arrive. It is possible you may receive the last being overland even after this. With regard to my plans, we are certainly off next packet, perhaps on Saturday. No farther can I aver. What use are plans? Did I dream 6 months ago of Andalusia where I have spent some of the most agreable hours of my existence? Such a trip! Such universal novelty and such unrivalled luck in all things. I must find time to send you at least a couple more letters from this place, to complete my sketch from Cordova. If I tell you more stories of men in buckram, do not smile. Literally a week ago we saved ourselves only by a moonlight scamper and a change of road. I gave all up, and only at Malaga two nights since with our feet in our stirrups, we were obliged to dismount and lay perdus till morn. When I reside at a place it is not very difficult to write home which is really always agreable, but if you co[ul]d form an accurate idea of the life of constant fatigue and excitement which I have experienced since I left you I do not think you wo[ul]d accuse me of neglect. What a country have I lived in! I am invited by "a grand lady of Madrid" I quote our host at Cordove to join her escort to Granada – twenty foot soldiers, four servants armed and tirailleurs in the shape of a dozen muleteers. We refused for reasons too long here to detail – and set off alone two hours before, expecting an | assault. I sho[ul]d tell you we dined previously with her and her husband, having agreed to meet to discuss matters. It was a truly Gil Blas scene. My Lord in an undress uniform, and highly imposing in appearance, greeted us with dignity, the Signora exceedingly young, and really very pretty, with infinite vivacity and grace. A French valet leant on his chair and a Duenna, such as Stephanoff[1] wo[ul]d draw, broad and supercilious, with jet eyes, mahogany complexion and cocked up nose, stood by my Lady, exercising[?] a large fan. She was most complaisant, as she evidently had more confidence in two thickheaded Englishman with their Purdeys and Mantons,[2] than in her specimen of the once famous Spanish Infantry. She did not know that we are cowards on principle. I co[ul]d screw up my courage to a duel or a battle, but I think my life worth five pounds, in the shape of ransom to Jose Maria. In spite of her charms, and their united eloquence which, as they only spoke Spanish, was of course most persuasive, we successfully resisted. The moon rises on our course; for the first two leagues, all is anxiety, as it was well known that a strong band was lying in wait for the "great lady". After two leagues, we began to hope, when suddenly our guide in-

1 Either Francis Philip Stephanoff (1790?-1860), London-born engraver and painter of popular pictures, or his brother, James (1788?-1874), famous mainly for his paintings of ceremonial scenes such as coronations and royal receptions.

2 James Purdy and Joseph Manton were both well-known gunsmiths of the day. Harold L. Peterson ed *Encyclopedia of Firearms* (1964).

146 | 95 forms us, that he hears a trampling of horse in the distance. Ave Maria! A cold
9 Aug 1830 perspiration came over me. Decidedly they approached – but rather an uproarious crew. We drew up out of pure fear, and I had my purse ready. The band turned out to be a company of actors travelling to Cordova. There they were, dresses and decorations, scenery and machinery, all on mules and donkeys, for there are no roads in this country. The singers rehearsing an Opera – the principal Tragedian riding on an ass, and the Buffo most serious looking as grave as night with a segar and in greater agitation than them all. Then there were women in sidesaddles, like sedans, and whole | panniers of children – some of the former chaunting an Ave, while their waists (saving your presence, but it is a rich trait) were in more than one instance encircled by the brawny arm of a more robust devotee. All this irresistibly reminded me of Cervantes! We proceed and meet a caravan (Corsario they call it, but I spell from sound) of armed merchants, who challenged us with a regular piquet, and I nearly got shot for not answering in time, being somewhat before my guide: then come two travelling friars who give us their blessing, and then we lose our way. We wander about all night; dawn breaks; and we stumble on some peasants sleeping in the field amid their harvest. We learn that we cannot regain our road and utterly wearied, we finally sink to sound sleep with our packsaddles for our pillows. This is the country for a national novelist. The alfresco life of the inhabitants induces a variety of the most picturesque manners, their semi savageness makes each district retain with barbarous jealousy their own customs and their own costumes. A weak government resolves society into its original elements and robbery becomes more honorable than war, inasmuch as the robber is paid, and the soldier in arrear. Then a wonderful ecclesiastical establishmt. covers the land with a privileged class who are perpetually producing some effect on society. I say nothing while dotting in these lines, which afterwards may be expanded into a picture, of their costume. You are waken from your slumbers by the Rosorio, the singing procession by which the peasantry congregate to their labours. It is most effective, full of noble chaunts and melodious responses, that break upon the still, fresh, air, and your even fresher feelings, in a manner truly magical. Oh! wonderful Spain! Think of this romantic land covered with Moorish ruins and full of Murillo! Ah! that I could describe to you the wonders of the painted temples of Seville, ah! that I could wander with you amid the fantastic and imaginative halls of delicate Alhambra! Why, why, cannot I convey to you more perfectly all that I see and feel! I thought that enthusiasm was dead within me, and nothing could be new. I have hit perhaps upon the only country which co[ul]d have upset my theory, a country of which I have read little, and thought nothing, a | country of which indeed nothing has been written and which few visit[.] I dare to say that I am better. This last fortnight I have made regular progress, or rather felt perhaps the progress which I had already made. It is all the Sun. Do not think that it is society or change of scene. This, however occasionally agreable, is too much for me, and ever throws me back. It is when I am quite alone, and quite still, that I feel the difference of my system, that I miss old aches, and am conscious of the increased activity and vitality and expansion of my blood. Write to me

when[eve]r you can – always to Malta, from whence I shall be sure to receive my letters sooner or later. If I receive 20 at a time, it does not signify; but write; do not let the chain of my domestic knowledge be broke for an instant – write to me about Bradenham, about dogs and horses, orchards, gardens – who calls, where you go. Who my father sees in London – what is said. This is what I want – never mind public news, except it be private in its knowledge, or about private friends. I see all newspapers sooner or later. I shall write from here overland. I forgot to say I wrote from Falmouth. I did not know that I had been long on the rock. They all complain of my angel visits.[3] I fear Ponsonby is not at Malta.[4] I am obliged for the letter to Hankey.[5] I have already made wadding for my pistols with six to that Gentleman, but this between ourselves. Keep on writing but dont *bore* yourself – mind this. A thousand, thousand loves to all. Adieu my beloved. We shall soon meet. There is no place like Bradenham, and each moment I feel better, I want to come back.

BD

The rain wo[ul]d have finished me for ever: even if the Sun had not revived me, and all had been fancy, I sho[ul]d not have known it then. I think the consequences on my mind would have been fearful. Two thunderstorms in the mountains. That is all we had. Each day cloudless, and the air like a furnace. The heat of the moon is unpleasant at night. Quelle pays!

96

TO GEORGE BARROW — Malta, [Friday] 20 August 1830

ORIGINAL: HM I

EDITORIAL COMMENT: *Sic*: agreable, Grenada, agreably, Tomata's.

Malta – August 20th. 1830

G. Barrow Esq[1]

Dear Barrow,

I have long been intending to write to you, not I assure you, for the purpose of availing myself of your kind offer, which I sho[ul]d do without ceremony, but really because I was desirous of expressing how very much I am obliged to you for your introduction to Broadfoot, which from certain circumstances, I found of no slight importance; for it so happened as I was standing on the deck of the Steamer and gazing on my country's lessening shores, it suddenly occurred to

3 'What though my wingèd hours of bliss have been, | Like angelvisits, few and far between?' Thomas Campbell *The Pleasures of Hope* II 377-8.

4 Maj Gen Sir Frederick Cavendish Ponsonby (1783-1837), second son of the 3rd Earl of Bessborough, was lieutenant governor of Malta 1826-36. In 1825 he had married Lady Emily Charlotte Bathurst (d 1877), youngest daughter of the 3rd Earl Bathurst. Ponsonby performed the office of governor but the position was styled 'lieutenant governor'. Unlike Don in Gibraltar, Ponsonby seems not to have had an absentee superior, but was apparently accorded the lower rank to justify a lower salary. A.V. Laferla *British Malta* (Valetta 1946) I 133.

5 Col Sir Frederick Hankey (1774?-1855), KCMG 1818, chief secretary to the governor of Malta 1825-38, formerly secretary to the high commissioner of the Ionian Islands. Hankey was not, it seems, popular with the Maltese population. Laferla I 158.

1 George Barrow (1806-1876), eldest son of John Barrow, had since 1825 been a clerk in the Colonial Office. He succeeded his father as baronet in 1848.

me, that Gibraltar, at which I intended to stop only a few hours, was anciently in the Kingdom of Spain, and that that romantic region had of late, been little visited. To be brief, I have only this moment arrived here where I intended to be in the middle of June, having wandered for two delightful months through Andalusia, and visited I believe every part of the South of Spain. Among the mountains of Ronda, in the wildest part of the Sierra, I met Colonel Batty, and only regretted, that we were companions for so short a time. I hope he has not been plundered, for we were in very wicked parts, and he bore with him sundry coats and chattels very tempting. Your brother arrived at this place in the Blonde a few days before me, but he is in long quarantine.[2] I have had a lengthy palaver however with him from a respectful distance, and from his looks I don't think, that he has got the plague. I offered to send any message, but he writes by this packet. As your father and yourself were fortunately almost the last two persons I saw in | England, it was in my power to give him a bulletin of your blooming looks.

I found Spain in almost the same state as in the time of Gil Blas: less rich perhaps, but with a social order almost as imperfect, and quite as picturesque. Robbers infest every road, and the whole government of the country exercising an authority, which is limited to the walls of the capital, the population are forced to take the law in their own hands, and travel with all the etiquette of warfare. Riding on, one night, before my servant, I was challenged by a piquet of some travelling toy dealers from Malaga, and all but shot because I was silent from astonishment. I travelled generally by night – *pour voir le pays*, you will add with a smile – but really the moon is so bright that one may use one's sight with as much advantage, and with more comfort, than in the daytime. It is more than bright, it is warm, it is hot. Carracioli's famous story about the moons of Naples has been misunderstood – he alluded, I feel confident, to the heat. There are no roads and you work your way on horseback, which is less pleasant than you wo[ul]d at first imagine. I have generally been ten hours in the 24 on my steed, and more than once saw the Sun set and rise without quitting my saddle, which few men can say, and which I hope never to say again. After this I need not aver that I am in fine condition, but my confounded brain comes round but slowly, and will, I fear yet give me much trouble. The mode of life in Spain is very agreable to a young man and wo[ul]d I think please you. The women without being strikingly | handsome, are highly interesting. Their countenances have all that charm which arises from excessive sensibililty. They have, when very young, a fine voluptuous gait, and what are called *speaking* eyes – but their ocular conversation is not the restless, fidgetty, chat of a Frenchwoman. Their large soft black eyes gleam rather than sparkle. Their fault is, that in too many cases, they too early indulge in the magnificence of embonpoint, but a very youthful Spanish girl, who has not exceeded sweet seventeen (equal in these climes to our

2 William Barrow (1810-1838) was John Barrow's youngest son. He was at this time a lieutenant in HMS *Blonde*, a 46-gun frigate commanded by Capt Edmond Lyons, which had just arrived at Malta.

27) dusk and lithe, is a very poetical heroine, and God knows, a very passionate one.

Cadiz is the most brilliant city you co[ul]d well fancy. Its white walls and verdant jalousies sparkle in the sun. Figaro is in every street, and Rosina in every balcony. I got up to Seville from this place by a Steamer (the only evidence I have met of the vaunted regeneration of Spain) up the Guadalquivir. The city is ancient and interesting moreover from being the Temple of Murillo's genius, an artist whom I have always greatly admired, but whom I now hesitate not to place above all the Italians. Indeed I am greatly inclined to consider the Spaniards as the first of all masters; particularly when I think Velasquez[3] by whose side Titian's portraits are dull – but we know nothing of these men. There is not a first rate Murillo in England, tho' we have some clever specimens of his early styles. We always consider him as a painter of beggar boys and courtesans because he once painted as a capriccio a varlet playing at chuckfarthing and a whore looking out of [a] window. I can also tell you that he once painted | a dead duck. The truth is, he was a mighty master of ideal grace. He beats the Romans in design and the Venetians in coloring. From Seville I repaired to Cordova skirting the Sierra Morena, and thence to Grenada. This delicious country was highly refreshing after the burning plains and barren mountains over which I had long wandered. I will not attempt to describe Alhambra, which is the most imaginative, the most delicate and fantastic creation that ever sprang up in a Summer night in a fairy tale.

My dear fellow, Spain is the only land for travel. After what I had seen I thought nothing co[ul]d greatly interest me; I have been agreably disappointed. In this country, the hedges are of aloes in bloom, fit company for the palm and the indian fig and the Sugar cane which flourishes all around Velez Malaga. Magnificent pictures by masters of whom we have never heard fill every temple, and splendid buildings which make you hourly regret the expulsion of the Saracens, attest their refined civilization, while they contribute to the pleasurable excitement which in this land never ceases. The manners of the people are poetical – their costume and their castanets, their alfresco habits which are constantly conducive of adventure, and which hourly show me what was the Studio of Cervantes, are all enchanting. I say nothing of Tomata's, Olla Podrida, and Bull fights, because my sheet deserts me. Remember me to your father. I often hear his name mentioned, and always with that honor, which it will ever command: to Batty also, and believe me with sincere regard,

faithfully yours

B. Disraeli

3 Velazquez was born in Seville.

97 TO ISAAC D'ISRAELI Malta, [Wednesday] 25 August 1830

ORIGINAL: QUA 207

PUBLICATION HISTORY: HL 48-64, dated 25 August 1830, with omission of any reference to the '*extraordinary*' letter, and with minor changes; M&B I 154-5, dated 27 August 1830, extracts from the second section of the letter

EDITORIAL COMMENT: *Sic*: 28 28th.; Ferdousi; Jeffrey Wyattville; guilding; this, To; agreable; Inclose; Bury; du Tencins; disagreable; Scirocc; Timboctoo; Burghesh; rissible.

Malta. August 25. 1830. Lazaretto.

My dear father,

We have at length arrived at what Major Rennell declares is *not*, the ancient Melita, in spite of all tradition,[1] but as I am not yet allowed to enter the city, but am imprisoned in a vast and solitary building, and shunned by all my fellow creatures, I can give you no account of it, except that the city, Valetta, looks extremely beautiful from the distance. I had wished to have written to you another Spanish letter or two from Gibraltar, but was in such a constant bustle there between calling on old friends and preparing for my new voyage, that I could not find time to collect my senses for a cool communication. I am very glad my letters please you. You know I hate writing such things, but to you it is indeed a pleasure. Literally they were scribbled almost like Erasmus' Encomium on horseback, and I can only regret, that they are so imperfect, and convey so feeble and hasty an expression of my adventures and feelings in the memorable and romantic land in which I wandered. I found all letters here up to the 28 28th. July and read them with lively satisfaction. Pray continue to write whenever convenient, and direct to me always at this place. They contribute greatly to my happiness. The "*extraordinary*" letter – Sarah rightly guessed the purport of – All however is settled on that point in another quarter, and even if it were not and a thousand other reasons did not sway, it sho[ul]d be, for it was concocted for that market, and is suited to it only. It is well however to have an opening in another region. I have spoke to you all thus frankly, because I never wish to have secrets from you, and if ever I have witheld it is because I have been somewhat obliged by your noble failing of being more frank than your neighbours, a splendid and honorable foible, if it be one, but inconvenient and injurious, and not suited to this vulgar and wary life. I am sure that I have only to express my absolute request that what has taken place, and what I have mentioned, sho[ul]d be confined to our *own hearth*, to find this my *great* wish complied with. Let it be buried in silence, and I entreat in case you meet the writer, that it make no difference in your carriage, and sho[ul]d he be so silly as to speak, *which he* | *will not*, I entreat that you know *nothing* of the affair.[2]

1 D was wrong. James Rennell (1742-1830), the geographer, *had* argued in a paper to the Society of Antiquaries in 1827 that Malta was mentioned in the Acts of the Apostles as the site of Paul's shipwreck.

2 The letter arrived under J.W. Croker's frank, but was not from Croker. Isaac and Sarah recognized John Murray's handwriting and they were curious, but their letters to D do not, in fact, contain speculations about the contents (H A/IV/E/3-4). Presumably this was Murray's answer of 29 May to D's letter of the 27th. See **86**n4. D's indifference was the result of *The Young Duke* having already been placed with Colburn, but, obviously, the family had not known that D had re-established communication with Murray 'to have an opening in another region'.

I parted with my friend Standish at Seville with regret. He is excessively fantastic and odd, but a good fellow. The Spaniards cannot make him out, and the few English that meet him set him down only as excessively affected. He is something more. The man of pleasure who instead of degenerating into a roué, aspires to be a philosopher, is to my mind certainly a respectable, and I think an interesting character.

I wish that I co[ul]d convey to you some idea of the Saracenic architecture in perfect and brilliant specimens of which the South of Spain abounds, but I feel it is impossible. Description is always a bore, both to the describer and to the describee. One thing however I will say, for it is a further and a stronger illustration of what I have long thought, that however there may be a standard of *taste* there is no standard of *style*. I must place Alhambra with the Parthenon, the Pantheon, and York Minster. The same principles of taste are there evident, but the combinations are different as they are different in the east[?]. On this principle you may equally admire Aeschylus, Virgil, Shakespeare and Ferdousi.[3] There never co[ul]d have been a controversy on such a point, if mankind had not confused the ideas of *Taste* and *Style*. The Saracenic architecture is the most inventive and fanciful, but at the same time the most fitting and the most delicate, that can be conceived. There wo[ul]d be no doubt about its title to be considered among the first inventions of men if it were better known. It is only to be found in any degree of perfection in Spain. When a man sneers at the Saracenic ask him what he has seen. Perhaps a barbarous tho' picturesque building called the Ducal Palace at Venice? What sho[ul]d we think of a man who decided on the buildings of Agrippa by the architecture of Justinian or judged the age of Pericles by the restorations of Hadrian – yet he | wo[ul]d not commit so great a blunder. There is a Moorish Palace – the Alcazar at Seville – an immense Mosque at Cordova turned into a cathedral only with partial alteration, Alhambra at Granada – these are the great specimens, and sufficient for all study. There is a shrine and chapel of a Moorish Saint at Cordova quite untouched, with the blue mosaic, and the golden honeycomb roof, as vivid, and as brilliant as when the Saint was worshipped. The materials are the richest, the ornaments the most costly and in detail the most elegant and the most novel, the most fanciful and the most flowing – but nothing at the same time can be conceived more just than the proportion of the whole, and more mellowed than the blending of the parts, which indeed Palladio co[ul]d not excel.

The great efforts of antique architecture are confined to Temples or Theatres, which at the best can be only a room. Alhambra is a palace, and the opportunity for invention is of course infinitely increased. It is not a ruin as I expected, scarcely in a state of dilapidation. Certainly under the patronage of our late Monarch, it might have been restored to all its pristine splendor, tho' I think a compliant Parliamt. wo[ul]d have been almost as necessary as Sir Jeffrey

3 Firdausî, Persian for 'garden', was the name employed by Aub'l-Qâsim Mansûr (934?-1020), author of the Persian classic *Shâhnâma*.

Wyattville.[4] Everything about it, tho exquisitely proportioned, is slight and small and delicate. Murphy makes the Court of Pillars too large and coarse.[5] Around this court are chambers with carved and purple roofs studded with gold, and walls entirely covered with the most fanciful relief, picked out with that violet tint, which must have been copied from their Andalusian skies. In these you may sit in the coolest shade, reclining upon cushions with your beads or pipe and view the most dazzling sunlight in the Court which assuredly must scorch the flowers, if the faithful lions ever ceased from pouring forth that element which you must travel in Spain or Africa to honor. Pindar was quite right.[6] | These chambers are innumerable. There is the Hall of the Ambassadors, always the most sumptuous, the Hall of Justice, the rooms of the Sultanas and of the various members of the family – quite perfect – not a single roof has given. What a scene – ah! that you were [here?], but conceive it in the times of the Boabdils[7] – conceive it with all its costly decoration, all the guilding, all the imperial purple, all the violet relief, all the scarlet borders, all the glittering inscriptions, and costly mosaics burnished, bright and fresh – conceive it full of still greater ornaments, the living groups with their rich, and vivid and picturesque costume, and above all, their shining arms – some standing conversing in groups, some smoking in sedate silence, some telling their beads, some squatting round a Storier. Then the bustle, and the rush, and the arriving horsemen all in motion, and all glancing in the most brilliant Sun. Enough of this, To add to the delights of Granada, it is situated in a most beautiful and productive country. Its fruit market is nearly as great a wonder as the Alhambra: but the route to Velez Malaga is through a land even fuller of milk and honey. Surrounded by aloes, and Indian figs, and for the first time, *sugar canes*, I co[ul]d have fancied myself in the Antilles. All this was very agreable after burning plains and barren mountains. All my adventures must be orally delivered. I have slightly sketched them in a hasty letter to Sarah from Gib. by the last packet. It was a life of perfect Romance, but the fatigue was sometimes appalling: yet I bore it all; and from the moment I wrote to my mother I have been progressively improving. Slow, but I now flatter myself – certain. It will not be | very quick work, but I am too grateful to grumble. It is all the Sun and the Western breeze. The least blow from the Levant and I partially relapse. Society has nothing to do with it. On the contrary, tho' very delightful, it retards, I am confident, my convalescence: for Temperance and Quiet are also most important, but it is impossible to escape. I do what I can to guard – you have yet to receive from me a letter from Seville – an

4 Sir Jeffry Wyatville (1766-1840), architect, is best known for his remodelling of Windsor Castle, and for the enthusiasm with which he applied stucco to buildings of earlier architectural periods.

5 The description of the Alhambra in *The Arabian Antiquities of Spain* (1815) by James Cavanah Murphy (1760-1814).

6 The opening line of 'To Hieron of Syracuse', Pindar's first Olympian ode – 'Best of all things is water.'

7 Boabdil, a corruption of the name Abu Abdullah, the last Moorish king of Granada, who lost his throne in 1492. D appears to be giving the term a generic meaning to cover all the kings in the final period of Moorish rule.

elephantine sheet from Granada to my mother and a letter from Gibraltar to Sa. I shall send this to George Barrow, and therefore shall make it a long affair, but stop for the present. While I remember it, a copy of the Y[oung] D[uke] must be sent to Lady Don. Tell Ralph to attend to it. Write in the Title – "Lady Don, by desire of the author". Inclose it to her and then put another cover addressed "*His Excell[enc]y General Sir George Don. G.C.B. Gib[ralta]r*"[.] You will be surprised at my sending a light novel and finding a muse in an old Lady of seventy, but in truth she is the cleverest and most charming woman I ever met, beating all the Lydia Whites, Mrs. Weddells[8] and Misses Bury[9] out and out, and the only person I know who gives me the least idea of the Madame du Tencins and the other brillantes, who flirted with Henault,[10] chatted with Montesquieu, and corresponded with Horace Walpole.

We sailed here with Captains Coffin and Nesham who have come out to join the Gloucester and Melville 74s in the place of the new Admirals Stuart and Schomberg.[11] They are very gentlemanly, agreable men, of a certain age, and I have already got an invitation to both their ships to eat sea pie etc! The latter has a very agreable daughter, who came out with him, and has lightened by her good humor the bore | of our quarantine,[12] and a son in the Rifle Brigade which is here. We are free tomorrow. The Blonde frigate in which Wm. Barrow is a Lieutenant has just arrived, but in a long quarantine from Turkey. Adieu for the present.

I forgot to say we had a very rough and disagreable voyage the wind, a devil of a Levanter, and sometimes Sirocc, full in our teeth half the time and not go-

8 Miss Lydia White (d 1827) was one of the well-known hostesses of the Regency. It was once claimed by a scholar that familiarity with her name indicated a command of the literary history of the period. William Prideaux Courtney *Eight Friends of the Great* (1910) 152. Lady Charlotte Bury describes dinner parties at Miss White's in 1819-20, when the hostess was apparently old and infirm. *The Diary of a Lady-in-Waiting* (1908) II 199, 226-7; see also the Earl of Ilchester ed *Elizabeth, Lady Holland to Her Son, 1821-1845* (1946) 58. Mrs Weddell (or Weddel) of Newby also belonged to this era. The sister of Lady Rockingham, she figured, sometimes amusingly, in fashionable society. Joseph Farington *Diary* ed James Greig (1923) I 125; V 177.

9 Although D spells the name 'Bury' it is probable that 'Berry' was intended. The Misses Berry, Mary (1763-1852) and Agnes (1764-1852), were both active in literary circles. Mary was the earliest editor of the *Works* of Horace Walpole.

10 Claudine Alexandrine Guérin (1681-1749), marquise de Tencin, French author. Charles Jean François Hénault (1685-1770), French historian and poet.

11 John Townsend Coffin (1789-1882) and Christopher John William Nesham (1771-1853), respectively captains of HMS *Gloucester* and HMS *Melville*, mounting 74 guns each. Both men retired with the rank of admiral. The officers whom they replaced were Rear Adm Henry Stuart (1767-1840) and Rear Adm Alexander W. Schomberg (1774-1850). *ER*; Boase.

12 Travellers were subject to an especially rigorous quarantine at Malta as, in the eyes of all European powers, the island served as a gateway for the whole Continent. Cholera was on the rise at this time, but any other disease deemed to be infectious was also cause for quarantine. Nor was quarantine limited to travellers returning from the East; those travelling out of Europe might also be subject to the regulations, depending upon conditions of health in their port of departure. For further details see Paul Cassar *Medical History of Malta* (1964) ch 31. Even so, Malta was then considered the best port in Europe for what was called 'performing quarantine'. Travellers were confined for a shorter period than was required elsewhere and living conditions were better. Sir Gardiner Wilkinson *Modern Egypt and Thebes* (1843) I 55.

On the evidence of this letter and that of **96**, D's quarantine on his arrival from Gibraltar via Algiers lasted one week, 19-26 August.

ing even with the steam, more than four knots an hour. I maintained my character as a sailor, but was otherwise very unwell in my head. The sky was covered with clouds nearly the whole time. This is the only disagreable weather we have had. The Summer is universally agreed to be unusually hot. I was howr. repaid for all this by a visit to Algiers. We did not land, but the town is built on the coast and on a hill, so we saw every house – we observed with interest that the Tricolor flag was flying.[13] I consider myself very fortunate in having seen this famous place. It is a very handsome white town, and the hills about well cultivated and covered with white houses. The harbour seemed a very fine one, and the mole is a strong piece of masonry. It was fortunately our only fine day. So ends my account of Algiers, which is about as long, and much more true, than Caille's description of Timboctoo.[14] |

Saturday. 27 –

I scribble until the return of the packet a daily bulletin. We landed yesterday for breakfast, and are quartered in a capital hotel – Beverleys.[15] I assure you I look forward to some repose here after all my exertions with great zest. We did not find this at Gibraltar where our quarters were horrid. To our surprise we find James Clay[16] here, immensely improved and quite a hero. He has been here a month, and has already beat the whole Garrison at Rackets and billiards and other wicked games, given lessons to their Prima Donna, and seccaturad[17] the primo tenore. Really he has turned out a most agreable personage, and has had that advantage of Society, in which he had been deficient, and led a life which for splendid adventure wo[ul]d beat any young gentleman's yet published in 3 vols pt. 8vo. Lord Burghesh wrote an Opera for him and Lady Normanby a farce.[18] He dished Prince Pignatelli[19] at Billiards and diddled the Russian Lega-

13 Meaning that the force which had carried the Bourbon fleur de lis to North Africa had now recognized the Revolution of 1830.

14 René Auguste Caillé (1799-1838), French traveller. He set off to explore Africa as a result of reading *Robinson Crusoe*, and became obsessed by the idea of reaching the fabled town of Timbuctoo. He arrived there in April 1828, and spent two weeks before returning to France where he was awarded a prize of 10,000 francs, a pension, and the Legion of Honour, for being the first traveller to bring back exact information. His *Journal d'un voyage à Temboctou ...* was published in Paris in 1830, and an English version, *Travels through Central Africa to Timbuctoo*, appeared in London the same year. There were initially some doubts (later dispelled) in English circles about the truthfulness of Caillé's description (II ch xxi), and presumably D was reflecting these.

15 The name of this hotel is not in Thomas MacGill's *Handbook to Malta* (1839), though the author purports to list the best establishments. However, Lord Lindsay records a stay at Beverley's in 1836. *Letters on Egypt ...* (1839) 18.

16 James Clay (1805-1873), Liberal MP for Hull 1847-53, 1857-73. He enjoyed some reputation as an authority on whist. Clay had been at Winchester with Ralph Disraeli and at Oxford with Meredith. Although Isaac, Maria and Sarah strongly disapproved of Clay, D's friendship with him was lifelong.

17 'Bothered', 'annoyed'. D has invented a verb from an Italian noun.

18 An opera by Lord Burghersh was first performed in Florence during June 1829. *The Private Diary of Richard, Duke of Buckingham and Chandos, KG* (1862) III 207-8. Maria Phipps (d 1882), eldest daughter of 1st Baron Ravensworth, had married in 1818 Constantine Henry Phipps, Viscount Normanby, after 1831 2nd Earl of Mulgrave. In her reply Sarah undercut the honour paid to Clay by observing that Lady Normanby had 'lost her reputation'.

19 Francesco Pignatelli (1775-1853), Prince of Strangoli. A general, patriot and historian, he was prominent in the struggle for a united Italy.

tion at Ecarté. I had no need of letters of introduction here – and have already "troops of friends". The fact is in our original Steampacket, there were some very agreable fellows, officers whom I believe I never mentioned to you. They have been long expecting your worship's offspring, and have gained great fame in repeating his third rate stories at second hand: so in consequence of these messengers, the Messiahship has answered, and I am received with branches of palm. Here the younkers do nothing but play rackets, billiards, and cards, race and smoke. To govern men you must either excel in their accomplishments – or despise them. Clay does one: I do the other, and we are equally popular. | Affectation tells here even better than wit. Yesterday at the racket court sitting in the Gallery among strangers, the ball entered, slightly struck me, and fell at my feet. I picked it up, and observing a young rifleman excessively stiff, I humbly requested him to forward its passage into the Court, as I really had never thrown a ball in my life. This incident has been the general subject of conversation at all the messes to day.

I call on the governor tomorrow. He is reputed a very nonchalant personage and exceedingly exclusive in his conduct to his subjects.[20] Clay had no letter to him, but his Exclly. is a great racketplayer, and so he addressed our friend one day with condescending familiarity, but did not ask him to dinner till he had been here some time, which so offended our friend who is excessively grand and talks of nothing but Burghesh, Normanby, Lady Williamson[21] and various Princes, that he refused and is in opposition[.]

The city is one of the most beautiful for its architecture and the splendor of its streets, that I know, something between Venice and Cadiz.

We dined yesterday with Clay to meet Captn. Anstruther[22] our principal steamboat friend and some other officers.

Sunday morn –

Yesterday I called on Ponsonby. He was fortunately at home. I flatter myself that he passed through the most extraordinary quarter of an hour of his existence – I gave him no quarter, and at last made our nonchalant Governor roll on the sofa from his rissible convulsions. Then I jumped up, remembered that I must be sadly breaking into his morning and was off: | making it a rule always to leave with a good impression. He pressed me not to go – I told him I had so much to do! I walked down the Strada Reale, which is nearly as good as Regent Street, and got five invitations to dinner (literally a fact)[23] and then betook my-

20 In this respect Ponsonby seems to have epitomized the attitude of the British official population to the Maltese. There were then some 700 resident British, exclusive of the military, and several writers of the time commented both on the cost of administration and on its apparent indifference to the welfare of the inhabitants. Andrew Bigelow *Travels in Malta and Sicily ... in MDCCCXXVII* (Boston 1831) 126, 151; James Webster *Travels Through the Crimea, Turkey and Egypt* (1830) I 293-7.

21 Anne Elizabeth Williamson (d 1878), third daughter of 1st Baron Ravensworth, had married in 1826 Sir Hedworth Williamson (1797-1861), 7th Baronet, and lived in Florence. She was the sister of George Liddell and of Lady Normanby.

22 Robert Anstruther (1805-1855), eldest son of Sir Alexander Anstruther, was then a member of the 73rd Foot.

23 D's rate of acquiring acquaintances may be judged by the fact that the Strada Reale in Valetta was three-quarters of a mile long, running through the centre of town. George Waring *Letters from Malta and Sicily* (1843) 73.

self to the Union Club. This is in every sense of the word not an inferior establishment even in the building, which is an old Palace to the London Union, and tho' there are only 80 members, yet as they are always there, even on this point, it does not seem inferior. You may dine here and everything. We are honorary members of it, which is most convenient and also of the Malta Sporting Club, which is a very exclusive establishment of recent date. Thus you see, not being in our own country, we are considered prophets.

When I arrived home I found an invitation for Tuesday which fortunately I can accept from the Gen and Lady Emily. Clay confesses my triumph is complete and unrivalled.

I stop the press to say that I dined at the mess of the 73rd. in an Andalusian dress. After such buffooneries I need not add, that I continue tolerably well.

Monday.

Sunday passed in a delightful far niente. I dine to day with an officer named Primrose.[24] I have been introduced to lots of men and among them little Lord Rothes – Lady Henrietta Murray's brother. He is the Marquess of Exeter | of Gibraltar and has a stud of fourteen horses, with regular jockeys, grooms, etc. etc. as at Newmarket.[25] Clay has offered to run any of his steeds if his Lordship will give him 100 yards start. The packet is announced in sight, and I am disappointed in my hope of sending you any further adventures at present. I am glad to hear that Jem is so efficient a member of the famille, which indeed I expected. I have great confidence in him. His Commission sho[ul]d be thought of. Pray have no hesitation in applying to Croker, who I am sure will be delighted to oblige you in a manner which costs him nothing.[26] Tell Ralph I shall write to him from this place, which after some time will, I dare say, afford matter for a separate epistle – before this, any thing to him wo[ul]d only have been a repetition. His handkerchief which he | brought me from Paris is the most successful thing I ever wore, and universally admired – a 1000 loves to all. Pray let me find long letters soon and direct always to Hunter and Ross.[27]

Your affec Son

BD

I have held a long parley with William Barrow at a respectful distance.

24 Lt Philip Primrose had joined the 73rd in 1823 and had left the service by 1832. Army List.

25 George William Evelyn Leslie (1809-1841), 15th Earl of Rothes. His sister, Lady Henrietta Anne Murray (d 1832), had married in 1827 Charles Knight Murray. In likening the Earl to the 2nd Marquess of Exeter (1795-1867), D meant that he was a sportsman and a man of fashion on a large scale.

26 It had first been hoped that John Wilson Croker could obtain a naval commission for James Disraeli. But Croker resigned his Admiralty post in November 1830, and the D'Israelis' attention shifted to other sources of influence. H A/IV/E/1, 17.

27 Bankers and merchants of Malta. Apparently D's dealings were with James Ross who, apart from his business interests, served for a time as the Dutch consul general at Malta. His son's correspondence indicates that the elder Ross was still alive in 1852. Janet Ross ed *Letters from the East by Henry James Ross, 1837-1857* (1902) 161-7. Donald Sultana has kindly supplied information about Ross from documents in his possession.

TO BENJAMIN AUSTEN Malta, [Tuesday] 14 September 1830 98

ORIGINAL: BL ADD MS 45908 ff31-2

COVER: [In D's hand]: Al Signor | Signor Benjamin Austen | ~~Poste Restante~~ | No. 4 Raymond Buildings | ~~Firenze.~~ | Gray's Inn | *Angleterre London.* [In another hand]: Recd your's yesterday and found this at the Post office all well – March 29th.

POSTMARK: [illegible]

PUBLICATION HISTORY: Layard 18, 19, 20, undated extracts; M&B I 143-4, 145, 156, undated extracts; Jerman 110-13, dated 14 September 1830

EDITORIAL COMMENT: Here D repeated much of what he had told Sarah in his letter to her of 9 August 1830 (**95**). This letter is written on both sides of very thin paper through which the ink has penetrated. It is particularly difficult to read. *Sic*: burthern, blanke, Coliseum, agreable, relieve.

Malta. Septr 14. 1830

My dear Austen,

I arrived at this place some ten days ago, and found your welcome letter among others, which had been awaiting me for months. You know of course that I changed my plans of travel after our parting, and that I have been wandering during the summer through the South of Spain. I have been greatly pleased with what I have seen of that interesting country. I visited it at a time which is not considered the most judicious for travellers, but I can bear I believe any degree of heat, and passed through a blazing summer in sight of Africa without any inconvenience. I travelled through the whole of Andalusia on horseback. I was never less than ten hours out of the twenty four on my steed, more than once I saw the sun set and rise, without quitting my saddle, which few men can say, and which I never wish to say again. I never saw anything more sublime than the straits of Gibraltar with Europe and Africa frowning on each other, but our sultry sister has the advantage in picturesque beauty tho' both are very fine. The contrast between a country where the hedges be of aloes in bloom and the iron bound coasts of Falmouth was of course striking. I have sometimes seen two or three hundred aloes in blooming company which wo[ul]d have delighted Mrs. Austen. I visited Cadiz, Seville, Cordova and Granada among many other cities which must not be named with these romantic towns. I sailed upon the Quadalquivir, I cheered at the bull fights, I lived for a week among brigands and wandered in the fantastic halls of the delicate Alhambra. Why sho[ul]d I forget to say that I eat an olio podrida? I will not weary you now with tales of men of buckram. They must be reserved for our fire side. I entered at Spain a sceptic with regard to their robbers and listened to all their romances with a smile. I lived to change my opinion——It is difficult to conceive a more brilliant city than Cadiz. Its white walls and verdant jalousies sparkle in the Sun. Figaro is in every street, | and Rosina in every balcony. I at length found a country where adventure is the common course of existence, and from necessity must be so. All travel by night, and in armed companies. A moon so brilliant that you might see for miles, lights up a country alternately formed of sierras, or mountain passes, and immense plains. Merchants in armed bands, muleteers defiling, a couple of friars secure in the sanctity of their character and their poverty, some lords and ladies of high degree with a military escort which always scampers off at the first shot, these with a few adventurous travellers like ourselves, form the interesting and constant groups. In the cities, the Church is still the

The first page of the manuscript of Letter 98
British Library ADD MS 45908 f31

Royal Exchange of Assignations, and through the whole warm night the constant castanet reminds you of the fascinating Fandango. From Gibraltar I arrived here, a place from which I expected little and have found much. Valetta surprises me as one of the most beautiful cities I have ever visited, something between Venice and Cadiz. I was very much obliged to you and Layard for your letter to Hankey, I gave it in preference to others which I had. Sir Fred is a fine fellow, and spoke of Layard with great regard but as he is at present in the country I have not seen much of him. Clay who is here, and whom I have not seen for 3 years, and who likes Layard very much, desires to be particularly remembered to him. With regard to myself I have certainly made very great progress, but not enough. I have still illness enough to make life a burthern, and as my great friend the Sun is daily becoming less powerful, I daily grow more dispirited, and resume my old style of despair. Had I been cured by this time I had made up my mind to join you in Italy. As it is, I go I know not where, but do not be surprised if you hear something very strange indeed.[1] |

I am very anxious to hear from you. I shall communicate again very soon, and sho[ul]d have done before, had I known more of your movements and had I not been leading such a restless life in countries where to find materials for letter writing is I assure you no easy matter. Even at Granada when I wanted to write home, I was obliged to apply to a notary for materials. The small pox rages here so desperately that they have put in a quarantine of three weeks at Sicily which has prevented my trip to an island I much desired to visit. I have a great deal to say to you of infinite small matters which will not tell in a letter. May we soon meet. As for myself, I hardly know what to say. All is uncertain and gloomy. Each day I feel more keenly that without health life is a blanke. Write to me about your movements, in order that if possible I may meet you and see the Coliseum by moonlight with Madame and all that. My letters from England which I found here in a regular bonanza are all very agreeable ones, which is something. I was told here by a person of consideration that my father was to be in the new batch of baronets, but I suppose this is a lie. If it be offered I am sure he will refuse, but I have no idea that it will. The Governor here is a very agreable person General Ponsonby, a brother of Lady Caroline Lamb.[2] Except to him and Hankey, I have never given any letters of introduction, as I find so many friends here, some travelling like myself, some quartered in regiments, and some on board ship and I have not recovered my gusto for society. We have a very good opera here, and altogether it is a sort of place which, particularly in winter wo[ul]d be a desirable residence tho' it has not a single tree, but the city is truly magnificent full of palaces worthy of Palladio. Talking of Art run my dear fellow to Seville and for the first time in | your life know what a great artist is –

1 In his next letter to Austen, on 18 November 1830 (**103**), D was to tell him of an earlier resolve 'to join the Turkish army as volunteer in the Albanian war'.

2 Lady Caroline Lamb (1785-1828), only daughter of the 3rd Earl of Bessborough, in 1805 had married William Lamb, after 1829 2nd Viscount Melbourne. She was notorious for her tempestuous affair with Byron, and had separated from her husband in 1825.

Murillo, Murillo, Murillo! After all, I believe these Spaniards are the top of the tree. I have become an inveterate smoker. Are you not surprised? Conceive me with a Turkish pipe seven feet long puffing on a sofa. Barrow,[3] who is a Lieutenant in the famous frigate the Blonde just arrived from Stamboul (I was on the frigate on board which they gave the grand entertainment to the Turkish authorities) presented me with this beauty with an amber mouth piece, and a porcelain bowl. I find it relieve my head. I have also a Meerschaum and one of Dresden china set in silver, both presents. Am I not fortunate? A thousand kind remembrances to Madame from

yours ever

BD

---

99 TO [RALPH DISRAELI] Malta, [Friday 17?] September [1830]

ORIGINAL: QUA 208

PUBLICATION HISTORY: HL 68-74, undated, with changes and omissions. RD prints this letter after **100** and before **101**.

EDITORIAL COMMENT: The MS of this letter was damaged by fire. The pages are charred and the top and left side of each sheet is cropped. Missing words and parts of words have been suggested where possible in square brackets. Ralph omits what he cannot read and censors other sections. *Dating*: the month is legible in the MS as is the second numeral of the date. In **100** of 10 October 1830, D told Isaac that he had left Malta 'nearly three weeks ago'. The date of Friday 17 September would be consistent with the intention stated here of leaving Malta 'next Wednesday' (22 September). *Sic*: relieve, Lieutt., fuzileer, agreable, Corfou, inclose.

Malta. September [1?]7 [1830]

Mashalla![1]

Here I am smoking in an easy chair a Turkish pipe [*si*]x feet long with an amber mouth piece and a porcelain bowl. [*W*]hat a revolution! But what if I tell you that I not only [*h*]ave become a smoker, but the greatest smoker in [*M*]alta! The fact is I find it relieve my head and therefore [*gi*]ve the Syriac, Latakia or Canastre[2] (for we have a [*Du*]tch Squadron in harbour) no quarter. Barrow who [*is*] here in the Blonde and a most knowing young Lieutt. [*w*]ho informed me the other night, when drunk, that [*he w*]as sure to be made a captain in 18 months, therefor[*e*] [*ther*]eby irresistably reminding me of John Falconer [...] in Patronage,[3] presented me with the Turkish, [*and*] has given me a Meerschaum, and Anstruther [*a*] most splendid Dresden, green china set in [*most*] massy silver, an extremely valuable pipe [*ind*]eed. But there is nothing like a Meerschaum. [*When I*] get into those parts where I am not at present [*I must*] pick one up for you, which when skilfully [*done*], will be worth as many pounds as [*nomi*]nally

3 See **96**n2.

---

1 See **93**n7 (and the portion of the text which that note annotates) for the circumstances possibly behind D's adoption of this term as a nickname for Ralph. RD's version adds an orthodox salutation not present in the MS and moves 'Mashalla' to the text (HL 68).

In one of his notebooks, however, D has entered: '*Marshalla* – a celebrated Jewish astron[ome]r at Bagdad.' H A/III/E/i/8.

2 Varieties of tobacco.

3 John Falconer is the head of the Falconer family in Maria Edgeworth's *Patronage* (1814).

cost shillings. I have spent some [*w*]eeks here. Ponsonby the Governor is a [*most*] charming fellow, and has been most courteous [*to m*]e. His wife is very ugly and not very popular [...] being grand, but I rather like her. I [*din*]ed there on the Tuesday and on the Sunday [*fol*]lowing when Meredith also dined there [*ha*]ving been presented by Sir John Stoddart.[4] [*We m*]et most of the best people in Malta [*ther*]e: Next day they left town for Mafra [*a sh*]ooting box which the Governor has sixteen [*mi*]les off, a considerable distance in these islands | [...] party have taken a box [*there*] in which is a great lounge.

Do you remember in ancient days in Windsor, the Royal Fusileers bei[*ng*] quartered there and James swearing that tw[*o*] young Subs. Liddell and Lord Amelius Pau[*let*] were brothers of his schoolfellows and all that.[5] How curious life is! That Liddell i[*s*] now quartered here (being Senior Capt on the Station in the absence of Fitzclar[*ence*] who has gone to see his Papa,[6] he comma[*nds*] the Regiment.), and has become my mo[*st*] intimate friend. He is the George Lid[*dell*] who acts all the Listonic parts at priv[*ate*] theatricals at Harrington House[7] and Nor[...] theatre, and is a most delightful party. He and another fuzileer by name Pery, the [*future*] Lord Limerick,[8] are my usual compa[*nions.*] They are both men of the world and g[*ood*] company forming a remarkable [*contrast*] to all their brother officers, for sooth to [*tell*] a visit to Gibraltar and Malta, our two c[*rack*] garrisons, has quite opened my eyes to [*the*] real life and character of a milita[*ire*]. By heavens I believe these fellows are boys till they are Majors, and sometimes d[*on't*] even stop then. Their ignorance of[*ten*] is astounding, only equalled by their e [...] | admiration of [rest of top line of second sheet missing]

The Society at Malta is very supe[*rior*] [*i*]ndeed for a Colony. I have received great attentions from everybody, but at present most families are what is called "in the country" that is living some dozen miles away in a site very much like a quarry without a tree to be seen, or shrubs [*e*]nough to feed their bees. Therefore I see little of them, as it is impossible to visit at this distance, [*b*]ut in winter all agree that it is extremely [*a*]greable.

A week ago, I knew not what I [*woul*]d do. All is now settled. On Wednesday

4 Sir John Stoddart (1773-1856), editor of *The New Times* 1818-26, chief justice of Malta and judge of the Admiralty Court there 1826-40. He was known for his confidence in the capacity of the Maltese to govern themselves. Harrison Smith *Britain in Malta* (Malta 1953) I 80. See also **36**n4.

5 The records do not reveal any Lord Amelius Paulet. The two young officers of whom James had spoken must have been Lord William Paulet (1804-1893), fourth son of the 13th Marquess of Winchester, and later a field marshal, and George Augustus Frederick Liddell (1812-1888), fifth son of 1st Baron Ravensworth, then a captain in the 3rd Regiment of Foot. Both had been lieutenants in the Royal Fusiliers in 1825, the period to which D is referring. Army List.

6 Lord Frederick Fitzclarence (1799-1854), illegitimate son of William IV, was a lieutenant colonel in the Royal Fusiliers.

7 The London residence of Charles Stanhope (1780-1851), after 1829 4th Earl of Harrington. He was a patron of the stage and in the following year, 1831, married a well-known actress, Maria Foote. As Viscount Petersham he had been one of the most prominent figures in society during the Regency and reign of George IV, and he may well have staged private theatricals of the kind to which D refers.

8 Edmond Henry Pery (1809-1844), after 1834 Baron Glentworth, then a lieutenant in the Royal Fusiliers. In 1836 he married Eve Marie Villebois, a sister of Lady Sykes. He died before his grandfather, and so never became Earl of Limerick.

[*m*]orning I quit this place where on the [*wh*]ole I have spent very agreable hours in [*the*] [*y*]acht which Clay has hired and in which [*he*] intends to turn pirate. The original [*pl*]an was to have taken it together, but [*as*] Meredith was averse to the plan, we [*have*] become his passengers at a fair [*rate*] and he drops us whenever and wherever [*we*] like. You sho[ul]d see me in the costume [*of a*] Greek pirate. A blood red shirt with [*silv*]er studs as big as shillings, an immense [*sca*]rf for girdle full of pistols and daggers, [*a*] red cap, red slippers, blue broad striped [...] jacket and trousers. Excessively wicked!

We shall touch at Corfou on [*pur*]pose to get the letters which come out by this [*pack*]et and which Ross will send on immediately. I | [first line missing at top of page] all letters must be sent on to Corfou. I will inclose a direction. This is the last regular letter you will receive, perhaps the very last in direct answer but do not on any account cease to write every packet, in order tha[*t*] the chain may be never broken, and that I may not return with the feelings of a stranger.

Sir John Stoddart is an ass. His Lady the most vulgar old washerwom[*an*] I ever met. She bored me to death a[*bout*] "*Miss Porson*" I could not conceive who she meant. At last it came out t[*hat*] it was something to do with old [...] Parsons, of whom I told her I h[*ad*] n[*ever*] heard. Mrs. Seymour Bathurst[9] [*is an*] interesting woman, but she has j[*ust*] lost her child, and has since gone [*to*] Naples. I sat next to old Mrs. Hankey[10] at dinner, whom they all make mu[*ch*] of, but who is rather an old fashioned affair. There is a Mrs. Pleydell Bouverie h[*ere*] with a pretty daughter. The father Cap[*t*] | commanding[11] [most of 1st line at top of page is missing] [*et cum m*]ultis aliis q.n.p.l.e.[12] I am sorry [*to say*] among them a beauty very dangerous to the peace of Your unhappy brother, but no more of that, and in a few weeks I shall be bounding, and perhaps seasick upon the blue Ægean, and then all will be over. Nothing like an emetic in these cases.

I find I have very little to tell you, for altho' each day brings an infinite deal of nothings which might authorize [*a*] record over a wood fire in the old [*h*]all, they are too slight to bear [*a*]ny communication but an oral [*one*]. So let us hope that that may soon [*tak*]e place. I often think of you all. [*How*] go on the Norrises,[13] and the Lord Abbot?[14] [*If yo*]u hear of my marriage (or death) don't believe [*it*]

9 Julia Bathurst (d 1877), daughter of John Peter Hankey (Sir Frederick's brother), who in 1829 had married Lt Col Thomas Seymour Bathurst (1793-1834), third son of the 3rd Earl Bathurst. At this time Seymour Bathurst was military secretary to the governor, his sister's husband.

10 As D is usually accurate in the way in which he refers to women, 'Mrs H' would probably be Sir Frederick Hankey's mother, Mrs Elizabeth Hankey, née Thompson.

D could be referring to Sir Frederick's second wife (although she would be 'Lady H'), who died in 1835 and was described in Burke's as 'a native of Corfu'. In 1827 Henry Fox described her as follows: 'His wife is a Greek. She is dreadfully fat ... but she is lovely; her eyes, her teeth, her complexion are the finest I ever saw almost.' The Earl of Ilchester ed *The Journal of the Hon. Henry Edward Fox ... 1818-1830* (1923) 243.

11 Duncombe Pleydell Bouverie (1780-1850), second son of the 2nd Earl of Radnor. He was later colonel of marines and vice admiral. In 1809 he had married Louisa May (d 1852). Their daughter Louisa (d 1898) married in 1832.

12 'Et cum multis aliis quibus non possum loqui ego' – 'and with many others too numerous to mention.'

13 See **191**n3. The Norrises then lived at Hughenden, which many years later was to become D's home.

14 D's nickname for Robert Smith (1752-1838), 1st Baron Carrington, whose residence, near Bradenham, was Wycombe Abbey.

any more than I shall our father [*be*]ing in the new batch of Baronets which [*is*] here currently reported.

Clay is immensely improved, and [*a*] very agreable companion indeed, with [*su*]ch a valet! Giovanni by name, Byron [*d*]ied in his arms, and his mustachios touch [*t*]he earth. Withal mild as a lamb, tho' | [*he has two*] daggers always about his perso[*n*].[15] Our yacht is of 55 tons, an excellent size for these seas, with a crew of 7 men. She is a very strong sea boat and bears the unpoetical name of Susan, which is a bore, but as we can't alter it we have painted it out. And now my dear boy adieu. I enclose a letter to Sa,[16] and Hankey has promised to send them free. I cannot say that I have made any great progress since my last, but I am not wor[*se*] and much better indeed than when I left. Le[*t*] us hope good things.

Your Most affec. bro[*ther*]

B. Disrae[*li*]

You will continue to send the letters on to Malta directed to Hunter & Ross.

TO ISAAC D'ISRAELI Corfu, [Sunday] 10 October 1830 **100**

ORIGINAL: QUA 209

COVER: I. Disraeli Esqre. | Bradenham House | Wycombe | Bucks. | [In another hand]: E Barrow

POSTMARK: (1) In circle: [illegible] | NO.[illegible] | 1830 (2) Small orange four-pointed star

PUBLICATION HISTORY: HL 65-7, dated 10 October 1830, with omissions

EDITORIAL COMMENT: Two-thirds of pages 3 and 4 of the MS have been torn off, and the top quarter of pages 5 and 6 is also missing. *Sic*: Corfou, disagreable, aide camps.

Corfou October 10. 1830

My dearest father,

I left Malta nearly three weeks ago and also left a letter for the packet which was then hourly expected and which we imagined wo[ul]d reach this island before us. To our infinite surprise and inexpressible mortification, it has not even yet arrived. Either it is wrecked, or put in port or else has been superseded by a sailing vessel – at all events I must quit this place without hearing from you, but in case it do arrive I write these hasty lines in addition to my monthly report. If it arrive in a few days, I will have the letters sent back to Malta and forwarded to Constantinople, but if not, they must remain at Malta. There is little communication between this place and the Levant, but pretty constant at Malta. On due consideration, I cannot alter my previous instructions about writing always to Malta, as I wo[ul]d infinitely prefer receiving all my letters months after their date, than losing one which breaks the chain. We had a stormy, but not disagreable, passage here. I like a sailors life much, tho' it destroys the toilette, and one never feels, or is indeed, clean. This, tho' a poor village, is a most lovely island, offering all that you can expect | from Grecian scenery, gleaming waters, woody

15 This is D's first reference to Giovanni Battista Falcieri (1798?-1874), otherwise known as Tita. Once Byron's servant, in the summer of 1830 he entered the service of James Clay, and, later, of Isaac D'Israeli at Bradenham. See also **212**n3. M&B I app A 383-5.

16 This letter has not been located.

isles, cypress, olive, vine, a clear sky, and a warm sun. Zante is I believe even more beautiful, with the remnants of a decent Venetian Town – Cephalonia not so fine. Santa Maura, the ancient Leucadia of Sappho[1] I hope to see, and the barren Ithaca must not be forgotten. I am disappointed in entering Albania, and visiting Yanina and the "monastic Zitza"[2] for the whole country is in a state of insurrection. I am glad to say the Porte every where triumphant. One of the rebel Beys, of Valona,[3] arrived here a fugitive the day before us, with many rich pipes and pistols but without his women. He fled in such haste. If the Grand Vizier with the Turkish army be at Prevesa, as is reported, I am to have the honor of bearing him a letter from the "Lord High" which I shall present with my two aide camps, Clay and Meredith, and hope to get a pipe at least. I am going up to the Palace now to learn | my fate and see if for once in my life I am to be an ambassador. All Nats[4] letters have been very good. Tell him so with my regards. Sir Frederick[5] received me most courteously. He has the reputation of great talents, tho' he looks like Bartley in the Innkeeper in the "£100 Note"[6] – Tomlinson[7] of the 18th who is much improved called on me and asked me t[o] | [two thirds of page three is missing] two dollars a day and held very cheap altogether here – described to me as a most asinine braggadocio, and a certain high personage hesitated not to say, that he had no doubt the Count had taken her in, with long accounts of his palace and villa, having neither. Sir John Franklin[8] is expected on this station. We may probably meet.

There is a very great thing which you [can do] for me | [two thirds of page four, and some lines at the top of page five are missing]

I continue much the same – still infirm, but no longer destitute of hope. I wander in pursuit of health like the immortal exile in pursuit of that lost shore which is now almost glittering in my sight. Five years of my life have been already wasted, and sometimes I think my pilgrimage may be as long as that [of] Ulysses.

Adieu my dearest friend. 1000 loves to all. I hope my letters duly arrived. I

1 Leucadia, one of the Ionian islands, has a high cliff from which, according to one legend, Sappho hurled herself to her death.

2 The expression is Byron's (*Childe Harold* II 425), incorrectly transcribed by Ralph Disraeli as 'romantic Zitza'. Zitza was the home of the monastery of St Elias. William Martin Leake *Travels in Northern Greece* (1835) IV 92.

3 As D clearly was to reveal in his letter to Austen of 18 November, he was under the misapprehension that there was such a person as *the* 'Bey of Valona'. However, there were simultaneously several beys, or nobles, of Valona. Two prominent ones of the previous decade were Ismael Bey and Bekir Bey. Gabriel Rémérand *Ali Tébélen Pacha de Janina, 1744-1822* (Paris 1928) 230, 240.

4 Nathaniel Basevi (1792-1869), D's cousin; he was the first Jewish-born barrister to practise in English courts. Basevi family tree, Jewish Museum; Blake 9.

5 Lt Gen Sir Frederick Adam (1781-1853). From 1824 to 1832 he was lord high commissioner to the Ionian Islands, and from 1832 to 1837 governor of Madras. He was also colonel of the 73rd Foot 1829-35, and he became a general in 1846.

6 *The £100 Note*, a farce by Richard Brinsley Peake (1792-1847), produced in 1827. Bartley is presumably the actor George Bartley (1782?-1858).

7 Nicholas R. Tomlinson was then a lieutenant in the 18th Foot.

8 Sir John Franklin (1786-1847), arctic explorer.

enumerated their respective dates in the last Malta letter. Write without ceasing.
BD

TO ISAAC D'ISRAELI Prevesa, [Greece], [Monday] 25 October 1830 **101**

ORIGINAL: QUA 210

COVER: I. Disraeli Esqr. | Bradenham House | Wycomb | Bucks.

PUBLICATION HISTORY: HL 75-95, dated 25 October 1830. The bulk of the letter was reproduced verbatim in *Contarini Fleming* part V chs 10, 14.

EDITORIAL COMMENT: D's enthusiasm for the culture of the Near East (Turkish, Jewish and Arab alike) steadily mounted throughout this tour. He had already emphasized the Moorish influence as underlying the fascinations of Spain, and his sympathies were further defined as he approached Greece. Undoubtedly the majority of Englishmen, educated to regard Greece as the cradle of western civilization and reinforced by the romantic example of Byron's death, would unhesitatingly have expressed their support for Christian Greece in its struggle for freedom from Mohammedan Turkey. D, equally unhesitatingly, took the opposite position. While the idea of Greece seemed occasionally to conquer, as in the last passages of this letter, the call of the East reasserted itself. He saw the Porte as the last bulwark of a civilization to which he seemed instinctively to respond, and whose continuing appeal extended far beyond these letters – to *Alroy*, *Tancred*, the 'Asian Mystery' and even to the Congress of Berlin forty-eight years later. *Sic*: Corfou, agreable, accomodation, Gazel, journeyd, sate, Moslemin, have drank, tipsey, rased, buzzeed, the the, Scheik, seiges, antichamber, groupes, Redschid, cheif, arabésques, St.James, lacqueys, the Peter the Great, Gulph.

Prevesa. October 25. 1830

My dearest father,

I wrote to Ralph from Malta, and to you from Corfou, and left the letters to be forwarded by the October packet when it arrived, if it ever did, of which today there is a report here. It was so late after its time that it was quite despaired of. Doubtless howr. you have received my letters by some source or other. I ment[ione]d in my letter to you that there was a possibility of our paying the Grand Vizier a visit at head quarters at Yanina, the Capital of Albania. What was then probable has since become certain. We sailed from Corfou to this place where we arrived on the eleventh Inst. and found a most hospitable and agreable friend in the Consul Genl. Mr. Meyer,[1] to whom Sir Frederick had given me a very warm letter. He is a gentleman of the old school, who has moved in a good sphere, and has great diplomatic experience of the East. He insists upon our dining with him every day, and what is even still more remarkable, produces a cuisine which wo[ul]d not be despicable in London, but in this savage land of anarchy is indeed as surprising as it is agreable.

As the movements of his Highness were very uncertain we lost no time in commencing our Journey to Yanina. We sailed up to Salora (I mention these places because you will be always able to trace my route in your new maps) and on the morning of the fourteenth, a company of six horsemen all armed, set off for Arta, where we found accomodation ready for us in a house belonging to the Consulate. Arta, once a town as beautiful as its situation, is in ruins – whole streets razed to the ground and with the exception of the Consulate House, re-

1 William R. Meyer was British consul in Albania. *ER* 1828, 1834.

built since, scarcely a tenement which was not a shell. Here for the first time I reposed upon a Divan, and for the first time heard the Muezzin from the Minaret, a ceremony which is highly affecting, when performed, as it usually is, by a rich and powerful voice. Next morning we paid a visit to Kalio Bey[2] the Governor once the wealthiest, and now one of the most powerful, Albanian nobles. He has ever been faithful to the Porte, even during the recent insurrection, which was an affair of the great body of the Aristocracy. We found him keeping his state, which in spite of the surrounding desolation, was not contemptible, in something not much better than a large shed. I cannot describe to you the awe with which I first entered the divan of a Great Turk, or the curious feelings with which for the first time in my life I found myself squatting on the right hand of a Bey smoking an amber mouthed chibouque, drinking coffee, and paying him compliments through an Interpreter. He was a very handsome, stately man – grave but not dull, and remarkably mild and bland in his manner, which may perhaps be ascribed | to a recent imprisonment in Russia where however he was treated with great consideration, which he mentioned to us. He was exceedingly courteous and would not let us depart, insisting upon our repeating our pipes, an unusual honor. At length we set off from Arta with an Albanian of his body for our escort, ourselves and guides six in number and two Albanians who took advantage of our company. All these Albanians are armed to the teeth, with daggers, pistols, and guns invariably richly ornamented, and sometimes entirely inlaid with silver, even the barrel. This was our procession

An Albanian of the Beys guard, completely armed,
2 Turkish Guides with the baggage,
Three Beyasdeers Inglases, or sons of English Beys,
armed, after their fashion.
Giovanni covered with mustachios and pistols
Boy carrying a Gazel
An Albanian completely armed.

The Gazel made a capital object, but gave us a great deal of trouble. In this fashion, we journeyd over a wild mountain pass, a range of the ancient Pindus, and 2 hours before sunset having completed only half our course in spite of all our exertions, we found ourselves at a vast but dilapidated Khan,[3] as big as a Gothic castle, situated on a high range and built as a sort of halfway house for the travellers by Ali Pacha[4] when his long, sagacious, and unmolested reign had permitted him to turn this unrivalled country which combines all the excellencies of Southern Europe and Western Asia to some of the purposes for which it is fitted. This Khan had now been turned into a military post and here we found a young Bey to whom Kalio had given us a letter in case of our stopping

2 He is the subject of the chapter 'The Bey of Arta' in *Contarini Fleming*.

3 Arabic word for the sort of inn which D described elsewhere by the Persian term 'caravanserai'.

4 Known as the 'Lion of Janina', Ali Pasha (1744-1822) was one of several overmighty subjects who challenged the Porte early in the nineteenth century. To Byron, he was 'Albania's chief' and a romantic figure. A more mundane and grimly explicit account of this remarkable man and his deeds is found in the Rev T.S. Hughes *Travels in Greece and Albania* 2nd ed (1830) II. Hughes visited Ali Pasha five years after Byron.

for an hour. He was a man of very pleasing exterior, but unluckily co[ul]d not understand Giovanni's Greek, and had no Interpreter. What was to be done! We co[ul]d not go on, as there was not an inhabited place before Yanina and here were we sitting before Sunset, on the same Divan with our host who had entered the place to receive us, and wo[ul]d not leave the room while we were there, | without the power of communicating an idea. We were in despair, and we were also very hungry, and co[ul]d not therefore in the course of an hour or two plead fatigue as an excuse for sleep, for we were ravenous, and anxious to know what prospect of food existed in this wild and desolate mansion. So we smoked. It is a great resource – but this wore out, and it was so ludicrous smoking, and looking at each other, and dying to talk, and then exchanging pipes by way of compliment, and then pressing our hand to our heart by way of thanks. The Bey sate in a corner, I unfortunately next, so I had the onus of mute attention and Clay next to me. So he and M. co[ul]d at least have an occasional joke, tho' of course we were too well bred to exceed an occasional and irresistible observation. Clay wanted to play Ecarté, and with a grave face, as if we were at our devotions, but just as we were about commencing it occurred to us that we had some brandy, and that we wo[ul]d offer our host a glass as it might be a hint for what sho[ul]d follow to so vehement a schnaps. Mashallah! had the effect only taken place 1830 years ago, instead of in the present age of scepticism, it wo[ul]d have been instantly voted a first rate miracle. Our mild friend smacked his lips, and instantly asked for another cup – we drank it in coffee cups. By the time that Meredith had returned, who had left the house on pretence of shooting, Clay, our host and myself had despatched a bottle of brandy in quicker time and fairer proportions than I ever did a bottle of Burgundy and were extremely gay. Then he wo[ul]d drink again with Meredith and ordered some figs, talking I must tell you all the time, indulging in the most graceful pantomime, examining our pistols, offering us his own golden ones for our inspection, and finally – making out Giovannis Greek enough to misunderstand most ludicrously every observation we communicated. But all was taken in good part, and I never met such a jolly fellow in the course of | my life. In the meantime, we were ravenous, for the dry round, unsugary fig, is a great whetter. At last we insisted upon Giovanni communicating our wants, and asking for bread. The Bey gravely bowed and sd. "Leave it to me – take no thought" and nothing more occurred. We prepared ourselves for hungry dreams, when to our great delight a most capital supper was brought in accompanied to our great horror by —— wine. We ate – we drank – we eat with our fingers – we drank in a manner I never recollect – the wine was not bad, but if it had been poison, we must drink, it was such a compliment for a Moslemin, we quaffed it in rivers – the Bey called for the Brandy – we drank it all – the room turned round, the wild attendants who sat at our feet seemed dancing in strange and fantastic whirls, the Bey shook hands with me, he shouted English – I Greek – "very good" he had caught up from us – "Kalo, Kalo," was my rejoinder – He roared – I smacked him on the back – I remember no more. In the middle of the night I woke. I found myself sleeping on the Divan, rolled up in its sacred carpet – the Bey had wisely reeled to the fire – the thirst I felt was like that of Dives – all were sleeping except two, who kept up during the night the great wood fire. I rose lightly stepping over my sleeping companions, and the shining arms that here and there informed me that the dark mass wrapped up in a capote was a human being. I found | Abraham's bosom in a flagon of water. I think I must have drank a Gallon at the draught. I looked at the wood fire, and thought of the blazing blocks in the Hall at Bradenham, asked myself whether I was indeed in the mountain fastness of an Albanian chief, and shrugging my shoulders, went to sleep and woke without a headache.

We left our jolly host with regret. I gave him my pipe as a memorial of having got tipsey together.

Next day having crossed one more steep mountain pass we descended into a vast plain over which we journeyed for some hours, the country presenting the same mournful aspect which I had too long observed – villages in ruins and perfectly uninhabited, caravanseras deserted, fortresses razed to the ground, olive woods burnt up. So complete has been the work of destruction, that you often find your horses course on the foundation of a village without being aware of it, and what at first appears the dry bed of a torrent turns out to be the backbone of the skeleton of a ravaged town. At the end of the plain immediately backed by very lofty mountains, and jutting into the beautiful lake, that bears its name, we suddenly came upon the City of Yanina – suddenly for a long track of gradually rising ground had hitherto concealed it from our sight. At the distance we first beheld it, this city once if not the largest, one of the prosperous and the most brilliant in the Turkish dominions, still looked imposing but when we entered, I soon found that all preceding desolation had only been preparative to the vast scene of destruction now before me. We proceeded through a street winding in its course, but of very great | length to our quarters. Ruined houses, mosques with their tower only standing, streets utterly rased – these are nothing. We met great patches of ruin a mile square as if a swarm of locusts had had the power of desolating the works of man as well as those of God. The great heart of the city was a sea of ruin. Arches and pillars, isolated, and shattered still here and there jutting forth, breaking the uniformity of the desolation, and turning the horrible into the picturesque. The great bazaar, itself a little Town, was burnt down only a few months since, when an infuriate band of Albanian soldiers heard of the destruction of their chiefs by the G[rand] Vizier.—— But while the city itself presented this mournful appearance its other characteristics were anything but sad. At this moment a swarming population, arrayed in every possible and fanciful costume, buzzeed and bustled in all directions. As we passed on, and you can easily believe not unobserved, where no "*mylords Ingles*" (as regular a word among the Turks as the French and Italians) had been seen for more than nine years, a thousand objects attracted my restless attention and roving eye. Every thing was so strange and splendid, that for a moment I forgot that this was an extraordinary scene even for the East, and gave up my fancy to a full credulity in the now obsolete magnificence of Oriental Life. Military chieftains clothed in the most brilliant colors, and most showy furs, and attended by a cortege of officers equally | splendid, continually passed us – now for the the first time a Dervish saluted me and now a Delhi with his high cap reined in his desperate steed as the suite of some Pacha blocked up the turning of the street – the Albanian costume too is inexhaustible in its combinations, and Jews and Greek priests must not be forgotten. It seemed to me that my first day in Turkey brought before me all the popular characteristics of which I had read, and which I expected I occasionally might see during a prolonged residence. I remember this very day I observed a Turkish Scheik in his entirely Green vestments, a Scribe with his writing materials in his girdle, and a little old Greek physician, who afterwards claimed my acquaintance on the plea of being able to speak English, that is to say, he could count nine on his fingers, no further (literally a fact). I gazed with a strange mingled feeling of delight and wonder. Suddenly a strange, wild, unearthly drum is heard, and at the end of the street a huge camel, to me it seemed as large as an elephant, with a slave sitting crosslegged on its neck and playing an immense kettle drum, appears and, is the first of an apparently interminable procession of his Arabian brethren. The camels were very large, they moved slowly, and were many in number – I sho[ul]d think there might have been between 60 and 100 one by one. It was an imposing sight – all immediately | hustled out of the way of the Caravan and seemed to shrink under the sound of the wild drum. This procession bore corn for the Viziers troops encamped without the wall.

It is in vain that I attempt to convey to you all that I saw, and felt this wondrous week. To lionize and be a lion at the same time is a hard fate. When I walked out I was followed by a crowd, when I stopped to buy anything, I was encompassed by a circle. How shall I convey to you an idea of all the Pachas, and all the Agas and all the Selictars[5] whom I have visited and who have visited me – all the coffee I sipped, all the pipes, I smoked, all the sweetmeats I devoured. But our grand presentation must not be omitted. An hour having been fixed for the audience, we repaired to the celebrated fortress palace of Ali, which, tho greatly battered by successive seiges, is still inhabitable, and yet affords a very fair ide[a] of its old magnificence. Having passed the gates of the fortress we found ourselves in a number of small streets like those in the liberties of the Tower or any other old castle – All full of life, stirring and excited – then we came to a Grand Place, in which on an ascent stands the Palace. We hurried through courts and corridors all full of guards and pages and attendant chiefs and in fact every species of | Turkish population, for in these countries one head does everything and we with our subdivision of labor and intelligent and responsible deputies have no idea of the labor of a Turkish Premier. At length we came to a vast, irregular apartment serving as the immediate antichamber to the Hall of Audience. This was the finest thing I have ever yet seen. In the whole course of my life I never met anything so picturesque and cannot expect to do so again. I do not attempt to describe it, but figure to yourself the

5 A 'pacha' or 'pasha' was originally the title of a military commander, but by this time various grades of senior administrators, including Europeans in the service of the Porte, were so described.

An 'aga' was a Turkish gentleman. Neither office nor nobility was implied. A 'selictar' was an official more senior than the literal meaning 'sword-bearer' would suggest.

largest chamber that you ever were perhaps in, full of the choicest groupes of an Oriental population, each individual waiting by appointment for an audience, and probably about to wait for ever. In this room we remained, attended by the Austrian Consul[6] who presented us about ten minutes, too short a time. I never thought that I co[ul]d have lived to have wished to have kicked my heels in a ministers antichamber. Suddenly we are summoned to the awful presence of the pillar of the Turkish Empire, the man who has the reputation of being the main spring of the new system of regeneration, the renowned Redschid,[7] an approved warrior, a consummate politician, unrivalled as | a dissembler in a country where dissimulation is the principal portion of their moral culture. The Hall was vast, built by Ali Pacha purposely to receive the largest Gobelin carpet that was ever made, which belonged to the cheif chamber in Versailles and was sold to him in the Revolution. It is entirely covered with gilding and arabésques. Here squatted up in a corner of the large divan I bowed with all the nonchalance of St. James St. to a little, ferocious looking, shrivelled, care worn man, plainly dressed with a brow covered with wrinkles, and a countenance clouded with anxiety and thought. I entered the shedlike Divan of the kind and comparatively insignificant Kalio Bey with a feeling of awe. I seated myself on the Divan of the Grand Vizier, who as the Austrian Consul observed, has destroyed, in the course of the last three months *not* in war, "upwards of four thousand of my acquaintance", with the self-possession of a morning call. At a distance from us, in a group on his lefthand were his secretary and his immediate suite – the end of the saloon was lined by lacqueys in waiting with an odd name which I now forget and which you will | find in the glossary of Anastasius.[8]

Some compliments now passed between us, and pipes and coffee were then brought by four of these lacqueys – then his H[ighne]ss waved his hand and in a instant the chamber was cleared. Our conversation I need not repeat. We congratulated him on the pacification of Albania. He rejoined that the peace of the world was his only object and the happiness of mankind his only wish – this went on for the usual time. He asked us no questions about ourselves or our country as the other Turks did but seemed quite overwhelmed with business, moody and anxious. While we were with him, three separate Tartars arrived

6 Some of the consul's correspondence of 1825-6 was intercepted by the British and is preserved in the Ionian Islands section of the records of the Colonial Office. C.W. Crawley *The Question of Greek Independence* (Cambridge 1930) 15n. The documents (PRO) indicate that the consul, at least immediately before D's visit, was Vincenzo Micarelli.

7 Reshid Mehmet Pasha, also known as 'Kutahia' (d 1836), was grand vizier of the Ottoman Empire, c 1829-34. After distinguished service in Greece and his successful suppression of the Albanian insurrection, he was himself defeated and taken prisoner by the Egyptians at the battle of Konieh in December 1832. He ended his career as commander-in-chief (seraskier) of the Sultan's forces in Asia Minor. This grand vizier is not to be confused with Reshid Mustapha Pasha, the reforming vizier of the 1840s. John Burke *The Official Kalendar for 1830* (1830) col 840; Peter J. Burke ed *The Royal Register ... for MDCCCXXXI* (nd) 186; J.B. Capefigue *L'Europe depuis l'avènement du roi Louis-Philippe* (Paris 1846) VII ch 3; Harold Temperley *England and the Near East: The Crimea* (1936) 10, 542.

8 The lackeys in question were 'Koords', mountaineers of Anadoly, said to be the bodyguards of the Asiatic pashas. Thomas Hope *Anastasius, or Memoirs of a Greek* (1820) II 237n.

with dispatches. What a life! and what a slight chance for the gentlemen in the antichamber.

After the usual time we took our leave, and paid a visit to his son Amin Pacha, a youth of eighteen, but who looks ten years older and who is Pacha of Yanina.[9] He is the very reverse of his father – incapable in affairs, refined in his manners, plunged in debauchery and magnificent in dress. Covered with gold and diamonds he bowed to us with the ease of a Duke of Devonshire and said the English were the most polished of nations. | But all these visits must really be reserved till we meet. We found some Turks extremely intelligent who really talk about the Peter the Great, and all that, with considerable gout. With one of these, Mehemet Aga, Selictar to the Pacha of Lepanto, and an approved warrior, we became great friends.[10] He showed us his new books of military tactics, and as he took a fancy to my costume, insisted upon my calling to see his uniforms, which he gets made in Italy, and which really wo[ul]d not disgrace the 10th.

I forgot to tell you, that with the united assistance of my English, Spanish and fancy wardrobe, I sported a costume in Yanina which produced a most extraordinary effect on that costume loving people. A great many Turks called on purpose to see it – but the little Greek physician, who had passed a year at Pisa in his youth, nearly smoked me – "*Questo vestito Inglese o di fantasia?*" he aptly asked. I oracularly replied "*Inglese e fantastica*"[.][11] |

I write you this from that Ambracian Gulph where the soft Triumvir gained more glory by defeat, than attends the victory of harsher warriors.[12] The site is not unworthy of the beauty of Cleopatra. From the sinuosity of the land, this gulph appears like a vast lake walled in on all sides by mountains, more or less distant. The dying glory of a Grecian Eve bathes with warm light a thousand promontories, and gentle bays, and infinite undulations of purple outline. Before me is Olympus, whose austere peak glitters yet in the Sun: a bend of the land alone hides from me the islands of Ulysses and of Sappho. When I gaze upon this scene, I remember the barbaric splendor, and turbulent existence, which I have just quitted, with disgust. I recur to the feelings, in the indulgence of which I can alone find happiness, and from which | an inexorable destiny seems resolved to shut me out.

Pray write regularly as, sooner or later, I shall receive all your letters – and write fully. As I have no immediate mode of conveying this safely to England, I shall probably keep it in my portfolio till I get to Napoli, and send it through Mr. Dawkins[.][13]

The Times (2 Oct 1830), in reporting a massacre of rebels at Janina, called him 'Emir Pacha'. Other sources render the name as 'Amir', but all versions agree that this person was the grand vizier's elder son, the younger being named Ibrahim.
Contarini Fleming part V ch 14 adds some details about this warrior.
'Is your costume English or the product of your own fancy?' 'It is both English and fanciful.'
Off the promontory of Actium, at the mouth of the Ambracian Gulf, where Octavian defeated the fleets of Antony and Cleopatra in 31 BC.
Edward James Dawkins was appointed British Resident in Greece, 11 November 1828. He served as minister plenipotentiary to Greece 1833-5, and then left the service. D. Dakin *The Greek Struggle for Independence 1821-1833* (Berkeley and Los Angeles 1973) 268.

A thousand loves to all,
yr m[os]t affec
BD

---

102 TO HENRY COLBURN [Nauplia, Greece], [Thursday] 18 November 1830

ORIGINAL: PRIN Parrish Collection AM 15767

COVER: Henry Colburn Esqre | Northumberland Place | New Road | *private.* London

POSTMARK: (1) In oval: 10.F.NOON.10 | 21.JA | x 1831 x (2) In packet: T.P | Charing Cross (3) Large numeral: 2

EDITORIAL COMMENT: Nauplia had been captured by the Greeks from the Turks in December 1822, and was used as the centre of Greek administration until it moved to Athens in 1833. It was still known by its old title of Napoli, to which D has appended its location in the old Turkish province of Romania.

Napoli di Romania | Nov. 18. 1830

Henry Colburn Esq
My dear Sir,

I send you by our Ministers bag an account of my visit to the head quarters of the Grand Vizier during the Albanian Insurrection – which will form an interesting article for the C[ourt] J[ournal].[1] I have written it in a manner as little egotistical as a personal narrative can well be, and I beg you will not make it more so. I have engaged with my two companions[2] a yacht which is the only mode of travel for this interesting sea. Tomorrow I sail to Athens, and intend, if wind will favor me, to pass my Christmas and the winter months at Constantinople.

I do not see by the newspapers, up to the 10th. Ulto:, that have reached me, that the Y[OUNG] D[UKE] is yet advertised.[3] I very much fear that you are injuriously procrastinating its appearance.

Believe me, dear Sir,
Yours truly
B. Disraeli

---

103 TO BENJAMIN AUSTEN [Nauplia, Greece], [Thursday] 18 November [1830]

ORIGINAL: BL ADD MS 45908 ff33-4

COVER: Benj: Austen Esqr | Raymond Buildings | Grays Inn | London | PRIVATE

POSTMARK: (1) In oval: 10.F.NOON.10 | 21.JA | x 1831 x (2) In packet: T.P. | Charing Cross

PUBLICATION HISTORY: Layard 21, undated extract; M&B I 158-9, undated; Jerman 113-15, dated 18 November [1830]

EDITORIAL COMMENT: There is no signature. *Sic*: Corfou, Spacteria, arabian nights, Pylus, Navarin, french.

---

1 'A Visit to the Grand Vizier' appeared in *The Court Journal* no 92 (29 Jan 1831) 66-7.

2 James Clay and George Meredith.

3 D had submitted his MS of *The Young Duke* to Colburn before he left England, but the novel was not published until April 1831.

Napoli di Romania | Nov. 18. **103** | 173
18 Nov 1830

My dear Austen,

As I have unexpectedly a mode of conveying letters to England I write you a few lines. I wrote to you at Florence from Malta, and was on the point of dispatching you another letter, when I accidentally met your friend Mrs. Christie[1] at Corfou who informed me that you had renounced your intention of travel. I was not surprised at this, tho' very sorry to hear it.

When I wrote to you last, I had some thoughts, indeed had resolved, to join the Turkish army as volunteer in the Albanian war. I found however on my arrival at Corfou, whither for this purpose I had repaired, instead of going on to Egypt, that the Grand Vizier, while all your newspapers were announcing the final loss of Albania to the Porte[2] had proceeded with such surprising energy, that the war, which had begun so magnificently, had already dwindled into an insurrection. I waited a week at Corfou to see how affairs wo[ul]d turn out, at the end of which came Schiem [?] Bey one of the principal rebels flying for refuge, and after him, the Bey of Valona[3] and some others. Under these circumstances, I determined to turn my intended campaign into a visit of congratulation to head quarters, and Sir Frederick Adam gave me a letter and with Meredith and Clay, our servants and a guard of Albanians, we at last reached Yanina the capital of the Province. |

I can give you no idea in a letter of all the Pachas and all the Selictars and all the Agas, that I have visited and visited me, all the pipes I smoked, all the coffee I sipped, all the sweetmeats I devoured. I must reserve until we meet matter for many a chat. Even the grand audience can only be glanced at. For a week I was in a scene equal to anything in the arabian nights – such processions, such dresses, such corteges of horsemen, such caravans of camels. Then the delight of being made much of by a man who was daily decapitating half the province. Every morning we paid visits, attended reviews, and crammed ourselves with sweetmeats, every evening dancers and singers were sent to our quarters by the Vizier or some Pacha.

We have hired a yacht which is the only mode of travel for this sea, where every headland and bay is the site of something memorable, and which is studded with islands which demand a visit. We were a week at the scene of Codrington's bloody blunder,[4] | Navarino, a superb, perhaps unrivalled harbour, with

1 Wife of James Christie II (1773-1831), of the well-known family of art and book auctioneers.

2 Reports in *The Times* came mainly from Belgrade and were about a month behind events. Thus the issue of 17 September carried two brief reports. The first, dated 4 August, anticipated the defeat of the Turks; the second, of 27 August, reported the massacre of four hundred of the rebels at Bitoglia, otherwise known as Monastïr.

3 Schiem Bey may well have been one of the beys of Valona. See **100**n3.

4 Sir Edward Codrington (1770-1851) was the admiral of the British force which, with French and Russian squadrons, entered the Greek harbour of Navarino on 20 October 1827 and destroyed the Turkish fleet. D's interpretation agreed with the ungrateful view held by Wellington and the Tories that it was an 'untoward event'. The Whigs and the Radicals had applauded Codrington's action. For a survey of political reaction to Navarino see Lady Bourchier ed *Memoir of the Life of Admiral Sir Edward Codrington* (1873) II 178-83.

the celebrated Spacteria on one side and old Pylus on the other.[5] Here we found the French in their glory. They have already covered the scene of Spartan suffering with cafés and billiard rooms, and make daily picnics to the grotto of Nestor.[6] Navarin looks exactly like a french Village. From Navarino, after visiting Modon, and sailing by the bay of Coron, the Promontory of Malea, Cerigo, a beautiful island, we reached Napoli. Here we have been three or four days and after visiting Argos, Mycenae and Corinth, we shall sail for Athens and if the wind favor us pass our Xmas at Stamboul. All this is pleasant enough, but I cannot say that I am advanced as much as I cd desire, but this is a subject of which it is vain to think. I drew upon you from Malta £100. and will write before I draw again.

A 1000 remembrances to Madame and Louisa who I trust are quite well. I am quite a Turk, wear a turban, smoke a pipe six feet long, and squat on a Divan. Mehemet Pacha told me that he did not think I was an Englishman because I walked *so slow*. In fact I find the habits of this calm | and luxurious people entirely agree with my own preconceived opinions of propriety and enjoyment, and I detest the Greeks more than ever. I do not find mere Travelling on the whole very expensive, but I am ruined by my wardrobe. You have no idea of the rich and various costume of the Levant. When I was presented to the Grand Vizier I made up such a costume from my heterogeneous wardrobe, that the Turks, who are mad on the subject of dress, were utterly astounded. Amin Pacha sent a Colonel to know whether my dress was English, and I | had a regular crowd round our quarters, and had to come forward and bow like Don Miguel and Donna Maria.[7] Nothing wo[ul]d persuade the Greeks that we were not come about the new King and I really believe that if I had 25000£ to throw away I might increase my headache by wearing a crown.[8]

---

104 TO ISAAC D'ISRAELI

Athens and Constantinople,
[Tuesday] 30 November 1830

ORIGINAL: QUA 211
COVER: I. Disraeli Esquire | Bradenham House | Wycombe | Bucks.
POSTMARK: (1) In circle: E? | JA20 | 1831
PUBLICATION HISTORY: HL 96-102, dated 30 November 1830, with omissions and changes
EDITORIAL COMMENT: The bulk of the letter was written in Athens and during the voyage to Constantinople, where D added a postscript and where he posted it. *Sic*: encreasing, french.

---

5 During the first phase of the Peloponnesian War, the Athenians at Pylos destroyed or captured several hundred Spartan hoplites on Sphacteria, the island that almost blocks the Bay of Pylos, scene of the Battle of Navarino.

6 According to Homeric legend Nestor was son of King Neleus of Pylos.

7 In 1828 Dom Miguel, brother of the Emperor of Brazil, usurped the crown of Portugal, depriving the child Queen, Donna Maria da Gloria. D's use of this stylistic device is of the same order as his earlier comparison of a young Turk to the Duke of Devonshire (**101**). Any member of a European royal family would serve to make the parallel.

8 Leopold of Saxe-Coburg had refused the throne of Greece in June of that year; Prince Otho of Bavaria had yet to accept it.

Athens. November 30. 1830 **104** | 175
30 Nov 1830

My dearest father,

I wrote you a very long letter from Prevesa, and forwarded it to you from Napoli through Mr. Dawkins bag. You have doubtless received it. As you probably wo[ul]d be disappointed, if you did not also receive one from the "city of the Violet Crown",[1] I sit down before we sail from the harbour of Piraeus, to let you know, that I am still in existence. We sailed from Prevesa through the remaining Ionian islands among which was Zante, preeminent in beauty; indeed they say none of the Cyclades are to be compared to it with its olive trees touching the waves, and its shores undulating in every possible variety. For about a fortnight we were for ever sailing on a summer sea, always within two or three miles of the coast and touching at every island or harbour that invited. A cloudless sky, a summer atmosphere, and sunsets like the neck of a dove, completed all the enjoyment which I anticipated from roving in a Grecian sea. We were obliged however to keep a sharp look out for Pirates, who are all about again – we exercised the crew every day with muskets, and their encreasing prowess, and our own pistol exercise, kept up our courage. We sailed round the coast of the Morea, visiting Navarino, which has become quite a little french town with cafés and billiard tables, Modon, and Napoli. From here we made excursions to Argos, Mycenae and Corinth. Napoli is a bustling place for Greece. Argos is rising from its ruins. Mycenae has a very ancient tomb or temple of the time of their old kings, massy as Egypt, and Corinth offered to us a scene which, both for its beauty and associations, will not easily be forgotten. From Napoli we had a very quiet passage to this memorable place. November here has been warmer than our best English summers, but this is unusual. Never was such a season known all agree. | On the afternoon of our arrival in Piraeus, which is about six miles from the city, I climbed a small hill forming a side of the harbour. From it I looked upon an immense plain covered with olive woods and skirted by mountains. Some isolated hills rise at a distance from the bounding ridge. On one of these I gazed upon a magnificent temple bathed in the sunset – at the foot of the hill was a walled city of considerable dimensions – in front of which was a Doric temple apparently quite perfect – the violet sunset, and to day the tint was peculiarly vivid, threw over this scene a coloring becoming its beauty, and, if possible, increasing its delicate character. The city was Athens, but independent of all reminiscences, I never witnessed anything so truly beautiful, and I have seen a great deal.

We were fortunate – The Acropolis which has been shut for nine years was open to us, the first Englishmen. Athens is still in the power of the Turks, but the Grecian commission[2] to receive it, arrived a short time before us. When we

1 Athens was first called the 'Violet-Crowned City' by Aristophanes. The name involved a comic play on words: Ion (ancient Greek for violet) was one of the early representative kings of Athens and the city became known as King Ion's city or 'the city with Ion crowned (its king)'. The pun, translated into English, became 'Violet-Crowned City' (or King Violet's city).

2 The body set up by Great Britain, France and Russia under the Treaty of London to establish the boundaries of the independent state of Greece. C.W. Crawley *The Question of Greek Independence* (Cambridge 1930) 204.

entered the city we found every house roofless, but really before the war, modern Athens must have been no common town. The ancient remains have been respected. The Parthenon and the other temples which are in the Acropolis, have necessarily suffered during the siege, but the injury is only in the detail – the general effect is not marred – we saw hundreds of shells and balls lying among the ruins.[3] The temple of Theseus[4] looks at a short distance, as if it were just finished by Pericles. Gropius, a well known character, was the only civilised being in this almost uninhabited town, and was our excellent Cicerone. |

We have just returned from an excursion into the country, to Marathon etc. I can give you no idea of the severe hardship and privation of present Grecian travel. Happy are we to get a shed for nightly shelter, and never have been fortunate enough to find one not swarming with vermin. My sufferings in this way are great, and so are poor Clays, but Meredith escapes. Our food must not be quarrelled with, for we lived for a week on the wild boar of Pentelicus,[5] and the honey of Hymettus, both very good; and I do not care for privation in this respect, as I have always got my pipe – but the want of sleep from vermin, and literally I did not sleep a wink the whole time I was out, is very bad, as it unfits you for daily exertion.

We found a wild boar just killed at a little village and purchased half of it – but it is not as good as Bradenham pork.

We have been at Egina for a couple of days. A favorable wind has risen, and we are off for Stamboul.

We have had a most splendid view of Sunium: its columns looked like undriven snow, and are now among the clustering Cyclades – sixteen islands in sight, and we are making our course east among the heart of them – our passage promises wonderfully.

We have reached the Dardanelles – a capital passage – what a road to a great city – narrower and much longer than the straits of Gibraltar, but not with such sublime shores. Asia and Europe look more kindly on each other, than Europe and her more sultry sister.

The breeze has again sprung up. We have yet one hundred and thirty miles to Constantinople.

It is near sunset and Const. is in full sight – it baffles all description, tho' so often described; an immense mass of buildings, cupolas, cypress, groves and minarets. I feel an excitement, which I thought was dead. |

10th. December. [Constantinople]

George Seymour,[6] I am sorry to say, left this place two months ago for Florence,

3 Having surrendered Athens in 1822, the Turks had recaptured the city in 1826 and the Acropolis in 1827.

4 The best preserved of the ancient buildings of Athens, the Temple of Theseus was built c 465 BC, and was thus older than the Parthenon.

5 This sounds like a mythical beast, but apparently it was quite real.

6 George Hamilton Seymour (1797-1880), diplomat, appointed minister resident at Florence in November 1830. He was later minister to the Belgian Court.

where he is appointed Minister but other friends promise, tho' this is provoking. The Ambassador's bag goes off in a few hours; this letter must therefore be shorter than intended.

I have just got a pile of papers. What universal gloom! but I think under no circumstances War. I can say no more at present, being pressed to the utmost, but will write very soon. I have received no letters since the Malta one, dated the end of July, nor could I – but they will all reach me very soon, and surely. Pray write regularly. I continue, I think mending, but have made no great move these last two months – which makes me low.

A thousand loves to all

Your most affec Son

B. Disraeli

105

TO ISAAC D'ISRAELI [Constantinople, Thursday 23? December 1830]

ORIGINAL: QUA 215

COVER: I. Disraeli Esquire | Bradenham House | Wycomb | Bucks.

POSTMARK: (1) In circle: D | JA.31 | 1831

PUBLICATION HISTORY: This letter was omitted from Ralph Disraeli's edition, its contents being redistributed to the conflated postscript of the printed version of **109**.

EDITORIAL COMMENT: *Sic*: inclose.

My dear father,

Meredith wishing me to inclose a letter, I add a few lines. I do not write by this opportunity because by writing too often I am unable to give any results – but will communicate fully before I leave this place, when I hope I may be able to speak satisfactorily about my return. You will be glad to hear that George Seymour's absence has been of no disadvantage to me, as the Ambassador has received me with a kindness which I shall always remember with gratitude. It is almost impossible for him to have done more, whatever ties existed between us.

I have just got thro' a pile of Galignanis. What a confusion! What a capital Pantomime "Lord Mayor's Day, or Harlequin Brougham!"[1]

Your most affec Son

BD

All your letters have been sent on to Alexandria. I long to be there. Continue to write regularly.

1 The British news of November centred on the resignation of Wellington's administration, the cancellation (owing to political unrest) of the King's traditional visit to the City on 10 November and the elevation of Henry Brougham (1778-1868) to the post of lord chancellor. This most brilliant and most difficult of Whig politicians thus became Baron Brougham and Vaux – a ludicrous turn of events, coming on the heels of his initial truculent refusal of the chancellorship. *Galignani's Messenger* (Paris) nos 4886-98 (11-25 Nov 1830). D was not one to waste a good line on a single correspondent. He used it again in **106** to Austen, and in **107** to Bulwer.

106 TO BENJAMIN AUSTEN Constantinople, [Monday] 27 December 1830

ORIGINAL: BL ADD MS 45908 ff35-36
COVER: Benjn. Austen Esqr | Raymond Buildgs | Grays Inn, | London
POSTMARK: (1) In oval: 10.F.NOON.10 | 1.FE | x 183[1] x (2) In packet: T.P | Charing Cross (3) Large numeral: 2
PUBLICATION HISTORY: M&B I 202, undated extract; Jerman 115-16, dated 27 December 1830.

Constantinople Decemr. 27th. 1830

My dear Austen,

I wrote to you from Napoli some six weeks or two months ago by the Minister's bag. You have doubtless received the letter. I wrote to Mrs. Austen a few days back, but it is probable you will receive this first as hers has been forwarded by a private hand, and this goes by an extraordinary bag. I do not therefore enter in to much detail about my whereabouts – but make this a letter of business, as I have not forgotten you impressed upon me, to give due notice of drawing. Since I wrote last, I have drawn upon you one hundred pounds, vizt. 75 on Hunter and Ross of Malta and 25£ on Messrs. Hanson of this place.[1] The last bill will eventually meet this in case, from most improbable circumstances, the debt is not previously discharged. It is probable that I may draw another hundred pounds upon you – *no more under any circumstances*. After what passed | between us upon this subject, I have no false delicacy in so doing, altho' I have not forgotten, and shall never forget, your generous friendship.

Let me hear from you directed to Hunter and Ross at Malta, who will forward the letter to any part of the Levant I may be in.

I hope to return soon. I sho[ul]d be glad to return immediately. What a confusion you are all in. I have just got thro' a batch of Galignanis. What a capital Pantomime it wo[ul]d make – "The Lord Mayor's day, or Harlequin Brougham".

I am entirely destitute of news from home – since July – in fact I know nothing, all my letters | having been sent on to Alexandria.

I scribble this at the Palace with scarcely a moment allowed me.

Ever Yrs

BD

1 D carried a general letter of introduction to a long list of financial houses in that part of the world, including 'Charles S. Hanson' at Constantinople. H A/IV/E/11.

A year previously, the press carried a notice of the marriage of Charles Simpson Hanson of Constantinople. Hanson & Co were the correspondents in Constantinople and Smyrna for J. & R. McCracken of London. *Murray's Handbook for Turkey* 3rd ed (1854).

TO EDWARD LYTTON BULWER Constantinople, [Monday] 27 December 1830

ORIGINAL: HCR D/EK/C5/1
COVER: Edward Lytton Bulwer Esq | 36 Hertford Street | May Fair | London.
POSTMARK: (1) On the back of the cover, in oval: 8.MORN. 8 | 1.FE | x 1831 x (2) On the front of the cover, in packet: [T.P] | Charing Cross (3) Large numeral: 2
PUBLICATION HISTORY: *Lytton* (1883) II 322-3, dated 27 December 1830
EDITORIAL COMMENT: *Sic*: boring of saloons, sooner that.

Constantinople. Decr 27. 1830

My dear Bulwer,

In spite of the extraordinary times and engrossing topics on which we have fallen, I flatter myself you will be glad to hear of my existence, and that that existence is in a state not quite so forlorn, as when I last had the pleasure of enjoying your society. Since then I have travelled through Spain, Greece and Albania, and am now a resident in this famous city.

I cannot easily express how much I was delighted with the first country. I no longer wonder at the immortality of Cervantes, and perpetually detected in the picturesque and al fresco life of his countrymen, the sources of his inspiration. The Alhambra and other Saracenic remains, the innumerable Murillos, and above all their olla podrida in | turn delighted me – I arrived at Malta time enough to name the favorite horse for their races "Paul Clifford",[1] and I have since learnt by a letter at this place, that he won the plate.

While at the little Military hot house,[2] I heard that Albania was in a flaming insurrection, and always having had a taste for a campaign, I hurried off with a couple of friends to offer our services to the Grand Vizier. We found the insurrection by the time of our arrival nearly crushed, and so turned our military trip into a visit of congratulation at | headquarters. I must reserve for our meeting any account of my visit. I certainly passed at Yanina ten of the most extraordinary days of my life, and often wished that you had been my companion.

Of all the places that I have visited, Athens most completely realized all that I co[ul]d have wished. The place requires no associations to render it one of the most delightful in the globe. I am not surprised that the fine taste of the dwellers in this delicate land should have elected the olive for their chosen tree, and the violet for their favorite flower.

I | confess to you that my Turkish prejudices are very much confirmed by my residence in Turkey. The life of this people greatly accords with my taste, which is naturally somewhat indolent and melancholy, and I do not think would disgust you. To repose on voluptuous ottomans, and smoke superb pipes, daily to indulge in the luxuries of a bath which requires half a dozen attendants for its perfection, to court the air in a carved caique by shores which are a continual scene and to find no exertion greater than a canter on a barb, is I think a far

1 After Bulwer's novel of 1830.
2 'Thou little military hothouse'. Byron's 'Farewell to Malta' 46.

more sensible life than all the bustle of clubs, and all the boring of saloons | – all this without any coloring and exaggeration is the life which may be here commanded accompanied by a thousand sources of calm enjoyment and a thousand modes of mellowed pleasure, which it wo[ul]d weary you to relate, and which I leave to your own lively imagination.

I can say nothing about our meeting, but pray that it may be sooner that I can expect. I send you a tobacco bag, that you may sometimes remember me. If ever you have leisure to write me a line, anything directed to *Messrs. Hunter and Ross Malta*, will be forwarded to whatever part of the Levant I | may reside in.

I mend slowly, but mend. The seasons have greatly favored me[.] Continual heat, and even here a summer sky, where the winter is proverbially severe.

Remember me most kindly to your brother[3] – and believe me
my dear Bulwer
Yours most faith[ful]ly
Benj. Disraeli

I have just got thro' a pile of Galignani's. What a confusion! and what an excellent Pantomime – "*Lord Mayor's Day, or Harlequin Brougham*" – Oh! for the days of Aristophanes and Foote, or even Scaramouch – Damn the Licenser.[4] |

I have just been informed that it is questionable whether I can forward these letters with the parcel. I therefore send them by the Ambassador's[5] bag, but I fear that you will receive them long before Mrs. Bulwer does her slippers.

---

108 TO SARA AUSTEN — Constantinople, [Sunday 9] January 1831

ORIGINAL: BL ADD MS 45908 ff37-8
COVER: Mrs. Austen | 32 Guildford Street | London
PUBLICATION HISTORY: M&B I 165, undated extract; Jerman 117-19, dated 9 January 1831
EDITORIAL COMMENT: *Dating*: the MS shows evidence of '10' having been written first, and of a heavier '9' having been written over the zero, the '1' remaining uncorrected. The date thus appears to be 'Jan 19'. However, comparison with **109** (which also stated D's intention of leaving Constantinople in the very near future) and with the itinerary reported in **110** would seem to rule out 19 January as being too late for this letter. Jerman's dating has therefore been adopted as the one most consistent with the known facts. *Sic*: Careatides, Bosphorous, Easter, Bythinia.

Constantinople Jan 19. 1831

My dear Mrs. Austen,
Some three weeks ago I sent you from this place a pair of slippers and a letter;

3 William Henry Lytton Bulwer (1801-1872), Whig MP and diplomat, Edward's elder brother, who, after his KCB in 1843, was known as Sir Henry Bulwer. The year before his death he was raised to the peerage as Baron Dalling and Bulwer. In 1830 he was an attaché at the Hague and was elected MP for Wilton in that year. Later he held a series of ambassadorial posts.

4 D was blaming the lord chamberlain's censorship for a decline in the liveliness of British theatre. It was not a time of great political satire on the stage and D obviously felt that the actionable satires of Samuel Foote (1720-1777), or even the milder fare of the *commedia dell'arte*, would enliven political comment.

5 Sir Robert Gordon (1791-1847), fifth son of George Gordon, Lord Haddo, presented his credentials at the Porte in July 1829 and was recalled because of poor health in September 1831. He later served as ambassador in Vienna 1841-6. His eldest brother, the 4th Earl of Aberdeen, was later prime minister. S.T. Bindoff *et al* eds *British Diplomatic Representatives, 1789-1852*, Camden Society (1947), 3rd ser, 50, 169.

the latter was some days after returned to me as its company might have rendered the receipt of the former problematical. I have kept it by me since, but as I have had no opportunity of forwarding it to you until so long after its date, I send this as a substitute. I have been here a month and like the place exceedingly, altho' the Franks[1] are unfortunately so gay, that instead of residing in an eastern city, you might really fancy yourself in all the bustle and bore of a London season. The Carnival has now commenced, and rages so terribly that I intend to leave this place immediately.

Of all that I have yet visited, nothing has more completely realized all that I imagined and all that I could have wished than Athens. Independent of associations, it is the most beautiful assemblage of all that is interesting in art and nature. Had any of the houses boasted a roof I should certainly have remained, but tho' the city yet makes an important feature in the distant landscape, successive sieges have rendered it quite an uninhabited shell. After being closed nine years to the curiosity of travellers, the Acropolis was opened not nine days before my arrival. When | you remember that besides the Parthenon, this height boasts the rich remains of two other temples, and among them the far famed Careatides,[2] you will be pleased at my good fortune. The ancient relics have been respected during the struggle by all parties and are little injured – as the old acropolis is the modern Citadel, and so strong that it is still in the possession of the Turks it has of course not escaped quite harmless. Many were the balls and shells I stumbled over, when wandering among its columns. These pillars are here and there a little chipped, but the principal features are not injured. The small but beautiful temple of Theseus without the walls has been quite untouched, and is altogether so perfect, that to my sight it looks just finished by Pericles.

Description is an acknowledged bore, therefore I say nothing of Constantinople, save that in this, as in all other instances, you can form no idea of the object in question but by sight. Cypress groves and mosquish cupolas, masses of habitations and minarets growing out of waters intersecting the city and covered with innumerable carved boats and all teeming with human beings in the brightest | and most fanciful costume, when grouped by your lively fancy will give you a better idea than half a dozen elaborate pages. The caique is not unlike a gondola but gayer and even more swift! The golden Horn is a branch of the Sea not unlike the Grand Canal, but the Bosphorous can be likened to nothing but itself. The view of the Euxine when near its termination is the most sublime and mystical affair that I remember. In short all here is very much like life in a Pantomime or Easter Tale of Enchantment, which I think very high praise.

I depart for Egypt in a few days, and if I make as much progress there as

1 In the Ottoman Empire, Europeans were generally so described. The term Frank ('el Frangi') was applied, it seems, to Russians as well as to western Europeans, but Greeks appear not to have come under the label. Charles MacFarlane *Constantinople in 1828* (1829) I 46; Capt Charles Colville Frankland RN *Travels to and from Constantinople in the years 1827 and 1828* (1829) II 181.

2 The six figures of maidens or 'caryatids' which support the porch at the southwest corner of the Erectheum on the Acropolis.

here shall not complain. The spring I trust will confirm my convalescence, and if so, will bring me back. I am quite in ignorance of your movements, as my letters have all been forwarded to Alexandria, but if you will write to me, care of Hunter and Ross, Malta, it will reach me – but write without any unnecessary loss of time.

This place is celebrated for its cold winters, but this year, summer will not end. Since I left England, nothing but cloudless skies and constant Sun.

Meredith left us to our great regret some days back, and is now wandering among the mountains of Bythinia. We shall probably meet him at Smyrna | but I am afraid we shall not induce him to join us to Egypt.

Pray write to me fully, and if you like, you may cross.[3]

Remember me most kindly to Austen and Louisa and believe me

Ever Yrs

B. Disraeli

---

109 TO ISAAC D'ISRAELI — Constantinople, [Tuesday] 11 January 1831

ORIGINAL: QUA 212

COVER: I. Disraeli Esquire | Bradenham House | Wycomb | Bucks

POSTMARK: (1) In circle: N | FE14 | 1831

PUBLICATION HISTORY: HL 103-10, dated 11 January 1831, adding a postscript of twenty-three printed lines which (with the exception of the first sentence) includes a version of **105** and a paragraph from a source not located. RD has also moved the final paragraph (eight lines) of the postscript in the MS to the body of the letter.

EDITORIAL COMMENT: D has used here for the first time a device consisting of a long dash crossed in the centre, which, it is assumed, indicated a new paragraph without incurring the loss of space on the sheet usually resulting from the normal paragraphing procedure. These are indicated by + before the new paragraph begins. In the MS the sentences are continuous. *Sic*: agreable, Bithynian, suburbe, swifte, Easter, turks.

Constantinople. Jany. 11. 1831.

My dearest father,

Having been here more than a month without communicating, you will be glad to receive a letter. I have been silent, because it is possible to write too frequently, which prevents you giving any results, or occasions you giving false ones. +

In the first place I can give a favorable bulletin of my health which continues improving: in fact I hope that the early spring will return me to Bradenham in very different plight to that in which I left it. I can assure you that I sigh to return, altho' in very agreable company: but I have seen and done enough in this way, and a mingled picture of domestic enjoyment and fresh butter, from both of which I have been so long estranged, daily flits across my fancy. +

Meredith quitted us to our great regret a fortnight ago, as he had always intended, and is now wandering among the Bithynian mountains, which are remarkable for being more devoid of interest than any hills in existence. We antic-

3 A practice common among nineteenth-century correspondents, intended to save postage. Having completed a page in the usual way, the writer would turn it ninety degrees and continue, with the new text crossing the old at right angles. Fortunately D never crossed in his own letters.

ipate meeting him at Smyrna, and if so, may probably find him not disinclined to renounce his ambitious intentions of being a discoverer. +

You will all be glad to hear that George Seymours absence occasioned me no inconvenience. Nothing co[ul]d be kinder to us than the conduct of the Ambassador. Since Meredith's departure in consequence of the unfavorable change in the weather we have left our ship and taken lodgings in Pera. H.E. has given us a general dinner invitation, so that if we wish to dine with him, we only send to the Palace in the morning: he has introduced us to all the other Ambassadors and invites us to every picnic, here a favorite expedition. We visited in his suite, the other day, the Seven Towers, which are never shown, probably because there is nothing to see – a more amusing affair was the departure of the Mecca Caravan from Scutari, the Asiatic suburbe. We were entertained here by one of the Ministers very sumptuously, smoked out of pipes with diamond mouthpieces, and sipped coffee perfumed with roses in cups studded with precious stones.

Description is an acknowledged bore. I dread it myself, and therefore sympathise with your already murmured fears. So | I leave Constantinople to your imagination. Cypress groves and mosquish domes, masses of habitations grouped on gentle acclivities rising out of the waters, millions of minarets, a sea, like a river, covered with innumerable long, thin, boats, as swifte as gondolas, and far more gay, being carved and gilt – all these and this, when filled with a swarming population in rich and brilliant and various costume, will afford you a more lively, and certainly not a more incorrect, idea than, half a dozen pages worthy of Horace Smith.[1] There are two things here which cannot be conceived without inspection – The Bosphorus and the Bazaar. Conceive the Ocean a stream not broader than the Thames at Gravesend, with shores with all the variety and beauty of the Rhine, covered with palaces, mosques villages, groves of cypress and woods of Spanish chestnut. The view of the Euxine at the end is the most sublime thing I can remember. The Bazaar wo[ul]d delight you however more than the Bosphorus. Fancy the Burlington Arcade or some of the Parisian passages and panoramas, fancy, perhaps, a square mile of ground covered with these arcades intersecting each other in all directions, and full of every product of the Empire from diamonds to dates. The magnificence, novelty, and variety of the goods on sale, the whole nation of shopkeepers all in different dress, the crowds of buyers from all parts of the world – are just to be hinted at. Here every people have a characteristic costume. Turks Greeks, Jews and Armenians are the staple population – the latter seem to predominate. The Armenians wear round and very unbecoming black caps and robes – the Jews a black hat | wreathed with a white handkerchief – the Greeks black turbans – the Turks indulge in all combinations of costume. The meanest merchant in the Bazaar looks like a Sultan in an Easter fairy tale. This is mainly to be ascribed to the marvellous brilliancy of their dyes, which is one of the most remarkable circum-

1 Horatio (Horace) Smith (1779-1849), poet, essayist and novelist. His popular *Gaieties and Gravities* (1826) contains Levantine themes.

stances in their social life, and which never has been explained to me. A common pair of slippers that you purchase in the street is tinged of a vermilion or a lake so extraordinary, that I can compare their color to nothing but the warmest beam of a southern sunset. +

We have seen the Sultan[2] several times. He affects all the affable activity of a European Prince, mixes with his subjects, interferes in all their pursuits and taxes them most unmercifully. He dresses like an European and all the young men have adopted the fashion. You see young turks in uniforms which would not disgrace one of our crack cavalry regiments, and lounging with all the listlessness of royal illegitimates. It is on the rising generation that the Sultan depends, and if one may form an opinion, not in vain. After all his defeats, he has now sixty thousand regular infantry excellently appointed and well disciplined. They are certainly not to be compared to the French or English line – but they would as certainly beat the Spanish or the Dutch, and many think with fair play, the Russians. Fair play their monarch certainly had not during the last campaign. Its secret history wo[ul]d not now interest, but it was by other means than military prowess that the Muscovites advanced so successfully. The Sultan had to struggle against an unprecedented conspiracy the whole time, and the morning that Adrianople was treacherously delivered up, the streets of Stamboul were filled with the dead bodies of detected traitors.[3] |

Kiss my mother and Sa. Tell my dearest Sa I shall soon have her letters. I saw Lingards coldblooded hand at work in the monthly which I of course expected.[4]

Adieu my dearest father,

Your most affec[tionate]ly

BD

I have been inside a Mosque – Suleimana, which is nearly as large and far more beautiful than Sophia. The most wonderful thing here are the burial grounds – but it is vain to write – I must return, if only to save you from reading these stupid letters. I expect in ten days to be in Egypt as the wind is most favorable.[5] From that country I shall return to Malta and then to Naples – at least these are my plans which may probably not be executed. I wish to get back for Bradenham races, but very much fear I shall not, unless I can somehow or other shuffle quarantine which is a month or six weeks from these awful parts. Esperons!

[***105*** *was inserted by Ralph Disraeli as a continuation to the first sentence of the postscript*

2 Mahmoud II (1785-1839) was Sultan of the Ottoman Empire 1808-39.

3 Hostilities between Russia and the Ottoman Empire broke out in April 1828 and were terminated by the Treaty of Adrianople in September 1829. The Sultan's military effort was certainly inhibited by concern about the loyalty of the Albanian troops under Mustapha Pasha.

4 Sarah and Isaac had been curious about the author of an attack on volumes III and IV of Isaac's *Commentaries on the Life and Reign of Charles the First.* H A/IV/E/10. The review called Isaac 'a jacobite of the old school' and proclaimed the demise of Toryism. *The Monthly Review* XV (Oct 1830) 193-212. In attributing the attack to John Lingard (1771-1851), a Roman Catholic historian engaged in a work even more ambitious than Isaac's, D was probably correct.

5 This was to prove an optimistic forecast. After Constantinople (on the evidence of **110**) D and Clay went to Smyrna for a ten-day reunion with Meredith, then to Cyprus, Jaffa, Jerusalem, back to Jaffa and finally, on about 12 March, arrived at Alexandria.

in his published version of the letter, followed by the paragraph printed below, the original of which has not been located]:

Tell Ralph we are very gay here, nothing but masquerade balls and diplomatic dinners. The Ambassador has introduced us everywhere. We had the most rollicking week at the Palace, with romping of the most horrible description, and things called 'games of forfeits.' Gordon, out of the purest malice, made me tumble over head and heels! Can you conceive anything more dreadful? There are only two attachés here: Villiers, a very clever and agreeable person; and Buchanan, a good fellow.[6]

TO SARAH DISRAELI Alexandria, [Sunday] 20 March 1831 **110**

ORIGINAL: QUA 213

COVER: Miss Disraeli | Bradenham House | Wycomb. Bucks | Inghilterra | [at right angles]: INGHILTERRA

POSTMARK: (1) In circle: 12 | AVRI[L] | 1831 (2) In circle: U | AP19 | 1831 (3) In dotted circle: FPO | AP [lower half missing] (4) P.I.[?]P. | MARSEILLE[S]

PUBLICATION HISTORY: HL 111-21, dated 20 March 1831, with omissions

EDITORIAL COMMENT: There is a small hole in page three of the MS, and the final page is badly stained. *Sic*: Alessandria, agreable, cock and a bull, Sphorades, Jafa, Beirout, Sour, confectionary, Ramle, Jehosaphat, there wanderings, asmodeus.

Alessandria March 20. 1831

My dearest Sa,

Your charming letters deserve a direct commendation and therefore I address the usual bulletin to yourself. I had directed Ross to send all my letters to this place, renouncing by this arrangement the agreable chance of occasionally receiving them, for the sake of the guarantee of not missing any. He has forwarded me here only two dated Sepr. and Ocr., informing me at the same time, that he has yet three more. Is not such stupidity inconceivable? Had not your two letters been so delightful, I think I sho[ul]d, have sunk under the disappointment. I arrived here on the twelfth and wrote a hurried line by a ship which went off next day to Malta, for the other letters which he may have, and am flattered with the hope that in six weeks they will reach me.

Here I am at last in the ancient land of Priestcraft and of Pyramids, about which howr I must at present say little. It is so long since I have written altho' I miss no reasonable opportunity of so doing, that I almost forget what I was about when I wrote to you last. I think on the eve of my departure from Constant[inopl]e, Meredith having already departed for his exploration of Asia Minor, respecting which he was very mad altho' I believe it to be a country equally unsatisfactory to the topographer, the antiquarian, and the man of taste.

6 Villiers was the family name of both the Earl of Jersey and the Earl of Clarendon. No Villiers appears on the diplomatic list for Constantinople at this time, but one of them could have been a military attaché. Andrew Buchanan (1807-1882) is said by *DNB* to have been at the embassy in Constantinople between October 1825 and 13 November 1830, when he went to South America. However, this would have meant that D could not have met him during his visit. Buchanan's career in the diplomatic service was long and varied. He was knighted in 1860, and was created a baronet in 1878.

Even Leake,[1] who owes whatever dry reputation he possesses to his researches in this region, warned me against it. We remained at Const. about a fortnight after Williams Departure, and were literally unable to make our escape from our friend Sir Robert, who at last in his desperation, offered us rooms in the Palace, when we complained of our lodgings, and finally, when all was in vain, parted from us in a pet. We came with a dashing breeze down the Dardanelles, but were becalmed between Lesbos i.e. Mitylene and Zea for three days. You cannot conceive anything more lovely than the scenery of the Gulf of Smyrna, which is vaster and more beautiful than the Ambracian. At Smyrna, where we intended only to touch for a day, we were detained ten, by our winter season, violent and unceasing rains, and terrible gales of wind. Here howr. we found Meredith in a very decent bivouack, so having much to say to each o[the]r, we got over the affair better than might have been expected. This is the only winter we have had, tho' this season at Constantinople is usually even severe. I ascribe to this continuance of fine weather and to smoking the continued improvement in my health, which is most satisfactory. Your letters are delightful. I did not send you a name for James' dog because you limited me to an appropriate one, and I co[ul]d not think of any thing or person who was white at the time. I suppose it was from being in sight of Africa. The missing of the Seville letter is unaccountable and | provoking. In the crowd of impressions I cannot now tell what it was about, but shall perhaps be able when we meet. Perhaps about Frank Hall Standish whose acquaintance I made at Cadiz, and whom I met again at Seville where he resides, and who received me very hospitably – but Heaven knows. With regard to general news, I am *au jour* by the aid of Galignani's excellent journal. What endless confusions! I long to get back.

At Smyrna I found that Mer[edith] began to indicate a wish to see Egypt. The fact is that he had got hold of some books there, Hamilton's Egyptiaca[2] etc., which had opened his mind upon the subject. The truth is, as I then discovered, he knew no more about Egypt than a child, and was quite surprised to learn that there were more remains there on one spot, than in all the rest of the globe united. I did the impossible to induce him to rejoin us, but he co[ul]d not make up his mind to give up an intended trip to the unseen relics of some unhea[r]d of cock and a bull city, and so we again parted. We found ourselves again in an Archipelago, the Sphorades, and tried to make Rhodes but a contrary wind, altho' we were off it for two days, prevented us. After some days, we landed at Cyprus, where we passed a day on land famous in all ages, but more delightful to me as the residence of Fortunatus, than as the rosy realm of Venus, or the romantic Kingdom of the Crusaders. Here we got a pilot to take us to Jafa. One morning with a clear blue sky and an intense Sun, we came in sight of the whole

1 William Martin Leake (1777-1860), topographer, author and traveller. Working with William Richard Hamilton, he made a general survey of Egypt. Leake published his *Journal of a Tour in Asia Minor* in 1824. D had contact with his family in London and he was to mention an Emily Leake in 1832. See **207**.

2 *Aegyptiaca: The Ancient and Modern State of Egypt* (1810) by William Richard Hamilton (1777-1859) contained the first translations of the inscriptions on the Rosetta Stone.

coast of Syria, very high and mountainous, and the loftiest ranges covered with Snow. We passed Beirout, Sour, the ancient Tyre, St. Jean d'Acre, and at length cast anchor in the roads of Jafa. Here we made a curious acquaintance in Damiani, the descendant of an old Venetian family, but himself a perfect Oriental. We had read something about his grandfather in Volney,[3] and as he had no conception of books, he was so appalled by our learning, that had we not been Englishmen, he wo[ul]d have taken us for Sorcerers. We found him living among the most delightful gardens of oranges, citrons and pomegranates, the trees as high and the fruit as thick as our English apple orchards; himself a most elegant personage in flowing robes of crimson silk etc. etc. I am obliged to hint, rather than describe, and must reserve all detail till our meeting. He wished us to remain with him for a month, and gave us an admirable Oriental dinner, which wo[ul]d have delighted my father. Rice, spices, pistachio nuts, perfumed rotis, and dazzling confectionary. |

From Jafa, a party of six, well mounted and armed, we departed for Jerusalem. Jafa is a pretty town, surrounded by gardens, and situated in a fruitful plain. After riding over this we crossed a range of light hills and came into the plain of Ramle, vast and fertile. Ramle, the ancient Arimathea, is the model of our idea of a beautiful Syrian village all the houses isolated and each surrounded by palm trees – the meadows, and the exterior of the village covered with olive trees or divided by rich plantations of Indian fig. Here we sought Hospitality in the Latin convent, an immense establishment, well kept up, but with only one monk. I co[ul]d willingly dwell in immense detail but cannot. The next day we commenced our Journey over the delightful plain, bounded in the distance by the severe and savage mountains of Judea. In the wild stony ravines of these shaggy rocks we were wandering the whole day; at length after crossing a vast hill, we saw the Holy city. I will describe it to you from the mount of Olives. This is a very high Hill, still partially covered with the tree which gives it a name. Jerusalem is situate upon an opposite height, which descends as a steep ravine, and forms with the assistance of the mount of Olives, the narrow valley of Jehosaphat. Jerusalem is entirely surrounded by an old feudal wall with towers and gates of the time of the crusaders and in perfect preservation; as the town is built upon a hill, you can from the opposite height discern the roof of almost every house. In the front is the magnificent mosque built upon the site of the Temple, with its beautiful gardens and fantastic gates – a variety of domes and towers rise in all directions, the houses are of a bright stone. I was thunderstruck. I saw before me apparently a gorgeous city. Nothing can be conceived more wild and terrible and barren than the surrounding scenery, [...] dark, stony and severe, but the ground is thrown about in such picturesque undulations, that the mind, [is] full of the sublime, not the beautiful, and rich and waving woods, and sparkling cultivation wo[ul]d be misplaced. The city on the other side is in the plain, the ravine not being all round. It is, as it were in a bowl of mountains. I have dotted down materials for description; I have not space to de-

3 The grandfather, Jean Damiani, is mentioned in Constantine, comte de Volney *Voyage en Syrie et en Ægypte pendant les années 1783, 84 et 85* (1787 Paris repr 1959) 256.

scribe. I leave it to your lively imagination to fill up the rest. Except Athens, I never saw anything more essentially striking – no city, except that, whose site was so pre-eminently impressive. I will not place it below the city of Minerva. Athens and Jerusalem in their glory must have been the finest representations of the beautiful and the sublime. Jerusalem in its present state, wo[ul]d make a wonderful subject for Martin[4] and a picture from him co[ul]d alone give you an idea of it. We sought Hospitality from the fathers of the famous Terra Santa Convent for an account of which see Clarke.[5] There were we were told 6000 pilgrims at Jerusalem – 4000 at the Armenian convent – 2000 at the Greek. | The Latins have left off there wanderings. I sho[ul]d have said that the road w[as] all full of these gentry. One of the best houses in Jerusalem, belong'd to the convent, and servants were allotted to us. They sent us provisions daily. I co[ul]d write half a doz. sheets on this week, the most delightful of all our travels. We dined every day on the roof of our house by moonlight – visited the Holy S[epulchre] of course, tho' avoided the other coglionerias;[6] the house of Loretto is probability to them, but the Eastern will believe anything. Surprised at the number of remains at Jer – tho' none more ancient than Herod. The tombs of the Kings very fine. Weather delicious – mild summer heat – made an immense sensation – received visits from the Vicar General of the Pope, the Spanish Prior etc. Never more delighted in my life – wretched passage from Jafa to this place – where I have been a week. Mr. Briggs the great Egyptian merchant, has written from England[7] to say, that great attention is to be paid me because I am the son of the celebrated author. The consequence is we dine every day with his partner, whose cuisine is excellent. This is substantial fame.

You have been unfortunate in a Tuscan asmodeus in Maria Slin[g]sby.[8] Her sharp voice, snub nose and intense and innate vulgarity must have given effect to her second hand scandal. I am surprised to find that Miss G de C. and her spouse figured in my epistles in an heroic point of view, as I was not aware that [I] had mentioned their names. I never heard anything of the gentleman except that he was a keen jockey who took in his friends, and that Mademoiselle was something as bad, who took in Perry.[9]

4 John Martin (1789-1854), English painter of visionary and apocalyptic landscapes on biblical themes.

5 Edward Daniel Clarke (1769-1822), traveller and antiquary. He visited the eastern Mediterranean in 1801 and his account of the convent occurs in his *Travels in the Holy Land* (Philadelphia 1817) 150-1.

6 From 'coglioneria', Italian for 'piece of foolishness', 'idiocy'.

7 Samuel Briggs, a long-time confidant of Mehmet Ali, was then functioning as his sole agent in England. Richard Robert Madden *Travels in Turkey, Egypt ... in 1824, 1825, 1826, and 1827* (1829) 216 and Madden *Egypt and Mohammed Ali* (1841) 56.

8 Maria Slingsby, sister of the Rev Henry Slingsby, in 1837 married Edward Peacock, a clergyman. GM ns IX (Jan 1838) 88. Miss Slingsby had just returned from two years in Italy, and Sarah, in her best form, commented on the experience: 'She has made several pleasant English acquaintances and not spoken to a single Italian.' H A/IV/E/17. Asmodeus is said to have spent much of his time sowing discord, particularly between newly-weds.

9 Sarah relayed the gossip from Miss Slingsby: '... she says Geraldine de Courcy was in want of a dinner and that young Perry lost all his money in horse-racing.' H A/IV/E/9.

The most surprising news! Meredith has just arrived as I understand in a Turkish Ship – after a horrid passage. He writes to me to come alongside directly as they threaten him with a months quarantine. This is the case and I believe there is no chance of Escape. He w[*ill*] go mad. I am going to the Gov[ernor] Gen[eral][10] to see what can be done. He is a very good fellow. I will w[*rite*] again soon. I shall leave this place in a day or two. I have a most knowing Cy[*prian*?] servant in the most delicate costume. God bless you all. I am afraid you [*will*] never get this, as I am out of the lands of regular posts, ambassadors, and public offices.

Your most affec.

BD

111

TO SARAH DISRAELI [Cairo, Egypt], [Saturday] 28 May 1831

ORIGINAL: QUA 214

COVER: Miss Disraeli | Bradenham – House | Wycomb. Bucks | Inghilterra | [at right angles]: INGHILTERRA

POSTMARK: (1) In circle: Y | AU30 | 1831 (2) In dotted circle: [FP]O | AU30 | 1831 (3) VERONA | 20.AGO (4) VERONA | 20.AGO (5) In rectangle: [LA]ZERET[TO] | [?]SO DIL[?] (6) In small rectangle: T.I.

PUBLICATION HISTORY: HL 122-37, dated 28 May 1831, with omissions

EDITORIAL COMMENT: There is a postscript written in the left margin of the first page of the MS. The first part, a phrase, is an insertion with its intended location marked in the text. It is transcribed following D's intention. The rest, a sentence, bears no relation to the first and is transcribed as a postscript.

The right margin of the last page of the MS has a small section missing. *Sic*: musquitoes, agreable, much bore, chàsseur, *a là 'Turque*, Naroli, Atar, Fitzroy, principle art, Lybian, Hadgees, Simoom, Sphynxs, to a death.

May 28. 1831.

My dearest Sa!

I have received all your delightful letters March packet inclusive, and one from Ralph, for which give him my warmest thanks. I wrote home, to whom I forget, from Alexandria, about ten weeks ago, giving an account of my Syrian adventures, and my visit to Jerusalem, which I trust you received, but we are out of the lands of diplomatic bags, and I tremble about our dispatches. I had intended to have written by this opportunity a long letter to my father, giving him a detailed account of my travels in this ancient country, and a miscellaneous sheet to yourself, but the wonderful news[1] which meets me here in a pile of Galignanis has really quite unsettled my mind for such an exertion, and there-

The lady in question was the second daughter of Lt Col Gerald de Courcy and married in 1830 William Perry (1801-1874). After serving as master of horse to the lord lieutenant of Ireland, Perry held a number of consular posts and was knighted in 1873. *BP* under Baron Kingsale; Boase.

10 Probably he meant the senior British representative in Egypt – the agent and consul general. See 111n14.

---

1 The introduction of the Reform Bill had raised D's hopes for a seat in Parliament. He assumed that, were the Bill to pass, there would soon be a general election under the new franchise; were it to fail, and the government then to resign, there would probably also be an election.

fore I write only to you, giving only a rapid sketch of my progress, which must be finished and colored when we meet. That meeting will I trust be speedy. In fact I am only waiting here for a ship to convey me to Malta, and in all probability, shall come home straight, but at any rate, if I arrive overland, it shall delay me very little. Circumstances may even render it the shorter way, and this consideration will entirely sway me. +

I am glad that you are not as astonished as the rest at Meredith and myself parting. Considering that Egypt and Syria formed two prominent objects of my travels, and that he had so positively arranged that certainly the last, and, in all probability, the second wo[ul]d not suit him I am surprised, I confess, at their marvelling. Had it not been for the affair of the yacht which held out to me the advantage of reaching Syria, which otherwise I sho[ul]d not have been able to accomplish, we must have originally parted at Malta. Meredith – who by the bye is looking excessively well – is now at Thebes, and I have no mode of communicating with him. His letters have arrived, at Cairo, but it will be most unsafe to forward them, which co[ul]d only be done by a chance boat etc. In fact I am strongly advised against it by all persons, to say nothing of his particular request to me, when I saw him last in Upper Egypt not to forward them. If he kept to his then plans, he will return in a few days to this place, but I fear he may be tempted to advance higher. I cannot convey in writing all the considerations etc. which occur to me, but my impression is, that three or four weeks may | elapse before I sail from Alexandria, and that therefore it is pretty certain that Willm. will have returned to Cairo and will depart with me. In case however I quit Egypt with[ou]t seeing him I shall leave a letter for him, and we shall certainly meet at Malta, as I shall have to pass my quarantine there. This is a very inelegant epistle but I am writing it at night, with at least fifty musquitoes buzzing about and biting me in all directions, which destroys sentences. Clay has got an intermittent fever, which in itself is bad enough, and as he has never been ill before in his life, he is exceedingly frightened. Luckily here is a very good Frank physician. I rather imagine he will go off in a day or two to Rosetta for change of air. I am very well indeed and find the climate of Egypt delicious – very hot, but always a most refreshing breeze. I am very sorry about my companion, as he has been to me a highly agreable one. I owe much to his constant attentions. It is a great thing to travel with a man for months and that he sho[ul]d never occasion you an uneasy moment which I can sincerely say of him. Indeed I am greatly indebted to him for much comfort. You know that tho' I like to be at my ease, I want energy in those little affairs of which life greatly consists. Here I found Clay always ready – in short he saved me from much bore. I am sorry also to say that his faithful servant Giovanni better known by the name of Tita (he was Byron's chàsseur of renown) who is a Belzoni in appearance and constitution, is also very ill of a dysentery, which is a great affliction. Thus you see the strong men have all fallen while I who am an habitual invalid am firm on my legs – but the reason is this, that I – being somewhat indolent and feeble, live *a là 'Turque* while Clay and Giovanni are always in action and have done nothing but shoot and swim from morning to night. As I am on the chapter of domestic troubles, you will hear with regret that my favorite servant, a Greek of Cyprus, gave me warning yesterday, his father | being very ill at Alexandria. He leaves me directly which is a great bore at this moment especially as I am about to be alone, and wo[ul]d annoy me at all times, because he wore a Mameluke dress of crimson and gold with a white turban thirty yards long, and a sabre glittering like a rainbow. I must now content myself with an Arab attendant in a blue shirt and slipperless. How are the mighty fallen!

I cannot sufficiently commend your letters. They are in every respect charming – very lively and witty, and full exactly of the stuff I want. If you were only a more perfect mistress of the art of punctuation, you might rival Lady Mary herself.[2] Thank my mother for her remembrance of me. I cannot write to say I am quite well, because the enemy still holds out, but I am sanguine, very, and am at any rate quite well eno' to wish to be at home. I shall enquire about Naroli,[3] but for perfumes I rather think Stamboul was the best place. Mustapha's shop there, the Imperial perfumer, was my daily lounge and I never went to the Bazaar with[ou]t smoking a pipe with him. I don't think I ever mentioned this character to you – remember when we meet. He never showed me Naroli howr., tho' he did everything to tempt me to daily expense. The great perfume among the Turks is Atar of Jasmine. I have some – which I sent to Malta with all my goods, some of which will ornament Bradenham in the shape of pipes nine feet long, and curious Oriental arms. I never bought anything, but with a view to its character as furniture. Everything is for Bradenham.

Jem's commission wo[ul]d occasion me much anxiety, if I did not know anxiety were useless. If Croker really wish to serve my father, he can, whether in or out, because Lord Hill is a creature of the Duke's,[4] and a whisper from him is enough, but my father must be explicit, and not let him suppose that he wants a commission for nothing. It was no use writing to Lord Fitzroy,[5] who probably | never saw the letter. All these men have private Secretaries who have a discretion to open all letters and to answer all matters of course which this was. Tell James, I am highly pleased with him, and have no doubt he will turn out an honor to the family, and that I shall always be his friend. +

I am quite delighted with my fathers capital progress. How I long to be with him, dearest of men, fleshing[6] our quills together, and opening their minds, "standing together in our chivalry", which we will do, now that I have got the use of my brain for the first time in my life.

Tell Ralph to write as often, and as much as he likes, and that I have become a most accomplished smoker, carrying that luxurious art to a pitch of refine-

2 Lady Mary Wortley Montagu (1689-1762) was the wife of Edward Wortley Montagu, who in 1716 was appointed ambassador in Constantinople. Her observations on the East and on English society – she was an inveterate gossip – established her fame as a letter-writer.

3 Neroli was an oil extracted from orange blossoms and used as a base for perfumes.

4 Rowland Hill (1772-1842), 1st Baron Hill, in 1842 1st Viscount Hill, commander-in-chief of the Army 1828-42, owed his appointment to the Duke of Wellington.

5 Lord FitzRoy James Henry Somerset (1788-1855), after 1852 1st Baron Raglan, youngest son of the 5th Duke of Beaufort. In 1827 he was appointed military secretary at the Horse Guards. He is best remembered as the commander of the British Army in the Crimea.

6 'Fleshing', drawn from the practice of inciting hounds by taste of blood; figuratively, the term means inflammation by the foretaste of success. RD's 'flashing' is wrong.

ment of which he has no idea. My pipe is cooled in a wet silken bag, my coffee is boiled with spices, and I finish my last chibouque with a sherbet of pomegranate. Oh! the delicious fruits that we have here and in Syria – orange gardens miles in extent, citrons, limes, pomegranates – but the most delicious thing in the world is a Banana, which is richer than a Pineapple. How I long for my dear father, and how he wo[ul]d wash his mouth in a country where the principle art of life is to make a refreshing drink. +

Your visit from the Guards is most amusing. Young officers purporting to be the son of Jekyll, and the nephew of Home must have been hoaxing you. Why the first is an Antediluvian, and the second a Pre-Adamite.[7]

I don't care a jot about the Y[oung] D[uke].[8] I never staked any fame on it. It may take its chance. I meant the hero to be a model for our youth, b[*ut af*]ter two years confinement in these revol[utionar]y [*times*] I fear he will prove old-fashioned. Goethe and V[ivian G[rey] of course gratifying. I hear the Patriarch is dead. Perhaps a confusion with his son.[9] I saw it in Galignani, an excellent publication which keeps, me *au jour*. I am of course very anxious to hear of the progress of the bill. I have heard up to the majority of one.[10] On examining the lists of the votes I am inclined to think | that it will be lost, tho' I see the papers take another view, and indulge in other anticipations.

The death of Max has cut me to the heart. The epitaph is charming and worthy of the better days of our poetry. Its classical simplicity, its highly artificial finish (I mean of style), and fine natural burst of feeling at the end are remarkable, and what I believe no writer of the day co[ul]d produce. It is worthy of the best things in the anthology. It is like an inscription by Sophocles translated by Pope.[11] +

7 Sarah wrote on 22 January 1831 of two officers of the Grenadier Guards – Col Home and Capt Jekyll – who had visited Bradenham. H A/IV/E/13. These were Lt Col John Home and Edward Jekyll, then apparently only a lieutenant. Home was identified as having an uncle who was 'the author of Douglas', and Jekyll was described as the descendant of one 'who lived in this house about 50 years ago'. The first was thus the playwright John Home (1722-1808), and the second, Joseph Jekyll (1753?-1837), politician, wit and sometime resident of Bucks. D's incredulity that men of the eighteenth century should be represented by youthful sons or nephews did not last: some years later he told Lady Blessington that Jekyll had a son of his own age (**347**).

8 On 1 May Sarah had written to report on the reception of *The Young Duke*: 'Where ever we go the Y.D. is before us, and its praises for ever resounding.' H A/IV/E/21. For details of the reviews see **117**n3.

9 Sara Austen had reported that a friend had just come back from Weimar and that 'the old man himself and Madame Goethe, his son's wife, were among the warmest admirers of *Vivian Grey*: they had it on their own particular book shelves, and they spoke enthusiastically of it as being after Scott the first of their English favourites.' Goethe, according to his daughter-in-law, 'considered that there was more true originality in the work than in any he had seen for years'. M&B I 176.

Goethe lived until the following year; however his son August had died in Rome in October 1830.

10 See **117**n1.

11 Isaac's elegy on the family pet, printed in HL 130, is as follows:

Max, true descendant of Newfoundland race,
Where once he sported, finds his burial place.
Few were his months, yet huge of form tho' bland,
Well tutored by our James with voice and hand.

The account in the C[our]t J[ournal] was written by your humble servant. I did not like to appear as furnishing anything to the Journal directly, so I wrote in a dull sort of Ollierish resumé style, as from a letter.[12] +

I never told you to *buy* horses of Rymell,[13] only to *borrow* them – however I don't see, that he has behaved very nefariously.

I have gossipped a great deal with you. It is impossible to say when I shall be home, but I sho[ul]d think in three months. I do not look upon Quarantine as a bore except that it keeps me from you. I want rest. From Alexandria from whence I wrote to you last, I crossed the desert to Rosetta. It was a twelve hours job, and the whole way we were surrounded by a mirage of the most complete kind. I was perpetually deceived, and always thought I was going to ride into the sea. At Rosetta I first saw the mighty Nile, with its banks richly covered with palm groves. A grove of palms is the most elegant thing in Nature. From Rosetta five days in a capital boat, which the Consul[14] had provided for us with cabins and every convenience and which recently he had had entirely painted and fitted up for Lord Clare,[15] took us to Cairo through the famous Delta. This greatly reminded me of the rich plains of the Pays Bas – quite flat with a soil in every part like the finest garden mould – covered with production but more productive than cultivated. The banks of the river studded with villages of mud, but all clustered in palm groves beautiful – moonlight on | the Nile indescribably charming and the palms by this light perfectly magical. Grand Cairo a large town of dingy houses of unbaked brick, looking terribly dilapidated, but swarming with population in rich and various costume. Visited the Pyramids and as-

Mild in his pensive face his large dark eyes
Talked in their silence to our sympathies.
His awful paw our fond salute would hail,
And pleasure fluttered in the o'ershadowing tail.
Vast limb'd, his step resounding as he walk'd,
The playful puppy like a lion stalk'd;
All clad in spotless snow he seemed to stand
Like faultless marble from the sculptor's hand.
Domestic friend, companion of all hours!
Our vacant terraces and silent bow'rs
No more repeat thy name, and by this urn
Not to love dogs too well we sadly learn.

2 Presumably this refers to the item which appeared in *The Court Journal* on 29 January, and is mentioned in the letter to Colburn of 18 November 1830 (See **102**). The account was said to have been from all three of the young travellers. Obviously D entertained no very high opinion of the style of the oriental romances of Charles Ollier (1788-1859), Shelley's publisher. For D's earlier relations with Ollier see **71**n3.

3 Sarah provoked this comment by writing that 'Your friend Rymell has taken us in ... we gave him £25 for a horse not worth £5.' H A/IV/E/14. Rymell was a local farmer.

4 John Barker (1771-1849) was consul general in Egypt, 1829-33. Previously he had been consul at Alexandria. His correspondence records the meeting: 'I was much pleased with the manners of Clay and Disraeli. They are gone up the country, and purpose on their return to pass the winter in Cairo.' Edward B.B. Barker ed *Syria and Egypt under the Last Five Sultans of Turkey* (1876 repr New York 1973) II 168. The spelling of D's name was probably modernized by the editor.

5 John Fitzgibbon (1792-1851), 2nd Earl of Clare, governor of Bombay 1830-4. He had no doubt stopped in Egypt en route to his post.

cended the great one, from the top of which some weeks afterwards a man, by name Maze, whom I had slightly known in Spain, tumbled, and dashed himself to a mummy.[16] Very awful – the first accident of the kind. A Voyage of three weeks in the same boat to Thebes – banks of the river very different. The Delta ceases at Cairo, and Egypt now only consists of a valley formed by a river running through a desert. The land is however equally rich the soil being formed by the Nile, but on each side at the distance of 3 or 4 miles, and sometimes much nearer, Deserts. The Lybian desert on the African side is exactly our common idea of a desert, an interminable waste of burning sand, but the Arabian and Syrian deserts very different; in fact what we call Downs. Landing on the African side one night, where the Desert stretches to the very banks, found a ship of Hadgees[17] emptied on the shore in the most picturesque groups, some squatting down with their pipes, some boiling coffee, some performing their devotions. It was excessively close, but had been a fine clear day. I walked nearly a mile from the shore – in an instant very dark, with a heat perfectly stifling – saw a column of Sand in the distance. It struck me directly what it was. I rushed to the boat with full speed, but barely quick enough. I cannot describe the scene of horror and confusion. It was a Simoom. The wind was the most awful sound I ever heard. Five columns of sand taller than the monument | emptied themselves on our party. Every sail was rent to pieces, men buried in the earth. Three boats sailing along overturned, the crews swam to shore – the wind, the screaming, the shouting, the driving of the sand were eno' to make you mad. We shut all the windows of the cabin, and jumped into bed, but the sand came in like fire. I do not offer this as a description, but as a mem. for further details. +

As for Dendera and Thebes and the remains in every part of upper Egypt, it is useless to attempt to write. Italy and Greece mere toys to them, and Martin's inventions common place. Conceive a feverish and tumultuous dream full of triumphal gates, processions of paintings, interminable walls of heroic sculpture, granite colossi of Gods and Kings, prodigious obelisks, avenues of Sphynxs and halls of a thousand columns, thirty feet in girth and of a proportionate height. My eyes and mind yet ache with grandeur so little in unison with our own littleness – there the landscape too was quite cha[*racteristic*], mountains of burning sand, vegetation unnatur[*ally*] vivid, groves of cocoa trees, groups of croc[*odiles*] and an ebony population in a state of nud[*ity*] armed with spears of reeds.

Having followed the course of the Nile for seven hundred miles to the very confines of Nubia, we returned. As an antiquary I might have been tempted to advance to have witnessed further specimens, but I was satisfied, and I wish[*ed*] not to lose time unnecessarily. We were a week at Thebes with the advantage of the society of Mr. Wilkinson[18] an Englishman of vast learning, who has devoted

16 A letter of 11 April 1831 from the consul-general told the story of 'the melancholy end of Mr. Maze, son of a Bristol merchant well known in Smyrna. I suspect a suicide, for there is no instance in the traditions of Egypt that a person has ever fallen off the Pyramids.' Barker *Syria and Egypt* II 168.

17 Hadjis, or pilgrims who had been to Mecca.

18 John Gardner Wilkinson (1797-1875), Egyptologist. He was knighted in 1839.

ten years to the study of hieroglyphics and Egyptian antiquity, and who can read you the side of an obelisk, or the front of a pylon, as we wo[ul]d the last number of the Quarterly. | This Cairo in spite of its dinginess is a luxurious and pleasant place. The more I see of Oriental life, the more I like. There is much more enjoyment than at Constantinople. I have seen the Pacha in a very extraordinary manner. Wandering in the gardens of his palace at Shubra, I suddenly came upon him one afternoon surrounded by his Court, a very brilliant circle, in most gorgeous dresses, particularly the black eunuchs in scarlet and gold, and who ride white horses. I was about to retire, but one of his principal attendants took me by the arm and led me to the circle. The Pacha is exceed[ing]ly fond of the English. His H[ighne]ss was playing chess with his fool, and I witnessed a very curious scene. I stayed about a quarter of an hour, and had I waited till his game was finished, I am informed that he wo[ul]d have spoken to me, but as I had no interpreter with me, and am pretty sure that he was in the same state, I thought it best to make my bow. My presentation has been delayed on account of Clay's illness, but it has been offered to me several times. I look forward to it rather as a bore than not – as he receives you quite alone and X [cross-] examines you to a death. | A thousand loves to all – Write to Malta until the July packet inclusive.

your most affec. brother

BD

Also you need not be alarmed about my locks.

TO ISAAC D'ISRAELI — Cairo, [Wednesday] 20 July 1831 — **112**

ORIGINAL: H A/IV/E/30

COVER: Read this first, and alone. | I. Disraeli Esq.

PUBLICATION HISTORY: M&B I 177-8, dated 20 July 1831, omitting the medical details

EDITORIAL COMMENT: A draft of this letter is in the Hughenden papers A/IV/E/29. This was the covering letter with which were enclosed the two following letters and the medical reports. *Sic*: (, I am; sate.

Cairo. July 20. 1831.

READ THIS ALONE

My dearest father,

If you were not a great philosopher, as well as a good man, I do not think, that I could summon courage to communicate to you the terrible intelligence which is now to be imparted by this trembling pen; but I have such confidence in your wisdom, as well as in your virtue, that it is your assistance to which I look in the saddest office that has ever yet devolved upon me, because I know that the joint influence of your experience and your benevolent soul will at the same time assist the sufferers in forming a juster estimate of their loss than can occur in the first pangs of affliction, and offer the only solace which is precious to a refined mind – the Sympathy of one as refined.

You have already guessed the fatal truth – our William is lost to us. I feel that I must repeat it. It is too terrible to believe. He returned to Cairo in the finest health and spirits. I had waited for him to return together. Our departure was postponed for a week or two for his sake. About nine or ten days ago (, I am too

| distracted to remember dates) on the very eve of departure he felt himself unwell, and called in a Frank physician of the name of Gaetani,[1] who has recently arrived in Cairo, to preside over the Pasha's hospitals. He is the best physician here. He was in every respect a man of skill, education and experience, quite unlike the medical characters that you meet in this country, and we had great confidence in him, particularly from the judicious manner in which he had treated Clay in a fever. Gaetani said there was inflammation in the bowels, bled him in the arm, and applied leeches to the part. The pain went off, but some fever remained, but not very great. Clay went off to Alexandria to see after a ship, and I remained with our friend. On the third day, the small pox developed itself in a copious eruption, but it was of a modified kind, and there was no dangerous symptom. Gaetani assured me that all wo[ul]d go well that it was a kind that never was fatal, | that it must take its course, that he wo[ul]d not even be marked. Our poor friend had no pain, and never lost his confidence for a moment. Each day the suppuration advanced, and yesterday the 19th. July Gaetani came as usual in the morning and examined him, and said that all was well, that in all probability tomorrow the eruption wo[ul]d commence disappearing. Our dear friend complained of an oppression in his chest from phlegm. Gaetani ordered him some squills and went away, perfectly easy; he said he was going on as well as possible, that he had not a dangerous symptom. About five o'clock one of his attendants came running into an adjoining room, where I was conversing with a son of Botta the historian,[2] a very scientific traveller and a surgeon, and told me that his master had fainted. I took Botta[3] along with me who opened a vein, the blood flowed, but not strongly, the body was quite warm in every part. The terrible truth – apparent to all, never occurred to me, but I will not dwell on my own horrible | sufferings. So much now depends upon me, that I feel I must not give way. I wo[ul]d willingly have given my life for his. I will send for the satisfaction of his family by this post if possible a report by his physician. I will also write to his sister to break the intelligence to his family, enclosing some lines to his father. I will enclose both of them to you open, that you may read them, and send them if you think proper.[4] My principal reason in

1 Dr F. Gaetani prepared, in Italian, a full report on Meredith's illness. D enclosed the report with this letter to Isaac to be sent to Meredith's family, together with an English translation, the full text of which is given in **113**n3. There is a postscript of 27 lines of comment added by D at a later date, possibly on his return to England, and certainly after his stay at Malta on the return voyage.

2 Carlo Giuseppe Gugliemo Botta (1766-1837), historian and surgeon. His principal work was a history of Italy between 1789 and 1814, which was published in 1824.

3 Paul Emile Botta (1802-1870), archaeologist, Assyriologist and (on the evidence of this letter) surgeon. In the 'Mutilated Diary' D described Botta as 'the man from whom I have gained most in conversation ... the most philosophic mind that I ever came in contact with. Hour after hour has glided away, while chibouque in mouth we have disserted together upon our Divan, in a country where there are no journals and no books. My mind made a jump in these higher discourses. Botta was wont to say that they formed also an era in his intellectual life.' H A/III/C. See app III. Letters to D from Botta are preserved in the Hughenden papers (A/IV/F).

4 It is probable that Isaac did not forward Gaetani's report, with its translation, to Georgiana Meredith with **113**, judging so much detail to be inappropriate at such an early stage of the Merediths' grief. It could well have awaited D's return and then been sent on with D's further comments as postscript (**113**n3).

writing them is that you should be quite unoccupied, and devote yourself solely to one who indeed requires solace.

Oh! my father when I think of this I am nearly mad. Why do we live? The anguish of my soul is great. Our innocent lamb, our angel is stricken. The joy of our eyes and hearts. Save her! Save her! I will come home directly. I think that I shall return in the September packet, which returns from Malta on the first Octr. | Let me have a line, if possible, by it as it comes out.

My dear father, I do not know whether I have said all that is necessary. It requires great exertion not to go distracted. I have sent off a Courier to Clay. Mr. Botta has been very kind to me, and sate up all night with me, as I could not sleep, and dared not be alone, as my anguish was very great. I wish to live only for my sister. I think of her all day and all night. It is some satisfaction that I was with our friend in his last moments. Oh! my father I trust a great deal to you and my dear Mother. I do not know what to write, what to think. I have not said anything that I wanted, yet I have said too much. God bless you my dear father. Embrace them all. I wish that I could mingle my tears with yours.

Your ever affectionate Son

B. Disraeli

I have written to his sister. I cannot, I cannot write to his father. I have begun a thousand times. There is not a single topic of consolation. His death they say was occasioned by intense internal inflammation of which there was no outward symptom as pain etc. ending in an internal hemorrhage which issued from the mouth. Botta says this is not uncommon.

T.O. |

They tell me I must send duplicates of all these letters for safety – I will do it.

TO GEORGIANA MEREDITH Cairo, [Wednesday] 20 July 1831 **113**

ORIGINAL: FE EJM 13

COVER: Miss Meredith

EDITORIAL COMMENT: There is a copy of this letter in the Hughenden papers (A/IV/E/31) which has slight variations, and which is doubtless the duplicate to which D refers in the postscript of his letter written to Isaac on the same day. At the time of the preparation of this edition, this letter and its accompanying medical reports were in the possession of Messrs Francis Edwards, London.

Cairo. July 20. 1831.

READ THIS ALONE

My Dear Georgiana![1]

There are crises in life which require all our energy to endure, and yet under which, when mellowed by Time, by Sympathy, by Reason, and by Religion, we are sometimes not ungrateful that a benevolent Nature has permitted us to sup-

1 Georgiana Esther Meredith, sister of William George Meredith, who married the Rev Edward Higgins on 7 February 1833. *The Times* (8 Feb 1833). The entry for her appears in Walford's *County Families* until 1900, but not in 1901.

port ourselves. One of these crises has now arrived for us all; and it will require all that strength of mind which I have ever observed in you, and all those delightful and amiable feelings, which we have long acknowledged with admiration, to support it yourself, to communicate its import to your family, and to strengthen and to solace them under its irresistible and overwhelming affliction.

The fatal quickness of an affectionate mind has already whispered to you the dreadful truth. Yes! my dear and much loved friend, it is indeed too true. Our William is lost to us. That friend of our lives, that joy, and hope, and expectation, can no more sweeten our existence with his society, enliven us with his presence, and gladden us with his promise. All is over, and he has yielded to his Creator without a bodily, or mental, pang, that pure, and honorable, and upright, soul, which we all so honored and esteemed: he has suddenly closed a life unsullied by a vice, scarcely by a weakness. Such a death is too awful but | for those who are virtuous as himself, and if we regret that the unconsciousness of his approaching fate has occasioned him to quit us without leaving some last memento of his affection, let us console ourselves by the recollection of the anguish, that the same cause has spared him.

I will endeavour, in spite of the distraction of my mind, calmly and shortly to trace to you the progress of this fatal result. He returned to Cairo in the finest health and spirits: never was he looking better, never more cheerful. I had waited for him in order that we might return together. Our departure was postponed a week or two for his sake. About nine or ten days ago, on the very eve of departure, he felt himself unwell, and called in a Frank physician by name Gaetani, who has recently arrived here to preside over the military hospitals. He is by far the best physician here. He is in every respect a man of skill, education and experience, quite unlike the medical characters that you meet in this country, and we had great confidence in him, particularly from the judicious manner in which he had treated Clay in a fever. Gaetani said there was inflammation in the bowels, bled him in the arm, and applied leeches to the part. The pain went off, but some fever remained but not very great. Clay went off to Alexandria to see after a ship, and I remained with your brother. On the third day the SMALL POX developed itself in a copious eruption, but it was of a modified kind, and there was no dangerous symptom. Gaetani assured me that all would go well, that it was a kind that never was fatal, that it | must take its course, that all that medical skill could now [do] was to watch its progress, and that he would not even be marked. Our poor friend had no pain, and never lost his confidence for a moment; he never supposed that it would be more than an affair of a few days. Each day the Suppuration advanced, and yesterday, the 19th. July, Gaetani came as usual early in the morning and examined him, and said that all was well, and that in all probability on the next day, the eruption wo[ul]d commence disappearing. Our dear friend complained of an oppression on his chest from phlegm. Gaetani ordered him some squills, and went away, perfectly easy: he said he was going on as well as possible, that he had not a dangerous symptom. About five o'ck one of his attendants came running into an adjoining room where I was conversing with a gentleman of the name of Botta, a very scientific traveller, and who has studied surgery, and told me that his master had fainted. I took Botta along with me who opened a vein. The blood flowed, but not strongly. The body was quite warm in every part, and remained so for some time. Every thing was done and tried. The terrible truth apparent to all never occurred to me, but I will not dwell on my own sufferings. After a night of horror I rise with the determination of doing my duty which is imperative. I write to you therefore without loss of time, because tomorrow I may be unable. I will not attempt to console you. Find consolation in your own heart. I would willingly have given my life for his, for his was much more precious.

I | write by this post to a family to whom he was scarcely less dear. Oh! there is one member of it, my dearest Georgiana, of whom I think with unutterable anguish – but let me not speak of others. I have tried to write to your Excellent father,[2] but cannot. Tender him my duty and my affection, and let him rest assured, that I will not neglect the corpse or the memory of the friend to whom I was devoted. I have ordered the Physician to draw up a report.[3] Farewell, farewell! What, what is life, if it lead only to such agony. Farewell! I wish that I could mingle the tears I am fast shedding with your own.

Your affectionate friend,

Benjn Disraeli

The rites of the English Church will be performed by a Protestant Missionary.

2 William George Meredith Sr.

3 Account of the last illness of W.G. Meredith Esqre

Mr. W.G. Meredith an English traveller of about 29 years of age who had for some months been living in the best health in this city (Cairo) was attacked on the 11th of July 1831 by sudden indisposition. Being sent for to attend him I proceeded to the house of the invalid whom I found with the following symptoms.

Fever of an inflammatory nature, throbbing pain in the head, eyes sunk, face flushed, animated, mouth dry, tongue whitish, the edges and tip red, thirst, pain in the epigastric region which was increased by pressure, retching, and vomiting a substance of a white mucous nature, pains in the loins, a feeling of weariness particularly in the great articulations of the body and limbs, constipation etc.

I immediately ordered 12 ounces of blood to be taken from him, and prescribed an enimma [*sic*] of decoction of mallows, | and a mucilligenous [*sic*] draught.

The same day towards evening Mr. Meredith informed me, he had perspired much during the day, that the pain in the head was a little diminished but that in other respects he found no alteration since the morning.

On the second day's illness the pain in the head stomach, and loins had decreased, but as pressure with the hand on the epigastric region was painful, and as the fever and throbbing continued, I had thirty leeches applied on the epigastric region, advising when these fell off, that the stomach should be covered with an emollient cataplasm, which should be changed every three, or four hours, with the intention both of promoting bleeding from the bites of these insects, and of fomenting the bowels, which were evidently so much affected.

The evening of this day there was no alteration – during the day the patient slept for some hours.

The third day all the symptoms had diminished, the fever was slighter, the pain nearly removed, the breathing almost natural, and every thing indicated a speedy recovery, when on the evening of this day, I observed on | the face of the patient an unusual redness like erysipelas in spots dispersed over it irregularly in which spots on closer examination I discovered the marks of pustules.

The period of the eruption the place where it first appeared, and the form it assumed, joined to the progressive cessation of the gastric symptoms as the eruption appeared, authorized me in characterizing the illness as small pox.

The fourth the fifth and the sixth days the eruption showed itself successively in the face, throat breast, arms, and the rest of the body, and the lower extremities. The eruption proceeded mildly, the pustules were full of limpid matter, nothing wrong was observed in the functions of the viscera, head, breast, and lower stomach, the fever was mitigated, and every thing promised a happy termination.

The seventh day the pustules on the face began to grow yellow, the period for suppuration having arrived. The evening of this day, the pulse was more frequent, | and the patient complained of a sensation of fullness on the stomach, and thick mucus which rising to the throat, was expectorated with difficulty. His mouth became dry, and the thirst increased; but as it is known to every medical man who is tolerably well acquainted with his profession, that in the commencement of the period of suppuration, the gastric symptoms are seen to re-appear and that they disappear of themselves after 24 or 36 hours, I only saw in this case the regular and constant progress of the disease.

Mr. Meredith asked for a refreshing drink, and I prescribed for him mineral lemonade slightly acidulated with sulphuric acid and sweetened with syrup of mallows.

The eighth day the pulse was quieter, every thing had returned to the former state except the mucus which annoyed the patient.

The ninth and last day of this illness Mr. Meredith complained more than ever of the difficulty of the expectoration of the above mentioned mucus on account of its being so glutinous; I prescribed three ounces of | Oxymel of Squills as an expectorant a tea spoon full to be taken occasionally. It is to be observed that there were no symptoms denoting the slightest derangement in the visceral functions.

It was 9 o'clock in the morning when I visited Mr. Meredith and I congratulated him sincerely on the mild progress of a malady in so many cases fatal. About 4 o'clock in the afternoon I was sent for very hastily Mr. Meredith having (as his servant informed me) fainted. I hastened immediately to the patient's abode; and found him pale, with his mouth open, deprived entirely of circulation either arterial, or of the heart. The eruption of the small pox was still on the skin, the pustules on the face and part of those on the neck in a state of suppuration, those on the breast, arms, and lower part of the stomach of a red colour and full of lymph, but those on the extremities had assumed a violet hue.

When I arrived at the house of Mr. Meredith I found that | Dr. Botta had attempted to bleed him, but could only obtain a few drops of blood.

A death so melancholy and unexpected can only be attributed by me to the afflusion of a quantity of mucus in the trachea by which suffocation was caused.

Signed Doctor F. Gaetani.

[D *added the following at the end of the document which contained Dr Gaetani's original report*]:

I think it proper to add that Dr. Gaetani only examined the body of my lamented friend immediately after the decease, that he was then obliged to go into the country, and that the funeral necessarily took place before his return next day.

The body was examined by Mr. Botta the following morning. The blood was flowing from the mouth, and from this, and from other symptoms, Mr. Botta was confirmed in his decided opinion, that the sudden decease was occasioned by an internal hemorrhage. As however he had not attended my friend in his lifetime, Mr. Botta declined giving any formal written opinion. I also submitted this statement to several of the most eminent military Surgeons at Malta, with whom I was acquainted. One of these, Mr. [George] Martin of the 73rd., had attended his own regiment at Malta when the Small Pox was raging in it. He was therefore particularly | qualified to decide. It was his conviction, as well as that of the others, that the decease was occasioned by an internal hemorrhage, which is not unusual. I mention these particulars, because from the rapid alteration after this fatal event, the body of my friend was not opened, altho' I had instantly expressed a desire that it sho[ul]d be.

Benj. Disraeli

TO SARAH DISRAELI [Cairo, Wednesday 20 July 1831] 114

ORIGINAL: H A/I/B/1

PUBLICATION HISTORY: M&B I 178-9: from draft, with omissions

EDITORIAL COMMENT: There is also a draft of this letter, H A/IV/E/29. There is no signature.

My own Sa!

Ere you open this page, our beloved father will have imparted to you with all the tenderness of parental love the terrible intelligence which I have scarcely found courage enough to communicate to him. It is indeed true. Yes! our friend of many years, our life, and joy, and consolation, is in this world lost to us for ever. He has yielded to his Creator without a bodily, or mental, pang, that pure and honorable and upright soul, which we all so honored, and so esteemed; he has suddenly closed a life unsullied by a vice, scarcely by a weakness. Such a death is too awful but for those who are virtuous as himself, and if we regret, that the unconsciousness of his approaching fate has occasioned him to quit us without leaving some last memento of his affection, let us console ourselves by the recollection of the anguish that the same cause has spared him.

Oh! | my sister, in this hour of overwhelming affliction my thoughts are only for you. Alas! my beloved! if you are lost to me, where, where, am I to fly for refuge! I have no wife, I have no betrothed, nor since I have been better acquainted with my own mind and temper, and situation, have I sought them. Live then my heart's treasure for one, who has ever loved you with a surpassing love, and who would cheerfully have yielded his own existence to have saved you the bitterness of reading this. Yes! my beloved! be my genius, my solace, my companion, my joy! We will never part, and if I cannot be to you all of our lost friend, at least we will | feel, that Life can never be a blank while illumined by the pure and perfect love of a Sister and a Brother!

TO BENJAMIN AUSTEN Alexandria, [Egypt], [Wednesday] 3 August 1831 115

ORIGINAL: BL ADD MS 45908 ff39-40

COVER: Benj. Austen Esq | Raymond Blgs Grays Inn | London | *Inghilterra* | PRIVATE | [at right angles]: INGHILTERRA | [In another hand]: Recd. and forwarded by Y.O.S. Jno. Rowlett & Co. | Malta 9th. Septr *1831*

PUBLICATION HISTORY: Jerman 127-8, dated 3 August 1831

EDITORIAL COMMENT: There is a small tear in the last page of the MS. *Sic*: unmitigable, agreable.

Alexandria. August 3 1831.

My dear Austen,

Ere you receive this you will be apprised of that miserable event, that will in all probability cast a gloom over the whole of my after life, and which, from your intimate acquaintance with the families, whom it will plunge, I fear, in unmitigable affliction, you cannot have learnt with[out] deep sorrow. I cannot write upon it, nor upon anything else. Thank Mrs Austen for her letter, which, tho' written long ago, I have not very long received. I was about to answer it, giving her a full account of all late adventures, | but these must now be reserved for future converse. I return instantly to England, and have drawn upon you here for no less a sum than two hundred pounds, which I hope you will pardon, as I shall arrive almost as soon as the bill. I wished to tell you the reason that I have thus troubled you, but I am not now equal to a long story. Suffice it to say, that your assistance at this moment prevents | me from putting myself under any obligation to Colburn, and I have reason to believe that it may be of the utmost importance to my success to find myself on my return, at least not obliged to such a publisher as our little fri[*end*].

Farewell my dear friend. You have assisted me so often that in this hour of affliction I feel, doubly feel, the value of a real friend. I hope that in future you will find me one more agreable, and less troublesome.

Ever Yrs

B. Disraeli

Supposing you may be absent, I have written a line to Percival[1] mentioning that I was about unexpectedly to draw.

---

116 TO ISAAC D'ISRAELI

Quarantine Station, Malta, [Wednesday] 7 [September] 1831

ORIGINAL: EGT 1

COVER: I. Disraeli Esqre. | Bradenham House | Wycomb. Bucks | *England*

PUBLICATION HISTORY: Sotheby's catalogue (12-13 Dec 1977) item 311, extracts

EDITORIAL COMMENT: The letter is written from the 'Lazaretto', or quarantine station, and the MS is slightly discoloured by three brown spots, possibly as a result of having been disinfected. *Dating*: D has dated this letter 'August', but at the top of the first page of the MS in Isaac's hand is: 'Recd 3/9 October[.] Should this not be *Septr.*?' Isaac is undoubtedly right. In **112** D expressed his intention of returning 'in the September packet, which returns from Malta on the first Octr.' As **115** to Austen made clear, he was still in Alexandria on 3 August, and speaks here of just arriving after a long passage of five weeks. The month therefore is certainly September.

Malta – Lazaretto | August. 7. 1831

My dearest father,

I arrived here last night after a long passage of five weeks and am placed nearly in double quarantine on account of the Cholera Morbus which has broke out in Egypt. In consequence however of having left my ship immediately, and other circumstances too long to detail, I am led to hope that my imprisonment may be shortened, and my conviction is that I shall be able to leave this port by the return September packet.

I can write no more. The harrowing suspense, which I must experience, until I learn in what manner my last dreadful notification has been received, deprives me of the power, and the desire, of communicating less | important affairs, or of noticing in detail your interesting letters, all of which I have received. For me, under the circumstances in which I am placed, my lamented friend dies again each day. Yet even under the pressure of this calamity, I am supported by the hope that I may administer to the consolation of those I love. I will not now talk of happiness, but Time may bring even this treasure.

Farewell my dearest father. I am in excellent health. Let us yet indulge in

1 A partner in Willis, Percival & Co, bankers at 76 Lombard Street.

Hope. Kiss my mother, and whisper to my beloved Sa, that my heart is entirely hers.

Your affectionate Son

Benj Disraeli |

Authentic intelligence has this moment been received here that the whole of Pera, with the Ambassadors Palaces etc. has been burnt to the ground.[1]

TO ISAAC D'ISRAELI Falmouth, Sunday 23 October 1831 **117**

ORIGINAL: H A/IV/E/32

COVER: I. Disraeli Esqre. | Bradenham House | Wycomb | *Bucks.*

POSTMARK: (1) In double circle: FALMOUTH | OC22 | 1831

EDITORIAL COMMENT: This letter was begun on Monday 17 October 1831, in the frigate HMS *Hermes* off Cape St Vincent, and the postscript, dated Sunday 23 October 1831, was added on her arrival at Falmouth. Although the postmark is for the preceding day, such endorsement was not uncommon for letters posted on Sundays, and it seems probable that D's dating is correct.

The paper is torn on the last page of the MS. *Sic*: unburthern, my my.

H.M.S. Hermes | off Cape St. Vincent | Octr. 17. 1831

My dearest father and friend,

No letter by the packet. I sometimes fear that you have not received the awful letter, particularly as I see no notice in the papers. I say nothing of my own sufferings. The Suspense is terrible, but I wo[ul]d willingly endure the sum of all human suffering, to alleviate those of my beloved Sister.

I hope to be in harbour on Sunday or Monday, in town by Thursday, when I will write to you again. Turning affairs every way, I do not see that I can be less than a week in town. You cannot conceive the state I am in; literally not a shirt to my back – and nothing but Turkish Slippers and a single coat – and I have no wish to return to town again.

Will you have a stall or two cleared out for me. I take it for granted your two stall stable is occupied. Do not suppose by this that I am about to bring a whole stud from Araby the blest, but I may require some accommodation, and in case I bring a groom, you will object to his sleeping in the house. The room over the stables had therefore better be cleared, and put in order. I am sorry to trouble you at this moment with such trivial matters, but it | [is] better not to take you by surprise.

If the Reform Bill pass,[1] I intend to offer myself for Wycomb. Henry Stanley, the brother of the Secretary,[2] whose acquaintance I made in Spain and who is at

[1] Pera, the European quarter of Constantinople, burned down on 2 August 1831. Some 20,000 houses were destroyed, including the residence of the British ambassador.

---

[1] Grey's Whig government had come to power in November 1830 and Lord John Russell had introduced the Reform Bill in the House of Commons on 1 March 1831. Second reading was passed by a majority of one on 23 March, but defeated in committee on 19 April. Following the dissolution on 22 April, the Whigs and their allies swept back with a majority of 140. The new Parliament met in June, and the Bill passed the Commons on 21 September, but on 8 October the Lords rejected it.

[2] Edward Geoffrey Stanley (1799-1869), after 1834 Baron Stanley, and after 1851 14th Earl of Derby, was chief secretary for Ireland from November 1830 to March 1833. He was colonial secretary 1833-4, 1841-5, and prime minister 1852, 1858-9, 1866-8.

His younger brother was Henry Thomas Stanley (1803-1875). He was Whig MP for Preston 1832-7. See also **124**n7.

present my fellow traveller, finds however a letter at Cadiz, which tells him it will be lost, but we can scarcely credit it.

I am very well indeed. My complaint seems almost suddenly to have quitted me. It is the hope of contributing to all your happiness that alone supports me.

The Y[oung] D[uke][3] is of course forgotten, or rather has never been remembered. He was indeed, a singing bird in a Storm, and the thunder crushed his chirp, but this I expected and it has not given me a moments uneasiness. I have some of the right stuff ready for them, but probably shall let a year at least pass over before I publish. I am at last going to attack them in good earnest.[4] I think you will agree that I have at length knocked | the nail on the head, but Time will show. Whatever may be the result, I shall at least unburthern my mind, which is absolutely necessary, whatever is to be my future occupation. You will be surprised, perhaps even astounded at the quantity I have planned and written – constant intellectual exertion is now my only resource. The [*fata*]l event has entirely changed [*my chara*]cter, or rather forced me to recur to my original one. I wish no more to increase the circle of domestic sympathies, since they lead to such misery – I will cherish what remain threefold.

Adieu my dearest Sir[e]. I leave this open for a line from Falmouth.

Sunday Octr 23.

Just arrived, found your letter. Shall be in town I think on Wednesday and Thursday. Let me find a letter at my my old Albergo, the Union, and write upon it, "to be *called* for."

BD

---

118 TO BENJAMIN AUSTEN Union Hotel, [London], Monday [31 October 1831]

ORIGINAL: BL ADD MS 45908 ff41-2

PUBLICATION HISTORY: Jerman 130-1, dated 'late October 1831'

EDITORIAL COMMENT: *Dating*: by comparison with **117** of 23 October, from Falmouth, in which D said that he would be in London by Wednesday or Thursday. This letter reported his delay at Exeter for two days en route, which would be consistent with his arrival in London on Sunday, 30 October 1831.

Union Hotel | Monday.

My dear Austen,

I arrived in town yesterday with the intention of staying a week, but a letter from Bradenham calls me off this morning. I shall return in a few days. We shall then meet, and I sho[ul]d have called even now for a minute, had I not

3 *The Young Duke* had been quite well received in some quarters, leading, for example, to the claim that D had fine powers although his judgement was deficient. *The Literary Gazette* no 743 (16 Apr 1831) 242-3. But some reviewers found the work repulsive because of its author's obvious fascination with the aristocracy. Stewart *Novels* 136-8. Monypenny describes a family tradition that Isaac, on first hearing of the book, said: '*The Young Duke*! What does Ben know of dukes?' M&B I 128.

4 The reading public.

been confined nearly to my | bed by an inflammation on my chest. I have been nearly, or rather above, a week getting up to town. It never ceased raining for six days from the moment of landing. I caught a cold, the severity of which made up for having been exempt from such inflictions so long, and was obliged | fairly to lie up at Exeter for two days – otherwise in famous condition, indeed better than I ever was in my life, and full of hope and courage, in spite of the overwhelming catastrophe. I am most nervous about my first interview today,[1] but any chance of tolerable existence for the great | sufferer depends upon my maintenance of self.

Adieu. A thousand good wishes to my dear friends. We shall meet in a very few days, and have much to say.

Yrs ever and truly

BD

119

TO GEORGIANA MEREDITH Bradenham, [Thursday] 3 November 1831

ORIGINAL: FE EJM 6-i
COVER: Miss Meredith | 5 Paragon Buildings | Bath Road | Cheltenham
POSTMARK: (1) In rectangle: Cheltenham | Penny Post (2) HIGH WYCOM[BE]
PUBLICATION HISTORY: M&B I 179, extract dated 1831
EDITORIAL COMMENT: The first page of the MS is edged in black.

Bradenham House. Novr. 3/31

My dearest Georgiana,

I have made a very slow progress to Bradenham, for the English climate saluted me with its most rigorous influence, and I found myself so knocked up at Exeter with a feverish cold, that I was obliged to remain there, and afterwards proceed by more moderate stages.

I am once more in England, and my first anxieties and enquiry after those faces which now surround me are for you, and for your hearth. I would have written to your dear father, but I was not sure, whether a letter might not disturb him, and you will therefore assure him that it is for this reason, and not because he is absent from my thoughts, which he has not been for a moment for many months.

Do you wish that we should meet? Say the word, and I will be with you at Chelten[ha]m | instantly, or join you in town, or do exactly what you wo[ul]d wish. Pray speak upon this subject with perfect frankness, and believe that I can never have a dearer pleasure than to contribute to your comfort and satisfaction.

I was obliged to forward by another ship, than that in which I reached Malta, the wardrobe etc. of our lost friend, but, acting as I have done throughout this business as his virtual executor, I have possessed myself of all his papers, trinkets and slight articles, which retain an interest from having been his constant companions. These I shall deliver to you at the first opportunity.

1 With Sarah.

His papers are very interesting. They consist of a journal, and an unfinished, but advanced, work upon Egyptian Architecture. I have sometimes thought, my dear Georgiana, that it might be consolatory, that the memory of one so ingenious, as well as so virtuous, sho[ul]d not | be permitted to die away without a record – and that, at least for private circulation, his principal productions, with extracts from the most interesting parts of his journals, might be printed, heralded by a memoir in which one who knew him well and long, might attempt to do justice to a life ennobled by virtue, and distinguished by talent. It wo[ul]d be the noblest monument and one which to the last hour of our existence wo[ul]d perhaps contribute to our consolation. It is yet too soon perhaps to think of that, which, at all events, would require great labor and much time, but in speaking of his papers, it seemed opportune to intimate what has, more than once, occurred to me, and in the prospect of achieving which, I have sometimes discovered a source of melancholy pleasure.[1]

I intend to remain here but a very few days, two or three at most. Pray let me have a line, if only a line, by return of | post. Sa is anxious to hear from you. I cannot trust myself to write of her, but her sweet and virtuous soul struggles under this overwhelm[in]g affliction. Adieu. A thousand kindest words to Mrs. Meredith,[2] your father and your Sister.[3]

your most affec friend

B. Disraeli

Pray write to Sa, as she seems very unwell to day, tho' my visit seemed at first to revive her.

120 TO BENJAMIN AUSTEN — Bradenham, [Thursday] 3 November 1831

ORIGINAL: BL ADD MS 45908 ff43-4

COVER: Benjamin Austen Esqre | Raymond Buildgs | Grays Inn.

POSTMARK: (1) In double circle: F | 4 NO 4 | 1831

PUBLICATION HISTORY: M&B I 203, undated extract; Jerman 133, extract dated 3 November 1831, and 140, extract dated early November 1831

EDITORIAL COMMENT: The first page of the MS is edged in black.

Bradenham House. Novr. 3 | 1831

My dear Austen,

I received your kindest letter this morning. I hope to be in town on Monday and certainly shall be, if I do not go to Cheltenham, which depends upon a letter I shall receive, I hope, tomorrow. Even then I shall probably be in town on Tuesday at the furthest.

You know I always laugh at the claims of family connections, because they are merely such. There is no person whose hospitality I wo[ul]d sooner accept than

1 Neither the BL catalogue nor the *NUC* lists any work by Meredith published posthumously (with the exception of 'Rumpel Stilts Kin', the juvenile work written in collaboration with D). During his lifetime his *Tour to the Rhine* (1825) and *Memorial of Charles, King of Sweden* (1829) were published.

2 Evelyn, wife of William George Meredith Sr.

3 Ellen Meredith (d 1879), who married Frederick W. Hope in 1835.

yours, but I shall be [in] town only for a very short time, and shall be full of bustling business, better suited to an Hotel. You will have all my spare moments. |

With regard to *drawing*, your generosity does not surprise me, because I know you well. I feel that I have already abused your goodness, but I feel also confident that you will perceive, that I have acted in a way which, while it demonstrated my confidence in your friendship, was also most conducive to my ultimate good fortunes. The fact is circumstances occurred which rendered it of the utmost importance to me, that I sho[ul]d not draw upon Colburn, who had promised to honor my draught to any discreet amount, and in supporting me at this moment, you have not only lent me a considerable sum of | money, itself a very, very, great favor, but exercised a most beneficial influence on my future fate.[1] All when we meet.

The times are damnable. I take the gloomiest views of affairs, but we must not lose our property without a struggle.[2] In the event of a new election, I offer myself for Wycombe But this is *entre nous*.

With love at home

Yours ever

BD

TO GEORGIANA MEREDITH Bradenham [Saturday] 5 November 1831 **121**

ORIGINAL: FE EJM 6-ii

COVER: Miss Meredith | 5 Paragon Buildings | Bath Road | Cheltenham

POSTMARK: (1) In rectangle: Cheltenham | Penny Post (2) HWYCOMBE | Penny Post (3) In rectangle: No. 1.

Bradenham House – Novr. 5 | 1831.

My dearest Georgiana,

You have acted I think most wisely in postponing our interview. I assure you I looked forward to it with great anxiety, but I thought it only dutiful to hold myself at your immediate service.

1 D had returned with most of the MS of *Contarini Fleming* completed. He had high hopes for this work, but felt that if he were to be taken seriously as a writer it would be necessary for him to free himself from association with Colburn and his stable of writers, who, in D's judgement, produced primarily light-weight entertainment. As Colburn had already published his first two novels he was particularly conscious of the danger of being so labelled permanently if yet a third were to come from the same source. D was determined to have his new book published with the added prestige that acceptance by a publisher of John Murray's standing would bring to it. He had already (**86**) re-established contact with John Murray before leaving England with exactly this end in view.

However, if D's chronic shortage of money could only have been alleviated by a loan from Colburn, the price Colburn would have exacted would doubtless have been the only collateral D possessed – his future manuscripts. Austen's financial indulgence thus would have been very important to D.

2 After the Lords had rejected the second Reform Bill on 8 October, riots broke out in Bristol. Parliament was prorogued on 20 October, and met again in early December, when a third Bill was introduced.

The obnoxious paragraph[1] caught my eye the moment of my landing, and I took some ineffectual steps in London to discover the author. There is no doubt from its mode of expression, that it was picked up in conversation. As, tho' very | distressing, it is not malignant, and as, any further notice wo[ul]d only increase the annoyance, I shall not persevere in following up the clue. We have succeeded in concealing it from our Sa: indeed she seldom looks at a paper.

I rejoice to hear your father is better. Command me at all times, and believe me

most entirely yours

BD

122

TO SARAH DISRAELI 15 Pall Mall East, [London], Friday 11 November [1831]

ORIGINAL: H A/I/B/2

COVER: Miss Disraeli | Bradenham House | Wycomb | *Bucks.*

POSTMARK: (1) In Maltese cross: C.H | 11NO1831 | X

EDITORIAL COMMENT: Five page-change indications appear in the last sentence because it runs across the bottom of two pages of the MS. *Sic*: en placer.

---

15 Pall Mall East. | Friday. Nov 11.

My dearest Sa,

The sight of your dear handwriting gives me the greatest delight. You showed your usual tact in informing me of Bulwer's letter.[1] I have not yet seen him, but will call tomorrow. I have seen B.E.L. who departs tomorrow for Brighton, and have had a long talk with John Hardwick.[2] I dine with the Austens to day to meet Ward alone, who is in town for a day and wished to meet me.

All your hints are very good, and you never commit impertinencies. In consequence of your criticism, I burnt the sketch I read to you, and have written something in another vein, which is said to be very witty and gaily slashing, though not at all ferocious.[3] I think you | would like, tho' I am not clear that it

1 Doubtless the following: 'The Mr. Meredith who died suddenly on the 19th July at Cairo was at the moment of his death, with his young friend Mr. D'Israeli, the author of "Vivian Grey", "The Young Duke" etc. They had been for some time travelling in the East and were contemplating their return to England. Meredith was a very accomplished young man, and heir to an immense fortune. – He had been betrothed to Miss D'Israeli (daughter of the literary *veteran*) who remains inconsolable at so sudden an event.' *CJ* no 130 (22 Oct 1831) 718. O'Connor 3n-4n gives additional information on Meredith's supposed fortune.

---

1 Bulwer had written welcoming D home: 'Pray let me not be the last – if I have not been among the first – to congratulate you on your safe return.' H B/20/Ly/7. In her letter to D of 10 November Sarah wrote: 'This morning a letter arrived to you from Ed. Bulwer.' H A/I/B/413.

2 John Hardwick (1791-1875) was then a stipendiary magistrate at Lambeth Street, Whitechapel, London. Boase; *ER*.

3 D published three items in *The New Monthly Magazine* in the summer of 1832: 'The Court of Egypt' XXXIV (June) 555-6, 'The Bosphorus, a Sketch' XXXV (Sept) 242 and the sketch to which D is here referring, 'The Speaking Harlequin' XXXIV (Aug) 158-63. See also **211**&n3.

will be published, for I have not succeeded in seeing Colburn. As Dr. Bowring[4] is said to have written the Review in the West[minste]r,[5] and there was a simultaneous and lighter attack in the Examiner by Fonblanque,[6] I have classed them together, and described the dull quack Doctor calling in the assistance of his gay and impudent Scaramouch. Ollier says it will have the best effect, and the book will receive fresh vigor from the skirmish.

I am exceedingly well, but shall never be really happy till I get to Bradenham. Tuesday will be my latest day. I struggle for Monday, but will write to you again. |

I have seen Bolton, who is richer than ever. "If you wish to know anything about politics I'll tell you. I have had the heads of all the parties dining with me this season several times" by whom I suppose he means Ld. Grey, the Duke, and Hunt.[7]

He says that one of the most beautiful girls in London, highborn, very rich, very clever, very accomplished, is dying in love with me.[8] I must not tell you the name, which of course wo[ul]d be a sad breach. You see I am in full luck.

John Hardwick has been again flung off his horse in Lambeth, and had his head hurled against the curbstone. His hat saved him, and he was bled 14 oz. and is now quite round again, but his luck, or his seat, is bad. I have not yet got a horse, tho' I am to see one tomorrow. | I have a serv[an]t with the highest character I ever heard. He is still en placer with Mr. Protheroe the M.P. for Bristol[9] who is obliged to curtail his establishment. He is only twenty, and promises to turn out excellently. Hudson[10] says my pipes are the finest that ever were in England, and tho' the times are so bad, I think he will give me a handsome price for them. He says the D[uke] of Sussex[11] wo[ul]d purchase | them directly, but that he dare not show him | them, as his account is so long against him. Love to | all |

Your faithful, loving brother
BD

John Bowring (1792-1872), LLD, linguist, writer, traveller and editor of Bentham's works. He was co-editor, with Henry Southern, of *The Westminster Review* when it was founded in 1824, and he wrote many articles on political and literary subjects for it. He was knighted in 1854.

There was a hostile review of *The Young Duke* in *The Westminster Review* XV (Oct 1831) 399-406.

The Examiner no 1232 (11 Sept 1831) 579. Albany Fonblanque was its editor. The 'lighter attack' had included the view that 'This is one of those books which sensible men only happen to read when they have fevers or broken legs.'

Charles Grey (1764-1845), 2nd Earl Grey, leader of the Whigs, and the current prime minister. He retired in 1834.

Arthur Wellesley (1769-1852), 1st Duke of Wellington, leader of the Tories, prime minister 1828-30.

Henry 'Orator' Hunt (1773-1835), the Radical MP for Preston 1830-2 who rose to fame at the time of the 'Peterloo' Massacre of 1819. He retired from politics in 1833.

This turned out to be Margaret Trotter. See **142**n7.

Edward Davis Protheroe (1798?-1852), Whig MP for Evesham 1826-30, for Bristol 1831-2 and for Halifax 1837-47. He was defeated in the general elections of 1832 and 1835. Stenton.

J. Hudson of 132 Oxford Street, tobacconist to the King.

HRH Prince Augustus Frederick, Duke of Sussex (1773-1843), sixth son of George III and brother of George IV and William IV.

123 TO SARA AUSTEN [London], Friday [11? November 1831]

ORIGINAL: BL ADD MS 45908 ff48-9

COVER: Mrs. Austen | B Disraeli

PUBLICATION HISTORY: Jerman 141, excerpt dated November 1831

EDITORIAL COMMENT: *Dating*: on 8 November 1831 Bulwer reported Colburn as asking: 'Mr. Disraeli, sir, is come to town – young Mr. Disraeli! Won't he give us a nice light article about his travels?' The Earl of Lytton *The Life, Letters and Literary Remains of Edward Bulwer, Lord Lytton by his son* (1883) II 324.

The context confirms Jerman's attribution of this letter to November 1831. The Fridays in that month were 4, 11, 18 and 25. On 4 November D was almost certainly at Bradenham as he wrote two letters to Georgiana Meredith from there, on 3 and 5 November (**119** and **121**). On 18 November he would not have said, as he does here, 'Tell Austen I sh[ou]ld have written to him ... ' for D did write to Austen on 17 November (**129**) just before leaving London. On 12 November D wrote to Sarah: 'I dined with Ward yesterday (ie, Friday the 11th) alone at Austens' (**124**). As D was in 'hourly expectation of seeing' Austen, it is reasonable to conclude that he went to the Austens on the evening of Friday 11 November and dined with Ward, and therefore that this letter was written earlier that day.

Friday afternoon

My dear Mrs. Austen,

I have just this moment arrived in town, and shall call upon you the moment I have a local habitation, as well as a name. I have come up very suddenly, and shall call upon nobody but yourself, as I have a great deal of business. Tell Austen I sho[ul]d have written to him, had I not been in hourly expectation of seeing him.

With regard to your kind letter – | I never write in Magazines or Annuals, for if you once do it, all peace is over.

"They stop your chariot, and they board yr barge."[1]

Mr Valpy has my thanks and my good wishes, but I regret that I cannot even yield him the feeble assistance of a single article, because I have refused that favor, if it be one, *more than once* since my return, to Lytton Bulwer, who is savage and sulky already, and were I now to contribute to a rival publication, and to accede to the request of one, who has less claims upon | my exertions – why he wd. be justly and deeply offended.

So much for Valpy. Between ourselves, the Metrop[olitan] is a dead failure, and has been a very losing concern from the beginning. Instead of giving "a very large sum for the copyright," I am credibly informed said Valpy has taken it as the only chance of getting his bill paid for work done as printer, and may in due time, with great energy, realize a shilling dividend.[2]

Farewell – may we meet soon!

BD

1 'What walls can guard me, or what shades can hide? | They pierce my thickets, through my grot they glide; | By land, by water, they renew the charge; | They stop the chariot, and they board the barge.' Pope 'Epistle to Dr. Arbuthnot' 7-10.

2 Abraham John Valpy (1787-1854) was initially just the printer of *The Metropolitan Magazine*, and D's account of the reasons for his assumption of the editorship was probably correct. However, D was wrong in his prophecy of early failure. The publication, which began in May 1831, ran for nineteen years, until 1850.

TO SARAH DISRAELI 15 Pall Mall East, [London], Saturday [12 November 1831] **124**

ORIGINAL: H A/I/B/3
COVER: Miss Disraeli | Bradenham House | Wycomb | Bucks
POSTMARK: (1) In Maltese cross: C.H | 12NO1831 | X.

15. Pall Mall East | Saturday.

My dearest Sister,

I write you tho' I have of course but little to tell you, and I am afraid our beloved Sire will justly grumble at the postage, but I hope some day to be a privileged correspondt. when I may even send you a billet doux by the Royal Mail.[1]

I shall not sacrifice the pipes as indeed there is no need. Had I fifty thousand a year, I should sell them, as really now I have quitted the land of splendor, they strike me as too magnificent for any Frank. I have not yet finally arranged about them, as I do not choose to appear in a hurry, but I have no doubt I shall satisfactorily.

I hope that Jem will not be in despair when I tell you, that I have resolved to bring down neither horse | nor groom at present. The fact is I am already touched by another cold, and I foresee, that I must be a very wary wanderer in the fields during this winter. I shall therefore postpone till the spring, the establishment of my stud. In coming to this resolution, I must however observe, that I have been influenced by the consideration, that my father always had two saddlehorses at my command, and at this time of the year, when William[2] is so little employed by you, even a groom. Jem's *fiasco*[3] howr is a blow to this arrangemt., but I hope we may recover, and put ourselves in our old, or a similar, position.

I hope to be with you on Tuesday, and sho[ul]d perhaps on Monday, but the most extraordinary thing has happened. My friend Henry Stanley,[4] who came over | very much involved, and to whom I gave very good advice etc. lost his good genius when I left London, and instead of having the courage to go to his father, is playing hide and seek and can nowhere be heard of. His family are in a state of frenzy. His father[5] has opened one of my letters addressed to Knowsley Park, and writes up to me full of heartrend[in]g apologies at the liberty and paternal exclamations to save his son. It was fortunately a letter of very good advice. Ld Stanley looks entirely to me for succour, and I am surrounded by Stanleys, all day long, full of despair, making researches and following clues. My col-

1 The practice of franking allowed members of Parliament to send up to ten letters a day without charge. The top of the cover had to set out the date (in words) and the signature of the MP, all in his own handwriting, but the system was subject to abuse. Before franking was abolished in 1840, up to one-ninth of all letters passing through the Post Office were franked. *Third Report from the Select Committee on Postage* (1838) XI 59.

2 One of the servants at Bradenham, mentioned throughout D's correspondence with his family.

3 James Disraeli's lack of judgement in buying horses, several of which went lame, was a constant theme in D's letters home.

4 See **117**n2. Knowsley Hall is the Derby family seat near Liverpool.

5 Edward Smith Stanley (1775-1851), Baron Stanley, after 1834 13th Earl of Derby.

league in all this is Col. Long of the G[uar]ds.[6] We have made some very extraordinary discoveries, and you cannot imagine what curious characters I am obliged to see. Under these circumstances, I cannot leave London until I receive Lord Stanleys answer to my letter of this evening, which will be Tuesday. I shall come down on that day, provided I am not anxiously | requested to remain. I think you will agree with me that it will be neither kind nor judicious to desert them. Is not this an adventure?[7] Ralph thinks an establishment may be procured at Sharpes in the Haymarket which will suit us.[8] I dined with Ward yesterday alone at Austens. He is quite himself again both in health and intellect, and was more than kind, but so deaf, that to me he is a dead man. Conversation is impossible. Love to all. How I long to be with you – and a thousand, thousand loves to my dearest Sa, from her devoted brother –

BD

125

TO FRANCIS DOUCE 15 Pall Mall East, [London], Sunday [13 November 1831]

ORIGINAL: BODL MS Douce d33 ff185-7

EDITORIAL COMMENT: *Dating*: D appears to have stayed at 15 Pall Mall East only between 11 and 17 November 1831. The only Sunday in this period was 13 November; the dating is confirmed by the reference to Douce in **126**. *Sic*: Desarts.

---

15 Pall Mall East. | Sunday

Francis Douce Esqr

My dear Sir,

Ever since I have returned to the white cliffs and the foggy skies of Albion, I have been almost confined to my chamber by a severe cold and inflammation on my chest. I can scarcely allow myself to go about for urgent and indispensable business, and almost fear, that | I must postpone the first of the many, long conversations I had anticipated holding with you, about all that I have seen from the Sierras of Andalusia to the Desarts of Araby the blest. I do not however leave London for two or three days, and will yet make an effort to reach Gower Street.[1]

My brother will deliver to you an Osiris | which I have brought you from Thebes, and which is a very fine specimen of the kind. These little pocket divinities are seldom found so sharp and fresh and defined. He will also give you a small collection, that I have made for you in the course of my travels, some articles of which are very curious and which I will explain when | we meet. They are Gods and Goddesses whose names are only recently discovered.[2] The Egyptian Pantheon is entirely reformed.

6 Lt Col Samuel Long (d 1881) who in 1825 had married Edward Geoffrey Stanley's sister, Louisa Emily. *BP* (1884), entry for Derby.

7 For an account of the affair and its significance for D's relations with the Stanleys see C.L. Cline 'Disraeli and Peel's 1841 Cabinet' *The Journal of Modern History* XI (1939) 509-12. See also Blake 71-3.

8 The only commercial premises in the Haymarket associated with the name Sharpe were those of one William Sharpe, a haircutter at number 65. Ralph appears to have enquired about lodgings.

---

1 Francis Douce lived at 15 Upper Gower Street.

Accept these my dear Sir, as evidences of my never ceasing regard, and gratitude for early kindness. Altho' I am one of your youngest, you are one of my oldest friends.

Vale!

Benjn. Disraeli

TO SARAH DISRAELI 15 Pall Mall East, [London], Monday 14 November 1831 **126**

ORIGINAL: H A/I/B/4
COVER: Miss Disraeli | Bradenham House | Wycomb | Bucks.
POSTMARK: (1) In Maltese cross: C.H | 14NO1831 | X
EDITORIAL COMMENT: *Sic*: St. James, Haibar.

---

15 Pall Mall East. | Monday. Novr. 14. 31

My dearest Sa,

I received your letter[1] this morning. A lawyers letter will do no harm. Nash[2] will tell you how far you can proceed without incurring expenses, and how far indeed it may be prudent to proceed at all. If the dealer be solvent, the warranty full, and the evidence of unsoundness perfect, your remedy will of course follow.

I have not yet called upon Douce, tho' I shall tomorrow, but I sent him yesterday by Ralph a very pretty collection of divinities and other trifles, which indeed will be a great addition to his "small specimens", among them an Osiris of great beauty and sharpness of execution.

The Cholera is little thought of here: indeed many persons are altog[ethe]r sceptical as to the fact. Rigid precautions are howr. taken against it.[3] All the alleys of London are visited and whitewashed: and raiment and food given to the naked and the hungry. It is at all events an excellent thing for the needy.

No news of Henry Stanley. I can do no | more. I have made great discoveries. I traced him to the new exclusive Hell in St. James St.[4] and after a mixture of diplomacy and courage, which I trust were worthy of Mr Pelham,[5] or any other hero of three volumes post 8vo, I made the leg,[6] who keeps it, make me strange and sad disclosures. Nothing can be done now but to call in the aid of the Police,

2 The opening decades of the nineteenth century were the era of the first professional Egyptologists. J.D. Wortman *The Genesis of British Egyptology, 1549-1906* (Norman, Oklahoma 1971).

---

1 Sarah wrote to D on 13 November 1831, seeking advice on the best means of recovering money that Jem had spent on a lame horse. H A/I/B/414.

2 John Nash (1780-1860), Isaac's solicitor in High Wycombe. *GM* 209 (July 1860) 103. For an account of his political activities see **199**n2.

3 The first cholera epidemic of the nineteenth century reached England in October 1831. Cases occurred in London a month or so later. In early 1832 it was still not unusual for people to allege that talk of cholera was being used to enhance the importance of the Metropolitan Board of Health. *The Court Journal* made fun of one J.B. Kell who had claimed the distinction of being 'the first to discover the disease and communicate it to the public'. *CJ* no 148 (25 Feb 1832) 119.

4 The establishment in St James's belonged to one Effie Bond. It appears that D owed him money. See **124**n7.

5 D is comparing his actions in helping Henry Stanley (**124**) to those of the hero of Bulwer's novel *Pelham* (1828), who also had adventures in the seamier parts of London.

6 'Blackleg', a gambling swindler.

but his brothers hesitate to adopt this plan, which I strongly urge, and will not, without the authority of their father, send Plank, or Ruthven,[7] after an officer in his Majesty's service. Tomorrow will bring me a letter from Lord Stanley, which of course may influence my proceedings, but as far as I can form an opinion, nothing can well prevent me from being with you on Wednesday. I have promised to dine with Col. Long on Tuesday, who expects that Lord Stanley will come up. Mr. Hornby arrived on Saturday night, but of course to no purpose, as he co[ul]d only enforce Ld S's first letter.[8]

I dined on Saturday with Bolton and met Angerstein,[9] Baron Haibar,[10] a noble spy, as I conceive, in the interest here of Charles 10, but who moves in the first circles, and is altog[ethe]r one of the most remarkable men I have ever met, and John Hardwick. Angerstein is not | at all a puppy of the present day, but a very gentlemanly, unaffe[c]ted, and intelligent man of thirty. He is the warmest admirer I ever met of your correspondent, who dines with him today, to meet Henry Vyner[11] who has just come from Egypt etc.

I am sorry to say that the Travellers will prove a complete failure.[12] There has been an addition of two hundred members since I have been on the books and I have not been elected. It is a club you cannot enter with[ou]t the permission of Lord Auckland.[13] I co[ul]d probably have obtained this, had I been in England, but as it is, the opportunity is lost. I am still on the books and may be for three years before I have another chance. Singer[14] says the canvassing was unrivalled: of course, as I was ignorant of the struggle, I went to the wall. I shall speak to Angerstein today about it, as he is a member, but I believe it is quite hopeless.

7 Sam Plank (1777?-1840), chief of the Bow Street Runners, was actually attached to the police office at Great Marlborough Street. Another police officer, George Ruthven (1792?-1844), would have been an appropriate choice for the mission, as he was himself apparently a heavy gambler. John L. Bradley ed *Rogue's Progress: The Autobiography of "Lord Chief Baron" Nicholson* (Cambridge, Massachusetts 1965) 75; Henry Goddard *Memoirs of a Bow Street Runner* (1956) 59n, 137n; *AR* (1840) app 165 and (1844) app 229.

8 Henry Stanley's uncle, Edmund Hornby (1773-1857), of Dalton Hall, Westmorland, was a magistrate and deputy- lieutenant of Lancashire. He was brother-in-law in a double sense to Lord Stanley, each having married the other's sister. *BLG* (1846; 1875).

9 John Angerstein (1773?-1858), son of John Julius Angerstein, captain in the Grenadier Guards and Whig MP for Greenwich 1835-7.

10 Baron Moritz von Haber (1798-1874), eldest son of the Karlsruhe banker Salomon Haber, who was ennobled in 1829. As the eldest son of a baron, the younger Haber assumed the title during his father's lifetime. Heinrich Schnee *Die Hoffinanz und der moderne Staat* (Berlin 1963) IV 68-85.

11 Probably Capt Henry Vyner (1805-1861) of Newby Hall, Yorkshire. *BLG*; *AR* (1832) app 171.

12 Founded in 1814, the Travellers' Club was established in its present home – in Pall Mall adjoining the Athenaeum – in 1832. Its formal requirement for new members was that they should have 'travelled out of the British Isles to a distance of at least 500 miles from London in a direct line.' The more daunting barrier was the informal one of high social status. Sir Almeric Fitzroy *History of the Travellers' Club* (1927).

13 George Eden (1784-1849), 2nd Baron Auckland, after 1839 1st Earl of Auckland, MP 1810-12 and 1813-14; president of the Board of Trade 1830-4 and 1835; first lord of the Admiralty 1834-5 and 1846-9; governor general of India 1835-41.

14 Samuel Weller Singer (1783-1858), editor and miscellaneous writer, was at the time secretary of the Travellers' Club. Sarah described him as 'a prince of toadeys'. H A/I/B/540.

We must make a push at the Committee of the Athenaeum.[15] I can write no more, save to say that I am very well and with my love to all, and especially to my Sa,

Believe me yr. dev[ote]d Br[other]. |

I paid for dining with Ward alone, by dining with Waller and Sams tog[ethe]r yesterday. The first whom I had never seen but in uniform, I now perceive, altho' fair, to be strongly marked. He is however a gentlemanly man but his brother so painfully vulgar, that I co[ul]d not even speak to him.[16] Ralph I see constantly. He will write and take up the parable, when I quit town. Geo. Basevi called upon me, but the interview had no feature. The fault of the Travellers is, that some friend did not inform my father of the additional two hundred. Had Singer done so, it wd. have been courteous.

127

TO SARAH DISRAELI [15] Pall Mall East, [London], Tuesday 15 November [1831]

ORIGINAL: H A/I/B/5
COVER: Miss Disraeli | Bradenham House | Wycomb | *Bucks.*
POSTMARK: (1) In circle: Q | NO15 | 1831
EDITORIAL COMMENT: *Sic*: neighourood, agreable, Mistivitch, Kosciusko, Viner.

Pall Mall East. | Novr. 15. Tuesday.

My dearest Sa,

I cannot receive a letter from Lord Stanley till tomorrow morning. It was a miscalculation of the Colonel. This will make no difference in my arrangements, unless something very particular occur. I shall be with you on Wednesday (tomorrow) evening by teatime, or on Thursday morning by breakfast.

I caught Foord Bowes[1] yesterday just out of the York mail and about to fly down to Brighton to his mother by the afternoon coach. I learnt from him that Henry Stanley was at Manchester on Monday week last. Colonel Long was down at Richmond, but | I had time to scribble off a line to Lord Stanley. He told Bowes that he sho[ul]d go on to Knowsley directly, but altho' he had not arrived there, some days afterwards, I still hope that he is only lingering in the neighbourood.

I have not yet parted with my pipes, but my negotiations with Hudson are anything but unsatisfactory. He says they are too magnificent for him, and that he cannot presume to make an offer. He says no one co[ul]d offer less than one hundred for the three great pipes, and even half is more than he has courage for – that if he values them betweeen gentleman and gentleman, he co[ul]d not

15 The Athenaeum, which was founded in 1824, appealed particularly to men of letters and to those interested in the fine arts. Its members included adherents of all political parties. Isaac was an early member and, after his move to Bradenham, continued to use its facilities on his visits to town. Ogden 130.

16 A confirmation of there being two brothers with different surnames is found in a letter of 1 May 1831 from Sarah. She noted how D had been great friends with a 'Capt. Waller' whose real name was Sams, which, she added enigmatically, 'he wisely drops'. H A/IV/E/20.

---

1 Capt Barnard Topham Foord Bowes of the 95th Foot. He was the son of Timothy Fish Foord Bowes, a clergyman who held a succession of positions at Court.

certainly say less than from 120 to 150£. He is very frank, and therefore I suppose will | not purchase, not at least in a hurry – but as I am not pressed for money I shall leave the case with Ralph who may see other dealers, or sell them separately. As they only cost me forty pounds, at any rate I shall not make any very great sacrifice. Every body is astounded with them. I shall bring a smaller, but still most beautiful one, down with me.

I dined yesterday at Angersteins, a most agreable party. Mistivitch[2] the Polish Poet, who talked to me of the "Curiosities". Angerstein has crammed this venerable Nestor of Literature and politics, the friend of Washington and Kosciusko,[3] and the Pres[ident of the] R[oyal] A[cademy] of Poland with "the Young Duke". It was ludicrous to hear his grey hairs and reverend lip perpetually quote such frivolity. At last I was obliged to stop him, and in pity let him know, that he sho[ul]d never have looked at such nonsense. Henry Viner, very elegant and kind. My friend the Baron, most original, wonderful, and Sir Francis Vincent,[4] a fashionable, handsome | Homfray,[5] with a dash of Ed. Bulwer. Vincent is more than six feet high, married, but I think a roué. It was a most agreable reunion, and Angerstein is the most courteous of hosts and the most unaffe[c]ted of men. We parted with great warmth, and I promised when I again visited town to make one of my earliest calls upon him. He encourages me about the Travellers, and, had he been cognizant, wo[ul]d have secured me, but he will attack the Committee. I leave it in his hands. Ralph, breakfasted | with me to day to meet Foord Bowes, who has | just gone off, | having failed yesterday.

Love to all, and especially to yourself
my dearest Sister.
BD

---

128 TO GEORGIANA MEREDITH [London?], Thursday [17 November? 1831]

ORIGINAL: FE EJM 6-v

EDITORIAL COMMENT: *Dating*: by comparison with **129** in which D implied that he planned to be at Bradenham the next day (the 18th). *Sic*: Brazenose.

Thursday. 11 ock.

My dear Georgiana,

I have just received your note. I very much desire to go down to day for Sa's sake, and if so, I must leave town by one. I fear therefore I may not reach you.

I enclose a note for your father.

It is unnecessary for you, and yours, ever to *explain*, as I always, and shall always, give you credit for the kindest intentions.

2 'Mistivitch' is what D wrote. However, he must have meant the poet Julian Ursin Niemcewicz (1757-1841), who accompanied Gen Kosciuszko to America in 1797 and there met Washington. The other details also correspond to facts known about Niemcewicz. J.A. Carroll and M.W. Ashworth *George Washington; a biography* (1957) VII 511n.

3 Gen Tadeusz Bonaventura Kosciuszko (1746-1817), Polish patriot.

4 Sir Francis Vincent (1803-1880), 10th Baronet, Whig MP for St Albans 1831-5.

5 The best-known people bearing this name were the families of Samuel Homfray (d 1822) of Monmouthshire and Sir Jeremiah Homfray (d 1833) of Glamorgan. The latter had five sons then living. *BLG*; Walford's *County Families*.

Never mind the case of which I have no want. Return it when I come up again. | Your father desired, that I wo[ul]d send him a copy of the simple inscription with which I have recorded our loss. A Friend who is resident there, has promised me to visit the tomb at least twice every year.

With regard to my suggestion,[1] I never supposed that it co[ul]d be executed ex[cep]t at a very considerable interval, and I only mentioned it, because I thought the anticipation of its future achievement might prove a source of consolation at the present | moment and might prevent the destruction of papers.

I ought to apologise for these rough coffee house notes.

Believe me
ever yrs
BD

T.O. |

Sacred

to the memory of William George Meredith Esq F.R.S. – A.M. of Brazenose College Oxford, only son of George Meredith of Berrington Court in the County of Worcester, Esquire, who died at Cairo on the nineteenth day of July, one thousand eight hundred and thirty one, on his return from Upper Egypt in the twenty ninth year of a life distinguished by his talents, and ennobled by his virtues.

TO BENJAMIN AUSTEN [London?], [Thursday] 17 November 1831 **129**

ORIGINAL: BL ADD MS 45908 ff45-6

COVER: *Private* | Benj. Austen Esqr | Grays Inn. | *B. Disraeli*

EDITORIAL COMMENT: As this letter was delivered by hand it is probable that D dispatched it in London immediately before leaving for Bradenham. Letter **128**, written at 11 A.M., expressed his intention of leaving at 1 P.M.

Novr. 17th. 1831

My dear Austen,

You will do me the greatest favor if you will give my brother a cheque for £31, and which I will send you up a draft from Bradenham for by tomorrows post.

I enclose you the letter of credit,[1] and I hope that I may soon settle your advance, tho' I shall never be able to clear the account of gratitude.

1 The suggestion in **119** that Meredith's papers be published.

---

1 The letter of credit (ff47-8) is appended to the original of this letter. It reads:

May 19th 1830

Benjn. Disraeli [*in D's hand, crossed by* 'London' *in another hand*]

To Messrs Hunter and Ross of Malta
To Messrs Irasiel and Jackson of Smyrna
To Messrs C.S. Hanson and Co. of Constantinople
Gentn,
We have great pleasure in introducing to your acquaintance the Bearer of these few lines Mr. Benjn Disraeli, who is about to leave England for the Levant. At his request we have given Mr. Disraeli a letter of Credit upon you collectively to the extent of £500 – say Five Hundred

Your much obliged and faithful
BD
The entry of the 75£ item is mine and I have no doubt is incorrect.[2]

130 TO UNKNOWN Bradenham House, Wycombe, [Wednesday] 21 December 1831
ORIGINAL: UTT 1.

Bradenham House - Wycombe | Decr. 21.1831.

My dear Sir,[1]

My mother sends you a quarter of pork, which is the only pork in the present day, that does not give the Cholera, it being born at Bradenham, and fed upon the milk and honey of that land of promise. Two fowls also fly away at the same time, and will fall dead at your feet. It is reported however, that they were killed this morning.

pounds Sterling and we shall feel obliged by your furnishing him with this or any part of the said amount against his drafts on Messrs. Willis Percival and Co. Bankers of this place, for the due payment of which we hereby give you our guarantee. |

As in all probability Mr Disraeli may not have occasion to draw to the full extent of the above Credit at either place, you will please for regularity' [*sic*] sake to state at the foot of this letter whatever sums you have been kind enough to furnish him with.

Annexed is the signature of Mr. Disraeli.

We remain Gent
Your Most Obedt. Servts
Hanson Brothers

[*Endorsements in another hand*]:

One Hundred pounds Sterling advanced by the undersigned to Mr. Disraeli on this letter of Credit.

£100 Stg — Malta 21st. September 1830.
Hunter and Ross.

[*Endorsements in D's hand*]:

£75. Drew on Messrs. Hunter and Ross. Decr. 1830
BD

£125. paid by C.S. Hanson and Co Constantinople

Clearly the endorsements in D's hand are contrary to the recording procedure laid down in the letter of credit. In his letter to Austen from Napoli di Romania of 18 November 1830 (**103**) D reported that he had drawn £100 in Malta from Messrs. Hunter and Ross. In his next letter, from Constantinople 27 December 1830 (**106**), he reported a withdrawal of £75 from Hunter and Ross of Malta, and £25 on Messrs Hanson at Constantinople, with the warning that there might be a further £100 (as there was) before he left the Turkish capital. The letter from Alexandria of 3 August 1831 (**115**) told Austen of a further £200, not noted in this letter of credit. The only official notation on this document is for £100 from Hunter and Ross at Malta on 21 September 1830. It appears evident that, before he returned to England, D had drawn up to the full £500 limit of the letter of credit.

2 This ambiguous postscript is perhaps explained by D's realization that on the final two endorsements, which are in his own hand, the only date to appear is December 1830, which would have been correct for the Constantinople entry but not for the Malta one, as he was not there at that time.

---

1 The recipient could be Sharon Turner or any one of a number of Isaac's friends. It is interesting to note that the handwriting of this letter is more carefully and precisely formed and the spacing more meticulously arranged than in any other Disraeli letter of this period – including the letters to the Duke of Wellington.

I seize this opportunity to congratulate you upon your flourishing condition. I hope, as the Spaniards say, "you will live a thousand years – " I have returned to | our blessed country, after a long absence, to witness its last expiring struggle. I ascribe the present melancholy state of affairs to the death of George the fourth, and the general giving up of punch drinking, which has taken place during the last half century.

When I see you, I will give you an idea of Turkish music, which possesses neither harmony nor melody, and therefore is most unlike your enchanting performance.

Believe me, my dear Sir,
Most faithfully yours
Benjn Disraeli

TO GEORGIANA MEREDITH Bradenham, [Thursday] 29 December 1831 **131**

ORIGINAL: FE EJM 6-iii
COVER: Miss Meredith | Nottingham Place | Portland Place | London
POSTMARK: (1) In double circle: F | 30DE30 | 1831
EDITORIAL COMMENT: The first page of the MS is edged in black.

Bradenham House | Decr. 29 1831

My dear Georgiana,
Sa requests me to acknowledge your letter, which Ralph duly delivered, and to thank you all for your kind recollection of her. Any offering from friends, so dear to her as yourselves, she must ever greatly appreciate, and as a testimony of your regard must, under any circumstances, ever afford her gratification, but a memorial[1] which only commemorates her greatest misfortune, | she finds it impossible to select.

For myself, whom you have so kindly recollected, I indeed require no memento to remind me of a friend, whose recollection is blended with all my past hopes, and all my future prospects, many of which must now fade away. At my time of life, it is difficult, perhaps impossible for a man, to find a new confidant. If I might be permitted to mention it, I know nothing that would afford me greater solace than to possess a favorite volume from his | library. I sho[ul]d esteem such a possession above all other memorials, and from his classical books, I might perhaps cull one without inconvenience to yourselves.

Unfortunately we possess none of his hair.

They are all grieved here to learn, that so long an interval must elapse before you can meet; but the expectations of affection are doomed to disappointment, for they are generally unreasonable. They must console themselves by the | anticipation of the future. With our kindest remembrances to Mrs Meredith and Ellen

Believe me, dear Georgiana
Ever faithfully yrs –
B. Disraeli

---

1 Ralph Disraeli wrote to D in January 1832: 'Your mother has a valuable diamond ring for you, in Memory – rather it be for our dearest.' H A/I/E/46. See also **137**&n1.

132 TO BENJAMIN AUSTEN Bradenham, [Friday] 6 January 1832

ORIGINAL: BL ADD MS 45908 ff50-1

COVER: Benjamin Austen Esqr | Grays Inn | B DISRAELI

PUBLICATION HISTORY: Jerman 142-3, extracts dated 6 January 1832

EDITORIAL COMMENT: *Sic*: underceived.

Bradenham House | Jany. 6. 1832

My dear Austen,

I acknowledge by our mutual Mercury[1] the receipt of yours enclosing note by which it correctly appears I am indebted to you £315.17.6 – for which I hope you will permit me to pay interest from the payment of the several bills. You will not refuse this slight favor, after having conferred such weighty ones.

With regard to the period of repayment, I believe you to be as frank as you are friendly, and therefore will avail myself of your kindness, if the detention be not inconvenient, and your confidence remain. If not, | I will, with readiness, request my Sire to repay you, and feel equally obliged.

I am ready to attack the public, but am obliged to watch the signs of the times before I move; altho', unless we have a new Revolution, I hope the immortal work will make its appearance in a few months. Probably from the Albemarle Press[2] – but all this is under the Rose.

We hoped to have had the pleasure of seeing you in a few days among our bowers, and Sa had commenced a letter to Madame, supposing that term did not commence till the 20th., but Ralph unfortunately underceived us. We hope therefore that you | will come down at its termination.

I am pretty well, having just left off a six weeks course of Mercury[3] – which has pulled me down, but head all right, and working like a Tiger.

It is no use of talking of other affairs. I fear that ours is one of the few cases in which Time can bear no consolation, but only embitter woe. But we exist and therefore we must endure. As for myself I look forward to solace in constant action, and if I cd. only induce the gentle Burgesses of Wycombe[4] to return me, sho[ul]d have my time too occupied for melancholy.

Vale

BD |

Would you like me to send you a bill?[5]

1 Ralph.

2 D had yet to write to Murray in Albemarle Street about the MS of *Contarini Fleming*. See **135**.

3 Mercury was very widely used in the first half of the century for the treatment of nearly every illness.

4 Before the Reform Bill was passed, Wycombe was a 'closed' borough, and the Corporation selected the MPs. The Corporation consisted of 'a Mayor, Recorder, two Bailiffs, twelve Aldermen, a Town Clerk, and an indefinite number of Burgesses, being freemen inhabiting within the borough; to which number the corporation have also thought fit to add several persons *not inhabiting* the same, by constituting them Honorary Freemen, or Burgesses.' The Mayor, Bailiffs and Burgesses (not receiving alms) were entitled to the 'rights of election'. In this period there were some fifty voters. T.H.B. Oldfield *The Representative History of Great Britain and Ireland* (1816) III 85.

5 An acknowledgement of his debt which would be legally enforceable.

TO BENJAMIN AUSTEN | The Red Lion, High Wycombe, [Thursday] 19 January [1832] | 133

ORIGINAL: BL ADD MS 45908 ff59-60

PUBLICATION HISTORY: M&B I 212, undated excerpt; Jerman 160-1, dated 29 June 1832

EDITORIAL COMMENT: *Dating*: the date on the MS appears to be January 19, although another hand has added '(June)' before the date, and '1832' after it. However, by June it was known that Baring was not going to the Lords, but that he might be moving to a Hampshire seat (Benjamin Lindo to D, 9 June 1832, H B/I/A/14). The matters discussed seem to follow from D's letter to Austen of 6 January 1832 (**132**), and reflect an early stage of his experience as a canvasser.

Although the first digit of the date could be either a 1 or a 2, the mid-January dating is consistent with the exchange between D and Robert Smith in February (**134**). Jerman's date for this letter as 29 June (160), three days after Grey's election, is inconsistent with the references to Baring.

Red Lion Wycomb. | Jan. 19

My dear Austen,

I write you a hurried note after a hard days canvass. Whigs, Tories, and Radicals, Quakers, Evangelicals, Abolition of Slavery, Reform, Conservation, Corn-laws, here is hard work for one, who is to please all parties. I make an excellent canvasser, and am told I shall carry it, if the Boro' be opened, of which there can be no doubt, but | within these few days we have understood, that Sir Thos. Baring is to be called up,[1] and then the question is, whether the Corporation will elect me, and whether I can accept the trust without compromising myself with the 10£rs.[2]

Under these circumstances, I cannot say when I shall be in town, tho' there is a chance of | my being there as *MP* in a fortnight for aught I know.[3] In the meantime, I cannot be absent an instant with[ou]t peril, and a few days since, being a little nervous about my condition, tho' without cause, I went up to town in the mail, and returned to Wycombe the next morning in time for a civic dinner where I harangued them.

I | do not enclose the bill, because I do not know what term to fix upon. It becomes not me to fix; and because I am in expectation of seeing you down here

1 Sir Thomas Baring (1772-1848), 2nd Baronet, who had been MP for Wycombe since 1806, was not 'called up' (elevated to the peerage). As it turned out, Baring resigned his seat in June 1832 to contest a vacancy for Hampshire. This in turn led to the by-election which D fought without success.

2 Owners or occupiers of property assessed at £10 or more a year were due to be enfranchised. D was thus planning to ingratiate himself with future constituents in anticipation of the passing of the Bill. There were some 250 'ten-pounders' in the constituency.

3 This sentence is probably the reason for Jerman's dating of the letter as June 1832. However, D's optimism was based on two assumptions: first, that in the event of a sudden vacancy, an election controlled by the closed Corporation would return him, and second, that it would be done so quickly that no serious opposition would have time to emerge.

in a few days. It is a long time since the families have met, and the bitterness of the past[4] must no longer be permitted to interfere with the course of friendship. Pray therefore make an exertion to come, w[hi]ch will do us here all good.

Vale

BD

134 TO ROBERT JOHN SMITH Bradenham, [Wednesday] 1 February 1832

ORIGINAL: CARR 1

EDITORIAL COMMENT: Endorsement on the first page of the MS in another hand: 'B: Disraeli | 1st: Feb: 1832'. *Sic*: neighbourood.

Bradenham House | Feb. 1. 1832

Hon: R. Smith[1]

Sir,

Your acquaintance with my father will excuse, altho' it may not justify this communication. I fear you will consider it an intrusion; I shall regret very much if you do.

Some | of my neighbours have flattered me by expressing a wish, that in the event of an anticipated vacancy in the representation of Wycombe, I sho[ul]d offer myself as a Candidate. No one, I trust, can be less desirous than myself, to obtrude upon society; no one, I am sure, can be more conscious of his very slender claims to the honor in question. But I cannot learn, that any gentleman in the | neighbourood is inclined to advance, and I am sure you wo[ul]d regret as much as myself, were you to find a colleague in a political adventurer.

In desiring to enter Parliament, I am actuated by no vulgar ambition. Looking forward to such a position, as a theatre of honorable exertion, I wo[ul]d never obtain it at the cost of honorable conduct, by the sacrifice of those feelings, which should | influence gentlemen, and by placing myself in collision with one, with whose political conduct I sympathise, and whose superior claims I gladly recognise, and greatly respect.

Am I too bold then, in wishing to be informed, as frankly as I request the information, whether you wo[ul]d consider any movement on my part an interference with your individual interests?

I have the honor to remain,

Sir,

with great consideration,

your faithful Servant,

Benjn Disraeli

4 The breaking of the engagement between Mrs Austen's sister, Louisa Rickett, and D's cousin, Benjamin Lindo (see **81**).

1 Robert John Smith (1796-1868), after 1838 2nd Baron Carrington, Whig MP for Wycombe 1831-8. His reply, dated 2 February, warned D that, as it was unlikely that Baring would be raised to the peerage, there might be no vacancy. H B/I/A/2. See **133**n1.

TO JOHN MURRAY Bradenham, [Friday] 10 February 1832 **135**

ORIGINAL: MM 19

PUBLICATION HISTORY: Smiles II 335, dated 10 February 1832

EDITORIAL COMMENT: In another hand, on the last page: '1832 Feby 10 | D'Israeli Benj Esq'.

Bradenham House | Wycombe | February 10. 1832

John Murray Esq

Sir

I have at length completed a work,[1] which I wish to submit to your consideration.

In | so doing, I am influenced by the feelings, I have already communicated to you.

If you retain the wish expressed in a note, which I received at Athens, in the autumn of | 1830, I shall have the honor of forwarding the MS. to you.

Believe me, Sir,
Whatever may be the result,
Very cordially yrs,
Benj Disraeli.

TO EVELYN MEREDITH Bradenham, [Friday] 10 February 1832 **136**

ORIGINAL: FE EJM 7.

Bradenham House | Feby. 10. 1832

My dear Mrs. Meredith,

Although I hope, in the course of a few days, personally to thank you for the magnificent memorial,[1] which you have presented me of my noble and beloved friend, I sho[ul]d grieve, were even this interval to elapse without my acknowledging | your considerate kindness.

Believe me, that while it hourly reminds me of his virtues and our affliction, it does not the less impress upon my memory, how much regard and duty are owing to those dear relatives he has left behind, and | most especially to yourself, whose wishes I shall ever consider commands, and whose good will I shall ever esteem one of my most precious possessions.

I had not an opportunity, when I last had the pleasure of seeing | you, of offering you a Rosary which I brought for you from Jerusalem. It is a rude, but perhaps not uninteresting, memento of a sacred, and celebrated, place.

Believe me, my dear Madam, with kindest regards to Georgiana and Ellen,
your affectionate, faithful,
Servant,
Benj Disraeli

1 *Contarini Fleming, A Psychological Auto-biography* (1832), published by John Murray. In Moxon's edition of 1834 the subtitle reverted to D's original and preferred name for the novel, 'The Psychological Romance'.

1 One of Meredith's books. See **131**.

137 TO GEORGIANA MEREDITH Bradenham, Saturday [11 February 1832]

ORIGINAL: FE EJM 6-iv

COVER: Miss Meredith | 6 Nottingham Place.

EDITORIAL COMMENT: *Dating*: by comparison with **136**. By the next Saturday, the 18th (as **138** shows), D was back in London.

Bradenham House | Saturday morn.

My dear Georgiana,

Our dear Sa was so violently affected by the receipt of your letter, that I have never ventured again even to allude to its subject, or to produce that cherished memorial[1] which you so kindly entrusted to me, and which is still in my poss[ess]ion. I cannot help thinking that it might be better that it sho[ul]d return to your hands, but I wo[ul]d not send it | by Ralph even, without your permission, lest you sho[ul]d misinterpret the motives which influenced me in so doing. I shall myself return in a week, and co[ul]d then bring it, if you all think that course advisable, which I cannot refrain from confessing that I do. For why sho[ul]d you be deprived of a memorial which might occasion you much satisfaction and which here seems only to have given rise to the wildest and most ungovernable grief. |

I told our dear Sa that I wo[ul]d write to you, and that you sho[ul]d not think her unmindful of your kindness, but I am so fearful that she may again lose her command of herself, that I have never approached the subject again.

I received the enclosed from Malta since my arrival here. It speaks of a subject which I apprehended had been neglected, and respecting which I have often written. If you will pay the amount to Ralph, he will save you further trouble, and hand it over to Mr Hunter.[2]

My kind regards to Mrs Meredith and Ellen

yours ever

BD

1 The ring for Sarah.

2 Presumably a bill connected with the costs of shipping home Meredith's effects, which D incurred through Hunter & Ross of Malta on his return voyage. See **119**.

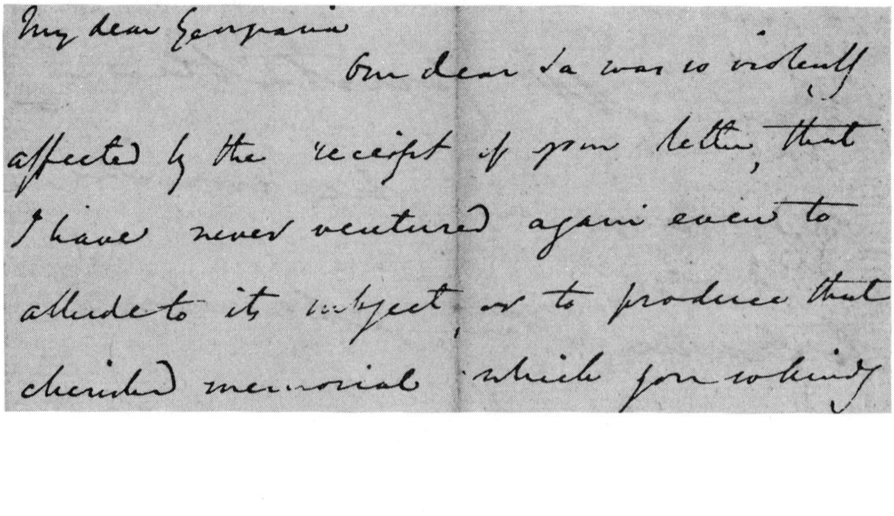
My dear Georgiana
Our dear Sa was so violently affected by the receipt of your letter, that I have never ventured again even to allude to its subject, or to produce that cherished memorial which you so kindly

TO SARAH DISRAELI 35 Duke Street, St James's, [London], [Saturday 18 February 1832] 138

ORIGINAL: H A/I/B/6

COVER: Miss Disraeli | Bradenham House | Wycombe | *Bucks.*

POSTMARK: (1) In circle: A | FE18 | 1832

PUBLICATION HISTORY: LBCS 1-2, dated 18 February 1832, presents a version of the second paragraph, the tenth ('my landlord'), and the twelfth, conflated with parts of **159**. M&B I 203-4, dated 18 February 1832, reprints this mixture.

EDITORIAL COMMENT: The return address on D's letters at this time indicates that he moved to 35 Duke Street, St James's, in mid-February 1832. *Sic*: St. James'.

35 Duke St. St. James'

My dearest Sa,

I write to you because I think you will prefer a stupid letter to none. My father of course duly recd. his power this morning, which he will return me by post.[1]

I have most comfortable lodgings and find the people very attentive.

Lord Stanley is at Knowsley, and will not return for ten days: the Longs are also away. I called on Ld. Eliot,[2] Sotheby,[3] Robert Smith, and Bulwer yesterday.

Mrs Bolton is still confined to her room, but they say mending. Haber called | on me – more mysterious than ever. He says that Russia will ratify the treaty in a few days, but that it is a ruse, and that there will be another invasion of Belgium[4] by the Prince; all is prepared.

People don't seem to think much of the Cholera.

I think I shall sell my pipes – and well. Toft[?] is most zealous.

I have seen the Merediths twice – very amiable. I met no one there.

I delivered, or sent, all my mother's letters. |

Ralph is very well.

My landlord tells me that Douce has just purchased the Vellum Pliny of Payne,[5] who procured it from Italy. It is the finest MS. in the world, and Douce gave 300 Gu[ine]as for it.

1 To enable him to act for Isaac in a number of business matters, D had drafted a power of attorney for Isaac to sign and return. See **141**.

2 Edward Granville Eliot (1798-1877), Baron Eliot, after 1845 3rd Earl of St Germans; Tory MP for Liskeard 1824-32 and for East Cornwall 1837-45. As envoy extraordinary to Spain in 1834 he induced the Carlists and the Queen's party to sign the 'Eliot Convention' for the humane treatment of prisoners.

3 Probably William Sotheby (1757-1833), author, playwright and translator, a member of the auctioneering family.

4 On 15 November 1831 the representatives of the powers had signed the treaty establishing the frontiers of Belgium. However, ratification remained a difficult business, for the northern powers – Russia, Prussia and Austria – were most reluctant to coerce the Dutch to observe pledges to the new state of Belgium. In the event, the Russians ratified the treaty on 4-5 May 1832 and the Prince of Orange did not again attack Belgium. However, Russian ratification was indeed a near thing and there is reason to suppose that, had the Grey ministry been defeated in the Lords a few days earlier – and not three days after the ratification – Russian ratification would not have occurred. Fl[eury] de Lannoy *Histoire diplomatique de l'indépendance belge (1830-1839)* (Bruxelles 1948) 38-9. Wellington and the Tories were much closer to Russia's position than were Melbourne and Palmerston, but Wellington was himself unable to form a government.

5 Presumably John Payne of Payne & Foss, booksellers at 81 Pall Mall. *LPOD* (1832).

My father never gave me a note for Rogers,[6] which we talked of. He might enclose it to me; as I sho[ul]d like it – an easy note it sho[ul]d be. You know.

The MS. most | graciously received is now passing the Albemarle St. ordeal.

Farewell my dearest – my nex[t] letter shall be more amusing – but as yet I have scarcely seen any one. 100 loves to yourself and all –

BD

139 TO JOHN MURRAY

35 Duke Street, St James's, [London],
[Saturday 18 February 1832]

ORIGINAL: MM 3
EDITORIAL COMMENT: In another hand on last page: '1832 (No date) | D'Israeli B. Esq – '. *Dating*: D told Sarah on 18 February 1832 (**138**) that Murray had received the MS, and on 20 February (**140**) that he had received it 'only on Saturday'. *Sic*: St. James'.

35 Duke Street | St. James'

John Murray Esq
Dear Sir,

I regret, that some unexpected County business should have occasioned any delay in the | transmission of the MS. of "The Psychological Romance", which you now receive.

I consign it to you with perfect confidence in your honor and impartiality, but while I express my trust and challenge severity, I deprecate neglect, and entreat candor. The | work is not divided into Volumes, as I do not wish it to appear in the hackneyed form. I wo[ul]d make one or two suggestions on this head with great deference to your experience, did I not consider them premature. |

My stay in town is uncertain, but I shall be here, I rather conceive, some time.

I have the honor to be
Dear Sir
Your obliged and obedient Serv[ant]
B. Disraeli

140 TO SARAH DISRAELI

35 Duke Street, St James's, [London],
[Monday 20 February 1832]

ORIGINAL: H A/I/B/7
COVER: Miss Disraeli | Bradenham House | Wycombe | Bucks
POSTMARK: (1) In Maltese cross: V.S | VFE20S | 1832
EDITORIAL COMMENT: There is no signature. *Sic*: St James', d Haussez.

35 Duke St St James'

My dearest Sa,

I received your welcome letter this morning, and the morning gown etc. duly on Saturday night. I shall attend to Mortimer[1] tomorrow and write if anything oc-

6 Presumably a letter of introduction to the poet Samuel Rogers.

1 The firm of E. Mortimer & Co, stockbrokers, at 7 Shorter's Court, Throgmorton Street, London. *LPOD* (1832).

cur. I have no fear in having the two hundred with me here, as it is not like a common lodging and plenty of drawers etc.

I have forbid the Globe.[2]

I have not been able to see any of the family – nor the Austens – but will make an effort. Tell Jem to send the cane by Taplin[3] with a direction tied onto it.

I | am busier than ever. I have got before me all the Cabinet papers of Charles the 10th.,[4] all the despatches of the Dutch Ambassador,[5] and a secret correspondence with the most eminent opposition member in France[6] – all from Haber, and Baron d Haussez[7] one of the Ex-Ministers – Such secrets! I am writing a book which will electrify all Europe.[8] I am perfectly uncontrolled, and, if I have time enough, I hope to produce something which will not only ensure my election, but produce me a political reputation, which is the foundation of everything, second to none. *This is the greatest of all great se[c]rets and must be confined to our hearth.*

I have seen no one, but | the Merediths and Mrs. Spence, who is very silly, trying to apologize for her husbands ratting, and all that.[9] She is full of Sir Wm Young[10] of course, and told me in confidence he was going to be married. He came up to London merely to tell her, and she was the only person who knew it. I, of course, floored her, and after having eulogised the Bart as the cleverest of men, as well as the most – delightful, I made her confess, he had only one idea in his head. Henry Young,[11] she says, is an object of universal abhorrence. "*He is the greatest brute,* and *the most horrid glutton*" and everything else abominable. Miss Lawrence[12] detests him as much as Mrs. Spence. I don't know what the poor devil has done.

2 Isaac had altered his choice of London newspapers, replacing *The Courier* with *The Globe*. After a month or so of *The Globe*, he regretted the decision. H A/I/C/18 19 24.

3 The proprietor of the Falcon Inn from which coaches left High Wycombe for London.

4 Charles X (1757-1836), King of France 1824-30.

5 Baron Hugo Zuylen van Nyevelt. See **163**n2.

6 As always, there was more than one opposition in France. Probably the centre of opposition before the July Revolution was Jacques Laffitte (1767-1844), the banker and politician. However, if by 'eminent' D referred to the office held, rather than to effectiveness in overt opposition, the grand référendaire, de Sémonville, might have been intended. See **141**&n1.

7 Charles Lemercher de Longpré, baron d'Haussez (1778-1854), minister of marine under Charles X. He found asylum in England after the July Revolution, although his *Mémoires*, published in 1896, record no events after 1830. He published some rather insipid impressions of England under the title *La Grande-Bretagne en 1833*, but this work is equally uninformative about his later political activities.

8 This was to be *England and France: or a Cure for the Ministerial Gallomania* (1832), henceforth referred to as *Gallomania*.

9 In 1819 Anne Kelsall had married George Spence (1787-1850), jurist and pioneer in Chancery reform, Tory MP successively for Reading and Ripon 1826-32. Spence's 'ratting' consisted in his support of the Reform Bill.

10 Sir William Lawrence Young (1806-1842), 4th Baronet, Tory MP for Buckinghamshire 1835-42. He married Caroline Norris of Hughenden.

11 Probably the 4th Baronet's brother, Henry Tuffnell Young.

12 Elizabeth Sophia Lawrence (1761-1845), the owner of Studley Park (which formed the township of Studley Royal) in Yorkshire. She was described in 1838 as a 'highly esteemed maiden lady, now in her 75th year, and generally styled Mrs. Lawrence.' *White's West Riding Directory* (Sheffield 1838) 805; Anon *The History of Ripon* (Ripon 1839) 100.

Of course nothing from Murray, who had the MS. only on Sat. I will write, if possible, every day, but at present can only say I love you and all – | Ralph saw the Trevors[13] yesterday, but sd. nothing about the fire. I will make enquir[i]es I left the note at Rogers' yesterday, as it was written, otherwise I am too deeply engaged to care for mere society.

---

141 TO SARAH DISRAELI

35 Duke Street, St James's, [London], Wednesday [22 February 1832]

ORIGINAL: H A/I/B/8
COVER: Miss Disraeli | Bradenham House | Wycombe | Bucks.
POSTMARK: (1) In circle: N | FE22 | 1832
PUBLICATION HISTORY: LBCS 2-3, dated 22 February 1832, followed by M&B I 204, which quotes from 'I am writing' in the second paragraph to 'And no more' in the third
EDITORIAL COMMENT: *Sic*: St James, anyway.

---

35 Duke St St James | Wednesday

My dearest Sa,

Tell my father I paid into his account this morning £212.13.6, and have kept the o[the]r 200£ as he instructed me, and shall keep it by me, until I clearly see my future movements. I went into the City yesterday, but it was necessary for the power to be lodged a day previously, which the stupid Mortimers had not informed me, and therefore gave me double trouble.

I continue enveloped in affairs. Ask my father, if he remember a curious scene of the Grand Ref[er]endary of France, Count de Semonville,[1] restoring some | colors etc. and the subsequent attack upon him in the Times, which made a great sensation, giving the substance of a conversation between the Ref[er]endary and one of the ministers. The Minister was d'Haussez, and the writer of the article Haber.[2] That article will give you an idea of the wonderfully curious, I may say, unprecedented, materials I have before me, and with which I may do what I like. I am writing a very John Bull book, which will quite delight you and my mother. I am still a Reformer, but I shall destroy the foreign policy of the Grey faction.

13 Presumably the family of Charles Trevor (1800-1880), who married Olivia Lindo, D's cousin. At this time Trevor held the office of solicitor for legacy duties; later he became the comptroller of legacy duties.

---

1 Charles-Louis Huguet (1759-1839), marquis de Sémonville, until 1834 grand référendaire, or keeper of the royal seal of France. He was also a count.

2 Sémonville had concealed some Napoleonic trophies – specifically, Austrian standards – in the Luxembourg. In the celebrations marking the first anniversary of the July Revolution these colours were displayed in the upper house. Unfavourable comment came in a *Times* leader of 30 July 1831 which contained, within quotation marks, a passage said to come from 'a person of honour who took an active part in the transactions of the last reign'. This was Haber's contribution. It quoted a conversation of 15 July 1830 which served to link Sémonville with those same arbitrary measures of Charles X which the référendaire had later denounced. D alludes to this business in *Gallomania* 123.

They seem firmly fixed at home, altho' | a storm is, without doubt, brewing abroad. I think peers will be created, and Charles Gore[3] has promised to let me have timely notice, if Baring be one. He called upon me, and said that Lord John[4] often asked how I was getting on at Wycombe. He fished as to whether I sho[ul]d support them. I answered they had one claim upon my support; they needed it. And no more.

I understand the St. Thomas affair[5] does not in anyway touch the Lindos.[6] The Jamaica business is considered very serious, and the last blow to the W.I. interest.

It is curious, that none of my friends have done me the honor to return my call, which is gratifying to my vanity. As it is, I wish to see no one. I think Bulwer is offended. I am credibly informed the Mag[azine] has sensibly declined in sale under his Editors[hi]p, and this combined with his now universally acknowledged | failure[7] in a more important place perhaps depresses him. I am sorry for him, but God is great. I saw Mrs. Austen. She says there is no such expression in Hohenlinden, or any of Campbells poems, as "*clouds of carnage*", and wishes my father to explain.[8] Tell him to send me a message, as the desire was reiterated, and, indeed I am informed, expressed in a letter I recd. at Bradenham, and which I co[ul]d not have carefully read. Tell me how my mother is. I have not seen the *MS*[9] since Sunday. I hope to write you some more amusing letters. Mrs. Bolton still very ill.[10]

Your m[os]t loving brother.

BD

3 Charles Alexander Gore (1811-1897), fifth son of Col William Gore and younger brother of the 4th Earl of Arran. From 1828 he was in the paymaster general's office, then in the Treasury. He was private secretary to Lord John Russell 1830-4 and 1835-9, and so was in a position to know the business of the Whig administrations. From 1839 to 1885 he was a commissioner of woods and forests. Greville IV 232n; Spencer Walpole *Life of Lord John Russell* (1889) I 323; Boase.

4 Lord John Russell (1792-1878), third son of the 6th Duke of Bedford, after 1861 1st Earl Russell. Whig and Liberal MP for various constituencies 1813-61, prime minister 1846-52, 1865-6. He was then paymaster general in Grey's government.

5 This refers to the state of affairs in the Jamaican parish of St Thomas during the slave insurrection of 1832. Although the abolition of slavery was still two years away, a false report was circulated in January throughout Jamaica that it had already been proclaimed. Resulting disappointment led to widespread rioting.

6 For evidence of Benjamin Lindo's Jamaican holdings see Isaac to D, H A/I/C/24. The family interest in Jamaica was established, it would seem, by Alexander (or Alexandre) Lindo (d 1818), slave dealer and merchant. See Philip Wright ed *Lady Nugent's Journal of Her Residence in Jamaica from 1801-1805* (Kingston, Jamaica 1966) 305.

7 Bulwer's novel *Eugene Aram*, which was published in January 1832, was savagely attacked in the February number of *Fraser's*. Sadleir *Bulwer* (276) and *The Wellesley Index* both attribute the review to William Maginn. D may also be referring to Bulwer's demonstrated incapacity to think on his feet in the House of Commons.

8 Sarah replied that the expression was a 'family tradition'. H A/I/B/415. Perhaps the joke was simply that one might expect to meet such language in the poetry of Thomas Campbell (1777-1844).

9 *Gallomania*.

10 Within a short time Clara Bolton was to become an invalid. Sarah Harriet Burney's description of her in 1835 was that she was 'very handsome, immoderately clever, an Astrologer' and had to be 'carried on an inclined plane to people's houses.' Joyce Hemlow *The History of Fanny Burney* (Oxford 1958) 476.

142 TO SARAH DISRAELI 35 Duke Street, St James's, [London],
Friday [24 February 1832]

ORIGINAL: H A/I/B/9
COVER: Miss Disraeli | Bradenham House | High Wycombe | Bucks.
POSTMARK: (1) In Maltese cross: V.S | VFE24S | 1832
EDITORIAL COMMENT: *Sic*: St James, wave, tete á tete, Beiroot, Salonicka, gallopping, St. James'.

35 Duke St. St James | Friday

My dearest Sa,

I received *this morning* a joint letter dated *Wednesday*, and yesterday the cane and Jem's agreeable note. Lord Eliot called on me yesterday, and Henry Bulwer, but I was out. I received on Wednesday evening a most affectionate letter from Edward, telling me that he had not called from perfect engrossment of time, and living out of town in a cottage 14 miles off with Madame[1] – but | begging me to wave all ceremony, and dine with him *quietly* on Wednesday in Hertford Street.[2] I like not the phrase *quietly* – it sounds like a tete á tete, which I wish to avoid, as I am not in the humor to be nicked. I do not like the way he is going on. He is, I am told, announced as a lecturer at the National Political Union.[3] Probably he has his eye on one of the Metropolitan Districts, but can such an object, or any other, justify such intrigue?

Peers will be created and in | any quantity – 50, 100, or 200. The Minister has carte blanche; I have written by a frank to Huffam;[4] as I wish to get in by the corporation. I have my inform[ati]on from the highest source. Tell Jem to make up a jar of tobacco for Carter,[5] with my compliments. Give him the Beiroot, and put about as much Salonicka tied up in a parcel neatly and put it in the same jar. Let Carter know that one is the finest Turkish, and the o[the]r the finest Syrian tobaccos, and impossible to obtain. Let him give it with my Comp[limen]ts *and without loss of time*.

The day before yesterday walking down King St., I perceived a Diana Vernon[6] looking personage gallopping thro' St. James' Sq: on a bay charger and

1 Rosina Doyle Bulwer, née Wheeler (1802-1882), had married Edward Lytton Bulwer in 1827. After a stormy marriage they were legally separated in 1836.

2 At this time the Bulwers' town house was at 36 Hertford Street, London.

3 A radical association founded in 1831 to press for parliamentary reform. Sir Francis Burdett, the MP for Westminster, was chairman. D.J. Rowe ed *London Radicalism, 1830-1843: Selections from the Papers of Francis Place* (1970) xi, xvi, 29-34.

4 John Hudson Huffam, a naval lieutenant on half pay, was one of D's Wycombe supporters. On 18 May 1832 Sarah wrote to D: 'Has Huffam written to you about the Pigeon match. They seem all to be talking of it in Wycombe and have formed a club.' H A/I/B/429 and Navy List.

5 John Carter, a tanner, was a Tory alderman of High Wycombe throughout the 1830s and in February 1832 was the Mayor. Ashford 261, 264-65.

In her reply Sarah wrote: 'Carter received the Tobacco most graciously. Jem flatters himself from his graceful manner of presenting it.' H A/I/B/416.

6 A character in Scott's novel *Rob Roy*. The image was then commonly applied to young ladies who were elegant riders. See, for example, William Archer Shee's use of the term in *My Contemporaries, 1830-1870* (1893) 32.

followed by a groom on a grey cob, whose tail swept | the ground. She stopped at Bolton's, as I quitted the door. I suspected it was the fair Margaret,[7] and the next day the puffer General[8] called upon me, and informed me that the lady's heart was equally prophetic – but as I understand from ano[the]r and more accurate source, that the lady has *down* only 20,000£, why, I am in no hurry. This is a hasty letter, but I have put off writing to the last moment. I shall write again soon. The Merediths are all well.

Your m[os]t *loving* brother |

My father's observations[9] are quite just; but they do not apply to the present instance. I hope I am not green enough to be taken in by secret agents, and as for parties, *I am for myself*. No one will ever make me a tool. I will tell you more about Haber when we meet.

In case I do not come in a day or two, I will send the 100£ tomorrow by a frank.

143

TO JOHN MURRAY — 35 Duke Street, St James's, [London], Sunday [26 February 1832?]

ORIGINAL: MM 8

PUBLICATION HISTORY: Smiles II 338-9, undated

EDITORIAL COMMENT: In another hand at the top of the last page: '1832 – (No date) | D'Israeli Benjn'. *Dating*: Murray had received the MS on Saturday 18 February (see **139**); on Monday 27 February D told Sarah (**144**) that he had written to Murray on the previous day. See also **145**, **148**, **149**.

---

35 Duke St | St. James | Sunday

John Murray Esq

My dear Sir,

It is with deep regret, and some mortification that I appear to press you.

It is of the highest importance to me that the *P[sychological] R[omance]* sho[ul]d appear without loss of time. I have an impending election in the county, which a | single, and not improbable, event may precipitate. It is a great object with me, that my work should be published before that election.

Its rejection by you will only occasion me sorrow. I have no desire that you sho[ul]d become its publisher, unless you conceive it may be the first of a series of works, which may support your | name and sustain your fortunes.

There is no question of pecuniary matters between us. I leave all these with you with illimitable trust.

Pray, pray, my dear Sir, do not let me repent the feelings which impel me to seek this renewal of our connection. I entreat therefore | your attention to this subject, and request that you will communicate your decision.

7 As letters from Mrs Bolton make clear, this is Margaret Trotter, the 'Amazon' of Grosvenor Square, daughter of Sir Coutts Trotter, who was the senior partner in the Coutts banking house. H A/IV/G/5-7. At the death of her father in September 1837 she was still unmarried, having recently broken off her engagement to vicomte de La Rochefoucauld. *CJ* no 437 (9 Sept 1837) 568.

8 Clara Bolton, who paraded eligible women before D.

9 Presumably admonitions by Isaac in the 'joint letter dated *Wednesday*'. The letter is not in the Hughenden papers.

Believe me, as I have already said, that what[eve]r that decision may be, I shall not the less consider myself

Very cordially yrs

B. Disraeli

144 TO SARAH DISRAELI

35 Duke Street, St James's, [London], Monday [27 February 1832]

ORIGINAL: H A/I/B/10

COVER: Miss Disraeli | Bradenham House | High Wycombe | Bucks.

POSTMARK: (1) In circle: V | FE27 | 1832

EDITORIAL COMMENT: *Sic*: St James, *chassèd*, baccularian.

35 Duke St St James | Monday

My dear, dear Sa,

A week having elapsed, and not hearing from Murray, I yesterday dispatched him a note. I received instanter, the most courteous letter possible, in which he says, that not liking to trust in such an affair to his own judgment, he had confided my MS. to "*a literary friend of the most accomplished class, and perfectly unknown to me, except by fame*" that the said critic was not in town, and that he was in hourly expectation, and that I might depend that not an instant sho[ul]d be unnecessarily lost. I, at first, thought Mitchell;[1] but on reflection, I do not think Murray has sufficient confidence in him, and I suspect Milman.[2] If so, I fancy I am in good hands, as I think he will enter into it. Of course, after this, I must not press him, and perhaps a few hours will settle it

I wrote to you on Friday. Tell my father I did not send him the £100, as I co[ul]d not conveniently | get a frank. The best way will be for him to draw, and I will pay tomorrow, or on Wednesday morning *at the furthest*, £100 into his bankers.

With regard to a certain subject,[3] I can, I think, positively state, that no one is in the field. I am thus in the height of favor on account of frequent calls, especially with Madame,[4] who is more than cordial. I am pleased to observe, that a certain youth in whom we take an interest, has been mentioned more than once by a certain damosel[5] with remarkable unction for her – such as "you must get poor – in Parliamt. too" ["]You must do something for him – do" etc. I think there is every hope, and if once they are down at Bradenham etc. I speak mystically, because I am not sure you will be up, and this letter may be opened. Give orders that our correspondence is sacred in future; seals never broke etc. Mad-

1 See **83**n2.

2 Henry Hart Milman (1791-1868), professor of poetry at Oxford 1821-31, dean of St Paul's, author of a number of dramas (1815-26), editor of Gibbon (1838), author of *History of the Jews* (1830), *History of Christianity under the Empire* (1840) and, his principal work, *The History of Latin Christianity* (1854-5).

3 Probably a reference to D's courting of Ellen Meredith.

4 Mrs Meredith.

5 There seem also to have been hopes that Ralph might marry one of the Meredith girls.

ame mentioned to me, that she considered my making her house an | exception in morning visits etc. very flattering (she knows I have not been anywhere) and said she had not ventured to ask me to dinner, as Day[6] was not there, and she supposed my time was too valuable. I instantly expressed my willingness to come, and I agreed for Friday; I believe the Bucks[7] are to be solicited.

Tomorrow, I dine with B.E.L. Wednesday with Bulwer. I have never been so well for years, altho' there is nothing but fog. I ascribe it in a great degree to the regularity of my diet – roast meat and brandy and water. I am wonderfully well; in real high feather.

So after all, Horace Claggett has never married Miss Day,[8] but on the contrary been *chassèd* by the prudent father *sans ceremonie*.

I have discovered that the Grand Priest or Pope of the new St. Simonian Religion, or Heresy, is a Jew; Rodriguez.[9] He writes to Haber every week. His communications are very curious, quite in an infallible demi-inspiration strain – *on dit* the affair spreads very much; it will, I think, take with the Hebrews, as it appears to me, they need reject nothing and adopt nothing.

Mrs. Bolton continues very unwell. B. is mortified that I have not yet met the Amazon,[10] but I am more baccularian than ever. The way he goes on, is supremely ludicrous. Every day he calls, and fetches away a pipe or a dagger to show Mrs. B. and always lets out when | he returns them, that they have been to Grosvenor Sq: –

Ld. Grey has certainly a carte blanche for Peers – but Haber has thrown a new light upon the subject. He says that many lords who voted for the bill, will vote against it on vital points such as metropol[itan] members[11] etc. and will send it down to the Commons so that they will reject it after all the creation of peers. The peers will not be pumped,[12] and the upshot is, with the carte blanche, the Minister does not know how to act. Peers howr. will be created, and I must get in with the Corporation. Adieu, my dearest, dearest Sa. Write to me, and give my love to all.

BD |

Tomorrow and Wednesday, I shall call upon the family, etc.

6 Probably William Day (see vol II, **384**n6). He was a member of a different family from the Charles Days about whom D gossips two paragraphs later. See also **152**n5.

7 Presumably the same with whom D dined a month later. See **160**n4.

8 Horace, third son of Horatio Claggett of Claggett & Pratt, a firm of American merchants. Miss Day was the daughter of Charles Day (d 1836) of Day and Martin's Blacking. The family was deemed distressingly nouveau riche but envied for their wealth. As one fashionable lady of the time wrote, 'it is *that* Day but his profits are enormous'. Hon J.H. Home ed *Letters of Lady Louise Stewart* (Edinburgh 1901) II 255-6. Despite Day's objection, the couple eventually eloped. *CJ* no 181 (13 Oct 1832) 682.

9 Benjamin Olinde Rodriguez (1794-1850) actually seems to have played the more mundane role of treasurer of the Saint Simonian movement. A mission was dispatched to England in 1832. H.R. d'Allemagne *Les Saint-Simoniens, 1827-37* (Paris 1930) 155-6.

10 Margaret Trotter.

11 The Reform Bill created eight new seats for London.

12 Speculation about the peers and their response to the Reform Bill had long been a favourite topic of conversation, and Henry Rich's pamphlet *What Will the Lords Do?* (1831) spawned many imitations.

145 TO JOHN MURRAY 35 Duke Street, St James's, [London], Thursday [1 March 1832]

ORIGINAL: MM 15

EDITORIAL COMMENT: On the fourth page in another hand: '1832 (No date) | D'Israeli Benj Esq.' *Dating*: D told Sarah on 1 March, 'I have not heard from Murray, but with all deference for his critic, have written to day for a definite and immediate answer.' **146**. Murray replied on the same day apologizing for the delay in the return of the MS of *Contarini Fleming* from his critic. H E/VII/C/5. *Sic*: St James, agreable.

35 Duke St. St James | Thursday

John Murray Esq
My dear Sir,

With deference to your critic,[1] and a due regard of your interests, pardon me for definitely stating that the publication of the *P[sychological] R[omance]* can no longer be delayed. I | must either be rejected or adopted, and at once. I hope therefore to receive, in a few hours, an agreable communication from you, but if this unhappily be not in your | power, I really must require you to return the MS. to its author, who has great pleasure in subscribing himself,

Your very faithful Ser[vant]
B. Disraeli

146 TO SARAH DISRAELI 35 Duke Street, St James's, [London], Thursday 1 March [1832]

ORIGINAL: H A/I/B/11

COVER: Miss Disraeli | Bradenham House | High Wycombe | Bucks

POSTMARK: (1) In circle: C | MR-1 | 1832

PUBLICATION HISTORY: LBCS 3-4, dated 1 March 1832, extracts from the first paragraph and all of the second, except for the last sentence

EDITORIAL COMMENT: There is no signature. *Sic*: St James, tete á tete, french, partiér quarré, champaign, ticketted, Ann, aid de Camps.

35 Duke St St James | Thursday Mar. 1.

My dearest Sa,

I received yours yesterday, and also the previous Friday epistle.[1] On Tuesday I dined tete á tete with our good cousin of Verulam,[2] and yesterday I called upon Mrs. Philip Hardwick[3] whom I co[ul]d not see, but whose boys are doing well, and the Trevors, and others, and dined with Bulwer. I met there a french no-

1 Milman. See **151**n1.

1 Sarah wrote to D on 24 February 1832 (H A/I/B/415), and on 29 February (H A/I/B/416).

2 Benjamin Lindo, whose address at this time was 4 Verulam Buildings, Gray's Inn.

3 Julia Tufnell Hardwick, née Shaw, was the wife of Philip Hardwick (1792-1870), architect, and brother of John Hardwick. Philip Hardwick is best remembered as the designer of Euston Station. For evidence of his friendship with the D'Israeli family see Sarah to D (H A/I/B/558) and Isaac to D (H A/IV/E/14).

bleman whose name I co[ul]d not catch, altho' he spoke good English. He is one of the Guizot school[4] paying a visit to this constitutional country, and Charles Villiers,[5] an intermediate brother of | Hyde Villiers, and my dear, and sulky, and neglected friend, Edward. He is a very intelligent and gentlemanly person. Frederick Villiers,[6] my old acquaintance, is no relation of these, but is now in the house, where he has distinguished himself by voting for the bill in all its stages, and then delivering a violent philippic against it. A certain coolness, in consequence, ensued between himself and his old ally, Edward Lytton. Lord Mulgrave,[7] who, according to my host, is "exceedingly anxious" to make my acquaintance, was to have formed the partiér quarré, but was unfortunately pre-engaged to Sir Geo Warrender, or rather | Provender.[8] Luttrell[9] says, that the two most disgusting things in the world, because you cannot deny them, are Warrender's wealth, and Croker's talents.

We had some amusing conversation, and our host, whatever may be his situation, is more sumptuous and fantastic than ever. Mrs. B. was a blaze of jewels, and looked like Juno, only instead of a peacock, she had a dog in her lap called Fairy, not bigger than a bird of Paradise and quite as brilliant. We drank champaign out of these [sketch of a very wide and shallow stemmed wine glass], a saucer of ground glass mounted on a pedestal of cut glass. The side board is now supported by a long row of ormolu pillars as big as those of the Theseum, and flamed with plate.

I saw the Merediths yesterday.

The | Days have returned. I paid £100 into Curtis'.[10] I have hitherto avoided dining with the Austens, but am at last ticketted for Saturday. I met Patmore,[11] who told me that he had just received a letter from Ward, that Ann[12] was given over, and that Tremaine, as High Sheriff,[13] co[ul]d not open the Assizes. According to P. the secret history of Gilston is very curious, but too long for present narration. The series of rows that took place there are beyond conception. The Wards say that Mad[am]e killed the girls, and the recrimination now is, that

4 There were many French noblemen among the followers of François Guizot (1787-1874), the liberal statesman and historian. Among them were the duc de Broglie (1785-1870) and the baron de Barante (1782-1866), but neither seems to have been in England at the time.

5 Charles Pelham Villiers (1802-1898), Whig MP for Wolverhampton 1835-98. He was the younger brother of Thomas Hyde Villiers (1801-1832), Radical MP for various constituencies 1826-32.

6 Frederick Meynell Villiers (c 1801-1871), Whig MP for Saltash 1831-2.

7 Constantine Henry Phipps (1797-1863), after 1831 2nd Earl of Mulgrave, prominent Whig politician, colonial governor and diplomat; governor of Jamaica 1832-4; lord lieutenant of Ireland 1835-9. He was created Marquess of Normanby in 1838.

8 Sir George Warrender (1782-1849), 4th Baronet, Whig MP for various constituencies 1807-32. Greville I 205n. The splendour of his dinner parties led to his nickname.

9 Henry Luttrell (1765?-1851), wit and man of letters who lived on a pension from the Irish government. Lloyd Sanders *The Holland House Circle* (1908) ch 13.

10 Robarts, Curtis and Co, bankers at 15 Lombard Street. Robson's *Directory*.

11 Peter George Patmore (1786-1855), journalist, miscellaneous writer and editor of the *The New Monthly Magazine* 1841-53. He was the father of Coventry Patmore, the poet.

12 Anne, youngest daughter of Robert Plumer Ward, died in 1835.

13 D sometimes referred to Robert Plumer Ward, who in 1830 became sheriff of Gilston, as 'Tremaine'.

the young Wards killed her.[14] Long before her death, Henry and his wife[15] had left the house, and did not speak to her, but resided in a neighbouring cott[ag]e at 30£ a year, on their own income, and that alone – etc. etc. etc. | A beautiful comb for my beloved has arrived from Spain. Don spent more than treble his income, but after paying everything, 60000£ will be the portion of her Lady[shi]p, to whom everything was left, not even a ring to his servile aid de Camps. Geo. Basevi has another son,[16] and is to raise a monument to the Gibraltar hero.[17] I have not heard from Murray, but with all deference for his critic, have written to day for a definite and immediate answer. I write by this to Huffam with a frank. I saw Douce, and at present, have escaped dining, altho' asked.

Write – and tell me whether I shall send the comb. It is of Tortoise, at least I suppose, plain, but delicate. God bless you all.

147

TO JOHN MURRAY — 35 Duke Street, St James's, [London], Friday [2? March 1832]

ORIGINAL: MM 9
PUBLICATION HISTORY: Smiles II 339, undated extract
EDITORIAL COMMENT: In another hand, inverted, on the final page: '1832 – No date | D'Israeli Benj.' *Dating*: by comparison with **145**. *Sic*: St. James.

---

35 Duke St St. James, | Friday

John Murray Esq
Dear Sir,
My stay in town is very precarious: my absence, from the present aspect of the political horizon, I should perhaps say, my immediate absence, *very probable*.

It would be highly gratifying to me to know, without | any unnecessary delay, your opinion of the *P[sychological] R[omance]*. I require only your *literary opinion*: all other arrangements can be left to your convenience, and I am sure, as far as I am concerned, in them your interests will be not | less studied than my own.

There is no work of fiction on whose character I could not decide in four and twenty hours, and your critic ought not to be less able than your author.

Pray | therefore communicate without loss of time, to
your obed. and faith[fu]l Ser[van]t
BD

14 In 1830, Julia and Catherine, Ward's daughters by his first marriage, had both died, followed by the death on 26 March 1831 of Mrs Plumer Ward. See H A/IV/E/8 & 21, in which Sarah reported that 'Mrs Plumer Ward has departed this life to Ward's infinite astonishment and has left him Gilston and about £8,000 a year.' The standard biography makes no reference to any scandal associated with the deaths, so the alleged killing was presumably not meant literally! Hon Edmund Phipps *Memoirs of the Political and Literary Life of Robert Plumer Ward* (1850) II 185-6.

15 Henry George Ward (1797-1860), son of Robert Plumer Ward, Whig MP for St Albans 1832-7, and for Sheffield 1837-49. In 1824 he had married Emily Elizabeth Swinburne, daughter of Sir John Swinburne, 6th Baronet. Ward was knighted in 1849.

16 James Palladio Basevi (1832-1871) was born on 23 February. Basevi family tree in the Jewish Museum, London.

17 A monument to Sir George Don was erected at Gibraltar.

TO JOHN MURRAY [London], [Sunday] 4 March 1832 **148**

ORIGINAL: MM 34

PUBLICATION HISTORY: Smiles II 336-7, dated 4 March 1832

EDITORIAL COMMENT: In another hand on the first page: '1832 March 4 | D'Israeli, Benj. Esq.' *Dating*: the MS clearly shows this to be written in the early hours of Sunday 4 March, notwithstanding the discussion here of details of the financial arrangements for *Contarini Fleming*, which would seem to place it after both D's request for the return of the MS on the following day, and his receipt of Milman's favourable report on 7th March.

Saturday night | 2 o ck. | Mar 4 1832

John Murray Esq

My dear Sir,

I wish that I could simplify our arrangements by a stroke, by making you a present of "the Psychological Romance" – but at the present you must indeed take the will for the deed, altho' I hope the future will allow us to get on more swimmingly. That work has, in all probability, cost me more than I shall ever obtain by it, and indeed I may truly say, that to write that work, I have thrown | to the winds all the obvious worldly prospects of life.

I am ready to make every possible sacrifice on my part to range myself under your colors. I will willingly give up the immediate and positive receipt of a large sum of money for the copyright, and by publishing the work anonymously renounce that certain sale, which, as a successful, altho', I confess, not very worthy author, I can command. But in quitting my present publisher,[1] I incur, from the terms of our last agreement, a *virtual penalty*, which I have no means to | pay except by the proceeds of my pen. Have you therefore any objection to advance me a sum on the anticipated profits of the edition not exceeding two hundred pounds?

It grieves me much to appear exacting to you, but I frankly tell you the reason, and as it is to enable me to place myself at your disposal, I hope you will not consider me mercenary, when I am indeed influenced by the most sincere desire to meet your views.

If this modification of | your arrangement will suit you, as I fervently trust it will, I shall be delighted to accede to your wishes. In that case, let me know, without loss of time, and pray let us meet to talk over the minor points, as to the mode of publication etc. I shall be at home all the morning; my time is very much occupied, and on Thursday, or Friday, I must run down, for a day or two to Wycombe, to attend a public meeting.

Fervently trusting that this will meet your wishes, believe me

Yours

Benj Disraeli

1 Henry Colburn.

149 TO JOHN MURRAY

35 Duke Street, St James's, [London], [Monday 5 March 1832]

ORIGINAL: MM 12

PUBLICATION HISTORY: Smiles II 337, undated

EDITORIAL COMMENT: In another hand on the last page: '1832 – (No date) | D'Israeli Benj. Esq.' *Dating*: this is clearly the request for the return of the MS referred to in D's letter to Sarah (**150**) of 5 March. *Sic*: St. James.

35 Duke St St. James

John Murray Esq.

My dear Sir,

I am very sensible, that you have conducted yourself, with regard to my MS., in the most honorable, kind, and judicious, manner, and I very much regret the result of your exertions, which neither of us deserve.

I | can wait no longer. The delay is most injurious to me, and in every respect very annoying. I am therefore under the painful necessity of requesting you to require from your friend the return of my work *without a moment's delay*, | but I shall not deny myself the gratification of thanking you for your kindness and subscribing myself,

with regard,

your faithful Serv[an]t

Benj Disraeli

150 TO SARAH DISRAELI

[35] Duke Street, [St James's, London], [Monday] 5 March [1832]

ORIGINAL: H A/I/B/12

COVER: Miss Disraeli | Bradenham House | Wycombe | Bucks.

POSTMARK: (1) In circle: O | MR-5 | 1832

PUBLICATION HISTORY: LBCS 4-5, dated 5 March 1832, includes the second paragraph without the last two sentences, and conflated with extracts from **151** and **152**.

Duke St. Mar. 5.

My dearest Sa,

I received yours[1] this morning. Nothing is settled, but it is not Murray's fault who has behaved in the most attentive manner. He has written this morning to the critic to say I require the MS. I dare say all will be properly accounted for, but I will wait no more.

I intend if possible to get down at the end of this week, Thursday or Friday for a few days to see my constituents – my constituents I hope they will be, although the Reform Bill is in a most crazy state, and now that the King has given the Earl a carte blanche, which he has undoubtedly, Ld Grey does not know what to do with it. I should not be overwhelmed with astonishment if the bill

1 Sarah wrote D on 4 March 1832. H A/I/B/417.

failed altogether. There will however be | a dissolution at all events. I have seen Forbes, who was most friendly and called upon me to day. Bulwer has just left me after smoking a Turkish pipe and a very long visit.

I do not think that Hope,[2] or anyone, is in the field more than myself, but Ralph has no chance, unless they come down to Bradenham.

Friday I dined with the Merediths, Saturday with the Austens. These domestic engagements destroy me, altho' I | avoid them. The Haberian book[3] goes on very well, and it is possible that some part of it in some shape or other, either as a vol. or a number, may soon appear.

I suppose I have a great deal to say, but really I am conscious of nothing except the postman's bell.[4] I shall write on Wednesday to say when I shall come down. In the meantime receive my love and offer it my dearest to all those around you.

BD

151

TO SARAH DISRAELI [London, Wednesday 7 March 1832]

ORIGINAL: H A/I/B/13

COVER: Miss Disraeli | Bradenham House | Wycombe | Bucks

POSTMARK: (1) In circle: U | MR-7 | 1832

PUBLICATION HISTORY: LBCS 4-5, dated 5 March 1832, prints the first paragraph (except for the last sentence), and the second (conflated with **150**) from the beginning to '... is not true', with several alterations. The version concludes with a paragraph from **152**.

EDITORIAL COMMENT: The first page of the MS is damaged.

My dearest Angel,

The critic has responded, and beyond all our hopes.[1] He was Milman, and the

2 Frederick W. Hope (1797-1862), curate and entomologist, who in 1835 married Ellen Meredith. He was not related to D's friend Henry Thomas Hope.

3 *Gallomania.*

4 It was not until the 1840s, with the introduction of prepaid postage and the installation of letter-boxes on each house, that letter-carriers ceased the practice of ringing the doorbell to deliver mail. Until 1846 there were also letter-carriers who rang bells in the streets and, for a fee of one penny per letter, collected mail after the post-office receiving-boxes had closed. Frank Staff *The Penny Post, 1680-1918* (1964) 77, 168-9; Howard Robinson *Britain's Post Office* (1953) 167; J.C. Hemmeon *The History of the British Post Office* (1893) 342.

---

1 Smiles (II 337-8) prints Milman's letter to Murray on *Contarini Fleming*:

My dear Sir, Reading, March 5th, 1832.

I have been utterly inefficient for the last week, in a state of almost complete blindness; but am now, I trust, nearly restored. Mrs. Milman, however, has read me the whole of the MS. It is a very remarkable production – very wild, very extravagant, very German, very powerful, very poetical. It will, I think, be much read – as far as one dare predict anything of the capricious taste of the day – much admired, and much abused. It is much more in the Macaulay than in the Croker line, and the former is evidently in the ascendant. Some passages will startle the rigidly orthodox; the phrenologists will be in rapture. I tell you all this, that you may judge for yourself. One thing insist upon, if you publish it – that the title be changed. The whole beauty, of the latter part especially, is its truth. It is a rapid volume of travels, a 'Childe Harold' in prose; therefore do not let it be called "a Romance" on any account. Let those who will, believe it to be a real history, and those who are not taken in, dispute whether it is truth or fiction. If it makes any sensation, this will add to its notoriety[.] 'A Psychological Auto-Biography' would be too sesquipedalian a title; but 'My Life Psychologically Related,' or 'The Psychology of my Life,' or some such title, might be substituted.

H.H. Milman.

reason of his delay was that from a disorder in his eyes he cannot read and therefore the work was read to him by Madame, which took time. I have not seen his letter, because Murray gave it to Lockhart, but am to. I can therefore only collect a general impression from M – who you know is very vague, but he said that there had been nothing like the descriptions and pictures of Oriental life since Bruce.[2] This is the only par[*ticu*]lar trait, that I co[ul]d extract, or rather obtained. M. said that he looked forward to it with the | same confidence as to Childe Harold in spite of the times. It is to be printed in four volumes, like Byrons collected works, as you have them.

Milman opposes the word *Romance* in the title. He says that nothing sho[ul]d disturb the reality of the impression, or make the common reader for a moment suppose that every word is not true. Think of a title. The Ps[ychological] *Biography* [*or*] *Memoir* – or *History*?[3]

I shall ride down on Monday, if it do not rain, and hope | to bring a proof. It is very inconvenient for me to leave town until I have finished the Haberian vol. in which I much miss your aid, but these 10 pounders must be looked after. I shall probably only stay till the middle of the week.

Adieu my dearest Sa – and believe your most
affectionate brother,
BD

---

152 TO SARAH DISRAELI [London], Friday [9 March 1832]

ORIGINAL: H A/I/B/14

COVER: Miss Disraeli | Bradenham House | Wycombe | Bucks.

POSTMARK: (1) In circle: A | MR-9 | 1832

PUBLICATION HISTORY: LBCS 4-5, dated 5 March 1832, presents a shortened version of the first paragraph (conflated with **150** and **151**), the first sentence of the second, and the first sentence of the third.

Friday

My dearest Sa,

I shall be at Gerards X[1] to bait about one on Sunday, and shall be happy to meet Jem. I shall send my portmanteau by the Coach. I shall be able to make a longer stay than I expected, and shall certainly be able to remain a week. I shall howr. be very busy, and employ you to your hearts content. |

With regard to politics, I flatter myself I know as much as *Bob*,[2] but I really cannot pretend to say what is going to happen, altho' I may ascertain before

2 James Bruce (1730-1794), author and traveller in Africa and the Middle East.

3 'Auto-biography' was the final choice for this edition.

---

1 Gerard's Cross, in Buckinghamshire on the road between London and Wycombe, where D planned to halt for refreshment.

2 Robert Smith.

tomorrow. I have the best means of information, for through Haber, I have become acquainted, altho' I have ment[ione]d the acquaintance to no other person but yourself, with the Editor of the Times by name Murray[3] | and who writes those freq[uent] art[icle]s which you read with wonder.

If Lord Grey do not make peers, he will go out, and perhaps finish his mortal, as well as political, career at the same time. I care very little, what[eve]r may be the result, as, under all circumstances, I hope to float uppermost.

Douce I saw yest[erda]y; fortunately, no more talk of dinner. Hardwick has just left the room very well. I dined in Nottingham Place yesterday en famille.[4] I think Mrs Day[5] much the most disgusting person I ever meet. I co[ul]d not have anticipated in the pres[en]t day, a young woman so offensive. We shall soon meet and I postpone all chat.

BD |

I have Jem's Dahlias and Bears Grease.[6]

TO [JOHN MURRAY JR] [London], Friday [9 March 1832] **153**

ORIGINAL: MM 28

EDITORIAL COMMENT: In another hand on the first page: 'March 9 – 1832 | Disraeli – Benj'.

Friday

My dear Sir,[1]

As I suppose your father is in the agonies of quarterly parturition,[2] I will not trouble him with the enclosed extract from a domestic letter, but I think it deserves attention.

"Few things are more difficult and nice than to fix on an homogeneous title to a work of imagination, and of truth. Certainly it were most desirable that the title should not disturb the illusion of Reality. The | *present one* has at least a striking novelty, which will excite the curiosity of a great body of readers. Nor do I see that the term *Romance* precludes the notion of a veracious History, for on more than one occasion, a fabulous designation has been given to a very authentic narrative. Till a more fortunate one can be discovered, I should consider that *Narrative*, *Memoir*, *History*, or *Biography* compared with the present, as heavy and

3 James Murray (d 1835) was not the editor of *The Times*, but its foreign director and a leader-writer. *History of The Times* (1935) I 419-20.

4 The Merediths lived at 6 Nottingham Place.

5 Probably the wife of William Day, a frequent visitor at the Meredith residence. See also (VOL II) 384n5.

6 Bear's Grease was a generic term for a men's hair pomade which was thought to nourish, strengthen and beautify the hair. Genuine bear's fat was alleged to possess special efficacy, but soon became scarce, and purified beef-marrow or other animal fats were usually substituted, mixed with almond oil and perfumes and sold under the same name. *Chambers's American Encyclopaedia* (New York 1885) II 206.

The initial 'B' in the MS could also be 'Sh' – in which case, joined with the reference to dahlias, Jem's commission might have been the much more mundane purchase of oil for garden shears.

---

1 John Murray Jr (1808-1892), eldest son of John Murray.

2 Murray would then have been preparing for the number of *The Quarterly Review* which appeared on 10 March. *MP* no 19,111 (10 Mar 1832).

| uninviting. I should not let go the bird in the hand, unless you were positive of the one in the bush.

Could not the title *Romance* be explained by some apt motto?"[3]

I shall leave town tomorrow night for Bradenham, where my stay will probably be short, but where it is uncertain. I think that if no proofs are ready before | my departure, they had better be forwarded to me, by the Bradenham Coach which leaves the Argyll St. Green Man and Still,[4] Mondays and alternate days at one, and which is a trusty conveyance.

Believe me

Very f[aithfu]lly yours

B. Disraeli

---

154 TO [JOHN MURRAY] [London, Saturday 10? March 1832]

ORIGINAL: MM 10

COVER: John Murray Esq. | [In another hand]: 1832 – (No date) | D'Israeli Benj Esq

PUBLICATION HISTORY: Smiles II 340, undated extract

EDITORIAL COMMENT: *Dating*: by comparison with **153**.

What do you think of "*The Psychological Memoir*"? I hesitate between this and *Narrative* – but discard *History* or *Biography*. Decide – and announce by the author of xxxxxx which | I think good.

On survey , I conceive the MS. will make four Byronic tomes, according to the pattern you were kind enough to show me.

Might it not be expedient, that the work sho[ul]d appear not in *boards*, but | in *paper* and *poetical covers*, but I submit this with all deference.

BD

---

155 TO BENJAMIN AUSTEN [London], Monday [19 March? 1832]

ORIGINAL: BL ADD MS 45908 ff52-4

PUBLICATION HISTORY: Jerman 149-50, dated early May 1832

EDITORIAL COMMENT: This is the first of a long series of letters in which D tried to persuade Austen that his future financial prospects were bright and that therefore there was no need for Austen to worry about repayment. For some time D's basic argument was that, of course, instant repayment was always possible, but that this would, somehow, wreak long-term disadvantage to him should Austen be so insensitive as to require it. *Dating*: the resumé of Milman's report of 5 March and of D's negotiations with Murray about the terms on which *Contarini Fleming* was to be published sets this letter almost certainly in March 1832.

D said (**152**) that he intended to come to Bradenham on Sunday 11 March to stay for a week. If he returned to London on the evening of Sunday 18 March, wrote this the next morning, and then returned to Bradenham the same day (as he said here he intended to do), the letter to Murray from Bradenham, also assigned the date 19 March, is not only possible but most consistent with D's known movements.

---

3 Isaac had made this suggestion to a letter sent by Sarah to D on 9 March 1832. H A/I/B/418.

4 A coaching inn at 335 Oxford Street.

Monday. **155** | 243

My dearest Austen, 19 Mar 1832

I arrived in town last night, and must return to day for a Tuesday meeting. On Thursday I come up to be a permanent visitor of the capital.

I should be grieved, my dear fellow, if for a moment you co[ul]d suppose that I was either neglecting you, or was in the slightest degree unworthy of your generous friendship. I can assure | you that this is not the case, but that both by the quantity, and I now can say by the quality, of my productions I have justified your confidence.

Mr. Murray's critic, who is no less a personage than Mr. Milman, of all men most capable of deciding, has written that I have produced a work "*in no way inferior to Childe Harold and equally calculated to arrest | public attention even in these times*."[1] Besides this work, which is in four volumes, I have another finished in my portfolio.[2] But Murray, while he is candid enough not to conceal all this, tells me that if I force him, as a tradesman to purchase my copyright at this moment, I must be prepared to make a very great sacrifice. He wishes me to publish an Edition at his risk, I | receiving my half of the calculated profits at once, and retaining the whole copyright which if it succeed, as he anticipates, will in fact become very valuable property.

In this cruel predicament, am I, and feeling that you ought to be considered above all others, I have not closed with his proposal, but am still negotiating, although not to lose time, we are printing as fast as possible.

This is the reason I have not | sent you the bill, which I did not wish to be a mere piece of paper, but an affair of regular business, on the punctuality of which you might rely.

My dear friend advise me: but do not doubt for a moment my trustworthiness, which I am not howr. for an instant suggest[in]g that you have done. In the course of the week, we will settle it one way or the other. I shall see Murray this morning – your balance has been more than once enclosed to you: but I was called down to Wycombe at a moments notice, and have come up to see a political friend with equal rapidity and want of preparation. You may rely upon receiving the balance on Friday morn[in]g as I receive my quarter in the course of the week. Most | annoyed am I, my dear friend, that you ever sho[ul]d have had to mention these affairs to me. But I co[ul]d not anticipate these extraordinary times, which howr. I hope will soon mend. They talk very much in the best informed circles of throw[in]g out the bill and the administration at once, and

1 See **151**n1. D's interpretation is very free indeed.

2 Not *Gallomania*, for, although it was nearing completion, it was not a novel, was short, had mixed authorship and, above all, was to be kept very confidential until publication, being designed by D to win political kudos rather than financial return. He probably meant *Alroy*, which he had put aside in 1830 while he wrote *The Young Duke* with the object of making money to pay for his tour. *Alroy* at this time was far from finished, but it served to make the point about his productivity, which D hoped would persuade Austen to cease pressing for repayment.

tog[ethe]r and bringing in Lord Harrowby.[3] Whatever occur, I fancy I shall secure a seat at the dissolution.[4]

I shall see you the first morning I am in town – in the meantime, with kind regards to all at home, –

Believe me, Your obliged and f[aithfu]l

BD

156

TO [JOHN MURRAY] Bradenham, Monday [19? March 1832]

ORIGINAL: MM 2

PUBLICATION HISTORY: Smiles II 341-2, undated

EDITORIAL COMMENT: On the fourth page in another hand: '1832 (No date) | D'Israeli Benj Esq.' *Dating*: see **155**ec. In his letter to Austen of this date D said that he was returning to London on Thursday (22 March). *Sic*: tomorrow.

Bradenham, | Monday night.

private.

Dear Sir,

By tomorrow coach, by your desire, I send you one half of the vol.[1] which howr. is not in the finished state I cd. have wished.

I have materials for any length, but it is desirable to get out without a moments loss of time. It has been suggested to publish a vol. periodically, and let this one come out as No 1., so to establish a journal of general foreign politics, for which there are | *ample sources of firstrate information.*

I have not been able even to revise what is sent, but it will sufficiently indicate the work.

I am to meet a personage on Thursday evening in town, and read over the whole to him. It is therefore absolutely necessary that the MS. sho[ul]d be returned to you on Thursday morning, and I will call in Albemarle St. the moment of my arrival which will be | about four o ck.

If in time acknowledge the receipt by return of post.

The remaining portion of the volume, consists of several more dramatic scenes in Paris, a view of the character and career of L[ouis] P[hillipe] a most curious chapter on the conduct of the Diplomatists, and a gen[era]l view of the state of Europe at the moment of publication.

Pray be cautious, and | above all let me depend upon your hav[in]g the MS. on Thursy., otherwise, as Liston says in Love, Law, and Physic, "*we shall get all shot.*"[2]

BD

3 Dudley Ryder (1762-1847), 1st Earl of Harrowby, had been lord president of the Council from 1812 to 1827. Given the prominence of Harrowby's position on the Reform Bill, there is no reason why such speculations should not have been abroad as early as March. The rumour that Harrowby might be asked to form a government seems not to have surfaced in the press until 9 May. *CJ* no 159 (12 May 1832) 303.

4 Parliament was not dissolved until December 1832.

---

1 The first instalment of *Gallomania* then consisted of three chapters written by D and a further three by Haber.

2 The comic actor John Liston played Lubin Log in *Love, Law and Physic* (1812), a farce by James Kenney (1780-1849).

TO JOHN MURRAY [London], Friday [23? March 1832] 157

ORIGINAL: MM 11
COVER: John Murray Esq [In another hand]: 1832 – (No date) | D'Israeli Benj. Esq
PUBLICATION HISTORY: Smiles II 342, undated
EDITORIAL COMMENT: *Dating*: by comparison with **155** and **156**.

Friday 11 o'ck

My dear Sir,
I much regret that I missed you yesterday, but I called upon you the instant I arrived . I *very much wish to talk over* the *Gallomania*, and will come on to you, if it be really impossible for you to pay me a visit. I have so | much at this moment on my hands, that I sho[ul]d esteem such an incident, not only an honor, but a convenience.
BD

TO [JOHN MURRAY] [London], Monday [26? March 1832] 158

ORIGINAL: MM 13
PUBLICATION HISTORY: Smiles II 342-3, undated
EDITORIAL COMMENT: In another hand on the first page: '1832 – (No date) | D'Israeli Benj. Esq.' *Dating*: the context requires this to have been written on the Monday before **162**.

Monday

Dear Sir,
I have a great respect for your judgment, especially on the subject of titles, as I have shown by giving up, in another instance, one which I shall ever regret.[1]

In the present, I shall be happy to receive from you | any suggestion, but I can offer none. To me the *Gallomania* (or, *Mania for what is French*,) appears to me one of the most felicitous titles ever devised. It is comprehensive, it is explicit, it is poignant, and intelligible, as I sho[ul]d suppose to learned and unlearned. |

The word *Anglomania* is one of the commonest on the other side of the channel, is repeated daily in almost every newspaper, has been the title of one or two works, and of the best farce in the French language. It is here also common and intelligible.[2]

1 D's proposal to use the subtitle 'A Psychological Romance' for *Contarini Fleming* had been vetoed earlier that month by Murray's reader H.H. Milman (**151**n1). D's alternative, 'The Psychological Memoir', also failed to please and so the subtitle came to be 'A Psychological auto-biography'. Smiles II 338, 340.

2 The terms 'Anglomania' and 'Gallomania' were both then relatively commonplace; both occur, for instance, in the political vocabulary of a non-European such as Thomas Jefferson. The disease of Anglomania surfaced at the time of the Seven Years' War, and Louis Charles Fougeret de Montbron, in his *Préservatif contre l'Anglomanie* (1757), was one of the first to use the term. The farce that D chose to overpraise in order to make a point must have been *L'Anglomane, ou l'orpheline léguée* (1772), a one-act comedy by Bernard Joseph Saurin. Nor was the companion term unfamiliar. In 1817, William Jerdan had published *Six Weeks in Paris: or, a Cure for the Gallomania*.

There is no objection to | erasing the epithet "NEW" if you think it loads the title.

At all events, I shall send you the MS. tomorrow morning, as we sho[ul]d not lose time.

Believe me
dear Sir
yrs
BD

---

159 TO SARAH DISRAELI

[35 Duke Street, St. James's, London], Monday [26 March 1832]

ORIGINAL: H A/I/B/28

COVER: Miss Disraeli | Bradenham House.

PUBLICATION HISTORY: LBCS 1-2, dated 18 February 1832, consists of paragraph two, the first sentence of paragraph three, paragraph four and paragraph five, conflated with part of **138**; M&B I 203-4, dated 18 February 1832, omits the first paragraph of the LBCS version, which was taken from **138**.

EDITORIAL COMMENT: There is no signature. *Dating*: the missing seal was found on 28 March 1832 (**160**). *Sic*: sent, Legh, 'said.

Monday morng

My dearest Sa,

I expect Papa in a few minutes and scribble some lines almost in bed. You already know that Murray has agreed to publish the Gallomania. I hope we may have it out in a week or ten days. I am almost positive that I left my seal at Bradenham – I want it very much. Tell Jem to look in the drawer of my dressing table, my writing table, desk etc., and sent it up if found in a packet.

We had a very brilliant reunion at Bulwers last night. Among the notables were Lords Strangford[1] and Mulgrave, with the latter of whom I had | a great deal of conversation, Count D'Orsay, the famous Parisian dandy[2] – my father has just come in and I must hurry. There was a large sprinkling of blues – Lady Mary,[3] Mrs. Norton,[4] L[etitia] E[lizabeth] L[andon] Mrs. Legh[5] etc. Bulwer came up to me and said there is one blue who insists upon an introduction.

1 Percy Clinton Smythe (1780-1855), 6th Viscount Strangford, diplomat and author. He was the father of George Smythe, who was later to be D's close associate in the 'Young England' movement.

2 Count Alfred Guillaume Gabriel D'Orsay (1801-1852) was acknowledged in London society of this period to be the quintessential dandy. He met the Blessingtons in 1821, and married Lord Blessington's daughter, Lady Harriet Gardiner, in 1827. In 1849 he fled to Paris to escape his creditors. Michael Sadleir *Blessington-D'Orsay: A Masquerade* (1933) provides a useful corrective to the unscholarly literature on this remarkable figure. See also **178**n6.

3 Probably Lady Mary Fox (1798-1864), second daughter of the Duke of Clarence and Mrs Jordan. She married in 1824 Charles Richard Fox, son of 3rd Baron Holland, born before the marriage of his parents. In May 1831 she had been raised to the rank of a marquess's daughter, and in the *DNB* article on her husband she is described as 'a woman of great social ability'. She may have earned the reputation of being a bluestocking from her friendship with Mrs Norton. At this time her husband was equerry to Queen Adelaide and she was state housekeeper of Windsor Castle. Surviving publications by Lady Mary date from later in the decade. They include *An Account of an Expedition to the Interior of New Holland* (1837). Jane G. Perkins *The Life of Mrs Norton* (1909) 81; Clare Jerrold *The Story of Dorothy Jordan* (1914 repr 1969) 422.

4 Caroline Elizabeth Sarah Norton, née Sheridan (1808-1877), poet and novelist. She was the granddaughter of Richard Brinsley Sheridan (1751-1816), the dramatist. In 1827 she married

"Oh! my dear fellow, I cannot – really, – the power of repartee has deserted me."

"I have pledged myself; you must come." |

So he led me up to a very sumptuous personage, looking like a full rich blown rose – Mrs. Charles Gore. I never recd. so cordial a reception in my life.[6] She sent for her husband after some talk, who 'said ["]we look upon you quite as an old friend. There is no person so often quoted in our house" – and so it turned out that little Charley Gore was their cousin, and has made a reputation this season on all the crumbs he has caught | from my table.

Mr. Albany Fonblanque[7] my critic was in the room, but I did not see him – the Mr. Hawkins who made a wonderful speech and who altho' he squinted horribly was the next day voted a Cupidon, and has since lost his beauty by a failure[8] – and many others, whom in this hurry I cannot recall – Charles Villiers, Henry Ellis etc. etc.

I avoided L.E.L. who looked the very personification of Brompton – pink satin dress and white satin shoes, red cheeks snub nose, and her hair a la Sappho.[9] |

Adieu my dearest. I will write you a more elegant letter soon.

My love to my mother.

Rimell[10] wo[ul]d take 25£ for the mare whom he warrants – Her crippling comes from bad shoeing during a country job. She was, and still is, one of the finest hunters in England.

She wants no firing or blistering[11] – 25£ is too much.

George Chapple Norton (1800-1875), formerly an MP and later a magistrate. An alleged liaison with Lord Melbourne created a scandal in 1836, when her husband brought an action for criminal conversation against the prime minister.

5 For Letitia Elizabeth Landon see n9. 'Mrs. Legh' was probably Augusta Mary Leigh, née Byron (1783-1851), half-sister of the poet. In 1807 she married Lt Col George Leigh. Certainly this Mrs Leigh was an intimate of the Bulwers, and D must have met her on other occasions at Hertford Street. One such occasion, on 11 April 1832, is recorded in Sadleir *Bulwer* 151.

6 Although D had corresponded with Catherine Gore (**75**), this was obviously the first time they had met.

7 Albany Fonblanque (1793-1872), journalist. In 1826 he became the principal leader-writer for *The Examiner*, and he had been an important contributor to *The Westminster Review* from its establishment. From 1830 to 1847 he was editor of *The Examiner*. Edward Barrington Fonblanque ed *Life and Labours of Albany Fonblanque* (1874). See also **122**n6.

8 John Haywood Hawkins (1802-1877), Whig MP for various constituencies 1830-41, had made an eloquent speech on 19 April 1831 in favour of the Reform Bill, which was apparently the apex of his political career. Years later it was still the feat by which he was identified. *The Assembled Commons; or Parliamentary Biographer* (1836) 927; *Hansard* III (1831) cols 1618-30.

9 Letitia Elizabeth Landon (1802-1838) was always identified in D's mind with Sappho – because of her poetry – and because one part of her poem *The Improvisatrice* (1824) was called 'Sappho's Song'. He also associated her with Brompton, an area then deemed to be Bohemian, because she had long resided there. Laman Blanchard *Life and Remains of L.E.L.* (1841) 24, 93. The presence of both comments in an article in *The Star Chamber* (1826) has led to renewed claims that D, despite his denials, must have written for it. Michael Sadleir ed *The Dunciad of To-Day, A Satire and the Modern Æsop* (1928) 10-11.

LEL published many volumes of poetry and, later, some novels. She was frequently a figure of fun, even to some contemporaries, and of course posterity has not acclaimed her sentimentality. She was particularly fond of deathbed scenes, and one of her novels has eight of them.

10 Spelled Rymell in **111**.

11 Cauterizing, often tried as a cure for spavined horses.

160 TO SARAH DISRAELI

Pay Office, [Whitehall, London],
[Wednesday 28 March 1832]

ORIGINAL: H A/I/B/16
COVER: Miss Disraeli | Bradenham House | Wycombe | *Bucks.*
POSTMARK: (1) In circle: W | MR28 | 1832
EDITORIAL COMMENT: There is no signature. *Sic*: Bucke's, Bucke.

Pay Office | alias Charley Gores

My dearest Sa,

The Egyptian letter was from Botta,[1] and very interesting, but not a line from Galloway,[2] to whom I shall write immediately. The seal is found.[3] I regret all your trouble. I dined yesterday at the Bucke's on the principle of always dining with a man the first time I am asked. It was the Alpha and Omega of my visiting in Cumberland St. | So many guests all equally awkward, so many servants all of different heights, and so many dishes and courses and wines, and such regular boredom, nothing omitted from two soups to two liqueurs. As for Bucke he is the most vulgar fellow in his own house I ever dined with, and the famous Miss H. in my presence, full of pretence and hesitation, and has lost all her insolent fluency.[4] And for the guests, a Genl. in blue and brass buttoned | up to the chin, bien poudré with a red face – just one of the Generals whom Bolton wo[ul]d not visit and Spence wo[ul]d. Divie Robertson[5] and his horrid family, droning Sir John Sewell[6] etc. and a stray officer or two worse than Foord Bowes. This morning I received another invitation for the 10th. so I suppose Miss H. rejoices in having a lion in her toils – but I soon settled that.

1 The letter, dated 3 December 1831, is in the Hughenden papers (A/IV/F/1). In February 1833 D apparently threw a letter from Botta across a dinner table to Lord Melbourne. Haydon 51. This was probably Botta's letter of July 1832 (H A/IV/F/2), which dealt, in considerable detail, with the peculiarities of native sexual practices in the Middle East.

2 The correspondence has not yet been found. Presumably D was referring to J. Galloway (d 1836), known after 1834 as 'Galloway Bey'. He spent a number of years in Egypt as an engineer, his last project being a railroad from Cairo to Suez. Still a young man at his death, he was one of D's companions in Egypt and is mentioned in letters from Botta. James Augustus St John *Egypt and Mohammed Ali* (1834) II 403, 424; *The Times* (22 Nov 1831); *GM* ns VI (Oct 1836) 446.

3 Sarah wrote to D on 27 March 1832: 'I ... wish I could also send your seal but alas it is no where to be found.' H A/I/B/419.

4 There was a George Buck then living at 13 Cumberland Street, Portman Square. Mr and Mrs Buck, accompanied by a 'Miss Buck' (possibly 'the famous Miss H'), were in evidence during that London season. *CJ* no 158 (5 May 1832) 284.

George Buck appears in the membership of the Carlton. *A List of the Members of the Carlton Club* ... (1836) 11.

5 The firm of Divie Robertson & Son, wine merchants, was then at 17 Villiers Street. Robertson was at one time a director of the Scottish Union Fire and Life Insurance Company. The family lived at 22 Bedford Square, and, as they were listed in *Boyle's*, were obviously deemed respectable.

6 Sir John Sewell (d 1833) was then one of the advocates in the ecclesiastical department. He had been a judge of the Vice-Admiralty Court of Malta. *ER* (1828); Shaw *Knights of England* (1906 repr Baltimore 1971) II 316.

I write this in a horrible hurry because I thought you wo[ul]d be disappointed, if you had no letter. All goes on well with the books[.] | The Gallom[ania] is finished and in the press,[7] and the 1st. Vol of the o[the]r is finished, and the 2nd and 3rd. advanced.

161

TO [JOHN MURRAY] [35] Duke Street, [St James's, London], Friday [30 March 1832]

ORIGINAL: MM 36
PUBLICATION HISTORY: Smiles II 343, dated 30 March 1832
EDITORIAL COMMENT: In another hand at the top of the fourth page: '1832 March 30 | D'Israeli Benj. Esq.'

In another hand, across the bottom of pages three and four: 'I sent you his note of yesterday – trusting that you would have told him instantly The Title w[hi]ch I preferred and have advertised it accordingly. | Have you not sent him the *proof* this Tuesday.'

Possibly in D's hand in superscription on page one: 'MARCH. 30 – '. *Dating*: the context confirms that the only Friday appropriate for this stage of the publication of *Gallomania* was 30 March.

Duke St. Friday

Dear Sir,

I am going to dine with d'Haussez, de Haber, *et hoc genus* to day, and must report progress, otherwise they will think I am trifling with them.

Have you determined on a title? What think you | of

A CURE
FOR THE
MINISTERIAL GALLOMANIA

and advertize dedicated to Lord Grey. Pray decide.

You are aware I have not yet received a proof. Affairs look awkward in France.[1] Beware lest we are | a day after the fait, and only annalists instead of prophets.

Believe me,
Your very f[aithfu]l Ser[van]t
B. Disraeli

162

TO [JOHN MURRAY] [35 Duke Street, St James's, London], [Friday 30 March 1832]

ORIGINAL: MM 37
PUBLICATION HISTORY: Smiles II 343, dated 30 March 1832
EDITORIAL COMMENT: In another hand on the first page: 'March 30 | 1832'. In another hand on the last page: '1832 March 30 | D'Israeli Benj. Esq'. It seems probable that Murray sent proofs and advertisement immediately in answer to **161**, and this note acknowledged receipt of these. *Sic*: Philip.

---

7 This was not literally true; D was still making alterations for the publisher. See **161**. *Contarini Fleming* was being printed.

1 A Carlist uprising had recently been quelled at Grenoble. D wished success to the cause and doubtless reasoned that a premature move could only have harmed it.

Dear Sir,

I think it does very well, and I hope you are also satisfied. I shall send you the rest of the MS. tomorrow morning. There is a very remarkable chapter | on Louis Philip[1] which is at present with Baron D'Haussez, and this is the reason I have not forwarded it to you.

BD |

I keep the advertis[e]m[en]t to show them.

163

TO JOHN MURRAY [35 Duke Street, St James's, London, Friday 30? March 1832]

ORIGINAL: MM 14

COVER: *immediate* | John Murray Esq | 50 Albemarle St.

PUBLICATION HISTORY: Smiles II 343-5, dated 30 March 1832

EDITORIAL COMMENT: In another hand on the first page: '1832 (no date) | D'Israeli Benj. Esq.' *Dating*: according to Smiles, this was written on the same day as **161** and **162**. If so, it was after D's dinner with his collaborators, and after he had had time to examine the proofs in detail.

---

confidential

My dear Sir,

In further answer to your note received this evening I think it proper to observe that I entirely agree with you that *I "am bound to make as few alterations as possible"* coming as they do from such a quarter – and I have acted throughout in such a spirit. All alterations and omissions of consequence are on this first | sheet, and I have retained in the others many things of which I do not approve, merely on account of my respect for the source from whence they are derived.

While you remind me of what I observed to your son, let me also remind you of the condition with which my permission was accompanied vizt: that everything was to be submitted | to my approval, and subject to my ratification. On this condition I have placed the proofs in the hands of several persons not less distinguished than your friend,[1] and superior even in rank and recent office. Their papers are on my table, and I shall be happy to show them to you. I will mention one: the Chapter | on Belgium was originally written by the Plenipotentiary of the King of Holland to the Conference, Baron Van Zuylen.[2] Scarcely a

1 It appears in *Gallomania* 179-226. Though the MS does not survive in the Hughenden papers, D himself was probably the author.

---

1 D must then have already known, or suspected, that Murray's reader was John Wilson Croker. Later, he mentioned the name (**169**).

2 Baron Hugo Zuylen van Nyevelt (1781-1853) was the Dutch spokesman at the conference on Belgian independence. He was naturally hostile to the Whig policy of joining with France to coerce the Dutch in the interest of the Belgians. After conspiring with the Tories to unseat Grey's government, Zuylen was recalled from London in March 1833. Sir Charles Webster *The Foreign Policy of Palmerston* (1951) I 105.

line of the original composition remains, altho' a very able one, because it did not accord with the main design of the book.

With regard to the omission p.12-13, I acknowledge its felicity, but | it is *totally at variance with every other notice of M. de Talleyrand in the work*, and entirely dissonant with the elaborate mention of him in the last Chap[ter]. When the reviser introduced this pungent remark, he had never even read the work he was revising.[3]

With regard to the authorship of this work, I | should never be ashamed of being considered the author. I should be *proud to be*. But I am not. It is written by Legion,[4] but I am one of them, and I bear the responsibility. If it be supposed to be written by a Frenchman, all its good effects must be marred, as it seeks to | command attention and interest by its purely British spirit.

I have no desire to thrust my acquaintance upon your critic. More than once I have had an opportunity to form that acquaintance and more than once I have declined it, but I am | ready to bear the *brunt of explanation*, if you desire me.

It is quite impossible that anything adverse to the general measure of Reform can issue from my pen or from anything to which I contribute. Within these four months | I have declined being returned for a Tory Borough,[5] and almost within these four hours, to mention slight affairs, I have refused to inscribe myself a member of "the Conservative Club".[6] I cannot believe that you will place your critic's feelings for | a few erased passages against my permanent interests.

But in fact these have nothing to do with the question. To convenience you I have no objection to wash my hands of the whole business and put you in | direct communication with my coadjutors. I can assure you that it is from no regard for my situation that Reform was omitted, but because they are of opinion, that its notice wo[ul]d be most unwise and injurious. For | myself I am ready to do anything that you can desire except entirely change my position in life.

I will see your critic if you please or you can give up the publication and be reimbursed, which shall make no difference in our other affairs. All I ask in this | and all other affairs, are Candor and Decision.

The present business is most pressing – at present I am writing a Chap[te]r on Poland[7] from intelligence just received, but it will be ready for the Printer tomorrow morning, as I shall finish it before I retire.

BD

I await your answer with anxiety.

It is but due to myself to remark that in the sheet hastily shown me by your son

3 D expressed admiration for Talleyrand's abilities, if not for his character. *Gallomania* 250-1. A more non-committal statement in the first chapter (6) must have been given an excessively negative turn by Croker.

4 D was receiving the assistance of a number of European diplomats and politicians who had reason to wish the Whig government discredited.

5 This may well be true, but D's correspondence of the time makes no other mention of the fact.

6 The Carlton Club, which grew out of the Charles Street Society of 1828, was often so described. The Conservative Club was, however, not founded until 1840. T.H.S. Escott *Club Makers and Club Members* (1914) 215-18, 230; Greville II 327-8.

7 *Gallomania* 236-41.

I observed no remarks on Reform, and that is the only sheet in which to any extent they can be introduced.

164 TO JOHN MURRAY JR [London], Saturday [31 March 1832?]

ORIGINAL: MM 33
COVER: John Murray Junr Esq
PUBLICATION HISTORY: Smiles II 345, dated 31 March 1832
EDITORIAL COMMENT: On the first page in another hand: 'March 31 | 1832'.

Saturday

confidential.

My dear Sir,

We shall have an opportunity of submitting the work to *Count Orloff*[1] tomorrow morning in case you can let me have a set of the proofs *tonight*. I mean as far as we have gone.

I | do not like to send mine, which are covered with corrections.

Yrs truly

BD

If possible by *nine o ck.*

165 TO SARAH DISRAELI [London, Saturday 31 March 1832]

ORIGINAL: H A/I/B/15
COVER: Miss Disraeli | Bradenham House | Wycombe | *Bucks.*
POSTMARK: (1) In circle: E | MR31 | 1832
EDITORIAL COMMENT: *Sic*: Frazer, flaggons, indian, Seldyneck.

My dearest Sa,

I received your note[1] by the 2y. p[os]t this morning. I wrote you before a very hasty letter, but I was pressed to save the post. I get on very well. The Gallom[ania] will be out next week and in very good time, but I have been obliged to modify the title to please that blockhead Murray who never co[ul]d understand it, and persisted that if it were not changed, it wo[ul]d consequently fall stillborn from the press. The novel[2] proceeds, nearly three volumes are finished.

There is a very good portrait of our Sire in Frazer,[3] and a very friendly no-

1 Gen Count (later Prince) Alexis Fedorovich Orlov (1787-1862). Orlov left the Hague late in March to attend the London negotiations on Belgium and arrived on the evening of 27 March. *Memoirs of the Prince de Talleyrand* (1891-2) IV 287. See also **138**n3. He was on a highly confidential mission for the Tsar, his instructions being to do all in his power to prevent 'a union of the British Cabinet with that of the Palais Royal'. Major John Hall *England and the Orleans Monarchy* (1912) 111, 114. With such instructions, Orlov had an obvious interest in collaborating with D's project.

1 Sarah wrote to D on 29 March 1832 (H A/I/B/420).
2 *Contarini Fleming.*
3 *Fraser's Magazine for Town and Country* V (Apr 1832), facing p 321. The portrait, by Daniel Maclise, accompanied an article on Isaac in William Maginn's 'Gallery of Literary Characters'.

tice, but unfortunately – you see the consequence of signing initials – he figures as *Israel D'Israeli* Esq – which leads to an observation or two, otherwise he is placed in | his right position as an author and treated with great respect. Seeing the advertisement, and conceiving from the name that it might be a lampoon, I called upon Mister Frazer,[4] and informed him that callous as I was to such things myself, I myself perceived no use in a son unless he prevented you from being insulted. He was frightened out of his wits and very civil, brought me the biography, and persisted, which I believe, that it was a mere error. It was too late to make a cancel – so the affair rests.

If my election co[ul]d come on now at the Travellers, I think I co[ul]d manage it. There is no disgrace in being blackballed as these things happen every night and to the first people. Ld. Sefton[5] the other night and among little | men poor Charley Gore – but they say that the Secretary Machin[6] can get in any man he likes, as he lends money etc. to Auckland and all the dandies. Haber introduced me to him, and I received an invitation to dinner at Pimlico yesterday, which of course I accepted. It was a most amusing scene. Besides being Secretary, he is a merchant, and has a mania *for distinguished men* at his table and all that. He has a rather pretty wife and a very pretty sister in law – and is himself a most goodnatured, vulgar, servile braggadocio, half Broadfoot and half Bolton.[7] We dined in a sort of Gallery with a skylight, the walls covered with splendid pictures, Italian and Spanish – the table and sideboard groaned with silver waiters and massy flaggons, the drawingrooms for China, bijouterie, and indian screens, like Baldock's shop.[8] The dinner very good, the wines exquisite – he showed us above twenty snuffboxes, one worth 250 Gu[ine]as. He brought down Peagreen Hayne's dressing case for which he had given 500 and which cost | 1200,[9] and finally there was no manservant. Haber dined there, and Baron de Seldyneck[10] just arrived, a morganatic brother of the G[rand] D[uke]

4 *Fraser's Magazine* was named after one Hugh Fraser, a barrister, but here D probably intended James Fraser, the publisher of the magazine between 1830 and 1841.
5 William Philip Molyneux (1772-1838), 2nd Earl of Sefton.
6 Mr R.A. Williams, the secretary of the Travellers' Club in 1977, was kind enough to check membership lists of the club from 1832 back to 1818. The club had no member or secretary of the name 'Machin', though *The Times* of 12 May 1830 referred to 'Mr. Machin of the Travellers' Club'. The secretary in 1832 was certainly S.W. Singer. A clue to Machin's identity is D's reference to his collection of objets d'art. There existed, until 1837, a firm of auctioneers at 26 King Street, Covent Garden, called Machin, Debenham and Storr. The senior partner, Nathaniel Smith Machin, then of 26 King Street, Covent Garden, died 16 April 1837, aged sixty-two. *The Times* (18 Apr 1837).
7 Dr George Buckley Bolton and Dr Alexander Broadfoot.
8 E.H. Baldock was a dealer in antique furniture and ornamental china at 1 Hanway Street, Oxford Street.
9 J.G. 'Peagreen' Hayne was a man of fashion, most prominent in the season of 1825. He owed his nickname either to his taste in clothes or to his gullible nature. Charles E. Pearce *Madame Vestris and Her Times* (New York nd) 105. Hayne once paid £1500 for a dressing case, probably the same that was auctioned in March 1826. As an auctioneer Machin would have been well situated to acquire the famous bauble, though he was neither the auctioneer nor the purchaser in the sale of 1826. After a period in debtor's prison, Hayne retired to Brussels, having dissipated a fortune of £120,000. *The Age* no 44 (12 Mar 1826) 352; *The Mirror of Literature, Amusement and Instruction* no 820 (11 Feb 1837).
10 As he was German, the 'de' is gratuitous. Spelling in printed sources varies, but the name appears to have been von Seldeneck. *CJ* no 149 (3 Mar 1832) and no 153 (31 Mar 1832).

of Baden, and his master of the Horse. It was very amusing. I understand that M. piques himself on having the first men of rank and fashion in London at his table. He told me that my conversation was the most fascinating that he had ever known, which seemed to console him for my not playing whist. He asked me to dine on Wednesday with him and with Tom Duncombe,[11] Charles Greville,[12] and D'Orsay, but | I refused. I have been so engaged that I have not seen the Merediths or called on any one, but in a day, or two I shall be free. Your violets were very acceptable.[13] Write my dearest to

your most affec brother.

166

TO [JOHN MURRAY] [London, Sunday 1 April? 1832]

ORIGINAL: MM 5

EDITORIAL COMMENT: In another hand: '1832 (No date) | D'Israeli Benj Esq.' *Dating*: on the assumption that this is 'the note of last night' to which D refers in **168**, and continues the discussion initiated in **163**.

My dear Sir,

I have just received your note which I have read with grief, but in a temper which I hope will prevent any disagreeable consequences. It is | impossible to write upon these points, but these indeed must be settled *at once*: even this evening I have an engagement for which it is absolutely necessary that I should know | *how I stand.*

Shall I come on to you? Indeed it is better. Delay under such circumstances may be most injurious. Let us always understand ourselves as soon as possible. The affair is | not so simple as you imagine.

BD

167

TO [JOHN WILSON CROKER] [London, Sunday 1 April? 1832]

ORIGINAL: PS 79

PUBLICATION HISTORY: Smiles II 348-9, undated

EDITORIAL COMMENT: Smiles introduces the text of this letter: 'The following announcement was published by Mr. Disraeli in reply to certain criticisms of his work'. The letter has not been found in published form, and publication seems inherently unlikely, as it was meant only for the eyes of the anonymous critic.

As D preserves the fiction of being unaware of the identity of his critic, it is probable that he forwarded this letter to Croker through Murray.

I cannot allow myself to omit certain observations of my able critic without remarking that those omissions are occasioned by no insensibility to their acuteness.

Circumstances of paramount necessity render it quite impossible that anything can proceed from my pen hostile to the general question of *Reform.*

11 Thomas Slingsby Duncombe (1796-1861), Radical MP for Hertford 1824-32, and for Finsbury 1834-61.

12 Charles Cavendish Fulke Greville (1794-1865), the famous diarist, and clerk to the Privy Council 1821-59.

13 Sarah wrote (H A/I/C/27): 'I am afraid my violets were not sweet.' The faint praise suggests that D agreed.

Independent however of all personal considerations, and viewing the question of Reform for a moment in the light in which my critic evidently speculates, I would humbly suggest that the cause which he advocates would perhaps be more united in the present pages by being passed over *in silence*. It is important that this work should be a work not of *party* but of national interest, and I am induced to believe that a large class in this country, who think themselves bound to support the present administration from a superficial sympathy with their domestic measures, have long viewed their foreign policy with distrust and alarm.

If the public are at length convinced that Foreign Policy, instead of being an abstract and isolated division of the national interests, is in fact the basis of our empire and present order, and that this basis shakes under the unskilful government of the Cabinet, the public may be induced to withdraw their confidence from that Cabinet altogether.

With this exception, I have adopted all the additions and alterations that I have yet had the pleasure of seeing without reserve, and I seize this opportunity of expressing my sense of their justness and their value.[1]

The Author of 'Gallomania.'

168

TO JOHN MURRAY [35 Duke Street, St James's, London], Monday [2 April 1832]

ORIGINAL: MM 4
COVER: IMMEDIATE | John Murray Esq | 50 Albemarle Street | [on the flap in another hand]: 1832. (No date) | D'Israeli, Benj. Esq
PUBLICATION HISTORY: Smiles II 346, dated 2 April 1832
EDITORIAL COMMENT: In another hand on the first page: '1832 – (No date) | D'Israeli Benj. Esq.' *Sic*: coadjuter.

Monday morn. | 9 ock.

Dear Sir,

Since I had the honor of addressing you the note of last night, I have seen the Baron.[1] Our interview was intended to have been a final one, and it was therefore absolutely necessary, that I should apprise him of all that had happened, of course concealing the name | of your friend. The Baron says that the insertion of the obnoxious passages is fatal to all his combinations, that he has devoted two months of the most valuable time to this affair, and that he must hold me personally responsible for the immediate fulfilment of my agreement, vizt. to ensure its publication when finished.

1 On 5 April Sarah was to write to D: 'We are all delighted that Croker has seen the proofs, now no responsibility can be with you!' H A/I/B/422.

1 Presumably D meant Haber, as his relations with d'Haussez were less close. Haber's letters to D beginning 16 March (H E/IV/C/2-7) all expressed great urgency. Haber's concern was not just that of a conspirator, hoping to disrupt the alliance between the Whigs and Louis Philippe, but that of a co-author; a draft of what was to become pages 57-141 of *Gallomania* is in his hand. H E/IV/C/1.

We dine at the same | house to day and I have pledged myself to give him a categorical reply at that time, and to have ensured its publication by some mode or other.

Under these painful circumstances, my dear Sir, I can only state that the work must be published at once and with the omission of all passages hostile to Reform, and that if you are unwilling to | introduce it in that way, I request from your friendliness such assistance as you can afford me about the printer etc. to occasion its immediate publication in some other quarter.

After what took place between myself and my coadjuter last night, I really can have for him only one answer or one alternative, and as I wish to give him the first, and ever avoid the second, I look forward | with confidence to your answer.

BD

---

169 TO SARAH DISRAELI [London], Monday 2 April 1832

ORIGINAL: H A/I/B/19

COVER: Miss Disraeli | Bradenham-House | Wycombe | *Bucks*

POSTMARK: (1) In Maltese cross: V.S | VAP2S | 1832

PUBLICATION HISTORY: LBCS 6-8, dated 28 April 1832, omits the first and second paragraphs, the last three sentences of the fifth and all of the sixth and seventh. M&B I 204-5, dated 28 April 1832, prints part of the LBCS text.

EDITORIAL COMMENT: There is no signature. *Sic*: blanch, soireé, Ramohun, waved.

Monday. April 2. 1832

My dearest,

I received your letter[1] this morning. I proceed very well. Murray showed the proofs to Croker[2] who was so delighted with them that he offered to read all the book and add if the author pleased what he thought necessary etc. I of course instantly gave him carte blanch to add and alter as he liked, subject to my ratification, and he has availed himself of my permission hitherto very fully.

Bulwer has made me a formal offer for my father to write – 25 Gu[ine]as pr sheet the publisher taking the copyright, and 16 gu[ine]as, the copyright withheld. I said I thought my father wo[ul]d not like to give up the copyright and that 16 gu[ine]as wo[ul]d not tempt him, but that I wo[ul]d communicate. I think my father cannot do better than empty his common place books into the Mag[azine],[3] by which he might make two or three hundred pr. ann. – and not materially interfere with a regular work, only somewhat delay it. I sho[ul]d take care however that my first two or three | articles were of a high quality, and I beg that he will send nothing without my revision. His History of Nonsense[4] etc. etc. and all his mass of unfinished works might be moulded into Magazine shape. Bulwer says that the Mag[azine] of the present month is perfect, and that he is confident that ultimately it will take the lead of all periodicals.

1 Sarah wrote to D on 1 April 1832. H A/I/B/421.
2 See **167**.
3 *The New Monthly Magazine*, then edited by Edward Bulwer Lytton.
4 Apparently it remained unfinished.

The soireé last night was really brilliant: much more so than the first night. There were a great many dames there and of distinction, and no blues. I sho[ul]d perhaps except Sappho who was quite changed; she had thrown off her Greco Bromptonian costume and was perfectly *a la francaise* and really looked pretty. At the end of the evening, I addressed a few words to her, of the value of which she seemed sensible. I was introduced "by particular desire" to Mrs. Wyndham Lewis,[5] a pretty little woman, a flirt and a rattle; indeed gifted with a volubility I sho[ul]d think unequalled, and of which I can convey no idea. She told me that she liked silent, melancholy, men.[6] I answered that I had no doubt of it.

I did not observe many persons that I had seen before: people address you with[ou]t ceremony. A lady of more than certain age, but very fantastically | dressed came up to me to ask my opinion about a Leonardo da Vinci dress. She had a contention with another lady etc. etc. She paid me the most ludicrous compliments. This was Lady Stepney.[7] I had a long conversation with Ld. Mulgrave, and a man talked to me very much who turned out to be Lord Wm. Lennox.[8] In the course of the evening I stumbled over Tom Moore, to whom I introduced myself. It is evident that he has read or heard of the Y[oung] D[uke], as his courtesy was marked. "How is your head?" he enquired – "I have heard of you as everybody has. Did not we meet at Murrays once?" He has taken his name out of the Athenaeum as "really Brooks is sufficient, so I shall not see your father any more."

Ramohun Roy[9] was there, and Hajji Baba Morier.[10] A man addressed me by name and talked to me for some time. I do not know who it was, and forgot afterwards to ask Bulwer, but I think Geo. Lamb.[11] The face I know, and he was evidently a man of distinction, a wit, and a fine scholar. – Henry Bulwer has been very ill for five weeks – it is too long a story to tell you, but worth knowing. He was for three days insensible. Mind I tell you.

My father is only mentioned allusively in the West[minste]r and a quotation from the pamphlet – , but the attack is very weak and commonplace, all about

5 This is D's first meeting with his future wife. Mary Anne Lewis (1792-1872) was the daughter of John Evans and Eleanor Evans, née Viney, after 1808 Eleanor Yate. In 1815 she had married Wyndham Lewis, Tory MP for Maidstone. Wyndham Lewis died on 14 March 1838, and Mary Anne married D on 28 August 1839.

6 Sarah responded: 'Captain Orange was a favourite protégé of Mrs. Wyndham Lewis on her principle of liking silent men – for silent read stupid.' H A/I/B/422.

7 Catherine Stepney, née Pollok (d 1845), had married in 1813 Sir Thomas Stepney, 9th Baronet, who died in 1825. In later life she acquired a modest literary reputation through her novels, and established her house in Cavendish Square as one of London's major literary salons.

8 Lord William Pitt Lennox (1799-1881), brother of the 5th Duke of Richmond, novelist, journalist and miscellaneous writer. He was Whig MP for King's Lynn 1831-5 and editor of *The Review*.

9 Romohun Roy (more correctly Ramanohana Raya), Indian administrator and scholar, who came to England in 1831. He died in December 1833. *AR* (1833) app 247-9.

10 James Justinian Morier (1780?-1849), author of *The Adventures of Hajji Baba of Ispahan* (1824).

11 George Lamb (1784-1834), younger brother of Viscount Melbourne, the future prime minister. He was Whig MP for Dungarvan 1820-34.

leaving slime and *brightest names* etc. *etc.*[12] Bulwer said that my father's pamphlet had advanced even *his* name, and that those who entirely differed with him on the subject co[ul]d but admire the ability of the treatment. Some of the sarcasm | at the end as good as anything we have had for a long time.

If the little horse get well, you had better sell him. I have not forgotten the Le Clercs.[13] Nash wrote to me about the other estate. I waved any more purchases, sd. my father was *very alarmed* at the times, and more inclined to invest in American Stock etc. I beg that he will maintain this dignified terror.

I remained in Hertford St. after the breaking up about one until four o'ck smoking. Colonel Webster who married Boddington's daughter[14] sd. to me – "Take care my good fellow. I lost the most beautiful woman in the world by smoking. It has prevented more liaisons than the dread of a duel or Doctors commons"[15] – "You have proved then" I rep[lie]d "that it is a very moral habit." You know altho' no Adonis, he is a terrible roué.

---

170 TO JOHN MURRAY JR

[35 Duke Street, St James's, London, Wednesday 4 April? 1832]

ORIGINAL: MM 44

COVER: John Murray Esq Junr | [In another hand]: April 4. 1832 | D'Israeli, Benjn.

EDITORIAL COMMENT: On the top of the first page of the MS, possibly in D's hand: '3d April 4.' *Sic*: the the.

My dear Sir,

Excuse this rough epistle. What I want most urgently is the the revise of *the alterations*. The Baron has sent to me several times to know when I can get a fair revise of the first sheets – as we | wish if possible to put them in the hands of a noble Lord[1] with[ou]t unnecessary delay, and I have some important additions to make *before*.

Urge then revises, and let them be sent with[ou]t a moments loss of time.

BD |

Everything promises but *Time* – but let us hope.

12 The comments appear in the review of Lord Nugent's *Some Memorials of John Hampden*. In an aside directed at Nugent's Tory critics, of whom Isaac was the chief, the reviewer condemned writers who 'fix upon some great action, some illustrious name and by dint of an epithet here and insinuation there ... contrive occasionally to leave a part of their slime ... upon the noblest deeds and the brightest characters of history.' *The Westminster Review* XXXII (Apr 1832) 508.

13 Sarah had made an enquiry about the family, noting that one of them was marrying a Miss Frankland. She had wondered if it were true that one Gen Le Clerc had married Napoleon's sister. It was. Charles Victor Emanuel Le Clerc (d 1802) married Pauline, Napoleon's youngest sister. The name was significant to the D'Israeli family, since it was this Le Clerc who caused great distress to the house of Alexander Lindo when Le Clerc's bank draft for £276,000 was dishonoured by the French government. James Picciotto *Sketches of Anglo-Jewish History* (1875) 274.

14 Henry Vassall Webster (1793?-1847) had been promoted to lieutenant colonel in 1831. Army List (1832) 42. In 1824 he had married Grace Boddington (1793-1866), daughter of Samuel Boddington (1767-1843), at one time MP for Tralee. Reginald Stewart Boddington *Boddington Pedigree* (1890). He was knighted in 1843.

15 Proceedings for divorce. Doctors' Commons was the short form for 'The College of Doctors of Law exercent in the Ecclesiastical and Admiralty Courts', within whose jurisdiction divorce had been placed by a royal charter of 1768. The College was abolished in 1857.

---

1 Lord Aberdeen. See **173**n1.

TO [JOHN MURRAY] [35 Duke Street, St James's, London], Thursday [5?] April [1832] **171**

ORIGINAL: MM 38

PUBLICATION HISTORY: Smiles II 346-7, dated 6 April 1832

EDITORIAL COMMENT: In another hand: '1832 April 6 | D'Israeli. Benj. Esq'. *Dating*: Thursday was 5 April, and D's emphasis on the day makes the 5th more probable than the 6th.

Thursday | April 6

confidential

My Dear Sir,

I have just received a note, that if I can get a set of clean proofs by Sunday, they will be put in the Duke's hands – preliminary to the debate.[1] I thought you would like | to know this. Do you think it impossible? Let this be between us.

I am sorry to give you all this trouble but I know your zeal, and the interest you take in these affairs. I myself will never | keep the printer, and engage when the proofs are sent me, to prepare them for the press within an hour.

Yours

BD

TO MARY ANNE LEWIS [London], Friday [6? April 1832] **172**

ORIGINAL: H A/I/A/1

COVER: Mrs. Wyndham Lewis

EDITORIAL COMMENT: *Dating*: D first met Mrs Wyndham Lewis on 1 April 1832; see **169**. On the assumption that D was more intrigued by Mary Anne than his comments to Sarah indicated, and that he initiated a correspondence at once, it is probable that he wrote on the first Friday following the meeting, which was 6 April. There is an endorsement in Mary Anne's hand: 'The first Note I ever received from dear Dizzy March or April 1832'. *Sic*: Provencale, Trobadour.

Friday

I have read your tale, which I admire exceedingly. It is very poetic and Provencale, and worthy of a Trobadour. I have found out the writer, and will tell you when we meet.

I | hope *la belle du monde* is quite well this morn!

Your true knight

Raymond de Toulouse.[1]

1 Debate on the second reading of the Reform Bill opened in the Lords on Monday 9 April. The success of the Bill – and of Whig domestic policy in general – was linked in the closest way to the London negotiations on Belgium. See also **138**&n3.

---

1 Scott had stimulated interest in the courtly tradition with his *Count Robert of Paris*, published November 1831, where Raymond is introduced as one of its exemplars.

173 TO SARAH DISRAELI [London, Saturday 7 April 1832]

ORIGINAL: H A/I/B/20
COVER: Miss Disraeli | Bradenham House | Wycombe | Bucks.
POSTMARK: (1) In circle: Y | AP-7 | 1832
EDITORIAL COMMENT: *Sic*: Brookes.

1/2 past 5

My dearest,

I write only to say I love you. My time is entirely engrossed with the Gallom[ania]. It is now with Lord Aberdeen.[1] I have made Lord Eliots acquaintance whom I like very much. I have received an offer to belong to the Anti-Brookes club,[2] but thought it expedient at present to refuse.

The Psyc[hological Romance] is nearly finished.

I | should not be surprised if the bill were thrown out in spite of all they say. It will certainly be finally Knocked up.

Ld Eliot says that he has never forgotten me at the Trav[e]ll[er]s and flatters himself much that I shall be in by the new house. All goes on well.

BD

174 TO SARAH DISRAELI [35 Duke Street, St James's, London, Tuesday 10 April 1832]

ORIGINAL: H A/I/B/21
COVER: Miss Disraeli | Bradenham House | Wycombe | Bucks
POSTMARK: (1) In circle: D | AP10 | 1832.

1/2 pt 5 –

My dearest angel,

Your note[1] has just come and the bellman is again ringing – yet all day I have wished to write to you. The books go on very well – the first only delayed by important intelligence. I know nothing about Mrs. G.B.[2] and be damned to her. All | these rumors are shots. I cannot tell you about Ld. Eliot at present. We are great friends. Lady Jemima[3] not in town. Henry Stanley is, and a great bore. He

1 George Hamilton-Gordon (1784-1860), 4th Earl of Aberdeen, prime minister 1852-5. He was the 'noble Lord' mentioned in **170**.

2 The Carlton Club, founded in 1832, was described by a contemporary as 'a counter-balancing meeting to Brookes' [*sic*], which is purely a Whig re-union'. Entry for 7 April 1832 in *A Portion of the Journal Kept by Thos. Raikes Esq. from 1831 to 1847* (1856) I 21. Brooks's Club was originally part of Almack's. In 1778 it had been established at 60 St James's Street under the management of Mr Brooks (or Brookes).

---

1 Sarah wrote to D on 9 April 1832. H A/I/B/423.

2 George Basevi Jr married in 1830 Frances Agneta Biscoe, fourth daughter of Joseph Seymour Biscoe. Basevi family tree in the Jewish Museum, London. Isaac and Sarah had both written to D on 6 April (H A/I/C/27) wondering how Mrs George Basevi had come to know that D was at work on the *Gallomania*. Sarah thought that the leak must have come through Murray.

3 Lady Jemima Eliot (1803-1856), afterwards Countess of St Germans, third daughter of the 2nd Marquess Cornwallis. She had married Lord Eliot in 1824.

asked me to go with him to Newmarket to the Craven[4] | but I refused. I shall come to you for Easter – *certain*.

I have not seen Bulwer, who was out of town for a few days.

Adieu

BD

The violets beautiful

TO JOHN MURRAY JR [35 Duke Street, St James's, London, Wednesday 11 April? 1832] **175**

ORIGINAL: MM 41

COVER: John Murray Junr Esq | BD | [In other hands]: (1) April 11. 1832 | Disraeli B – (2) Benjamin Disraeli (3) 50 Albemarle St | April 11

EDITORIAL COMMENT: Uncharacteristically, the first page is headed by a 1, and the second by a 2.

I think I may as well send you all the proofs I have. The report and the rem[ainde]r of the Chap[te]r that lead to it are ready for Press. Ancona and Poland[1] are ready as far as I am concerned, but I imagine have not been seen by Mr. – . It is probable he will make little alteration in them – and if they be mere verbal and slight ones, the Printer may go to press with[ou]t send[in]g me a revise. These chap[te]rs are calculated to make a sensation, and with the one on Belgium[2] | are the best in the book. I suppose I shall have a revise of Bel[gium] to night – and the other proofs wh[ic]h I am anxious to see.

They kick very much at giving up the Chap[ter] of the Epochs,[3] which came from the Duc de Blacas[4] but I have insisted upon it.

I commend everything to your diligence. We have missed the Debate,[5] but there is plenty of opportunities behind hand, and I think I can secure its being well brought forward.

BD

4 The Craven Stakes was a race meeting which in 1832 was held late in April. It marked the traditional opening of the racing season. *CJ* no 102 (9 Apr 1832) 256.

---

1 In February of that year a French fleet had occupied Ancona to check the reactionary influence of Austria on Italian affairs. In *Gallomania* (227-35) D condemned the passivity of the British government. A similar theme informed the chapter on Poland (236-41).

2 The chapter on Belgium (242-56) saw the culmination of D's argument that the British government had done the bidding of Louis Philippe uncritically.

3 According to D's original plan (H E/I/218-9), the fourth chapter was to have been called 'Five Epochs at which the Bourbon family might have succeeded in forming a strong government'. In the final text it was deleted.

4 Pierre Louis Jean Casimir (1770-1839), duc de Blacas, Charles X's ambassador to Naples, who accompanied him into exile. Charles was then at Holyrood House in Edinburgh and did not leave for Prague until the autumn, so Blacas would have been in Britain in the spring of 1832.

5 The Lords debated the Reform Bill all week, but it was obvious that publication would come too late to affect the outcome.

176 TO JOHN MURRAY JR

[35 Duke Street, St James's, London, Thursday 12 April 1832]

ORIGINAL: MM 42
COVER: John Murray Junr Esq | Albemarle St.
EDITORIAL COMMENT: There is no signature. In another hand on first page: 'April 12'.

I enclose them for Press. Let swaggering ruffians of course stand.[1] I shall stay at home the whole morning with the hope of receiving proofs which I will always return by bearer.

You of course recd. the Dedication yesterday for Mr.B.'s perusal.[2] It is most important.

N.B. I must tell you that Mr.——, in one of his alterations, has made a great error, which I did not observe. It is at *Page 69*. He has written the numbers of the division *wrong. 212 sho[ul]d be 181*.[3] But if it be too late to alter it, I will send an *adroit erratum*.

177 TO JOHN MURRAY JR

[35 Duke Street, St James's, London], [Thursday] 12 April 1832

ORIGINAL: MM 32
COVER: *private* | John Murray Esq Junr | 50 Albemarle Street | [Crossed in another hand]: April 12, 1832 | D'Israeli Benj | King puts | Secrets of Cabinet | at my disposal.

April 12 | 1832

My dear Sir,

I enclose the proof. I have been obliged to make one or two *slight erasures*, because as the King[1] puts the secrets of his Cabinet at my disposal, I am bound in *honor and otherwise* not unnecessarily to injure the feelings of the Royal family. I never go out of my way to eulogise them. You can tell Mr—— this if you like, as he of course when he made the observ[ati]on was not aware of it. I shall continue at home all day.

BD

1 The expression 'desperate ruffians' appears in *Gallomania* (138).

2 Given the libellous nature of the dedication – among other pleasantries, it accused Grey of displaying 'an indubitable characteristic of insanity' in mistaking friends for enemies – 'Mr. B.' was perhaps a solicitor. However, the Turners, father and son, appear to have handled most of Murray's legal business.

3 This referred to a report of a vote of the French Chamber, in the spring of 1830, deploring the appointment of the Polignac ministry. In D's correction confusion was confounded, for the printed text put the vote at '221 to 216' (69) and there was then an erratum which changed 216 to 209 and which distinguished between the 'absolute' and the 'actual' majorities. The passage is not a model of clarity.

1 Charles X.

Lady Blessington
by Sir Thomas Lawrence

178 TO SARAH DISRAELI

[35 Duke Street, St James's, London], Thursday [12 April 1832]

ORIGINAL: H A/I/B/22
COVER: Miss Disraeli | Bradenham – House | Wycombe | Bucks
POSTMARK: (1) In circle: A | AP12 | 1832
EDITORIAL COMMENT: There is no signature. *Sic*: Brooke's, party-colored.

Thursday.

My dearest,

Henry Stanley has just brought me the ministerial list made up at Brooke's this morning, which gives a majority of *12* to the Cabinet. He says they will make *twenty* peers, perhaps *thirty* – but can say nothing for certain about Baring.[1] This is the Governmt. st[andin]g from the highest authority. We shall soon see.

I have seen B.E.L. who tells me my father complains of my not acknow[le]d[ging] the receipt of draft, but it arrived after I had written.

I long much to see you – my labors are drawing to a close. The Gallomania will be out in a day or two. It has been delayed by Croker who has taken great | interest in it.

Lord Eliot was Secretary to Lord Heytesbury[2] at the time of the Brazilian Portuguese Charter[3] and I wrote to him thereon, and he called. We have become great friends. I like him very much indeed and see a good deal of him.

The last vol. of the other work[4] will finish printing this evening. Murray is in good spirits and thinks that both will appear at a favorable time – considering all things.

Your violets are my great delight.

I am very well, and long to see you all.

Has my father heard from Bulwer? |

I called on Mrs. Gore and her husband returned the said visit. He is a pleasant fellow eno' and has lost his *rouerie* sufficiently.

I mean to make a rush at the family these next two or three days.

I feel quite dozy now with[ou]t an object, and have cleared my table preparatory to again filling it.

I have read E. Aram[5] at Bulwers request. It is his best thing, and very clever indeed. He says it has sold even in these times better than all his works. So I

1 Sir Thomas Baring was not made a peer.

2 William A'Court (1779-1860), 1st Baron Heytesbury. He was ambassador at St Petersburg 1828-32 and lord lieutenant of Ireland 1844-6. As ambassador to Portugal in 1824 he would have been involved in the negotiations between Portugal and Brazil.

3 In March 1824 the Emperor of Brazil proclaimed a new, more liberal, constitution. Negotiations were opened in London between Brazilian and Portuguese representatives on the subject of Brazilian independence from Portugal. In August 1825 a treaty was signed by which the Portuguese king, John VI, assumed the title 'Emperor of Brazil', and immediately abdicated in favour of his son, acknowledging Brazil as an independent empire.

4 *Contarini Fleming*.

5 See **141n7**.

have some hopes for myself. D'Orsay attacked me yesterday in Bond St. attired with a splendor I cannot describe, so dishevelled were his curls, so brilliant his bijouteries and the shifting tints of his party-colored costume. He knows who I am, and has I suppose been | crammed by Lady Ble[s]sin[g]ton.[6] I have been so engaged that I have not seen any of our friends. I hope I shall get into the Travellers as they mean to make a batch of new Members, some of whom will be appointed by the Committee and Ld E[liot] is very zealous indeed.

How is the little horse? I am sorry for the Disneys,[7] but perhaps the loss may make them more domestic. Have you a new Rector?[8]

TO SARAH DISRAELI — [35 Duke Street, St James's, London], Saturday 14 April [1832] — 179

ORIGINAL: H A/I/B/23

COVER: Miss Disraeli | Bradenham House | Wycombe | Bucks

POSTMARK: (1) In circle: P | AP14 | 1832

EDITORIAL COMMENT: There is no signature. There is a small hole in the second sheet of the MS. *Sic*: Heyday, bretheren.

Ap. 14 ~~Friday~~ | Saturday

My dearest,

I shall be with you on Saturday if fine. Ralph's movements are very doubtful, as in consequence of the alterations of the terms,[1] which are now fixed instead of being moveable, it is probable he may be busy in what were heretofore the holidays.[2]

I hope to send you a copy of the Gallom[ania] on Monday but am not sure. The other I will bring with me.

The bill as you know by this time was carried this morning by a majority of eight (nine), that is (as proxies do not count in Committee) virtually only *two*,

6 Marguerite Gardiner, née Power (1789-1849), Countess of Blessington, married in 1804 Capt Maurice Farmer (d 1818) from whom she soon separated; in 1818 she married Charles John Gardiner, 1st Earl of Blessington (d 1829). She travelled on the Continent with her husband and Count D'Orsay, and came to know Byron. On her husband's death she settled in London, continuing a notorious liaison with D'Orsay which lasted for the rest of her life. She published her first novel in 1833, and she was editor of *The Book of Beauty*. As a result of financial difficulties she retired to Paris in 1849 and died there. After D'Orsay's death in 1852, his brother-in-law, the duc de Gramont, constructed on his estate a joint tomb and monument to them both.

7 Sarah referred frequently to a Captain Disney, who lived on Bradenham Green. The Disneys' child had just died. H A/I/B/423.

8 They had; it was Isaac King Jr. **205**n6.

---

1 1 Wm IV *c* 70 fixed the law terms and the meetings of the Quarter Sessions, effective from 1831.

2 The beginning of Ralph's legal studies was marked by Sarah in a letter of 30 October 1830: 'Ralph left this day for Law and London.' H A/IV/E/10. However, his name does not appear in the *Law List* until 1842, when he is recorded as a clerk to the registrars in Chancery, so it is not even clear in what branch of the law he was reading. An early biographer of D claimed that Jem succeeded Benjamin in the office of Swain, Stevens, Maples, Pearse and Hunt. John M'Gilchrist *The Life of Benjamin Disraeli* (1866) 10. Perhaps he meant Ralph. Other sources place Ralph in Benjamin Austen's office.

therefore they must make | peers, and probably a great number. I am, as Eugene Aram says, "*equal to either fortune*" – that is am sure of a Boro' if the Tories ultimately succeed, w[hi]ch I doubt, and have a fair chance the other way. And really do not care about it, as I am more desirous of writing than ever.

I look upon the Gallomania, viewed as a piece of political writing, "as perfect" accord[in]g to the Bulwerian phrase. You will be astonished how it has been worked up. A great noise will be made about it in the Times; and if my political career here finishes, at least I have done something. All are very sanguine of its success. |

I shall be very glad to have some fresh air, and smell some violets on their native banks.

Bulwer will be in town on Monday or Tuesday, and I shall see him.

I wish to know whether you wo[ul]d like any inscription on the book Heyday[3] is binding and which I shall bring down with me, and where the inscription sho[ul]d be. On the side? Or only the initials on the back? Write and tell [*me*] my dearest.

I dined with the Trevors yesterday to see Louisa,[4] and went to the house afterwards. I have written a dedication to Lord Grey, which will make him stare; even Ld E[liot] says "*it is admirably pungent and pithy, and must produce effect*"

Talk[in]g to Murray of the Times who is really a most kindhearted, thoro' John Bull, and secretly a Tory[,] he sd. "*Oh! you must come in. If the Duke be in power, the Gallom[ania] will settle it. And if not,* | *I shall write an article and tell the Wycombites to elect you.*" *Nous verrons.* In the meantime, we must now think of Contarini and his shadowy bretheren who are yet in embryo.[5]

Half the Whigs who voted for the bill are in despair at its passing. This I know. Lord Darnley[6] told Bolton that we sho[ul]d all rue it, and looked as if he had just taken one of his surgeon's blackdoses. This *entres nous.* Times Murray sd. "*Now we must have the* | *Duke in directly its all settled*[.]" The Baron knew nothing about the Le Clercs particularly, but sd. he wo[ul]d enquire. I suppose he has forgotten in all this agitation. I have had no personal intercourse with *J.W.C.*.[7] I do not care about the Ath[enaeum] which must be left to chance, but certainly I cannot belong to the Conservative *now.*

3 Though both D and Sarah spelled the name 'Heyday', they presumably meant James Hayday (1796-1872), the bookbinder, Lincoln's Inn Fields. Boase; Ruari McLean *Victorian Book Design* (1963) 64.

4 Charles Trevor's wife, Olivia, was the sister of Louisa Lindo.

5 The 'shadowy bretheren' may include Alroy, Iskander and the heroes of the oriental tales which D wrote for Bulwer's *New Monthly Magazine* in 1832. For a list of these see Stewart *Writings*.

6 Edward Bligh (1795-1835), 5th Earl of Darnley; Whig MP for Canterbury 1818-30. *BP* (1884). The Lords had passed the second reading of the Reform Bill (agreement in principle) on 14 April by nine votes. Thirty-nine peers had either changed their votes to support the Bill or had abstained from opposing it.

7 John Wilson Croker. According to Monypenny, the D'Israelis thought that Croker was responsible for D's failure to gain membership in the Athenaeum. A modern biographer of Croker disputes this, arguing that D's reputation and 'outlandish behaviour did not appeal to the other members of the club'. M&B I 206; M.F. Brightfield *Life of J.W. Croker* (Berkeley 1940) 234-40.

TO JOHN MURRAY JR [35 Duke Street, St James's, London, Monday 16? April 1832] **180**

ORIGINAL: MM 30

COVER: IMMEDIATE | John Murray Jun Esq | 50 Albemarle St. | [In another hand]: April 17 – 1832 | Disraeli B.

EDITORIAL COMMENT: *Dating*: despite the endorsement by Murray's clerk, the context requires this to have been written on the morning of Monday 16 April. D is exhorting Murray to print the *Gallomania* by the end of that day. **181** shows that this was done, and the advance copy was despatched to Bradenham (**182**) the next morning.

My deference for your critic is so great that if his letter had arrived yesterday, I wo[ul]d have endeavoured to comply with its suggestion altho' against my conviction. *It is now too late.* The Dedication *must* appear, as it was shown to the Duke of W[ellington] in the house, and all concerned in the work count very much upon it, especially because since Mr—— has seen it, it contains a most important *prophecy*.[1] I see he does not like these last speculations, but you may rest assured that nothing of | the Kind is admitted in the work, but on the highest information. We are better acquainted with Metternichs cabinet than any other, and know what the Austrians are about.[2]

The Dutch Ambassador sends off a special vessel to night to his King[3] with the result of the debate. We can send a copy to his Majesty thereby: in the meantime the Baron gave the other to the Duke last | night in the house.

Pray let the Printer go to press *immediately*, and let me have a copy or copies in the afternoon if possible with the dedication[.] Most earnestly I request you to exert yourself with your usual vigor.

BD

Pray let no further discussion take place about the Dedic[ati]on, as to be very frank, I have already had on such subjects rather warmer debates with my friends than I admire.

1 The prophecy was: 'Although we have not heard much of Germany lately, I think I can assure your Lordship ... that you will soon be apprised that its interesting inhabitants are not entirely deprived of their share in the universal felicity which your golden rule appears to have generally occasioned.' *Gallomania* vi. Clearly D must have been in possession of advance knowledge of the Austrian effort to check the progress of reform in Germany. The Whigs were not entirely out of sympathy with Metternich's aims, but found his repressive methods distasteful.

2 No Austrian officials were numbered amongst the international cabal responsible for *Gallomania*. Prince Paul Esterhazy was then Austrian ambassador to the Court of St James's, but his name was never mentioned by D in connection with the conspiracy against the Whigs.

3 William I (1772-1848) was proclaimed King of the Netherlands in 1815 and abdicated in 1840.

181 TO JOHN MURRAY JR [35 Duke Street, St James's, London, Monday 16? April 1832]

ORIGINAL: MM 6
COVER: J. Murray Junr Esq. [In another hand]: 1832 (No date) | D'Israeli Benj Esq
PUBLICATION HISTORY: Smiles II 347, undated
EDITORIAL COMMENT: *Dating*: this seems to have been written late on the same day as **180**, and is acknowledging receipt of the advance copy of *Gallomania* which was sent on to Sarah the next morning (**182**). Reviews appeared in *The Morning Post* on 19 April, and in *The Times* on the following day.

My d[ea]r Sir,
I am *very glad* to receive the copy. I think that one sho[ul]d be sent to the Ed[itor] of the Times as quickly as possible, that at least he sho[ul]d not | be anticipated in the RECEIPT, even if in the *notice* by a Sunday paper – but I leave all this to your better judgment

BD |

You will send copies to Duke St as soon as you have them.

182 TO SARAH DISRAELI [35 Duke Street, St James's, London], Tuesday [17 April 1832]

ORIGINAL: H A/I/B/24
COVER: Miss Disraeli
PUBLICATION HISTORY: LBCS 5-6, dated 7 April 1832, prints the first sentence from each of the first two paragraphs, and all of paragraphs three and four.
EDITORIAL COMMENT: *Sic*: peice, carcase.

Tuesday morning

My dearest,
Herewith you receive what was not in time for yesterdays coach – the Gallomania. If I obtain another copy in time, I shall send you two.

I long to be with you. It is a great pleasure at last to come down with an empty head, and to feel that both works are completed. M[urray] thinks this considering all things a very good time to publish.

Washington I[rving]'s works have been of late only read by the author who is daily more enamoured of these heavy tomes. He demanded for the new one a large price. Murray murmured – W. talked of Posterity and the badness of the | public taste, and Murray said that authors who wrote for Posterity must publish on their own account.

In the last Omnibus is an alphabetical-poetical list of Authors
"I is Israeli a man of great gumption,
To leave out the D is a peice of ass-umption."[1]

My fathers old enemy the Catholic Monthly is defunct. Bentley has bought

1 The passage was misquoted from *The National Omnibus and General Advertiser*, a satirical newspaper of 1831-3. The original was: 'I leaves D'Israeli, a man of much gumption, | The D being dock'd is a piece of assumption.' no 42 (13 Apr 1832) 118.

the carcase on his own account, and under his influence it is to become the startler of the town.[2] This is all in embryo. He came and offered me the editorship, which was very kind and considerate of him. |

I think the Merediths are very much inclined to take Bradenham parva.[3] I shall see them today or tomorrow. They asked the terms. Madame thinks they will not be able to be much there. The girls are for it. Tell me the terms.

Tell my father to read the Gallom[ania] and write me his *real opinion*. I shall be down on Saturday – but shall write again. He can let me have a letter by Friday morning. On second thoughts, I do not think he will have time.

I saw Louisa who is very well.

Farewell my dearest, with love to all

BD

I have never seen Bulwer who will not be in town until the end of the month.

183

TO SARAH DISRAELI — [35 Duke Street, St James's, London], Friday [20 April 1832]

ORIGINAL: H A/I/B/25
COVER: Miss Disraeli | Bradenham House | Wycomb | Bucks.
POSTMARK: (1) In Maltese cross: C.H | 20AP1832 | X
EDITORIAL COMMENT: *Dating*: Good Friday in 1832 was 20 April.

Good Friday

My dearest,

I write you a hasty line to say that I shall be down if tolerably fine tomorrow, but not to dinner, as I have a great deal to do – and must gain the morning.

I know nothing of the book since Wednesday when the sale was very brisk, but none of the notices in the papers had then appeared which are all favorable | and important especially the one in "the Times" this morning which must produce an effect.[1]

I have *a most satisfactory* letter to my father from Bulwer which I shall bring down with his MSS.[2]

2 *The Catholic Miscellany and Monthly Repository of Information* began in 1822 and ceased publication with the number of May 1830. Richard Bentley, who had begun his career in publishing in 1829, did not, in fact, succeed in reviving the *Miscellany*. The periodical seems never to have taken direct notice of Isaac's work, but its persistent hostility to Southey may account for Isaac's feelings about it.

3 This was the Disneys' house, which they wished to sub-let until the lease expired at the end of the year. H A/I/B/424.

---

1 *Gallomania* was reviewed in *The Times* of 20 April 1832. The reviewer called the book a '*piece de circonstance*', probably aimed at the Reform Bill, and certain to be a 'hit' with the Tories. The final observation was more damning: 'When we have recommended the work on the ground of cleverness and curious information, we have said nearly all we can say in its favour. It is coloured with absolutism from beginning to end.'

2 These were articles for Bulwer's *New Monthly*. One of them is mentioned in a letter from Isaac to D (H A/I/B/424). It later appeared in three parts – 'Our Anecdotage'. *NMM* XXXIV (1832) 541-4; XXXV (1832) 154-7; 440-5.

Lady Jemima is in town and I have been introduced to her.

I shall see the Merediths to day if possible. |

My coming tomorrow is uncertain – I have so much to do – but I shall make every possible exertion.

BD

184

TO SARA AUSTEN — Bradenham, Saturday [28 April? 1832]

ORIGINAL: BL ADD MS 45908 ff148-9

PUBLICATION HISTORY: Jerman 146, extract dated April 1832

EDITORIAL COMMENT: *Dating*: attacks on *Gallomania* appeared in *The Globe* on 23 April and in *The Courier* on 26 April.

Brad Ho: | Saturday morng.

My dear Mrs Austen,

I write you a hasty line to thank you for your kind letter. I am anxious that my name sho[ul]d not be mentioned in reference to the work you have been lately reading, and that any reports | or opinions which may be formed from the internal evidence of style and the circumstantial evidence of a 1000 and 1 nothings sho[ul]d not receive authority or confirmation from the | conversation of those who are supposed to have my confidence.

I know nothing about the book.[1] I suppose you saw the Art[icle] in the Times of Good Friday.[2] So favorable notice in the chief Min[isteria]l paper doubtless piqued Min[iste]rs and | gave rise to these attacks from the Treasury Scribes in the Globe and the Courier,[3] which I hope will be repeated.

Yrs

BD

185

TO SARA AUSTEN — [35 Duke Street, St. James's, London], Thursday [3? May 1832]

ORIGINAL: BL ADD MS 45908 ff146-7

PUBLICATION HISTORY: Jerman 147, extracts dated April 1832

EDITORIAL COMMENT: *Dating*: D intended to go to Bradenham on 21 April (**183**); the context suggests that Sara Austen had answered **184** and that this, in turn, was a reply to her.

---

1 *Gallomania* was published anonymously and, as D had undertaken its compilation as a means of furthering his own credibility as a political writer, this insistence on secrecy might seem quixotic. As the letters have shown, the Tory leaders were aware of the authorship, and it is probable that, drawing on the experience of *Vivian Grey* in 1826, D wished general speculation to add to the debate he hoped the book would stimulate. Disclosure of D's name, he was shrewd enough to realize, might prevent the work from being taken seriously, particularly as its publication coincided with that of a novel, sponsored by the same publisher. Association with such a reactionary publication as the *Gallomania* would have ruined the credibility of one who was still to fight two elections in 1832 on a radical platform. Consequently D chose rarely to acknowledge his part in the book, although he did so in 1835. See (vol II) **409**.

2 The review of *Gallomania* in *The Times* on 20 April.

3 For these assaults on *Gallomania* see *The Globe* no 9,203 (23 Apr 1832) and *The Courier* no 12,708 (26 Apr 1832).

Thursday

My dear Mrs Austen,

I have left town this fortnight, and am now only passing thro'. I hope I may catch you before I leave again, but | I must be off on Monday at the latest; I will take my chance of seeing you on Sunday.

Of course I | meant you to keep the book; and am glad it is in the possession of one so familiar with my writings that you will not | give me credit for every idiotism you meet in its columns.[1]

yours ever

D

TO JOHN MURRAY Bradenham, Sunday 6 May [1832] 186

ORIGINAL: MM 39

COVER: John Murray Esq | 50 Albemarle Street | London | [In another hand]: 1832 May 6 – | D'Israeli Benj. Esq

POSTMARK: (1) In double circle: F | 7 MY 7 | 1832 (2) In small rectangle: No. 1 (3) HWYCOMBE | Penny Post

PUBLICATION HISTORY: Smiles II 340, dated 6 May 1832.

Bradenham House | May 6th. Sunday

Dear Sir,

From the notice of "C[ontarini] F[leming]" in the Lit[erary] Gaz[ette] which I received this morning, I imagine that Jerdan has either bribed the printer, or purloined some sheets. It is evident that he has only seen the last volume.[1]

It is unnecessary for me | to observe, that such premature notice, written in such complete ignorance of the work, can do no good. I think that he sho[ul]d be reprimanded, and his petty larceny arrested. I shall be in town on Tuesday.

BD

TO SARAH DISRAELI [London], Wednesday [9 May 1832] 187

ORIGINAL: H A/I/B/26

COVER: Miss Disraeli | Bradenham House | Wycomb | Bucks.

POSTMARK: (1) In circle: A | MY-9 | 1832

PUBLICATION HISTORY: LBCS 8, dated 9 May 1832, with omissions.

---

5 o'ck. | Wednesday

My dearest Sa,

I write to tell you that the Ministers were turned out this morning at 1/2 past twelve, and that the King has sent for Lord Harrowby – at least all this I have been just informed.[1] I | have not time to write more. What is going to happen no one can predict.

Ralph is well,

BD

1 The varying styles in *Gallomania* reflected the multiple authorship.

---

1 *The Literary Gazette* no 798 (5 May 1832) 277-8 contained a disappointingly brief notice of *Contarini Fleming*. However the journal made up for it the following week. See **188**n7.

---

1 On 8 May cabinet decided to resign unless the King at once created as many peers as might be

188 TO SARAH DISRAELI

[35] Duke Street, [St James's, London], Saturday [12 May 1832]

ORIGINAL: H A/I/B/27
COVER: Miss Disraeli | Bradenham House | High Wycomb | Bucks.
POSTMARK: (1) In Maltese cross: C.H | 12MY 1832 | X
PUBLICATION HISTORY: LBCS 8-9, dated 12 May 1832, the first three paragraphs with omissions
EDITORIAL COMMENT: *Sic*: Edinburg, Berri, neighbourood.

Duke St Saturday | 1/2 pt 5.

My dearest angel,

I received your welcome letter[1] this morning. I have written to Huffam by this post which I intended to have done. This morning will settle the fate of the Ministry. I dine at Lord Eliots "sans facon"[2] and shall hear the results. He also asked me yesterday, and is more than friendly.

The Duke is Premier hav[in]g once refused on account of his unwillingness to pass a Ref[orm] Bill. Peel will not join them for the same reason, but is to work for them in the Low[e]r House.[3] Baring Chanc[ello]r of the Excheq[ue]r Ld.

needed to pass the Reform Bill in its entirety. On 9 May the King refused. After nine days it became evident that neither Wellington nor Peel could form a government. The King did not send for Harrowby. On 18 May Grey was back in office with the King's reluctant promise to create peers if necessary. In the event, it was not.

1 The local opponents of the Reform Bill were alarmed lest the obstruction of the Tory peers should provoke incitement to revolution. Sarah wrote to D on 11 May 1832:

> You can imagine the astonishment and consternation of old and young Wycombe. All screwing up their courage to the sticking point, some to have their throats cut, some to cut. Parker as white as a sheet says "WE have gone too far." Huffam came over yesterday morning. I do not exactly know the purpose of his visit. Whether to find out what you were going to do, or for us to convey to you his feeling. He seemed in a great fright, that you were going to betray him by proving | yourself a Tory after he has for so many months sworn to all Wycombites that you were not one – what will happen? I should be sorry to give up the plan of regenerating and turning them all unconsciously into Tories.
>
> ... I hope we shall get a letter from you tomorrow. Huffam burnt that which you sent him, he was | afraid to carry in his pocket anything which smelt so of Toryism.

[In Isaac's hand]: The charming Expression which he read to me, before he burnt it, was that "We must not be made a Catspaw by the Whigs". [H A/I/B/426]

2 Informally.

3 The Duke was not 'Premier', having only been asked to form a ministry. Nor was D's inference correct, for Wellington would have been willing to pass a reform bill. J.R.M. Butler *The Passing of the Great Reform Bill* (1914) 388-91. There was, however, considerable agitation in the country at the prospect of Wellington's return. Sarah's worries (n1) were reflected in the local press:

> We learn that the Duke of Wellington consents to be Premier again! We learn, too, that HE will go on with the Reform Bill, and that he proposes to make very little alteration in it!! ... Parliament will, it is believed, be dissolved immediately, therefore, let the people prepare forthwith. Stocks have fallen one per cent more! ... The greatest alarm is entertained lest the 100,000 men at Birmingham should not be kept from an outbreak. It is felt to be the duty of the Tories to take their post without delay, so that if there should be a conflict between the government and the people, it may not be between the people and Earl Grey ... There is panic in the city. [*BG* no 1,033 (12 May 1832)]

Sir Robert Peel (1788-1850), 2nd Baronet, was then Tory MP for Tamworth, and the Duke's principal lieutenant in the Commons.

Carnarvon[4] probably President, Leach[5] Chancellor | Croker I have not heard, but if anything important occur to night, I will send you a parcel by a stage.[6]

Contarini published next week. The review in the Lit[erary] Gaz[ette] is by L[etitia] E. L[andon],[7] so Bulwer says, whom I met this morning.

In spite of the great sensation which all agree the Gallomania made, it has not sold the Edit. It was to have been reviewed in the Edinburg, but in the chaos of agitation in which we now exist, most probably will be omitted.

The Spence's party dull as usual. Old Genl. Maitland and his wife.[8] Sir George and Lady Rose and the eternal Miss Pouncey,[9] Donald and his lady who is no longer pretty, tho' agreeable.[10] I sat next | to her. A stray member or so, Mr Mackinnon,[11] an ass, and some horrid lawyers, old and young. I escaped early, disgusted, and shall cut the concert, to night in all probability.

They intend to decapitate the Duchess de Berri;[12] at least I fear so – having violated the law of nations in her capture, for she was under the protection of a friendly flag – and there is no proof of any design on her part. It is suspected that the flag was raised by the ministry at the moment they knew she wo[ul]d depart from Leghorn to Barcelona as an excuse for seizing her.

God bless you, my dear love

BD T.O. |

I forgot to say that Williams the coach proprietor says that a farmer (I think) in our neighbourood Phelps or Phipps[13] has a horse that wo[ul]d just suit us. Tell

4 Henry George Herbert (1772-1833), 2nd Earl of Carnarvon.

5 Sir John Leach (1760-1834), Tory MP for Seaford 1806-16.

6 This is one of the many circumstantial accounts which circulated during the nine days in which the King was trying to replace Grey. No such cabinet was ever formed.

7 *The Literary Gazette* (12 May 1832) made up for its non-committal initial notice of *Contarini Fleming* on 5th May (see **186**n1) by the publication of a full and highly favourable review. Letitia Landon's comments included the soothing judgement, 'we know no writer of the present day to whom the word "genius" may be more truly applied' (289-91).

8 Gen Frederick Maitland (1763-1848), grandson of the 6th Earl of Lauderdale. He held a wide variety of military and administrative posts in Europe and the West Indies, and had been promoted to full general in 1825. In 1790 he had married Catherine Prettijohn of Barbados, who survived him.

Sir George Rose (1782-1873), KC, writer on law and, after 1840, a master in Chancery. Lady Rose was the daughter of Capt Robert Pouncey and so Miss Pouncey must have been Lady Rose's sister.

From the context, George Spence would appear to have been the host. His eldest son was named Harry Donald Maurice and, although D seldom used first names for men, he may have been the Donald referred to here.

William Alexander Mackinnon (1789-1870), Tory MP for various constituencies 1819-65. He was the author of *On Public Opinion in Great Britain and Other Parts of the World* (1828), a pioneering work in the field.

Caroline de Bourbon (1798-1870), duchesse de Berry, mother of the Pretender to the French throne. The failure of her son's hopes during the Vendée revolt in 1832 attracted much interest in England, where the Duchess had lived in exile in 1830-2.

The Times of 10 May had reported her capture in Marseilles aboard a Sardinian steamboat. Only later was it discovered that the prisoner was not the Duchess but her maid. The Duchess was ultimately captured but, being with child, was later released. H.N. Williams *A Princess of Adventure* (1911) 304-11.

A newspaper report of disorder caused by unemployment made incidental mention of one James Phelps of Temple Farm near High Wycombe. *The Times* (22 Nov 1830).

Jem to enquire of Williams. They have done nothing here. If Phelps won't do, I will get something and am looking out. | It is a real edit of Ld N[ugent][14] but they printed a very small one – certainly not more than 750 and I *suspect 500.*

---

189 TO SARAH DISRAELI [London], Tuesday [15 May 1832]

ORIGINAL: H A/I/B/29

COVER: Miss Disraeli | Bradenham House | Wycombe | Bucks.

POSTMARK: (1) In circle: Q | MY15 | 1832

PUBLICATION HISTORY: LBCS 9, dated 15 May 1832, paragraphs one and two, omitting the first sentence of paragraph one; M&B I 205, dated 15 May 1832

EDITORIAL COMMENT: *Sic*: Whig's, frowsy.

Tuesday. 5 o'ck –

My dearest Sa,

I missed the post yesterday in all the excitement in which we here live. I very much fear that the Whig's are again in, and on their own terms. Such indeed is the report, but that is only a shot founded on last night's debate – but it is I apprehend a conjecture, that will turn out to be a prophecy.

I dined at Eliots on Saturday and met Col. and Captain A'Court,[1] brothers of Lord Heytesbury, and Lord Strangford. We had some delightful conversation and remained till a late hour. Strangford is an aristocratic Tom Moore. His flow is incessant and brilliant. The A'Courts very unaffected, hearty fellows. |

Lady Jemima improves. She is very courteous, and, dressed, looks really pretty. In the evening dropped in the Marchioness, and I suppose an unmarried sister[2] on their way to an assembly. Miladi['s] mother something between Lady Wynford[3] and Mrs. Davenport late of Covent Garden.[4] I like Eliot better every day. His kindness is very great. I call upon him every day to talk over affairs, and he conceals nothing from me. In my position at this moment such a *liaison* is invaluable. I ought not to forget the children who are the most wonderful devils – but of them when we meet.

I dined at Forbes on Sunday a trio with John Hardwick. I called on | Mrs. Phil[5] as I heard she was going out of town. Mrs. Spence's at home had broken up when I left Eliots, but I looked in – a frowsy affair.

14 George Nugent Grenville (1789-1850), 2nd Baron Nugent, younger son of the 1st Marquess of Buckingham, Whig MP for Aylesbury 1812-32, a lord of the Treasury 1830-2. On 11 May Isaac had written to ask, 'Is it a real *second* Edn of Lord Nugent?' H A/I/B/426. *The Times* of 10 May had advertised as 'just published' a new edition of '*Memoirs* [sic] *of Hampden, his Party and his Times* by Lord Nugent.' See **169**n12.

---

1 Capt Edward A'Court (1783-1855), later vice-admiral and Tory MP for Tamworth 1837-41. Col Charles Ashe A'Court (1785-1861), afterwards lieutenant general. *BP*, under Heytesbury.

2 Lady Jemima Eliot's mother, Lady Louisa Cornwallis (1776-1850), Marchioness Cornwallis, daughter and co-heiress of the 4th Duke of Gordon of the first creation, and widow of the 2nd and last Marquess Cornwallis. *BP*, under St Germans. Unmarried sisters of the period rarely excited the attention of genealogists.

3 Mary Ann Best, née Knapp (d 1840), married in 1794 William Draper Best (1767-1845), 1st Baron Wynford, chief justice of the Court of Common Pleas. *BP* (1884).

4 Mary Ann Davenport, née Harvey (1765?-1843), famous actress. Her active career ended in 1830; hence D's remark that she was 'late of Covent Garden'.

5 Probably Julia Hardwick, wife of Philip Hardwick.

From your letter you dont seem to think much of the Lit[erary] Gaz[ette].[6] I assure you it has produced no slight effect. I heard of it everywhere. It seems agreed that I have got the laurel crown, but the book is not published until to-morrow.

Tell Jem I want a Blenheim puppy. I suppose I can get one at Wycombe which is I believe famous for such brutes. Let him enquire and communicate the result. How can it be sent up to me? I gave Lady Jemima the book, but made a great favor of it, and I told her that my father was not authorized to give the other and that I had | reprimanded him. She wrote me a letter. I dined with the Austens yesterday, but was there only an hour as I had to go back to the house where there was an awful debate. There has been a wonderful scene at Devonshire House.[7] Lady Lyndhurst[8] fainting etc., but too long to tell.

Love to my mother who I hope is better.

BD |

N.B. I have seen my father.

190

TO SARAH DISRAELI — [35] Duke Street, St James's, [London], [Friday] 18 May [1832]

ORIGINAL: H A/I/B/30
COVER: Miss Disraeli | Bradenham House | High Wycombe | Bucks
POSTMARK: (1) In circle: Z | MY18 | 1832
EDITORIAL COMMENT: *Sic*: St James.

Duke St St James | May 18.

My dearest,

I did not write to you yesterday, because my father anticipated my news. Lord Strangford called on me on Thursday, and Col. Long who has just come up to town after five months absence and has found out from the Lit[erary] Gaz[ette] that I am a great author. Yesterday Henry Stanley called on me. He was going to the drawing room with his sister[1] and also that worthy Foord Bowes who was also going to make his bow to her majesty. He is to be married this month with his father's consent but | alas! not to the unhappy Helen Brackenbury![2]

6 Sarah had written to D on 14 May 1832: 'We cannot for a moment doubt that L.E.L. | is the contriver and part-writer of the review of *Contarini Fleming*, it is so charmingly interspersed with Brompton slip-slop. "*As if* Mr. D. ever did such wonderful things." Who but L.E.L. would call Contarini and Alceste "a young couple" as if they had just married at Kensington or Chelsea.' H A/I/B/427. See also **188**n7.

7 The London residence of the Duke of Devonshire, located at 78 Piccadilly, was a centre of London fashion for a century.

8 Sarah Garay Copley, née Brunsden (d 1834), married in 1819 Lord Lyndhurst, who was then Sir John Copley.

---

1 Henry Thomas Stanley had two living sisters at this time: Charlotte Elizabeth (d 1853), who in 1823 had married Edward Penrhyn; and Eleanor Mary, who in 1835 married the Rev Frank George Hopwood, rector of Winwick, Lancs. *BLG*, under Derby.

2 Helen Brackenbury (d 1883), later Talavera, second daughter of John Brackenbury. The comment was no doubt prompted by the announcement of Bowes's forthcoming marriage to one Margaret Rice which took place 7 June 1832.

The same day (yesterday) I met Bulwer and passed a good part of the morning with him. He has asked me down to Pinner[3] to spend tomorrow and Sunday with a bevy of beauties, but I fear that I shall not be able to go.

Lord Eliot has invited me for next Wednesday to meet Sir Robert Peel.

I beg that James will be very cautious with the Wycombe people and not appear at all interested | about the pigeon shooting.[4] He is very young and no diplomatist at present. Leave everything to Huffam who is acquainted with my feelings. Any encouragement from James is bad. They certainly, if anything, will have a cup.

In politics all is unsettled, but the Baron[5] has just come in, and I must finish
dearest
this scrawl
BD[6]

Buy the lady dog for me – and let me know about Phelps horse. I shall enquire.

191

TO SARAH DISRAELI

35 Duke Street, St James's, [London],
Monday [21 May 1832]

ORIGINAL: H A/I/B/31
COVER: Miss Disraeli | Bradenham House | Wycombe | *Bucks.*
POSTMARK: (1) In circle: E |MY 21 | 1832
EDITORIAL COMMENT: *Sic*: St James.

---

35 Duke St St James | Monday

My dearest angel,

Immediately that I received your letter I sent off an answer to the Athenaeum but my father never returned. You have no cause for annoyance. When a horse is warranted sound, and during its trial any injury occurs to it in consequence of its unsoundness, the vendor must take the consequences, and had any ill hap-

3 Now a suburb of London, near Harrow.

4 Political enthusiasts at Wycombe determined on a pigeon shoot, an elaborately structured precursor to clay-pigeon shooting. Sarah in an earlier letter mentioned the enthusiasm of the butcher, the plumber, the carpenter, the chairmaker, the tailor and the coach proprietor, but at the same time acknowledged that 'it would do mischief if great expectations are raised which cannot be fulfilled.' H A/I/B/429. Further correspondence reveals that there was great difficulty in obtaining pigeons in June, when they sold at twenty shillings a dozen, and it is not certain that a shoot was held at that time. However on 27 January 1833 Sarah wrote to say that her brother's cup had been shot for, generally 'very badly'. H A/I/B/451.

5 Haber.

6 There is a postcript written by Ralph Disraeli which reads:

Literary Union.

Ben wanting wax. I seal this. The Governor was quite well yesterday. Every thing is unsettled altho' much is expected this evening. Let me hear from you. When do the Merediths go to Bradenham. The Spences party was the old regular set. Starkies were there of course, and the Daughter – an uncommon pretty girl is the Daughter!! Contarini is not yet in the shops. I suppose we shall hear of it on Sunday. No reviews yet except the Lit[erary Gazette] and Ath[enaeum]. Give my best to my Mother and Jem. Always your affect. br[other]
RD

Nothing but speculation in the evening papers.

'A Radical Conservative'
from the diary of Blanche Norris, 1832

pened to Jem, he might have had recourse against the vendor. I recommend you therefore to return the horse to the man and at the same time offer him £2. Let some disinterested person accompany William in order to prove the tender, provided, as I anticipate, the man do not accept it. Then let him bring his action, if he dare. |

Strangford called on me again on Friday, and we had a long oriental coze,[1] which ended with him doing me out of a copy of Contarini, of which howr. I made a great favor.

My cut[2] was no great affair, and is now well. I did not go to Bulwers on Sunday howr. partly in consequence. I felt disinclined, and it perhaps just dissuaded me. Going to consult Bolton upon it, I found Lord Darnley, a most agreeable, unaffected, intelligent personage with whom I had a long conversation which ended by his saying that he sho[ul]d have the pleasure of calling upon me on his return to town. I like him very much and am inclined to cultivate his acquaintance. |

I know nothing of course of Contarini, as I avoid Albemarle St. until it be published a fortnight or so.

I shall send the portrait, done up of course in a parcel for you, to the Merediths, as it is so safe a mode of conveyance. I mention this that you may know what it is, as I shall say nothing to them.

I am extremely well. Tell Blanche[3] that I called on Fletcher[4] about her watch, but he had already sent it to Hughenden. Since then it has been returned, and will be finished in a week. He has orders to send it to some lady in town, but I will bring it down if they like, as I shall be at Bradenham I suppose at the end of the month.

No news in politics. Tonight will settle how many of | the Tories choose to retire. There is a rumor to day that they will rally and join the Crown to make peers.[5] Lord Carnarvon sd. to Strangford, summing up the affair, that "it was a choice bet[wee]n assassination and suicide, and that for his part, he preferred the former."

Yours very lovingly,

BD

Write about the horse of Phelps. Buy the lady dog for 30/-. I shall not write until Thursday. Write if possible, in the interim.

1 A friendly chat.

2 Sarah wrote on 20 May 1832: 'I hope you have not seriously hurt yourself. Papa says you have cut your lip ...' (H A/I/B/430).

3 Blanche Norris (1814?-1903) was the fifth daughter of John Norris (1773-1845) of Hughenden House. In 1841 she married Philip Wroughton of Ibstone House, Bucks. *BLG*. She kept a diary which chronicled the doings of their neighbours, especially the D'Israelis. It is now in the possession of Mr and Mrs Philip Wroughton, of Woolley House, near Wantage, Oxon. Sarah's comments on the family were not unfriendly, but decidedly condescending. She described the father as 'a good old Tory of the Ultra school' and the girls as 'pretty, good-natured, and profoundly ignorant'. H A/IV/E/10.

4 S. Fletcher, engraver and jeweller, at 34 Great Marlborough Street. *LPOD* (1832).

5 In this context, to 'join the Crown' meant acquiescing in the King's grudging agreement to create peers, if necessary, in order to pass the Reform Bill.

TO SARAH DISRAELI [London], Thursday 24 May [1832] **192**

ORIGINAL: H A/I/B/32

COVER: Miss Disraeli | Bradenham House | High Wycombe | *Bucks.*

POSTMARK: (1) In Maltese cross: C.H | 24MY1832 | X

PUBLICATION HISTORY: LBCS 9-10, dated 24 May 1832, omitting the first two paragraphs. M&B I 205, dated 15 May 1832, with omissions and conflated with **189**

EDITORIAL COMMENT: The cover bears in another hand (possibly Sarah's) across the top: 'London – May 24th. 1832.' and at the lower left: 'B Disraeli.' The pattern is close to the way the cover would have looked had D franked it as a member of Parliament (although the '24th' should have been written out in words). Sarah was, perhaps, anticipating. *Sic*: York, disagreable.

Thursday May 24

My dearest Sa,

I received yours[1] this morning. Let me know about the horse as I have seen one here which might suit, but I have not had it examined in consequence of Phelps.

I am rejoiced to hear you like the frame, which is I think at once novel and beautiful.

Yesterday I dined at Eliots – a male party consisting of eight. I sat between Peel and Herries,[2] but cannot tell you the names of the other guests altho' they were all members of one or other house, altho' at last I detected among them Captain York[3] whom I had | met in the Levant. Peel was most gracious. He is a very great man indeed, and they all seem afraid of him. By the bye I observed that he attacked his turbot most lustily with his knife, so Walker's[4] story is true. I can easily conceive that he co[ul]d be very disagreable but yesterday he was in a most condescending mood and unbent with becoming haughtiness.[5] I reminded him by my dignified familiarity both, that he was an Ex-minister, and I a present Radical. Herries, old grey headed financial Herries, turned out quite a literary man – so false are one's impressions. The dinner was sumptuous and the day very agreeable. We broke up late. Several parties came in in the evening, altho' Lady Jemima | herself went off to Lady Salisbury's.[6]

I can write no more.

Yrs ever,

BD

1 Sarah wrote to D on 23 May 1832. H A/I/B/431.

2 John Charles Herries (1778-1855), writer on economic subjects and Tory MP for Harwich 1823-41, and for Stamford 1841-53. He became secretary at war in Peel's first government.

3 Capt Charles Philip Yorke (1799-1873), after 1834 4th Earl of Hardwicke, Tory MP for Reigate 1831-2, and for Cambridgeshire 1832-4. He eventually became a vice-admiral.

4 Thomas Walker (1784-1836), writer on political economy; he was appointed police magistrate in Lambeth Street in 1829, there joining John Hardwick. Walker edited the periodical called *The Original* (1835).

5 Many years later Eliot is recorded as having had a very different memory of the dinner: 'From his appearance or manner Sir Robert Peel seemed to take an instinctive dislike to him. He "buried his chin in his neck cloth" and did not speak a word to Disraeli during the rest of the meal.' Sir William Fraser *Disraeli and His Day* (1891) 187; Blake 87.

6 This was probably Mary Amelia Cecil (1750?-1835), dowager Marchioness of Salisbury. She entertained more frequently than the current Marchioness, Frances Mary, née Gascoyne (1802-1839), who had become in 1821 the first wife of James Brownlow William Cecil, 2nd Marquess of Salisbury, who on the marriage assumed the surname Gascoyne-Cecil.

193 TO SARAH DISRAELI [London], Saturday [26 May 1832]

ORIGINAL: H A/I/B/33

COVER: Miss Disraeli | Bradenham House | High Wycombe | Bucks.

POSTMARK: (1) In Maltese cross: C.H | 26MY1832 | X

PUBLICATION HISTORY: LBCS 10-11, dated 26 May 1832, the first two paragraphs with changes; M&B I 191, extract dated 26 May 1832

EDITORIAL COMMENT: *Sic*: Montague, Czartoriski, Atwood, organization, vitious, drank.

Saturday.

My dearest Angel,

I received yr letter yesterday and sent Ralph a note, but have not seen him. The letter *was* from Beckford[1] to whom I sent a copy, as I like to do astonishing things. His answer is short, but very courteous. It commences with four exclamations "How wildly original! How full of intense thought! How awakening! How delightful!"

This really consoles one for Mr. Patmore's criticism in the C[our]t J[ourna]l.[2]

On Thursday I dined at the Polish Club[3] with Montague Gore[4] - Campbell in the Chair and the guests Prince Czartoriski,[5] Mr. Thom. Atwood[6] and the rest of the Birmingham | Deputation. Altho' domestic politics are forbidden, on this day they co[ul]d not refrain from breaking into them, and there was a consequent tumult. The Prince is a dignified and melancholy looking man, with a fine head.

None of the Birmingham heroes are above par, altho' there is a simplicity about Atwood which is pleasing. His organization very inferior – his voice good, his pronunciation most vitious and Warwickshire – altog[ethe]r a third rate man. His colleague Scholefield[7] quite devoid of talent, and the rest poor things. The

1 William Beckford (1759-1844), the Gothic novelist. He greatly admired D's novels, especially *Contarini Fleming* and *Alroy*. The letter from which D quotes has not been located.

2 Patmore, if indeed he was the reviewer, professed himself quite mystified by the book: 'To describe it were easy enough; for it were simply to construct a string of antitheses, half as long as the book itself. But to describe it intelligibly, and with any view to the information of the reader, is quite beyond our limited faculties.' *CJ* no 161 (26 May 1832) 349-50.

3 The Literary Association of the Friends of Poland, founded in 1831 by Thomas Campbell, the poet. A famous line from Campbell's *The Pleasures of Hope* affirmed his commitment to the Poles: 'And Freedom shrieked – as Kosciusko fell!' (I 382). Britain accepted some 500 Polish refugees following the revolution of 1830. Jerzy Zubrzycki *Polish Immigrants in Britain* (1956) 33.

4 Montagu Gore (1800-1864), Whig MP for Devizes 1832-4; Tory MP for Barnstaple 1841-7.

5 Prince Adam Czartoryski (1770-1861), president of Poland after the revolution of December 1830. He resigned in 1831 and from 1832 until his death he lived mainly in Paris. Chambers.

6 Thomas Attwood (1783-1856), Radical MP for Birmingham 1832-40; supporter of O'Connell, and later prominent in the Chartist movement; founder of the Birmingham Political Union. Asa Briggs 'Thomas Attwood and the Economic Background of the Birmingham Political Union' *The Cambridge Historical Journal* IX (1948) 190-216.

7 Joshua Scholefield (1744-1844), banker and merchant, Radical MP who sat, with Attwood, for the two-member constituency of Birmingham, from 1832 to his death, aged ninety-nine.

Revd Dr Wade,[8] a drunken parson with[ou]t an idea, but with the voice of a bullock which they mistake for oratory. |

I have seen Ralph who cannot come for Tuesday, altho' probably he will be able to get down by Wednesday or so.

I forgot to say, that Peel speaking about the S[tate] P[aper] Office, and the facility etc. I attacked him about my father[9] and made him look extremely small.

Angerstein returns next month. He is a great friend of Gore (Montagu) who is a very gentlemanly fellow. I had my health drank by the Poles, and made a speech. Campbell was quite idiotic. Among the guests was little Fox the Unitarian min[iste]r who is a capital fellow, and likes my novels which for a Radical, an Unitarian, and a Utilitarian, is pretty well.[10]

In the greatest haste,

Yrs ever,

BD

194

TO SARAH DISRAELI [London], Monday [28 May 1832]

ORIGINAL: H A/I/B/44

PUBLICATION HISTORY: LBCS 11-12, dated 28 May 1832, includes parts of the first two paragraphs with alterations, conflated with an extract from **197**; M&B I 191, dated 28 May 1832, reprints an extract from RD's text.

EDITORIAL COMMENT: *Dating*: the review of *Contarini Fleming* in *The Atlas* had appeared the day before – 27 May.

Monday | 6 o'ck.

My dearest angel,

I send you a parcel of criticism which I received from Ralph. Amid abundance of praise and blame, one thing, which we all expected, is very evident, that not one of the writers has the slightest idea of the nature or purposes of | the work. As far as I can learn howr. it has met with decided success and is making as much sensation as we co[ul]d desire, more than we co[ul]d expect.

Among o[the]rs, Tom Campbell, who, as he says, never reads any books but his own, is delighted with it. He is reading it in a most analytical manner, preparatory to | "a psychological review."[1] "*I shall review it myself and it will be a psy-*

8 The Rev Arthur S. Wade (1789?-1845), DD, the Owenite vicar of Warwick. Already prominent in Radical circles in 1832, he later became a Chartist. Such conspicuous militancy was still rare among the clergy of the Church of England, and Wade was consequently a figure of some notoriety. For an account of some of his early political activities see Alfred Plummer *Bronterre O'-Brien 1804-1864* (1971). See also Venn VI part ii.

9 In his memoir of his father, written in 1848, D mentioned that the secretary of state had refused to allow Isaac to consult records in the State Paper Office when he was writing his *Charles the First*. *Curiosities of Literature* new ed (1863) xxviii. Isaac confirmed this in a comment in the work itself. *Charles the First* III 61. At the time (1825) Robert Peel was home secretary.

10 William Johnson Fox (1786-1864), a radical preacher and journalist, was one of Bulwer's friends, and a noted orator on behalf of the working classes. D is reported to have written to Fox, boasting that his *forte* was sedition. The report continues: 'Most clever young men who are not born to fortune, and who feel drawn into political life, fancy too that their *forte* is sedition.' Justin McCarthy *A History of Our Own Times* (1879) I 257. See also **263**n1.

---

1 The word 'psychological' was then relatively new. Isaac D'Israeli had taken pains to explain it in his *Calamities of Authors* (1812).

chological review" he exclaims. Campbell of course quite comprehends it. "Don't be nervous about the sale, that's nothing. Nothing sells, but this will *last*. Its a philosophical work Sir!"

About the fair, what are you going to do? | Write to me and let me know something definite.

I am going this very moment to b[u]y a horse which I hope will suit you, and if I think it will, I shall send you it down for a week with Ralph.

Yrs

BD

I have seen my fathers name quoted in several places. Soc[iet]y for Diff[usi]on of Knowledge[2] etc. |

It is curious that the Atlas evidently believes that *Psychol[ogica]l* means *Amatory*.[3]

195 TO SARAH DISRAELI

[35 Duke Street, St James's, London], Tuesday [29 May 1832]

ORIGINAL: H A/I/B/17
COVER: Miss Disraeli | Bradenham House | Wycombe | Bucks
POSTMARK: (1) In Maltese cross: C.H | 29MY1832 | X
EDITORIAL COMMENT: *Sic*: Montague.

Tuesday | 1/2 past 6

My dearest,

I received your letter this morning. I have a horse which I think will do and if it do not rain Ralph will bring it down tomorrow. 'Tis on hire for a week, and the price demanded is 40 gu[ine]as.

If the Merediths will not stay for the fair, and you have no other arrangements, I sho[ul]d like Mrs. Bolton to be asked to Bradenham for many reasons, first because I don't think it possible for her to come[,] 2ndly. because she is of great service[1] to me and I know she wo[ul]d highly prize the attention and 3rdly. | because if she do come she wd. not bore you, as you wo[ul]d rather like her. She is so very much improved. In this case (supposing you have no regular

2 The Society for the Diffusion of Useful Knowledge began its work of popular education late in 1826. The prime movers were Lord Brougham, Matthew Hill, the legal reformer, and Charles Knight, writer and publisher. It is not clear in which of the numerous publications of the Society Isaac's name appeared.

3 *Contarini* was reviewed in Robert Bell's Sunday paper *The Atlas* no 315 (27 May 1832) 347-8. After quoting several passages relating to the hero's love for three different women, the reviewer commented: 'These specimens will show how the psychological portion of the work is treated.'

---

1 Mrs Bolton seems to have been privy to D's political plans and to have provided him with useful contacts amongst her circle of acquaintances. Her letters to him are full of advice against alienating the High Tories and Haber, and she obviously made every effort to present D's radical leanings to others in a sympathetic light. The men with whom she most frequently discussed D's political ambitions – and from whom she derived information – were Marcus Hill, Montagu Gore and Haber. H A/IV/G/2-9.

family and therefore room) I shall in all probability bring down a man or two, Montague Gore or so.

I co[ul]d write more but I have delayed to the last minute to see Ralph.

All praise Cont[arin]i. I harp | at the Athenaeum.[2]

Lady Blessin[g]ton never travels with[ou]t the Lit[erary] Char[acters].

BD

If you do not *disapprove* of Mrs. B. it wo[ul]d be well for you to write to her. I much wish to pay her attention.

196

TO SARAH DISRAELI [35 Duke Street, St James's, London, Wednesday 30 May 1832]

ORIGINAL: H A/I/B/18
COVER: [In Ralph's hand]: Miss Disraeli | *RD*
EDITORIAL COMMENT: *Dating*: by reference to the letter of the day before. *Sic*: Montague.

My dearest,
I scribbled you a most hurried letter yesterday, and as I sent it to the post at the tenth hour, and by a strange hand, it is doubtful whether you have received it. Ralph was at a ball last night and therefore may not come down; he called on me this morning, but I was unexpectedly out. His calling again is doubtful.

The dog must be called Alcesté – short Cesté.

Ralph has come and I can therefore only write a line.

I said in the letter that I wished | Mrs Bolton to be asked for the various reasons I have therein mentioned. If you have not received the letter let me know by return of post, and I will write again. Speak to Ralph about it.

All I hear about the book is good. I had a long convers[ati]on with Bulwer yesterday. I meant to get down for a day but cannot. I am engaged every day – today, tomorrow | Friday Bulwer, Saturday Hardwick; if no o[the]r engage[me]nt, Sunday Montague Gore.

Ralph won't stay.

BD

197

TO SARAH DISRAELI [35] Duke Street, St James's, [London], [Friday] 1 June [1832]

ORIGINAL: H A/I/B/34
COVER: Miss Disraeli | *Bradenham House*| *BD*
PUBLICATION HISTORY: LBCS 11-2, dated 28 May 1832, includes most of paragraph four, conflated with **194**; M&B I 191, dated 28 May 1832, extract from LBCS conflation
EDITORIAL COMMENT: *Sic*: St James, Montague.

Duke St St James | June 1

My dearest Angel,
Mrs. Bolton cannot venture to pay us a visit at present, but will postpone it till the end of July or so. The compliment is paid, and that is enough.

2 Meaning that he continued to seek election to the Athenaeum. See **179**n7.

I shall invite a man but who I know not. Montague Gore tho' he has an opera box[1] and £10000 per ann – wo[ul]d just do, being very modest amiable and awkward and rather intelligent – but | unfortunately he is obliged to leave town this morning suddenly for the Berkshire election[2] and I consequently do not dine with him on Sunday.

We shall see.

I suppose you have read the Review in the Monthly[–]Where I am accused of Atheism, because I retire into Solitude to write novels.[3]

Bulwer is quite up | to it. He will review it himself in the next Mag[azine].[4] I hear nothing but high praise from the cognoscenti, but know nothing of the sale. Bulwer says it will not have a great sale for three, perhaps 6 months.

I intend to be with you in a very few days.

Adieu dearest

BD

Send up the dog, giving me notice that I may send to the Stage.

198

TO BENJAMIN AUSTEN [London], Saturday [2? June 1832]

ORIGINAL: BL ADD MS 45908 ff55-6

COVER: Benjn Austen Esq

PUBLICATION HISTORY: Layard 26, extracts dated 10 June 1832; M&B I 211, undated extract; Jerman 155-6, dated 10 June 1832

EDITORIAL COMMENT: *Dating*: by context. This is the beginning of D's active campaign; by Monday 4 June (**199**) he was already actively canvassing in Wycombe, and on the following Saturday he made the first of his famous 'Red Lion' speeches there. Although the letters from O'Connell, Hume and Burdett were described here as though they were already in his possession, they were not yet written, and this represents a good example of D's habit of endowing expectation with actuality. Hume's letter, for example, was written on 2nd June; D's letter of thanks, composed immediately on receiving it, was written from Wycombe on the 5th. **200**.

---

1 A box at a major theatre was a significant piece of property. At about this time, Thomas Duncombe was offered Lord Carrington's box, for which the going rate was £400 per season. T.H. Duncombe ed *The Life and Correspondence of Thomas Slingsby Duncombe, late M.P. for Finsbury* (1868) I 185.

2 The polls opened that day for the last by-election before the Reform Bill received royal assent. Gore was an elector in the Sonning hundred of Arborfield parish, where he owned property. Information kindly supplied by the Berkshire Record Office from *The Register of Electors, Berkshire, 1832*.

3 The author of the review of *Contarini Fleming* in *The Monthly Review* ns II (June 1832) 281-99 said: 'What are we to understand by exemption from "sectarian prejudices"? The absence of religion. What is meant by the "flowing spirit of creation"? Simply that there is no God' (283).

4 Bulwer's enthusiastic review, under the pseudonym 'Asmodeus at Large', appeared in the July 1832 number of *The New Monthly Magazine* 26-8. 'Mr D'Israeli is a writer of very great genius, and "Contarini Fleming" is so vast an improvement on "Vivian Grey" and "The Young Duke", that it is difficult for me to believe it written by the same man ... ' He went on to defend the profundity of the work: 'The mass of readers will not perceive its object, and therefore it seems to them bizarre, merely because its meaning is not on the surface. In fact, "Contarini Fleming" is a delineation of abstract ideas, in which, as in "Wilhelm Meister", the Author is often allegorical and actual at the same time.' Bulwer concluded with a generous boost for D's political aspirations: 'By the way, I see he is standing for Wycombe: – joy be with him! A man of such talent and such knowledge ought to be in Parliament, more especially when the powers he possesses are pledged to the advance of those Great Truths which are now so firmly rooted in the Hearts of the People.'

Saturday | 1/2 pt 10. 198 | 285
2 Jun 1832

Dear old fellow,

I have just received a dispatch from Wycombe informing me that the crisis has commenced, and I must go down, declare, and canvass. Baring is my opponent. In seven days I shall know the result, and either he or myself I hope will be shelved.

I start on the high Radical | interest, and take down strong recommendatory epistles from O'Connell, Hume, Burdett[1] and *hoc genus*. Toryism is worn out, and I cannot condescend to be a Whig.

I wished to settle our account before I quitted town this time, and I am prepared; but I suppose I shall be up in a week.

I want a horse and if | you will let me, will purchase yours. In that case, let it

1 This was in anticipation of Bulwer's success in his offer to obtain for D letters of support from Hume and O'Connell, and of Charles Gore's in obtaining one from Burdett.

Daniel O'Connell (1775-1847), the Irish Radical leader, known as 'the Liberator', had already spent twenty-five years in vigorous political action outside Parliament before he was elected MP for County Clare at a by-election in 1828. As stormy a petrel inside Parliament as he had been outside it, he continued to represent successively various Irish constituencies until his death. In 1832 he was MP for Waterford.

Joseph Hume (1777-1855) was at this time Radical MP for Middlesex.

Sir Francis Burdett (1770-1844), 5th Baronet, was the Radical MP for Westminster; later he sat as a Tory.

O'Connell gave the following reply to Bulwer's solicitation of support on D's behalf:

Parliament-street, June 3rd, 1832.

My dear Sir,

In reply to your inquiry, I regret to say that I have no acquaintance at Wycombe to whom I could recommend Mr. D'Israeli. It grieves me, therefore, to be unable to serve him on his canvass. I am as convinced as you are of the great advantage the cause of genuine Reform would obtain from his return. His readiness to carry the Reform Bill into practical effect towards the production of cheap government and free institutions is enhanced by the talent and information which he brings to the good cause. I should certainly express full reliance on his political and personal integrity, and it would give me the greatest pleasure to assist in any way in procuring his return, but that, as I have told you, I have no claim on Wycombe, and can only express my surprise that it should be thought I had any.

I have the honour to be,
My dear sir, yours very faithfully,
Daniel O'Connell. [Beeton 67]

For Hume's letter of 2 June, and its retraction on the 6th, see **200n1**.

When asked by Gore for a letter of recommendation on behalf of D, Burdett sent the following reply:

St. James' Place, June 3rd, 1832.

Dear Sir,

I am sorry not to have it in my power to promote Mr. D'Israeli's return to Parliament, but I have not the least connection with, or even acquaintance at, Wycombe.

I can, therefore, express my regret at having no power to aid a person of so much merit.
I remain, dear sir, yours sincerely,
F. Burdett. [Beeton 68]

be in Duke St tomorrow at 1/2 past 11. Excuse this abrupt style. Time is valuable.

Give me your prayers and believe me
Ever
BD

---

199 TO JAMES GEORGE TATEM Red Lion, Wycombe, [Monday] 4 June [1832]

ORIGINAL: OSER 1

COVER: PRIVATE | J.G. Tatem Esq | etc. etc. etc. | wait for | answer.

Red Lion Wycombe | June 4.

J.G. Tatem[1]
etc. etc. etc.
private
Sir,

You may perhaps not be unaware that it is my intention to offer myself as a Representative for this Boro'.[2] In doing so, I come forward on principles the most *decidedly liberal*, and supported by the sanction, the recommendation, and the personal interest of the | most illustrious of our public men.

I bear with me letters from Sir Fras. Burdett, from Mr Hume, from Mr O'Connell, and many others,[3] expressing the deep interest they feel in my success. I am desirous of submitting these documents to yourself as the most influential, the most | able, and the most sincere reformer in Wycombe, and if it be not considered an intrusion, I shall have the honor of waiting upon you at once, or receiving you here.

I have the honor, to remain
Sir
with great consideration,
Your faithful Servant,
B. Disraeli.

1 James George Tatem was a London merchant who had retired to High Wycombe. He was a Whig reformer who took a very active part in the life of the community, first as an alderman and a churchwarden, and later, in 1836, as the first mayor of the new municipal council. He was, most decidedly, a political opponent of D. Ashford 257, 267, 278.

2 For a treatment of D's electoral activities in 1832, especially during the June by-election, see C.L. Cline 'Disraeli at High Wycombe: The Beginning of a Great Political Career' *University of Texas Studies in English* 22 (1942) 124-44.

D's election agent was John Nash, well known as an associate of the Marquess of Chandos. This fact dismayed D's Radical supporters and lent credence to Whig claims that D was a Tory in disguise. Sarah to D, 5 April 1832, H A/I/B/422. *BG* no 1038 (16 June 1832) and no 1040 (30 June 1832).

3 See **198**n1 and **200**n1. Bulwer wrote to D on 3 June telling him that Hume's letter had been forwarded to Bradenham and should reach him on 5 June. After summarizing Hume's words, Bulwer associated himself with cordial support for D as a reformer. The letter, formally signed 'E. Lytton-Bulwer, M.P. for St. Ives' was clearly intended as an additional document of support for D to use in his campaign. Beeton 66-7.

TO JOSEPH HUME Bradenham, Tuesday 5 June 1832 200

ORIGINAL: PS 30

PUBLICATION HISTORY: O'Connor 139, dated 5 June 1832, quoting Hume's letter in *The Globe* (11 Jan 1836).

Bradenham House, Wycombe, | Tuesday, June 5th, 1832.

Joseph Hume, Esq., M.P.

Sir,

I have had the honour and gratification of receiving your letter[1] this morning. Accept my sincere, my most cordial thanks.

1 Bulwer had obtained for D the following letter of support from Hume:

Sir, Bryanston Square, 2nd June, 1832.

As England can only reap the benefit of reform by the electors doing their duty in selecting honest, independent, and talented men, I am much pleased to learn from our mutual friend, Mr. E.L. Bulwer, that you are about to offer yourself as candidate to represent Wycombe in the new Parliament.

I have no personal influence at that place, or I would use it immediately in your favour, but I should hope that the day is arrived when the electors will consider the qualifications of the candidates, and, in the exercise of their franchise, prove themselves worthy of the new rights they will obtain by reform.

I hope the reformers will rally around you who entertain liberal opinions in every branch of government, and are prepared to pledge yourself to support reform and economy in every department, as far as the same can be effected consistent with the best interests of the country.

I shall only add that I shall be rejoiced to see you in the new Parliament, in the confidence that you will redeem your pledges and give satisfaction to your constituents if they will place you there.

Wishing you success in your canvass, I remain your obedient servant,

Joseph Hume

To – D'Israeli, Esq. [Beeton 68-9. See also **199**n3.]

Hume's offer of support was later withdrawn in the following letter addressed to Smith and Baring:

Dear Sirs, – Bryanston Square, June 6th, 1832.

A handbill has just been put into my hands, containing an abstract of a letter of mine sent to Mr. B. D'Israeli, in which I express my hopes that, as a reformer, I should be happy to see him a Member of the new Parliament; but, at the same time I wrote that letter, I was not aware that he would come in opposition to either of you, to disturb you in your present seats, and I feel concerned that I should in any way, by my statement in favour of Mr. D'Israeli, have tended to disturb the seats of two gentlemen with whom, for so many years, I have had the pleasure to sit in Parliament. I am anxious to state to you that it would really give me considerable pain to have inadvertently done anything to weaken the confidence which your constituents ought to have in you both, who have, for so many years, supported Liberal measures, and in particular during the last eighteen months, given such important support to the cause of reform, now near its completion.

I have this day written to Mr. D'Israeli, stating to him the cause of the mistake, by which my name has been used against you, and expressing my hope that he will not attempt to disturb the seats of two gentlemen who have given their aids to bring about that reform for which the country has so long been in need.

Hoping that you may neither of you suffer any inconvenience by the manner in which my name has been used,

I remain, your obedient servant,

Joseph Hume.

To the Hon. Robert Smith, M.P., and

Sir Thomas Baring, Bart., M.P. [Beeton 69-70]

It will be my endeavour that you shall not repent the confidence you have reposed in me.

Believe me, Sir, that if it be my fortune to be returned in the present instance to a reformed Parliament, I shall remember with satisfaction that that return is mainly attributable to the interest expressed in my success by one of the most distinguished and able of our citizens.

I have the honour to be, Sir,

Your obliged and faithful servant,

B. DISRAELI

---

201 TO SARA AUSTEN

Bradenham, Sunday [10 June 1832]

ORIGINAL: BL ADD MS 45908 ff57-8

COVER: Mrs. Austen | 32 Guildford Street | London

POSTMARK: (1) In double circle: F | 11JU11 | 1832 (2) [H]WYCO[MBE]

PUBLICATION HISTORY: Layard 26, dated June 1832; M&B I 213, dated 10 June 1832; Jerman 157, dated 12 June 1832

EDITORIAL COMMENT: *Dating*: considering the subsequent notoriety of D's so-called 'Red Lion' speech, it is curious that there has remained some confusion about the date on which it occurred. Jerman (156) gives Monday 11 June; O'Connor (51) says Wednesday 13 June, while M&B, Meynell and Blake do not give an exact date.

There were, in fact, two 'Red Lion' speeches: one on Saturday 9 June when Charles Grey was present, and a second on Wednesday 13 June, when Grey was absent. The events of each have often been conflated to make it seem that there was only one event. *The Bucks Herald* on 16 June reported the speeches of both Grey and D from 9 June. D's contribution on that day had been a spontaneous interruption of the official beginning of Grey's canvass. D's own parade took place on Wednesday 13 June 1832, when he entered town, accompanied by his two brothers and some friends, and he was again moved to speak from the Red Lion. *BG* no 1,038 (16 June 1832). The Whig *Bucks Gazette* reported Grey's speech on 9 June, without referring to D at all.

We are hard at it. Sir Thomas[1] you know has resigned. His son[2] was talked of, I have frightened him off, and old Pascoe Grenfell,[3] and St. Buxton.[4] Yesterday

1 Sir Thomas Baring had been MP for Wycombe since 1806 and resigned to contest a vacancy in Hampshire.

2 At this time there were five members of the Baring family in Parliament: Sir Thomas Baring; his son Francis Thornhill Baring; Alexander Baring, brother of Sir Thomas; and Alexander's sons William Bingham and Francis.

Thomas Baring, younger son of Sir Thomas, did not enter Parliament until 1835. Rumours of a younger Baring running in High Wycombe might have referred, not to Francis Thornhill Baring, comfortably ensconced in a Whig seat at Portsmouth, but to one of Alexander's sons, both of whom had apparently alienated their father by voting for the Reform Bill. Alexander was the one member of the family to vote against the bill. Thomas George Baring, Earl of Northbrook ed *Journals and Correspondence from 1800 to 1852 of Sir Francis Thornhill Baring afterwards Lord Northbrook* (Winchester 1905) 70, 87n, 101, 276-7.

3 Pascoe Grenfell (1761-1838), formerly MP for Great Marlow 1802-20.

4 Thomas Fowell Buxton (1786-1845), the great opponent of slavery in the British Empire, was Whig MP for Weymouth. His memoirs record no interest in changing constituencies in 1832, at which time he was preoccupied with the cause of abolition. Charles Buxton ed *Memoirs of Sir Thomas Fowell Buxton Bart* 4th ed (1850) ch 18.

The Clapham Sect, the evangelical reforming group to which Buxton belonged, was known, derisively, as 'the Saints'. Ernest Marshall Howse *Saints in Politics* (Toronto 1952) 9n.

In a letter to D, dated 11 June 1832, Bulwer stated that Edward Ellice had assured him that 'Pascoe Grenfell ... had never once dreamt or could be persuaded to stand, much less Buxton ...' H B/I/A/15.

the Treasury sent down Colonel Grey[5] with a hired mob and a band. Never was such a failure. After parading the town with his paid voices, he made | a stammering speech of ten minutes from his phaeton – all Wycombe was assembled. Feeling it was the crisis; I jumped up on the Portico of the Red Lion and gave it them for an hour and 1/4. I can give you no idea of the effect. I made them all mad.[6] A great many absolutely *cried*. I never made so many friends in | my life or converted so many enemies.[7] All the women are on my side – and wear my colors, pink and white. Do the same. The Colonel returned to town in the evening absolutely astounded out of his presence of mind, *on dit* never to appear again. If he come I am prepared for him –

BD

Sunday

TO [HENRY GWILLIM] Bradenham, [Friday 22 June 1832] **202**

ORIGINAL: PS 47

PUBLICATION HISTORY: Sotheby's catalogue 1153 (4 Nov 1898) item 66

EDITORIAL COMMENT: The catalogue described the letter as: 'A.L.S. 3 pp., 4to. Bradenham House, June 22, 1832, to Henry Gwellim [*sic*], early letter'.

The letter was endorsed, presumably by Gwillim: 'In proof of the sincerity of Mr. Disraeli as a reformer, he at the County election which took place soon after the date of this letter became the most active canvaser [*sic*] and strenuous supporter of that Ultra Conservative the Marquis of Chandos.' The sale copy of the catalogue notes that the letter was 'Sold to Hare'. It has not been located. *Dating*: Gwillim's reference to 'the County election' is confusing and may well have been added long after the event. D's text obviously refers to the Borough election, which was to take place 'on Tuesday morning'. The June vote for the Borough was held on a Tuesday, while the December one was held on a Wednesday. The attributed date is therefore probably correct.

---

5 Lt Col Charles Grey (1804-1870), second son of the prime minister and Whig MP for Wycombe 1832-7. He was then on half pay, for he acted as his father's private secretary between 1830 and 1834. He later developed strong links with the royal family, having been appointed private secretary to Prince Albert from 1849 to 1861, and to the Queen from 1861 until his death. He was promoted to lieutenant general in 1861 and to general in 1865.

6 D was undoubtedly an arresting speaker, but it is no doubt also true that his flamboyance left some voters uneasy. An unfriendly biographer described the Wycombe electorate 'who, good wondering people, tried all they possibly could to understand him. But they were completely puzzled by this Oriental apparition.' George Henry Francis *The Right Honourable Benjamin Disraeli, M.P. A Critical Biography* (1852) 23.

There is evidence for D's growing ability to sway an audience in sympathetic reports of his canvassing in the Taunton campaign of 1835. John Dix *Pen and Ink Sketches* ... (1846) 257-61.

7 The opposition press lost no chance to ridicule D's style of campaigning. One report said that his 'principal merit, pretension, or whatever else it is to be called, is, that he has written a novel ... it is said that this Adonis of the sable cheek found many amongst the other sex who, being "easy" in their politics, were his zealous partisans and most eager to exhibit their devotion. He who at an election time challenges attention to himself by adorning his wrists with cambric, his bosom with lace, who puts a blue band round his hat, where the vulgar wear a black one, who carries a black cane with a gold head, whose coat is lined with pink silk and who before he essays to speak on the hustings, formally adjusts his ringlets whose duty is assigned them on his brow ... such a man ... we had almost said such a popinjay ... appears to deliver himself symbolically something as follows ... "Look on my antagonist, and look on me. See him, plain in his attire, plain in his speech. Behold me. Will you not vote for a person of my blandishments and the author of a novel?" ' *BG* no 1,040 (30 June 1832).

27 Jun 1832

[Sir,][1]

I have the honour to enclose you my address[2] to the future Constituency of the Borough of Wycombe in consequence of the Mayor[3] and the great majority of the resident members of the Corporate body having declared that they shall be influenced at the ensuing election which takes place on Tuesday morning by the sense of that Constituency, the future electors held a public meeting at which it was agreed to recommend me to their notice ... I shall be proud to count you among my supporters in this struggle for the independence of our Borough and for the furtherance of principles of true Reform.[4]

---

203 TO THE FREE AND INDEPENDENT ELECTORS OF WYCOMBE

Bradenham, [Wednesday] 27 June 1832

ORIGINAL: H B/I/A/16

EDITORIAL COMMENT: A printed sheet. On the day before, at the declaration of the poll, D had made a long and indignant speech. He accused Sir Thomas Baring and Sir John Dashwood King of having promised him neutrality and of then having voted against him. Defending himself against the charge that he was a Tory in disguise – a charge frequently made by *The Bucks Gazette* – he accused the paper of being in the employ of the government. Pointing to Lord Nugent, a lord of the Treasury who came down to help Grey, D said that the 'nearest thing to a Tory in disguise was a Whig in office.' *BG* no 1,040 (30 June 1832). Nugent was furious and challenged D to a duel. The seconds, however – Lord Ebrington for Nugent and Capt Angerstein for D – met and succeeded in arranging a truce. The terms of the settlement appeared in *The Times* on 3 July 1832 and in *The Bucks Gazette* of 7 July:

'An impression having arisen in Lord Nugent's mind that some phrases used by Mr. D'Israeli on the hustings at the late election at High Wycombe were intended to bear a personal application to him, and some correspondence having taken place in consequence between them, Mr. D'Israeli has expressed his willingness to remove any such unpleasant impression by an entire disavowal of any intention to apply those phrases in an offensive or personal sense to Lord Nugent; and Lord Nugent,

---

1 Henry Gwillim (d 1855) of 319 Strand, London, was a grocer and tea-dealer who owned property in Wycombe and thus was eligible to vote in the county election. County Poll Book, Guildhall; will, Somerset House; directories. Whether or not Gwillim had a vote in the borough election – perhaps as one of the honorary freemen – D was presumably asking him to use his influence.

2 The address, no copy of which has been located, was circulated by D's supporter, Huffam. *BG* no 1,038 (16 June 1832).

3 The mayor was then John Carter. Ashford 261.

4 There was some ambiguity about the meaning of the principle of 'true reform', and even Bulwer wrote to D, distressed at the slogan 'Grey and Reform; Disraeli and the People'. Having supported D's candidacy, Bulwer now feared that his own 'public character' would suffer if his friend opposed progressive measures. Bulwer had written to D on 11 June 1832:

> You don't mean it seriously or publicly to countenance the idea – that you consider the cause of the People an antithesis and opposition to the cause of Reform. In that case you will have placed me in a most singular position. You cannot suppose that my name can be employed against the Bill I have voted for and helped to secure. [H B/I/A/15]

on his part, is equally ready to withdraw the terms which he applied to those phrases under the supposition that they were directed personally to him; and Captain Angerstein on the part of Mr. D'Israeli and Lord Ebrington on the part of Lord Nugent have considered it right, under these circumstances, that all the letters which have passed between the parties should be destroyed.

J.J.W. Angerstein
Grenadier Guards
Ebrington'.

London July 2nd, 1832

For other repercussions of the speech of 26 June see **219**.

Bradenham House,
June 27th, 1832.

TO THE

FREE AND INDEPENDENT ELECTORS OF WYCOMBE.

GENTLEMEN,

My grateful thanks are due to those Electors who afforded me on Tuesday their free and unbiassed support in our first struggle for the independence of this Borough.[1]

Gentlemen, there are instances in which defeat is no disgrace, and victory no triumph.[2] My opponent has been returned by the suffrages of electors whose foreign franchise the law of the land, introduced by his own father, has already declared to be pernicious.[3]

For some decades, Wycombe had been controlled by Lord Carrington and the Dashwood family. Despite Carrington's fluctuating political loyalties, this arrangement had secured a succession of Whig members. D, however, exaggerated the plight of the electors, who as recently as 1831 had displayed great independence in requiring Sir John Dashwood King, a Whig who opposed reform, to stand down in favour of a supporter of the Reform Bill. D was to repeat the accusation of this letter in the second of Wycombe's 1832 elections. See **223**.

D's implication here, as it had been in his speech of the previous day, was that Grey had won through the votes of those who lived outside Wycombe. However, press reports stated the residents' vote was: 'Grey 11, D'Israeli 7'. *BG* no 1,040 (30 June 1832).

The result of the Wycombe poll on 26 June 1832 was Grey 23, Disraeli 12.

Although the Reform Act had already become law on 7 June 1832, the changes did not come into force until the next general election (in December 1832). As a result, the by-election was held under the old franchise.

A contemporary account describes it thus: 'The election was really an odd affair. One half of the proceedings was on the old rotten borough principle. The other half was popular. The mayor and burgesses allowed themselves to be influenced by the popular feeling ... but on the other hand they could not forego ... all their ancient privileges. Accordingly though the novelty of a hustings appeared in front of the Town Hall, where, a greater novelty still, the nomination was to take place, we heard that the candidates were in the first instance nominated in the Town Hall, in the exclusive presence of the mayor and burgesses.' *BG* no 1,040 (30 June 1832). See also **132**n4.

The Wycombe election has sometimes been described as the very last one to be conducted under the unreformed system. Beeton 74. However, there were other by-elections before the general election in December, and at least one of them – Winchelsea in July – was in a constituency that disappeared as a result of the Reform Act. Hence one must suppose that the unreformed electoral machinery was used.

I appeal once more to emancipated Wycombe, and I appeal without apprehension. Rest assured, Gentlemen, that as long as I enjoy the felicity of residing among you, the good cause shall never need a champion.

I have the honor to remain,
GENTLEMEN,
Your devoted Servant,
B. DISRAELI.

E. KING, PRINTER, WYCOMBE.

---

204 TO JOHN MURRAY

[35] Duke Street, [St James's, London], [Thursday] 5 July [1832]

ORIGINAL: MM 31
COVER: *John Murray Esq* | 50 Albemarle St. | [In another hand]: 1832 – July 5 | D'Israeli Benjn Esq
PUBLICATION HISTORY: Smiles II 341, dated 5 July 1832.

Duke St. | Wednesday | July. 5.

Dear Sir,

I have just returned to town and will call in Albemarle St. as soon as I can.

Tita, Lord Byron's faithful servant and who | was also my travelling companion in the East, called upon me this morning. I thought you might wish to see one so intimately connected with the | lost bard, and who is himself one of the most deserving creatures in the world.[1]

Yrs f[aithfu]lly
B. Disraeli

---

205 TO SARAH DISRAELI

[London, Thursday 5 July 1832]

ORIGINAL: H A/I/B/35
COVER: Miss Disraeli | Bradenham House | Wycombe | Bucks.
POSTMARK: (1) In circle: S | JY-5 | 1832
PUBLICATION HISTORY: LBCS 12, dated 5 July 1832, parts of paragraphs three, four and five, conflated with extracts from **207** and **208**; M&B I 216, extract dated 5 July 1832. Ralph Disraeli adds 'from Ripon' after the names of Spence and Petit.
EDITORIAL COMMENT: *Sic*: chasséd.

My dearest love,

I have seen Charles Gore but not had the desired conversation as we were disturbed.

I dined at Angersteins with Lord Deerhurst,[1] Sir Francis[2] and two Colonels in

1 See **99**n15.

---

1 George William Coventry (1808-1838), Viscount Deerhurst, son and heir of the 8th Earl of Coventry. He predeceased his father.

2 Sir Francis William Sykes (1799-1843), 3rd Baronet, whose wife Henrietta was to become D's mistress. As these letters will show, Sir Francis enjoyed an increasing reputation for unpredictable eccentricity.

the Guards, Ellison and Fergusson.[3]

Mrs. Lawrence has turned violent Tory and chasséd Spence | and Petit.[4]

Giovanni[5] called on me (announced by the servant *Don Giovanni*); he has left Clay and brought me a lock of Lord Byron's hair from Venice, which he cut himself off the corpse at Missolonghi. Clay is somewhere in the country. |

Pray write. I can say no more at present. Old Murray is out of town. Contarini is universally liked, but moves slowly.

In great haste,

BD

I have written to Isaac King.[6]

206

TO SARAH DISRAELI [London], Wednesday [18 July 1832]

ORIGINAL: H A/I/B/36
COVER: Miss Disraeli | Bradenham House | *High Wycombe*
POSTMARK: (1) In circle: Y | JY18 | 1832
EDITORIAL COMMENT: *Sic*: gallopping, Legh.

Wednesday

My dearest,

I received your letter this morning. Ralph's expedition was most senseless.[1] Among other things, he lost a very agreeable reunion at Mrs. Boltons on Monday. I don't understand your letter, and the one to Ralph which I have just opened in consequence, is still more mysterious; however I shall pay today £50 to Trevor.[2] Of course if Jem be in any scrape and want this money, it is very much at his service, but if it be a family affair, I beg that | it may be repaid, as my bankers' account is in the last agonies of a gallopping consumption.

I dined yesterday *en famille* with Bulwer, with Henry, who has come to life

3 Robert Ellison was promoted lieutenant colonel in the Grenadier Guards in 1824, and Henry Robert Ferguson achieved the same rank in the same regiment in 1828.

4 As patroness of the borough of Ripon, Mrs Lawrence was able to choose its representatives, even after the Reform Bill. George Spence and Louis Hayes Petit (1774-1849) ended their parliamentary careers by supporting the Bill against her wishes. Both men retired to their legal practices. T.H.B. Oldfield *The Representative History of Great Britain and Ireland* (1816) V 309; Godfrey Richard Park *Parliamentary Representation in Yorkshire* (Hull 1886) 63-4; and obituary of Spence, *AR* (1850) app 286. This formidable lady also dismissed those of her tenants who subsequently voted against her candidates. Gash *Politics* 221-3.

5 Tita.

6 Isaac King (1804-1865), son of Isaac King of Lee, Bucks, was the new rector of Bradenham. He remained there until his death. Foster II 795.

---

1 In her letter of 16 July Sarah had written:

> Just imagine Ralph getting into a postchaise with Charles Ellis at the Club, on Sunday night, and going on to sleep at his house at Tetsworth. What between drinking egg flip, and porter, and talking, they never arrived there until four o'clock in the morning. Ralph was afraid of getting into the bed they gave him, and had to walk six miles before he could get here yesterday, want of rest, over-exertion, and indigestion added to his pre-disposition to Cholera, have quite knocked him up ... [H A/I/B/439]

2 'The object of my note to him was to say that Trevor had lent James £50, and to know if you would pay it into Coutt's house, or if Papa should give Trevor a draft here, which he can very readily do.' Sarah to D, H A/I/B/440.

'The D'Israelis at home' (a) Isaac (b) Sarah – insets: Isaac, Maria, James (Ben in the lamp)
from the diary of Blanche Norris, 1833

again, L.E.L. and Mrs. Legh; very pleasant indeed. On Friday I join a water party attaché to the fair Rosina.

Bulwer will send my father's proofs to him, which he, B, received last night, I think.

I am not yet married, tho' | Henry Bulwer has promised to introduce me to 7000£ per ann – but "he is not mercenary", therefore I suppose the dame is not too agreeable. I fear a certain damsel has not more than 25000 tho' otherwise satisfactory in all respects.

Henry B. is mad for Contarini, which he thinks the finest thing ever written.

Yrs

BD

T.O. |

I have paid Trevor.

The water party is put off.

Isaac King is in town and called upon me today. He will write to you about coming to Bradenham, but I think you may expect him for *Monday*.

TO SARAH DISRAELI [London], Saturday [21 July 1832] 207

ORIGINAL: H A/I/B/37

COVER: Miss Disraeli | Bradenham House | Wycombe | Bucks.

POSTMARK: (1) In circle: H | JY21 | 1832

PUBLICATION HISTORY: LBCS 12, dated 5 July 1832, includes paragraph four with extracts from **205** and **208**. M&B I 191, dated 5 July 1832, extract from LBCS conflation

EDITORIAL COMMENT: *Sic*: D'Arblay, poneys.

Saturday

My dearest,

I have seen Ralph but only en passant, and have not yet consulted about the carriage – No time sho[ul]d be lost in finally arranging about your equipage. Has Jem any ponies in view, that he talks so confidently? If not, and I can get a horse, the opportunity sho[ul]d | not be lost.

All my father has to do for the Magazine[1] is to write for it, and not to bother himself or other people about matters respecting which they sho[ul]d be ignorant. I do not think B[ulwer] has the remotest intention of retiring. Yesterday I was at Vauxhall with Mrs Bulwer – the Websters etc., a fragment of | the intended water party.

I hope to be down permanently in a few days.

The staunchest admirer I have in London, and the most discerning appreciator of Contarini, is old Madam D'Arblay.[2] I have a long letter which I will show you; capital.

Emily Leake[3] says that it is the finest work ever produced, but of course can-

1 *The New Monthly Magazine*, edited by Bulwer.
2 Fanny (or Frances) Burney (1752-1840), the novelist and diarist. In 1793 she had married Gen Alexandre d'Arblay, a French refugee in England.
3 D was acquainted with William Martin Leake, a neighbour of the Merediths in Nottingham Place (see **110**). However, there was no Emily recorded as a member of his family.

not be appreciated by the generality. Think of this! What next. I told you I met Charles Grey – very friendly. I have seen a | good deal of the family in the course of the last week or so. I have nothing to say of import. Write about the equipage, whether you have, or want poneys.

BD

208 TO SARAH DISRAELI [London], Friday [27 July 1832]

ORIGINAL: H A/I/B/38

COVER: Miss Disraeli | Bradenham House | *High Wycombe*

POSTMARK: (1) In Maltese cross: C.H | 27JY1832 | X (2) four-pointed star

PUBLICATION HISTORY: LBCS 12, dated 5 July 1832, includes parts of paragraphs seven and four (in that order), with extracts from **205** and **207**.

EDITORIAL COMMENT: *Sic*: croney.

Friday

Dearest,

Had Jem called in Duke St before his departure which I expected, he wo[ul]d have brought you down a letter which I left for him. I co[ul]d not send it by the post, both on account of the lateness of the hour and its being enveloped.[1]

I saw Murray Wednesday, who sd. Cont[arini] was quite alive, and sold better than when it was first published.

We shall soon meet. I wish the Trevors had fallen to my lot instead of the Reynolds.[2]

Mind I tell you a story about myself | and Tom Ashburnham,[3] a story of resemblance and mistakes as good as the Dromios.[4] It is very good, but too long for a letter.

The landlord never heard of wafer paper being used by bookbinders, and stared immensely. I will get some.

I am anxious to hear what you think of the carriage and horse. I have not seen the latter, but if it be as good as the first, *bene, molto bene.* |

The Cheque was duly received this morning. Tell my father to keep working at the Mag[azine] with[ou]t ceasing. I hope to be down in a very few days. I have been very idle, the natural consequence of former exertion, but am very well, and shall soon buckle to among our beeches.

Marcus Hill[5] is on the new Travellers Committee, and appears a very ardent

1 Envelopes, as opposed to integral covers, were rarely used before the introduction in 1840 of the initially unpopular Mulready envelope. Until this change an envelope counted as a separate sheet, making the cost of postage excessively expensive unless one could use a frank.

2 Vincent Stukey Reynolds (1796?-1843) of Canonsgrove, Somerset, married Maria Basevi (1798-1861), daughter of George Basevi the elder. The family sometimes visited Bradenham. On 31 July Sarah wrote that the Reynolds were not coming. She knew that this news would please D. H A/I/B/443.

3 Thomas Ashburnham (d 1872) was the fourth son of the 3rd Earl of Ashburnham. He was then a captain in the Coldstream Guards, rising later to the rank of general. Boase.

4 Dromio of Ephesus and Dromio of Syracuse are twin brothers in Shakespeare's *Comedy of Errors*.

5 Lord Arthur Marcus Cecil Hill (1798-1863), third son of the 2nd Marquess of Downshire; Whig MP for Newry 1832, and for Evesham 1838-52.

friend of mine. He says he cannot doubt he shall succeed in effecting my election somehow or other. And he is one of those who always mean more than they say. He is Charles Gore's prime croney and Charley is very devoted. |

Mrs. Bolton, if well eno', will probably leave town on Monday on a visit to the Lamberts at Chertsey[6] where the fair Margaret[7] is also staying. I have a sort of an invitation also there, which it may be expedient to comply with for a day or two, but I shall wait to hear Madame's bulletin. This is the only thing that may keep me from Bradenham for a day or two,

in great haste

your most affectionate

BD

TO SARAH DISRAELI [London], Saturday [4 August 1832] **209**

ORIGINAL: H A/I/B/40

COVER: Miss Disraeli | Bradenham House | High Wycombe | Bucks

POSTMARK: (1) In circle: T | AU-4 | 1832

PUBLICATION HISTORY: LBCS 13, dated 4 August 1832, paragraphs three and six, and part of seven; M&B I 216, extract dated 4 August 1832

EDITORIAL COMMENT: *Sic*: McClise, Frazer.

Saturday

My dearest Sa,

Mrs. Bolton has at length fairly departed for Chertsey, but she has delayed her trip so long that I do not think I can contrive to join her and shall therefore by the next post in all probability announce my coming. I am sorry to have lost all this time from Bradenham for what you will call a freak, but I am easy tempered, and have been somewhat consoled for the affair by the great progress I have of late made in Alroy, who flourishes like a young cedar of Lebanon. |

My father may exercise his judgment as to sending me up Jackson[1] on Monday, and I will if I think fit, forward it to Bulwer. Indeed this appears the best plan.

Town is fast emptying. I have been lately at the House of Commons and one night had a long conversation with my late antagonist and present representative[2] – we are more than friendly.

At Mrs. Bolton's we always command if necessary an evening re-union . Marcus Hill and Charley Gore, the Ongleys[3] etc. We all agree it is better than a club. But even this is over. |

6 Francis John Lambert (1798-1876), younger son of Sir Henry Lambert, 4th Baronet, lived in Chertsey, Surrey.

7 Margaret Trotter.

---

1 Isaac D'Israeli's article, 'A Psychological Memoir of a Provincial Man of Genius: Jackson of Exeter', by 'Atticus' *NMM* XXXV (Sept 1832) 256-62. William Jackson (1730-1803), known as Jackson of Exeter, was a composer; his opera 'The Lord of the Manor' (1780) was immensely popular.

2 Charles Grey.

3 The 2nd Baron Ongley died in 1814 and the 3rd was a bachelor, one of four bachelor brothers. Frances Ongley, née Burgoyne, was the widow of the 2nd Baron, and she and her daughter Charlotte (b 1813) may be the people to whom D refers. For a reference to these two in society see *The Times* (21 June 1833).

I met Maginn and had a long conversation. He likes Contarini much.

Did I tell you I saw a good deal of McClise[4] who is very amusing and tells me much about L.E.L. and the Bromptonian coteries. There in no doubt that Lockhart has been a principal contributor to Frazer and one of the assailants of Bulwer.[5]

How speeds the horse? I hope well. It is a promising beast in its present situation. Write and tell me. I shall have plenty of work for you when I come down. My love to all and especially to yourself.

BD T.O. |

Crossing over from Greenwich, I called in on Miss Dowding,[6] who is very well and sends her love.

---

210 TO SARAH DISRAELI

[35] Duke Street, [St James's, London], Tuesday [7 August 1832]

ORIGINAL: H A/I/B/41

COVER: Miss Disraeli | Bradenham House | High Wycombe | Bucks.

POSTMARK: (1) In Maltese cross: C.H | 7 AU1832 | X

PUBLICATION HISTORY: LBCS 13, dated 8 August 1832, includes part of paragraph three interpolated with parts of **211**, and an extract from **212**; M&B I 216-17, extracts dated 8 August 1832.

Duke St. Tuesday

My dearest,

I am sorry you are in such trouble but I hope to extricate you.[1] The mare I know to be a most sweet tempered creature, perfectly sound and very powerful, with[ou]t a single trick. Being yet in her prime, she wo[ul]d last you a dozen years. I know her well. I think her present failings may wear off in a fortnight, at any rate she is worth running the chance, and I shall therefore send you some quiet regular beast, probably the stout gentleman you had before for the nonce – and give the mare a fortnights trial. Emmott[2] will not charge for the

4 Daniel Maclise (1806-1870), Irish painter and caricaturist.

5 In the August 1832 number of *Fraser's* (VI 67-8) appeared a satire on Bulwer's *Eugene Aram*, entitled 'Elizabeth Brownrigge, a tale; dedicated to the author of *Eugene Aram*, a Novel'. In his 1931 edition of *Bulwer* (280), Sadleir attributed the article to Thackeray. Miriam M.H. Thrall, in *Rebellious Fraser's: Nol Yorke's Magazine in the Days of Maginn, Thackeray, and Carlyle* (New York 1934) 62-4, argues that it was by Maginn 'possibly with the help of Lockhart'. In the same issue appeared a hostile essay on Bulwer in Maginn's series the 'Gallery of Literary Characters' (XXVII). For an account of *Fraser's* vendetta against Bulwer, see Sadleir *Bulwer* 195-7, 202, 261, 276, 281, 283.

6 A Miss Dowding lived at 24 Mecklenburgh Square, London, close to the D'Israelis' old Bloomsbury Square address. Robson's *Guide* (1833). She may have been related to the London bookseller of that name.

---

1 Sarah wrote to D on 31 July: 'We seem fated to be always an annoyance, the new horse has already gone lame, and is I suppose a cheat.' H A/I/B/443.

2 Emmott's Livery Stables, Davies Street, Berkeley Square. When Sarah lost her dog, the advertisement in *The Times* (18 June 1833) requested that it be returned to that address in London.

week past, and £45 is really 15 less than she wo[ul]d be worth at any other season.

As my mare wants work, let William mounted on her be at Uxbridge | at the Crown Inn on Thursday, and Emmott's man will meet him with a horse. Emmott's will be there by twelve – William shd: set off from Ux. by two. He sho[ul]d be there himself at ten or 11, and give the bay mare sufficient rest.

I dine with Bulwer to day and intended to have come down to Bradenham on Thursday, but I think Bulwer may accompany me, and I shall therefore postpone it until next day, that your domestic arrangemts. as to horses etc. sho[ul]d be settled. He wants to come for absolute retirement, really to write and all that. He is to do what he likes, feed if he choose alone, and wander about the woods like a madman. I will write tomorrow positively as to this. I gave him | Jackson with some verbal alterations. The faults are radical, and I co[ul]d not alter them. The writer has thought too much with the pen in his hand, so there are many carts before the horse. It is ingenious but inconsistent, but on the whole highly interesting.

If Wm. cannot come on Thursday, let Richard Lacy. If Bulwer and I come on Friday I sho[ul]d like the carriage to meet us at Beaconsfield, but more of this by and bye.

B.E.L. I understand from Ralph has recovered the price of the horse – £40.

What is the matter with James?

Tell Phelps I have attended to his son, and will get him a place as Captains clerk or so if possible, but I must have his name, age, and also an assurance of character etc.

BD

TO SARAH DISRAELI [London], Wednesday [8 August 1832] **211**

ORIGINAL: H A/I/B/39

COVER: Miss Disraeli | Bradenham House | High Wycombe | Bucks.

POSTMARK: (1) In Maltese cross: V.S | VAU8S | 1832

PUBLICATION HISTORY: LBCS 13, dated 8 August 1832, includes the first paragraph, with part of **210** interpolated, and part of **212** as the concluding paragraph; M&B I 216-17, extract dated 8 August 1832.

EDITORIAL COMMENT: *Sic*: Carlisle.

Wednesday

My dearest angel,

On Friday I shall pitch my tent in the green retreats of Bradenham. Bulwer accompanies me. I am anxious that he and my father sho[ul]d become better acquainted. Our sire never had a warmer votary. B. has but recently become acquainted with his works. He sd. yesterday, "if I were to fix, I shd. say your father was decidedly now at the top of the tree. I tell you where he beats us all, – in style. There's nothing like it." |

We shall leave town about three and dine with you. Suppose your hour is half p[as]t 6. On second thoughts the carriage had better not meet us, as I do not wish to be mobbed through Wycombe.

Put in Bulwer's room all the translations of German tales and traditions we have – Grimm, Carlisle, Gillies etc. I think something of Thirlwall.[1]

I am very well; in fact my health seems firmly established. You will be surprised to hear (at least I am) that the Speaking Harlequin[2] is considered the best hit of the season, and | makes a great noise. All my father's papers are highly praised. I saw the Globe[3] and the National Omnibus, which last speaks of the authors as "*most eloquent*", but by a hand "*they ken not*". More fools they![4]

God bless you my love. I shall embrace you with fervor.

BD

Where do you think I dine to day? At my old friend Ellis; a bachelor establishment in Spring Gardens.[5] |

I don't think Mrs. Bolton will come for a fortnight. You might give Bulwer the blue room, as it is more still and the scenery more inspiring, but you know best. Ralph talks of Saturday.

---

212 TO SARAH DISRAELI

[35] Duke Street, St James's, [London], Friday [24 August 1832]

ORIGINAL: H A/I/B/42
COVER: Miss Disraeli | Bradenham House | High Wycombe | Bucks.
POSTMARK: (1) In circle: R | AU24 | 1[832]
PUBLICATION HISTORY: LBCS 13, dated 8 August 1832, includes the first part of paragraph four, with extracts from **210** and **211**; M&B I 216-17, extract dated 8 August 1832.
EDITORIAL COMMENT: *Sic*: St James, Windham, your's.

Duke Street St James | Friday

My dearest,

Mrs Bolton is in town, and quite recovered, altho' with a slight scar. I have not yet seen her.

Bulwer called on me yesterday at 1/2 past 6, just as I arrived and I dined with him, Henry and Madame, in the evening Mrs. Windham.[1] He retains a most

1 The fairy tales of the Brothers Grimm were already well known in England by 1832. Thomas Carlyle had translated Goethe's *Wilhelm Meister* in 1824. Robert Pearse Gillies (1788-1858), writer, journalist and friend of Scott, had published a number of tales translated from German in *Blackwood's*, while Connop Thirlwall (1797-1875), later bishop of St David's and author of a *History of Greece*, was in 1832 chiefly famous for his translations of Niebuhr's *The History of Rome* in 1828, and of Tieck's *Novellen*.

2 See **122**n3.

3 *The Globe* commented favourably on 'Asmodeus at Large', 'The Speaking Harlequin' and 'Our Anecdotage'. Judgement on the article 'Of the Three Earliest Authors in Our Vernacular Literature' was more restrained, noting its 'curious information'. *The Globe* no 9,294 (7 Aug 1832). The first was Bulwer's column, the second was by D, and the last two were by Isaac.

4 'The "Spirit of Death" is a mere fragment but, of the three earliest authors in our vernacular tongue, somebody, whose name comes not within our ken has been unusually eloquent.' *The National Omnibus* no 58 (3 Aug 1832) 243. The praise was moderate perhaps because the Tory *Omnibus* was hostile to Bulwer's *New Monthly*.

5 George Henry Ellis, a solicitor, lived at 7 Spring Gardens.

---

1 Mrs Wyndham Lewis; at this early stage of acquaintance with his future wife, D was inconsistent in his spelling of her name.

grateful recollection of Tusculum,[2] and seems to have talked of us a great deal. He is off on Saturday. |

I have corrected a proof of Jackson – and improved several phrases.

I saw Tita today, who suggests that he shall return with me to Bradenham and try the place for a month,[3] which will be most satisfactory to both parties. Amy[4] who will be there will be a good initiator.

I began my letter to tell you that I understand from Bolton that Madame wo[ul]d rather postpone her visit for the | present to which I assented. It is therefore adjourned *sine die.*

Mind if B.E.L. come down on Saturday, and I do not succeed in previously seeing him, that you speak about young Phelps.

Since I began writing, I have seen Sub-Editor Hall,[5] who tells me that he has sent you a proof of Jackson. As I think my alterations are important I have told him to go to press with them and not wait for your's.

This last paragraph is addressed to our father.

Vale!

BD T.O. |

It was not Harman the shoemaker who votes for us, but Harman the Constable who votes for Grey who called upon me and expressed his intention to support me if possible. He was in attendance on his duty, and converted by my speech.[6] |

Mrs. B. attacked me about you, and coming to stay next season and all that. She says she hears of nothing else but your eyes and your dog. I hypocritically assured her that it was nothing like Fa.

213

TO SAMUEL CARTER HALL — [35] Duke Street, St James's, [London], Friday [24 August? 1832]

ORIGINAL: NYPL Montague 7

EDITORIAL COMMENT: In another hand: 'Mr. D'Israeli | written about 1850 | S.H.' *Dating*: D moved into Duke Street in mid-February 1832, and *The Amulet* for 1833 appeared in late 1832. The year, therefore, is certainly 1832. Assignment to 24 August is, however, based only on probabilities. The deadline for submission of material to the annuals, assumed here to be not far off, was usually in the early autumn. **212** to Sarah on 24 August noted that D had met Bulwer the evening before, and that he had seen Hall in connection with Isaac's contribution to *The New Monthly Magazine*. The conjunction of all these circumstances, coupled with D's preoccupation with minor journalistic endeavours, makes 24 August the most probable Friday in 1832 for this letter. *Sic*: St James.

---

2 Clearly a fanciful reference to Bradenham. It would be well within the ambit of D's imagery to equate the D'Israeli family home with the capital of the Etruscans.

3 Tita stayed at Bradenham from that time until Isaac's death in 1848. He then became a confidential messenger in India House. Mrs William Pitt Byrne *Gossip of the Century* (New York 1892) I 123.

4 A servant at Bradenham.

5 Samuel Carter Hall, who was sub-editor of *The New Monthly Magazine* under Bulwer in 1831-2, and then was editor between 1832 and 1836. His *Retrospect of a Long Life* (1883) 182 contains a brief but telling description of *The New Monthly Magazine* under Bulwer.

6 The name Harman was a common one in Wycombe. In the early 1830s local directories record no fewer than three shoemakers of that name, but the constables were not listed.

23 Sep 1832

Duke St St James | Friday

S. C. Hall, Esq[1]

Sir,

Mr Bulwer some time back mentioned to me your desire that I sho[ul]d contribute to "the Amulet", a desire by which I feel honored. I did not act upon his intimation, because, to be candid, | I have a great dislike to this sort of desultory composition, and indeed have invariably refused any contributions of the kind. I should be sorry however, if indeed it be in my power, not to serve an ingenious man, and therefore if you will have the | kindness to inform me how late I may send in my quota, I will, if time permit, prepare you a dozen pages.

I have the honor
to remain, Sir,
Your very obed S[ervan]t
B Disraeli

---

214 TO SAMUEL CARTER HALL — Bradenham, Sunday [23 September? 1832]

ORIGINAL: JW 1

COVER: *S.C. Hall Esqr.*

EDITORIAL COMMENT: *Dating*: during September and early October 1832 D was frequently back and forth between London and Bradenham. After the first week of October he became increasingly concerned with political activities. Late September, therefore, seems consistent with his undertaking to Hall in **213**.

Bradenham House | Sunday

private

I send you corrected Proof of the Pilgrimage.[1] *Pray be very careful with the corrections.* I entirely trust to you.

Also accompanying this, is a paper for the next | number of the *N.M.M.*[2]

In future, have the kindness not to send any proofs to Bradenham by the post. There is a Thame Coach which goes from the Green Man and Still Argyll St. every day through | Bradenham and will leave any parcel at our gates. I am sorry to give you this trouble.

I hope you have quite recovered.

Have the kindness to acknowledge the receipt of this.

D

1 Samuel Carter Hall was the editor of *The Amulet* from 1826 to 1837. D's sketch 'Pilgrimage to the Holy Sepulchre' appeared in *The Amulet* for 1833 (61-72). Andrew Boyle *An Index to the Annuals* (Worcester 1967) 81.

---

1 See **213**n1.

2 A sketch entitled 'Egyptian Thebes' by 'Marco Polo Junior' appeared in the October number of *The New Monthly Magazine* (333-9).

TO THE INDEPENDENT ELECTORS OF THE BOROUGH OF CHEPPING WYCOMBE Bradenham, [Monday] 1 October 1832

ORIGINAL: PS Times 8

PUBLICATION HISTORY: *The Times* (5 Oct 1832)

EDITORIAL COMMENT: Following his normal practice, D published this political announcement as if from Bradenham, but this provides no guarantee that he was there at this date. *Sic*: and and.

Bradenham House, Oct. 1, 1832.
To the INDEPENDENT ELECTORS of the BOROUGH of CHEPPING WYCOMBE.[1]

Friends and Neighbours,

A Dissolution of Parliament, notwithstanding the machinations of those who have clogged the new charter of your rights which you have won with so much difficulty, with all the vexatious provisoes of a fiscal enactment, being an event which cannot be much longer delayed, I think fit to announce my readiness to redeem the pledge which I made to you at the close of the late contest on the hustings of our borough, and to assure you of my resolution to go to the poll to make another, and I doubt not, triumphant struggle for your independence.

I warned our late masters of the dangerous precedent of electing a stranger merely because he was the relative of a minister. I foretold as the consequence of their compliance, a system of nomination as fatal as those close corporations of which you are relieved. The event has justified my prediction. Wycombe has now the honour of being represented by the Private Secretary of the First Lord of the Treasury. A few weeks back Aylesbury was threatened with the Private Secretary of the Lord Chancellor.[2] The men of Aylesbury rejected with loathing that which it appears suited the more docile digestion of the late electors of Wycombe. The Private Secretary of the Lord Chancellor was withdrawn, and in his place was substituted an unknown youth, whose only recommendation is, that he is the very young brother of a very inexperienced minister, and one who has obtained power merely by the renunciation of every pledge which procured him an entrance into public life.[3]

Gentlemen, I come forward to oppose this disgusting system of factitious and intrusive nomination which, if successful, must be fatal to your local independence, and which, if extensively acted upon throughout the country, may even be destructive of your general liberties. I come forward wearing the badge of no

1 Chepping Wycombe was, and is, a municipal borough co-extensive with the parish of High Wycombe. As D was addressing the electors of the borough who chose the parliamentary representative, he used the name of the borough rather than that of the constituency.

2 The principal secretary to Lord Brougham was Denis Le Marchant (1795-1874), after 1841 1st Baronet, chief clerk of the House of Commons 1850-71. He had been announced as a candidate in Aylesbury, but did not run.

3 Thomas Benjamin Hobhouse (1807-1876) unsuccessfully contested Aylesbury in 1832 and 1835. He was the half-brother of Sir John Cam Hobhouse (1786-1869), 2nd Baronet, Radical (later Whig) MP for Westminster 1820-33, for Nottingham 1834-47 and for Harwich 1848-51. He was appointed secretary at war in February 1832. His support in office for authoritarian policies alienated him from his former Radical colleagues. In 1851 he became 1st Baron Broughton de Gyfford.

party and the livery of no faction. I seek your suffrages as an independent neighbour, who, sympathising with your wants and interests, will exercise his utmost influence in the great national council to relieve the one and support the other.

But, while I am desirous of entering Parliament as an independent man, I have never availed myself of that much abused epithet to escape an explicit avowal of my opinions. I am desirous of assisting in the completion of the machinery of our new constitution, without which perfection I am doubtful whether it will work. I am prepared to support that ballot[4] which will preserve us from that unprincipled system of terrorism with which it would seem we are threatened even in this town.

I am desirous of recurring to those old English and triennial parliaments of which the Whigs originally deprived us, and by repealing the taxes upon knowledge,[5] I would throw the education of the people into the hands of the philosophic student, instead of the ignorant adventurer.

While I shall feel it my duty to enforce on all opportunities the most rigid economy and the most severe retrenchment, to destroy every useless place and every undeserved pension, and to effect the greatest reduction of taxation, consistent with the maintenance of the public faith and the real efficiency of the government, I shall withhold my support from every ministry which will not originate some great measure to ameliorate the condition of the lower orders, to rouse the dormant energies of the country, to liberate our shackled industry, and re-animate our expiring credit.

I have already expressed my willingness to assist in the modification of our criminal code. I have already explained how I think the abolition of slavery may be safely and speedily effected.[6] With regard to the corn laws, I will support any change the basis of which is to relieve the consumer without injuring the farmer, and for the church, I am desirous of seeing effected some extensive commutation which, while it prevents tithe from acting as a tax upon industry and enterprise, will, I trust, again render the clergy what I am always desirous of seeing them, fairly remunerated because they are valuable and and efficient labourers, and influential because they are beloved.

And I now call upon every man who values the independence of our borough, upon every man who desires the good government of this once great and happy country, upon every man who feels he has a better chance of being faithfully served by a member who is his neighbour, than by a remote representative,

4 The secret ballot.

5 The repeal of the stamp duty on newspapers and periodicals was a standard Radical plank.

6 D's support for the abolition of slavery was a qualified one and he was accused of involvement with 'proprietors of colonial estates'. The flat denial made on his behalf that he had 'any interest either directly or indirectly in Colonial estates' was technically correct. *The Wycombe Sentinel* no 8 (7 Dec 1832). But the Lindos were cousins, and they held property in the West Indies. *The Representative* had also been linked to the West India interest (**23**n1). Furthermore, D's connection with the Marquess of Chandos could not fail to be embarrassing, as Chandos was then the chairman of the Society of West India Planters and Merchants. L.J. Ragatz *A Guide to the Study of British Caribbean History, 1763-1834* (Washington 1932) 436; *BG* no 1,039 (23 June 1832), no 1,054 (6 Oct 1832), no 1,063 (8 Dec 1832).

who like the idle wind no man regardeth, comes one day we know not whence, and goes the next we know not whither, to support me in this struggle against that rapacious, tyrannical, and incapable faction, who having knavishly obtained power by false pretences, sillily suppose that they will be permitted to retain it by half measures, and who in the course of their brief but disastrous career have contrived to shake every great interest of the empire to its centre.

Ireland in rebellion, the colonies in convulsion, our foreign relations in a state of such inextricable confusion, that we are told that war can alone sever the Gordian knot of complicated blunders: the farmer in doubt, the ship owner in despair, our merchants without trade, and our manufacturers without markets, the revenue declining and the army increased, the wealthy hoarding their useless capital, and pauperism prostrate in our once contented cottages – Englishmen, behold the unparalleled empire, raised by the heroic energies of your fathers, rouse yourselves in this hour of doubt and danger, rid yourselves of all that political jargon and factious slang of Whig and Tory, two names with one meaning, used only to delude you, and unite in forming a great national party which can alone save the country from impending destruction.

I have the honour to remain,

Your obliged and devoted servant.

B. DISRAELI.

TO BENJAMIN AUSTEN — Bradenham, [Saturday] 6 October [1832] — 216

ORIGINAL: BL ADD MS 45908 ff61-2

COVER: Benjamin Austen Esquire | Paragon | Ramsgate | ~~Sussex~~ [in another hand]: Kent

POSTMARK: (1) In double circle: F | 6 OC 6 | 1832 (2) In rectangle: No. 1 (3) HWYCOMBE | Penny Post

PUBLICATION HISTORY: Jerman 162, extracts dated 6 October 1832.

Bradenham House | Octr. 6.

My dear Austen,

I did not receive your letter (from absence in London) until Tuesday, and was obliged to write up to town before I co[ul]d give you a satisfactory answer. I expect in a few days to have £150 paid into me, which altho', I will confess, bespoken, I shall immediately hand over to Willis.[1] I had intended to have requested you to have permitted me to pay up the interest and to have renewed the bill for the proceeds of my new book,[2] which will be | published on the 1st. of January. Accept my thanks for all your confidence and kindness. I shall never forget that you supported me at a moment when I most needed, and I also trust, most deserved it, as I really am most active, and I believe work harder at this moment than any man in the kingdom.

The revising barrister will complete his list by the end of the month,[3] and

1 See 115n1.

2 *Alroy.*

3 One of the most important innovations of the 1832 Reform Act was the establishment of official electoral registers. Revising barristers held annual courts to hear applications for inclusion on, or omission from, these lists, and this was a contributory factor in the development of party organization.

then I imagine our contest will be virtually decided. In spite of your informant, the general opinion here is that I have the best of it. I might even use a bolder phrase.

I | did not answer your first letter, because I wished to do so in person, and kept postponing it accordingly. Independent of the pleasure of seeing you and Mrs. Austen, a week of sea air and relaxation wo[ul]d do me an infinity of good, but I cannot leave this place for a month at least owing to the election. You have no idea of the constant toil and effort, but if we win, which I little doubt, the triumph will indeed be great. Look in the Times of this day for my address.

My best regards to Mrs. Austen. We shall have a good deal to talk about when we meet.

Believe me ever
your obliged friend
BD

217

TO THOMAS MULLETT EVANS Bradenham, Wednesday 24 October [1832]

ORIGINAL: H A/V/A/14

COVER: Thomas Mullett Evans Esqr | 81 Stamford Street | Blackfriars Road | London

POSTMARK: illegible

PUBLICATION HISTORY: A.C. Ewald 'Two letters from Disraeli to T.M. Evans' *The Athenaeum* no 2,845 (6 May 1882) 568-9; M&B I 220 prints the second-last sentence.

EDITORIAL COMMENT: Part of the second sheet of the MS is missing.

Brad. House | Oct. 24. | Wednesday

My dear Tom,

I am obliged to write you a hasty line to say, that I am unexpectedly prevented coming up to you tomorrow by the sudden arrival of my old friend and fellow traveller, Clay, whom I have never seen since his return. I suppose you imagine I am not going to pay you my visit; but this is not the case. I am tied to this place by the impending contest. I calculate that the battle will be fought | and as I believe won, by the beginn[in]g of December; in that case if convenient to you, I wo[ul]d propose coming down for a day or two after the triumph or the catastrophe. If the dissolution be postponed for some weeks after the beginning of Decr., I must postpone the visit, as I must spend the winter at Bradenham, but I do not anticipate this result.[1] At any rate I shall pay you | a visit in the course of a couple of months or so. I have lots to tell – writing is humbug. My position most critical, but promising. If I gain my election, I think I [*ha*]ve doubled the Cape of my destiny.

1 Canvassing for the expected general election had begun as early as July. Parliament was dissolved on 3 December, and D was nominated at a meeting on 10 December by John Carter, who had recently completed his term of office as mayor of High Wycombe. Polling continued until 12 December, when the results were declared.

D's agent at this time was Archibald White, who seems to have been an admirer of the Reform Act and was no Tory. *BG* no 1,065 (22 Dec 1832). The course of the campaign was reflected in D's election-sheet, which he called *The Wycombe Sentinel*, and which appeared between 19 October and 7 December.

I will write agai[*n*]. My kindest remembran[*ces*] to Mrs. Evans.
Yrs aff[ectionate]ly and ever
BD

TO BENJAMIN AUSTEN Bradenham, Saturday [3? November 1832] **218**

ORIGINAL: BL ADD MS 45908 ff63-5

COVER: *private* | Benjamin Austen Esq | Raymond Blgs | Grays Inn | by RD.

PUBLICATION HISTORY: Jerman 163-4, undated

EDITORIAL COMMENT: *Dating*: Austen answered this letter on Monday 12 November (H B/XXI/A/23), having had time both to send Ward a letter about D's request, and to receive a reply. Saturday 3 November appears to be the most probable date for this letter. Although the letter ends with an injunction to T[urn] O[ver], the back of page three of the MS is blank. *Sic*: inclose, recal.

Bradenham H. | Saturday

My dear friend,

Herein I inclose a draft for £300 and will send you the interest by return of post, if you will kindly inform me its amount. I have no data to make the calculation, but I hope you will make it most punctiliously, by which you will add to the favors I have already experienced. Your confidence at this moment of my life is of inexpressible service to me, and I shall always recal it as an act of the greatest friendship. I repay you the loan now, because I wish you to feel that I have maintained my engagement to have it ready at a few days notice, but I confess to you that I am rather pressed with the election. I hope therefore that if at the beginning of the year a little assistance for a specific time of a few months be very serviceable to me, I may count on it. This letter is made up with | part of one I wrote you some time back, and did not send.

I certainly go to the poll and with the belief that I shall be successful. I can say no more but ought not to say less. If my men are true, and I have no reason to doubt them, I have a sufficient majority.

I am very desirous of gaining a qualification in the next Parliamt. *in another County*. This arrangement is most important. The one I at present hold is for Bucks.[1] Can you assist me. You wo[ul]d in so doing effect me | essential service. Would Ward for auld lang syne grant me one. He understands the thing, and knows there is little or no risk, as the deed which grants it need not be in my possession. *Let me entreat your attention* without loss of time to this very important point. I have no objection to give it up in one year. I wo[ul]d not write to Ward, but thought it better that the application sho[ul]d be made through you, but will write if you like.[2]

1 Until 1858, MPs had to own property worth £600 a year to be eligible to hold a county seat, and £300 a year for a borough seat; the requirement could be circumvented by nominal transfers of property, as D here suggested.

In implying that property had to be in the county which one represented, D was following convention and local prejudice. The law (9 Anne *c* 5) made no such stipulation. Helen E. Witmer *The Property Qualifications of Members of Parliament* (New York 1943) 52; Gash *Politics* 105.

2 Austen's application to Robert Plumer Ward was well received and on 12 November he reported to D that Ward would provide a qualification 'if he can'. H B/XXI/A/238. There is no evidence that Ward ever did so, and Austen's letter went on to suggest obstacles relating to Ward's properties in London, Surrey, Herts and Suffolk.

I hope to run up to town for a few days before the election and pay you and Mrs. Austen a visit.

With kind regards to herself and Louisa believe me

Ever yrs

BD

T.O.

219 TO THE EDITOR OF THE TIMES Bradenham, [Sunday] 11 November [1832]

ORIGINAL: PS Times 2

PUBLICATION HISTORY: *The Times* (13 Nov 1832)

Bradenham-house, Nov. 11.

Sir,

I trust to your spirit of justice to insert a single observation on a report in your journal of Saturday, of a dinner given at Wycombe to Colonel Grey.[1] The gallant Colonel is there represented as saying "that he was sure that the electors of Wycombe had not forgotten what Mr. Disraeli said in the anguish of disappointment at the result of the last election, in the hour-and-a-half speech which he made them, along with his bow at parting – 'The Whigs have cast me off,' said he, 'and they shall repent it.'"

I cannot take upon myself to answer for an accurate reminiscence of every expression in an extemporaneous "hour and a half speech" which it appears that Colonel Grey has required several months to answer, but I am sure that I never used the expression in question, because it would have been not only very intemperate, but quite nonsensical. Whatever may be the disposition of the Whigs to me, they never could have "cast me off," since I never had the slightest connexion with them. I believe that the phrase I did use, and I am sanctioned in my recollection by every person to whom I have applied, was the following: – "The Whigs have opposed me, not I them, and they shall repent it."[2]

I am in nowise ashamed of this observation, and I adhere to my intention.

I will not venture to trespass further on your valuable columns. Colonel Grey seems to complain of his reception at Wycombe during his canvass, and accounts for the want of popular courtesy by the usual story of a mob hired by his opponent. Colonel Grey has been misinformed. I have hired no mob to hoot him. The hooting was quite gratuitous.

I am, Sir, your obedient servant,

B. Disraeli

220 TO BENJAMIN AUSTEN [London], Friday [23 November 1832?]

ORIGINAL: BL ADD MS 45908 f173

EDITORIAL COMMENT: 'Friday' written over 'Thursday'. *Dating*: by comparison with **218**.

1 *The Times* (10 Nov 1832).

2 D's speech of 26 June 1832 was not so reported at the time, even by the Whigs. He did, however, attack Sir Thomas Baring and Lord Nugent. See **203**ec.

Friday

221 | 309
12 Dec 1832

My dear Austen,
I have great pleasure in sending you the desired amount and cannot write the dr[af]t with[ou]t feeling renewed gratitude for your confiding friendship, which you I hope will | never repent. I am on the wing, but shall make another effort to see you and Mrs A. before I go. I failed unfortunately yesterday w[hi]ch I much regret.

Ever yr oblg friend

D

221

TO THE ELECTORS OF THE COUNTY OF BUCKS Bradenham, [Wednesday] 12 December 1832

ORIGINAL: H B/I/A/23

PUBLICATION HISTORY: M&B I 221, extract dated 12 December 1832

EDITORIAL COMMENT: A draft of an election address. The High Wycombe poll in the general election was declared on 12 December. The results for the two-member constituency were: Smith 170, Grey 140, D 119. See **223**. From the evidence of this draft, on hearing of his defeat in Wycombe, D must have at once prepared to continue his campaign. He transferred his efforts to the county election, which was still in progress. See **225**.

Brad. He. | Decr. 12. 1832

To
the Electors of the County of Bucks.

Gentlemen,
I am encouraged by a requisition now in progress,[1] and signed in a few hours by several hundred of your constituency, to offer myself as a candidate for the high honor of representing you in Parliament. I come forward as the supporter of that great interest which is the only solid basis of the social fabric, and convinced that the sound prosperity of this country depends upon the protected industry of the farmer, I wo[ul]d resist that spirit of rash and experimental legislation which is fast hurrying this once glorious empire to the agony of civil convulsion.

With regard to my general political | views, a recent and arduous struggle for the independence of one of your most important towns, has of late placed them so often before your notice, that it is perhaps necessary for me only to remark that I shall continue to oppose, as I ever have done, that rapacious, tyrannical, and incapable faction, which by a species of political sleight of hand has of late unhappily contrived to seat themselves in the ~~royal~~ council chamber of the Sovereign.

~~While I express that deep gratification~~ I feel that the first return I can make

1 Though unknown to the electoral laws, the term 'requisition' seems to have been used to refer to an expression of support signed by prominent electors. A candidate coming forth in response to a requisition might have engineered it in the first place. For an example of a spontaneous requisition in 1830 see Charles Stuart Parker ed *Sir Robert Peel from his Private Papers* (1899) II 162.

for the ~~great honor which~~ unsought, unexpected and numerous offers of support I have received is to assure you that I shall go to the Poll and give every elector an opportunity of record[in]g his opinion.

I have the honor to remain, Gentlemen

your very obed and f[aithfu]l Ser[van]t.

---

222 TO THE ELECTORS OF THE COUNTY OF BUCKS

Aylesbury, [Thursday] 13 December [1832]

ORIGINAL: PS 72

PUBLICATION HISTORY: *The Bucks Herald* no 50 (15 Dec 1832); also printed in *The Bucks Gazette* no 1,064 (15 Dec 1832)

Aylesbury, 1 o'clock, Dec. 13.

To the Electors of the County of Bucks.

Gentlemen,

When I announced my intention to solicit your suffrages, for the honour of becoming your Representative, it was in deference to the repeated requisition of a very numerous and respectable body of your Constituency, and with the impression, that no supporter of the Agricultural Interest was inclined to advance. I have since learned that a Gentleman, with whom it would be arrogance in me for a moment to place myself in competition, has been simultaneously induced to come forward.[1] I, therefore, without hesitation, withdraw my pretensions and the tender of services, which I never could have been induced to offer, had not I conceived that the extremity of the case, and the urgency of the appeal, authorised, even on my part, a readiness to assume the arduous duties of your Representative.

I have the honour to remain,

Gentlemen,

Your obliged and faithful servant,

B. DISRAELI

1 Charles Robert Scott Murray was the second Tory candidate in the election, joining Lord Chandos who eventually headed the poll. Chandos and the two Whigs, John Smith and George Henry Dashwood, were all elected. Murray was not successful.

According to an account in *The Bucks Gazette*, Charles Murray had arrived in town almost at the moment when D made his address, and Lord Chandos had appeared at the same time as Murray. 'Whether the Marquis and the two gentlemen had an interview we have not troubled ourselves to enquire, but certain it is that Mr. D'Israeli within a short time after his arrival resigned in favour of Mr. Murray.' *BG* no 1,065 (22 Dec 1832).

TO THE INDEPENDENT ELECTORS OF WYCOMBE Bradenham, [Monday] 17 December 1832 223

ORIGINAL: PS 48
PUBLICATION HISTORY: *The Bucks Herald* no 51 (22 Dec 1832)
EDITORIAL COMMENT: The text is taken from the printed advertisement.

Bradenham House | Dec. 17, 1832

TO THE INDEPENDENT ELECTORS OF WYCOMBE.

GENTLEMEN,

Although I believe that I have expressed my thanks to every one of you individually for the courageous support which you afforded me during the late contest, it may be expected that I should have recourse to this formal expression of my gratitude. I feel confident that no Elector who yielded me his suffrage can regret the course which he pursued, and I can assure you that, although defeated, I shall ever look back to our struggle for the Independence of Wycombe as one of the most gratifying incidents of my life.

Gentlemen, we have been defeated, but we are not disgraced. We have been defeated by means the most unjust and the most unfair. We have been defeated by an unprincipled Coalition, by local tyranny,[1] and by Treasury gold.

The good cause will yet prosper, and while I live shall never need a champion. Assure yourselves of the friendship and of the fidelity of

Your obliged and devoted Servant[2]
BENJAMIN DISRAELI

FINAL CLOSE OF THE POLL

Smith	170
Grey	140
Disraeli	119

PLUMPERS.[2]

Smith	7
Grey	1
Disraeli	85

TO [JOHN GIBSON LOCKHART] [Bradenham?, Saturday 22? December 1832] 224

ORIGINAL: H B/XXI/L/243
PUBLICATION HISTORY: Blake 82; from the beginning to 'in that work', dated December 1832
EDITORIAL COMMENT: A fragment of a draft. The following is written at the top of the first page: 'and Young Dukes no longer "*wine*" with Marchionesses of Bucklersbury.' There is no signature. *Dating*: by context, and by comparison with Lockhart's reply dated one week later.

1 See **203**n1.
2 Each voter in Wycombe had the right to vote for two candidates. A 'plumper' was a voter who chose to cast only one vote. In showing separately the votes of the plumpers, D was emphasizing the large proportion of the electors who could not bring themselves to vote for either of his opponents.

Sir,

I have long been aware of the hostile influence (to use no harsher term) which you have exercised over my literary career, but I have hitherto passed it by unnoticed because I have a g[rea]t distaste to literary squabbling and because I feel confident that if I possess any genuine power I must ultimately prevail against even my most ungenerous opponents.

In the recently published no. of the Quarterly Review you have by one of those sidewind sneers for which I have been often indebted to you held me up to ridicule as using a phrase in a book called the Young Duke which is not to be found in that work.[1] I have deserved | severe criticism, I have certainly experienced it, and I hope to have profited by it. This howr. is not criticism and considering the quarter from whence it emanates I can only view it as a personal and offensive allusion and one which to pass over in silence wo[ul]d not so much indicate that spirit of patient resign[ati]on becoming a youthful writer, but rather a degree of cowardice unbefitting one who has any regard for the respect of society of himself.

I am therefore under the very painful necessity of request[in]g an explanation from you upon this subject.[2]

I have etc.

---

225 TO THE EDITOR OF THE TIMES

Bradenham,
[Wednesday] 26 December [1832]

ORIGINAL: PS Times 3
PUBLICATION HISTORY: *The Times* (27 Dec 1832)
EDITORIAL COMMENT: *Sic*: servaant.

Bradenham House, Dec. 26.

Sir,

I know too well the value of your columns ever to trouble you but with great reluctance. As however you have unintentionally circulated a caricature account of the proceedings of our county election, under the specious title of an abridg-

1 *QR* XLVIII (Dec 1832) 391-420; a review of J.J. Morier's *Zohrab the Hostage*. The offending phrase appears on page 392: '"Young Dukes" will not again be caught inviting Marchionesses of Bucklersbury to "*wine*" with them.'

2 Lockhart's reply of 29 December 1832 made no apology:

Sir,

If the reviewer of Zohrab in the last No of the Quarterly has ascribed the phrase you mention to *one* of your heroes in place of *another of them*, and if on reflection you wd. wish the I am sure involuntary mis-statement to be corrected – it shall be done in the next number of the Review.

As to myself I disclaim entirely the feelings with respect to yourself which your letter seems to impute to me. I am unconscious of having exerted any influence, one way or another, on your literary career and am of opinion that you must have been grossly misinformed as to some transaction of which I knew nothing [H B/XXI/L/244].

For D's relations with Lockhart see C.L. Cline 'Disraeli and John Gibson Lockhart' *Modern Language Notes* 56 (Feb 1941) 134-7.

ment from the *Bucks Gazette*,[1] in which I figure, I am sure your spirit of justice will permit me for a moment to trespass upon you.

It is unnecessary to contradict the *Bucks Gazette* in Buckinghamshire, and unless your columns had been adorned by the liveliness of its factious invention, I should have passed it over without a comment. I did not attend the meeting in the Town-hall of Aylesbury for the purpose of supporting an Ultra Tory candidate, but to explain to the assembled county the reasons which had induced me to withdraw my pretensions to its representation,[2] after having been honoured by a requisition, which received, in less than 48 hours, the unexpected and unsolicited signatures of nearly 600 freeholders.[3] I am assured that I did this to the satisfaction of the county, and therefore I will not trouble you with detail, which must be uninteresting.

With regard to "the uproar of the most extravagant description, which arose on my presenting myself,"[4] there was certainly a band of individuals in a cautious corner, whose exertions on that day may well entitle them in future to perform the part of the infernal chorus in Der Freischutz[5] in any barn in the county; but after half an hour's most amusing yells, their exhausted lungs failed them, and I had the pleasure of addressing, for a considerable time, an audience consisting of 2,000 persons, and was listened to with an attention which, it would appear, was more gratifying to the orator than to the reporter, since the veracious editor of the *Bucks Gazette*[6] has not found sufficient room even to allude to the circumstance.

As for "John Abel Smith, Esq., (son of Mr. J. Smith),[7] who rushed forward, and apparently under the influence of a feeling of strong indignation, went up to Mr. Disraeli, etc.," I have a perfect recollection of a young gentleman, who, as it appeared to me, and as I believe to others, with most uncalled for zeal, demanded if I had made use of a personal allusion to him, which, as I was perfectly unacquainted with him, either by name or person, it was scarcely necessary for me to disclaim, even had I read the choice expression culled by the

1 *The Times* (24 Dec 1832) printed an abridged account, taken from the *The Bucks Gazette* of 22 December, of the nomination meeting for the county of Bucks, held at Aylesbury on 17 December.

2 At the nomination meeting Murray failed to speak, *The Bucks Gazette* noting that 'the honorable gentleman was so much excited by the novelty and difficulty of his situation that he fainted.' D then arose and had great difficulty in making himself heard. The same publication recorded with some relish that D 'assumed several of his best attitudes, and exerted his lungs to the utmost, but to no purpose ...' He received 'a volley of such epithets as "Tory Radical", "Radical Tory", "Mountebank orator" etc.' *BG* no 1,065 (22 Dec 1832).

3 In D's speech the figure was 'upwards of 500'. *BH* no 51 (22 Dec 1832). See also **221**.

4 From newspaper reports, it would appear that D was provoked by barracking on the part of Whig supporters, and that he gave offence by calling his tormentors 'cowardly'.

5 Weber's opera was first performed in London at the English Opera House in 1824.

6 The Whig *Bucks Gazette* was published by James May, a printer of Aylesbury. Possibly he doubled as editor, as was common with weeklies.

7 John Abel Smith (1801-1871) had first entered Parliament in 1830, and was subsequently Whig MP for Chichester. He was head of the firm of Smith, Payne and Co. His father, John Smith (1767-1842), sat as county member for Bucks 1831-5, and was the brother of Robert Smith, 1st Baron Carrington.

faithful memory of the editor of the *Bucks Gazette*, and embalmed in the classic columns of *The Times*, which I did not.

There were good reasons why a certain party, whom I had met on the hustings of Wycomb, should be anxious to prevent me from being heard on the hustings of Ayle[s]bury, and the certain party signally and ridiculously failed. I returned from Aylesbury with feelings of perfect satisfaction to my "ardent admirers and supporters, the ultra radicals of Wycomb," who consist, as the event of the election proved, of a large portion of the electors, who, however they might have differed on particular points of politics, agreed in the necessity of exerting themselves to prevent their town from becoming a Whig-ridden, a nomination borough, and whom the means by which they were defeated in their virtuous intention, bribery, debauchery, and intimidation, midnight canvassing and noonday orgies, have, I rejoice to say, made sincere advocates of the only mode of election which can preserve at least the smaller constituencies from being demoralized by the exercise of what the constitution has intended as one of the most solemn trusts reposed in a subject.

I am, Sir, your faithful servaant,

B. DISRAELI.

226

TO JOHN MURRAY [Bradenham?], Sunday [30 December 1832?]

ORIGINAL: MM 7

COVER: John Murray Esqre. | 50 Albemarle Street | B. DISRAELI | [In another hand]: 1832 – No date | D'Israeli B. Esq.

EDITORIAL COMMENT: *Dating*: assuming that Murray's clerk was correct in assigning this letter to 1832, there is no Sunday in that year which fits. D had to be out of London at a time when 'the decision' could refer to one of D's two works published in 1832, *Contarini Fleming* or *Gallomania*. The circumstances of Sunday 30 December 1832 would fit, however, if the hypothesis is accepted that D had submitted *Alroy* to Murray (who refused it) before the work was accepted by Saunders and Otley. See **228**.

Sunday

My dear Sir,

I shall be in town on Wednesday, and wish to stay there as short a time as possible. You | will greatly convenience me by having your decision prepared by that or the following day.

Yours truly

B. Disraeli

227

TO [JOHN GIBSON LOCKHART] [Bradenham?], Tuesday [1? January 1833]

ORIGINAL: H B/XXI/L/245

PUBLICATION HISTORY: Blake 83, undated extract

EDITORIAL COMMENT: A draft reply to Lockhart's letter of 29 December 1832 (H B/XXI/L/244). The draft is written on the back of a cover addressed to D, postmarked 29 December 1832. There is no signature.

Tuesd

Sir,

My unavoidable absence from town and some neglect in forwarding my letters prevented me from receiv[in]g yr. comm[unication] until this morng.

Even had the mistatement of which I complained been of a more glaring nature I shd. not have required a public correction of it in the manner you offer. Public satisf[actio]n is not what I aimed at. The repu[tati]on that depends upon such punctilios must indeed be delicate.

As I feel I have the assurance of the writer of the reviewal of Zohrab that the mistatement was involuntary, I am of course precluded from say[in]g ano[the]r word. I applied to you with the conviction that the critic who to attack a recent work of a writer quoted a phrase in a very distant and juvenile prod[ucti]on, co[ul]d only have been influenced by a very ungenerous, not to say malignant, motive. It appears I was mistaken.

I am etc.

228

TO SARAH DISRAELI — [35] Duke Street, St James's, [London], Saturday [12 January 1833]

ORIGINAL: H A/I/B/45
COVER: Miss Disraeli | Bradenham House | High Wycombe | Bucks.
POSTMARK: (1) In circle: Q | [J]A12 | 1833
EDITORIAL COMMENT: *Sic*: St. James.

Duke Street St. James | Saturday

My dearest Sa,

With frozen fingers I write to you to say that I am quite well and that I have made an excellent arrangement with S. and O.[1] who "out of sight" are the best fellows I ever dealt with. An edition of only one thousand and a bill at very short date of £300,[2] as much as Bentley wo[ul]d have given me for the copyright, and a thousand apologies in addition for the badness of the times and the lowness of their offer, which in truth is two 3rds of the profits. The fact is they are longsighted | fellows and do not care for a miserable immediate profit. They seem quite beside themselves with the connection, and assure me they can sell much more of a book than any other house. I told Saunders, I sho[ul]d give up Literature unless I co[ul]d ensure myself £3,000 pr. ann. He answered with a smile "Well, Sir, let us hope[.]" This is all nonsense to be sure, but it is a great contrast to the other gentlemen I have had to do with. They said they co[ul]d have made a great card of C[ontarini] F[leming] and Murray had entirely | ruined it by his bad management etc. My father bid me say he is very well, and in tolerable spirits in spite of the infernal Docks of which you see in the Times.[3] But for this, he sho[ul]d never be better, but we hold up our heads notwithstanding and beg you to take heart. My father has seen a great many people of

1 Saunders and Otley, publishers at 50 Conduit Street. They published *Alroy* the following March.

2 Saunders and Otley had issued a promissory note to be honoured within two or three months. As the current market for fiction was depressed, these were favorable terms. J.A. Sutherland *Victorian Novelists and Their Publishers* (1976) 12-13, 155.

3 It would appear that Isaac D'Israeli held stock in the West India Dock Company. *The Times* of 12 January 1833 reported a dramatic decline in the value of the stock following the announcement of a lower half-yearly dividend than was anticipated.

whom he will write or tell, among them Van de Weyer (the Belgian Minister)[4] who has read all his works etc. I dined on Wednesday with the Bulwers, and went to Cov[en]t Garden in a private box with them, Mrs Wyndham, L.E.L. and Lowther beat at York by Bayntun,[5] and a good fellow. On Thursday dined alone at B's and went tog[ethe]r to Madame Vestris,[6] but disappointed. I have got an invitation from Lady Stepney for Tuesday to meet Lady Aldborough[7] etc. – but am going to Bath for a week | with E.L.B. on various adventures political and literary, tomorrow. S and O have put me in high spirits. They encourage me to the utmost. The Wycombe news, funny – Keep them up, but do not go out of the way, as my return to the next Parliament may be considered certain. In the meantime, make money, make money.

There are some small private bills of mine at Wycombe. Wootton the saddler, Lockey for 8 doz: of port, Ball (sent in) – Thomas slippers, 15.9, Nicholl slippers 9/- etc.[8] Let Jem collect these and I will send a draft on my return. I owe my mother about 12£ provided she pay Lockey's *spirit*-bill. Rosalie is published.[9] I shall perhaps write from Bath.

Ever thine,

BD |

The umbrella arrived.

The Duke of Bucks[10] is about as ill as Ld. Carrington.[11]

Abbotsford a dead failure.[12]

4 Sylvain Van de Weyer (1802-1874) was Belgian minister to London 1831-67. He negotiated on behalf of Belgian independence at the London Conference of 1831. *ER*; Greville II 179n.

5 Samuel Adlam Bayntun (1804-1833), Whig MP for York 1830-3. One of his defeated opponents in the general election of December 1832 was John Henry Lowther (1793-1868), Tory MP for York 1835-47.

6 Lucia Elizabeth Vestris (1797-1856), actress and theatre proprietor. Her professional name, Vestris, was that of her first husband. In 1838 she married Charles James Mathews. She was rumoured to have been at one time a mistress of the Prince Regent.

7 Elizabeth Stratford, née Hamilton (d 1846), widow of John Stratford, 3rd Earl of Aldborough. *BP*.

8 Abraham Wootton, saddler and harness maker, Paul's Row; Oliver Lockey, wine and spirit merchant, Temple Place; James Thomas, boot- and shoemaker, Paul's Row. There were several High Wycombe merchants named Ball: a William Ball, baker and confectioner, High Street; William Ball, watch- and clockmaker, White Hart Street; and Ball & Belson, tailors, Church Square. No tradesman named Nicholl is listed. *Pigot and Co.'s National Commercial Directory* (1830).

9 'Poor Rosalie', a story by Amelia Opie (1769-1853), appeared in *The Amulet* for 1833, 256-95. The annuals, intended for the Christmas market, normally appeared some months before their nominal date, further supporting the assumption that this is the work to which D refers. He would certainly also have known Mrs Norton's book *The Sorrows of Rosalie*, which had appeared in 1829, but there is no sign of any subsequent edition. The same issue of *The Amulet* contained the sketch 'Pilgrimage to the Holy Sepulchre' (61-72), described as 'by the Author of "Contarini Fleming"'. See **213**.

10 Richard Temple Nugent Brydges Chandos Grenville (1776-1839), 1st Duke of Buckingham and Chandos, and father of the Marquess of Chandos.

11 Lord Carrington was a prominent Bucks Tory, whose son was one of the Whig MPs for Wycombe. The death of either the Duke of Buckingham and Chandos or Lord Carrington would have created a vacancy in the House of Commons.

12 The plan to raise by public subscription enough money to lift the mortgage from Sir Walter Scott's Abbotsford estate as a memorial to him failed to gain its object. Sadleir *Bulwer* 283.

TO SARAH DISRAELI Bath, Friday [18 January 1833] **229**

ORIGINAL: FE EJM 1

COVER: [In Bulwer's hand]: Bath January ~~E.L. Bulwer~~ nineteen ELB 1833 | [In D's hand]: Miss Disraeli | Bradenham House | High Wycombe | Bucks | [In Bulwer's hand]: Free Edw Lytton Bulwer

POSTMARK: (1) In double circle: BATH | JA 19 | 183[3]

PUBLICATION HISTORY: LBCS 14-15, extracts dated 19 January 1833, conflated with part of the fourth sentence of **230**; M&B I 222-3, dated 19 January 1833, reprints extracts from the LBCS conflation.

EDITORIAL COMMENT: The cover was franked by Bulwer.

Bath. Friday.

My dearest Sa,

We arrived here on Monday and I have found the change very beneficial and refreshing. Such is the power of novelty that the four or five days seem an age. We have a lodging at 2£ pr. week in an unfashionable part of the town, with no servant, and do every thing but cook our own dinners to which Bulwer was very inclined. We have two sitting rooms and scribble in solitude in the morning until two. I have written about fifty pages of a pretty tale about Iskander[1] which will be a fine contrast to Alroy, and which I want, to make it a guin[ea] and half work[.] | The type and page of Alroy is most original, striking and beautiful.[2] We are great lions here as you may suspect, but have not been anywhere though we have received several invitations, preferring the relaxation of our own society and smoking Latakia,[3] which is a source of amusement w[hi]ch I suppose will last a week. We intended to return on Sunday next, but Bulwer is anxious to remain and if he can contrive, we shall perhaps stay till Wednesday. I will write to you again.

E.L.B. has written a work in two volumes on "The present State of England",[4] grave and philosophical, in which he tells me he has written a great deal about my father, and at length put him in his right place as the first writer of the day. It will be published soon. |

I like Bath very much. When we meet, which will be soon, I shall have a good deal to tell you, which will not occur in letters. Write to me instantly, under cover to E.L.B. MP. Post Office Bath.

I hope all the family are well. When does Georgiana marry?[5] and do the Merediths remain in London after the ceremony? I wish to know. You have got Rosalie?

Farewell, my dearest Sa,

BD

1 Since *Alroy* is a relatively short work and would not have filled up the standard three-volume format, *The Rise of Iskander*, a short tale, was added.

2 The first edition had a handsome, though standard, binding. The size of the print was unusually large.

3 A Turkish tobacco produced near Latakia, a Syrian seaport.

4 Bulwer's *England and the English*, book IV, entitled 'View of the Intellectual Spirit of the Time', is inscribed to Isaac D'Israeli, who is compared favourably with Hazlitt, Lamb and Southey.

5 Georgiana Esther Meredith married the Rev Edward Higgins (d 1884), later rector of Eastnor in Hereford, on 7 February 1833. *The Times* (8 Feb 1833); *BLG* (1846).

Maria, Ralph and James
from the diary of Blanche Norris, 1833

TO [SARAH DISRAELI] Bath, Thursday [24 January 1833] 230

ORIGINAL: PS 35

COVER: The printed source notes that the cover was 'franked by Bulwer Lytton'.

PUBLICATION HISTORY: A.M. Broadley *Chats on Autographs* (New York 1910) 189-90

EDITORIAL COMMENT: This is a reply to a letter from Sarah dated Monday 21 January 1833. H A/I/B/450. *Sic*: Bayntums.

BATH, Thursday

MY DEAREST,

You ought to have recd my letter on Sunday and I should have answered your's immediately, but it is almost impossible to get a frank out of Bulwer and I thought my father wd go quite mad if he received an unprivileged letter[1] under present circumstances. We quit this place tomorrow and shd have done so today, but dine with a Mr. Murray[2] here. I like Bath very much. At a public ball I met the Horfords,[3] Hawksleys[4] etc. Bulwer and myself went in very late and got quite mobbed.

I have nearly finished Iskander, a very pretty thing indeed, and have printed the 1st Vol of Alroy.

I have answered the agric[ultural] affair which was forwarded to me from London.[5]

Directly I am in town I will write about the bills.

The Horfords (father and brother here) asked us to dine, but were engaged.

Met the Bayntums, but not Clementina.[6] Rather think I may to day.

yrs ever

B.D.

Let me have a letter in Duke St. Bulwer is getting on immensely and I shd not be surprised if we shortly see him in a *most eminent* position,[7] but this not to be spoken of. Met Ensor.[8]

1 Letters, neither franked nor prepaid, had to be paid for by the recipient, and the rate charged was based on distance. A letter from Bath to High Wycombe would have cost Isaac 6d. *LPOD* (1832).

2 It is not clear from the context whether Murray was a resident or, like D, a visitor. William Murray of 5 Ebenezer Terrace, Bath, was a printer. *Pigot and Company's Royal National and Commercial Directory of the Counties of ... Somerset* (1842).

3 Possibly the name in the original is Harford; Henry Harford was a local solicitor. *Law List.*

4 Probably William Hawksley of Bath, who married Rosetta, daughter of Coningham M'Alpine of County Tyrone. *BLG* (1846).

5 The Buckinghamshire Agricultural Association had been formed at a public meeting held in Aylesbury on 23 January 1833. D had been sent an advance notice of who was to be at the meeting by Joseph L. Howard (d 1865?) of Aylesbury, the secretary of the association. H B/XXI/H/693 and A/I/B/450.

6 Vice Adm Sir Henry William Bayntun (1766-1840) and his wife. Their daughter, Clementina, described by Sarah as one of D's 'admirers', married in 1834 John Christian Boode. H A/I/B/525; *GM* ns II (1834) 101.

7 No such position materialized, though some recognition came when Melbourne offered Bulwer a lordship in the Admiralty in 1835.

8 When Isaac referred to 'Ensor' in later correspondence, he meant George Ensor (1769-1843), the political writer. H A/I/C/59: letter of December 1835.

231 TO SARAH DISRAELI [London], Tuesday [29 January 1833]

ORIGINAL: FITZ Disraeli A1

COVER: Miss Disraeli | Bradenham House | High Wycombe | Bucks.

POSTMARK: (1) In circle: G | JA29 | 1833

PUBLICATION HISTORY: LBCS 15, dated 29 January 1833, part of paragraph one; M&B I 223, dated 29 January 1833, extract from paragraph one

EDITORIAL COMMENT: *Sic*: soireé, bible.

Tuesday -

Sweet Sa!

I am so busy with "*the ungrateful rebel*"[1] that I missed the post to you yesterday, I have almost done so today. I think I have made a capital story of it, and a fine relief to Alroy. I have finished 120 pages and forty more will complete it with[ou]t hurry. Nothing particular has happened. I dined with Bulwer en famille on Sunday "to meet some truffles" very agreeable company. His mother in law Mrs. Wheeler was there not so pleasant, something bet[wee]n Jeremy Bentham and Meg Merrilies, very clever but awfully revolutionary.[2] She poured forth all her systems upon my novitiate ear – and while | she advocated the rights of woman, Bulwer abused system mongers and the sex, and Rosina played with her dog. Today I dine with the Merediths, a sort of party I believe. Tomorrow a soireé at the Bulwers.

Ixion is considered very marvellous. What will they say to the impending part?[3] Did I tell you that I had run up a very good notice of Ibrahim Pacha for the next No. in consequence of the row he is making?[4]

I wish that you wo[ul]d send me *with[ou]t loss of time* a Turkish mirror. It must be one of *the best*, that is one of | those the embroidery of which is sharpest. "Domesticity" is in the next No. and also "Anne of Austria".[5]

Send me also my bible and the small English Dic[tionar]y.

Clay has written to me to come *a la turque* to a fancy ball at Brighton etc. – but I shall not leave London again exc[ep]t for Bradenham. About my movements I

---

1 *The Rise of Iskander.*

2 Anna Doyle (d 1848), youngest daughter of Archdeacon Doyle, married Francis Wheeler of Ballywire, County Limerick. She left him in 1812 when Rosina was ten years old. Mrs Wheeler was herself a great beauty but suffered from what her daughter called 'philosophical nerves'. D's composite description of her, which emerges from linking Scott's aged gypsy in *Guy Mannering* with the great utilitarian philosopher, defies annotation beyond noting that Jeremy Bentham, who had died 6 June 1832, and some of whose opinions she may have endorsed, had been one of her acquaintances. Louisa Devey *Life of Rosina, Lady Lytton* ... (1887) 3-4, 8, 9, 305.

3 Part one of 'Ixion in Heaven' had appeared in *The New Monthly Magazine* no 35 (Dec 1832) 514-20; part two appeared in no 37 (Feb 1833) 175-84.

4 'Ibrahim Pacha, the Conqueror of Syria, by Marco Polo Junior'. *NMM* 37 (Feb 1833) 153-4. Ibrahim Pasha (1789-1848), son of Mehemet Ali, had just defeated the Turks at Konieh.

5 'Domesticity; or, a Dissertation on Servants' by Atticus. *NMM* 37 (Feb 1833) 200-13; and 'The Aigulets of Anne of Austria (A Secret Anecdote)' 171-4. Both are by Isaac D'Israeli.

know not. I must print my book – I like what I see of Saunders and O[tley] very much. E.L.B. wants *all* the Governors works published in monthly volumes.

I opened a strange novel called Glen Moubray[6] the other day, a | great many of the mottoes of the Chapters were from Vivian Grey. It is a Scotch book, with a sort of cleverness and imitation of "our style" but unreadable. How is my mother and the gout and all?

T[out] a V[ous]

BD

TO SARAH DISRAELI [London], Thursday [31 January 1833] **232**

ORIGINAL: H A/I/B/47

EDITORIAL COMMENT: The lower half of the first sheet of the MS is missing. *Sic*: Buckes, Miss., soireé, Legh.

---

private! | Thursday night.

My dearest,

I fear you will have been disappointed at not receiving the Mag[azine] by this night's mail, but as the night is stormy and I wish to make up a parcel, I delay it until tomorrow morn[in]g. At the Merediths I met the Buckes who were at Bath "with us". Miss. H. much disappointed she did not meet the favorite son of her patroness Mrs. Bulwer Lytton.[1] Great rows in Nottingham Place and Higgins most horribly in the black books.[2] The wedding supposed to be next Thursday. I am asked. [*The lower half of the first page is missing.*] | my father and mother at intervals wo[ul]d of course even contribute to my happiness. I shall act prudently and cautiously. What do you think?

Last night, a small and agreeable soireé in the Library at Bulwers after a dinner party. Lady Charlotte,[3] Gally Knight,[4] Mrs Legh, my friend Lady Stepney, who turns out to be a very young old woman indeed, and appeared in the longest ringlets, the Fitzgeralds,[5] Webster etc. etc. Miss Bury, by name Blanche,[6] was

6 *Glen Moubray, A Tale*, three volumes, of unknown authorship, was published in October 1831 by Simpkin.

---

1 Elizabeth Barbara Bulwer, née Lytton (1773-1843), Bulwer's mother.

2 Georgiana's suitor, the Rev Edward Higgins, was not then in the good graces of the Meredith family.

3 Lady Charlotte Susan Maria Bury (1775-1861), youngest daughter of the 5th Duke of Argyll, had married in 1818 her second husband, the Rev Edward John Bury (d 1832). Lady Charlotte Bury was a minor novelist and a slightly indiscreet diarist.

4 Henry Gally Knight (1786-1846), writer, especially on architecture, and Tory MP for various constituencies both before and after the Reform Bill.

5 Probably Maurice Fitzgerald (1774-1849), Knight of Kerry, who was known to D. See D's 'Mutilated Diary' under 1836. Vol II app III. Fitzgerald's first wife died in 1829; it is not clear when he remarried. William Vesey Fitzgerald (1783-1843), 2nd Baron Fitzgerald, was also among D's acquaintances, but he was a bachelor, thus making the term 'Fitzgeralds' inappropriate.

6 Blanche Bury, daughter of Lady Charlotte Bury and the Rev Edward Bury. Described as 'a child of great promise and beauty', she served as the model for the Countess of Argyll in Wilkie's picture 'The Preaching of Knox'. *CJ* no 162 (2 June 1832) 368; no 164 (16 June 1832) 405.

also there. Very young, but a model for a sculptor, and cold as marble. Lady Charlotte, who by the bye *was* in a sort of weeds, is a perfect idiot [*The lower half of the page is missing.*] | nothing like marriage! Before 6 months are over we shall hear of her third hero, who will probably combine both qualifications. Mrs. Legh as usual never spoke a word, altho' she is particularly intimate at the Bulwers. Lady Stepney conceives that she is the only person who fully comprehends C[ontarini] F[leming] a propos to which she made me the confidant of her own work, originally named "Ubiquity" and changed by the publisher, as usual and to her great indignation, to its present trashy title. It is a work of genuine genius according to her L[adyshi]p. "Nothing but originality exc[ep]t its simplicity." But I hear *entre nous* that it is ridiculously bad, and that Ollier has been several months doing it into English.[7] I called on her today to see her Spanish pictures. She has a very poetical house, and as she has the reputation of giving the most agreeable parties in town, I endure her admiration.

Send the enclosed. If you are forwarding | to London, there is a new pair of boots which might come. All the things arrived very safe and the handk[erchie]fs very a propos.

Send the enclosed parcel by coach or o[the]rwise to Howard at Aylesbury.

I will write to my father at my leisure.

Thine

BD

233

TO [SARAH DISRAELI] [London, Thursday 7 February 1833]

ORIGINAL: PS 1

PUBLICATION HISTORY: LBCS 15-16, dated 7 February 1833; M&B I 223, extracts dated 7 February 1833

EDITORIAL COMMENT: *Dating*: *Hansard* verifies Bulwer's two contributions on 5 and 6 February, 1833.

February 7, 1833.

Tuesday I went to the new opera at Drury Lane, and was introduced to the Brahams,[1] on whom I have promised to call. Went to the House of Commons afterwards to hear Bulwer adjourn the House; was there yesterday during the whole debate – one of the finest we have had for years. Bulwer spoke, but he is physically disqualified for an orator,[2] and, in spite of all his exertions, never can

In 1842, apparently still unmarried, she lived in Rome with her mother. George Douglas Campbell, 8th Duke of Argyll *Autobiography and Memoirs* (1906) I 194. Later, she married one David Lyon. Lady Charlotte Bury *Diary of a Lady-in-Waiting* ed A. Francis Steuart (1908) ix.

7 Lady Stepney's novel, first entitled 'Ubiquity', appeared in 1833 as *The New Road to Ruin*. Charles Ollier acted as a reader for Bentley the publisher.

---

1 John Braham (1774?-1856), popular tenor, less successful as a theatre proprietor, married in 1816 a Miss Bolton of Ardwick. Their daughter, Frances Elizabeth Anne (1821-1879), was, after 1840, Countess Waldegrave, and a friend of D's.

2 Bulwer recognized his own deficiencies, but flattered himself that he had prevailed. 'If I have any ability less inconsiderable than another ... any one in which I surmounted the disadvantages of nature and acquired the powers of art, it is the talent of public speaking.' Letter of 6

succeed. He was heard with great attention, and is evidently backed by a party. Heard Macaulay's best speech, Sheil and Charles Grant.[3] Macaulay admirable; but, between ourselves, I could floor them all. This *entre nous*: I was never more confident of anything than that I could carry everything before me in that House. The time will come....

Grey spoke highly of my oratorical powers to Bulwer, said he never heard 'finer command of words'. *Ixion* is thought the best thing I ever wrote, and two vols. of *Alroy* are printed. Maclise is making a noise. His Mokanna[4] is exhibiting at the British Gallery, and is *the* picture of the year.

[D]

TO SARAH DISRAELI — [35] Duke Street, St James's, [London], Thursday [14 February 1833] 234

ORIGINAL: MNHP 1
COVER: Miss Disraeli | Bradenham House | Wycombe | *Bucks.*
POSTMARK: (1) In circle: W | FE 1[illegible] | 18[33]
PUBLICATION HISTORY: LBCS 16-17, dated 28 February 1833, a paraphrase of parts of the original
EDITORIAL COMMENT: Note 9 refers to a Liberal MP instead of to a Whig. For a full explanation of our practice in the use of party names see **323**n1. *Dating*: *Alroy* was published 5 March 1833. The only Thursday in February consistent with the postmark is the 14th. *Sic*: St James, age, checque, Matthews, soireé, Ossulton.

Duke St. St James. Thursday

My dearest,

Why are you so silent? It is more than a week since I heard from you. I think Alroy may be subscribed on Tuesday. There was a notice in the age of Ixion and the author, very much praising the talent of the thing.[1] I sent a checque for 5£ to the Bucks Agric[ultural] Soc[iet]y.[2] Did it appear in the list last week? On Friday last, I dined with Nat Basevi[3] and met Charles Matthews who was exceedingly amusing. On Saturday, I was invited to a soireé by Mrs. Bulwer, but

September 1826 in Louisa Devey ed *Letters of the late Edward Bulwer, Lord Lytton, to his Wife* (New York 1889) 66. The exaggerated bodily movements that accompanied his oratory detracted from the substance. William White *The Inner Life of the House of Commons* (1904) I 10. Palmerston was credited with saying that 'the House had *seen* the speech of the right hon. gentleman'.

3 These speeches all occurred during the debate in reply to the Speech from the Throne. Thomas Babington Macaulay (1800-1859), Whig MP for Leeds, defended himself against the charges by Bulwer Lytton and Richard Lalor Sheil (1791-1851), Whig MP for Tipperary, that he was inconsistent in his argument in favour of the existing legislative union with Ireland. Charles Grant (1783-1866), long-time Whig MP for Inverness, and after 1835 1st Baron Glenelg, defended Macaulay. *Hansard* XV (5-6 Feb 1833) cols 238-44, 250-64, 264-77.

4 'Mokanna Unveiling his Features to Zelica' by Daniel Maclise was exhibited at the gallery of the British Institution in 1833 and attracted much attention.

The reviewer called 'Ixion in Heaven' both cleverly written and elegant, but he also noted that it was not 'very Christian-like', a failing attributed to the author's being 'of the Jewish persuasion'. *The Age* (10 Feb 1833) 45.

Sarah sent him *The Bucks Herald* for the list of subscribers. D's name does not appear in the lists for that month. H A/I/B/453; *BH* nos 57-60 (2, 9, 16, 23 Feb 1833).

Nathaniel Basevi lived at 19 Lincoln's Inn, Old Square.

was in arrear with Iskander and obliged to stay at home. On Sunday a dull dinner at Guildford St. where I endeavoured to make my peace.[4] On Monday I dined at John Hardwicks with the Nortons,[5] Walker J.,[6] Charles Matthews and Phil. Hardwick. I sat next to Madame,[7] who was very agreeable and seemed to me then the handsomest person I had ever met with./ At ten o'ck we went off to see Miss Kelly,[8] whom they thought very clever, but I thought it a degrading imitation of Matthews. Yesterday I dined with the Nortons, and spent a most pleasant day. It was her brother's birthday, Brinsley, the eldest, who is "the only respectable one in the family, and that is because he has a liver complaint." There were there sd brother, a junior one Charley,[9] old Charles Sheridan, (the uncle),[10] a Mr. Pigou,[11] Henry Baring, who married Lady Augusta Brudenell,[12] J.H[13] and one or two others. The only lady besides Mrs. Norton, her sister Mrs. Blackwood,[14] also very handsome and very Sheridanic. She told me she was nothing "You see Georgy's the beauty and Carry's the wit, and I ought to be the good one, but then I am such a liar." I must say I liked her exceedingly. Besides she knows all | my works by heart, and spouts whole pages of V[ivian] G[rey] and C[ontarini] F[leming] and the Y[oung] D[uke] and all. In the evening, but very early, came the beauty Lady St. Maur[15] and anything so splendid I never gazed upon. Even the handsomest family in the world, which I think the Sheridans are all looked dull. She is the most dazzling person in the world. Clusters of the darkest hair and the most brilliant complexion, a contour of face perfectly ideal. There came also Lord Ossulton,[16] a very fine singer, and amiable, unaffected, goodlooking person. In the evening, Mrs. Norton sang and acted

4 The Austens had complained that D was neglecting his old friends. They lived at 33 Guildford Street, which Mrs Austen and some directories rendered as 'Guilford'.

5 Caroline and George Norton.

6 Thomas Walker, a magistrate but hardly entitled to the 'J'.

7 Julia Hardwick, the hostess.

8 Frances Maria Kelly (1790-1882), actress and opera singer. Her 'Dramatic Recollections' ran from February to October 1833 at the New Strand Theatre.

9 Caroline Norton had three brothers living at this time: Richard Brinsley Sheridan (1809?-1888), the eldest, and grandson of his namesake, was later Liberal MP for Shaftesbury 1845-52 and for Dorchester 1852-68; Francis Cynric Sheridan (d 1843) was later treasurer of Mauritius; and Charles Kinnaird Sheridan (1817-1847), the youngest, was later an attaché at the British Embassy in Paris.

10 Charles Sheridan (d 1843), Caroline Norton's uncle, Richard Brinsley Sheridan's son by his second marriage.

11 Either Charles Pigou of Clarges Street or Robert Pigou of Gloucester Place. Robson's *Guide* (1833). This member of the Sheridan circle is probably the one whose name was transcribed as 'Pigore' in Haydon's recollections of an evening at Lady Seymour's in July of that year. Haydon IV 110.

12 Henry Bingham Baring (1804-1869), Tory MP for Marlborough 1832-68, had married in 1827 Lady Augusta Brudenell (d 1853), fifth daughter of the 6th Earl of Cardigan.

13 Presumably John Hardwick.

14 Helen Selina Blackwood, née Sheridan (1807-1867), sister of Mrs Norton, married in 1825 Cmdr Price Blackwood (1794-1841), after 1839 4th Baron Dufferin and Clandeboye.

15 Jane Georgiana Seymour, née Sheridan (1809-1884), sister of Caroline and Helen, had married in 1830 Edward Adolphus Seymour (1804-1884), Baron Seymour, and after 1855 12th Duke of Somerset. 'St Maur' was an alternative spelling for the Seymour family name.

16 Charles Bennet (1810-1899), Baron Ossulston, after 1859 6th Earl of Tankerville, Tory MP for Northumberland North 1832-59.

and did everything that was delightful. I like them all, even Norton, who is very hospitable. We did not break up until 3 o'ck:!

My greatest admirer is old Mrs. Sheridan,[17] the authoress of Carwell, who by the bye is very young and pretty. But she was unwell. She sent me a message. The truth is the | whole family have a very proper idea of my merits, so I have tried to do them justice.

T[out] a. V[ous]

BD

I am exhausted by printing this book. I shall probably run down in a week or so.

TO HELEN SELINA BLACKWOOD 35 Duke Street, St James's, [London], Saturday [16 February? 1833] **235**

ORIGINAL: NIPR D1071B/E3/9B [2]

EDITORIAL COMMENT: *Dating*: **234** records D's enthusiasm about the Sheridans, and as his custom was to lose no time in initiating correspondence with people to whom he was attracted, it is reasonable to assume that this Saturday was the one immediately following the Wednesday he had spent with them. *Sic*: St James.

---

35 Duke St St James | Saturday

Mrs. Price Blackwood

Dear Madam!

I only received the book[1] from Bradenham last night, or I should not have required your agreeable reminiscence. I send it you because I promised, but the observations | are really so exceedingly futile, that they can afford no gratification to the accomplished author of Carwell, and reflect such little credit on the unhappy scribbler of the present note, that I | trust to your generosity to return the book.

I hope you are as well as you are witty, and as happy as you are beautiful; and with this compliment worthy of Ispahan,[2] I subscribe myself in Spring Gardens[3] phrase,

Your faithful Ser[van]t

B. Disraeli

17 Caroline Henrietta Sheridan, née Callander (1779-1851), mother of the Sheridan sisters, married in 1805 Thomas Sheridan (1775-1817), son of Richard Brinsley Sheridan. Mrs Sheridan achieved a minor literary reputation as the author of the novels *Carwell* (1830), *Aims and Ends* (1833) and *Oonagh Lynch* (1833).

1 D's annotated copy of *Carwell*; see **236**.

2 Alternate form of Isfahan, the capital of Persia in the sixteenth century.

3 The London address of Lord Seymour, husband of the third Sheridan sister, was 18 Spring Gardens.

236 TO CAROLINE HENRIETTA SHERIDAN

35 Duke Street, St James's, [London], Wednesday [20 February? 1833]

ORIGINAL: NIPR MIC22R54:6

EDITORIAL COMMENT: *Dating*: the Wednesday after **235**. *Sic*: St James, desarts.

Duke St. St James | Wednesday

Mrs. Sheridan

Dear Madam,

If you will permit me to call you so. I learn with great pleasure from your elegant note, that my battered copy of Carwell has afforded you some gratification. Had I imagined, when I dotted down those rambling thoughts, | in the desarts of Africa, that the book, by one of those singular combinations of circumstances which are the charm of life, was eventually to find its way into the hands of its accomplished author, I would have endeavoured to have made them worthier of her perusal; I would have written more about the author, and less about myself.

I assure you I have not yet sufficiently expressed the high estimation in which I | hold Carwell. I flatter myself, with all my many faults, that I am at least free from any feeling of literary jealousy, and believe me that it is with cordial feelings of delight, that I anticipate in your forthcoming work,[1] a production which will command the admiration of the many, as much as Carwell | has already secured you the sympathy of the refined few.

Believe me, dear Madam,
with sincere consideration,
Your obedient Serv[an]t
and admirer
Benjn Disraeli

237 TO [HELEN SELINA BLACKWOOD]

[London?, Thursday 21 February? 1833]

ORIGINAL: NIPR D1071B/E3/9B/5

EDITORIAL COMMENT: *Dating*: before **240** with which D is to send Mrs Blackwood a complete proof copy of *Alroy*. The repository lists this letter as one to Caroline Henrietta Sheridan. However, it is certainly addressed to Helen Selina Blackwood in response to a letter from her (NIPR D1071F/A4/2).

I send you the Song[1] – with regard to other music, listen! Alroy is full of fine things for music. Among many others I think there is a Drinking Song, a love song, and a chorus[2] (the return of the Caravan from Mecca to Bagdad) which

1 *Aims and Ends* and *Oonagh Lynch* were published together in a single three-volume edition, in February 1833.

---

1 Mrs Blackwood in her letter, to which this is a reply, had written: 'You require to be reminded of your promises very often! – where is the song I am to sing, and where are the song*s* I am to set to music? – oh vile *Shuffle*! – I will be a viler *Screw*. If you really will send me some songs, I will make the most edifying Psalm tunes on purpose for them, – and if you really won't – why – I shall "say nothing – but look upon myself, as a very ill-used gentlewoman"! – '. NIPR D107lF/A4/2A.

2 For once, D understated his case. Chapters 1, 7 and 10 all contain choruses.

might perhaps inspire you. These perhaps | are better subjects for you than any I co[ul]d write now, for I can never repress my feelings when composing, and you wo[ul]d of course ridicule them.

The moment a copy is attainable, the book shall be sent. I fear howr. it will be some days yet. You will have the first copy.

I say nothing about your | note. I think it very unkind, and I am very unhappy. I shall certainly not give up my pipe, which is now my only friend.[3]

I do not believe a word about your coming to town, or that I shall ever see you again,[4] and I subscribe myself, as you desire it,

Your obedt Ser[van]t[5]
Benj Disraeli

TO SARAH DISRAELI [London, Friday 22 February 1833] 238

ORIGINAL: PS 37

PUBLICATION HISTORY: Clarence I. Freed 'A New Sheaf of Disraeli Letters' *The American Hebrew* CXX (15 Apr 1927) 834

EDITORIAL COMMENT: The article cited above, pages 820, 834, 836, 838, 854-5, describes a collection of 'twenty-five letters recently purchased by Mr. Lloyd W. Smith of New York at a literary disposal of part of the collection of Mr. Harry Glemby. They were penned by Disraeli between the years 1833 and 1850. All, except two, are addressed to his Sister Sarah ... One of them is addressed to his father, Isaac D'Israeli' (820).

The Anderson Galleries, catalogue 2099 (New York 1926) item 17, had listed these letters as 'A collection of 25 Autograph Letters all except two signed "D" or "BD", and several with seal, comprising 115 pages, written from 1833 to 1850. Twenty-three of the letters are addressed to his sister Sarah – the famous "Sa" – and one to his father Isaac'.

This collection has not been located and, as complete letters were not transcribed, either in the Anderson catalogue or by Freed, the extracts which were quoted are here reproduced. The accuracy of some of the texts for **238**, **259**, **270** and **286** is highly suspect: for example, Freed discusses what purports to be a letter of 29 June 1833, quoting a text identical to Ralph's text in LBCS (20-1) which is itself a conflation of at least two letters in the Hughenden papers. *Sic*: Louise, Gwynn.

I was at Lady Stepney's on Monday, a very splendid soirée, tho' not many of my set. The finest woman in the room was Lady Tullamore, very tall and fair, with a classical face.[1] I talked a great deal to a nice person, who turned out to be Lady Charlotte Capel, a St. Albans, and her sister Louise, who looked like Nell

3 Mrs Blackwood's advice about using the chibouque was addressed to a fictitious Mr Halifax. She meant D.

4 In her postscript she expressed the hope she would soon see Mr Halifax's friend Mr Disraeli, but without 'his amber-mouthed chibouque'.

5 Mrs Blackwood had said: 'There were three mystical letters at the end T.A.V. which I suppose mean the same thing as Q.E.D. at the end of my Brother's problems, – don't they?' She ended her own letter: 'I can't remember the "*shut sesame*" with which one gets out of a letter – it is something about "obedt. Servant."'

D's use of this subscription – T.A.V. – had initially puzzled the editors too (see **231**). They are relieved to find Helen Blackwood in their company.

---

1 Harriet Charlotte Bury, née Campbell (d 1848), married in 1821 Charles William Bury (1801-1851), Baron Tullamore, after 1835 2nd Earl of Charleville.

Gwynn.[2] I don't think Alroy will be published until the first of March. Send me up my small dagger, and my talisman, which enclose in some little fanciful cover, as I intend to wear it, having mentioned it in the notes of Alroy.[3]

[D]

---

239 TO MACVEY NAPIER

35 Duke Street, St James's, [London], [Saturday] 23 February 1833

ORIGINAL: BL ADD MS 34616 ff45-6

COVER: *private and immediate* | The Editor of the | Edinbro' Review. | B. DISRAELI | [On the flap in another hand]: Benjn Disraeli Esq | Feby 23 | 1833

PUBLICATION HISTORY: Andrew Lang *Life and Letters of John Gibson Lockhart* II 77, extract

EDITORIAL COMMENT: *Sic*: St James.

---

35 Duke Street, St James | Feby. 23. 1833

confidential

Sir,[1]

I have just been reading "Zohrab the hostage" in consequence of Mr Lockharts panegyric of it in the Quarterly Review.[2] With a great reluctance to hurt the feelings of so gentlemanlike a fellow as Morier, I must say that I have a great desire to show the public the consequence of having a tenth rate | novelist[3] at the head of a great critical journal, for really a production in every respect more contemptible than Zohrab I have seldom met with. My acquaintance with Oriental life would not disqualify me for performing the operation, and if you are not disinclined to receive | the article, I will send you something poignant, and not too long, for your next No.

2 D must have meant Lady Caroline Capel (1804-1862), third daughter of the 8th Duke of St Albans. In 1825 she had married Arthur Algernon Capel (1803-1892), after 1839 6th Earl of Essex. Her younger sister Louisa (d 1843) married in 1835 Thomas Hughan of Airds. She may well have looked like Nell Gwyn, who was, of course, the mother of the 1st Duke of St Albans. Their elder sister, Lady Charlotte Beauclerk (1802-1842), died unmarried.

3 '*A cornelian Talisman covered with strange characters* (Note 9 – Page 68). Talismans have not in any degree lost their influence in The East. Most that I have seen have been cut upon cornelian. A very precious one of this nature, obtained at great cost and peril, of the most celebrated Sorcerer in Cairo, lies at this moment by my side. It secures to its possessor a constancy of good fortune. Unfortunately its present holder is the exception that proves the rule.' *Alroy* I 276.

---

1 Macvey Napier (1776-1847), editor of *The Edinburgh Review*. Napier encouraged D in a reply on 27 February, saying that he would be pleased to receive a review of *Zohrab the Hostage*, but only on condition that it not give rise to the charge that 'Zohrab had been cut up, as the phrase is, in the Edinburgh because extolled in the Quarterly; or not as to appear to bear any direct allusion to the literary merits of the Editor of that Journal.' H B/XXI/N/13. Perhaps Napier had shrewdly anticipated D's motive for his offer, for D did not respond, prompting a reminder from Napier on 6 March. See **252**n1.

2 See **224**.

3 Lockhart had written two novels: *Valerius, a Roman Story* (1821), and *The History of Matthew Wald* (1824).

I have, the honor to be,
Sir,
Your faithful Serv[an]t
Benjn Disraeli

240

TO [HELEN SELINA BLACKWOOD] [London], Saturday [23 February? 1833]

ORIGINAL: NIPR D1071B/E3/9B:9

EDITORIAL COMMENT: There is no signature. This letter is listed by the repository as one to Mrs C.H. Sheridan; however, the reference to '*chere Maman*' makes it clear that it is to Helen Selina Blackwood. *Dating*: by Saturday 2 March D had told Sarah that some copies of *Alroy* were in circulation. Here they are in proof only, suggesting the week before. It was written after **237**, but still just before the publication of *Alroy*.

Saturday

Dearest Lady!

I am so anxious that you should read "Alroy" before you enter the whirlwind of London existence, that, despairing of getting you a copy in time, I have made up one with my own rough proofs – you will read it under some disadvantage as the rough proofs are not | corrected, and I have not time this morning to correct them.

You tell me I must never trust to your generosity.[1] Let me appeal then to your honor. Seriously no one must see these pages (always excepting *chere Maman* if she like) or I may get embroiled not only with my publishers and my public, but with the only people | I care for, my own family, who will look unhappy and remonstrate, as they have not yet been favored with them.

I am not very sanguine as to the work which I think is too strange for the million, *mais nous verrons*!

When you have finished, you must return me/ these sheets and I will replace them with a complete copy wherein I will venture to inscribe thy fair and adored name!

241

TO BENJAMIN AUSTEN [London], Monday [25 February? 1833]

ORIGINAL: BL ADD MS 45908 ff66-7

EDITORIAL COMMENT: *Dating*: *Alroy* was published on 5 March 1833.

Monday | ——

My dear Austen,

I was sorry that I could not reach you yesterday, and am still more so that you cannot receive me to day. Is it convenient to | you to discount my bill accepted payable at Drummonds[1] for £100 for one month, the 21st. April? As the whole of Alroy is nearly published, I co[ul]d, if necessary, draw upon S. and O. in antici-

1 Mrs Blackwood had told him: 'Don't trust anything to my *generosity* – you have unfortunately hit on the *only* virtue I do not possess!' NIPR D1071F/A4/2B.

1 Drummond and Co, bankers, 49 Charing Cross.

pation of | part proceeds of the next Edit which they always pay by a bill in advance, but I do not wish to appear in anyway *pressed* to them, as the idea may affect the projected negotiation for the absolute sale | of the work. I generally find that the liberality of publishers is in exact proportion to your apparent independence.

T[out] A V[ous]
Disraeli

If it hold up, I may perhaps reach Guildford St. this morning.

---

242 TO SARAH DISRAELI [London], [Saturday] 2 March [1833]

ORIGINAL: FITZ Disraeli A2

COVER: Miss Disraeli | Bradenham House | Hh. Wycombe | *Bucks*

POSTMARK: (1) In Maltese cross: CH | 2MR1833 | X

PUBLICATION HISTORY: LBCS 17-18, dated 6 March 1833, prints the last sentence of paragraph two and an altered version of the latter part of paragraph four with an extract from **243**.

EDITORIAL COMMENT: There is a hole in the second sheet of the MS. *Sic*: french, Lewe's, Maurozeni, Philpotts.

Mar: 2

My dearest,

Not having received any proofs from Moxon,[1] I called and found that he had forwarded them direct to my father in order he said "to gain time". I hope that none will go to press with[ou]t my seeing them; howr. I said nothing to Moxon respecting that.

Nothing has happened until recently, which is the reason I have not written. We have sold nearly two hundred more of Alroy and S and O. seem very sanguine. The book is only just in circulation, barely.[2] Beckford has sent me a large paper copy of Vathek in french, only 25 printed.

The | Albion turns out a very capital club – Few in number, but not at all the set I anticipated – a great many M.P.s and tho' not fashionable, distinguished. The grub and wines the best in London, and all on a finished scale.

Thursday, a large and agreeable dinner party at the Wyndham Lewe's[3] – The

1 Edward Moxon (1801-1858) published Isaac D'Israeli's *The Genius of Judaism* (1833).

2 According to **243** of 6 March, the publication date of *Alroy* was 5 March 1833. Presumably these sales were advance subscriptions, though possibly review copies were in circulation.

3 Wyndham Lewis (1778-1838), partner in the Dowlais ironworks, and Tory MP for Maidstone from 1835 until his death. After the 1837 General Election D joined him in representing the constituency. In 1815 Lewis had married Mary Anne Evans, after 1839 D's wife.

Poulett Scropes,[4] the Dawsons,[5] Mrs. uglier than Madame Crewe,[6] but the same style of face, Fairlie with his new wife, the Speaker's dau[ghte]r,[7] who is extremely pretty, and many others whom I did not discover, among them my friend Lowther[8] – Mrs. Poulett | a strong Contarinite. Yesterday at Forbes – Maurozeni,[9] Castlereagh,[10] Ward,[11] Sir Jno. Maclean[12] and Sir John Waters,[13] two generals and former warriors in Egypt. I like Castlereagh who is full of animal spirits, unaffected, and amusing, but with no ballast. He asked me to call upon him – and we parted g[*ood*] friends.

The Review in the C[ourt] J[ournal] doubtless by Mrs Gore.[14]

There is plenty of time for the Genius, as the subject will be before the Public for these months yet.[15]

I hope all are well. Write my angel to yr
affec Brother.

Lady Stepneys house is a great | lounge in the morning, as she never goes out. Yesterday I met there Philpots of Exeter[16] – and Lord Strangford among others. His L[ordshi]p addressed me as if we had been brother friends from our cradles and exhibited his useless | heartless brilliancy[17] – "I am buried in Alroy. Have you seen the Eliots lately?" etc.

4 Emma Phipps Scrope, heiress and only child of William Scrope, married in 1821 George Julius Poulett (1797-1876), brother of Charles Edward Poulett Thomson, after 1840 1st Baron Sydenham, governor general of Canada. On his marriage Poulett assumed his wife's name. He was a geologist and Whig MP for Stroud 1833-67. Emma was a cousin and close friend of Mary Anne Lewis.

5 George Robert Dawson (1790-1856), under-secretary of the Home Department 1822-7, secretary to the Treasury 1828-30, first secretary to the Admiralty 1834-5, Tory MP for Londonderry 1815-30 and for Harwich 1830-2. His wife was the sister of Sir Robert Peel.

6 Harriet Crewe (d 1856), eldest daughter of 1st Baron Carrington, had married in 1819 Col John Frederick Crewe. See Sarah to D of July 1832 (H A/I/B/438), where she described Mrs Crewe's support for D's political career.

7 John Fairlie had married in 1831 Louisa Purves (d 1843), Lady Blessington's niece and step-daughter of Charles Manners-Sutton, Speaker of the House.

8 Probably John Henry Lowther.

9 Jean de Mauregini (or Maurojeni) was the Turkish chargé d'affaires at the Court of St James's between December 1832 and November 1833.

10 Frederick William Robert Stewart (1805-1872), Viscount Castlereagh, after 1854 4th Marquess of Londonderry, Tory MP for County Down 1826-52. He was the only child of his father's first marriage and a step-son to Frances Anne, Marchioness of Londonderry.

11 Either Robert Plumer Ward or his son.

12 Sir John Maclean (d 1846) of the 27th Foot, promoted to major general in 1825. *AR* (1846).

13 Sir John Waters (1774-1842) had served at Waterloo; he was made a major general in 1830 and lieutenant general in 1841.

14 The review was friendly if discursive. The only note of disapproval came at the end: 'One word respecting the "style" of this work, which the author regards as "a new one", and as an invention of his own. We do not regard it in this light: it's [*sic*] principle, or rather the philosophy of its principle, is good; but it is carried to a wild excess. This is not the age in which "prose" may be allowed to "run mad", even in a work of fiction.' *CJ* no 204 (23 Mar 1833) 202-3.

15 Isaac was seeking assurance that his *The Genius of Judaism* would appear in time to benefit from the interest in the renewed (but until 1858 unsuccessful) proposal to remove civil disabilities from Jews in Britain.

16 Henry Phillpotts, Bishop of Exeter 1830-69. He was described by *The Court Journal* no 156 (21 Apr 1832) 246 as 'one of the very first conversationalists of the time'.

17 If *Alroy* was indeed not yet generally available, Strangford's insincerity is sufficiently documented.

243 TO SARAH DISRAELI [London], Wednesday [6 March 1833]

ORIGINAL: FITZ Disraeli A3

COVER: Miss Disraeli | Bradenham House, | High Wycombe | Bucks.

POSTMARK: (1) In circle: V | MR-6 | 1833

PUBLICATION HISTORY: LBCS 17-18, dated 6 March 1833, includes the first sentence and part of paragraph four with an extract from **242**.

EDITORIAL COMMENT: *Sic*: Melborne, Melbornes, Clarke.

Wednesday

My dearest,

Alroy was published yesterday, subscribed 1/2 the Edit: in these times very good. I am in a long arrear to you, but you have other correspondents when they are in town.

Last Tuesday week I dined at B.E.L.'s a great gorge and large party of bachelors: a very capital banquet indeed. Wednesday the Nortons; Lord Melborne,[1] Charles Norton[2] and Mrs. Charles his wife more beautiful even than the three sisters,[3] Charles Sheridan etc. very pleasant and lively as it ever is there.

Thursday a very dull dinner at | the Spences. I am quite wearied of their eternal plate, and will never enter the house again. Friday repose. Saturday Merediths, Sunday Trevors, Monday, John Hardwick, who gives regular dinners now every week and very good. There was that Young three [there], Melbornes private Sec[retar]y,[4] Walker[5] whom I like, Major Clarke of the U.S.J.[6] who likes me etc.

1 William Lamb (1779-1848), 2nd Viscount Melbourne, was at this time home secretary in Grey's government. Legend has it that on this occasion, their first meeting, Melbourne asked the young D, 'Well now, tell me, what do you want to be?' and D replied, 'I want to be Prime Minister.' Melbourne patiently explained why that would be impossible. A further story has it that Melbourne, before his death in 1848, on hearing of D's impending elevation to the Tory leadership in the House of Commons, exclaimed: 'By God! the fellow will do it yet.' M&B I 255.

2 Charles Francis Norton (1807-1835), brother of Caroline's husband George Norton, captain 52nd regiment, MP for Guildford 1831-2; he married in 1831 Maria Wellesley Campbell (d 1888), daughter of Maj Gen Sir Colin Campbell. She married secondly in 1838 Edmund Phipps (1808-1857), brother of Lord Mulgrave.

3 The Sheridan sisters. See **234**.

4 The MS says clearly 'Young three'; however, the sense of the passage, considering the ages of the participants, is only consistent with assuming Young to be a proper name, and 'three' to be 'there'.

Tom Young, the son of a Nairn farmer, had been the purser on the Duke of Devonshire's yacht before becoming an unofficial private secretary to Melbourne. Greville described him as 'a vulgar, familiar, impudent fellow, but of indefatigable industry and a man who suits Melbourne'. He added, 'Tom Young was commonly known as "Ubiquity Young", because you saw him in every place you might happen to go to.' III 76n. 'Through him', Melbourne is supposed to have said, 'I am able to look down below; which for me is more important than all I can learn from all the fine gentlemen clerks about me.' Philip Ziegler *Melbourne: A Biography of William Lamb, 2nd Viscount Melbourne* (1976) 138. Most of Melbourne's biographers follow Greville's portrayal of Tom Young; for a more sympathetic account see Abraham Hayward *Sketches of Eminent Statesmen and Writers* (1880) I 372-4.

5 Possibly Thomas Walker.

6 Maj Thomas Henry Shadwell Clerke (d 1849). *AR* (1849), app 232; Army Lists. *The United Service Journal and Naval and Military Magazine* was published, under that title, 1829-43.

Yesterday I dined with my new friend Mr Munro,[7] a bachelor of immense fortune | who lives in Park St. – We dined in a gallery of magnificent pictures; the company, Lord Arthur Lennox,[8] Genl. Phipps,[9] Poulett Scrope, Wilkie,[10] Westmacott,[11] Turner[12] and Pickersgill[13] – A costly banquet. I like Munro much and mean to bring him down to Bradenham. We are great friends. He is about 40.

In great haste

BD

TO [HELEN SELINA BLACKWOOD] [London], Thursday [7 March? 1833] **244**

ORIGINAL: NIPR D1071B/E3/9B:13

EDITORIAL COMMENT: The tone of the letter is in the idiom of *Alroy*; see n5. *Dating*: the most probable Thursday, by the context, is the first after the publication of *Alroy*.

Thursday

Madame!

When I am a Despot,[1] I shall be revenged on all my enemies, and you will suffer. I shall decapitate you, and place your head upon Storeys Gate[2] as an example. I shall also, in the true Oriental style, order your hands to be cut off which I shall embalm and | keep as a memento of my justice.

I am glad you like the Prison scene, as I do myself. In the N[ew] M[onthly] Magazine I have just read the first attack upon "the New Style",[3] but I don't care for that.

The battles are very good battles, and according to the best receipts of the Art Military. |

7 Hugh Andrew Johnson Munro was best known to society as the owner of some fine paintings, including a Rembrandt. Records of his appearances, as late as 1849, suggest that he remained a bachelor. He had a country house in Ross-shire, and in London he lived at 113 Park Street, Grosvenor Square. *CJ* no 169 (21 July 1832) 492; Charles Eastlake Smith ed *Journals and Correspondence of Lady Eastlake* (1895) I 186, 239.

8 Lord Arthur Lennox (1806-1864), seventh son of the 4th Duke of Richmond and Gordon.

9 Gen Edmund Phipps (1760?-1837), uncle of the 2nd Earl of Mulgrave. He was a member of the Consolidated Board of General Officers and Tory MP for Scarborough 1794-1832 (except for 1818-20, when he sat for Queenborough).

10 Possibly David Wilkie, since 1830 painter-in-ordinary to the King.

11 There were two sculptors named Richard Westmacott active in London at this time. The father (1775-1856) was knighted in 1837, having executed many public sculptures in the city, including the Hyde Park Achilles and the pediment of the British Museum portico. His son (1799-1872) was professor of sculpture at the Royal Academy 1857-67.

12 In this company, most likely Joseph Mallord William Turner (1775-1851), the landscape painter.

13 Henry William Pickersgill (1782-1875), portrait painter.

---

1 Mrs Blackwood had whimsically asked D to make her a duchess when he became England's despotic monarch. NIPR D 1071F/A4/2C.

2 Storey's Gate (or 2 Prince's Court, Storey's Gate), Westminster, was the London address of George and Caroline Norton.

3 The review of *Alroy* in *The New Monthly Magazine* was generally laudatory. 'New style' is a term that did not appear in the review, but obviously D had carried it over in his mind from the comments he believed to be by Catherine Gore in *The Court Journal*. See **242**n14. *NMM* 37 (Mar 1833) 342-6.

Advices from Bagdad apprise me that your copy will probably arrive tomorrow.

I am sorry you do not like Schirene,[4] for I think she has some points of resemblance to yourself, particularly in person.

And so farewell.

I made an ineffectual attempt | to pay you a visit to day, but got drowned at Messrs. Drummonds and was obliged to put back to refit. As I believe nobody is ever at home at your house, I armed myself with the accompanying packet.

"Alp Arslan"[5]

---

245 TO [HELEN SELINA BLACKWOOD] [London, Thursday 7 March? 1833]

ORIGINAL: NIPR D1071B/E3/9B:14

EDITORIAL COMMENT: *Dating*: this letter is in D's handwriting, and is by him, although it is ostensibly an answer to Mrs Blackwood's note to Isaac which had been enclosed with her letter to D (NIPR D 1071F/A4/2C). Presumably it was sent together with **244**, and is assigned to the same date.

Mr. Disraeli Senior[1] to
"Helen, or Nelly",
greeting –

My dear Madam,

Your note is very flattering. My son I know has a vast number of odd acquaintances. He has been in a series of scrapes ever since he was fourteen, but he has just promised me to reform.

Your | grandpapa[2] was certainly "a very amusing old gentleman", and I had the honor of his acquaintance, but my familiar was your father,[3] whose gaiety, which like a fountain, was at the same time sparkling and ceaseless, I have not forgotten. |

4 The daughter of the Caliph, who marries Alroy.

5 The king of Karasmé who defeats Alroy in battle and then beheads him. The book ends: '"By my beard," exclaimed the enraged Arslan, "I am answered. Let Eblis save thee, if he can;" and the King of Karasmé, the most famous master of the sabre in Asia, drew his blade like lightning from its sheath, and carried off the head of Alroy at a stroke. It fell, and as it fell, a smile of triumphant derision seemed to play upon the dying features of the hero, and to ask of his enemies, "Where now were all their tortures?"' *Alroy* III 105-6.

---

1 Mrs Blackwood's enclosure, nominally to Isaac, to which this letter was the putative reply, read:

To Mr Disraeli [*sic*] Senior – greeting.

Dear Sir!

I wish I had the pleasure of your acquaintance – I should take such pains to please you that I am sure you would like me. I am what Doctor Johnson would call a "compendious epitome" of all the virtues, – in one vol. very neatly bound, and very *rare*, – there being but one copy extant. Sir! – I wish you joy of your son, – he is a *very* "rising young man" – mais il ment – comme dix – you should have taught him better! Have you read any of his works? I dare say not! Vivian Grey is something like himself. – Good bye, My dear Sir, – I am Mrs Carwell's daughter, and my Grandpapa was an amusing old gentleman, who had the honour of knowing you – I believe.

Your obedt. humble Servant
Helen
called by her friends and familiars
Nelly.

2 Richard Brinsley Sheridan, the famous dramatist and statesman.

3 Thomas Sheridan, colonial treasurer at the Cape of Good Hope.

Once we were to have written a book together upon Pugilism – I was to have supplied the history of ancient boxing, and he was to have been the historiographer of Gully and the Game Chicken,[4] for which duty, I will do him the justice to observe, he was well qualified. | But this plan came to nothing, altho' I have some very lively letters of his at Bradenham upon the subject.

If ever I have the pleasure of meeting you, which is not probable, as I have become of late years quite an Eremite, I will tell you many an amusing anecdote of your father, for whom I entertained a sincere regard.

I.D.

TO CAROLINE HENRIETTA SHERIDAN [London], Thursday [7 March? 1833] **246**

ORIGINAL: NIPR D1071B/E3/9A:18
EDITORIAL COMMENT: Transcribed from typed copy. *Dating*: by comparison with **244** earlier the same day, and with **247** two days later. *Sic*: Dears.

Thursday night

Dears Mrs Sheridan,

Mrs Blackwood flew away as usual like a capricious bird of Paradise, otherwise I had intended to have tied under her wing a note to my most valued correspondent.

Dear Mrs Sheridan, I hope you have quite recovered from your indisposition, which I heard of with great sorrow.

Everybody says that Oonagh is the most charming heroine of Romance, and I am sure that the Editor of the Quarterly Review,[1] if he have not lost his love for the excellent and fair, will in a few days agree with the world.

Your faithful

D

TO [CAROLINE HENRIETTA SHERIDAN] [London, Saturday 9 March? 1833] **247**

ORIGINAL: NIPR D1071B/E3/9A:20
EDITORIAL COMMENT: Transcribed from typed copy. *Dating*: by context. *The Athenaeum* appeared 9 March.

My dear Madam,

I picked up the accompanying journal,[1] which I send to you because it contains

4 John Gully (1783-1863), prize-fighter. In 1805 he fought the then English champion, Henry Pearce, known as the 'Game Chicken', but lost. When Pearce retired, Gully became the champion by defeating Bob Gregson in 1808. He then retired from pugilism, made a fortune from horse-racing, became an MP, representing Pontefract as a Reformer 1832-7, and finally was the owner of a colliery.

1 John Gibson Lockhart. *Aims and Ends* and *Oonagh Lynch* were reviewed in *The Quarterly Review* XLIX (Apr 1833) 228-47.

1 *The Athenaeum* no 280 (9 Mar 1833) reviewed Mrs Sheridan's *Aims and Ends* and *Oonagh Lynch* (147-8) and D's *Alroy* (150-1). It also printed a letter from Isaac D'Israeli.

reviews of both our works. I cannot say much for our critics, though I have no cause to complain, who am prepared for universal reprobation. Everywhere I hear praises of "Oonagh Lynch".

I am sure that the presence of Mrs Blackwood must have already charmed away your indisposition. Her flight from Storey's Gate to Hampton Palace[2] is the most disastrous event since the Hegira.

Your faithful,

Disraeli.

---

248 TO THE ELECTORS OF THE BOROUGH OF MARYLEBONE [London] [Saturday] 9 March [1833]

ORIGINAL: PS Times 12

PUBLICATION HISTORY: *The Times* (11 Mar 1833)

EDITORIAL COMMENT: The issue of *The Times* in which this appeared carried similar paid advertisements addressed to the Marylebone electors by: Samuel B. Whalley, Gilbert Ainslie Young, James Johnston, Henry Gahagan and 'A Brother Elector'. *Place of Origin*: although the text bears Bradenham as its nominal address, doubtless to impress prospective supporters, D was in London on this day, as he makes clear in **251**.

Bradenham-house, Bucks, March 9

To the ELECTORS of the BOROUGH of MARYLEBONE.

Gentlemen,

I am emboldened by a requisition, signed by a considerable number of your constituency, to offer myself as a REPRESENTATIVE of your important district in Parliament.[1] In so doing, I come forward with no other object but that of representing your interests in the spirit of integrity and truth. I come forward with the hope of assisting in that great system of amelioration which all honest men must desire, but I never can believe that that system can really be advanced by supporting a body of men who, after having obtained power by the pretence of advancing the principles of liberty, have pleged themselves to a violation of the Constitution.

I have the honour to be, Gentlemen,

Your obedient servant,

BENJAMIN DISRAELI

---

249 TO [HELEN SELINA BLACKWOOD] [London], Sunday [10 March 1833]

ORIGINAL: NIPR D1071B/E3/9B:17

EDITORIAL COMMENT: There is no salutation. The repository cites 'Caroline H. Sheridan' as the recipient; it is, however, clearly a letter to Helen Selina Blackwood, and in answer to her letter of Friday [8 March? 1833]. See also **246**.

---

2 After the death in 1817 of her husband, Thomas Sheridan, at the Cape of Good Hope, Mrs Sheridan had been given a grace-and-favour apartment at Hampton Court Palace by the Prince Regent.

1 Marylebone, a two-member constituency, was then held by Edward Berkeley Portman and Sir William Horne, both Whigs. On the resignation of Portman a by-election was called for 20 March.

Sunday

You are irresistible – I have often told you so: you cannot complain that you are resisted. At least it appears to me, that I am docile and devoted enough, altho' you sometimes indeed call me despotic.

As I never diplomatise, I confess that it was with rapture last night, long | past the witching hour, that I again recognised the handwriting of my inspiring Sylph. Before I went out I had despatched a newspaper to the Palace – I believe only that I might have the happiness of writing about you, if not to you.

I have not yet recovered | the fatal shock of your sudden departure. I called at Storeys Gate on Thursday to show Caroline, that my visits were not paid merely to you, but as she was not aware that I knew of your absence, and of course I did not tell | her that I did, the visit, as far as that object was concerned, was a failure however agreeable in other respects, and I have not ventured to repeat it, altho' my faithful steed, like the reindeer, will track his way down the wastes of | Parliament Street.

As for Oonagh,[1] the truth is, one has leisure to find fault only in Nubia, and I have despatched the dear heroine to my dearer little sister, to whom I ever send anything, that I think very good indeed. There were no notes, except one | at the end, a ! of Patagonian size.

I value your *cadeau* infinitely beyond my chibouque, that was given me by the Pacha of Acre,[2] and which some day you shall see. It is nearly twelve feet long and | the amber mouthpiece is really a magnificent glare of amber and enamel.

Farewell brightest of bright creations! If you are indeed "the most amiable of human beings," remember that it is in your power, with very little exertion, | mainly to contribute to the felicity of one of your fellow creatures. For indeed as, without any affectation, your presence is the charm of my existence, so the only consolation for not beholding you is sometimes to be reminded that I am not forgotten.

D

TO THE ELECTORS OF THE BOROUGH OF MARYLEBONE [35] Duke Street, St. James's, [London], Tuesday 12 March [1833] 250

ORIGINAL: PS Times 13
PUBLICATION HISTORY: *The Times* (13 Mar 1833)

---

1 The heroine of *Oonagh Lynch.*

2 D did not visit Acre in 1831, but Ibrahim Pasha took the city on 27 May 1832. D gives an account of his meeting in Cairo with Ibrahim Pasha in 'An Interview with a Great Turk, from the Book of a Recent Traveller, by the Author of Vivian Grey'. *CM* IV (Jan 1834) 11-12.

In her letter of 8 March Mrs Blackwood had said: 'I send you my amber-mouthed chibouque, or my idea of one; – you may smoke it or keep diamond pins and tooth-picks in it, as it seemeth good in your eyes; I certainly *am* the most amiable of human beings! – ' NIPR D107/F/A4/2D.

14 Mar 1833

Duke-street, St. James's, March 12.

To the ELECTORS of the BOROUGH of MARYLEBONE.

Gentlemen,

When I consented, in deference to the wishes of a considerable portion of your constituency, to become a candidate for the honour of representing you in Parliament, I did so because I was willing to become the humble instrument of opposing the conspiracy to convert your important district into a nomination borough of the present arbitrary Administration. Believing that a result so important to the liberties and good government of this empire as the defeat of the ministerial nominee can only be secured by concentrating as much as possible the elements of opposition, I retire from the impending contest;[1] but I retire with a deep sense of gratitude for the numerous promises of support which you have already made to

Your obliged and faithful servant,

BENJ. DISRAELI.

---

251 TO SARAH DISRAELI

[London], Thursday 14 March [1833]

ORIGINAL: H A/I/B/48

COVER: Miss Disraeli | *Bradenham*

EDITORIAL COMMENT: The last sentence of the text appears on the cover above the name and address of the recipient. *Sic*: Montague.

Thursday. 14th. Mar.

My dearest,

Tell my father that the accompanying arrived last night.

Ralph has written you about Marylebone,[1] which was a shy that might have succeeded.

I dined last Saturday at Lady Stepneys and met Lady Charlotte Bury, and Mrs. Bertie Matthews[2] – on Sunday at Montague Gores.

I am writing a very odd book in one vol.[3] which will be out in May I expect.

T[out] a V[ous]

1 By 12 March there were already four other candidates, three supporters of the government – Sir Samuel Whalley (moderate Radical), Charles A. Murray (Whig) and Thomas Murphy (extreme Radical) – and one Tory, Henry Thomas Hope. The Whigs and Radicals were reported to be aligning themselves behind Whalley as a means of keeping out Hope. D therefore retired to avoid splitting the anti-Whig vote. *The Morning Post* three days later commended D for his unselfish action. See **255**n1. At the election held 18-19 March the results were: Whalley 2,869, Hope 2,055, Murray 791, Murphy 172.

---

1 See **250**.

2 She was the widow (née Naylor) of Brownlow Bertie Matthews. Mrs Bertie Matthews appeared frequently at Court with her four daughters and *The Court Journal* reflected its confusion by ignoring the compound surname.

3 "*What is He*?" published in April 1833 by James Ridgway.

I found the MS. of the Dedication[4] which I enclose. I have reason to believe that the success of Alroy is most decided. |

The shoes are not finished – perhaps tomorrow.

TO MACVEY NAPIER [London], [Friday] 15 March 1833 252

ORIGINAL: BL ADD MS 34616 ff53-4

COVER: [In Gore's hand]: London March fifteen 1833 | [In D's hand]: Macvey Napier | Edinburgh | [In Gore's hand]: M.Gore

POSTMARK: (1) Double circle surmounted by crown: FREE | 15 MR 15 | 1833 (2) In circle: MR | C17A | 1833

EDITORIAL COMMENT: The cover is franked by Montagu Gore, MP for Devizes. In another hand on the flap of the cover: 'B. Disraeli | March 14th | 1833 | Review'.

Mar. 15 | 33

Dear Sir,

I am afraid you will consider me a very troublesome person – but since I received your last letter,[1] I have received an invitation to stand | for Marylebone, and although for various reasons I shall not persevere in the contest, still the affair has taken up so much of my time, and still threatens | to be so engrossing for some days, that I think it wisest to renounce at once the hope I entertained of becoming a contributor to your | classic journal. But I renounce it only for a season, and perhaps, next time, I may solicit yr. attention to a more important subject.

Assure yourself,
dear Sir,
of my great consider[ation] and my sense of your courtesy in this affair.
Benj. Disraeli

4 The MS of D's dedication of *Alroy* to Sarah reads:

To
** ********

> Sweet Sister! as I wandered on the mountains of Sion, behold! a gazelle came bounding o'er the hills! It perceived me, it started back, it gazed at me with trembling surprise. Ah! fear not! fair creature, I fondly exclaimed, fear not, and flee not away! I too have a gazelle in a distant land; not less beautiful in her airy form than thine, and her dark eye not less tremulously bright!
>
> Ah! little did I deem, my sweetest friend, that ere I pressed that beauteous form again, Sorrow sho[ul]d dim the radiance of thy smile, and charge that brilliant eye with many a tear! Yet trust thee, dearest, in a brother's love, | the purest sympathy of our fallen state! If I recall one gleam of rapture to thy pensive cheek, not in vain I strike my lonely lyre, or throw these laurels at thy fairy feet! [H E/I/III, and *Alroy* (1833) v-vi]

D had sent Sarah a pre-publication copy of *Alroy* without having previously mentioned the Dedication. She was overcome, and replied on 28 February:

> My darling brother what can I say for all the beautiful expressions of love you have poured out to me. I who am nothing, so utterly unworthy of belonging to you. Yet I am indeed proud of your love and tenderness, for which all mine is but a poor return – but they are all I have to give. I had grown so impatient for Alroy that | had he not appeared last night I am sure I should have gone quite mad, and then to come with such an introduction how kind you are, how much too good. H A/I/B/457.

---

1 D had not replied to Napier's letter of 27 February (see **239**), and Napier had written again on 6 March, asking if D wished to go on with the matter. H B/XXI/N/14. D never did write for *The Edinburgh Review*.

253 TO SARA AUSTEN [London], Saturday [16? March 1833]

ORIGINAL: BL ADD MS 45908 ff68-9

COVER: wait | Mrs. Austen | 33 Guildford Street | Russell Sq | B Disraeli

PUBLICATION HISTORY: Layard 28, undated extract

EDITORIAL COMMENT: *Dating*: by reference to Mrs Austen's letter, 9 March 1833, H A/IV/D/27. *Sic*: yrs., Scirok, Simoone.

Saturday

My dear friend,

I have been in such a bustle, that I co[ul]d not answer yrs. charming letter until yesterday, and then did not venture to write to Brighton,[1] anticipating your previous return. It is delightful to be understood and appreciated. I have received a great many | letters, but none are to be placed with yours except one from Beckford in which you will rejoice.[2]

As far as I can infer in so early a stage of his career, Alroy is pre-eminently successful.

I am anxious to hear about Austen. It has been a trying week | for him, and not only for him. I have myself nearly sunk under the fatal blast, worse than the Scirok or Simoone.[3]

Let me have a line, and believe me

Ever thine

D

254 TO GEORGE HENRY DASHWOOD 35 Duke Street, St James's, [London], Monday [18] March 1833

ORIGINAL: H B/I/A/39/1

PUBLICATION HISTORY: *The Bucks Herald* no 64 (23 Mar 1833). A note is printed *below* the letter heading: 'The following correspondence has been forwarded to us, as having passed between these two Gentlemen.'

EDITORIAL COMMENT: The texts for the D-Dashwood correspondence come, not from MSS, but from *The Bucks Herald*. The Hughenden number refers to a newspaper clipping preserved in the collection. The letter is dated 13 March (a Wednesday); this is presumably a misprint for 18.

The newspaper heading is: B. DISRAELI, Esq., and G. DASHWOOD, Esq. M.P.

1 The Austens were at Brighton in the early part of March 1833. Jerman 176, 180.

2 Before receiving his copy of *Alroy*, Beckford had praised *Contarini Fleming* in a letter of 5 March 1833, saying: 'If readers capable of appreciating works of genius are rare, Authors to whom the "pomp and prodigality of Heaven" have been imparted are rarer especially in the days of mud and tinsel upon which we are fallen.' H E/VI/M/4.

In a letter to his friend George Clarke, written on 14 March, Beckford bestowed the same high praise on *Alroy*: 'I have slowly and reluctantly finished the truly wondrous tale of Alroy, which I wish had been extended to 20 volumes. I did not hurry on, fearful of expending the treasure too fast, for a treasure I consider it to be, and of the richest kind ... What appears to be *hauteur* and extreme conceit in Disraeli is consciousness, uncontrolable [*sic*] *consciousness* of superior power.' H E/VI/M/5.

3 On the same day Sara Austen wrote to D describing the weather at Brighton, some of which presumably reached London: 'The sea air always disorganizes me and between the Salt, the Blast and the Frost I am pretty nearly in a state of crystallization.' H A/IV/D/28.

D had a life-long fear of the east wind and of its effects on his spirits. See **255**. In this attitude he was following a well-established tradition. Voltaire, for example, held the east wind in London responsible for many of the suicides there. E. Aubert de la Rue *Man and the Winds* trans Madge E. Thompson (1955) 71.

35, *Duke-street, St. James's, March* 13, 1833. | *Monday, One o'Clock, p.m.* **254** | 341
Sir,[1] 18 Mar 1833

A copy of the County paper, has this morning been forwarded to me, in which I find a report[2] of a dinner given to yourself and Mr. Smith[3] at Wycombe, wherein Mr. Dashwood is represented as observing that 'no degradation in his opinion, was more contemptible than political prostitution of character, when there is a marked absence of all integrity of purpose and consistency of conduct – a character which party disowns though factions support; when self aggrandisement is the object sought, and a seat in Parliament the mode of pursuing it – when the capability for swallowing pledges exceeds even the cormorant in appetite, and the performance of them (if it were possible) would exemplify the veriest harlequinade ever exhibited on any stage – secure him, perhaps, a seat in Parliament, by the sacrifice of character, principle, and a deluded constituency – a reformer, if such a one there were, he admitted

'Him, thus exalted, as a wit I own,
And hail him the first fiddler of the Town.'

but, in the language of the poet he said, 'Let no such man be trusted.'

If in this passage you only indulged in an imaginary political portrait for the purpose of illustrating an abstract moral opinion, – devoid of any personal allusion, you will regret to be informed, that, through the indiscretion of your friends, it has been supposed that in this passage you referred to your present correspondent – I am therefore under the necessity of requesting from you an explanation upon this point.[4]

I have the honor, etc.,
BENJAMIN DISRAELI.

1 George Henry Dashwood (1790-1862), Whig MP for Buckinghamshire 1832-5, and for Wycombe 1837-62.

2 The report – consisting of an extensive description of the dinner held on 4 February – appeared in *The Bucks Gazette* no 1,074 (23 Feb 1833).

3 Robert John Smith, son of Lord Carrington and Whig MP for Wycombe 1831-8.

4 Dashwood replied with the following letter:

Sir, – If you have *red* [*sic*] through the speech alluded to you must have observed my expression of congratulations to my friends in our having steered clear of all electioneering personalities both on their parts as well as my own. When, therefore, I depicted a character of political profligacy, you must perceive the inconsistency I should have been guilty of, had I made an individual application of it. I only got your note this morning on my return from the House, which will account for any delay in my answer.

I have the honor, etc,
G.H. DASHWOOD.

42, *Park-street, Grosvenor-square, March,* 19, 1833. *BH* no 64 (23 Mar 1833).

255 TO [HELEN SELINA BLACKWOOD] [London], Monday [18? March 1833]

ORIGINAL: NIPR D1071B/E3/9B:23

EDITORIAL COMMENT: There is no superscription or subscription. *Dating*: by comparison with Mrs Blackwood's letter to D of 16 March, from Hampton Court, in which she asks, 'What have you been doing to that poor borough of Stafford?'

Monday

Your blessed handwriting fell like an Iris on the dark cloud of life, but I yield you a gloomy tribute for such a brilliant gift. I am overwhelmed with a deep, a terrific, and an invincible melancholy (I see, as usual, you laugh | – some day or other, you will find that all this is not affectation) – your continued absence, the conviction that if even in town, I could only, by wretched fits and starts, enjoy your inspiring presence, fill me with uncontrollable sadness. I feel that the only and the last chance of felicity | is for ever lost. Enough of this, as I cannot bear being ridiculed.

I suppose by the *Stafford* Election, you mean the *Marylebone*. I should have been supported by a very strong party had I stood, but the prevalence of the Easterly wind and a poetical fit, | damped my ambition, and I would not go to the Poll without a certainty. The Tories consider that I have given them a turn by resigning, and the Morning Post indulged in a "leader" of great length on the certainty of Mr Hope's return on account of Mr Disraeli's manful resignation, | and the "respectability" of Mr Disraeli's party etc. etc. who were also very "*sagacious*" and Heaven knows what besides.[1]

London has been very dull this last week, at least I think so. I dined once with your friend Namik Pacha[2] and talked to him about you and Caroline,[3] whom I told him were the most | beautiful women in England, and that I had written a poem about you in which I compared one to Night, and the other to Day, which he said was quite Persian. I sent a copy of *C[ontarini] F[leming]* to the Sultan,[4] and Namik promised that the Chapter about his H[ighne]ss sho[ul]d be | translated in full divan.[5] He will send me of course the crescent in brilliants, but Namik suspected me of being an Egyptian, and was perhaps right.

Alroy I am told is a great hit – and sells better than anything I have published since *V[ivian] G[rey]*. | I find it on the whole well received by the critics, which in my opinion is greatly against it. Howr. I care little for the commendation or the censure of the despicable. Clarke in Mount St.[6] has shown me, and has allowed

1 *The Morning Post* discussed the Marylebone by-election in four successive issues, 13-16 March 1833. The leader mentioned here was not of great length, but it did comment on D's having 'manfully' sought the good of the constituency. It also noted the 'respectable' and 'independent' quality of his supporters. *MP* no 19,428 (15 Mar 1833).

Henry Thomas Hope (1808-1862) was also a candidate in the Marylebone by-election. He was later Tory MP for Gloucester 1833-41.

2 Then Turkish ambassador. Appointed at the age of twenty-eight, he presented his credentials in late December 1832. Greville II 338. He left England in late April 1835. *The Times* (30 Apr 1835).

3 Caroline Norton.

4 Mahmud II.

5 The Ottoman Council of State.

6 George Clarke (d 1835), bookseller, 11 Mount Street, Berkeley Square, long-time confidant of Beckford.

me to make a copy of a series of letters on | Alroy from Caliph Vathek[7] *himself* which ought to satisfy or rather to satiate any love of fame. I have shown them to no one, but shall of course to you, if indeed I ever have the opportunity.

I need not say that I am anxious to hear that you are much better and that | Mrs. Sheridan is convalescent.

I am afraid, nay I am sure I have written you a very stupid letter. Pardon me, pity me.

Your devoted –

TO GEORGE HENRY DASHWOOD 35 Duke Street, St James's, [London], Tuesday 19 March 1833 **256**

ORIGINAL: H B/I/A/39/3
PUBLICATION HISTORY: *The Bucks Herald* no 64 (23 Mar 1833)
EDITORIAL COMMENT: Newspaper heading: 'B. DISRAELI Esq., to G. H. DASHWOOD, Esq.'

35, *Duke-street, St. James's, March* 19, 1833. | *Tuesday,* 11 *o'Clock, a.m.*

Sir,

I regret extremely the provisional style in which your answer to my letter[1] is (I am sure unintentionally) couched, and that the only security against my being insulted, is the impossibility of your being inconsistent. Nevertheless, as I deprecate above all things a lengthened correspondence, I willingly infer from your note that you did not allude to me in the passage in question either directly or indirectly, and with this inference, it is of course unnecessary for me to characterise the passage in question as unjust, unfounded, and impertinent.

I have the honor, etc.,

BENJAMIN DISRAELI.

TO SARAH DISRAELI [London, Tuesday 26 March 1833] **257**

ORIGINAL: PS 3
PUBLICATION HISTORY: LBCS 18, dated 26 March 1833; Maggs catalogue 230 (1907) item 48
EDITORIAL COMMENT: The material from the Maggs catalogue is enclosed within square brackets. When Maggs and LBCS texts overlap, the Maggs version has been used.

[March 26, 1833.

I received the proofs yesterday morning, and despatched them to Moxon within a couple of hours. The ending is good and altogether it is a work of rare and remarkable merit, and I should not be surprised that it made a sensation....

....Of Alroy I hear hourly golden opinions, and I doubt not its success will be

7 William Beckford. In one of his letters to Clarke, Beckford regretted the quality of D's French but proclaimed his English 'the loveliest and most superior I ever met with'. Beckford also mentioned some 'short and rapid reflections' upon D's writings which he invited Clarke to show to the author. Melville 337. See also **253**n2.

1 See **254**&n4.

brilliant. I send you the review in the Atlas.[1] There was also one in the Town[2] still more Eulogistic,] I hear no complaints of its style, except from the critics. The common readers seem to like the poetry and the excitement. Mrs. Jameson[3] told Otley that 'reading it was like riding an Arab'. Slade, the traveller,[4] said 'it was the most thoroughly Oriental book he had ever read.'

[D]

258

TO SARAH DISRAELI Albion Club, [London], Thursday [28 March 1833]

ORIGINAL: H A/I/B/50

COVER: Miss Disraeli | Bradenham House | High Wycombe | Bucks

POSTMARK: (1) In circle: A | MR28 | 1833

EDITORIAL COMMENT: *Sic*: Buckes, Frazer.

Albion | Thursday

My dearest,

The Merediths I think there is no doubt will not come, but nevertheless I think it better that you should ask them, which I wo[ul]d do at once.

I don't know when I shall come, i.e. what day. I told Munro to day that we had better go on Thursday, wh[e]r[e]upon | he stared and said that he thought it wanted yet two months to Easter, did not know whether he co[ul]d leave town now, howr. I left him making arrangements which I have little doubt will permit him – a stupid party at the Buckes on Tuesday is all of which I have to speak. I shall call at Moxon's and | see after the book.[1] This fine day puts everyone in good humor, otherwise there have been grievous complaints.

I suspect I shall be the hero of Frazer.[2] I am proof against anything. I suppose all are well. As far as I can judge, you have ruined my mare, and broken Violets knees.[3] Instead of the cab, I think it will be expedient to bring down a

1 The review was not as eulogistic as Sarah might have been led to expect. It remarked: 'The wondrous tale of *Alroy* is the most splendid specimen, perhaps, in the English language, of great abilities lavished and wasted in search of a chimera.' *The Atlas* no 8 (24 Mar 1833). Sarah, however, apparently found nothing objectionable. On the next day she replied: 'Thanks for the Atlas, and for all the delightful things you tell us of Alroy.' H A/I/B/458.

2 A weekly edited by Samuel Carter Hall, *The Town* appeared between 1832 and 1834. (Nicholson's later gossip-sheet of the same title was unrelated to Hall's respectable publication.) *Alroy* was first described as 'prodigiously fine' – a judgement endorsed by a long review two weeks later. *The Town* no 63 (10 Mar 1833) 75; no 65 (24 Mar 1833) 91.

3 Anna Brownell Jameson (1794-1860), author, best known for her *Shakespeare's Heroines* (1832).

4 Adolphus Slade (1804-1877), author of *Records of Travels in Turkey, Greece, etc* ... (1833). He was knighted in 1858.

---

1 *The Genius of Judaism.*

2 D was soon to appear in the 'Gallery of Literary Characters' and was described as follows: 'The plain fact then is, that Ben D'Israeli is a clever fellow, who has written some striking books, in which we think he has shown great indications of talent, but nothing more ... Benjamin's politics are rather preposterous; but he is young and may improve. There is one good thing about him, viz., that he can never be a Whig; and while that can be said of any man, there is hope for him. Only, we beseech our friend not to write any more of that sounding Fustian which infests the wonderous tale of "Alroy".' *Fraser's Magazine* VII (May 1833) 602.

3 Sarah often lamented to D the successive ailments which beset the horses at Bradenham, and detailed the treatments undertaken to cure them.

couple of | riding horses. The postman is ringing the knell of this letter.

ever thine,

BD

259

TO SARAH DISRAELI [London, March 1833?]

ORIGINAL: PS 40

PUBLICATION HISTORY: Clarence I. Freed 'A New Sheaf of Disraeli Letters' *The American Hebrew* CXX (15 Apr 1927) 834; Anderson Galleries, catalogue 2099 (1926) item 17

EDITORIAL COMMENT: See **238**ec. *Dating*: conjectural, and based on the fact that D dined most frequently with Lady Stepney during the London season of 1833. Freed described it as 'undated' and 'in all probability' belonging 'to the year 1833'. The Anderson catalogue quotes a longer passage from this letter and the additional material from this source has been interpolated, inside square brackets, in Freed's text.

I dined yesterday at Lady Stepney's; a very agreeable little party [... old Lady Charlotte Lindsay (Lord North's daughter),[1] the Duke of St. Albans, Lady Fitzroy Somerset, Bulwer and myself. And] afterwards a soirée whereat H.R.H. of Cambridge[2] attended; a most noisy, rattling, swearing Prince, who rushed into the room, and as he forgot to sit down, we were all obliged to stand for some time, until Lady Stepney forced him into a chair.

[D]

260

TO SARAH DISRAELI 40 Brook Street, [London], Thursday [4 April 1833]

ORIGINAL: H A/I/B/51

COVER: Miss Disraeli | Bradenham House | High Wycombe | Bucks.

POSTMARK: (1) In Maltese cross: V.S | VAP 4S | 1833.

40 Brook Street | Thursday.

My dearest,

Do not suppose that I have changed my lodgings, because I am writing this at the Ottleys.[1] I have delayed writing to you these several days because I have wished to write you a long letter, but that has been and is impossible, because I am sitting for my portrait which entirely engrosses my morning.

I have an immense deal to *tell* you, but it must be | *told*; Remember I begin with last Saturday. I have been out every day and really have lived in a blaze of society. I have had invit[ati]ons from Genl Phipps,[2] Lady Charleville,[3] Lady

1 Lady Charlotte Lindsay (d 1849), third daughter of the 2nd Earl of Guilford (better known as Lord North, George III's prime minister between 1770 and 1781). She married in 1800 Lt Col John Lindsay (d 1826).

2 Adolphus Frederick, 1st Duke of Cambridge (1774-1850), the seventh son of George III.

---

1 William Young Ottley (1771-1836), amateur artist and writer on art, was then painting D's portrait. At this time Ottley was keeper of prints in the British Museum. However, he was listed as living at 31 Devonshire Street, Portland Place, and Mrs Ottley was described as the occupant of 40 Brook Street, Grosvenor Square. Robson's *Guide* (1833).

2 Gen Edmund Phipps.

3 Catherine Maria Bury (1761?-1851), widow of James Tisdall, who had married in 1798 Charles William Bury (1764-1835), 1st Earl of Charleville.

Floyd[4] etc. In short I have a great deal to say.

On Sunday, in case it do not pour cats and dogs, I and Munro will appear.

BD |

Why Moxon sent the trash called the Critic I know not. I believe it is already defunct.[5]

---

261 TO SARAH DISRAELI [London], Saturday [6 April 1833]

ORIGINAL: H A/I/B/52

COVER: Miss Disraeli | Bradenham House | High Wycombe | *Bucks.*

POSTMARK: (1) In circle: X | AP-6 | 1833

PUBLICATION HISTORY: LBCS 18-19, dated 8 April 1833, prints a version of the first two sentences, with extracts from **262**, and the following paragraph, the original of which has not been located: 'I have heard nothing more from [Dashwood?], who appears to have pocketed more than I should like to do. It was impossible to pass over attacks from such a quarter in silence. The only way to secure future ease is to take up a proper position early in life, and, show that you will not be insulted with impunity.' M&B I 224 follows the LBCS conflation.

EDITORIAL COMMENT: *Sic*: expences, Glocester.

Saturday –

My dearest,

I have this morning agreed to stand for Marylebone,[1] with every prospect of success. I shall not go to the poll unless I am certain, or very confident: there is even a chance of my not being opposed. All this wonderful work has happened within a few hours. It will delay our visit, which howr we | shall pay. Munro is not very sorry, as he co[ul]d only have remained 2 or 3 days at present.

If I go to the poll (and I repeat I shall not go unless I feel very certain) I can *guarantee* my expences to a very trifling amount. If I do not go to the Poll, I need not spend fifty pounds.

Rumor is flying that Hope stands for Glocester[2] with a good chance: Murray[3] has none here: I have been closeted the whole | morning with the leader of the

4 Either Anna Floyd (d 1844), widow of Gen Sir John Floyd, 1st Baronet, or her daughter-in-law Mary Floyd (d 1879), who had married in 1821 Lt Col Sir Henry Floyd, 2nd Baronet.

5 *The Critic, A New, Liberal, Impartial and Independent Literary Journal* had but two issues. It strongly dissented from the praise given to *Alroy* in *The New Monthly Magazine*. *The Critic* no 1 (1 Mar 1833) 10.

---

1 The Radical MP for Marylebone between 1833 and 1838 was Sir Samuel Whalley (1800-1883). A petition from a number of electors, complaining that he had not been duly elected in the by-election of 18-19 March 1833, was presented in the House on 2 April. For fifteen days there was a flurry of electioneering. With Hope no longer a competitor D decided to try again. See **263**. However, on 17 April the House voted to discharge the order to consider the petition, and Whalley's occupation of the seat was not again challenged. *The Mirror of Parliament* (1833) II part i 1161, 1266.

2 Rumours of Hope's intention to contest Gloucester first appeared in *The Times* of this day. He won the seat. *The Times* (6 Apr 1833).

3 Charles Augustus Murray (1806-1895), the defeated Whig candidate for Marylebone, was the second son of the 5th Earl of Dunmore. He became master of the Household to Queen Victoria, and later held a series of diplomatic posts.

Whalley party.[4] I profess moderate radical principles in contradistinction to the Murphyites.[5] I profess only what I announced at Wycombe.

Circumstances have occurred which render it not impossible, that the Whigs will not oppose me.

I will endeavour to write every day.

Your devoted

Brother. T.O |

I expect a letter at Bradenham. Pray forward *instantly*, any that may arrive.

262

TO SARAH DISRAELI [London], Monday [8 April 1833]

ORIGINAL: H A/I/B/54

COVER: Miss Disraeli | Bradenham House | High Wycombe | Bucks.

POSTMARK: (1) In circle: A | AP-8 | 1833

PUBLICATION HISTORY: LBCS 18-19, dated 8 April 1833, prints the postscript between extracts from **261** and the paragraph transcribed in **261**ph; M&B I 224, dated 8 April 1833, reprints part of this conflation.

EDITORIAL COMMENT: The second sheet of the MS is torn.

1/2 past 5 | Monday ~~Saturday~~

My dear,

I sent the parcel enclosing a letter to you this morning. I write again to say that the Steward of the Albion co[ul]d find us a cook,[1] but you have given me no details. As to | wages, and the assistance she has, and what to do – I said I believe dairy. Write up by return on all these points and others you deem necessary, and I will communicate to him, and if anybody occur, | send her to Mrs. Trevor[2] or whom you like for X[cross]examination.

BD

In the Town of yesterday[3] as, I am tol[*d*] "Some one asked Disraeli, in offering himself for Marylebone, on what he intended *to stand* – "On my head" was the reply."

4 It appears from this comment that D was not only assuming that Whalley would be unseated on petition, but that it would be possible to persuade Whalley's adherents to adopt him as their candidate instead. If they did indeed spend a morning hearing D defend his qualifications as a radical, the possibility must have existed.

Their leader may have been a Mr Hibbell, who was described as having made a vigorous appeal to the electors on 18 March, half-way through the polling, in support of Whalley. *The Times* (19 Mar 1833).

5 Named for Thomas Murphy. He twice contested Marylebone together with Sir Samuel Whalley. Murphy was unsuccessful on each occasion. D had a habit of creating ideological labels out of proper names; others appear not to have referred to Irish Radicals in this way.

---

1 In a note added to a letter from Sarah of 7 April Isaac wrote: 'There's one thing which is perfectly ludicrous, but which you will be really concerned in when you bring your friend down here. That's a good Cook. Adams has sunk into childishness – we of course after writing to several advertisements get no answers. The great difficulty is to get one who will *live in the Country*. Perhaps some stray personage might inform you of one – the Waiter who keeps the new Hotel.' H A/I/B/467. The Albion was in Cockspur Street. See **278**.

2 Olivia Trevor, née Lindo, wife of Charles Trevor.

3 *The Town* no 67 (7 Apr 1833) 109.

263 TO THE INDEPENDENT ELECTORS OF THE BOROUGH OF MARYLEBONE [London], [Tuesday] 9 April 1833

ORIGINAL: FE EJM 2

PUBLICATION HISTORY: *The Times* (10 Apr 1833)

EDITORIAL COMMENT: Despite the nominal Bradenham address, D did not leave London in this period. The pages of the MS are numbered in D's hand. *Sic*: burtherns.

Bradenham House – Bucks | Apl. 9th. 1833

To the Independent Electors
of the Borough of Marylebone

Gentlemen,

A speedy vacancy being generally anticipated in the representation of your Borough, I have the honor to announce my determination to solicit your suffrages on the first occasion that offers.

Although supported by neither of the aristocratic parties, I appeal to you with confidence as an independent member of society, who has no interest, direct or indirect, in corruption or misgovernment, as one of a family untainted by the receipt of public money, and which can prefer no claims to | public consideration but those that are founded on public sympathy.

I claim your support as a man who has already fought the battle of the people, and as one who believes that the only foundation on which a beneficent and vigorous government in this country can now be raised is an unlimited confidence in the genius of the British nation.

With this conviction, I am desirous of completing the machinery of the constitution by two measures which will invest the people with a power which was once their birthright, and | with a security which I hope their children will inherit. These measures are Triennial Parliaments, and Election by Ballot, and unless these measures be conceded, I cannot comprehend how the conduct of the government can ever be in harmony with the feelings of the people.

Because I am of opinion that those who are invested with power should be qualified for its exercise, I wo[ul]d support the abrogation of those stamp duties which eventually act as Taxes upon Knowledge.

Believing that unless the | public burtherns are speedily and materially reduced, a civil convulsion must occur, I am desirous of seeing a Parliamentary committee appointed to revise the entire system of our Taxation, with the object of relieving Industry from those encumbrances, which Property is more capacitated to endure – and I especially pledge myself to exert all my energy to obtain the repeal of the assessed taxes, a repeal which, from the state of the constituency of your Borough, is as necessary as a measure of constitutional privilege, | as of financial relief.

Opportunities will soon occur for me to express to you my opinions upon all those subjects which engage the attention of a man who aspires to be a representative of the people. It is sufficient for me now to observe that I shall ever be found a supporter of that system which consults the great interests of general happiness, and that I shall promote every measure which elevates the moral or improves the physical condition of the people of England. With | these views, Gentlemen, I solicit your attention – I hope soon to acquire your confidence.

I have the honor to
subscribe myself
your faithful Ser[van]t
Benjamin Disraeli[1]

264

TO SARAH DISRAELI [London], Sunday [14 April? 1833]

ORIGINAL: H A/I/B/53

COVER: [D used a cover sheet addressed to himself and altered it for his letter to Sarah]: 1st. letter | ~~B.~~ Miss Disraeli ~~Esqre~~ | ~~35 Duke Street~~ | ~~St. James'~~ | Bradenham

EDITORIAL COMMENT: *Dating*: letters H A/I/C/40 and H A/I/C/41 from Isaac and Sarah reveal that D was ill from Friday 12 April until Sunday 21st; therefore 14 April seems the most probable date for this letter.

Sunday

My dearest Sa,

On Friday evening I was seized with the Influenza at present raging in London, and have ever since been in bed, very ill. Yesterday so ill that I cd. not write, and wd. not let anybody else. Bolton does all that skill and att[enti]on can, but is himself slowly recov[erin]g from a very sharp and similar attack.

I can write no more.

BD

265

TO [HELEN SELINA BLACKWOOD] 35 Duke Street, St James's, London], Wednesday [17 April? 1833]

ORIGINAL: NIPR D1071B/E3/9b:27

EDITORIAL COMMENT: There is no superscription, and the letter is endorsed by NIPR as a letter to 'C. H. Sheridan'. However it is clearly part of the correspondence to Helen Selina Blackwood. *Dating*: by D's illness. See **264**ec. *Sic*: St James.

Duke St St James | Wednesday

I can sympathise with your illness, having been myself a severe sufferer, and confined to my room almost since I had the pleasure of seeing you.

1 Although the letter has not been located, it is evident that D wrote to William Johnson Fox, asking for his help in the Marylebone campaign. Fox replied on 11 April cordially wishing D well and referring him to a Marylebone elector who might have more influence in the constituency than he had himself. Fox concluded with the following advice: 'The great obstacle to yr success is that, if not yr sincerity, certainly yr earnestness, is doubted by very many persons. That this shd be the case need not, I think, either surprise or offend you. It may perhaps gratify you, as a difficulty wh you have to put forth power to overcome. For myself, I rely on yr talent for yr truth, holding all false men to be fools.' H B/I/A/54.

I do not send you my pamphlet,[1] because the politics will not please you, altho' I am not a Tory, and never intended to | be one. I saw "Starry Night"[2] yesterday, and am going to write something for her Mag[azine].[3] I wo[ul]d do it for none else but your sister. It is the last testimony of my affection, as I have a melancholy presentiment that horrible politics will ultimately, if not very soon, dissolve that agreeable acquaintance which has been the consolation of my life. We met a year too late – | but it is useless to regret, and now impossible to do anything else.

I will write you no more Persian letters, but on this condition that you will believe everything that I have written. Forget it, if you please.[4]

Farewell, dearest lady –

Your very faithful

Disraeli

---

266 TO CHARLES MATHEWS [London?, Sunday 21 April 1833?]

ORIGINAL: PS 56

PUBLICATION HISTORY: Sotheby's catalogue (24 Mar 1970) item 472

EDITORIAL COMMENT: Sotheby's described the letter as: 'Early A.L.s., *one page, 4to, Sunday,* 21 *April* [*paper watermarked* 1832], to the actor Charles Mathews, *with integral address leaf, remains of seal, original seal-tear, postmark, torn in folds.*'

[Dear sir][1]

... A fair lady of my acquaintance is very desirous of making your acquaintance and wishes you to dine with her on Friday next. You will meet the best people in London at her house[2] ...

1 *"What is He?" By the author of "Vivian Grey"* was published in April, at the time of the anticipated vacancy at Marylebone. The advertisement of the pamphlet occasioned the following comment by Mrs Blackwood: 'I see in the newspaper a six-penny question of yours advertised, and I mean to go to the expense of its purchase. Of course you are "*He*", – and if so – I hope you answer your own query, for the benefit of your readers, *me* especially who have great curiosity on the subject. I see your existence *must* be a political one, but alas and alack! how many things are required beside first-rate talent to succeed in that career, – so many little actions and mean considerations – though to be sure one doesn't mind them, with such a *great, big fat end in view*! (excuse the sublimity of my language,) but somehow it strikes me that if you don't end by being *all* you wish, (and moderate success would not content you,) you are the sort of man to sit down with your hands in your pockets, and be good for nothing all the days of your life; et ce serait dommage! I am persuaded one ought not to set one's heart *earnestly* on any one pursuit in this world, if one wishes to preserve any of the energy of youth beyond its first years.' NIPR D071B/E3/9B:26.

2 Caroline Norton.

3 Begun by John Bell in 1806 as *La Belle Assemblée; or Bell's Court and Fashionable Magazine*, *The Court Magazine and Monthly Critic* was edited by Mrs Norton from 1832 to 1837. A few months later, D's 'Walstein; or A Cure for Melancholy' appeared in it. *CM* III (3 July 1833) 3-8.

4 Mrs Blackwood had written: 'In my present fragile state of health you should not write me such *Persian* letters, for who knows that my excellent judgement may not share (for a time) in my physical weakness, and I might by accident take it all in earnest!'

---

1 Probably Charles Mathews the elder. D had met him in February 1833. See **234**.

2 Later letters in the same vein to other people were written by D on behalf of Lady Sykes, and it is probable (if the Sotheby's dating is correct) that this is the first of them. Alternatively, in **269** of 30 April 1833 he was to tell Sa that he had been to a lively 'political dejeuner' at the Wyndham Lewises on Friday 26 April (which was the day for which this invitation was issued), so his action could have been on behalf of Mary Anne.

TO SARAH DISRAELI Albion [Club, London], Tuesday [23 April 1833]

ORIGINAL: H A/I/B/55

COVER: Miss Disraeli | Bradenham House | High Wycombe | Bucks

POSTMARK: (1) In circle: N | AP 23 | 1833

EDITORIAL COMMENT: *Sic*: Windham.

Albion[1] – | Tuesday

My dearest,

I am again on the Pavé – and have been paying a round of visits to my suffering friends. Scarcely one has escaped. Both Mr and Mrs. Bulwer still indisposed. Mrs Windham[2] a ghost, Lady Stepney convalescent. The Charlevilles so so. Nobody has escaped except old Lady Cork.[3] I | thought you would like to know how I am, therefore I write, tho' I have of course little to say. I am going to dine to day with your old acquaintance Lady Sykes[4] – and Sir Francis.

Send me the MS. of the Sunday School Cat[echism] | by Ralph.[5]

I recovered under the hospitable roof of B.E.L. They sd. in Duke St to all my enquiring friends that I had gone for change of air to Grays Inn Lane![6] The Beau Monde stared.

BD

1 The club at 85 St James's Street, not the hotel mentioned in **262**. See **242**. A copy of *The Rules and Regulations of the Albion Club* (1828) is among the Hughenden papers (H A/IV/M/1).

2 D's spelling of the name remained eccentric, but Mary Anne's latest biographer takes for granted that she was the person intended. Molly Hardwick *Mrs Dizzy* (New York 1972) 47.

3 Mary Boyle (1746-1840), daughter of John Monckton, 1st Viscount Galway, had married in 1786 Edmund Boyle, 7th Earl of Cork and Orrery (d 1798). In the course of her forty-two years of widowhood, Lady Cork's house at 6 New Burlington Street became one of the centres of fashionable society. She is said to have been a model for Lady Belair, the society hostess in *Henrietta Temple* (1836), and for Mrs Leo Hunter in *The Pickwick Papers* (1836-7).

4 Henrietta Sykes (d 1846), eldest daughter of Henry Villebois of Marham Hall, Norfolk. She married Sir Francis William Sykes in August 1821. Sarah's response does little to clarify the nature of the acquaintance. She wrote on 26 April: 'How came you to be such great friends with Lady Sykes? Is she agreeable?' H A/I/B/471.

5 Sarah was apparently composing a Sunday school catechism, and D was dealing on her behalf with the publishing firm of Rivington. She wrote several essays and stories intended for *The New Monthly Magazine*. In March 1834 she and D published a novel, *A Year at Hartlebury, or The Election*, under the pseudonyms of 'Cherry' and 'Fair Star'. See **304**n1. H A/I/B/505, 506, 511.

The only attempts to record Sarah's life are silent about her writing. See F.E. Bailey *The Perfect Age* (1946) ch v; Sarah Gertrude Pomeroy *Little-Known Sisters of Well-Known Men* (Boston 1912) 225-49.

6 Benjamin Lindo's address appears in directories as 4 Verulam Buildings, Gray's Inn.

268 TO SARAH DISRAELI Albion [Club, London], Thursday [25 April 1833]

ORIGINAL: H A/I/B/56

COVER: Miss Disraeli | Bradenham House | High Wycombe | *Bucks*

POSTMARK: (1) In circle: U | AP25 | 1833

PUBLICATION HISTORY: LBCS 19, dated 25 April 1833, prints most of the third paragraph as a separate letter, omitting references to Lady Sykes and to Mrs Spence. LBCS 19, dated 30 April 1833, prints parts of the second and third sentences of the fourth paragraph, ending at 'very disagreeable', and adding an extract from **269**; M&B I 227, dated 30 April 1833, reprints an altered version of the last paragraph, taken from LBCS.

EDITORIAL COMMENT: There is no signature.

Albion – Thursday

My dearest,

I continue in very good condition. If Ralph could contrive to bring up my mare I sho[ul]d like it. As the ride might be too long for him, it co[ul]d be sent up to Uxbridge the day before, and then he co[ul]d ride it up cool and fit, for next days use.

Two pamphlets from Southey[1] | one of which I shall keep and send the other by the first opportunity. Honorable mention of my father and three piquant extracts from his "dignified rebuke"[2] to Milor.

I have very little to tell you except that I am well and love you. I have done nothing but go to the play, one night with Lady Sykes, | one with Madame Spence, and last night with Mrs Norton to see Sheridan Knowles' new play[3] which was successful. Public amusements are tedious but in a private box, with a fair companion, less so. Tomorrow a great breakfast at the Wyndham Lewis' when magnificent plate is to be presented from Maidstone to our host | the defeated Conservative.[4]

I have little to say except that I love you. There was an attack in the Morning Herald on "What is He" when the author was advised to adhere | to the Regions of Romance where he wields undisputed supremacy, or something to that effect.[5] Such attacks are not very disagreeable, but everybody says that "What is He?" is very clever. O'Connell told a friend that it was the best thing ever written. It has sold, which no pamphlets ever do.[6]

1 The two were obviously copies of *A Letter to John Murray Esq 'touching' Lord Nugent, in a reply to a letter from his Lordship, touching an article in the Quarterly Review, by the author of that article* (1833), written by Robert Southey (1774-1843). Isaac referred to the two copies in a letter to Southey dated 3 May 1833. H G/I/1377.

2 The expression is Southey's description of Isaac's criticism of Nugent in *Eliot, Hampden, and Pym, or, a Reply* ... (Colburn and Bentley 1832). Southey *Letter to John Murray* ... 16. In response to Nugent's judgement on his *Charles I*, Isaac had written: 'I would compare Hampden in these "Memorials" [Nugent's book] to what is usually termed "the lady in the lobster" – an almost invisible delicacy not always to be found when looked for.' *Eliot, Hampden, and Pym* 48-9.

3 James Sheridan Knowles (1784-1862), actor and playwright; the new play was probably *The Wife: A Tale of Mantua*, first performed at Covent Garden on 24 April 1833. Allardyce Nicoll *British Drama: An Historical Survey* (New York 1925) 339.

4 Lewis was defeated at Maidstone in the general election of December 1832.

5 The reviewer commented that D's proposals for instant repeal of the Septennial Act, the institution of election by ballot and the immediate dissolution of Parliament 'would be very appalling if the writer possessed one atom of that influence in the field of reality, which he wields with so much force in the regions of romance.' *The Morning Herald* no 15,820 (23 Apr 1833).

6 For confirmation that the sale of pamphlets rarely recovered the costs of their production see [James Grant] *The Great Metropolis* second series, 2nd ed (1838) I ch 4.

TO SARAH DISRAELI [London], Tuesday 30 April [1833]

ORIGINAL: H A/I/B/57

PUBLICATION HISTORY: LBCS 19, dated 30 April 1833, prints a version of the second and third sentences, conflated with an extract from **268**; M&B I 227, dated 30 April 1833, reprints the LBCS version.

EDITORIAL COMMENT: *Sic*: Frazer, over head and years, Talks, *societé*.

Tuesday – Ap 30

My dearest,

I am scribbling this with the hope that I may send it you down in company with Frazer wherein, as it appeareth, we exhibit.[1] I can give you no idea of the success of "What is He?" which is as much a favorite with the Tories as the Rads. The recent exposé of the Whigs proves me a prophet. I send you a copy of the new Edit. and we look forward to publishing a third at the end of the week. Ridgway[2] keeps it standing. I am sadly behind hand in giving you the detail of my life, but it is impossible in mere correspondence. It will afford conversation for our summer solitude. Great enquiries are made everywhere after you, and I can assure you I hear of many albums wherein "the Dedication is copied."[3]

Yesterday I dined at the Charlevilles[4] – a very agreeable party. The | Tullamores, Lord Downes,[5] old Lady Cork, Lady Charlotte Crofton,[6] Ibid Bury, Mr Scrope and one or two others whom I knew not. I sat between Lady Cork and Lady Tullamore, a large round table. I had made Lady Cork's acquaintance previously at Lady Sykes, who is her niece, that is Sir Francis is her nephew.[7] She is really one of the cleverest and most diverting persons in the world, but it is quite impossible except in chat to convey the slightest idea of all her sayings and doings and her singular mixture of sarcasm and benevolence. My beauty, Lady Tullamore turned out rather insipid, and is not much more intellectual than her mother. "Mr. Disraeli" Cork loquitur "do you know Lady Charlotte Bury?" – "I have that pleasure" "Very well?" – "I meet her a great deal." "Ah! I don't know her much myself – not | brilliant I believe, only good natured etc." "And somewhat sentimental" – "Ah! yes over head and years[8] in debt – upon my honor I think it much more honest to have gone on the highway at once" – "and much more brave." "He, he, he, and much more brave."

"Mr Disraeli, have you read Lady Stepneys book?" "I never read." "Thats what Dr Johnson used always to say. Madam when I want to read a book, I write

1 A portrait of D by Maclise appeared in *Fraser's Magazine* accompanying the article on D by Maginn in his 'Gallery of Literary Characters'. See **258**n2

2 The publisher James Leech Ridgway (1801-1862). His business was located at 169 Piccadilly.

3 The Dedication to *Alroy*; see **251**n4.

4 The Charlevilles lived at 14 Cavendish Square.

5 Ulysses Bagenal Burgh (1788-1863), 2nd Baron Downes, Tory MP for Carlow 1818-26, and for Queenborough 1826-30.

6 Lady Charlotte Crofton (d 1842), fifth daughter of the 7th Earl of Galloway and widow of Sir Edward Crofton (1778-1816).

7 The relationship was more complicated than D suggested. Lady Cork's niece (Elizabeth Monckton) had married Sir Francis Sykes's uncle (John Sykes).

8 The 'y' is quite clear in the MS. This is one of Lady Cork's more successful aphorisms.

Benjamin Disraeli (1833)
by Daniel Maclise

one." ["]Poor Lady Stepney, 'tis a sad business – all her friends deceive her – I tell her so, I tell her so. My dear, I said to her the other day, you have made yourself ridiculous[.]"

"Mr Disraeli, I see some of these things that are published, but fortunately I have no memory. I forget them the next day. Now I remember every word of V[ivian] G[rey]. That's my work. They say your last book is perfectly exquisite. I am going to read it. Now I tell you what, you *can* write. | Writing is not merely putting words tog[ethe]r which these people think, and Mrs. Gore, she can write too, only poor creature she writes for her bread – and Mr Bulwer he can write – why does everybody abuse him so?" etc. etc. etc.

In the evening I adjourned to a weekly ball at Lady Sykes "I suppose you are going to Lady Sykes Mr Disraeli" "I may perhaps" " – She is my favorite of all the young women in London and I have left her my china. I have left it her because she has got a heart, and she is very beautiful too. I would not if I were you leave this house too soon. Here you have *bon societé*, there you have only amusement.["] "I detest amusement." "I am glad to hear it. I can't understand why you go to Lady Sykes then. I have done all I could to put her in bon societé, but she will | not. She lets her sisters lead her away. Nothing but dancing, dancing, dancing. Do you dance?" Never. "I am glad to hear it. Now mind, never go out of bon societé. You can go where you like now, if you are wise. I can't ask you to dine with me on Wednesday, because my favorite niece, 150 miles off, is in danger, and I will have no parties till she has recovered." etc. etc. etc.

I am sorry I can give you no sketch now of the political dejeuner on Friday at the W[yndham] L[ewise]s[9] which was most splendid and amusing. By the bye my friend Lord Eliot has come to life, and called on me yesterday – symptomatic.

If Jem come to town, which I hope he will soon with my mare, which I much want, he may st[a]y a few days with B.E.L. who wishes it much. Ralph has just arrived.

in haste

BD |

True Sun Talks of a vacancy next week in Marylebone.[10]

TO SARAH DISRAELI [London, April 1833] 270

ORIGINAL: PS 38

PUBLICATION HISTORY: Clarence I. Freed 'A New Sheaf of Disraeli Letters' *The American Hebrew* CXX (15 Apr 1927) 836; LBCS 20, dated 29 June 1833, includes the first sentence of the second paragraph. M&B I 233 reprints the same sentence.

EDITORIAL COMMENT: *Dating*: '*What is He?*' was published in April 1833. See **238**ec.

We did nothing but catch trout, and wander in beautiful woods, eat cold pasties, and drink iced champagne. The only books taken were my works. Add to this a

9 The Wyndham Lewises lived at 1 Grosvenor Gate, Park Lane, D's future address.

10 'We understand upon good authority that Sir Wm. Horne will vacate his seat for Marylebone next week; the arrangement for his elevation to the Bench having been completed.' *The True Sun* no 362 (30 Apr 1833). Horne did not, in fact, resign.

most engaging companion, and you can easily fancy a very picturesque and Watteau like week. We arrived in town last night at half-past ten and were dressed and at the opera in time for the new ballet.

My table was literally covered with invitations and some from people I do not know, 'What is He?' a great hit. My love to all. Thine ever, dearest...

[D]

---

271 TO SARAH DISRAELI [London], Monday [13 May 1833]

ORIGINAL: H A/I/B/58

COVER: Miss Disraeli | Bradenham House | *Bucks*

EDITORIAL COMMENT: *Dating*: by comparison with **269**, and from Isaac's complaint of 'nearly a fortnight' of silence.

Monday Morng.

My dearest,

I wrote you the enclosed yesterday. Ralph ought to have told you that I had gone out of town. I gave him instr[ucti]ons to that effect. I am most grieved at yr. annoyance.[1] I never was better in my life, and shall soon embrace you. I have not seen Ralph | since my return, as we have constantly missed. He has been turned out of his lodgings. I will communicate with him directly, and also see after Tita.

God bless you my love.

Your own

D

Let Jem come up and call on B.E.L.

---

272 TO HELEN SELINA BLACKWOOD [London, Monday 13 May 1833]

ORIGINAL: NIPR D1071B/E3/9B:33

COVER: Mrs. Price Blackwood | Palace | Hampton Court

POSTMARK: (1) In oval: 4.EVEN.4 | 13.MY | X 1833 X (2) In double oval: NIGHT.7 | MY13 | 1833 (3) In packet: T.P | Grenville St

EDITORIAL COMMENT: A fragment.

---

not as beautiful as *your* copy, *should* have been, but I was too unwell to attend to it.

My affection to the most beautiful of Mammas. I am only reconciled to not having been summoned to the Adm[iralt]y[1] by the recollection that I was not in town.

Your devoted

Disraeli

1 Sarah wrote on 12 May: 'Your silence ... gives us much pain and anxiety.' Isaac added: 'You cannot imagine how greatly I am distressed by your unaccountable silence. I never ask for idle letters – but nearly a fortnight has elapsed and we do not know where or how you are!' H A/I/B/477. D's departure from his previous habit of openly documenting all his movements for the family marks almost certainly the intensification of his affair with Henrietta Sykes.

---

1 Spring Gardens was near the Admiralty. See **235**n3.

TO SARAH DISRAELI [London], Wednesday [22 May 1833]

ORIGINAL: TEXU [25]
COVER: Miss Disraeli | Bradenham House | High Wycombe | *Bucks.*
POSTMARK: (1) In circle: L | MY22 | 1833
PUBLICATION HISTORY: LBCS 20, extracts dated 22 May 1833
EDITORIAL COMMENT: *Sic*: the Sykes, Sydney, dinners.

Wednesday

My sweet,

Order dinner tomorrow at 7. We have altered our plans and shall now bring nothing save a stanhope and horse and no servants what[eve]r. Jem tells me that the Merediths would rather, he fancies, come on Monday. I would give much that they wo[ul]d postpone their visit to that day. They want to go he says to the Opera, but this may be Jem's fancy. Howr. if you can put them off to Monday, *do* – Munro will be off on that day and I wish that we sho[ul]d have him alone. His sister[1] who has been absent in Italy for nine years wrote this morning to say, that she was at Dunkirk and wo[ul]d arrive with[ou]t loss of time. He is howr. so anxious to come that we were nearly coming off today.

On Friday last there was a grand Review in Hyde Park, and the Wyndham L[ewise]s gave a most sumptuous dejeuner, which was attended by the very best set. I was there. I afterwards dined with the | Sykes with the Ludolfs,[2] Hennikers,[3] Hudson Gurneys,[4] Lord A. Chichester,[5] William Lennox, Manners Sutton,[6] Digby, Lady Ell[enborough]s brother,[7] Felix Bedingfield[8] Lady Cork, and Col. Poten.[9] I never saw such a service of plate in my life. The Spences' pla-

1 Isabella Margaret Munro (d 1873), only daughter of Sir Alexander Munro of Novar, Ross-shire. In May 1834 she married Henry Butler-Johnstone, third son of the 13th Baron Dunboyne, at the house of her brother, D's friend. *CJ* no 264 (17 May 1834) 345.

2 Count Guiglielmo di Ludolf (1757-1839), Sicilian minister to London 1827-39, and his wife.

3 Sir Augustus Brydges Henniker (1795-1849), 3rd Baronet, married (secondly) in 1826 Elizabeth Henniker-Major (d 1882), youngest daughter of John Minet Henniker-Major, 3rd Baron Henniker.

4 Hudson Gurney (1775-1864), antiquary and poet; MP for Shaftesbury 1812-13 and for Newtown 1816-32. In 1809 he married Margaret Barclay (d 1855), daughter of Robert Barclay, MP, of Ury, Kincardineshire.

5 Lord Arthur Chichester (1808-1840), fourth son of the 2nd Marquess of Donegall. He was Whig MP for Belfast 1832-4.

6 Charles Manners-Sutton (1780-1845), Tory MP for Scarborough 1806-32, for the University of Cambridge 1832-5, Speaker of the House of Commons 1817-35. He was knighted in September 1833, and in 1835 was created 1st Viscount Canterbury.

7 Probably Edward St Vincent Digby (1809-1889), later 9th Baron Digby, son of Adm Sir Henry Digby. Edward's sister Jane (d 1881) married 2nd Baron Ellenborough in 1824; they were divorced in 1830.

8 Felix William George Richard Bedingfield (1808-1884), youngest son of Sir Richard Bedingfield, 5th Baronet; barrister and colonial administrator; CMG 1869. References to him as a young man are found in *The Jerningham Letters (1780-1843); being the Excerpts from the Correspondence and Diaries of the Honourable Lady Jerningham and her daughter Lady Bedingfield* (1896) II 140, 152.

9 Frederick, Baron von Poten (d 1847). At this time he was an equerry in the household of the

teau was like one in a baby house to it. Three invit[ati]ons for the evening – Misses Blackwell,[10] Lady Charleville, and Mrs. Austen. The first was only practicable, and I am of course damned with the last. On Saturday I was at the Opera with Lady Sykes and Lady Charlotte Bertie. By the bye wo[ul]d you like her for a sister in law? Very clever, | £25000 and domestic. It is feasible.[11] On Sunday I dined with Munro to meet an amateur Mr Lowndes[12] who is writing an Opera from Alroy. Monday with the Sykes and Bertie to Mad. Dulcken's concert[13] – in

Duke of Cumberland. The colonelcy was a German rank; his rank in the British army was that of a captain on half-pay. Poten was a member of the Royal Hanoverian Guelphic Order and was a familiar figure in London society. Army List; *ER* (1828, 1834); and various numbers of *The Court Journal*.

10 Robson's *Guide* for 1833 lists a Miss Blackwell at 6 Seamore Place, Mayfair.

11 Lady Charlotte Elizabeth Bertie (1812-1895), second daughter of the 9th Earl of Lindsey, was very soon to become Lady Charlotte Guest. In just over two months, on 29 July, she married a man more than twice her age, Josiah John Guest (1785-1852), ironmaster and after 1838 1st Baronet, Whig MP for Merthyr Tydvil 1832-52. She was a writer, mainly known for her translation of *The Mabinogion* (1838-49), and, in later life, a noted collector of objets d'art. Her English china was to become the basis of the National Collection in the Victoria and Albert Museum. Her first husband was a partner of Wyndham Lewis in the Dowlais Ironworks which Lady Charlotte managed after her husband's death. In 1855 she married Charles Schreiber (d 1884).

Sarah took D seriously and was much alarmed by her brother's comment. On 23 May she responded with energy: 'Beware! oh beware of 25,000 which belongs to a young lady who can spend | the greatest part of it on herself, and who will expect from you sooner or later three times that sum. Remember what improvident blood more than half fills her veins. Are you sure too there is even that? Mrs Austen says that her mother wanted to make a match between her and Plumer Ward which if true makes the money seem doubtful.' H A/I/B/479.

At that opening performance of Rossini's *Tancredi* at the King's Theatre, Lady Charlotte recorded her impressions of D in her journal for 18 May: 'The younger Disraeli was in the box. He and I soon got acquainted. We talked about several things. He is wild, enthusiastic, and very poetical. His "Contarini Fleming" was written in Egypt – He knew Ibrahim Pasha and gave me anecdotes of him. He told me he thought Southey the greatest man of the age. He was *really* a great man, he said. The brilliancy of my companion infected me and we ran on about poetry, and Venice, and Baghdad, and Damascus, and my eye lit up and my cheek burned, and in the pause of the beautiful music (Tancredi) my words flowed almost as rapidly as his ... He tells me that repose is the great thing and that nothing repays exertion. Yet noise and light are his fondest dreams, and nothing could compensate to him for an obscure youth, – not even glorious old age. I cannot understand his trying to get into Parliament. It was beautiful to hear him talk of Southey. With all his enthusiasm and contradictions he pleased me and we were very good friends I think.' Montague J. Guest ed *Lady Charlotte Schreiber's Journals* (1911) I xx, entry for 18 May 1833; Jerman 187-8.

12 It is unlikely that this was Lowndes the bibliographer, though he lived in London. There was, however, a Lowndes family prominent in Buckinghamshire at this time, and several of that name served in public offices and were active Tories. Robert Gibbs *Worthies of Buckinghamshire and Men of Note of that County* (Aylesbury 1888) 262-6. In 1836 D was a steward for a Tory dinner, where William Selby Lowndes (Whaddon Hall), William Lowndes (of Chesham) and E. Lowndes (of Salden) were fellow stewards. *BH* no 256 (26 Nov 1836).

13 Louisa Dulcken, née David (1811-1850), German-born pianist who had settled in London and there become a major figure on the musical scene. The concert, known as 'The Morning Concert', was held on Monday 20 May 1833 at two o'clock. *CJ* no 213 (18 May 1833) 352.

Lady Charlotte also recorded this meeting: 'Mr. Disraeli, who had brought me flowers, sat by me and was most agreeable. He had less of eccentricity than on Saturday. Perhaps he then thought, by his brilliancy, to take my imagination by storm. I liked him better today – we agreed on very many points and his details interest me. If I had time I would put down much of his conversation.' She also noted that Lady Sykes had lent her a copy of *Alroy*. Guest *L.C.S. Journals* I xx-xxi, entry for 20 May 1833; Jerman 188.

the evening Mrs. Mitford.[14] Yesterday I went on a roving expedition with Lady Cork and Lady Sykes to Hampton Court to see Mrs Sheridan – a delicious day but I did not return till 11. being engaged to meet Lady Sophia Sydney[15] at dinners at Lady Stepney's. I am in a scrape. General Phipps has asked me to dinner Lady Sitwell[16] and Hon Mrs. Burton.[17]

We shall soon embrace.

Put the Merediths off till Monday if possible.

BD[18]

TO SARAH DISRAELI [London], Wednesday [22 May 1833] **274**

ORIGINAL: H A/I/B/49

COVER: Miss Disraeli | Bradenham House | High Wycombe | *Bucks*

POSTMARK: (1) In Maltese cross: VS | VMY2[2]S | [illegible]

EDITORIAL COMMENT: *Dating*: Sarah's letter to D of 23 May 1833 (H A/I/B/479) is clearly an answer to this letter.

2nd. letter | Wednesday | 6 o'ck.

My sweet Sa!

I hope you will not be very disappointed, but this instant the unhappy Miss Munro has arrived. I assure you Munro is more annoyed than myself and I have promised him the moment he has settled her, which will take only a few days[,] to come down with him. I cannot afford at this moment | to pay you two visits for particular reasons, and I very much wish to accompany Munro.

I have no desire to meet the Merediths. Let their visit be over and we will come down. I scribble this off at a moments notice. I dine with Munro today and his *damned* sister – and the result | of our conversation shall be communicated to you with[ou]t loss of an instant. We will meet soon, and for a long holiday.

Your m[os]t affec
brother
D

14 Probably Letetia Mitford (d 1844), wife of Robert Mitford of the Audit Office, Somerset House. At this time she lived at 64 Upper Berkeley Street. London directories; *GM* ns 21 (Oct 1844) 444.

15 Lady Sophia Fitzclarence (d 1837) was the illegitimate daughter of William IV. In 1825 she married Philip Sidney, after 1835 1st Baron de L'Isle and Dudley.

16 Susan Sitwell, née Tait (d 1880), married in 1818 Sir George Sitwell (1797-1853), 2nd Baronet.

17 Anna-Maria Plunkett (d 1856), fourth daughter of the 13th Baron Dunsany, married secondly in 1822 Capt Ryder Burton RN. *BLG* (1846).

18 There is a postscript on the cover and on the first page in James Disraeli's hand:

Dr Sa,

Put out the orange tree, just before the Damask rose bed, the sun dial, (get the pillar at Wooster's) [James Worcester, Bradenham chairmaker] in the little round bed with Balsams and put a Fucia [*sic*] in the Vase and set the Vase half way in the ground. The Vase is to stand between the campanula bed. [*sic*] If you think these arrangements not good do not do them, but have the Orange tree put out in a warm spot at any rate.

J. D. |

I will do all the Governor tells me.

Have the beds done before Munro comes.

275 TO SARAH DISRAELI [London], Monday [3 June 1833]

ORIGINAL: H A/I/B/59

COVER: Miss Disraeli | Bradenham House | High Wycombe | *Bucks*

POSTMARK: (1) In circle: O | JU-3 | 1833

PUBLICATION HISTORY: LBCS 20-1, dated 29 June 1833, prints parts of the third and fourth paragraphs, omitting reference to Mrs Bolton, conflated with extracts from **283** and **288** and with the two paragraphs in **283**ec.

EDITORIAL COMMENT: *Sic*: Champaigne, soireé.

Monday

My dearest,

Munro and I come on Sunday next *positively*. I will take care of the Claret and the Champaigne. Lady Sykes wants to come as Sir Fras is going down in the yacht for a week.[1] She knows Munro, and will bring us down in the carriage, which will be very convenient. My mother need not be alarmed as it is impossible for anyone to be more perfectly unaffected, and give less trouble.

I wish my mother wd. write her a note, and say that I had mentioned that she might be tempted to pay our dull place a visit etc. etc. you know what sort of note to | write. *Pray attend to this, my dearest, with[ou]t loss of time. It will be most amusing, and I am sure will do us all good.*[2]

On Friday after all I went to the Caledonian Ball[.][3] Mrs. Bolton made me a dress from my oriental collections which exceeded in splendor anything in the room. Particulars when we meet.

Yesterday at Mrs. Wyndhams at a large soireé I met Joseph Buonaparte | and his beautiful daughter.[4]

I have read your letter with attention and will answer it tomorrow.

The more I reflect, the more I feel I have acted in a perfectly justifiable and proper manner. Mrs. M[eredith] will have no cause to complain of me, but I think Ellen has deceived her.[5] I will write fully by tomorrows post.

Your most affect.

D

1 A week earlier an advertisement in *The Morning Post* had announced that the Sykeses' country seat, Basildon House, was to let. *MP* no 19,490 (27 May 1833).

2 As Blake (98) has noted, this sudden addition of Henrietta Sykes to the postponed Munro house-party threw Bradenham into a flutter. Sarah replied promptly with the requested invitation to Lady Sykes on 4th June, but there was trouble with the cook, wines had to be ordered, and what if it rained? H A/I/B/481.

3 The Grand Caledonian Ball was held at Willis's Rooms on Friday 31 May. *CJ* no 215 (8 June 1833) 398.

4 Joseph Bonaparte (1768-1844), eldest brother of Napoleon, King of Naples and Spain. He came to England in the fall of 1832. The 'beautiful' daughter was no doubt Zenaïde (1801-1854), who later married her cousin, the 2nd Prince of Canino. David Stacton *The Bonapartes* (New York 1966) 252.

5 Ellen Meredith's account of D's courtship obviously differed from his version of their relations.

TO SARAH DISRAELI [London], Wednesday [5 June 1833] 276

ORIGINAL: H A/I/B/60

COVER: Miss Disraeli | Bradenham House | High Wycombe | Bucks | B.D.

POSTMARK: (1) In circle: U | JU-5 | 1833

PUBLICATION HISTORY: LBCS 20, dated 22 May 1833, prints the third paragraph (taken from context) with an extract from **273** which makes it appear that D's comments on love were prompted by the possibility of his marrying Lady Charlotte Bertie (described as 'Lady Z – '). As this letter makes clear, they were in response to Sarah's comments on Ellen Meredith. See n1. M&B I 232, dated 22 May 1833, reprints part of the LBCS version.

EDITORIAL COMMENT: There is no signature.

Wednesday

My dearest,

My conduct to the Merediths was occasioned by believing that there was a sudden and unauthorised change in their demeanour to me. I may have been wrong, and as far as Mrs M. is concerned I am willing to believe I was. As for Ellen enough has passed bet[wee]n her and Salmon with regard to myself in my presence, tho' of course supposed by them unperceived, to justify a much more icy temperament than I have thought fit to assume.[1]

You had better write to Mrs. M. to say that I shall call as | usual etc. but that I deprecate all explanations, which never do good. You may say to her, as tenderly as you please, all that I say to you.

As for "Love", all my friends who married for Love and beauty either beat their wives or live apart from them. This is literally the case. I may commit many follies in life, but I never intend to marry for "love", which I am sure is a guarantee of infelicity.

As for "companionship", the phrase is so vague I do not know | what it means. I shall always be with my wife at proper times and in proper places.

So this affair ends. I am not conscious of having behaved throughout in any other than a becoming manner.

1 Thomas Stokes Salmon (b 1803?) of Berkshire was an exact contemporary of William George Meredith at Brasenose College, Oxford. In the 1830s he was a barrister of Lincoln's Inn. *Brasenose College Register, 1509-1909* (Oxford 1909) I 463. Salmon was Ellen Meredith's suitor, and in a long letter on 31 May 1833 Sarah had described the result of a conversation with Mrs. Meredith:

'Mrs. M seems most annihilated by your behaviour. She knew that you were not in love, but she believes that you are so entirely a man of honor that you would not propose to any woman (and especially Ellen) for whom you did not feel kindness and friendship, but she can scarcely reconcile that with your "cutting indifference." ... She admires you more than any man in the world, but she feels that all Ellen's happiness in marriage would consist in being her husband's companion, and she put it to me, could she ever be such to you? ...

'She [Mrs. M] assured me that she [Ellen] was not going to be married to Salmon, or to any one else ... She did not say however that Salmon had been refused ... I think the game *is still yours* if you should ever be inclined ... If she [Ellen] be sincere [,] for love of me save her from Clay ... Pray *burn* this *instantly*.' H A/I/B/480. Ellen did not marry Salmon.

I keep the letter open to answer yours of this morn[in]g.

I must write tomorrow as to all details. I suppose Lady S[ykes] will bring her page and maid: we nobody, exc[ep]t perhaps my groom who if he cannot sleep at home, may sleep out.

277 TO SARAH DISRAELI [London], Friday [7 June 1833]

ORIGINAL: H A/I/B/61
COVER: Miss Disraeli | Bradenham House | High Wycombe | Bucks
POSTMARK: (1) In circle: 1833 | 7JU7 | C[X?].

Friday

My dearest,

I received yours[1] this morn[in]g. We come on Saturday, but at what hour very doubtful. I sho[ul]d think about 3. Lady Sykes will venture to bring her only daughter[2] aged 3, but no nurserymaid. I assured her my mother wo[ul]d not disapprove of a pretty child. For the rest, her page and soubrette, Munro no serv[an]t or horses, but I shall send my groom with my horse in Munro's | gig. Be not alarmed about amusement: our guests are indolent and loungy. Lady S will not be able to stay beyond Thursday, and if the resources of Brad[enham] are exhausted, we must make an excursion to Velvet Lawn,[3] in the small carriages.

I have not yr. letter by me, but I believe I have attended to all yr. remarks.

BD

278 TO SARAH DISRAELI [London], Monday [17 June 1833]

ORIGINAL: H A/I/B/62
COVER: Miss Disraeli | Bradenham House | High Wycombe | Bucks.
POSTMARK: (1) In circle: Z | JU 17 | 1833
EDITORIAL COMMENT: The visit of Munro and Lady Sykes to Bradenham went off well. They arrived Saturday 8 June and stayed until Thursday 13 June. It did rain, however. Sarah asked D on 15 June 'if you were drowned before you reached London.' H A/I/B/483.

Monday

My dearest,

Before I received your letter, I had already made enquiries here, and prepared an advertisement which is now sent to the papers, and which will be in the Times tomorrow. Let us hope. You may depend upon my constant exertions.[1]

1 Sarah wrote to D on 6 June 1833: 'I am somewhat nervous at the idea of entertaining our visitors whose tastes I cannot even guess at'. H A/I/B/482.

2 Eva Sykes (1830?-1885), daughter of Sir Francis and Lady Sykes. She died unmarried.

3 A portion of the grounds of Chequers Court, now the prime minister's country residence, was so called from the texture of its mossy turf. James J. Sheahan *History and Topography of Buckinghamshire* (1862) 125.

1 Sarah's dog was missing. She wrote to D on 15 June 1833: 'We have no news of poor Pop ...' H A/I/B/483. *The Times* for 18 June 1833 announced a reward of five guineas for the return of a spaniel named Pop, lost in the neighbourhood of High Wycombe.

I co[ul]d not summon up strength to go to the Brahams on Thursday. On Friday Lord Charleville's, where were Lord Oxmantown,[2] Tom Campbell, Miss Porter,[3] Miss Flaminius Knight,[4] and Lady Stepney. Charleville's cuisine is first rate | and celebrated. In the evening Lady Cork's, which was amusing. I met Mrs. Blackwood there, and calling in the morning on Mrs Norton, I was introduced to Mrs Sheridan and her friend, Lady Westmorland.[5]

Saturday I was at the opera. Lady Aldboro' sent me an invitation to dinner for Wednesday next, but I am engaged to Lady Cork. I do not know Lady A. save by reputation. You know she is a great wit and the English Ninon.[6] |

The political horizon lowers. The leading art[icle] of the Chronicle was full of my pamphlet on Friday – whole sentences, "Federal and feudal" and all that.[7] I sho[ul]d not be surprised at a dissolution, perhaps a convulsion.

Tell my father that Barnett's Hotel appears to be done up and that I therefore recommend him to go to the Albion in Cockspur St. formerly Morleys[8] and now kept by Charles, the literary waiter of the Union[9] who will be very attentive.

Munro, that strange mule does nothing but talk of | Bradenham. He gave us a dinner yesterday – Lady Ashburton,[10] Lady Sykes, the Cranstouns,[11] Arthur Lennox and myself.

I will write again soon.

Your devoted

D

2 William Parsons (1800-1867), Baron Oxmantown, after 1841 3rd Earl of Rosse. He was Whig MP for King's County 1831-5 and president of the Royal Society 1848-54. An amateur astronomer of note, he was at this time building on his estate the largest telescope in Great Britain at a cost of £20,000.

3 Jane Porter (1776-1850), author of two successful novels, *Thaddeus of Warsaw* (1803) and *The Scottish Chiefs* (1810).

4 Ellis Cornelia Knight (1757-1837), unwilling member of the Nelson-Emma Hamilton household, author of *Flaminius, a View of the Military, Social and Political Life of the Romans* (1792).

5 Jane Fane, née Huck-Saunders (d 1857), in 1800 had become the second wife of John Fane, 10th Earl of Westmorland. While this was probably the first occasion on which D had met Lady Westmorland, he had certainly met Mrs Sheridan before. See **273**.

6 Anne Lenclos (1620-1705), known as Ninon de Lenclos, a Frenchwoman noted for her beauty and wit.

7 *The Morning Chronicle* on the preceding Saturday (not Friday) had included a leading article which lamented the obstructive tactics of the Tory peers, but neither D nor his pamphlet "*What is He?*" was mentioned specifically. The leader-writer asked 'Can they [the Tory peers] blind themselves to the fact, that the aristocratic principle is essentially destroyed in this country, and that all Europe is in a state of rapid transition from feudal to federal principles of Government?' *MC* no 19,907 (15 June 1833). D had also made a similar statement on the last page of *Contarini Fleming*.

8 'Morley's Albion Hotel' was at 22 Cockspur Street.

9 Presumably the Union Club (founded in 1824) in Trafalgar Square.

10 Ann Dunning, née Cunningham (d 1835), widow of Richard Dunning, 2nd Baron Ashburton of the 1st creation, who had died in 1823. *BP*.

11 James Edward Cranstoun (1809-1869), 10th and last Baron Cranstoun, did not marry until 1843. His brother, Charles Frederick Cranstoun (1813-1869), died unmarried. Perhaps one of them accompanied his widowed mother, or the two brothers may have been there together.

279 TO SARAH DISRAELI Cocoa Tree [Club, London], [Wednesday 19 June 1833]

ORIGINAL: H A/I/B/63

COVER: Miss Disraeli | Bradenham House | High Wycombe | Bucks

POSTMARK: (1) In circle: F | JU 19 | 1833.

Cocoa Tree[1] | 6 o'ck

My dearest dear,

I have only time to say how much I love you, and how much I sympathise with you. We were all doing out [our] utmost in your cause here, but it is now in vain further to speak. You must let me send you a pretty little stranger which you must love for my sake.[2]

My father is comfortably settled at Morley's Hotel – I have seen him every day. | This one he dines with Douce.

There is no news. Tomorrow I shall see Rivington,[3] and will let you know the result.

I write because you desired it.

Lady Sykes says she is in debt for a chair; I have promised to discharge the amount. Her cough has got worse and worse, and is now | very bad. She sends her love to you all.

Mine especially to my mother. Bulwer wants me to lay siege to *Miss Jervis*,[4] which he thinks practicable, a great heiress and clever. I have met her at Lady Corks. She is pretty also.

Thine,

D

280 TO MESSRS. RIVINGTON 35 Duke Street, St. James's, [London], [Thursday 20 June 1833?]

ORIGINAL: UCLA D100 Box42

EDITORIAL COMMENT: A copy. The handwriting is close to D's, but the spelling of the surname makes it certain that it is not his. There is no signature. *Dating*: on 19 June D promised Sarah he would see Rivington about publication of her Old Testament catechism, which had been sent to D in April (**267**). On Sunday 23 June he told her that Rivington had the MS (**281**). This letter is assumed to be a substitute for the personal delivery of the MS anticipated in **279**. *Sic*: St James, D'Israeli, DIsraeli.

1 In the eighteenth century, the Cocoa-Tree Chocolate House had been a gathering place for Jacobites. It became a club at 64 St James's Street, and lost its distinctive political tone. Byron had been a member. By the 1830s its character was more equivocal. Three years later *The Satirist* (1 May 1836) observed: 'There is a low filthy gambling house in St. James's Street called the *Cocoa-Tree* which has recently been re-opened by the notorious Acland, in connection with a gang of French pickpockets. It is we are assured, not only to be used for the purposes of a common hell, but is also fitted up for other purposes, on the principle of the brothel pest house in Piccadilly.' It was still functioning as a club in the 1840s.

2 Clearly D was offering a replacement for the dog that had been found dead in West Wycombe wood. H A/I/B/484.

3 Francis Rivington (1805-1885), of the famous Rivington publishing family. See **280**.

4 Mary Ann Jervis (1813-1893), daughter of the 2nd Viscount St Vincent. In the decade before her marriage in 1840, she was known as a talented amateur musician and composer. *CJ* no 113 (25 June 1831) 445. For a portrait, see *CM* IV (Jan-June 1834) 163-4.

35 Duke St | St James

Mr D'Israeli presents his compliments to Messrs. Rivington,[1] and forwards them the MS. which has been entrusted to his care. Mr DIsraeli had wished to have accompanied it by a short preface which he promised the fair author | to supply, but he has been prevented by indisposition. He would have shown that the New Testament is always first put into the hands of children, and that the difficulty of explaining many parts to them from their ignorance of | the preceding Scriptures occasioned the present work, which has been found to produce the best effect. It is learnt by rote during the time the children are reading the N.T. and assists their comprehension by explain[in]g the history of the peculiar people of God, and the connection | of the prophecies from the time of Abraham to their completion in the coming of our Saviour.[2]

Mr. D'Israeli solicits the honor of an early answer from Messrs. Rivington as illness has occasioned him to neglect his commission.

281

TO SARAH DISRAELI [London], Sunday [23 June 1833]

ORIGINAL: H A/I/B/64

COVER: Miss Disraeli. | *Bradenham*

EDITORIAL COMMENT: *Dating*: this letter answered Sarah's of Thursday 20 June 1833 (H A/I/B/485). There is no signature. *Sic*: Paulett, soireé, Gwynn.

Sunday

My dearest,

I did not write to you yesterday, because I had not seen Bolton. I have called upon him again to day, and with[ou]t success.

I have taken steps about the Windsor ticket[1] which I shall get from the Duke of Devonshire[2] and will send you, if not by my father, with[ou]t loss of time.

I should like to write something for the Bazaar,[3] but it appears difficult.

It sho[ul]d be of local interest. Brevity | only renders it more difficult.

1 C.J.G. and F. Rivington, booksellers, had premises at 3 Waterloo Place, and at 62 St Paul's Churchyard.

2 This summary of the purpose of Sarah's catechism contains the seeds of the famous chapter 24 in Disraeli's *Lord George Bentinck* to be published nineteen years later, in which he argued the organic unity of the Old and New Testaments.

---

1 Sarah had asked on 20 June: 'Can you get an order from Wyatville to see | Windsor. Mamma wishes it so much that I should be glad if you could contrive it.' H A/I/B/485.

2 The 6th Duke of Devonshire was at this time lord chamberlain of the Household, and his office was responsible for issuing tickets for members of the public to visit certain areas of the Windsor Castle grounds and the Great Park.

3 Sarah asked: 'Will you write "a story" for the Bazaar? if you think it worth taking | any trouble, about, a couple of pages will do. It must be entirely finished by the 15th of next month.' D's response to this was *Velvet Lawn: A Sketch Written for the Benefit of the Buckinghamshire Infirmary*, which was published at Wycombe by E. King in 1833. Sarah had 75 copies printed (H A/I/B/490), but the only one located is in the Hughenden papers (H E/III/15); the MS is in the Royal Archives at Windsor.

Rivington has your MS.[4] and I shall send you an answer by Tuesday or Wednesday.

Storrs[5] have not sent your pen home.

Lady Cork was delighted with everything.[6] I dined with her on Wednesday. Lady Wm. Paulett,[7] the Capels who asked me to them on Thursday, but I was engaged, the Gally Knights, the Duchess of Cleveland,[8] | Sir Geo. Talbot,[9] Lady Eastnor,[10] Sir Rd. Bromley:[11] in the evening a soireé in which Lady Morgan[12] made her appearance, but I was unaware of it. The D[uche]ss of Hamilton[13] dined at Lady Aldboro's. I was sorry to miss her as she much wishes to become acquainted, having heard so much of me from Beckford. I called on Lady Aldboro' who is very witty, but cares not | what she says, in any sense.

To day my father dines with Lady Sykes. I am afraid he will be bored. I shall finish this tomorrow morning, and send it by him.

I like the Capels. Lady Caroline is like Nell Gwynn,[14] but not clever: Capel himself very handsome, dark and a rich dresser like a fine Titian. I have met them | before at Lady Stepneys. Sir Geo. Talbot is a fine gentleman. He never speaks to anyone until he has ascertained their position. "No feeling" says Lady Cork "only fashion." He has decided in my favor – at least Lady Clarendon[15] called on Lady Cork yesterday and asked her to introduce me because Sir Geo. said that no person that he had ever met with had more | the talent of society.

4 See **267**n5 and **280**.

5 Paul Storr (1771-1844) was deemed the greatest goldsmith of the period.

6 On 13 June D had brought with him from Bradenham a chair and some cheeses as presents for Lady Cork.

7 Lady Grace Caroline Powlett (d 1883), youngest daughter of the 1st Earl of Lonsdale, had married in 1815 Lord William John Frederick Powlett (1792-1864), second son of the 1st Duke of Cleveland, and himself later 3rd Duke.

8 Elizabeth Vane, née Russell (1777-1861), in 1813 had married William Henry Vane, 3rd Earl Darlington, who had been created 1st Duke of Cleveland of the second creation in January 1833.

9 Sir George Talbot (1761-1850), 3rd Baronet.

10 Lady Caroline Harriet Cocks (1794-1873), fourth daughter of the 3rd Earl of Hardwicke; married in 1815 John Somers Cocks (1788-1852), Viscount Eastnor, after 1841 2nd Earl Somers; Tory MP for Hereford 1820-32, and for Reigate 1832-41.

11 There was no Sir Richard Bromley among either the baronets or the knights in 1833. It is probable that D meant Sir Robert Howe Bromley (1778-1857), 3rd Baronet of Stoke Hall, Notts. Sir Richard Broun *The Baronetage for 1844* (1844) 121. The participants at the Waterloo Dinner (see n17) were not listed in the press, but 'Sir R.H. Bromley' was noted later in the week as having attended the Queen's Drawing-room on 20 June. *The Times* (21 June 1833).

12 Sydney Morgan, née Owenson (1783-1859), the Irish novelist, who had married, in 1812, Sir Thomas Charles Morgan, a physician and later commissioner of fisheries. Lady Morgan recorded the occasion, an evening at Lady Cork's, in her diary entry for 28 June and reported that Disraeli 'ran off' as she arrived. Lady Morgan's impressions of other people at this gathering were more vivid than D's. For instance, she described Lord Oxmantown as 'an impersonation of the Committee of the House'. W.H. Dixon ed *Lady Morgan's Memoirs: Autobiography Diaries and Correspondence* 2nd ed (1863) II 360.

13 Susan Euphemia Douglas (1786-1859), second daughter of William Beckford, the novelist; she married in 1810 the Marquess of Douglas, after 1819 the 10th Duke of Hamilton.

14 D continued to be struck by the family resemblance. See **238**n2.

15 Maria Eleanor Villiers, née Forbes (1759-1844), wife of John Charles Villiers, 3rd Earl of Clarendon.

"Not so flattering as a female conquest" sd. Lady Cork "but worth more in the long run – He will talk of you at Whites."[16] Sir Rd. Bromley had dined the previous day with the Duke at the Waterloo feast.[17] He says the King made a terrible long speech. It was the most gorgeous | banquet ever known. The Gally Knights rather bores – the Duchess "tasted you more than I expected" sd. Lady C.

282

TO BENJAMIN AUSTEN — 35 Duke Street, St James's, [London], Monday [24 June 1833]

ORIGINAL: BL ADD MS 45908 ff70-2
COVER: *private* | Benjamin Austen Esqre | Raymond Buildgs | Grays Inn
POSTMARK: (1) In oval: 4.EVE[N.4] | 24.JU | 1833 (2) In packet: St. James's St.
PUBLICATION HISTORY: Jerman 182-3, dated 24 June 1833
EDITORIAL COMMENT: This letter contains one of the few allusions made by D to a third person which could refer to his affair with Henrietta Sykes.

---

35 Duke St | St James | Monday

My dear Austen,

Will you have the kindness to send me a line here to say on what day the bill | is due and whether it be payable at Drummonds.

I deeply grieve, among many other things, that you and I have seen so little of each other of late. I assure you the neglect, to which I fully plead | guilty, is not peculiar to you and Mrs. Austen who must always be considered my best friends, but all, even my own family, alike complain.[1]

The truth is, my dear fellow, but | this is an explanation which I offer only to you, I have for the last ten weeks been only *nominally in town*. The engrossing nature of my pursuits I | leave to your imagination, but pray continue to me, what I shall ever be to you,

a faithful friend

B.Disraeli

16 A gaming club, largely Tory in clientele, at 38 St James's Street. See the Hon Algernon Bourke *The History of White's ... The Betting Book* 2 vols (1892).

17 On 18 June every year a dinner was (and still is) held to commemorate the Battle of Waterloo.

1 Isaac's letters to D in this period reflect the concern of Bradenham. In one of them Isaac wrote, more in sorrow than in anger:

> You may imagine that my distress was not less than my surprise, at learning this morning of your sudden departure – without giving last night the slightest hint to any of us.
>
> All such violent movements in the quiet of domestic habits alarm one. I would ease my mind by the hope that nothing of any painful nature has drawn you off so unexpectedly, but I cannot conceal from myself that they betray that unsettled state of your mind which occasions me the greatest anxiety.
>
> If this however should only prove to be a freak, you will easily forget the few words I have written – and perhaps | hereafter, you may yet discipline your mind, too long the creature of Imagination. [H A/I/C/46]

283 TO SARAH DISRAELI [London], Saturday [29 June 1833]

ORIGINAL: H A/I/B/65

COVER: To | Miss Disraeli | Bradenham House | High Wycombe | Bucks.

POSTMARK: (1) In circle: F | JU29 | 1833

PUBLICATION HISTORY: LBCS 20-1, dated 29 June 1833, prints the first sentence of the fifth paragraph, and the seventh and eighth paragraphs, conflated with extracts from **275** and **288** and with the following material, the original for which has not been located:

> Bulwer has written to me to say that understanding that I give my opinion in society that he is 'Godolphin', and that is quite enough from our intimacy to convince everyone, he solemnly assures me he is not the author, etc. etc. There now can be no doubt of it.
>
> I was at 'the cream of blueism' the other night, at Madame la Marquise de Montalembert's [see **325**n6], but can hardly tell you who was there, as I was instantly presented to Lady Lincoln, Beckford's granddaughter, and she engrossed my attention. Handsome, brilliant, and young, but with one great fault, a rabbit mouth.

See **324**n7. M&B I 233, dated 29 June 1833, reprints part of the LBCS version.

EDITORIAL COMMENT: The two paragraphs of the postscript are headed respectively '1' and '2'. *Sic:* developes, soireé.

Saturday.

My love,

I have not yet received a final answer from Riv[ington] but I have no reason to believe that it will be unfavorable.

The parcel was sent to Nichols[1] and the letters put in the post. The pen will be home from Storrs on Monday – and I believe will cost nothing.

The evening papers are full of great news from the Delmontes and good from the Bolanos – Delmontes 32 to 34. Bol. 140. 145 or so.[2]

I did not send Madden.[3] |

I intend to write a short tale, and will let you have it in a week or so. All the things you send sho[ul]d have "Bradenham. I.D. and the date" worked or marked upon them.

1 Nichols and Son, printers, with premises at 25 Parliament Street and 10 King Street. Some directories spell the name 'Nicholls'. The son, John Gough Nichols (1806-1873), corresponded with Isaac on various occasions. H G/I/742.

2 Delmontes and Bolanos were two companies for mining Mexican silver that had been established in 1824-5. They were under the same management and had been condemned as dangerously speculative ventures. Anon *The Real del Monte Mining Concern Unmasked* (1833). The family probably lost money on the stocks, since the mines never realized their promise. The period between July 1833 and January 1834 was one of the most productive for the Mexican mines. The companies were not dissolved, however, until 1848-9. Robert W. Randall *Real del Monte: A British Mining Venture in Mexico* (Austin 1972) 45, 91, 206.

3 Sir Frederic Madden (1801-1873), antiquary and paleographer, who was appointed assistant keeper of manuscripts of the British Museum in 1828, and head of the manuscript department 1837-57. Sarah had asked on 28 June 1833: 'On Friday the Govr. received a copy of Madden's book. Did it come from you?' (H A/I/B/486). The book may be *Illuminated Ornaments Selected from Manuscripts and Early Printed Books from the Sixth to the Seventeenth Centuries* drawn and engraved by H. Shaw, with Descriptions by Sir F.M. (1833).

I don't know what a crocus is –

"Hocus Pocus
Conjurocus
Here's a crocus!"
will that do?[4]

I dined yesterday with the St. Maurs[5] to meet Mrs. Sheridan an agreeable party. The other guests, Lady Westmorland, very clever, Mrs. Blackwood, Lord | Clements[6] and Brinsley.[7] Ld St Maurs great talent, which developes itself in a domestic circle, tho' otherwise shy and bad manners.

In the evening a good soireé at Lady Charlevilles. I met Lady Aldboro' but the lion of the evening was Lucien Buonaparte, the Prince of Canino.[8]

I ought to have gone to a Beulah Spa[9] party with Lady Sykes today, but got off being really quite lazy, tho' very well.

I am yr affec and devoted

brother. |

Mrs. Dawson[10] told me the other night at the Opera, that my pamphlet was sent to the King by "a great personage."

Escott[11] told Lady Westmorland that it was the best thing yet published of the brochures. Lady W: a furious politician, but philosophical.

TO SARAH DISRAELI [London], Saturday [6 July 1833] 284

ORIGINAL: H A/I/B/66

COVER: Miss Disraeli | Bradenham House | High Wycombe | *Bucks*

POSTMARK: (1) In circle: X | JY-6 | 1833

EDITORIAL COMMENT: The last sheet of the MS sustained minor damage when the seal was broken. *Sic*: Matthews.

Saturday

My dear Sa,

I write to you lest you sho[ul]d be disappointed at not hearing. You will have the Pot pourri etc. by tomorrow's coach in good time. I sho[ul]d have sent it to day, but postpone[d] it with the hope of getting the pen, but have just called at

4 Sarah was preparing a collection of mounted dried plants, appropriately annotated, to be sent to the Aylesbury sale, and in her letter of 28 June asked D: 'Write me two lines on the crocus.'

5 Mrs Sheridan's youngest daughter, Jane Georgiana, and her husband, Edward Adolphus Seymour.

6 Robert Bermingham (1805-1839), Baron Clements, heir to the 2nd Earl of Leitrim, whom he predeceased.

7 Richard Brinsley Sheridan, grandson of the dramatist, was a magistrate in Dorsetshire. For mention of this occasion and others see Percy Fitzgerald *The Lives of the Sheridans* (1886) II 366-8.

8 Lucien Bonaparte (1775-1840), Prince of Canino, was the younger brother of Napoleon. A fragment from another letter also mentions the social activities of the Bonapartes: 'All the Buonapartes were at Lady Cork's and walked about the room in procession, Joseph first and the Prince of Canino bringing up the rear ...' Anderson Galleries, catalogue 2,099 (New York 1926) item 17.

9 Pleasure gardens in Upper Norwood, opened to the public in August 1831.

10 Mary Dawson, née Peel (d 1848), sister of Sir Robert Peel, married George Robert Dawson.

11 Bickham Sweet Escott (1801?-1853), Tory MP for Winchester 1841-7.

Storrs and see little chance thereof, for the truth is they have | either quite forgotten the business, or mislaid it. I will send you also the C[our]t Mag[azine] in which there is something of mine.[1]

Nothing very particular has happened. The St Maurs asked me to go with them to the Duke of Somerset's[2] breakfast at Wimbledon, but I co[ul]d not. On Thursday I dined at Genl. Phipps with Lincoln Stanhope,[3] Sir Willoughby Cotton,[4] James Smith[5] and Augustus Phipps.[6] Lady Cork says that James Smith is worn out but I thought him very amusing. He said | many good things, and some original. Talking of young Matthews,[7] Stanhope asked what he was; one sd. an architect, another a lawyer. "If he be an architect" sd Smith "all I hope is he may draw as many houses as his father." Sir Willoughby gave a longwinded description of some place in Jamaica which was "a general lounge, where everybody went, where you met everybody, a place wh[*ere*] people went to get an appetite for their dinner." "Ay" sd Smith "and to get a dinner for their appetite." I hate men parties, exc[ep]t for eating, but on the whole this was amusing. I might go everywhere, but am not very *repandu*.[8] The Stepney has a soirée tonight. She has pardoned me with[ou]t my apologising. I will if possible write a line tomorrow, and | give you some account of the progress of the tale,[9] not a word of which by the bye is written. What are your plans as to Oxford and all that? I cannot speak with any decision for the next week of mine, but the sooner I can now sit down and write, the better. My love to all and especially to thee, dearest Sister,

D

285

TO [SARAH DISRAELI] [London, Saturday 20 July 1833?]

ORIGINAL: PS 4

PUBLICATION HISTORY: LBCS 22, dated 20 July 1833; M&B I 234, dated 20 July 1833

EDITORIAL COMMENT: *Dating*: in the absence of a reliable text, Ralph's dating is followed, though there are doubts about its accuracy.

July 20, 1833.

I am putting my house in order and preparing for a six months' sojourn and solitude amid the groves of Bradenham. As far as one can form any calculations

1 ' "Walstein; or, A Cure for Melancholy", by the author of "Vivian Grey", "Contarini Fleming" etc.' appeared in the *The Court Magazine* III (July 1833) 3-8.

2 Edward Adolphus Seymour (1775-1855), 11th Duke of Somerset.

3 Maj Gen Lincoln Edwin Stanhope (1781-1840), second son of the 3rd Earl of Harrington.

4 Sir Willoughby Cotton (1783-1860), governor of Jamaica 1829-34.

5 James Smith (1775-1839), solicitor with the Board of Ordnance, but better known as a writer and humorist. He was the brother of Horace Smith.

6 The Rev Augustus Frederick Phipps (1809-1896), younger brother of 2nd Earl of Mulgrave and nephew of Gen Phipps. *BP* under Normanby.

7 Charles James Mathews (1803-1878), son of Charles Mathews the famous actor. Initially an architect, he later became a theatre manager, actor and playwright.

8 D's use of French idiom was often inexact. The expression 'répandu dans le monde' does not quite serve his purpose here.

9 *Velvet Lawn*.

in this sublunary world, I shall pitch my tent among you the end of July, but this need not interfere with your visit to Oxford, as, with deference be it spoken, I am not frightened at being alone. London is emptying fast, but gay. Lady Cork had two routs. 'All my best people, no blues.' At a concert at Mrs. Mitford's I was introduced to Malibran,[1] who is to be the heroine of my opera.[2] She is a very interesting person.

[D]

286

TO SARAH DISRAELI [London, Friday 26 July 1833]

ORIGINAL: PS 39

PUBLICATION HISTORY: Clarence I. Freed 'A New Sheaf of Disraeli Letters' *The American Hebrew* CXX (15 Apr 1927) 834, 836, dated 26 July 1833. LBCS 22, dated 8 July 1833, ends with the sentence: 'I have been introduced by Mrs. Norton to a rival poetess, Lady Emmeline Wortley, her person more beautiful than her poetry'.

EDITORIAL COMMENT: *Dating*: by the opera, and by Lady Charlotte Bertie's marriage.

On Saturday at opera.[1] Introduced to rival poetess – her person more beautiful than her poetry.[2] She is young, beautiful and interesting. I have always forgotten to tell you that my flame lady Charlotte is going to be married to a Croesus of the forge, Guest, the member for Merthyr. Mrs. Wyndham arranged it and is proud as Punch, or rather Judy, – an affair of three weeks. He is older than Wyndham, much uglier and very vulgar. So much for a romantic lady.[3]

[D]

287

TO SARAH DISRAELI [London], Wednesday [7 August 1833]

ORIGINAL: H A/I/B/68

COVER: Miss Disraeli | Bradenham House | High Wycombe | Bucks

POSTMARK: (1) In circle: B | AU-7 | 1833

EDITORIAL COMMENT: *Sic*: Phipps's.

Wednesday

My dearest Sa,

I have delayed writing to you day after day in order that I might speak positively of my intended arrival, which you seem to wish. This then is "the truth":[1]

1 Maria Felicita Malibran, née Garcia (1808-1836). The famous mezzo-contralto made her London début in 1825. From January 1833 until the autumn she was in England, engaged for the season at Drury Lane. Countess de Merlin *et al* *Memoirs of Mme Malibran* (1840) I 177-8.

2 Mrs Blackwood had written to D about making *Alroy* into an opera.

---

1 On 20 July 1833 at the King's Theatre a new opera opened: *I Montecchi e Capuleti* by Vincenzo Bellini.

2 See publication history. Lady Emmeline Stuart-Wortley (1806-1855) was the second daughter of the 5th Duke of Rutland. In 1831 she married Charles Stuart-Wortley, second son of 1st Baron Wharncliffe. Her earliest poems appeared in 1833, and for the next eleven years she published annually a volume of verse. She edited *The Keepsake* in 1837 and 1840, and was a close friend of Lady Blessington and of Mrs Norton, who were also editors of annuals.

3 See **273**n11.

---

1 On Sunday 4 August Sarah had asked D for '*the truth*' about when he was coming to Bradenham. H A/I/B/495.

that I shall arrive at "the lettered bowers" tomorrow week. I cannot before as I have a great many things to attend to which I have neglected. | Arrange about Oxford as you deem best. Either postpone your visit a week, if you wish very much to see me, or go on Monday, *which I wo[ul]d advise,* as I dislike postponements; and wish my father very much to go.

By this night's mail, Lady | Sykes sends him some venison. Genl. Phipps is talking with that peculiar voice which Phipps's only have and I can write no more at this moment, except to tell Jem, that it is quite impossible to get him pointers, and he had better speak to Triggers. A long letter with my box on Friday probably.

BD |

Lady Sykes has written you a note, which I have mislaid, but will send with the box.

288

TO SARAH DISRAELI [London, Saturday 10 August 1833]

ORIGINAL: H A/I/B/67

PUBLICATION HISTORY: LBCS 21, dated 29 June 1833, prints the first two sentences of the seventh paragraph, conflated with extracts from **275** and **283** and with the two paragraphs noted in **283**ec.

EDITORIAL COMMENT: *Dating*: this is an answer to Sarah's letter of Friday 9 August 1833. H A/I/B/496. *Sic*: Sykes'.

---

12 o'ck.

My sweet,

I have just received your note, and am about to send the box off to Taplin. Do not hurry your visit at Oxford. I shall be down on Thursday with[ou]t fail. Some solitude is what I want, and meditation.

Lady Sykes' note is of no consequence.[1]

I mentioned the subject of pointers to Sir Francis, who has now gone off to the moors, but he did not bite, making sundry observations that a brace of good pointers were worth 20 gu[ine]as and that of all dogs in the world he hated Newf[oundlan]ds which were of no use at all exc[ep]t as Retrievers etc. etc. Perhaps Miladi, if she go to Basildon before his return may do something.

I certainly cannot gallop off to Worcestershire or Herefords[hir]e for any consideration. I am dying to write. I look forward to 6 months of constant composition.

I visit the Tavistocks,[2] but have been no where of late exc[ep]t a few water parties and | such like. I have been to Richmond or Twickenham almost every day.

I send you all the invitations I co[ul]d scrape up, but I fear there are few anterior to the Influenza when Mrs. Lewis made a great burning.

Have you read "England and the English"?[3] I think it delightful. I hope Tita

1 D had lost the note from Lady Sykes, and Sarah did not want to be blamed for not answering it. H A/I/B/496.

2 Francis Russell (1788-1861), Marquess of Tavistock, after 1839 7th Duke of Bedford, married in 1808 Lady Anna Maria Stanhope (1783-1857), eldest daughter of the 3rd Earl of Harrington. Their London residence was at 8 Spring Gardens.

3 See **229**n4.

has got some wine for me, as it is not impossible that E.L.B. might come with me, *but very improbable.*

Tell Jem I will remember him and, Ralph is very well and about to come down – perhaps with me.

Ever yr attached
and faithful
brother
BD

Some cold cream in my room – and pens and ink.

TO [WYNDHAM LEWIS] [London, September? 1833] 289

ORIGINAL: H A/I/A/407

EDITORIAL COMMENT: *Dating*: the Bulwers went abroad in October 1833 and were rarely together in England thereafter. D first met the Wyndham Lewises in 1832 but did not achieve the degree of intimacy which this letter suggests until 1833. D had left for Bradenham on 15 August 1833 and stayed there until mid-November with occasional excursions to town.

---

6 o'clock

My dear Sir,

You are very kind indeed to remember me, and I should have been quite delighted to have dined with you, and our good friends, the Bulwers, had I | not unfortunately engaged myself this morning.

I have only this moment received your note, and must offer many apologies for not replying to it sooner. I am only a bird of | Passage through town, but I hope to see Mrs. Wyndham before I return to Bradenham.

Ever, my dear Sir,
your faithful Ser[van]t
B. Disraeli

TO SARAH DISRAELI [The Grange, Southend, Essex], Tuesday [12 November 1833] 290

ORIGINAL: H A/I/B/69

COVER: Miss Disraeli, | Bradenham House, | High Wycombe, | *Bucks*

POSTMARK: (1) In double circle: [B?] | 13[?]NO13[?] | 1833 (2) In rectangle: P[en]ny Post (3) In circular form: ROCHFORD

PUBLICATION HISTORY: LBCS 21-2, dated 8 July 1833, prints paraphrases of parts of the first and the sixth paragraphs, omitting references to the Sykeses, and with a sentence which appears to be a version of one in **286**.

EDITORIAL COMMENT: *Dating*: Sarah received this on Thursday 14 November, and answered it at once: 'Mamma will not retract her opinion, but in spite of all the Southenders still thinks you in danger of Ague.' H A/I/B/501. *Sic*: The Sykes, Sykes'.

Tuesday

My dearest Sa,

The people of Southend are very indignant with my mother for her general abuse of the place in which however they confess many mistaken persons join. Ague is quite unheard of, and the situation is remarkably high. I can only answer for the place being very pretty. The Sykes have here an old Grange[1] with gable ends and antique windows which Ald. Heygate[2] turned into a very comfortable residence and which is about 1/2 a mile from the town, or row of houses called a town.

I am very well and have got | two rooms together, so that I tumble into my sitting room as at home and breakfast alone. The muse has favored me very much. The third book[3] goes on with a giants pace and is I think very effective.

Ralph is I suppose in London, where I shall see him as I go through.

There is not a human being here, either in this house or the watering place. Sykes' yacht is here, and he is painting my portrait.

I have nothing to tell you. |

The sea air agrees with me – I am much in it. Sir W. Heygate passing thro' dined here yesterday. He says that he received upwards of 1200 letters in one year in consequence of Ady the Quaker[4] describing him in his circulars as his "Voluntary Referee", letters from all classes, Bps, generals even Royalty, the P[rince]ss Augusta.[5]

All I hope are well. Let me hear by return of post if possible directed to me at

Sir F.S. Bt.
The Grange
Southend
Essex

I | think of giving up my rooms in London, on the Screw system[6] on which I mean now to act.

Your m[os]t affectionate
Brother

1 In 1833 the Sykeses rented Porter's Grange – familiarly known to D as Brick House – in Southend. It was here, between November 1833 and February 1834, that D wrote much of *The Revolutionary Epick*. Sarah's letters to D, H A/I/B/499-512.

2 Sir William Heygate (1782-1844), 1st Baronet, London alderman for some twenty years; MP for Sudbury 1818-26, and a director of the South Sea Company.

3 See **291**.

4 Joseph Ady (1770-1852), a 'confidence man' whose method of fraud involved chain letters. His being a Quaker would appear to be unconnected with this way of earning a living.

5 Augusta-Sophia (1768-1840), second daughter of George III.

6 Attempts to economize.

TO SARAH DISRAELI The Grange, Southend, Essex, Friday [15 November 1833] 291

ORIGINAL: H A/I/B/70

COVER: Miss Disraeli, | Bradenham House, | High Wycombe, | *Bucks.*

POSTMARK: (1) In double circle: B | 16NO16 | 1833 (2) In rectangle: No. 1 (3) In circular form: ROCHFORD (4) In rectangle: Penny Post

EDITORIAL COMMENT: On the lower flap of the cover there is a long passage written in pencil which is illegible. There is a small hole in the last page of the MS. *Sic*: Sir Sykes.

The Grange. Southend | Friday

My dearest Sa,

Your two post office letters arrived this moment, as not expecting you to direct there, I had never enquired – you have received mine? I have nothing to tell you, or I wo[ul]d write oftener. I am very well and this is a very healthy place. The weather has been invariably fine and I have taken a long walk every day. I get up every morning bet[wee]n 7 and 8. and write till 1. The muse has | favored me. I hope to bring home two thirds of the third book, but I shall write with greater unction if I think that the bowers of Bradenham are more serene. I shall be home the day I told you, i.e. tomorrow week, not tomorrow as your letter seems to imply, but which you co[ul]d scarcely mean.

Sir Sykes has bought the copy of Flim Flams[1] out of the circulating library here. At Southend ague is unknown, which is not the case with | W[es]t Wycombe. As I only read the Morning Post, I saw nothing about the new[s] you mention, tho' three days back there was a flaming account of the Reals.[2]

Life is so monotonous here, tho' very agreeable, that not an incident ev[*er*] occurs – You wo[ul]d like Southend very much. It is just the place to suit you.

Sykes is going to initiate me in wildfowl shooting. He has begun my portrait and it promises to be both a splendid likeness and a splendid picture, and if he can be induced to finish it, which is not his forte, Lady S. intends to give it to my father, and it is to be hung up where the cross is. | The yacht is put up, therefore no sailing, tho the sea here is splendid and from the variety of the coast, more like the Ægean than our channel usually is. The post here goes out at three o'ck or so by which I missed writing to you last Monday. I shall soon be with you all, and [*ye*]t hope you will give me a good account of yourself and | the book. My father I hope is firm. As for myself I have conquered 1/2 Italy[3] almost with[ou]t fighting a battle. My love to him, my Mother and Jem, who I hope continues mending but who must be very careful.

your affect brother. |

1 Isaac D'Israeli *Flim-Flams! Or, The Life and Errors of My Uncle, and the Amours of my Aunt!* 3 vols (Murray 1805).

2 Sarah wrote to D on 12 November 1833: 'I suppose you see the papers you will therefore have read the bad accounts from Mexico. I hope not so bad as Papa thinks, for he is very much cut up by it.' H A/I/B/499. At this time fighting was going on between the forces of Santa Anna and Arista in the Mexican mining towns of the Real del Monte region. Hence Isaac had good reason to worry about his investment in the silver shares known as 'Reals'.

3 In book III of the *Revolutionary Epick*.

I found no note from G.Trevor,[4] and therefore did not consider the appointmt. binding.

292 TO SARAH DISRAELI Southend, [Essex], Wednesday [20 November 1833]

ORIGINAL: H A/I/B/43

COVER: Miss Disraeli | Bradenham House | High Wycombe | Bucks –

POSTMARK: (1) In double circle: B | 21NO21 | 1833 (2) In circular form: ROCHFORD (3) In rectangle: No. 1 (4) In rectangle: Penny Post.

Southend | Wednesday

My dearest,

In a few days I shall be with you. I have written to Ralph by this post not to leave my rooms, but to remain in London if he be there, as I wish to see him, tho' it is unnecessary for that purpose for him to leave Bradenham again, if he have returned.

I have nothing to say, my life is more monotonous here, even | than at home. I am very well, and have written a great deal. I rise at seven, I take regular exercise, and occasionally a sea bath. The third book far surpasses my most sanguine expectations.

The weather is magnificent. I continue to think this place both pretty and healthful. |

Probably tomorrow's post will bring me a letter from you. If Ralph is at Brad. and Jem is going up, do not let my movements interfere with his going to Duke St. as I shall only be in town for a night or so, and wo[ul]d rather find a bed for myself than disturb either of them.

I hope all are well, and all goes well – and that you will give as good an account of yourself in all respects when we meet as I have in this letter of

yr *affec: brother*

293 TO SARAH DISRAELI The Grange, Southend, Essex, Friday [22 November 1833]

ORIGINAL: H A/I/B/71

COVER: Miss Disraeli, | Bradenham House, | High Wycombe, | Bucks.

POSTMARK: (1) In double circle: B | 23NO23 | 1833 (2) In rectangle: Penny Post (3) In circular form: ROCHFORD (4) In rectangle: No. 1.

The Grange | Friday

Dearest Sa,

This is such an out of the way place, that I fear I cannot make any arrangement by which you can receive this before Sunday; but from the tone of my last letter you co[ul]d have hardly expected me home tomorrow. I shd. come on to you at once, on my arrival in town which will be tomorrow eve or Sunday morn – were

4 Probably George Trevor (1809-1888), clerk at East India House 1825-35. He later became a clergyman. *DNB* credits him with being an acquaintance of D's, and there is a letter from him to D dated 31 October 1833 (H B/I/A/51). He was a younger brother of Charles Trevor.

it not for | Ralph whom I wish to see, and I may be kept in town two or three days, but that depends upon circumstances. I doubt whether I shall be down till Tuesday, but I shall lose no time unnecessarily.

I have nothing to say. I am well, and shall be happy to find | you all so, when I have the pleasure of embracing you.

I am sorry to write so uncertain as to the moment of my arrival, but I cannot help it. I have written to Ralph, who will of course have received my letter tho' directed to Duke St.

Your affec
D

294

TO BENJAMIN AUSTEN [London?, Monday 25? November 1833]

ORIGINAL: BL ADD MS 45908 ff176-7

EDITORIAL COMMENT: *Dating*: the probable date for this letter is between the time Sarah informed D of Austen's accident, on 14 November 1833, and D's letter to Austen on 30 November 1833. D told Sarah that he was intending to leave Southend for London on Saturday 23 November. On the assumption that he did so, this letter is a reply to one from Austen which he found waiting for him. He returned to Bradenham on Wednesday 27 November, having had time first to visit Austen and (as **296** makes clear) to borrow money from him.

My dear Austen,

I am most surprised and sorry to receive yr. note. Such thoughts as those you allude to never enter my head, and I am perhaps wrong in supposing that they never enter the heads of my friends. The | letter you mention I received on Saty morning, having arrived on the preceding midnight, but being immediately summoned out as the second of Mr. Charles Villiers in an affair of honor[1] | of the most disagreeable and difficult nature, which engrossed my attention for several days, I must frankly confess that I omitted to send an answer at the time, and have ever since | intended to have the pleasure of making a personal explanation, which the arrear of business has prevented.

I have heard from several quarters howr. that you had recovered, which I trust is the case.[2] |

Believe me
Ever yrs
BD

1 No confirmation of this alleged duel has been located.

2 In the autumn of 1833 the Austens travelled to the Continent, intending to return on 26 October. Austen's travel diary is in the British Library (ADD MS 58197 f90). On 14 November Sarah reported to D that Austen had 'tumbled down stairs at Zurich and *almost* broke his back.' H A/I/B/501.

295 TO SARAH DISRAELI [London], Tuesday [26 November 1833]

ORIGINAL: H A/I/B/72

COVER: Miss Disraeli | Bradenham House | High Wycombe | *Bucks.*

POSTMARK: (1) In circle: Y | NO26 | 1833 (2) In rectangle: PARK STREET

PUBLICATION HISTORY: LBCS 22, dated 4 August 1833, prints the first paragraph; M&B I 234, dated 4 August 1833, reprints the LBCS version.

Tuesday

Dearest Sa,

My letters are shorter than Napoleons, but I love you more than he did Josephine. I shall be down tomorrow, but very likely by the mail, as I have a great many things to attend to.

London is foggy and frosty. Ralph will give me the watch etc. which I will take care of.

hurriedly.

D

296 TO BENJAMIN AUSTEN Bradenham, Saturday [30 November 1833]

ORIGINAL: BL ADD MS 45908 ff73-5

COVER: Benjamin Austen Esqre | 33 *Guildford Street*

PUBLICATION HISTORY: Jerman 204-5, dated 30 November 1833

EDITORIAL COMMENT: Surely only D, in defending himself against Austen's demands for swift repayment of £300, could, at the same time, ask for another £1,200. *Sic*: following-one, expences.

Bradenham House | Saturday

private

My dear Austen,

I am overwhelmed with difficulties. Do not think I have deceived you. I never have, and never will. When I borrowed money from you the other day, I believed that it was in my power to make arrangements, which wo[ul]d give me six months of quiet, all that is necessary to settle my affairs, and leave me, I hope, a considerable balance. This is not the case, your money is untouched, and shall be returned to you instantly, if, after this letter, you desire it.

I have | engaged with Saunders and Otley for two works, the Epic poem, and a novel to be delivered this year, both far advanced.[1] The least sum that I can receive for these is £1000. Alroy is in a second edition, which will be published immediately. All my copyrights (save the Y[oung] D[uke] which I shall catch up this year) are now mine, and it is my intention to publish a complete edition of my romances if possible this year, or at anyrate the following-one,[2] by which if we sell 4000 in monthly volumes I shall make 1500£. This is the state of my credits: my debts amount to £1200, all pressing. They are not occasioned by

1 The first part of *The Revolutionary Epick* (book I) was published not by Saunders and Otley but by Moxon on 25 March 1834, the second part (books II and III) on 16 June 1834. Stewart *Writings* 139. The novel could have been *A Year at Hartlebury* which was published by Saunders and Otley in March 1834.

2 The first British collected edition of D's novels was published in 1853 by Bryce. A two-volume American edition (excluding *Popanilla*), called *The Works of D'Israeli the Younger*, was published by Carey and Hart of Philadelphia in 1839.

personal expenditure, or trifling | vanity. I have given up my rooms in London, or rather shall when the year is out, I have no servant, my personal expences are reduced to the lowest ebb. There is nothing to prevent me from being at the end of the year perfectly solvent, but the anxiety, which any urgent demand always creates in me, and consequent disturbance of mind which mars effective exertion, which in short destroys my energy. I have no doubt that were I to come up to London I might by the sale of my unpublished and published MSS. raise this sum, but the arrangement wo[ul]d take great time, and in the meanwhile the child of my fancy from which I cannot spare | an hour, night or day, wo[ul]d receive a fatal blow, yet write I cannot in the present state of things – therefore I appeal to you, a friend often tried and never found wanting, and whom I know by long experience to be capable of great and generous actions.

Will you advance me the money for a year and take a formal assignment of my copyrights? Were I to die, you wo[ul]d be secured over and over again. I assure you most solemnly of this. If I live, you will find me as punctual in this matter, as you have I trust in all others. I entreat you, my dear friend, not to look upon this letter in the light in which such appeals are usually and justly viewed. I assure you it is no common feeling that induces me to make | it, but an unconquerable desire, which now seems near at hand, of producing something great and lasting, and the cruelty of having my power of creation marred at such a moment. I repeat therefore my entreaty that you will not view this letter in an odious light, but what[eve]r may be your determination, that you will ascribe the appeal only to the anxiety which activates a right mind to do a right action. Assist me now, and for my future career I shall in fact be indebted to you.[3] If you refuse me, the remembrance of past favors will not alter my feelings towards you, but I candidly declare that the injury which it will occasion me, will, tho' I hope not irreparable, be very great.

Your faithful and obliged friend

B. Disraeli

I did not know of the new Edit: of Alroy until Thursday noon.[4]

297

TO SARA AUSTEN — Bradenham, Sunday [1 December 1833]

ORIGINAL: BL ADD MS 45908 ff77-8

COVER: Mrs. Austen | 33 Guildford Street | Russell Square | *London*

POSTMARK: (1) In double circle: F | 2 DE 2 | 1833 (2) In rectangle: No. 1 (3) HWYCOMBE | Penny Post

PUBLICATION HISTORY: Layard 29, extracts dated 2 September 1833 and January 1834; M&B I 238, 238-9, 239, extracts dated 1 December 1833; Jerman 206-7, extracts dated 1 December 1833

EDITORIAL COMMENT: There is no signature.

Bradenham House | Sunday.

You appear to be the only person in the world, except myself, who have any energy. What wo[ul]d I give to have you always at my right hand! Are you sure that a Creole is dark?[1] No matter I will make her brunette. But see the Bona-

3 D's indebtedness was exactly what Austen was afraid of. He turned down the plea. See **298**n1.

4 Colburn published a second edition in 1834.

1 While writing *The Revolutionary Epick* D was concerned with the accuracy of his descriptions of Napoleon and the Empress Josephine. Although Mrs Austen was able to establish that Josephine was, indeed, a Creole, she was unable to consult a portrait. H A/IV/D/29, 30.

parte or the artist if you can. I was introduced to the King of Spain, and the Prince of Canino (Lucien) last year, but do not like to write to them.[2]

Now for the Epic! It appears to me that all great works that have formed an epoch in the history of the human intellect have been an embodification of the spirit of their age. An heroic age produced in the Iliad an *heroic* poem. The foundation of the Empire of the Caesars produced in the Æneid, a *political* poem. The revival of letters produced in the Divine Comedy a *national* poem. The Reformation and its consequences produced in the Paradise Lost a *religious* poem.[3]

Since the revolt of America a new principle has been at work in the world to which I | trace all that occurs. This is the *Revolutionary* principle, and this is what I wish to embody in "*The Revolutionary Epic*".

I imagine the Genius of *Feudalism*, and the Genius of *Federalism* appearing before the almighty throne and pleading their respective and antagonist causes. The pleading of the Feudal Genius, in which I can say all that can be urged in favor of the aristocratic system of society, forms the first book: the pleading of the Federal, the second: The decree of the Omnipotent is mystical. It declares that a man is born of supernatural energies, and that whichever Side he embraces, will succeed, or to that effect. The man is Napoleon just about to conquer Italy. The spirits descend to earth to join him. He adopts the Federal or Democratic side. The Feudal stirs up the Kings against him. Hence my machinery! The next two books contain the conquest of Italy: very little vulgar fighting | but highly idealized. This is all, about 4000 lines, that I shall now venture to print; tho' the whole of it is matured in my mind, tho' probably it co[ul]d not be completed under 30,000 lines. What do you think of it? The conception seems to me sublime. All depends on the execution. I have finished the three first books. The two first cost me much the most trouble; the rest is playwork. It ought to have been out in Feby. but many petty annoyances disturb the serenity of my mind, and I cannot write unless I am fairly inspired.

Thank you for remembering Eastlake.[4] I have made up my mind never to buy anything of any description. I never do things by halves, as you know, and I intend to turn miser. I am serious. I live here like a hermit, and have scarcely seen my family. I rise at seven, my day passes in study and composition. Breathe

2 D met Joseph Bonaparte, the former King of Spain, at Mrs Wyndham Lewis's on 2 June 1833 (**275**), and Lucien Bonaparte, the younger brother of Joseph, at Lady Charleville's on 28 June 1833 (**283**).

3 D was to include many of these comments in the preface to *The Revolutionary Epick*: '... the Poet hath ever embodied the spirit of his Time. Thus, the most heroic incident of an heroic age produced in the Iliad an Heroic Epick; thus, the consolidation of the most superb of Empires, produced the Æneid a Political Epick; the revival of Learning, and the birth of vernacular Genius, presented us in the Divine Comedy with a National Epick; and the Reformation and its consequences called from the rapt lyre of Milton a Religious Epick.'

4 Sara Austen had written to D on 30 November 1833: 'Do you wish to have a Proof of Eastlake's Byron's Dream'. H A/IV/D/29. 'Byron's Dream' is a painting by Charles Lock Eastlake (1793-1865), exhibited in 1829.

| not a word of the contents of this, to anyone – Austen of course if you like, and let me know your general impression of the plan.

Yrs ever

Alroy in a second edit: most unexpectedly. It will be out in 2 or 3 weeks, and no alterations of any consequence.

TO BENJAMIN AUSTEN Bradenham, Tuesday [3 December 1833] 298

ORIGINAL: BL ADD MS 45908 ff79-81

COVER: *private postpaid* 1/3 | Benjamin Austen Esqr | Raymond Buildgs | Grays Inn | London | [in another hand]: *Paid* 1/3

POSTMARK: (1) In double circle: F | 4 DE 4 | 1833 (2) In double tombstone: P | PAID | 4 DE 4 | 1833 (3) In rectangle: No. 1 (4) HWYCOMBE | Penny Post (5) In circular form: HIGH WYCOMBE

PUBLICATION HISTORY: Jerman 208-11, dated 3 December 1833

EDITORIAL COMMENT: The cover reveals that D prepaid one shilling and threepence to send this letter by express delivery. This form of postage was then rarely used except for emergencies, costing as it did fifteen times the charges of ordinary penny post. It would appear that the fourth postmark (see above) had been applied in error. *Sic*: either works.

Bradenham House – Tuesday

My dear Austen,

I received your letter this morning, which I read with very great pain.[1] If it only

1 Austen had sent a swift reply to D's plea of 30 November:

Sunday Evg. 1 Dec 1833

My dear Disraeli

Your Packet reach'd me early this morning. Your Letter has distressed and worried me and I have given to its Contents many Hours of most anxious and painful Consideration.

It would be very inconvenient for me to advance you such a Sum and tho' most unwilling to damp the sanguine Expectations you have formed of the value of the property you allude to, I cannot but think the secur[it]y would be a very uncertain one.

Tho' I have no Family myself I have very many and serious Ties upon me and I am not justified in ever putting in Jeopardy so large a Sum as you name unless urged by the strongest and most Irresistible Claims upon my Friendship.

I have asked myself have you now such claims and I am compelled to come to the Conclusion that you have not. Perhaps you may think I have now said enough but I cannot thus conclude my Letter. You say in yours you appeal to me as a Friend often tried but never found wanting. I am sorry to say, my dear Disraeli, that you have tried me too often, and more so to add that I have felt for some time past that Your Recollections of it ceased with the Necessity. I have not hesitated to tell you this in former Letters. However let that go by. I am unwilling to suppose that you have disguised from me the real Extent of your difficulties – but when you say you are overwhelmed with them – how unsatisf[actor]y is the Statemt without also ment[ionin]g how they can have arisen or how you are situated with your Father and your many Relations and Friends all able most certainly to relieve you. Believe me | I have come to the Resolution I have above expressed with great pain and Sorrow, because I know well how much your Energys [*sic*] and Exertions are disturbed by such a state of Things – but I cannot justify it to myself to comply with your Request. With respect to the £300 the use of it is at your Service and I would not wish to withdraw it, being assured you will not place it in Jeopardy. I cannot disguise from you, that I have long looked on with fear and trembling for you, but did not think myself suff[icient]ly in your Friendship and Confidence to offer a warning Voice, believing or at least hoping, that you saw your own way clear. I will add no more – it has suff[icient]ly pained me to write what I have.

Believe me I shall be most glad to hear that you have surmounted your difficulties – and now my dr Disraeli

I will subscribe myself

Your most sincere Friend

BA [BL ADD MS 45908 ff76-7]

alluded to money affairs, I wo[ul]d not have troubled you with a reply. I awoke from a dream. Rest assured that had I indeed supposed that I had troubled you "too often", you never wo[ul]d have been troubled again. I really thought you wo[ul]d have done anything for me, and that's the truth. You have indeed sometimes given way to an irritable expression about our decreased intimacy, but this I thought only the humor which will sometimes break from a friend, who is your senior, and who is not exactly leading the same life as yourself, and as my heart and conscience were quite clear of any intentional neglect, and as I have always entertained for you and yours the greatest affection, I looked forward to your friendship as one which twenty years hence might flourish with the same freshness, so these little ebullitions have never rested on my mind.

For these eight years I have considered you my friend, with me no idle word, what[eve]r you may think. That the close intimacy of our earliest years has not been maintained is sad, but | not surprising. Illness, different countries, different pursuits and circles, all these are causes which may render men *little intimate*, who are nevertheless *great friends*. It appears to me that last season is the only one in which you may certainly have some cause to find fault with my conduct, but the very fact that I, with[ou]t hesitation, asked from you, the other day, the greatest favor which a man can ask another, proved that I was conscious of no want of heart. I was so circumstanced last year that my acquaintance I utterly neglected, the relations to whom you allude I never went near, and I disregarded an entrance which offered itself to me to the most brilliant society of the metropolis. I am sorry to be forced to say all this – but really when one's friends turn against one in this wretched world, one does not like to be deserted with[ou]t a struggle.

As for my debts, they are *entirely* | and *altogether* electioneering debts, for which I have given bills to my agent, as is customary in these affairs, due this Xmas and early spring. I calculated that I co[ul]d produce money enough to meet them, and my calculation is virtually correct. My publishers pay me £600 in bills at the beginning of the year; 400 more I shall obtain in May. In this statement I do not reckon on second edit[ion]s of either works.[2] If the poem reach a 2nd Ed, the sum I shall receive this spring will be ab[ou]t £1400. If both books reach a 2nd. Ed: certainly 1700£. If the Poem have brilliant and decided success which is not impossible, the profits will be proportionate. "Overwhelming difficulties" was certainly a very strong phrase, but allow for a poet suddenly disturbed in the midst of the rapture of creation by something like a dunning letter. In sight of port, I was frightened by the wind setting against me, and poured out my unpremeditated feelings. In my haste, I also offered you much worse terms than were | in my power. For I co[ul]d at once have offered you an assignment not only of the copyrights of my published works, but also of the

2 D already knew that a second edition of *Alroy* was in preparation (**296**n4), but *The Revolutionary Epick* did not appear again until 1864.

copyright of my poem, as I do not part with it, so that if I were to die tomorrow, with[ou]t any "sanguine" calculation, you wo[ul]d surely be securely guarded, since for the unpublished poem, with[ou]t the copyright, my publishers will give me 600£, the new Edit: of Alroy will be out in a month. Cont[arini] F[leming] in Apl., and all these bills wo[ul]d be delivered to you as well as all others as they came in. In fact I expected at the end of the year for the first time in my life to be solvent some hundreds. It is not money at this moment I am so much struggling for, as two serene months to finish all off.

Now for my father. In the most important step of a man's life, tho' this sho[ul]d be breathed scarcely to you, I have opposed his Earnest wishes, and I have based my dutiful opposition upon my independence. I do not wish | by extraord[inar]y money applications, to one who is always very generous to me, to revive a most painful subject. As for my relations, I have never been on any terms of intimacy or friendship with a single member of the whole brood. I ask favors, and such favors only of friends. Friends, my dear Austen, are not made every day, nor do the habits of my life which are either passed in the dazzle of existence, or in complete solitude, allow me to make them. It is in youth only that these connections are formed, and yours was my last. Had the friend who in his gloomier hours never found me wanting, been spared to me, I sho[ul]d not have been forced to write this humiliating letter. Farewell! I am grateful for the past, and for your generous kindness which I have often experienced. It has never burthened my heart, for I thought you were delighted to assist me; it is with bitterness I at length discover my mistake. No one is more *devoted* to his own family than myself; yet last year I received their upbraidings for my "neglect", because I was seven months with[ou]t seeing them; now I receive yours. There is much to bear in this world yet nothing is more painful than *misconception*. I repeat my gratitude for your kindness. Once I thought that the day might arrive when you wd. look back to your assistance with pleasure, perhaps with pride. As for the future, I have no fears, but for your present loan, if I do not see my instant way perfectly clear, it shall be returned. I accept the compliment of your signature – but I am too shrewd an observer not to feel that that is all now over, and that as far as friendship is concerned, I am now alone in the world, and always shall be.

yours truly

Benjn Disraeli

PS. As I have a literary correspondence going on with Mrs. Austen, perhaps you had better conceal our personal one from her, as it may occasion annoyance and constraint.

299

TO BENJAMIN AUSTEN Bradenham, [Saturday] 7 December [1833]

ORIGINAL: BL ADD MS 45908 ff84-5
COVER: Benjamin Austen Esqr | Raymond Blgs | *Grays Inn*
POSTMARK: (1) In circle: F | 7 DE 7 | 1833 (2) In circular form: HIGH WYCOMBE
PUBLICATION HISTORY: Jerman 214, dated 7 December 1833
EDITORIAL COMMENT: *Sic*: thee past, evey.

31 Dec 1833

Bradenham House | Decr. 7

My dearest fellow,[1]

The only way to put an end to a painful correspondence is to forget it; to erase it from our minds. I willingly believe, I readily confess, that the fault entirely is on my shoulders. It never shall be "lend your money and lose your friend" with me. What cut me to the quick was my believing that you thought and expressed that I was not your friend. I repeat again you have labored under a perfect misconception, and I shd. be quite miserable if I thought there was any chance of that friendship terminating. | This damned money causes much mischief. I am more prudent than you imagine, and really had no idea when I spoke to you that I was involved. I wrote to you too hastily, but I act too often from impulse. In the matter in question, since I communicated with you last, I have made an offer to my publishers so advantageous to them, that if they have the capital, they must accept it. In that case I will repay you the £300 immediately, that there never shall be anymore money | affairs bet[wee]n us, and then you will believe the truth, that I am your disinterested friend.

I am most grateful for thee past. I have always believed and always shall think that no conduct on my part can evey repay you and Mrs. Austen for your fidelity to me. Believe me that there is not a person in the world who, if it came to the trial, wo[ul]d more cheerfully hazard everything he valued for your united service. If I am sometimes deficient in the little attentions of existence, remember | that my habits are irregular. I neglect my family much more than yours, and I wo[ul]d die for them tomorrow if necessary.

Believe me, my dearest Austen,
your faithful, grateful and
affectionate friend
Ben. Disraeli

---

300 TO RICHARD BENTLEY [London?] see ec, [Tuesday 31? December 1833]

ORIGINAL: LC Ac. 8033 12

COVER: Richard Bentley Esqre | *B Disraeli*

EDITORIAL COMMENT: *Dating*: the first page is endorsed in another hand: 'Dec 1833 | Declined | Jany 23 | 24 | WS.' D was not in Southend at all during December 1833, but he left Bradenham after Christmas, wrote to Austen on 1 January 1834, and was back in Southend by 5 January. It is probable that, during his stay in London *en route*, D wrote this letter to Bentley on 31 December in London, but gave the Southend address, as he was on his way there.

---

private at Sir Fras Sykes Bart | The Grange | *Southend*

Dear Sir,

I forward you an MS.[1] worthy of your *particular attention*. It will make two vol-

1 Austen had answered D's letter of 3 December on the next day. The surviving draft shows how carefully he wrote and rewrote what amounts to a long-renewed defence of his own position, while maintaining a conciliatory undertone which gave both of them the opportunity to remain friends without loss of face should D choose to do so. BL ADD MS 45908 ff82-3.

---

1 This is probably *A Year at Hartlebury, or The Election*, in two volumes, which D had written with Sarah. On 5 January 1834 D had to tell her that he had not yet found a publisher for the MS. This would be consistent with the dated endorsement, noted in the editorial comment, that after a month the MS had been declined. See also **304**n1.

umes equal to the first series of "Vivian Grey." I recommend you to read it, and read it *completely*. I am very much mistaken, if it do not possess the elements of very great | popularity.

Favor me with as early answer as possible, directed as above, and believe me

Yours truly

Benjn Disraeli

TO BENJAMIN AUSTEN [London], Wednesday [1 January 1834?] **301**

ORIGINAL: BL ADD MS 45908 ff86-7

COVER: *private* | Benjamin Austen Eqr | *Benj Disraeli*

PUBLICATION HISTORY: Jerman 219, summary dated January 1834

EDITORIAL COMMENT: Probably written *en route* from Bradenham to Southend. See **300**ec. On finding Austen to be out, D wrote this at Austen's chambers and left it for him. *Dating*: as the letter begins, in a leisurely fashion, the arrangements which were to lead to the dinner at Austen's on Thursday 16 January, 1 January appears reasonable as the date to suggest for this Wednesday. New Year's day was not then a public holiday.

There is a small blot in the first sentence of the second paragraph.

Wednesday

My Dear A[usten],

I have vexatiously missed you by two minutes. I have just made the following bargain with two booksellers.

An edit: of the Arabian Nights[1] to be published in 6 or 8 monthly volumes and similar [*to*] Murrays Byron, very splendidly illustrated with notes etc. by [']the "Author of V.G." who is to prefix a preliminary essay on the Work and on Oriental Life. The Editor to receive for each vol. £100 – and for the first vol £200. The Editor to contribute if he please a supplementary vol. consisting of an original tale called "An Arabian Night's entertainmt" by the author of V.G. etc.' and to receive for the cop[yrigh]t of this vol. as many hundred pounds as the work may be selling 1000s. Three thousand of the first vol. | printed and a sale of 5000 of the subsequent ones counted on.

This is certainly a job, but it will not take up a month of my time, and I may sack 12 or 1500 by it and am certain of 7 or 900. I don't think the edit: will appear until the 1st. of next year, but I shall have an agreement to bind them down. If I were now disengaged the edit: might be got out on the 1st. of June. I hope you will approve of the arrangement.

With regard to other affairs, perhaps you will have the kindness to | drop me a line to "the Post Office"
Southend
Essex

When it may be agreeable to you to fulfil yr. kind intentions. The 15th. or 16th.

---

1 Nothing further was heard of this proposal, nor of the one for the publication of the novels in monthly parts, which D mentions at the end of this letter.

wo[ul]d be most agreeable to me, but as I shall only be a day in town, I sho[ul]d like some day when you are disengaged and I might dine with you. Therefore I shall await your bidding.

I hope to get out my poem in the first week of March. If it prove a swan and not a goose, my novels are to be published on the 1st. Jany. next in monthly vols. So much is at stake.

yours ever and f[aithfu]lly

Benjn. Disraeli T.O. |

Do not bruit about the Arabian nights or we may be *anticipated.*

---

302 TO SARAH DISRAELI [Southend, Essex], Sunday [5 January 1834]

ORIGINAL: FITZ Disraeli A4

COVER: Miss Disraeli | Bradenham House, | High Wycombe, | *Bucks.*

POSTMARK: (1) In double circle: B | 6 JA 6 | 1834 (2) In rectangle: No. 1 (3) In rectangle: Penny Post (4) In circular form: ROCHFORD

EDITORIAL COMMENT: *Sic*: Sykes', talked off.

Sunday

My dearest Sa,

I received yours this morning and answer it by return. Let Moxon do what he likes.[1] I see no harm in the portrait being on the prospectus. A prospectus with a portrait attracts more attention. You had better not interfere with Moxon, what[eve]r his plans may be. Do not give him the opportunity of accounting for any failure by interference. I do not, I confess, share my mother's objection.[2]

I hope you have applied Oxalic acid to the inky deluge.[3] |

There is a very good quizzical quotation from Mr Disraeli in the Comic annual proving the misery of authors "Butler" says Mr D "lived in a cellar, and Goldsmith died in a Deserted village. Savage ran wild – Gays gaiety was quite fabulous"[4] etc. etc. etc.

1 Edward Moxon was bringing out a revised edition of Isaac's *Curiosities of Literature* and had retained Stephen Poyntz Denning, the miniaturist, to paint a portrait of the author. H A/I/B/504; H G/I/1285-90.

2 Maria D'Israeli was reported by Sarah to be 'in a perfect fever' because a portrait of Isaac was due 'to be sent round with the Prospectus', and 'Mr. Denning', the artist who was to complete it, had been so busy that he had not even begun. H A/I/B/504.

Denning turned up at Bradenham on 8 January and stayed three days until the portrait was finished. Sarah found his visit a trial, but confided to D that he was 'a quick sort of blackguard' who 'detected during the first evening the *great defect*, and when we were alone in the breakfast room | for five minutes the next morning, he said to me "You must be so good as sometimes to sit by your father and keep him in conversation, for I notice he has in common with other men of genius, Dr. Johnson etc. a manner of dropping the underjaw which entirely destroys every ray of intelligence in the face".'

Maria and Sarah liked Denning's work, and withdrew their objection to the prospectus. H A/I/B/505.

3 Sarah had written: 'Nothing has occurred since your departure excepting a scene in the study, in which the whole contents of a full ink stand were emptied on [Sharon] Turner's Henry 8th.'

4 Thomas Hood, in *The Comic Annual* (1834) 133, attributed these pleasantries to 'Mr D'Israeli'.

Isaac D'Israeli (1834)
by Stephen Poyntz Denning

I have nothing to tell you – all here is quieter even than Brad[enham] which suits me, as I have a great deal to do. The poem rather expands, but I have much enriched many parts. I cannot help feeling great confidence.

I have breakfasted every day | off Boars head stuffed with truffles, which my father wo[ul]d like.

The Sykes' have just bought the two series of the Cur[iosities] which is a pity.[5]

As to the commission we talked off, I think an opportunity may soon occur, and therefore do not leave me unprovided with instructions.

Give me due notice before you send to S and O. that I may write to them.[6]

My love to all,

Your m[os]t affect. Brother,

BD

---

303 TO BENJAMIN AUSTEN and SARA AUSTEN

Southend, [Essex], [Monday] 13 January [1834]

ORIGINAL: BL ADD MS 45908 ff90-1

COVER: *private* | Benjamin Austen Esqre. | Raymond Buildgs | Grays Inn | London.

POSTMARK: (1) In double circle: B | 14JA14 |183[4] (2) In rectangle: No. 1 (3) In rectangle: Penny Post (4) In circular form: ROCHFORD

PUBLICATION HISTORY: Layard 29, letter to Sara Austen, dated 15 January 1834; M&B I 239, letter to Sara Austen, undated; Jerman 219-20, letter to Benjamin Austen, dated 13 January 1834

EDITORIAL COMMENT: There is a small hole in the second sheet of the MS. *Sic*: Daniel.

Southend | 13th. Jany.

My dear Austen,

Your kind letter did not I imagine require an earlier and formal reply. I intend to avail myself of your invitation to dinner on the 16th: and shall come up on that day, and be with you on six o'ck precisely. I shall put a canto of my work in my bag, and if we are alone will perform the part of the Importunate Author and bore you with a grand recitation.[1] I | get on to my hearts content. I shall

5 Because there was to be the new edition.

6 The commission was certainly the search for a publisher for *Hartlebury* (see **300**n1). Sarah intended to send the MS of their jointly written novel, as yet unnamed, to Saunders and Otley. On 12 January she wrote: 'I hope to send the M.S. to S. and O. by the early Coach on *Tuesday* the 14th.' H A/I/B/505.

---

1 D dined with the Austens on 16 January 1834 and read to the assembled guests the first canto of his epic poem. Sir Henry Layard gave the following account of the event: 'Standing with his back to the fire, he proceeded in his usual grandiloquent style and with his usual solemn gesture to ask why, as the heroic age had produced its Homer, the Augustan era its Virgil, the Renaissance its Dante, the Reformation its Milton, should not the revolutionary epoch in which we live, produce its representative Poet? The scene was not to be forgotten by those who witnessed it. There was something irresistibly comic in the young man dressed in the fantastic, coxcombical costume that he then affected – velvet coat of an original cut thrown wide open, and ruffles to its sleeves, shirt collars turned down in Byronic fashion, an elaborately embroidered waistcoat whence issued voluminous folds of frill, and shoes adorned with red rosettes – his black hair pomatumed and elaborately curled, and his person redolent with perfume – announcing himself as the Homer or Dante of the age! After he had left the room, a gentleman who excelled as a mimic, assuming the attitude and voice of the poet, declaimed an impromptu burlesque of the opening lines, which caused infinite merriment to those present.' *QR* 168 (Jan 1889) 29-30. See also (vol II) **373**n9 and **375**n3.

however be anxious to receive the impression of your circle. If you have made, or anticipate making, other arrangements about dinner, and have asked, or intend asking, ano[the]r guest or so, don't let my boring plans interfere in any way, as another opportunity will occur.

your obliged and affec friend

BD

For Mrs. A,

I have got a grand simile about a S[ou'] Wester, I think they call it: | and am perfectly ignorant of the geography of the wind, and have no atlas here. I mean that wind that blows I think about the Cap[*e*] and knocks the Hon[ourable] Com[pany's] Ships about[.] Daniel has a famous picture about it – consisting of one ship and one wave. Is it a S[ou'] W[este]r that I mean, and whence does it blow? and all about it?[2] Get it up for the 16th. for

Your faithful scribbler

at command

D

TO SARAH DISRAELI [Southend?, Tuesday 14 January 1834] 304

ORIGINAL: PS 59

PUBLICATION HISTORY: Sotheby's catalogue (9 May 1961) item 273

EDITORIAL COMMENT: The material in the text within square brackets is part of the printed source. *Dating*: the Sotheby's description of the letter includes '*Tuesday* [*postmark*: 15 *January* 1834]'. *Sic*: Smyth, the Sykes.

... Do what you like with the end [of the poem]. I will have nothing to do with the suicide or anything else. Poetical justice is all stuff. I think you will spoil the

2 The picture shows a ship in a southeast wind. 'Gale off the Cape of Good Hope', unnumbered plate in Thomas Daniell and William Daniell *A Picturesque Voyage to India; By the Way of China* (1810).

D's image, in its final form, is a compromise. Canto XL is an attack on current demands for equality, and D catalogues instances to show that the principle of equality is unknown in nature. The fifteen-line description of the giant wave is the longest of these:

What time some wave like to a ridgy hill
Tipped with the snow, long, dark, and desolate,
Save where the cresting waters whitely foam,
Ere yet they break and burst into despair,
What time some wave, some solitary wave,
Itself an ocean, with the lowering sky,
Blending its rising form, its mighty wings
South-east, south-west extending, from the Cape
Where valiant Vasco and his pallid crew
The giant genius of the storm invoked,
Sweeps its fell course, while mid the darkened world
The thick slab gloom a single flash reveals,
Struggling with forky light, the shriek insane
Of moaning sea-birds tell the direful fate
Of those that brave the tempest!

The Revolutionary Epick (Moxon 1834) Book I canto XL 21-35

book, but you are Lady Paramount....[1]

Lady Drummond Smyth[2] is *in extremis* & the Sykes are in all the agitation of people expecting an addition of something like 3000£ a year....

305 TO SARAH DISRAELI

[The Grange, Southend, Essex], [Saturday] 25 January 1834

ORIGINAL: PS 76

PUBLICATION HISTORY: G. Michelmore catalogue 3 (1922) item 43

EDITORIAL COMMENT: The catalogue entry combines paraphrase and direct quotation. The paraphrasing has been included within square brackets. The letter is described as: '*A.l.s.*, 3 pages, 4to, 25 January 1834. To his sister.'

---

1 D was co-author, with Sarah, of a novel, not the poem which the printed source has assumed in its editorial additions. Sarah had written on 12 January: 'I wrote yesterday evening the important chapter and therefore read to the family the conclusion, which has created a great sensation. Unanimous is the feeling of horror, and unanimous is the cry for justice on G.G. I had already given the idea that the heroine had taken a great disgust to him, but still they cannot bear that he should remain quietly in the neighbourhood, and are very urgent with you to make him commit suicide in a Postscript on the discovery of the bond by Col. Neville. *Do you not think something might be done?*' H A/I/B/505.

The manuscript was submitted to Saunders and Otley, for Sarah wrote on 12 February: 'Talking of changes S and O seem to have been crucifying my poor Helen. I hope her name is to be preserved. They have *at last fixed on Aubrey Bohun* for the name. I have never written untill [*sic*] today that I might not interfere, in the hope that you would settle it. If it be not too late what do you think of "A Year at Hartlebury or the El[ectio]n" ' [H A/I/B/511].

Her suggestion was accepted, for, in March 1834, Saunders and Otley published a novel in two volumes, *A Year at Hartlebury, or The Election*, written by 'Cherry' and 'Fair Star'. The change must have occurred during printing, for in volume one the first 71 pages all bear 'Aubrey Bohun' at the top. On page 72 'Aubrey Bohun' appears for the last time and thereafter for the rest of the novel 'A Year at Hartlebury' replaces it.

Cherry and Fair Star were the leading characters in a popular 'melodrame' of that name, of unknown authorship, presented by Charles Farley at the Theatre Royal, Covent Garden, in 1822. It was revived in 1832.

Sarah wrote a preface for the novel: 'Our honeymoon being over, we have amused ourselves during the autumn by writing a novel. All we hope is that the Public will deem our literary union as felicitous as we find our personal one.' She complained later that Saunders and Otley were not doing enough to 'advertise the little preface to show in what relation Cherry and Fair Star stand to one another.' H A/I/B/513. Many other letters record the production of the book. H A/I/B/505, 506, 507, 509, 511, 513, 519.

The novel was published in March 1834 and received favourable reviews (particularly for the larger part of the second volume, on the election, which had been written by D). *NMM* XLI (May 1834) 100; *The Examiner* no 1,369 (27 Apr 1834) 259-61. See also **306**n2.

The first volume is certainly nearly all by Sarah, and the bulk of volume two by D. However, once the election is over, the abrupt last chapters at the end of *Hartlebury*, obviously by Sarah, are distinctly odd. At breakneck speed the hero, Aubrey Bohun, is transformed from a successful newly elected MP, set fair to win the hand of a Sarah-surrogate, the heroine Helen Molesworth, into a thoroughgoing cad, blackmailed by George Gainsborough who threatens to expose the fact that Bohun already has a wife. Bohun is shot and killed on his way to a questionable rendezvous with a tavern-keeper's wife. No killer is identified and loose ends are everywhere. The reviewer in *The Examiner* justly commented on this: 'A mystery, à la Byron, is cast around him [Bohun], which is left unelucidated at the end of the book, where he is murdered. As the story cannot consistently with humanity to the curiosities conclude thus, we reckon on many more years at Hartlebury' (260).

2 Elizabeth Smith, née Monckton-Arundell (d 1835), daughter of 2nd Viscount Galway, married first Sir Francis Sykes, 1st Baronet, and then in 1805 Sir Drummond Smith (d 1815), 1st Baronet. She was Francis Sykes's grandmother.

['Wants quiet to complete his famous book, the "Revolutionary Epic." Disraeli claims his sister's consideration. If anything approaching to importance occurs in which his aid can be of use to her he will cheerfully be with her "in 4 and 20 hours," but] you must not forget my own situation. Every time I move terribly distracts me, and altho' I have worked very successfully since I have been down here, I cannot say that I am even in sight of port, for altho' I have written 800 lines here what with additions and alterations the affair is so transmogrified that I calculate I have something like 1,500 lines yet to write. If blotting will make a perfect poem, mine ought to be eternal.[1] [If his health continues as it is he will have finished the Poem by the end of February. Does not contemplate being much in London during the year.] If you go to town for a short time, I should like to be with you and to print my poem at the same time, if you do not go I shall have the proof sent home to me.... Be not alarmed that I have not yet ratified any agreement about the Novel,[2] I understand Bksellers, [etc.]

306

TO SARAH DISRAELI [Southend, Essex], Wednesday [29 January 1834]

ORIGINAL: FITZ Disraeli A5

COVER: Miss Disraeli | Bradenham House | High Wycombe | Bucks.

POSTMARK: (1) In double circle: B | 31JA31 | 1834 (2) In rectangle: No. 1 (3) In rectangle: Penny Post (4) In circular form: ROCHFORD

EDITORIAL COMMENT: *Sic*: Capel, Buccleugh.

Wednesday

My dearest,

I am most anxious that James sho[ul]d go to Brummagem at all events.[1] Such a step I have long meditated for him. I entirely set my face against his farming speculations, which ere long he will himself repent.

Papa's letter was certainly most furious – but I am used to them. Such an abuse of the meaning of words has been seldom met with – "your strange and dead silence has filled us with the most heartrending affliction" – "Poor Sa, ever the last to complain, has at length sunk under repeated disappointment" – "All we hope is that it is sheer neglect." etc. etc.

1 Henry Sotheran unnumbered catalogue (1912) item 408 lists a letter from D to Sarah dated '1834' and quotes from it one sentence: 'I think of nothing but my poem, which improves every day.'

2 *A Year at Hartlebury*. See **304**n1.

---

1 James Disraeli was to visit William Broomhead in search of a job. The firm of Broomhead and Thomas, merchants, was located in Great Charles Street, Birmingham. H A/I/B/510; H G/I/130; Wrightson and Webb *Directory of Birmingham* (Birmingham 1835).

Do not be nervous about the MS. as ere long I shall make a good arrangemt. I am in the greatest rage with S and O. They have no opinion of the work at all, but especially the second volume. All the Election part they think most weak. I longed to tell them that I wrote it.[2] Before you go to Brighton we shall have made an arrangemt. They have only sold 150 of Cecil Hyde,[3] and this has sickened them. I only wonder they have sold so much.

Had not my father a letter of agreemt from Colburn about the Comm[entarie]s wherein it was specified | no commission was to be charged? Let me know the real state of the acct. and the No. of copies in hand of all the vols. which he does not tell me.

I am most anxious about James. What more co[ul]d you expect than the offer of introduction now made? It may lead to everything. I advise him strongly to go. His specul[ati]on does not sound very promising, but of course I am no judge. What is worse, at present I cannot assist him with anything more substantial than advice.

I have Muller with me and Capel.[4]

2 *A Year at Hartlebury; or the Election* clearly reveals its mixed authorship. Most of the second volume is a lively account of an election campaign in a small town not unlike High Wycombe, and clearly is D's work. However, the distinction obviously was not as clear to contemporary reviewers. After comparing the novel to those of Mrs Gore and of Lord Mulgrave, one of them referred to the preface (**304**n1):

> The title-page and preface would give us to understand that it is the joint production of a newly-married couple, but there are characters and incidents which could neither have been imagined by a bride nor submitted to her approval ... Indeed there is no trace of a female hand in the book, and Cherry has obviously had the whole matter to himself.
>
> The story is slight; a mere vehicle for the sketch of a contested election for a Whig borough, which is excellently described, and is almost a drama in itself.

The reviewer accurately isolates the characteristics of the protagonist, Aubrey Bohun, who has 'wealth, talent and accomplishment' and who decides to oppose both Whig and Tory at the Fanchester borough election. In many ways Bohun embodies a clear projection by D of his own aspirations at Wycombe, and many of the characters and incidents may be seen to be based on the 1832 campaigns. The reviewer noted, 'Mr Bohun stands for the borough of Fanchester upon Radical professions, which the author, grudging them to one of such wealth, station, and genius, gives us to understand are accordant with a subtle contrivance of Ultra Toryism, that would carry reform beyond the ground upon which the Whigs have found their coigne of vantage.' The reviewer thought that the description of the election itself (which fills some three-quarters of the second volume) was 'extremely well-managed' and devotes the rest of his review to the reproduction of the long climactic scene in which the hero wins by one vote. *The Examiner* no 1,369 (27 Apr 1834) 259-61.

3 *Cecil Hyde: A Novel* by Sir Martin Archer Shee (1769-1850), a portrait-painter and president of the Royal Academy 1830-50. As the novel had been published only that month, there had been little time for a substantial sale.

4 D was probably referring here to two books which he used in writing *The Revolutionary Epick.* The first was *An Universal History* (1818) by Johannes von Müller (1752-1809), the third volume of which deals in detail with European history of the seventeenth and eighteenth centuries. In 1836 D asked Sarah to send him Müller's *History.* The second book was *L'Origine et progrès de l'esprit révolutionnaire par un ancien ministre du roi de France* (LaHaye 1833) by Guillaume Antoine Benoit Capelle (1775-1842), minister of public works in the government of Charles X. Capelle was a signatory to the infamous July ordinances. In August 1830 he fled to England. Haydon mentions his presence at Lady Blessington's in April 1834. Ernest Daudet *Le Procès des ministres (1830) ...* (Paris 1877) 80, 302; Haydon IV 182.

Sykes has bought the Duke of Buccleugh's yacht the Owen Glendower 110 tons, the finest in the club.[5]

I am anxious to hear of Jems determination – I can only repeat my earnest advice.

I wish you co[ul]d postpone your visit to London for a month. But more of | this anon.

Love to all. Write soon –

Your

BD

My poem is to my satisfaction. Very rich and strong – but one proceeds slowly.

307

TO SARAH DISRAELI — The Grange, [Southend, Essex], Thursday [13 February 1834]

ORIGINAL: BEA [201]

COVER: The | Miss Disraeli, | 10 Cavendish Place, | Brighton, | *Sussex*

POSTMARK: (1) In double circle: B | 14FE14 | 183[4] (2) In circular form: ROCHFORD (3) In rectangle: Penny Post (4) In rectangle: No. 1

PUBLICATION HISTORY: LBCS 23, dated 15 February 1834, prints the last paragraph, with alterations and omissions, conflated with part of **308**; M&B I 245-6, dated 13 February 1834, with omissions

EDITORIAL COMMENT: *Sic*: altho', Sykes, Devises, Smythe's, Sykes'.

The Grange – Thursday

My dear child,

altho' I have only 1/2 sheet in my desk, you shall not be a loser thereby. I expected ere this to have had a line from Brighton. I continue here quite alone my only companion little Eva,[1] who with her golden locks and rosy cheeks is a most beautiful child and prattles with[ou]t ceasing. The Sykes have not returned, and their return is indefinite, for the Bart: is very unwell, and confined to his room.

Solitude at this moment suits me very well. The book surpasses all my hopes, but so little of the original sketch remains; that you will scarcely recognize it. Assure my father that it is not now at all like Pye,[2] which he seemed to fear. I think of dedicating it to the Duke in a long political prose: if so, I shall request his permission; but upon this dedi[cati]on I have not determined.[3]

Montagu Gore has accepted the Chiltern Hundreds[4] and asked me to stand for Devises, which I have refused. Any place but Parliamt. at present. The time

5 Walter Francis Scott (1806-1884), 5th Duke of Buccleuch and 7th Duke of Queensberry, lord privy seal 1842-6. The 5th Duke's income was said to be over £1,000,000 per year. He was a member of the Royal Yacht Club and owned, at various times, several well-known yachts, including the ocean-going *Flower of Yarrow*. CJ no 172 (11 Aug 1832) 537; no 219 (6 July 1833) 469; no 220 (13 July 1833) 483.

---

1 Eva Sykes, daughter of Sir Francis and Lady Sykes.

2 Henry James Pye (1745-1813) became poet laureate in 1790 and was the constant butt of contemporary ridicule.

3 See **312**.

4 Montagu Gore resigned his seat (Devizes) in early February 1834 and his successor, Sir Philip Durham, a Tory, was returned on 17 February. See also (vol II) **391**n3.

will howr. come, and is coming speedily. Gore, according to his address, resigns for two reasons, his health, and also because he has recanted and turned Tory! His health and head seem equally weak. He is an ass, who has terminated an asinine career with a very characteristic bray.

I hunted the other day with Sir Henry Smythe's[5] hounds, and altho' not in scarlet was the best mounted man in the field, riding Lady Sykes' arabian mare which I nearly killed, a run of 30 miles and I stopped at nothing. I gained great kudos. The only Londoner I met was Henry Manners Sutton, who had come over to cover from Mistley Hall: He asked me to return with him, but as Lady Manners[6] was not there, I saw no fun and refused. Write directly.

Love to all
your affec
D

I have heard several times from Ralph, and today from Jem. I told you I believe that Mrs. Norton had given me her portrait.

308

TO [SARAH DISRAELI] Southend, [Essex], [Monday 17? February 1834]

ORIGINAL: PS 49

PUBLICATION HISTORY: LBCS 23, dated 15 February 1834, conflated with a version of the last paragraph of **307**

EDITORIAL COMMENT: Fragment. *Dating*: from the Tregaskis quotation. See n1.

Write and tell me what you are doing. As for myself, I pass my days in constant composition. I live solely on snipes, and ride a good deal. You could not have a softer climate or sunnier skies than this much abused Southend. Here there are myrtles in the open air in profusion.[1]

309

TO SARAH DISRAELI [Southend, Essex], Friday [21 February 1834]

ORIGINAL: H A/I/B/46

COVER: Miss Disraeli | 10 Cavendish Place | Brighton | *Sussex.*

POSTMARK: (1) In double circle: B | 22FE22 | 1834 (2) In circular form: ROCHFORD (3) In rectangle: No. 1 (4) In rectangle: Penny Post.

---

5 Sir George Henry Smyth (1784-1852), 6th Baronet of Upton, Essex, Tory MP for Colchester 1826-30 and 1835-50.

6 John Henry Manners-Sutton (1814-1877), later Tory MP for Cambridge, was the second son of Sir Charles Manners-Sutton, the Speaker. Mistley Hall, Manningtree, Essex, was their country house. Lady Manners-Sutton, née Ellen Power (1791-1845), was the widow of John Home Purves. She had become Sir Charles's second wife in 1828, and was a sister of Lady Blessington.

1 James Tregaskis catalogue 758 (27 Apr 1914) item 796, dated '17 Feb 1834', quotes a longer version of the second sentence: 'I have my days in constant composition, sometimes I think I have written the most extraordinary book in the world, sometimes I think it is a delusion and dream.'

Friday

My dearest,

I received yours[1] this morning, and as there is no post tomorrow, I write you at once. My plans like yours are tending homeward. I shall follow you in a very few days. I cannot exactly fix the day, nor is it of any importance; sufficient that the first week in March will find me at Bradenham.

I am very busy. I think there is no doubt that I shall get my book out in the first week of April, which is of importance to me. Indeed I can think of nothing else.

Jem wrote to me the day before yesterday, ie. | I received his letter on that day. All well. This cursed steel pen is most plaguing. I have nothing to tell you except that I love you and that I hope you will be pleased with what I have done.

Yrs

D

TO EDWARD MOXON — Osborns Hotel, Adelphi, London, Monday [24 February? 1834] **310**

ORIGINAL: HUNT HM 20305-(34)

COVER: *immediate* | Mr. Moxon | *45 Dover Street*

PUBLICATION HISTORY: *The Rowfant Library: A Catalogue* (1886) 202 prints brief extracts from this letter.

EDITORIAL COMMENT: *Dating*: in his letter to Sarah of 7 March (**313**) D told her that on Monday 10 March he would be visiting Moxon, and hoped to find half his book printed. On 12 March Sarah told him 'we have seen the RE advertised' (H A/I/B/515). In this letter D was arranging to give Moxon the MS while asking for a separate publication of part I. The most probable date is two weeks before the printing was completed.

Osborns Hotel. Adelphi. | Monday. Nine *o'ck*

My dear Sir,

I am here *incog.* with Sir Francis Sykes, and leave London at *12*: having arrived last night. I wish if possible to see you immediately, but cannot come to you. Circumstances have occurred which render it of the utmost importance that the 1st. Part of "the | Revolutionary Epic" sho[ul]d be brought out at once, and I have brought up the MS. and wish to consult you on many points. Come on to me, at 11, or when you can bet[wee]n this and 12 at which hour we leave. Exert yrself to come.

Yours truly

B. Disraeli

I think there is a chance of making a great hit.

1 In her letter of 19 February Sarah had said: 'We are beginning to think of moving homewards.' H A/I/B/512.

311 TO SARAH DISRAELI [Southend, Essex, Monday 3 March 1834]

ORIGINAL: PS 50

PUBLICATION HISTORY: Maggs catalogue 333 (Spring 1915) item 15

EDITORIAL COMMENT: The text is presented as it appears in the printed source.

I have altered my plans about my book,[1] which will be published almost immediately: all about it when we meet.

I hope my father is not discouraged by the subscrip. of the Cur. which Moxon tells me is 1,000, because I know as a fact that Murray did not subscribe more than 5,000 of the 1st vol of Byron and 20,000 of the last....

You shd change your paper for the Morning Post,[2] whc. has doubled its cicuton (circulation) and is written with great power and the best informon.....

The Ep. Dedic.

to the Duke will be 50 Quarto pages. I only bring out the first book – 1,500 lines. I hope to bring you down the proofs.

312 TO THE DUKE OF WELLINGTON [Southend, Essex], [Monday] 3 March 1834

ORIGINAL: APSY 1

EDITORIAL COMMENT: Wellington added, at right angles, below D's signature: '13 1834 March 3 | From | Mr. Disraeli | Wants to dedicate | his Epic Poem | Ansd Wellin'.

Although the letter is addressed as if from Bradenham, D's movements make it probable that this letter was written from Southend. He did not return to Bradenham until the third week of March.

Bradenham House | Wycombe, Bucks | March the third 1834

To

His Grace, the Duke of Wellington. K.G.

etc. etc. etc.

My Lord Duke,

Being about to publish the first part of an | Epic Poem, devoted to the celebration of those mighty wars terminated by your victorious sword, and of those antagonist principles of government, which may yet call upon you to unsheathe it; I am desirous of inscribing this | work to your immortal name. And as such inscription, without your Grace's permission, might be considered a liberty, that permission is now solicited by one, who has the | honor to subscribe himself,

1 Book I of *The Revolutionary Epick*.

2 At this time the editor was Charles Eastlake Michele, who held the office from 1833-49. The passage of the Reform Bill forced the Tories to reconsider their attitude to the press, and in November 1832 an ad hoc committee of the party was formed with the aim of restoring the party's influence over public opinion. As a result, it was decided that *The Morning Post* would be rejuvenated to serve as the party's principal organ. A. Aspinall *Politics and the Press: 1780-1850* (1949 repr 1973) 328-30. However by 1836 the kindest thing a Tory critic could say about the paper was that it was 'the pet of the petticoats, the darling of the boudoir, the oracle of the drawing room and the softrecorder of ball room beauties and drawingroom presentations.' Quoted in H.R. Fox Bourne *English Newspapers* (1887) II 95-6.

My lord Duke,
with profound consideration,
Your Graces obliged, and
obedient faithful,
Servant,
Benjamin Disraeli[1]

TO SARAH DISRAELI Harwich, [Essex], Friday [7 March 1834] 313

ORIGINAL: H A/I/B/73
COVER: Miss Disraeli | Bradenham House | High Wycombe | *Bucks*
POSTMARK: (1) In circle: V | MR-7 | 1834.

Harwich | Friday

My dearest,
Let me have a line by return to the Albion Club – which I shall find I hope on Monday, and be with you the following day – i.e. if Moxon will let me. I hope to find half my book printed. I want to publish it before Easter: if it succeed, "the Plea of Lyridon" on the 1st. May – "the Conquest of Italy" being the ~~3rd~~ 2 and 4 Bks of the "R[evolutionary] E[pick]" on the 1st. July.[1] |

Keep moving!
Love to all.
Let my pipes be cleaned.
BD

1 Wellington drafted his reply at right angles across the first two pages of D's original letter:

S.S. March 7 1834

Sir,
I am really very much flattered by your desire to dedicate to me by Permission your Epic Poem.
Unfortunately I found myself under the necessity twenty years ago of determining that I would never give a formal Permission, that any work should be dedicated to me. I will not trouble you with the Reasons for this determination. They were founded upon a Sense of the necessity for this Course or for the adoption of another viz that I should peruse every work which it was wished that I should give permission that it should be dedicated to me before I should grant the required Permission. This last alternative was impracticable and I therefore have found myself under the painful necessity in many instances as in this of declining to give such formal permission.
If however you should | think proper to dedicate your Poem to me without such formal permission you are at full liberty to take that course assuring you at the same time that I feel greatly flattered by the expression of your desire that I should permit it.
Wellington [H B/XXI/W/156]

The Revolutionary Epick appeared without a dedication.

---

1 There was no fourth book. 'The Plea of Lyridon' and 'The Conquest of Italy' form books II and III of *The Revolutionary Epick*, published together in June as part II.

314 TO SARAH DISRAELI [Park Street, London], Tuesday [11 March 1834]

ORIGINAL: H A/I/B/74

COVER: Miss Disraeli | Bradenham House | High Wycombe | *Bucks*

POSTMARK: (1) In circle: B | MR11 | 1834

EDITORIAL COMMENT: There is no signature. *Sic*: who I met, poneys.

Tuesday

My dearest,

I had intended to have been with you this evening and had made my arrangemts. accordingly – but hear[in]g from Ralph that you are not to be alone,[1] I cannot venture down, as I am literally oppressed with business, Moxon wishing to get out the 1st book immediately.

Tell Jem to send me all my letters which are not obvious bills to 34 Grosvenor St.[2] I wo[ul]d rather have them sent there than the Club, as I am lodging in P[ar]k St.

If you wish me par[ticu]larly to | come down, say so – and I will obey with[ou]t hesitation.

My best love to my mother. I have picked up for her some old China – 3 cups and saucers, and three single figures.

The Curio[sitie]s[3] are more lively than I expected. I have yet hope. On Saturday Longman and Whittaker[4] sent for more. There are none in the Trade. They have passed the 1200.

I have seen and had long convers[ati]on with Bulwer. He is anxious to know how the Lit[erar]y History[5] goes on. |

Ralph tells me that he has attended to all yr comm[issi]ons.

Clay, who I met to day, tells me that we can have the horse that drew his four wheel car in the country – strong and perfectly quiet – but very old, that is above 12 yrs. an old hunter that once sold for 180 gu[ine]as to a friend of his. He thinks it worth 5 & 40£ – but gave little for it himself, and we may have it for less – 15£. It is not perfectly sound, a little touched in the wind, but all right on its legs. He is not anxious to sell it. Write by return of post your desires. Ralph saw the poneys; someth[in]g they asked under 40£ I think: not taxable.[6]

1 The Basevis were due to visit Bradenham. H A/I/B/515.

2 Sir Francis Sykes's town house. *Boyle's* (1835).

3 The first and second series of Isaac's *Curiosities of Literature* had been combined in a six-volume set published by Moxon, and it was selling better than expected.

4 Longman, Rees, Orme, Brown and Green, booksellers at 39 Paternoster Row; and Whittaker, Treacher and Co, booksellers at 13-16 Ave Maria Lane. *LPOD* (1832).

5 Isaac's proposed history of English literature was never completed. Two volumes of the proposed six were published in 1841 under the title *Amenities of Literature*.

6 The owners of horses used for pleasure or display were subject to an annual tax, not unlike the modern motor-vehicle registration fee. Presumably the horses seen by Ralph qualified as agricultural animals, which were not taxable. Stephen Dowell *History of Taxation and Taxes in England* (1884 repr New York 1965) III 225-9.

TO ALBANY FONBLANQUE Bradenham, [Sunday] 16 March 1834 315

ORIGINAL: PS 23

PUBLICATION HISTORY: E.B. de Fonblanque *The Life and Labours of Albany Fonblanque* (1874) 36, dated 16 March 1834

Bradenham House, Wycombe, Bucks, | March 16, 1834.

Sir,

I only learnt within these few days from our mutual friend, Mr. Bulwer,[1] that there was a mode, through the co-operation of your friends and admirers, of rendering by some mechanical arrangements your journal more effective.

I am sure at the present day even talent distinguished as yours must struggle in vain against machinery – a power which it is as well certainly to have on our side.

I believe that I am the last person who ought to bear witness to the candour or the justice of your strictures; but I am very willing also to believe that my case is the exception that proves the rule of your impartiality. I hope therefore you will permit me to inscribe my name in the list of the acceders to your proposition.[2] My friend Mr. Clay,[3] at present on a visit to us here, begs me on his behalf to express the same claim.

Believe me, Sir, with great respect,

Your obedient Servant,

BENJAMIN DISRAELI.

TO BENJAMIN AUSTEN Bradenham, Sunday [23 March 1834] 316

ORIGINAL: BL ADD MS 45908 ff94-5

COVER: *private* | Benjamin Austen Esqr. | Raymond Buildgs | Grays Inn | London.

POSTMARK: (1) In double circle: F | 2[4]MR[2]4 | 1834 (2) In circular form: HIGH WYCOMBE

PUBLICATION HISTORY: M&B I 240, undated extract from the second paragraph. Jerman 223-4, excerpts dated March 1834

EDITORIAL COMMENT: *Dating*: the preface to the first part of *The Revolutionary Epick* is dated 16 March 1834.

Bradenham. Sunday.

My dearest Austen,

I had hoped that a copy of my poem wd. have reached you on Saturday night, but altho' I gave instructions that the very earliest sho[ul]d be sent to Guildford St., I am disappointed. Monday however I doubt not will bring it to Mrs. Austen, and on Tuesday it will be published. I have ordered three copies to be taken off on large paper; one for Bradenham, one for myself, and one for you. You will not howr. receive this copy immediately.

1 Bulwer's letter to D dated 5 March 1834 is in the Hughenden papers. H B/XX/Ly/20.

2 It had been proposed that friends of *The Examiner* – edited by Fonblanque – pay their subscription ten years in advance to provide capital for the purchase of new equipment. *Life and Labours* 35; Fonblanque to D 21 March 1834 (H A/XXI/F/186); see also **317**.

3 Although Fonblanque (*Life and Labours* 36) identifies this as William Clay, letters from Sarah in this period make it clear that it was William's cousin and D's friend James Clay who had been staying at Bradenham. H A/I/B/516.

I have executed the work | to my satisfaction, and what is of more importance to the satisfaction of my father,[1] a critic difficult to please. I await the great result with composure, tho' I am not sanguine of its pleasing the million. I feel that I have now done enow for my reputation, and that I am at length justified in merely look[in]g to my purse. I have plenty of work carved out for me.

Let me hear from you. We shall soon meet, and I hope with joyful | faces. My kindest remembrances to Mrs. Austen (who is to write me a long criticism, as she did on Alroy) and to Louisa – and believe me,

my dearest Austen,
Affectionately yrs.
Benj. Disraeli

317

TO ALBANY FONBLANQUE — Bradenham, Sunday [23 March 1834]

ORIGINAL: BENT 1

COVER: Albany Fonblanque Esqr. | 5 Pine-Apple Place 5 | *Edgeware Road*

POSTMARK: (1) In oval: 10.F.NOON.F | MR.24 | 1834 (2) In double circle: F | 24MR24 | 18[34] (3) In circular form: HIGH WYCOMBE (4) In rectangle: T.P | Baker St

EDITORIAL COMMENT: *Sic*: checque.

Bradenham House | :Sunday

Dear Sir,

I am sorry my absence from home prevented me replying by return of post. I wd. thank you to give orders for the Examiner to be sent here, and I take the liberty of writing a checque. Mr. Clay unfortunately quitted us before the receipt of your letter, nor do I at this moment know his whereabouts, but | I have sent him a flying epistle which will find him sooner or later, and you may rely instantly upon hearing from him, as he is a very punctual man.

I am flattered by your wish of forming my acquaintance, and if an opportunity offer, I am sure I shall avail myself of it. As for my works, it is five years, a long period in my career, since I have indulged in the frivolities you allude to:[1] Certainly if | success be a justification of conduct I may plead it, for since I have aimed at higher things, and have written works, which I sometimes wd. believe, will not die; my popularity has been greatly on the wane. In a few days, I shall have the hardihood to publish an Epic Poem, but as this announcement has al-

1 Isaac had offered his comments on the first part of *The Revolutionary Epick* in a letter to D of 14 March: 'I am struck by the sublimity of the theme, by the many vigorous passages exquisitely poetic – highly original ... You have now fairly and boldly put to the test the public attention for a mode of writing, and even of form of publication, which had become obsolete. You will atchieve [*sic*] a durable triumph if you atchieve [*sic*] this great object. It is indeed a noble effort and I feel it is pregnant with sublime matters, congenial with the | Spirit of the age. I therefore do not despair of its attraction for the Few. A Poem which leaves the mind of its reader musing, is a great poem – and one which engages the Passions on its side, has also the chance of being read.' H A/I/C/47.

1 Fonblanque had written to D on 21 March: 'Your great sin in my sight has been keeping fashion in countenance, the imitation of which makes such fools and serviles of your middle classes.' H B/XXI/F/186.

ready in all probability dimmed your astonished sight, I will at present no more than subscribe myself,

Your very faithful Ser[van]t

Benj Disraeli

TO SARAH DISRAELI [London], Wednesday [9 April 1834] 318

ORIGINAL: HUNT RB 32006 vol 2 app 99

COVER: Miss Disraeli | Bradenham House | High Wycombe | Bucks.

POSTMARK: (1) In circle: Z | AP-9 | 1834

PUBLICATION HISTORY: Maggs catalogue 306 (Mar-Apr 1913) item 818, extracts dated 9 April 1834

EDITORIAL COMMENT: *Sic*: reseaches, pair, wants wants.

Wednesday

My dearest,

I hope to be with you tomorrow one p[m],[1] but perhaps Friday. I cannot understand Bulwers conduct, who howr. has I suppose written to you. He almost arranged to come down with me tomorrow. This was on Sunday, and I have heard nothing of him since, tho' I have called and written.

I have made great reseaches for lodgings and can give you all information.

Lady Sykes has two pair of carriage horses in town, and only uses | one. She *particularly* wants wants you to use the other while in town. *I would.*

I have called several times at Moxon's, four or five times, and it is a positive fact that exc[ep]t once, I have found people purchasing "Curiosities". Young Moxon[2] says the sale is more lively than ever. His first acc[oun]t of the sale was not a misapprehension of mine. He says that both vols. are in full sale, and work togr. | Of the Epick: three copies this week, which Moxon thinks 3 more than he expected.

Yours

D

Just recd. a note from Bulwer. He cannot come until Saty. and as Parliamt. meets so soon, not worth while.

TO BENJAMIN AUSTEN [31a Park Street, Grosvenor Square, London], Saturday [24 May? 1834] 319

ORIGINAL: BL ADD MS 45908 ff96-7

PUBLICATION HISTORY: Jerman 228, excerpts dated May 1834

EDITORIAL COMMENT: D had taken lodgings in Park Street, just around the corner from the Sykeses' town house in Upper Grosvenor Street.

1 The MS shows 'one' or 'eve' with a superscript 'p' over the first letter.

2 See **314**n3. 'Young Moxon' was probably Edward's younger brother Alfred, who worked in the shop and who was particularly interested in poetry. Harold G. Merriam *Edward Moxon: Publisher of Poets* (New York 1939) 190.

26 May 1834 Saturday

My dear Austen,

I hope to see you tomorrow in Holles St:. I have wished to reach you every day, but as I never go out until three, with[ou]t which resolution I find work impossible, I have been prevented hitherto | that pleasure, having, in consequence of my family being in town, had great claims on my spare moments and being cabless.

The success of the Epick has exceeded my most sanguine expectations, and I am busy | preparing for the press the two ensuing books.

I shall of course be prepared to take up my bill, but shall feel obliged by your letting me know when it is due, that there may be no mistake, as my bookseller's bill is | not yet cashed, tho' in course of being done.

Believe me, my dear Austen, that every morning that I rise to my great work, I feel more sensible of the invaluable friendship that has permitted me to prosecute it.

Yours ever and f[ai]th[fu]lly
BD

---

320 TO BENJAMIN AUSTEN

31a Park Street, Grosvenor Square, [London], [Monday 26 May 1834?]

ORIGINAL: BL ADD MS 45908 f92
COVER: Benj Austen Esqre. | 33 Guildford Street | *Russell Square*
POSTMARK: (1) In oval [largely illegible]: 8 MORN 8 | MY[?] | 1834 (2) In packet: Park St. G.S.
PUBLICATION HISTORY: Jerman 228 summary, assigned to May 1834.

31.A Park St. Grosr. Sq:

Mon cher Austen,

I NEVER received yr. last note. My direction is peculiar and little known. Observe the No. and the *letter* as above. But it *must* have come back to you. I misread yr. former epistle, which I did not apprehend required an answer, and I have it not by me to refer to. The money is *of course* ready, and I concluded the bill was pd. by this time. I must make a *1000* apologies for the stamp.[1] I suppose I was in a poetical fit, and did not read yr. letter with sufficient attention. As I have, like Jeremy Diddler, "not so much in my pocket at present",[2] I am obliged to send you a dr[af]t for the 3£. My poem turns out a terrible labor. I hope nevertheless to get it out in a fortnight. We never meet. My mornings are sacred, and you are of course much engaged, but any day you chance to dine at home, I wish you wo[ul]d let me dine with you.

Yours ever
BD

1 Austen had been left to pay the stamp duty on a bill, the debtor's responsibility.
2 Jeremy Diddler is a chief character in James Kenney's farce *Raising the Wind* (1803). His habit of borrowing money in small amounts, which he never intended to repay, gave rise to the slang expression 'to diddle', meaning to cheat on a small scale.

TO BENJAMIN AUSTEN [31a Park Street, Grosvenor Square, London, Wednesday 28 May? 1834] 321

ORIGINAL: BL ADD MS 45908 f93
PUBLICATION HISTORY: Jerman 228, extract assigned to May 1834
EDITORIAL COMMENT: *Dating*: by reference to Henry Ward's motion in the House of Commons.

My dear A[usten],
1000, 1000 thanks and apologies – for all yr. constant kindness and what I fear you will call my constant carelessness. I think the M.P. of St. Alb[ans] has distinguished himself and made up for old blunders.[1] As for Politics, I think it is "*la commencement du fin*"

Yours ever
BD

I am hard at the Epick.

TO SARA AUSTEN [31a Park Street, Grosvenor Square, London?], Wednesday [28 May? 1834] 321A

ORIGINAL: St Lawrence University, Canton, New York [1]
EDITORIAL COMMENT: *Dating*: by context and by comparison with **321**. D continued to use Sara Austen as his research assistant and, while the dating is necessarily conjectural, during May 1834 he was working on the section of *The Revolutionary Epick* where Josephine appears.

Wednesday

My dear Mrs. Austen,
Excuse this dirty note, and remember it is written by a poet in his garret. I give you a literary commission, *secret and confidential*, which you, I doubt not will conduct with your usual goodness and talent.

I cannot get anywhere in my hitherto researches, | which have however been very limited, a *definite* idea of the person of Josephine – was she tall or short? blond or brunette? The color of hair, eyes etc.

See what you can do for me, and if you can get me the information, | which contrive to do with[ou]t letting any one suspect for whom it is desired, send it to me to Bradenham.

Your faithful friend
BD

Tell Austen I have sent him a note to Chambers.

1 Henry George Ward, Whig MP for St Albans. On 27 May Ward introduced a motion in the House to appropriate part of the church property in Ireland. The cabinet could not agree on an Irish Church policy and in July Lord Grey resigned and the great 'Reform Ministry' had come to an end. D seems to imply that, by embarrassing the Whig government, Ward had atoned for failures to do so earlier. Ward had introduced annual motions of this character, but never before with such dramatic results. Contemporaries assumed that the timing was intended to complete the breach in the ministry. The Rt Hon Edward John Littleton *Memoir and Correspondence Relating to Political Occurrences in June and July 1834* ed Henry Reeve (1872) 8.

322 TO SARAH DISRAELI [31a Park Street, Grosvenor Square, London], Wednesday [28 May 1834]

ORIGINAL: H A/I/B/79

COVER: Miss Disraeli | Bradenham House | High Wycombe | *Bucks*

POSTMARK: (1) In circle [upper half missing]: 1834

PUBLICATION HISTORY: LBCS 24, dated May 1834, prints parts of the second and sixth paragraphs, and the postscript, with two sentences from **323**; M&B I 247, dated May 1834, prints extracts from the LBCS version.

EDITORIAL COMMENT: *Dating*: a Drawing-room was held by the Queen on Wednesday 28 May 1834. D did have dinner with O'Connell on Saturday 31 May (**323**). This answers Sarah's letters of 25 and 26 May 1834. H A/I/B/516, 517. *Sic*: Moskova, Lafitte.

Wednesday.

My dearest,

I was disappointed very in not rec[eivin]g the Brummagem Epistle,[1] for which, of course I had my frank prepared. I always believed, and always shall, that something wo[ul]d turn up from it. You none of you have an idea what a place Brummagem is.

I am so busy with my poem,[2] that I scarcely go anywhere. I even missed the Opera last night. We have got on immensely; finished the 2nd. Bk. I sho[ul]d think 700 lines more than you have seen; and yesterday I | sent the 1st. 1/2 of the 3rd Bk to the Printer. I hope to be out in a fortnight, if things are quiet. But the Ministry at present are quite broken up. There is no Governmt. and perhaps there will be a dissolution. I hope not. On Sunday I was at Lady Dudley's:[3] a very choice circle; among them Lady Strachan,[4] whom I had never seen before; certainly a very fine woman. On Monday I dined with Lady Bless[ington] the Prince of Moskova,[5] Charles Lafitte,[6] Lords Cas[tlereagh][7] Elphinstone[8] and Allen;[9] Mr Talbot[10] and | myself. Lord Wilton[11] was the absent guest, but he was

1 D did not receive the letter because James did not go to Birmingham. On 5 May 1834 Sarah told D: 'Farming is at a discount, this cold wind dried up the ground, and the ponds, the grass does not grow and the cattle are starving; with these troubles James will not get to Birmingham ... It is so very near hay time that if he do not go this week, it is not possible for him to go at all until all hay making is over.' H A/I/B/517.

2 The second part of *The Revolutionary Epick*.

3 Lady Dudley Crichton-Stuart, who lived at 16 Wilton Crescent. See **324**n3.

4 Lady Strachan, née Louisa Dillon (d 1868), widow of Sir Richard Strachan (d 1828). Greville V 19n.

5 Joseph Napoleon Ney, Prince de la Moskowa (1803-1857), son of Napoleon's marshal, Michel Ney.

6 Charles Laffitte (1803-1875), nephew of the financier Jacques Laffitte, was a relative by marriage of the Prince of Moskowa. Laffitte became an industrialist and railway promoter, served in the National Assembly 1844-8, and rose to considerable prominence under Louis Napoleon. Paul Duchon ed *Mémoires de Laffitte (1767-1844)* (Paris nd) ix.

7 Frederick William Robert Stewart, Viscount Castlereagh.

8 John Elphinstone (1807-1860), 13th Baron Elphinstone; captain in the Royal Horse Guards, later governor of Madras and subsequently of Bombay.

9 Joshua William Allen (1781?-1845), 6th Viscount Allen, soldier and dandy. He served under Wellington in the Peninsular War as an officer in the Guards and, according to Gronow, was 'one of the most famous dandies of his day'. Capt R.H. Gronow *Celebrities of London and Paris* (1865) 108.

10 No doubt Mansel Talbot, of whom D'Orsay made a portrait in that year. He is described

obliged to dine with the King and came in the evening. He is very handsome. A most agreeable party, and a capital cook.

I have got £100 from Colburn which is very good.

Have my "Examiners"[12] duly arrived?

Your letters were put in the Post.

Mr. Hopes[13] ball on Monday was the finest thing this year. Lady Sykes was there. They supped off gold and danced in the Sculpture Gallery. To day is the draw[in]g room ; but nobody thinks | of anything but politics. I am obliged to attend to my own affairs, and do not even step out.

Vale!

BD

I dine with O'Connell on Saturday.

TO SARAH DISRAELI [London, Monday 2 June 1834] 323

ORIGINAL: H A/I/B/75

COVER: Miss Disraeli | Bradenham House/ High Wycombe | Bucks

POSTMARK: (1) In Maltese cross: [illegible]s | [illegible]2 s | [illegible]

PUBLICATION HISTORY: LBCS 24, dated May 1834, prints the first two sentences of the fifth paragraph, with part of **322**; LBCS 25-6, dated 16 June 1834, prints a version of the fourth paragraph with parts of **329**.

EDITORIAL COMMENT: *Dating*: on 1 June 1834 (H A/I/B/519) Sarah asked D: 'What did O'Connell say yesterday, I hope you safely escaped his toils.' *Sic*: Sevre.

---

6 o'ck.

My dearest,

Everything here is confusion and I have delayed writing to the last moment, with the hope of sending you some authentic intelligence. The Ministry cannot exist: perhaps to night may finish them. It is certainly possible they may crawl on to a prorogation. I think it must end either way in a dissolution, and that ultimately the Ultra-Liberal party will carry everything before them. I think myself, and I hope so, that a Conservative[1] Governmt. may be formed | for a short

guardedly as 'a drowsy-eyed youth whose abode was more fixed than his occupation'. Willard Connely *Count D'Orsay, The Dandy of Dandies* (1952) 213.

11 Thomas Egerton (1799-1882), 2nd Earl of Wilton, soldier and diplomat.

12 See Sarah to D of 1 June 1834 (H A/I/B/519): 'Your Examiners arrived in due order.'

13 Henry Thomas Hope held a ball at his mansion at the corner of Duchess and Mansfield streets on 26 May 1834. *CJ* no 265 (24 May 1834) 355; no 266 (31 May 1834) 380.

---

1 The term 'Conservative', as an alternative to 'Tory', was introduced in *The Quarterly Review* of January 1830, and soon became widely used. Often, however, the term was employed as the opposite of 'Radical', not as a synonym for 'Tory'. In this sense 'Conservative' enjoyed very favourable connotations in the mid-1830s. See, for example, *NMM* XLII 168 (Dec 1834) 506, and Sir John Walsh *Chapters of Contemporary History* 3rd ed (1836) 70. The Peelite wing of the party came to be known as 'Conservative', though as late as 1837 it numbered no more than one quarter of the parliamentary party. The others were designated (depending on the beholder) as either 'Tory' or 'Ultra-Tory'. Norman Gash *Reaction and Reconstruction in English Politics, 1832-1852* (Oxford 1965) 148.

'Liberal' encountered more resistance, though already current in the early 1820s as a label for advanced Whiggism. However, its foreign associations – the term was first introduced in

time, as we are certainly not matured sufficiently, tho' gaining gigantic strength every hour. But the Tories give up the game in despair.

O'Connell I found as agreeable as I had often previously heard. I am not in his toils, and wish I were, for every one seems to lean to him in this storm.

Ld. Hertford was at Lady Cork's dejeuner on Monday.

I have a great many engagements. | Lady Blessington's house is a great focus of the Durham party.

I breakfasted with Castlereagh a few days back. He has the finest collection of Turquoise Sevre in the world. What is the correct name for that Cabinet we saw at Stanleys?

In great haste, I will write tomorrow.

B[2]

324

TO SARAH DISRAELI [London], Wednesday [4 June 1834]

ORIGINAL: H A/I/B/76

COVER: Miss Disraeli | Bradenham House | High Wycombe | *Bucks*

POSTMARK: (1) In circle: R | JU-4 | 1834

PUBLICATION HISTORY: LBCS 24-5, dated 4 June 1834, prints the first paragraph with minor omissions and alterations; M&B I 261, dated 4 June 1834, reprints part of the LBCS version.

EDITORIAL COMMENT: *Sic*: soireés.

Wednesday.

My dearest,

There is a lull in the terrible storm.[1] It is supposed that the session will now be hurried over quietly; and then something must be determined on. The Whigs cannot exist as a party with[ou]t taking in Lord Durham;[2] and the King will not consent to it. Durham is not anxious to hurry his avatar; and becomes each day more violent in his demands. Triennial Parliamts. to be a cabinet measure, and an extension of the Constituency. The ballot to stand on its merits. In short a revolution; for this must lead to a fatal collision with the house of Lords. The

Spain – gave it a pejorative flavour in some quarters. The ministerial party of the 1830s, known to others as 'Whigs', called itself the party of 'Reformers'. The designation 'Liberal' was not adopted until the election of 1847. Elie Halévy *A History of the English People in the Nineteenth Century* III *The Triumph of Reform* (1950) 180n.

In referring to the party affiliation of politicians who began their careers in the 1830s or earlier, we have used the terms 'Whig', 'Tory' or 'Radical'. For those who entered Parliament at a later date, it has seemed more sensible to replace the first two designations by 'Liberal' and 'Conservative'. No effort has been made, however, to record the fact that politicians beginning as, say, 'Tories' later accepted the description 'Conservative'.

2 Almost invariably D signed letters to his familiars BD or D. This is one of the very few signed B – an initial which he was not to use again until his elevation to the peerage in 1876.

---

1 Lord Stanley (the secretary for war and the colonies), Sir James Graham (first lord of the Admiralty) and the Duke of Richmond (postmaster general) – the nucleus of the group that in 1835 came to be known as 'the Derby Dilly' – had resigned from the cabinet on the night of 27 May as a result of dissension among the Whig ministry in the face of Henry George Ward's motion to appropriate part of the property of the Irish Church. See **321**n1.

2 John George Lambton (1792-1840), 1st Earl of Durham, had been lord privy seal in Grey's cabinet but had resigned on 14 March 1833 in protest against the compromises made by the reform ministry. After resigning he became the leader of the more radical Whigs.

Tories will not take office, unless the Whigs give it up in despair: That is; they will not turn the Whigs out, which they can do, if they like. My own opinion is that in the recess the King will make an effort and try to form a conservative Governmt. with Peel and Stanley; but the Tories themselves really think that Durham will have his way. I fear a dissolution must be the end of it. | I have been so busy, that I have not been much out. I was at Lady Dudley Stuarts[3] on Sunday, and made the acquaintance of Lord Hertford,[4] on whom I called on Monday, as he intends giving some fetes. I like Lady Dudley's soireés very much. They are very recherché indeed. I dine with lady Cork today. I believe I shall meet the Mulgraves[5] and Tavistocks[6] and Lincolns.[7] It is her best party, she told me.

A mad poet named Edmund Reade[8] called upon me with a letter from Lady Cork yesterday, to request the honor of dedicating "a great work" to me. He is the maddest person I ever met – but I must tell you all about him when we meet.

The chief bookseller in New York[9] will give my father as much money for the copyright | of any new work of his as the bookseller in London. If you receive 400£ for a novel in England, and will send over a MS. copy to America so that it may appear there before a printed copy can arrive from England, and the Am[erican] publishe[r] consequently obtain the copyright, he will give you £400. This I had from an American poet at Lady Blessington's, Willis[10] by name who offered to make the arrangemt. for me. They sell 5000 of an English novel of any name. I think it worth attention and shall make further enquiries. My father sho[ul]d certainly do it. He is very popular in America. I met Morier at Lady Dudleys. He is an ox in appearance; but the Moriers contrive to be first rate in fashion. Bulwer is very close with Lord Durham. O'Connell told me | that he did not sleep for the two nights previous to the Clare Election;[11] not a single wink.

3 Presumably Christiana Alexandrine Egypta Crichton-Stuart (d 1847), daughter of Lucien Bonaparte, Prince of Canino; she married in 1824 Lord Dudley Coutts Crichton-Stuart (1803-1854), fifth son of the 4th Earl and 1st Marquess of Bute.

4 Francis Charles Seymour (1777-1842), 3rd Marquess of Hertford. He is generally regarded as the original both for Lord Monmouth in *Coningsby* and for Lord Steyne in *Vanity Fair*.

5 Constantine Henry Phipps, 2nd Earl of Mulgrave, and his wife, first referred to by D as Lady Normanby.

6 Francis Russell, Marquess of Tavistock.

7 Henry Pelham Pelham-Clinton (1811-1864), Earl of Lincoln, after 1851 5th Duke of Newcastle, married in 1832 Susan Harriet Douglas-Hamilton (1814-1889), only daughter of the 10th Duke of Hamilton. She was the granddaughter of William Beckford.

8 From D's scorn it is probable that this was John Edmund Reade (1800-1870), already known as a writer and due for at least equal fame as a plagiarist. Isaac received various literary offerings from Reade and took his time about acknowledging them. H G/I/814-18.

9 Presumably Harper's was intended, for that firm led the efforts of New York publishers to supplant Philadelphia as the publishing capital. Henry Walcott Boynton *Annals of American Bookselling, 1638-1850* (New York 1932) 145. Isaac's correspondence is silent on the matter.

10 Nathaniel Parker Willis (1806-1867), American poet and author. Reaching England in May 1834, Willis sent home periodical dispatches – describing life in fashionable English society – to *The New York Mirror*. These were later published by Macrone as *Pencillings by the Way* in 1835. For his description of D in May 1834 see III 125-6. The later one-volume edition included fuller references to D. *Pencillings by the Way* (New York 1852) 471-2, 491-7, 510-16.

11 Daniel O'Connell's election for County Clare at a by-election in 1828 precipitated the debate which culminated in Catholic Emancipation the following year.

He felt that everyth[in]g was [at] stake, and that if he failed, he had made himself ridiculous for life. When he was 2000 ahead, a flaw was found in the registration which wo[ul]d have disfranchised all *his* votes; had they not polled. Love to all. What is my father doing?

BD

325

TO SARAH DISRAELI [London], Saturday [7 June 1834]

ORIGINAL: H A/I/B/77

COVER: Miss Disraeli, | Bradenham House, | High Wycombe. | *Bucks.*

POSTMARK: (1) In circle: Y | JU-7 | 1834

EDITORIAL COMMENT: *Sic*: Ossulton, soireé, MtAlembert.

Saturday

My dearest,

I hope to hear by return of post some better tidings of my mother. Your letter otherwise is very amusing. Poor Miss Landon – to be cut by Miss Pardoe![1] And my friend *Mrs. Skinner!*[2] I nearly died.

Lady Corks dinner on Wednesday very good. The Mulgraves very lively; the Tavistocks good-natured but stupid; Lady Frederick Bentinck[3] – spirituelle; Lord Ossulton, the Marquis of Douglas[4] etc. A good soireé.

Last night I was at | Lady Corks, Lady Essex,[5] and Mad[ame] MtAlembert.[6]

---

1 Julia S. Pardoe (1806-1862), writer of travel books, histories and novels. Major Pardoe and his family became neighbours of the D'Israeli family in 1833. Samuel Carter Hall in *A Book of Memoirs of Great Men and Women of the Age* (1877) 376 described Julia Pardoe as 'a laughing sunny girl'. Sarah was distinctly out of step with general opinion. On 1 June 1834 she told D: 'We have seen nothing of our new neighbours who Papa was | so dreadfully afraid of, thinking that the young lady had only taken the cottage to live by him, or you. They appeared at Church last Sunday. We called on Monday, and the whole week has passed and they have never returned our visit. They appear very common sort of people and with only one servant that I should much doubt James' receiving any rent.' H A/I/B/519.

Of the contretemps between Miss Landon and Miss Pardoe, Sarah had written to D on 5 June 1834: 'As I wished to make myself agreeable and bring myself down as nearly as possible to her level I enquired if she knew Miss Landon who I supposed was the Queen Bee of her acquaintance. To my utter surprise she made answer "I have seen her at Mrs. Skinner's in Portland Place where you know one meets everybody, but I refused to be introduced, there are so many objections, on the whole I thought I ought not." I made a delicate attempt at explanation "Is she then," I innocently asked, "very disagreeable in society." "Oh dear no, very agreeable indeed I believe too agreeable I should think." I was in wandering mazes lost, but all this time the Major is entertaining Papa, who probably may have asked the same sort of leading questions, with a less mysterious account of the affair, he roundly asserting that it is very well known to every one that L.E.L. has no less than three children by [William] Jerdan. I strongly suspect that | the two ladies must have been rivals for Jerdan's favors.' H A/I/B/520.

2 Mary, wife of the nabob Samuel Skinner, was a leader of fashionable society; her residence at Shirley Park, Surrey, and her town house at 23 Portland Place attracted many of the well-known writers of the day. H.A. Beers *Nathaniel Parker Willis* (Boston 1893) 160-3.

3 Lady Mary Cavendish Bentinck (d 1862), daughter of the 1st Earl of Lonsdale, and widow of Lord Frederick Cavendish Bentinck (1781-1828), youngest son of the 3rd Duke of Portland. Lady Mary was a sister of Lady Grace Caroline Powlett.

4 William Alexander Douglas-Hamilton (1811-1863), Marquess of Douglas, after 1852 11th Duke of Hamilton.

5 Sarah Coningsby, née Bazette (1761-1838), who in 1786 had married George Capel Coningsby, 5th Earl of Essex.

I dine with Lord Durham at Lady Blessington's on the 15th.

I have invit[ati]ons from the Duchess of St. Albans;[7] Lord Lonsdale[8] (to dinner), but am very unfortunately engaged, etc. etc.

Clay has sent a pound of snuff here for my father; but as he is coming to town, I do not think proper to send it. |

He cannot have a bed here at present, but will be able perhaps in a day or two. It is howr. a great way from his club. It will howr. I think be best that we sho[ul]d be together.

Love to my mother and all.

Ever Yrs

BD

The poem will I hope be published on Saturday next. I have finished it some days and to my entire satisfaction.

326

TO SARAH DISRAELI [London], Monday [9 June 1834]

ORIGINAL: TEXU [22]

COVER: Miss Disraeli | Bradenham House | High Wycombe | Bucks.

POSTMARK: (1) In circle: A | JU-9 | 1834

PUBLICATION HISTORY: C.L. Cline ed 'Five letters from Benjamin Disraeli to his sister Sarah' *Library Chronicle, University of Texas* VIII (Spring 1967) 13-18

EDITORIAL COMMENT: *Sic*: french.

Monday

My dear Sa,

I apprehend that the letter from Italy has been in town some days. A registered letter arrived for my father by the french mail merely directed "London". All registered letters must be deliv[ere]d to the person addressed or to their order. After some little delay notice was sent to my father directed to Moxon. I recd. it on Saturday but co[ul]d not send into the city then. I have today, but my messenger has not returned, and I can wait at home no longer. |

I will attend to Culverwell[1] immediately.

I met Mr Willis the American poet yesterday at Lady Blessingtons – a very young man, highly polished and even elegant in his manners. I will introduce

6 Eliza Rosée, comtesse de Montalembert (d 1839), was born Eliza Forbes and married Montalembert when he was an émigré in England. The comtesse was an occasional writer but is best remembered as the mother of Charles, the famous defender of Liberal Catholicism. D's use of 'Madame' was in no way a denial of her title, and Harriet, Countess Granville also referred to her in this way in 1825. Greville I 370; *AR* (1839). Hon F. Leveson Gower ed *Letters of Harriet, Countess Granville, 1810-1845* (1894) I 333.

7 Harriet de Vere, née Mellon (1777-1837), widow of Thomas Coutts, the banker, had married in 1827 William Aubrey de Vere, 9th Duke of St Albans.

8 William Lowther (1757-1844), 1st Earl of Lonsdale of the second creation.

---

1 Richard Culverwell, tailor and draper at 53 Great Marylebone Street, was D's tailor as well as one of his creditors. D went far beyond the gentlemanly habit of not paying his tailor, and actually borrowed money from him. There is extensive correspondence with Culverwell in 1835. Sarah had said on 8 June 1834: 'Culverwell has behaved in the oddest way to James, for your own credit you must enquire into it.' H A/I/B/521.

my father to him when he comes up. I think my father had better sleep here, if we have a bed, as anything is better than running after me.

After Lady B. I went to Lady Salis[bur]y[2] with whom I revived my acquaintance, at Lady Corks and | also to Lady Dudley Stuart.

I have nothing part[icul]ar to say at this moment, as I write in a hurry.

BD

5 o'ck. My messenger has not returned.

At present you can have a very good bed room in this house 3/- per night.

327

TO WILLIAM BECKFORD 31a Park Street, [London], [Friday 13 June? 1834]

ORIGINAL: BECK 19

COVER: William Beckford Esqr | 127 Park St

PUBLICATION HISTORY: Melville 340, undated

EDITORIAL COMMENT: The upper right corner of page three of the MS is torn off. *Dating*: D lived at 31a Park Street between March 1834 and May 1835. Guy Chapman in his *Beckford* (1937) believes that the letter was written immediately after D met Beckford for the first (and probably the only) time at the opera on 12 June 1834.

31.A Park Street.

William Beckford Esq.

Dear and honored Sir,

I send you some tribute in the shape of a piece of marble which I myself brought from the Parthenon. It may be sculptured into a | classical press for the episodes of Vathek,[1] which otherwise may fly away with[ou]t the world reading them.

I think it very unfair that I sho[ul]d | hear of t[*he great*] Beckford only [*from*] my friends, and that I am not permitted personally to express to him how very much he has obliged

Disraeli[2]

328

TO LADY BLESSINGTON 31a Park Street, [Grosvenor Square, London], Saturday [14? June 1834]

ORIGINAL: PFRZ Misc Ms. 900

PUBLICATION HISTORY: Morrison 13

EDITORIAL COMMENT: *Dating*: Rossini's *L'Assedio Di Corinto* was performed at the King's Theatre on Saturday 14 June 1834. On Monday 16 June D reported to Sarah on the opera (**329**). Sir Francis Sykes thanked D for the Dresden introduction in a letter from Hamburg which arrived in London Saturday 21 June 1834 (Foreign Post Office postmark). H A/IV/H/90.

---

2 The dowager Marchioness of Salisbury gave a conversazione on the evening of Sunday 8 June, and D was listed as one of the guests. *MP* no 19,814 (10 June 1834).

---

1 Beckford's novel *The History of the Caliph Vathek*, written originally in French, was first published in English in 1786.

2 Apparently the reason that Beckford wished to avoid personal contact with D was his strong disapproval of D's smoking. He told George Clarke that '[D's] Pipe-ry would not suit me. It is a great pity that the fire of such genius should evaporate in smoke – it is a filthy habit, and I am apt to think, a noxious one, more likely to muzzify than to invigorate.' On another occasion he wrote to Clarke: 'I am *sorry* to hear that Disraeli and Co. are smoking away like vulgar Factories.' Oliver 299.

31*a* Park St. | Saturday

Dear Lady Blessington,
Sir Francis Sykes who is at present at Copenhagen,[1] has written to me to send him out some letters for various cities in Germany, which he intends to visit. Among them is Dresden, where I know no one. He is a person I wish much | to oblige; and if you co[ul]d assist me with a letter to the capital of Saxony, you would be very amiable. I wo[ul]d not solicit this favor; were he not in every respect a very recommendable personage; being young, very goodlooking and very | accomplished. I am desirous, if possible, of sending him his letters by Tuesdays post.

I hope to have the pleasure of seeing you to night at the Opera. I cannot afford to miss it even for Madame B[ulwer?] as I have never heard | L'Assedio before.

Your friend
Disraeli

TO SARAH DISRAELI [London], Monday [16 June 1834] **329**

ORIGINAL: H A/I/B/78
COVER: Miss Disraeli | Bradenham House | High Wycombe | Bucks
POSTMARK: (1) In circle: M | [J]U16 | 1834
PUBLICATION HISTORY: LBCS 25-6, dated 16 June 1834, prints parts of the first and second paragraphs, and the fourth paragraph with the interpolation of one sentence from **323**. LBCS 26, dated 19 June 1834, prints parts of the second and third paragraphs.
EDITORIAL COMMENT: *Sic*: developemt., developement, develope, *Mei*noun, *Ley*la, Landsdowne, Conynham.

Monday

My dearest,
I went into the city after the missing letter[1] on Saturday, but the office is closed after two. Tomorrow I will repeat my visit. I made Beckfords acquaintance at the Opera[2] on Thursday. He told me that he shd send a copy of his Travels[3] to my father as well as one to myself; but neither has yet arrived. He says

1 Sir Francis Sykes left England in March 1834 for the Continent. He returned briefly in the spring of 1835, and then permanently in the fall of 1836. According to his own remarkably uninformative account of his tour, he undertook it to rouse himself 'from a slumbering fireside and a monotonous coterie'. Francis Sykes *Scraps from a Journal* (1836) 3. See also his letters to D (H A/IV/H/89-106).

---

1 A letter to D from his father and Sarah, dated 12 June 1834, mentions a 'curious letter of Angelo L[indo?]' and another earlier one from him which was, according to Isaac, 'missing'. Sarah adds: 'After all Papa is no nearer coming to London than he was before the letter arrived; for the letter is not the right but a very odd one. It is but a few lines dated the 18th of May written in addition to a long letter of the 16th to which it refers ... Can we obtain it by sending to the Post Office? And moreover where is the other letter with the power of attorney which Papa begins strongly to suspect you did not properly put into the post.' H A/I/B/522.

2 On Thursday 12 June a variety benefit performance – including a shortened version of Rossini's *Semiramide* – was held at the King's Theatre. *The Times* (12 June 1834).

3 *Italy; with Sketches of Spain and Portugal* (1834).

"Despotism"[4] is capital, full of the real stuff. I said it wanted developemt. He sd. *damn developement* – I can develope if a man gives me ideas – *Mei*noun and *Ley*la,[5] as he called it, capital. He has all his works in his tower at Landsdowne. | He amused me very much; but details must wait until we meet.

I dined yesterday at Lady Bless[ington]s with Durham, Albt. Conynham,[6] Massey Stanley,[7] Sir Wm. Somerville,[8] and Bulwer. A very agreeable party, and admirable dinner. Durham talked to me the whole evening. In the ev[enin]g but as late as 1 o'ck I was at Lady Salisburys. Today I dine with Bulwer *seul.*

I called on the Austens yesterday, and must dine there tomorrow and on Saturday with the Merediths whom I co[ul]d not refuse. |

Thus I have had three interviews of late with three remarkable men who fill the public ear at present; O'Connell; Beckford; and Lord Durham. The first is the man of the greatest genius; the second of the greatest taste, and the last of the greatest ambition.

Beckford's feeling for the fine arts is beyond all conception. His sight is marvellous; he can detect with[ou]t a glass a picture that has been painted over; and he is a perfect musician, deciding | on the merits of an Opera by reading the score. By the bye the "Siege of Corinth" by Rossini is very gorgeous and martial.

In the greatest poss[ible] haste

D

---

330 TO [WILLIAM BECKFORD?]

31a Park Street, Grosvenor Square, [London], [Monday 16 June 1834?]

ORIGINAL: HARV 4

EDITORIAL COMMENT: There is no indication of the recipient or the date, but the address and tone are consistent with D's letters to William Beckford in June-July 1834.

31a Park St | Grosr Sq

My dear Sir,

Colburn is going to publish a very beautiful Edit: of V[ivian] G[rey] with plates.[1] I therefore postpone send[in]g you a copy of | that book, but have sent you a copy of Contarini Flem[in]g for the present, which is a work of which I am not so much ashamed.

yrs f[aithfu]lly,

BD

4 *Despotism; or the Fall of the Jesuits* (1811), a novel by Isaac.

5 Isaac D'Israeli's *Mejnoun and Leila: The Arabian Petrarch and Laura* (1797).

6 Lord Albert Conyngham (1805-1860), third son of the 1st Marquess Conyngham, Whig MP for Canterbury 1835-41 and 1847-50. On inheriting the property of his maternal uncle in 1850, he assumed the surname of Denison, and at the same time became 1st Baron Londesborough. In 1833 he had married Henrietta Maria Forester (d 1841), daughter of the 1st Baron Forester.

7 William Thomas Stanley-Massey-Stanley (1807-1863), Whig MP for Pontefract 1837-41.

8 Sir William Meredyth Somerville (1802-1873), 5th Baronet, Whig MP for Drogheda 1837-52, chief secretary for Ireland 1847-52. In 1832 he had married Lord Albert Conyngham's sister Harriet. He was created 1st Baron Athlumney in 1863, and 1st Baron Meredyth in 1865.

1 No such edition ever appeared.

TO SARAH DISRAELI [London, Thursday 19 June 1834]

ORIGINAL: BEA 202

COVER: Miss Disraeli | Bradenham House | High Wycombe | *Bucks*

POSTMARK: (1) In circle: S | JU19 | 1834

PUBLICATION HISTORY: LBCS 26, dated 19 June 1834, prints four sentences from the second paragraph and three from the third; M&B I 250-1, extract dated 19 June 1834

EDITORIAL COMMENT: There is no signature. *Sic*: Grantly Berkleys, Aylesbury, Dorien Magins.

My dearest,

I think it very improbable that you will find room or rooms next week at the Union and Trafalgar[1] from which I have just returned, or any other hotels. The bedroom at my lodgings is very good, and the bed a four post. My father might breakfast with me, and wo[ul]d I make no doubt be very comfortable, as my landlady and her family are highly respectable; but the distance is considerably more than a mile from the Clubs. The nearest Coachstand in his route wo[ul]d be where Davies St. intersects Lower Gros[veno]r St.

I was at the Duchess of St. Alb[an]s on Monday, but rather too late for the fun. It was a most brilliant fete. The breakfast a real banquet; but I missed the Morris dancers etc.[2] In | the evening at Lady Essex where the coterie consisted of the new Postmaster Genl and his lady,[3] the Chesterfields,[4] George Ansons[5] and Albert Conynghams and Cas[tlereagh]. Tuesday after the Opera, I supped with Cas: who gave me a very recherché party. Ossulston, myself, Massey Stanley and a Forester; not Cecil.[6] Wednesday, a good dinner at Lady Sykes: the Grantly Berkleys,[7] the Charles Tollemaches and daughter, sister of Lady

1 See Isaac to D 10 June: 'I think I could get into the *Spring Garden* Hotel (the Trafalgar I think is the new name) it could be better for us both.' H A/I/C/48.

2 The Duchess of St Albans gave on 16 June what was described in the press as 'a farewell fete' at Holly Lodge, her London residence. 'Her Grace gave an Entertainment on Monday last which will long be remembered in the annals of pleasure as a *divertissement* of peculiar taste and refinement ... a promenade ... military band of the Guards ... morris dancers ... a sumptuous supper concluded all the festivities.' *MP* no 19,821 (18 June 1834).

3 Francis Nathaniel Conyngham (1797-1876), 2nd Marquess Conyngham, a general in the army. He was gazetted as postmaster general 5 July 1834. In 1824 he had married Lady Jane Paget (d 1876), daughter of 1st Marquess of Anglesey. See **329**n6.

4 George Stanhope (1805-1866), 6th Earl of Chesterfield, had married in 1830 Anne Elizabeth Forester (d 1885), daughter of 1st Baron Forester. Stanhope was master of the buckhounds in Peel's first government.

5 George Anson (1797-1857), son of 1st Viscount Anson, had married in 1830 Isabella Forester (d 1858), daughter of 1st Baron Forester. Anson was Whig MP for Great Yarmouth 1818-35, for Stoke-upon-Trent 1836-7, and for South Staffordshire 1837-53. He was killed in the Indian Mutiny.

6 Presumably one of the younger brothers of George Cecil Weld Forester, after 1874 3rd Baron Forester. They were: Charles Robert Weld Forester (b 1811), a major in the army and assistant military secretary in Ireland; Orlando Watkin Weld Forester, who entered the church, after 1886 4th Baron Forester; and Emilius John Weld Forester (b 1815), a colonel in the army.

7 George Charles Grantley Fitz Hardinge Berkeley (1800-1881), younger son of the 5th Earl of Berkeley. In 1824 he had married Caroline Benfield (d 1873). He was MP for West Gloucestershire 1832-52, and the major accomplishment of his parliamentary career appears to have been the sponsoring of the admission of ladies to the visitors' gallery. His memoirs claim friendship with D. *My Life and Recollections* (1866) I 357-8; III 223.

Aylesbury,[8] the Dorien Magins,[9] Lady Cork, Cas. and Ridley Colborne:[10] to night after paying my respects to their Maj[estie]s at the Opera[11] I am going to the Duchess of Hamilton's.[12]

I have had great success in society this year in every respect. I am as popular with the Dandies as I was hated by the second rate men. I make my | way easily in the highest set, where there is no envy, malice etc., and where they like to admire and be amused. Yest[erda]y Lord Durham called upon me, being the first day he has been in town since we met. I was not at home; but this Lady Bles[sington] told me. I am also right in pol[itic]s as well as society, being now backed by a very powerful party; and I think the winning one.

A good story! On Monday, I think; Lady Sykes was at Lady Cork's, and Lord Carrington paid her a visit.

Lady C: "Do you know young Disraeli?"

Lord C: "Hem!, why! eh!"

Lady C: "Why he is yr. neighbour isn't he, eh?"[13]

Lord C: "His father is – "

Lady C: "I know that. His father is one of my dearest friends. I dote on the Disraelis."

Lord C: "The young man is a very extraord[inar]y sort of person. The father I like; he is very quiet and respectable."

Lady C: "Why do you think the young man extraord[inar]y? I sho[ul]d not think that *you* co[ul]d taste him."

Lord C: "He is a great agitator. Not that he troubles us much *now*. He is never amongst us now. I | believe he has gone abroad again."

Lad[y] C literatum: "You old fool! Why he sent me this book this morning. You need not look at it; you can't understand it. It is the finest book ever written. Gone abroad indeed! Why he is the best ton in London! There is not a party that goes down with[ou]t him. The D[uche]ss of Hamilton says there is nothing like. Lady Lonsdale[14] wo[ul]d give her head and shoulders for him. He

8 Charles Tollemache (1775-1850), third son of Louisa Manners, who in 1821 had become Countess of Dysart in her own right. In 1803 he had married Gertrude Gardiner. Their elder daughter, Marie Elizabeth Brudenell-Bruce (1809-1893), had become the second wife of the 1st Marquess of Ailesbury in 1833, and the younger, Frances Louisa Tollemache, is the one to whom D refers.

9 Either Magens Dorrien-Magens (d 1849) of Hammerwood and Brightlingsea and his wife Henrietta Cecilia Dorrien-Magens (d 1849), eldest sister of 3rd Baron Dynevor, or their son John (b 1796), who married in 1830 Mary Stephana Riedsdell. Father and son were both doubtless connected with the well-known banking firm of that name.

10 Nicholas William Ridley Colborne (1779-1854), Whig MP for Wells 1834-7. In 1839 he was created 1st Baron Colborne.

11 The King and Queen attended a performance of Rossini's *The Siege of Corinth* at the King's Theatre on 19 June. Although D had seen the opera five days before (**328**), obviously he was planning to go again.

12 12 Portman Square was the London address of the Duchess of Hamilton.

13 Lord Carrington lived at Wycombe Abbey, only a few miles from Bradenham.

14 Lady Augusta Lowther (1761-1838), daughter of the 9th Earl of Westmorland, who in 1781 had married William Lowther, after 1807 1st Earl of Lonsdale of the second creation.

wo[ul]d not dine at yr. house, if you were to ask him. He does not care for people because they are lords; he must have fashion, or beauty, or wit, or something; and you are a very good sort of a person, but | you are nothing more." The old Lord took it very good humoredly and laughed. Lady Cork has read every line of the new books. I do not doubt the sincerity of her admiration, for she has laid out 17/- in crimson velvet, and her maid is binding it.

I have sent the book to the Lindos. |

Angelo's letter[15] cost me 7/-

332

TO MARIA D'ISRAELI and SARAH DISRAELI — 47 Gower Street, London, [Monday 23 June 1834]

ORIGINAL: FITZ Disraeli A6
COVER: Miss Disraeli | Bradenham House, | High Wycombe | *Bucks*
POSTMARK: (1) In Maltese cross: V.S | VJU23S | 1834
EDITORIAL COMMENT: The first twelve lines of the letter are addressed to D's mother; the rest, with the envelope, is addressed to Sarah. *Sic*: accomod[ati]on.

---

47 Gower St.[1] | 5 o'ck

My dear Mother,

You must come to me; as they cannot receive you at any hotel. You can have here a very good drawing and sleeping room, and accomod[ati]on for Wells. You need not bring William as my little boy will wait upon you. I have taken the rooms and everything will I think be very good, as the people are very respectable. Altho' distant from the club, it will be pleasant to be tog[ethe]r.

To Sa.

I have not got Mignet[2] –

Taylor is a hack of the Quarterly | and a creature of Lockharts.[3]

Beckford's book awaits my father.[4] The 2nd Vol. is delightful.

There are rev[iew]s in the Lit[erary] Gaz[ette] and the Athenaeum[5] – very fa-

15 See **329**n1.

1 Throughout the period, 47 Gower Street was listed as the address of George Falconer. However it seems clear that D's uncle Ephraim Lindo and his family lived there.

2 D used François Mignet's *Histoire de la révolution française depuis 1789 jusqu'en 1814* (Paris 1824) as a principal source in writing *The Revolutionary Epick*.

3 In a letter of 16 June 1834 (H A/I/B/523) Sarah had asked: 'Who is this Taylor that is so puffed up?' Henry Taylor (1800-1886), knighted in 1869, served in the Colonial Office and simultaneously pursued literary ambitions. He was a regular contributor to *The Quarterly Review*. In June 1834 he published his closet drama, *Philip van Artevelde*, and in 1836 *The Statesman*, an ironical account of how to succeed in politics. The lasting success of the latter suggests that D was being rather hasty in dismissing Taylor as a mere hack.

A review of *Philip van Artevelde* and one of *The Revolutionary Epick* appeared soon after, on the same page of *The Court Journal* 270 (28 June 1834) 457. The *Epick* received faint praise and Taylor's work was acclaimed as one of the most 'original works of our time'. This cannot have soothed D's feelings.

4 William Beckford's *Dreams, Waking Thoughts and Incidents* (rev ed 1834). D had offered to review it for *The Edinburgh Review*.

5 *The Revolutionary Epick* was reviewed in *The Literary Gazette* no 909 (21 June 1834) 427-8. Another review in *The Athenaeum* no 347 (21 June 1834) 468-9 has been ascribed to H.F. Chorley.

vorable. Gen[era]l impression that it will be more popular than the others; for which I care nothing, as I am certain that I must publish yet more, before the attention which I require can be obtained. |

in great haste.

My uncle sends his love to Emily; the girls are out and will soon write to her.[6]

BD

333

TO HENRY COLBURN [Bradenham?, June 1834?]

ORIGINAL: PS 52

PUBLICATION HISTORY: Maggs catalogue 349 (Autumn 1916) item 1171, described as 'A.L.S. "B.D." to Henry Colburn, 1 page, 4to. Bradenham House. 1834.'

EDITORIAL COMMENT: *Dating*: by reference to the first instalment of 'The Infernal Marriage' which appeared in the July number of *The New Monthly Magazine*.

I shall send you my article very early on Monday morning.[1] It is a very amusing one, and will make I think about 12 pages. I think your Mag: is improving.

334

TO LADY BLESSINGTON [London], Wednesday [2 July? 1834]

ORIGINAL: PRIN Parrish Collection AM 19732

PUBLICATION HISTORY: Madden II 216 prints the first paragraph without date.

EDITORIAL COMMENT: *Dating*: by comparison with **336**.

Wednesday

Dearest Lady Blessington,

Ever since your most agreeable dinner party ("after pleasure comes pain") I have been a prisoner with the Influenza; a most annoying infirmity in these | troublous times, when one likes to lounge about and gather all the chit-chat which is always wrong. I wish you would write me a little confidential note and tell me what the | Opposition mean to do, and what is to happen.[1]

I am going to indulge in a drive, but I fear I shall not gather strength eno' to crawl to you | altho' I am very anxious to have the honor of presenting my

Henry G. Hewlett ed *Henry Fothergill Chorley: Autobiography, Memoirs and Letters* (1873) I 96. *The Gazette* noted D's tendency to 'The mistaken use of odd expressions for poetry and of strong epithets for power', adding that the poem gave the impression 'of great labour' without being 'highly polished'. Nor was *The Athenaeum* laudatory, noting that 'the taste of the day is not for allegory', although the reviewer allowed that the poem improved as it went along.

6 Ephraim Lindo and his four daughters: Cecilia, Emily, Louisa and Olivia. Emily was presumably visiting Bradenham at the time.

---

1 Probably the first part of 'The Infernal Marriage', published in NMM XLI (July 1834) 293-304. On 24 May D had concluded an agreement with Colburn to supply material for use in *The New Monthly Magazine* in return for a stipend of £100. See H E/VII/D/16.

---

1 The Copley MSS held at the Pforzheimer Library in New York suggest that Lord Lyndhurst and Lady Blessington were close friends. For other evidence of their friendship see Derek Hudson ed *The Diary of Henry Crabb Robinson: An Abridgement* (1967) 136, entry for 2 December 1834. As the Tories had only recently been defeated, perhaps D was hoping for information from Lyndhurst via Lady Blessington. D seems not yet to have known Lyndhurst. See **338**.

friend Villebois[2] to you who has passed several years at the Northern Courts and whom you will like very much.

Yours, dr Lady Bless[ington]
Ever
B. Disraeli

TO WILLIAM BECKFORD [London, Thursday 3 July 1834] **335**

ORIGINAL: BECK 3
COVER: William Beckford Esqr. | Landdown Place | *20 Barth* | from *Mr. Disraeli*
POSTMARK: (1) In circle: EX | 3 JY 3 | 1834
PUBLICATION HISTORY: Melville 338-9, dated 3 July 1834
EDITORIAL COMMENT: The second and third lines of the cover are not in D's hand, so he cannot be credited with the highly original spelling of both elements of the address to which the letter was forwarded.

I am very sorry! I hope you will not fall into the hands of a Pict.
Thy ever faithful
Disraeli
If you have time, read "The Infernal Marriage" in the New Monthly.[1]

TO SARAH DISRAELI [London], Friday [4 July 1834] **336**

ORIGINAL: H A/I/B/80
COVER: Miss Disraeli | Bradenham House | High Wycombe | *Bucks*
POSTMARK: (1) In circle: R | JY-4 | 1834
EDITORIAL COMMENT: *Sic*: MtAlem[bert']s.

Friday

My dear Sa,

I got about yesterday morn[in]g but felt so exhausted, that I co[ul]d not go to Mad[ame] MtAlem[bert']s in the evening. I am now suffering only from extreme lassitude. I have not been doctored at all; but I shall now take some stimulants and in a few days shall be quite myself. The Influenza rages here: everyone is blind.

2 Probably Henrietta Sykes's brother, Henry Villebois, eldest son of Henry Villebois of Marham Hall, Norfolk. Her father, the elder Villebois, was a partner in a brewery. The brother married in 1831. *BLG* (1846).

---

1 In June D wrote to Macvey Napier, editor of *The Edinburgh Review*, offering to review Beckford's *Italy, Spain and Portugal.* When his offer was declined, D attached this note to Napier's refusal of 24 June (BECK 1) and sent both on to Beckford.

Beckford replied: 'So then I am doomed to fall into Picts' hands and certain therefore of being daubed or skinned. Praise or censure from tribes worse than savages is to me perfectly indifferent. I shall probably not find time to read their ravings, but I have snatched a moment to read the I.M. and bless the hour when I snatched it.' BECK 3.

'The Infernal Marriage', a series of satirical dialogues in the manner of Lucian, appeared in four issues of *The New Monthly Magazine*: XLI (July and Aug 1834) 293-304, 431-40; XLII (Sept and Oct 1834) 30-8, 139-44. Beckford did read 'The Infernal Marriage', and conveyed his appreciation through his friend George Clarke: 'Pray tell Disraeli that I have read, enjoyed, and admired his Infernal Marriage. The sly, dry humour of that most original composition is to me delightful.' Oliver 302.

The buckle has arrived and shall be forwarded at the first opportunity.[1]

Send the papers with[ou]t loss of | time. I have nothing to tell you for I have seen no one and heard nothing; but I will write when things are vice versa.

Thine,

D

---

337 TO SARAH DISRAELI [34 Grosvenor Street, London], Monday [7 July 1834]

ORIGINAL: BEA 203

COVER: Miss Disraeli | Bradenham House | High Wycombe | Bucks

POSTMARK: (1) In circle: V | JY-7 | 1834

PUBLICATION HISTORY: M&B I 251-2, dated 7 July 1834, with omissions

EDITORIAL COMMENT: *Sic*: Frank's, Cholmely, champaigne, Lewis'.

Monday morng.

My dearest,

I have just received your parcel. I have quite recovered, but I am taking quinine, and shall yet for a few days. I shall be sending you a parcel in a day or two when I will enclose my mothers buckle and the book for my father. I was very unwell unto Friday Ev[enin]g. I had promised to join a water party in Sir Frank's yacht which has returned with[ou]t its master,[1] to witness the Royal embarkation on Saturday morng,[2] and the exertion which I dreaded, cured me. It was almost the only party of pleasure that ever turned out pleasant. Lady Sykes[,] Sir M. and Lady Georgiana Cholmely,[3] the | Burdett daughters,[4] Castlereagh, Ossulston and myself. The day was beautiful. The ladies went off the night before. Ossulston drove me down in his cab. We arrived just in time, 1/2 past 9, in spite of a long debate on Tithes which had kept him and Cas. up till two.[5] Cas. rode down and arrived covered with dust and sulky but just in time also: and regained his good humor after breakfast. After the show we breakfasted, and sailed up to Greenwich. After lionising the Hospital[6] and sentimentalis-

1 Sarah had asked D on 3 July 1834: 'Has Mamma's buckle come from Howell and James. Tom was to call for it.' H A/I/B/526.

---

1 See **328**n1.

2 'Her Majesty, accompanied by the Duke of Saxe Meiningen, and attended by the Earl and Countess of Denbigh, the Earl and Countess Brownlow, Miss Bagot, Lord Frederick Fitzclarence, and Mr Davies, left the Palace of St James's at a quarter before 9 o'clock on Saturday morning in a carriage and four, with an escort of light cavalry, for Woolwich.' *The Times* (7 July 1834).

3 Sir Montague John Cholmeley (1803-1874), 2nd Baronet, married in 1829 Georgiana Beauclerk (d 1880), daughter of the 8th Duke of St Albans. Sir Montague was Whig MP for Lincolnshire 1847-52 and again 1857-74.

4 The daughters of Sir Francis Burdett were: Sophia (b 1794), married in 1833 Robert Otway-Cave, MP; Susannah (b 1800), married in 1830 John Trevanion; Joanna Frances (b 1804); Clara Maria (b 1806), married in 1850 James Money; and Angela Georgina (b 1814), after 1871 Baroness Burdett-Coutts in her own right.

5 The Irish Tithe Bill – an amendment to the Church Temporalities (Ireland) Act – was debated in the Commons on Friday 4 July, and the debate continued into Saturday morning. *The Times* (5 July 1834).

6 Greenwich Hospital, now the Royal Naval Hospital.

ing in the Park,[7] we had a magnificent banquet on deck, and had nothing from shore exc[ep]t white bait piping hot. Ossulston was our minstrel and a most musical one; and we all arrived in town in time for the | ballet.[8] I never knew a more agreeable day, and never drank so much champaigne in my life. I woke quite well, and after a very dull dinner party at the Wyndham Lewis' went to Lady Salisbury's. So you see I am on my legs again. On the receipt of this I sho[ul]d feel much obliged to you, if you wo[ul]d pack up my daggers and send them to town and also my old shawl. If they co[ul]d arrive at No. 34 Grosr. St.[9] directed to Lady Sykes in the course of the day, I shd. be very glad. I am sorry for dear Jem, but he has many fellow sufferers. The Influenza howr. is not so severe as last year.

My love to all.

Your own

D T.O. |

Ossulston asked me to allow him to put me up for Crockfords.[10] I told him that I was sure I shd. be blackballed, but he was sanguine of the reverse, and is to consult his friends. |

When have you a dinner party?

338

TO [SARAH DISRAELI] [London, Friday 11? July 1834]

ORIGINAL: PS 5

PUBLICATION HISTORY: LBCS 26-7, dated 11 July 1834; M&B I 252, extracts dated 11 July 1834

EDITORIAL COMMENT: *Dating*: Lord Grey announced his resignation in the House of Lords on Wednesday 9 July 1834. *The Times*; Greville III 53ff.

July 11, 1834.

We remain here in breathless agitation.[1] I can give you no idea of the state of excitement. At this moment nothing is settled. Lords Lansdowne and Melbourne were with the king all yesterday.[2] Massey Stanley brought the news to the opera[3] on Tuesday at nine o'clock. I was in Lady B's box. No one would be-

7 Greenwich Park, site of the Royal Observatory.

8 Rossini's *Semiramide* was performed at the King's Theatre on Saturday 5 July 1834, followed by *Le Pouvoir de la Danse*, a new ballet by M. Taglioni. *The Times* (5 July 1834). D had met Beckford at a performance which included a one-act version of this same opera on 12 June. See **329**n2.

9 The Sykeses.

0 Founded by William Crockford in the 1820s, Crockford's Club – located at 50 St James's Street – was one of the most famous gambling houses of the era. D, however, did not become a member until 1840. A.L. Humphreys *Crockford's or The Goddess of Chance in St. James's St, 1828-1844* (1953) 105.

---

1 On 9 July 1834, Grey resigned, having alienated O'Connell who felt betrayed by the news that the Irish Coercion Bill was to be renewed. Grey's growing sense of isolation within his own cabinet was perhaps the fundamental cause.

2 Melbourne became prime minister on 16 July 1834. Sir Henry Petty-Fitzmaurice (1780-1863), 3rd Marquess of Lansdowne, had been lord president of the Council in Grey's government and continued in that office under Melbourne. A moderate Whig, he favoured the abolition of the slave trade and other liberal measures.

3 Donizetti's opera *Anna Bolena* was playing at the King's Theatre.

lieve it. On Wednesday at Lady Cork's was the Duke of Wellington, in high spirits, but saying everywhere the Tories would not take office. Fonblanque, who was there, said the Tories were like a woman who fancies herself *enceinte* and goes about saying it is not yet her time.... I made my *début* at Almack's[4] with a subscription from Lady Tankerville,[5] but it was not a very brilliant reunion. Yesterday I met Lord Lyndhurst,[6] whom I like very much. The next time he goes the Norfolk circuit he is to sleep at Bradenham. He says the Duke of Wellington never reads any book but the 'Commentaries', and assured me it was a positive fact!

[D]

---

339 TO SARAH DISRAELI [London, Wednesday 16 July 1834]

ORIGINAL: FITZ Disraeli A7
COVER: Miss Disraeli | Bradenham House | High Wycombe | *Bucks*
POSTMARK: (1) In circle: M | JY 16 | 1834
EDITORIAL COMMENT: There is no signature. *Sic*: fro.

My dearest,

I intend to wake at Bradenham on the morning of the 1st of August. The horse howr. may be turned out, as I do not wish to move for the 1st. week at least out of the grounds, and I have a horse in London which I shall perhaps bring down with me.

The price outside to Exeter is £2. and there are coaches to and fro Bath and Exeter daily.

It is by no means settled that the Ministry is patched up even | yet; but as all parties apparently desire this temporary arrangement, I think it must take place. The Tories are lost for ever.[1]

4 Almack's Assembly Rooms, in King Street, St James's, served as the semi-official focus of the London season. Assemblies and subscription balls were usually held on Wednesday nights – since that day was considered a light one for Parliament. This institution was controlled by seven patronesses, all of noble rank, and long dominated by Lady Jersey and by Princess Lieven, wife of the Russian ambassador. There were also provincial equivalents, modelled on that of the metropolis. *CJ* no 196 (16 Jan 1833) 50 and no 287 (25 Oct 1834) 274; E. Beresford Chancellor *Memorials of St. James's Street together with the Annals of Almack's* (1922) 195-279.

5 Corisande Armandine Sophie Bennet (d 1865), daughter of Antoine, duc de Gramont, had married in 1806 Charles Augustus Bennet, 5th Earl of Tankerville. She was D'Orsay's niece (his sister Ida's daughter).

6 John Singleton Copley (1772-1863), 1st Baron Lyndhurst; solicitor general in 1819, attorney general 1824-6, chief baron of the Exchequer 1831-4, and three times lord chancellor, 1827-30, 1834-5, 1841-6. This seems to have been D's first encounter with Lyndhurst, to whom he later became an unofficial private secretary.

---

1 This was the first of a series of occasions when the Tories seemed unable to take sufficient advantage of the fragility of the Whig-Radical alliance. A possible coalition of Tories and Whigs was proposed by the King at this time, but Peel declined the opportunity. Some form of coalition continued to be bruited during successive crises in 1834-5. Sir Theodore Martin *A Life of Lyndhurst* (1884) 316; Greville III 137-8.

My Macclesfield letter was from one Mr Siddeley,[2] a great literary admirer, impressing the necessity of a cheap edit: of the Rev[olutionary] Epick for the manufacturing districts etc. etc. I wrote about Jem, but perhaps (tho' I think not) he is the Editor of a news[pape]r and not a manufacturer. |

I think your story may be in the next No. but it arrived *late*. I thought very well of it[.][3] The *I[nfernal] M[arriage]*[4] – is the most successful thing I ever wrote – I hear something of it every day.

I hope I may just escape the Shepherds,[5] which I think I shall. I called on B.E.L. the day after his arrival. I have 3 invit[ati]ons today, all of which I sho[ul]d like to accept – a birth day fete in honor of Margaret Purves[6] at Lincoln Stanhope's villa at Putney;[7] a white bait dinner with D'Orsay and the dandies at Blackwall; and a dinner at Lady Combermere's.[8] I have decided for the | middle affair, or rather Fate did for me. Adieu! I shall go to Almacks tonight, not to appear only to go once, but its Room is over this season. Castlereagh is off for Ireland on Thursday. Ossulston on Sunday week to the Duchess of Bedford's in the Highlands.[9] All talk of moving; yet there are rumours that Parlt. may sit thro' Augt.[10] Chalon has made the most exquisite portrait of Lady Sykes (full length) I ever saw.[11] It is marvellous, quite his chef d'oeuvre.

2 One Samuel Siddeley was a householder in Sunderland Street, Macclesfield. *The Poll at an Election of Representatives in Parliament for the Borough of Macclesfield in the Year 1835* (Macclesfield 1835) 21.

3 On 3 July Sarah had written: 'Do you think there is any chance of getting anything into the N.M. for the next time if I send it to you in three or four days. True Stories a series, this is No. 1 The Birth-day. It is a *very good story* indeed, quite as good as any Balaam I ever read, and much better than most – he may have it for anything.' H A/I/B/526. If the story did appear in *The New Monthly Magazine*, however, it was not under this name and has not yet been located.

4 See **335**n2.

5 The family of the Rev Dr George Shepherd (1767?-1849), then of Russell Square, London. He was a friend of Isaac. Foster IV; H G/I/861-62; A/I/B/527, 530.

6 Marguerite Purves (d 1896), niece of Lady Blessington, married in 1846 William Augustus Tollemache (1817-1911).

7 The villa, one supposes, was 'The Cedars'. See **340**.

8 Caroline Cotton (d 1837), second daughter of William Fulke Greville, married in 1814 Sir Stapleton Cotton, 5th Baronet, and later 1st Viscount Combermere. She was her husband's second wife, and for the last seven years of her life she lived apart from him at 8 Hereford Street, Oxford Street.

9 Lady Georgiana Russell (d 1853), fifth daughter of the 4th Duke of Gordon of the first creation, and, after 1803, second wife of the 6th Duke of Bedford. She usually spent part of the summer at 'The Doune', in the Forest of Rothiemurchus, Inverness-shire. Her lover, Edwin Landseer (1802-1873), painted a number of well-known pictures of the area. Campbell Lennie *Landseer: The Victorian Paragon* (1976) 43, 107.

10 By the beginning of August many members of the Commons had left town. The Lords suddenly came to life, threw out the bill for the admission of Dissenters into the universities by 187 to 85, and, with mounting enthusiasm, went on to reject the government's Irish Tithe Bill on 11 August by 189 to 122. Two days later the session ended.

11 Alfred Edward Chalon (1780-1860) was a member of a family of émigrés who had come to England in 1789. He became a very fashionable portrait-painter and was the first to paint Queen Victoria after her accession. Jerman (99) has a reproduction of a portrait of Lady Sykes by Chalon taken from the 1837 *Book of Beauty*.

340 TO SARAH DISRAELI [London], Wednesday [23 July 1834]

ORIGINAL: H A/I/B/81

COVER: Miss Disraeli | Bradenham House | High Wycombe | Bucks

POSTMARK: (1) In circle: X | JY23 | 1834

PUBLICATION HISTORY: LBCS 27-8, dated 23 July 1834, prints, in random order, six sentences from the first paragraph, and part of **341** (see n1).

EDITORIAL COMMENT: There is no signature. *Sic*: Matthews, almost, champaigne.

Wednesday

My dearest,

I have been expecting Jem in town every morng. and it has only just occurred to me that he has found his way to Dawlish with[ou]t passing thro' London. Tell Tita to get my pipes in good order, as I look forward to a batch of smoking with great zest. I still adhere to my plan of being down in a week or ten days. The season here will not be over for a fortnight. I go every day to fetes and water-parties. I was at Lady | Tavistock's at Richmond on Saturday: it rained dreadfully, with[ou]t ceasing. On Sunday I dined at the Seymours with the Nortons, Lord Mulgrave and Frank Sheridan; but it was such a dreadful night that I co[ul]d not make my final bow, as I had intended at Lady Salisburys. Monday another party to Blackwall with D'Orsay: the afternoon was fine: To day Lady Sykes has a grand water-party. Lincoln Stanhope has | lent her "the Cedars", the most beautiful villa on the Thames. She may consider herself fortunate in the weather, tho' there is a lowering look about the skies. Think of us at 4 o ck: when we embark at Whitehall stairs. I suspect a shower.[1] Tomorrow [I] go to Lord Hertfords; and Lady Cork has a party this evening, but I doubt whe[the]r we shall return in time. There are only twenty persons asked, and there is a large 8-oar boat that carries us all down tog[ethe]r, all the ladies are beauties, and all the men wits, so I suppose it must be a failure. | Margaret Purves, who is going today, now they say is about to marry Mortimer Ricardo;[2] rather a change from Lord Douro,[3] but a very good match for her all the same. There are two Miss Kings, dau[ghte]rs of Hon: Genl King,[4] and Miss Elliot of the Admiralty.[5]

1 LBCS 27-8, dated 23 July 1834, includes a passage from **341** of 26? July, describing the 23 July water-party at the 'Cedars' after it had taken place.

2 Mortimer Ricardo (1807-1876), third son of the economist, and then a captain in the 2nd Life Guards, did not, in fact, marry Miss Purves.

3 Arthur Richard Wellesley (1807-1884), Marquess Douro, after 1852 2nd Duke of Wellington.

4 Maj Gen Henry King (d 1839) was the fourth son of the 2nd Earl of Kingston. He was formerly governor of Heligoland, was awarded the KCB and gazetted lieutenant general in 1838. His first wife, Mary Hewitt, whom he had married in 1802, had died in 1821, and he had married in 1832 a widow, Catherine Richardson, née Philips (d 1847). He had four daughters by his first marriage – Caroline, Louisa, Sidney and Alicia – and those who were referred to as 'the daughters of The Hon Mrs King' in the social notes of the time were the two younger ones. *CJ* no 208 (20 Apr 1833) 264.

5 Georgiana Maria Elliot (d 1874) was the eldest daughter of George Elliot (1784-1863), second son of the 1st Earl of Minto, and first secretary of the Admiralty between 1830 and 1834. She married in 1843 the 8th Earl of Northesk.

Men: Oss[ulston] Landseer, Matthews,[6] Captn. Phipps,[7] F[rancis] Sher[idan]: Linley[,][8] Arthur Chichester, Henry Bathurst[9] and myself. almost all sing, and there is a quantity of guitars and champaigne. My love to all. The cold cream I very good; and your waistcoat *universally* noticed and admired.[10]

The last Almacks was much better. My subscrip[tion] of 3 tickets is out. I thought it useless to apply again.

TO [SARAH DISRAELI] [London, Saturday 26? July 1834] 341

ORIGINAL: PS 75

PUBLICATION HISTORY: Anderson Galleries, catalogue 2099 (1926) item 17; LBCS 27-8, extract dated 23 July 1834; see also **340**n1; M&B I 253, extract dated 23 July 1834

EDITORIAL COMMENT: *Dating*: by comparison with **340** (23 July 1834) in which D told Sarah that 'to day Lady Sykes has a grand water-party'. On 25 July Sarah had observed that they had not heard from D for three days. H A/I/B/531.

The passages from LBCS 27-8, of 23 July 1834, which seem to belong to this letter have been inserted in square brackets. *Sic*: Sykes'.

[I find the end of the season more fatiguing than the beginning, owing to the morning festivities.]

Lady Sykes' party on Wednesday was the most delightful I ever was at. We embarked at 5, the heavens very favourable, sang all the way down, wandered in beautiful gardens worthy of Paul Veronese [, full not only of flowers, but fountains and parroquets: the dinner first-rate and much better than cold miserable picnics, in which all bring the same things.] On Thursday I dined en famille with the Bulwers and went to Lord Hertford's[1] in the evening where I found a scene worthy of Caliph Vathek.[2] By the by, Beckford, who has long left town, has written a letter to Bentley and says there never was anything like 'The Infernal Marriage' and all people say the same ...

[People are still in town, but Goodwood[3] will, I think, clear us.]

6 Probably Charles Mathews, son of the comedian. The elder Mathews was, however, in England at this time. He departed on his tour to America one month later. Mrs Mathews *Memoirs of Charles Mathews, Comedian* (1839) IV 288.

7 Capt Charles Beaumont Phipps (1801-1866), second son of the 1st Earl of Mulgrave. He was at this time a captain in the Scots Fusileer Guards.

8 William Linley (1771-1835), the great-uncle of Francis Sheridan, was the composer of light operas and similar entertainments. Linley would have been older than the rest of the party but he was both a bachelor and a noted singer.

9 Presumably Henry George Bathurst (1790-1866), Baron Apsley. Four days after D's letter the 3rd Earl Bathurst died, and Lord Apsley, who had been Tory MP for Cirencester 1812-34, succeeded as the 4th Earl.

10 Sarah had made him one a month earlier: 'Your waistcoat is finished, I am all impatience to learn if it be a failure. I am half afraid of it, as it is my first attempt in that line.' H A/I/B/525.

1 Lord Hertford lived at Dorchester House, Park Lane.

2 See **327**n1.

3 The race meeting held annually in July near Chichester.

342 TO LADY BLESSINGTON [London?, Tuesday 29 July? 1834]

ORIGINAL: NYPL Kohns 35

COVER: The | C[ounte]ss of Blessington | Disraeli

EDITORIAL COMMENT: *Dating*: the 'tale' is almost certainly 'The Carrier-pigeon' which appeared in Lady Blessington's *The Book of Beauty* for 1835, published 15 November 1834. The date has been arbitrarily assigned to late July from the internal evidence of this sequence of letters to Lady Blessington.

Tuesday

My dear Lady Blessington,

I send you the tale, which I beg you to accept as a mark of my sincere regard; and to reject *with[ou]t hesitation*, if, on perusal, you do not consider it suitable to your wishes. I shall be glad indeed if you may consider it such, as it | must always afford me lively satisfaction to be of service, however slight, to one whom I so much esteem.

Yrs f[aithful]ly

D |

I fear the MS. is not as fair as I cd. wish. My amanuensis is too busy to help me, and I broke down in the copying. Let me have a proof.

343 TO [SARAH DISRAELI] [London], [Friday] 1 August 1834

ORIGINAL: PS 80

PUBLICATION HISTORY: J. Pearson catalogue 188 (nd) 33

EDITORIAL COMMENT: The catalogue describes this letter as being to Sarah, 'August 1st, 1834. 3 *pages*, 4to. An interesting early letter on a projected visit of Lady Cork to Bradenham.' The text is a mixture of paraphrase and quotation.

She had fixed on next Thursday for her visit and never even hinted it to 'the young man.' She did not care whe[the]r he was there or not, as she went to visit his father. Thro' the good offices of Lady Sykes I rejoice to say that the storm has at present blown over. 'He who gains time, gains everything', and therefore we will not anticipate future movements on the part of the old lady, ...[1]

344 TO LADY BLESSINGTON [London?, Saturday 2 August? 1834]

ORIGINAL: PFRZ Misc Ms. 913

COVER: The Countess of Blessington | Disraeli

PUBLICATION HISTORY: Morrison 13

EDITORIAL COMMENT: *Dating*: D left for Bradenham Sunday 3 August 1834 (**345**), and this has the tone of a note sent immediately before that departure.

My dear Lady Bless[ing]ton,

I venture to enclose you the letter for Botta, and a note which I shall feel obliged by your giving Count D'Orsay. I shall then be sure that it reaches him. I wish you wo[ul]d enforce the favor I ask of him.

I fear you will find my correspondence very monotonous; but I shall be too delighted to hear from you, to omit a claim for your answers.

1 There is no evidence that Lady Cork ever did descend on Bradenham; possibly the cause of her annoyance with D was his failure to come to her party on 23 July. See **340**.

We live at "Bradenham House, High Wycombe".

Pray let me have a proof of my little story, sent to Brad: The post, you know, will carry a proof sheet, if so certified on the direction. It shall be returned instantly.

In haste

Yr f[aithfu]l

D

TO LADY BLESSINGTON Bradenham, [Tuesday 5 August 1834] 345

ORIGINAL: PFRZ Misc Ms. 890

COVER: The | Countess of Blessington | 8 Seamore Place | London

POSTMARK: (1) In double circle: F | 5 AU 5 | 1834 (2) In rectangle: No. 1 (3) HWYCOMBE | Penny Post

PUBLICATION HISTORY: Morrison 13-14; Meynell 295-6; Madden II 219, excerpt

EDITORIAL COMMENT: There is no signature. *Sic*: Sandt.

Bradenham House | High Wycombe

My dear Lady Blessington,

I was so sorry to leave London with[ou]t being a moment alone with you but altho' I came to the Opera the last night on purpose, Fate was against us. I did not reach this place until Sunday, very ill indeed from the pangs of parting. Indeed I feel as desolate as a ghost, and I do not think that I ever shall be able to settle to anything again. It is a great shame, when people are happy together, that | they sho[ul]d be ever separated; but it seems the great object of all human legislation that people never shd. be happy tog[ethe]r.[1]

My father I find better than I expected, and much cheered by my presence. I delivered him all your kind messages. He is now very busy on his "History of English Literatu[re]"[2] in which he is far advanced. I am mistaken if you will not delight in these volumes. They are full of new views of the History of our Language, and indeed of our country, for the history | of a state is necessarily mixed up with the history of its literature.

For myself I am doing nothing. The western breeze favors an alfresco existence, and I am seated with a pipe under a spreading sycamore, solemn as a Pacha.

I wish you cd. induce Hookham[3] to entrust me with Agathon,[4] that mad Byronic novel.

What do you think of the modern French novelists? and is it worth my while to read them? And if so what do you recommend me? What of Balzac? Is he better than Sue[5] and Geo: Sandt Dudevant?[6] And are these inferior to Hugo? I

1 Lady Blessington was one of the few to whom D confided the details of his affair with Henrietta. The extravagance of his feelings was occasioned, not by any permanent break, but by the temporary separation brought about by his return to Bradenham for the autumn. See **346**n1.

2 See **314**n5.

3 Thomas Hookham, bookseller and publisher, 15 Old Bond Street, London.

4 *Agathon*, a romantic tale by Christoph Martin Wieland, was published in Germany in 1767. An English translation was published by T. Cadell in London in 1773.

5 Marie Joseph Sue (1804-1857), French novelist and author, who wrote as 'Eugène Sue'.

6 George Sand was the nom de plume of baronne Dudevant, née Amandine Lucile Aurore Dupin (1804-1876).

ask you these questions, because you will give me short answers, like all people who are masters of their subject. | I suppose it is vain to hope to see my dear D'Orsay here. I wish indeed he wo[ul]d come. Here is a cook by no means contemptible. He can bring his horses if he like, but I can mount him. Adieu dr. Lady Blessington. Someday I will try to write you a more amusing letter, at present I am in truth ill and sad.

---

346 TO LADY BLESSINGTON — Bradenham, Friday 15 August [1834]

ORIGINAL: PS 73

PUBLICATION HISTORY: M&B I 257-8, dated 15 August [1834]; Madden (II 217) prints two paragraphs which have been added here within square brackets. The similarity of subject supports the hypothesis that it is the material omitted by Monypenny as indicated by his ellipsis. R. Atkinson catalogue 58 (1924) item 55, includes extracts from this letter.

EDITORIAL COMMENT: There is a copy, in another hand, of the first page of this letter in the Berg Collection of the NYPL (no 8). The text, with minor changes, runs from the beginning to 'much pleased'. We have followed Monypenny's text, with additions from Madden. See ph. *Dating*: Lady Blessington replied 20 August: 'I knew you would like Agathon even thro' the diluting medium of a translation.' H A/B/XXI/B/557.

BRADENHAM HOUSE | *Friday, Aug 15.* [1834.]

My Dear Lady Blessington,

I have been very unwell, or I should sooner have acknowledged the receipt of your kind letter. I can assure you that your friendship is a great consolation to me. The change of life was too sad and sudden. Indeed I am quite at a loss how to manage affairs in future as I find separation more irksome than even my bitterest imagination predicted. God however is great, and the future must regulate itself, for I can't.[1] I have done nothing but scribble one day a third part of *The Infernal Marriage* with which fantasy Colburn pretends now to be much pleased. I suppose your letter is at the bottom of his rapture.

I am delighted with *Agathon*. It left me musing which is a test of a great work. I invariably close one in a reverie. Wieland indeed always delights me. I sympathise with him much. There is a wild Oriental fancy blended with his Western philosophy which is a charming union. I like a moral to peep out of the wildest invention, to assure us that, while we have been amused, we have also all the time been growing a little wiser. The translation of the *Agathon* is very clumsy. I wish I could read it in the original but I have no talent for languages and invariably lose my command over English in an exact proportion as I gain any hold over another tongue....

[I think the 'Manuscrit Vert'[2] sad stuff. The author's constant efforts to be reli-

1 Lady Blessington had written to D on 5 August, comforting him on his temporary separation from Henrietta:

> Partings are sad things, but yet this bitterness has a consolation, for we know they will be repaid by the happiness of meetings ... I saw that you were suffering (in anticipation,) for some days before you left Town, and if sympathy could have aught availed, be assured you had mine ... I am but now, 1/2 past twelve, returned from the Opera, where I saw "The Lady of your Love" looking as handsome as usual, and *much less* gay, this is all as it should be. [H B/XXI/B/558]

2 A novel by Gustave Drouineau (1800-1878), published in two volumes in 1832. By 1834 it had reached a third edition.

gious are very unfortunate. I fear that faith is not his practice. His hero seizes every inopportune occurrence to assure us that he believes in God. His evident conviction is the general one, that even this article of faith is by no means common in France. His hero and heroine are moulded in the German school, and are personifications of abstract ideas. The hero, because he believes in God, represents spiritualism; the heroine, because she instantly knows every man she meets, is materialism, forsooth! The lady is not a Philina,[3] and altogether the author is a fool.

I have not made up my mind about Pickersgill and the Three Brothers. When I see more, more I will say.[4] *At present, I am inclined to believe that the work is a translation from the German.* Altogether, in a season of sorrow, your kind parcel has much amused me. Shall I send the books back to Hookham?]

My kind regards to his Highness, King Alfred:[5] a wise man though not a Saxon.

Your faithful

D

TO LADY BLESSINGTON   Bradenham, Tuesday [2 September? 1834]   347

ORIGINAL: PFRZ Misc Ms. 895

COVER: The | Countess of Blessington | Disraeli

PUBLICATION HISTORY: Morrison 14-15; Madden II 218, excerpts; Meynell 296-7, excerpts

EDITORIAL COMMENT: *Dating*: Lady Blessington wrote to D on 20 August 1834 (H B/XXI/B/557) asking for the books D had borrowed to be returned to her rather than to Hookham's. D's apology for having 'so long omitted' a reply suggests Tuesday 2 September as a more probable date than the Tuesday before. Lady Blessington acknowledged this letter and receipt of the books on 4 September. H B/XXI/B/559. *Sic*: Parris'.

Bradenham House | Tuesday

Dearest Lady Blessington,

I have intended to return the books and send you these few lines every day, and am surprised that I cd. have so long omitted doing anything so agreeable as writing to you. We are all delighted with the portraits: my sister is collecting those of all my fathers friends; her collection will include almost every person of literary celebrity from the end of the Johnsonian aera. So your fair face arrived

3 Philina (or Philine) is a character in Goethe's *Wilhelm Meister's Apprenticeship*. She is a frivolous actress, a whimsical light-of-love, who nevertheless entrances Meister and most readers.

4 Joshua Pickersgill's *The Three Brothers* (1803) is said to have been the basis for Byron's *The Deformed Transformed* (1822). Madden (II 217n) claimed that he introduced the novel to Lady Blessington, adding that he had tried to obtain information about the author from the publisher, Stockdale, but with no success. Lady Blessington had sent D only the first volume. H B/XXI/B/558.

5 D'Orsay sent D a message through Lady Blessington on 4 September saying that he was 'half-affronted', and asking D to be '*less* ceremonious and *more* friendly' in his references to him. H B/XXI/B/559.

just in time. | I am particularly delighted with Parris' port[rai]t w[hi]ch I had never seen before.[1]

I have read the art[icle] on Coleridge in the Quarterly; but do not agree with you in holding it to be written by Lockhart. It is too good. L's style has certainly the merit of being peculiar. I know none so meagre, harsh and clumsy; or more felicitous in the jumble of common-place metaphors. I think the present reviewal must be by | Nelson Coleridge, a nephew of the poet, and a cleverish sort of fellow, tho' a prig.[2]

You give me the same advice as my father ever has done about dotting down the evanescent feelings of youth:[3] but like other excellent advice I fear it will prove unprofitable. I have a horror of journalising, and indeed of writing of all description. With me execution is ever a labor, and conception a delight. Altho' a great traveller, | I never kept a diary in my life.[4]

Do you really think that Jekyll is ninety?[5] He has a son, I believe of my standing.

As you are learned in Byron do you happen to know who was the mother of Allegra?[6]

I gave all yr. kind messages to my father, who returns you others equally amiable. He will c[all] upon you in the course of the month if he visit town. We have had a | very good harvest here, and our second crop of hay, like second love, has proved more satisfactory than our first.

My kindest remembrance to Count D'Orsay. Believe me, dearest Lady Blessington

Your affectionate
humble servant
D

1 Edmund Thomas Parris (1793-1873), painter and engraver, was well known during the 1830s for his portraits of fashionable people. Many of his engravings appeared in the *The Keepsake*, a competitor of Lady Blessington's *Book of Beauty*, and in the other annuals. Parris had prepared a portrait of Lady Blessington as the frontispiece for the 1834 *Book of Beauty*.

2 In the August issue of *The Quarterly Review* (LII 1-38) there was a review of *The Poetical Works of S.T. Coleridge* (1834). *The Wellesley Index* supports D's attribution of the review to Henry Nelson Coleridge (1798-1843), nephew and literary executor of S.T. Coleridge. He edited his uncle's *Literary Remains, Aids to Reflection* and *Confessions of an Inquiring Spirit*. His transcriptions of Coleridge's conversations were published in 1835 under the title *Table Talk*. During the 1830s Nelson Coleridge was a frequent contributor of articles to *The Quarterly Review*, especially on classical Greek poetry.

3 Lady Blessington had written on 20 August: 'I wish you would make a practice of writing down your feelings and sensations as they occur, you will find them a treasure hereafter, when they become blunted as alas! they will, and they will serve as beautiful views drawn from nature in some fine Country where we passed our youth, and which bring back to us some of its faded happiness.' H A/XXI/B/557.

4 The first date in the 'Mutilated Diary' is 1 September 1833. H A/III/C. See app III.

5 Joseph Jekyll died in 1837, aged eighty-four.

6 The daughter of Byron and Claire Clairmont. She was born in 1817, and lived with Byron for nearly three years. Despite her mother's opposition, she was placed in a convent near Ravenna, where she died in 1822.

TO LADY BLESSINGTON [Bradenham], Wednesday [3 September? 1834] 348

ORIGINAL: PFRZ Misc Ms. 907

COVER: The | C[ounte]ss of Blessington | [Also in D's hand]: This morng I forwarded you the books and a letter

EDITORIAL COMMENT: *Dating*: by comparison with **347**; the books referred to on the cover of the present letter are almost certainly the same ones referred to in **347**.

Wednesday Eve

Your entreaties are to me commands. I received the proof this afternoon, | which I now return. I wish, instead of sending it by the Oxford coach, | I cd. tie it under the wing of Mignon![1]

TO BENJAMIN AUSTEN Bradenham, [Tuesday] 7 October [1834] 349

ORIGINAL: BL ADD MS 45908 ff98-9

COVER: Benjamin Austen Esqr. | 10 Lansdown Crescent | *Cheltenham*

POSTMARK: (1) In circular form: HIGH WYCOMBE (2) In rectangle: Cheltenham | Penny Post

PUBLICATION HISTORY: Jerman 236, excerpt dated 7 October 1834

EDITORIAL COMMENT: There is a small hole in the second sheet of the MS. *Sic*: 7.th, St Thomas', here, Smythe.

Bradenham House | Octr 7.th

My dear Austen,

This golden and smiling autumn has been a very gloomy season for us here. I am myself slowly recovering from a most severe illness which has nearly confined me to my room for twó months. My brother James has had a rheumatic fever; and in the midst of all this confusion, our most able servant among the womankind has had a fit. Such a combination of domestic misfortunes | never before occurred to us. A few days back, I made a great effort and reached Aylesbury to call upon our friend Layard.[1] What was my grief and astonishment to find our friends there in almost as bad a plight as ourselves. Layard in bed, and really dangerously ill, and your sister[2] a terrible sufferer. It really was like a visit from St Bartholemews to St Thomas'.[3] Your nephew[4] was there, and promised to write me a bulletin of his father's state, which he has not performed, and I have therefore dispatched him a line | by this post. I hope that you and yours have escaped all similar sufferings and really enjoyed yourselves in your beautiful county in this unrivalled season. My sister desires her kindest remembrances to Mrs. A. and begs me to say that she wo[ul]d have written, now that our sufferings are on the wane, had she not found that I was performing the same office. Pray let us here [*of*] your doings. I have nothing to tell you. My life here is always uneventful, and during this season has been literally a blank.

1 Mignon is the name of the pigeon in D's tale 'The Carrier-pigeon'.

1 Henry Peter Layard, Austen's brother-in-law, had died the day before, 6 October. *The Times* (11 Oct 1834).
2 Marianne, Layard's wife.
3 Both are hospitals in London.
4 Austen Henry Layard.

What do you think of affairs? Had you any Spanish?[5] Lord Auckland[6] I hear is to go to India, and Sydney Smythe to be the new Bishop.[7] My kindest regards to Mrs. Austen and Louisa. Write soon to

yours ever,

B. Disraeli

---

350 TO LADY BLESSINGTON — Bradenham, Friday [17 October 1834]

ORIGINAL: PFRZ Misc Ms. 891
COVER: The Countess of Blessington | 8 Seamore Place | Curzon Street
POSTMARK: (1) In double circle: F | 18OC18 | 1834 (2) In circular form: HIGH WYCOMBE
PUBLICATION HISTORY: Morrison 15; M&B I 259, excerpt dated [17 October 1834]; Meynell 297-8
EDITORIAL COMMENT: *Sic*: sheathe.

Friday | Bradenham House

My dear Lady Blessington,

My absence at Quarter Sessions,[1] where I was bored to death, prevented me instantly answering your letter. I hope however you will receive this before your departure. I sympathise with your sufferings; my experience unhappily assures | me how ably you describe them. This golden autumn ought to have *cured* us all. I myself in spite of the *sunshine*, have been a great invalid. Indeed, I know not how it is, but I am never well save in action, and then I feel immortal. I am ashamed of being "nervous". | Dyspepsia always make me wish for a civil war. In the mean time, I amuse myself by county politics. I received yesterday a letter most spritely and amusing from E.L.B.[2] dated Limerick. He is about to return to Dublin, and talks of going to Spain. I am ashamed that I must confess to him that I have not read Pompeii,[3] but alas! a London bookseller treats us provincials with great contempt and in spite of reiterated epistles and promises as numerous I | have not yet received the much wished tomes. My father sends his kindest regards. As for myself, I am dying for action, and rust like a Damascus sabre in the sheathe of a poltroon. Adieu! dear friend. We shall meet on your return.

D

5 The price of Spanish bonds (known as '5 percent Spanish stock') jumped in London and Paris during the first week of October 1834 following the news from Madrid that the new Cortes had agreed in principle to honour the financial obligations contracted by King Ferdinand VII between 1823 and 1833. *The Times* (2-10 Oct 1834). For other evidence that 'Spanish' meant 'Spanish bonds' in the argot of the Stock Exchange see [James Grant] *The Great Metropolis* 2nd ser, 2nd ed (1838) II 36.

6 Lord Auckland was at this time first lord of the Admiralty. He was not officially appointed governor general of India until the next year.

7 Sydney Smith (1771-1845), the noted wit, had been a canon of St Paul's since 1831, but he did not become a bishop.

---

1 The autumn session opened 14 October. An account of the proceedings makes no mention of D's presence. *BH* no 146 (18 Oct 1834) 2, 3.
D did not become a JP until 5 August 1836, though that would not have prevented his attending. H A/I/miscell and Bucks County Record Office: Q/RRO33.

2 Though invited, D had felt unable to accompany Bulwer on his trip. Bulwer reassured him he had not missed much: 'You had no loss in Birmingham – a sort of kitchen covered with red flock paper.' H B/20/Ly/24.

3 Bulwer's *The Last Days of Pompeii* had been published in July 1834.

TO BENJAMIN AUSTEN — Bradenham, [Friday] 24 October 1834 — **351**

ORIGINAL: BL ADD MS 45908 ff100-1

COVER: *private* | Benjamin Austen Esqr. | Raymond Buildings | Grays Inn | London

POSTMARK: (1) In circle: F | 25OC25 | 1834 (2) In rectangle: No. 1 (3) In rectangular form: HWYCOMBE | Penny Post

PUBLICATION HISTORY: M&B I 259, dated 24 October 1834, extracts from the third paragraph; Jerman 236-7, extracts dated 24 October 1834

EDITORIAL COMMENT: *Sic*: capitally, Your.

Bradenham House | Oct. 24. 1834

My dear Austen,

Layard's death[1] greatly affected me. I agree in your estimate of his character, and had he been spared I make no doubt his career would have been that of an amiable and regular man. He was still young; I had no idea that he was only 50. I anticipated the pleasure of cultivating his acquaintance now that he was a neighbour, and my first visit brought | me almost to his deathbed! Such is life! I sent over to Aylesbury yesterday, to enquire after the family, and received a good report of Mrs. Layard and all of them.

I intend to be in town in the course of ten days or so, when we shall meet and when I hope to find you and yours all well and prospering.

The pen has been very busy and everything in that department looks capitally. I have been howr. prevented in bringing out a novel,[2] as I hoped in Novr. by a strange illness which kept me to my sofa, exactly two months. It was something of the kind of attack that you experienced at Fyfield | great pains in the legs and extraord[inar]y languor. It came upon me suddenly. I struggled against it for some time, but mounting my horse one day, I had a slight determin[ati]on of blood to my head, and was obliged to throw myself on the floor of the hall. This frightened me remembering old sufferings, and I laid up. Quiet, diet and plenteous doses of Ammonia (heavenly maid!) not only restored me, but I have felt better and more hearty this last fortnight than I long remember.

With regard to your kind and never to be forgotten loan, I feel myself bound not only by law, but by honor, to repay it at the beginning of the year, if you require it. I wo[ul]d howr. myself propose that it shd. be paid in the course of the ensuing year in two equal portions or moieties, if not disagreeable to you. I really can hold out no inducement to you to grant me this fresh favor, for I cannot affect to feel more obliged to you than I already do. The act of friendship was | one which it is painful for me to attempt to express my sense of by words. When we meet, I will give you the reasons which induce me to make this proposal: at present I have not room.... Sa has written to Mrs. A. but directed to Cheltenham. I am sorry I did not visit you: the truth is I was meditat[in]g the very step when the mournful event took place that called you to Aylesbury. I

1 See **349**n1.
2 Presumably *Henrietta Temple*, which was begun in 1834 but not published until December 1836.

speculated on yr. letter perhaps mak[in]g me the offer, which I hardly | ventured to propose myself, as I was still weak and nervous. All possible kind regards to all.

Your aff[ectionate]ly

BD

We have no hope of Del Montes:[3] we try to forget such things. Ah! for Spanish![4] I rejoice you had a crumb; if not a slice!

---

352 TO [SARAH DISRAELI] [London, Tuesday 4 November? 1834]

ORIGINAL: PS 6

PUBLICATION HISTORY: LBCS 28, dated 4 November 1834; M&B I 262, dated 4 November 1834

EDITORIAL COMMENT: *Dating*: Denvil appeared in *Manfred* at the Theatre Royal, first on 29 October 1834, then nightly until 14 November.

Quaritch catalogue 289 (May 1910) item 7 lists an extract, the last sentence of which is to be found in the second paragraph of RD's text: 'Lad[y] B[lessington] with an Italian greyhound not as big as Muff, quite white with a red collar and gold bell ... I went to see the new actor ... '

November 4, 1834.

I dined on Saturday with Lyndhurst *en famille*. A more amiable and agreeable family I never met. The eldest daughter, 'Sa,' is just like her mother,[1] and although only thirteen, rules everything and everybody – a most astounding little woman.

Yesterday I went to see the new actor, Denvil.[2] He is deplorable, has not the slightest feeling, nor one physical or mental qualification for the stage. I saw Chandos[3] to-day and had a long conversation with him on politics. He has no head, but I flatter myself I opened his mind a little...D'Orsay has taken my portrait.

3 The silver-mining stocks had been grossly overpriced, according to contemporaries. Anon *The Real del Monte Mining Concern Unmasked* (1833). Though their value would continue to fluctuate with news of fresh discoveries, the trend was downward. The aggregate value of the various silver stocks was £4,375,000 in 1825. A decade later the market value was £620,000. *The Circular to Bankers* no 394 (5 Feb 1836) 7.

4 See **349**n5.

---

1 Lyndhurst's wife (see **189**n8) had died ten months earlier. There were three daughters: Sarah Elizabeth (1821-1865), who married Henry John Selwin in 1850; Susan Penelope (1822-1837); and Sophia Clarence (1828-1911), who married Hamilton Beckett in 1854.

2 Henry Gaskell Denvil (1804-1866), who played the leading role in Byron's *Manfred* at Covent Garden. *The Times* (3 Nov 1834).

In her letter to D of 6 November, Sarah described the Pardoes' reaction: 'Our Bradenham authoress has been to see Manfred and is quite enchanted with it. Papa happening to call there had her letter read to him which of course he thought very clever, so now the Major and his Lady run about the green saying "Manfred transcends, Manfred transcends." As their memories no further carry them I cannot tell you what it transcends!' H A/I/B/535.

3 Richard Plantagenet Temple Nugent Brydges Chandos Grenville (1797-1861), Marquess of Chandos and, after 1839, 2nd Duke of Buckingham and Chandos. At this time Chandos was the nominal head of the Bucks Tories, and a power for D to placate in his attempts to establish his political credentials in his home county. There are eighty-one letters between 1834 and 1861 from Chandos to D in the Hughenden papers (H B/I/A/28-31, 57-9; H B/XXI/B/1119-93), but D's letters to him have not been located.

Benjamin Disraeli (1834)
by Count Alfred D'Orsay

353 TO LORD DURHAM [London?] see ec, Monday 17 November [1834]

ORIGINAL: LAMB 1

PUBLICATION HISTORY: S.J. Reid *Life and Letters of the First Earl of Durham, 1792-1840* (1906) I 408-9; M&B I 267, dated 17 November 1834

EDITORIAL COMMENT: Although this letter is written *as from* Bradenham, all the evidence points to D's still being in London on this date. Three days later Sarah wrote that they had been expecting him and asking when he would be coming. H A/I/B/536.

Bradenham House | High Wycombe | Monday Nov. 17th.

private

My dear Lord Durham,

My electioneering prospects look gloomy. The Squires throughout my own County look grim at a Radical – and the liberal interest is so split and pre-engaged | in our few towns, that I fear I shall fail. At present I am looking after Aylesbury, where young Hobhouse[1] was beat last time and will be beat this, if he try, but where, with my local influence, your party wo[ul]d succeed. If you have influence with Hobhouse, counsel him to resign in my favor, and not of another person, as 'tis rumored | he will. At the same time if Nugent[2] return, he will beat us all. So, my dear Lord, my affairs are black; therefore remember me, and serve me if you can. My principles you are acquainted with; as for my other qualifications, I am considered a great popular rhetor.

What do you think of the Tories! At a moment, when decision and energy wo[ul]d be pearls and diamonds to | them, they have formed *a provisional government*![3] "The voice of one crying in the wilderness, Prepare ye the way of *the Lords*!" such is Wellington's solitary cry; a Baptist worthy of such a Messiah as – Peel.[4]

In great haste,
Dear Lord Durham
Your faithful
Benj Disraeli

1 See **215**n3.

2 In July 1832 Lord Nugent had been named lord high commissioner to the Ionian Islands. When he returned from this posting he ran unsuccessfully for Aylesbury in 1837 and 1839. See also **188**n14.

3 Viscount Althorp, chancellor of the Exchequer and leader of the Whigs in the House of Commons, was translated to the House of Lords on 10 November, on the death of his father, 2nd Earl Spencer. This provided the King with an excuse for dismissing Melbourne. Wellington was asked to form a provisional government pending Peel's return from Italy, which took place on 9 December. Kitson Clark 193-6.

Clearly, D favoured the alternative strategy of coalition between the Tories and some elements of the Whigs.

4 This apparent disloyalty was no barrier to the enlistment of Wellington in D's efforts to enter Parliament (see **358**). It was just as well, for in his answer Durham had little comfort to offer: 'I have not sufficient acquaintance with Hobhouse to authorize me to offer him any advice on the point to which you refer.' He then added conventional good wishes to D in his endeavours. H B/XXI/D/448 (20 Nov 1834).

TO SARAH DISRAELI [London], Monday [24 November 1834] 354

ORIGINAL: H A/I/B/82

COVER: Miss Disraeli | Bradenham House | *High Wycombe*

POSTMARK: (1) In circle: B | NO24 | 1834.

Monday

My dearest,

I have so much to tell you, that I can write nothing. My affairs on the whole have a very favorable aspect, but this aspect is liable to change every day, and at present all is uncertainty. I received yr. welcome packet, which contained | a friendly letter from Durham. The Lord Chancellor[1] is my *staunch friend*, nor is there anyth[in]g for my service w[hi]ch he will not do. Chandos[2] wrote to me this morning, saying he shd. be up in town in a very few days. When he comes, probably | something may be settled.

In gt haste,

Yr own

BD

TO SARAH DISRAELI [London], Saturday [29 November 1834] 355

ORIGINAL: NYPL Kohns 19

COVER: Miss Disraeli | Bradenham House | High Wycombe

POSTMARK: (1) In circle: M | NO29 | 1834.

Sat.

Dearest,

I hope to be at Brad[enham] tomorrow for certain.

It was not *Bulwer* who made the speech but *Buller*,[1] an ass.

Lady B[lessington] has given me a fine waistcoat for the Book of B[eaut]y.[2]

D'O[rsay] has taken my portrait. | All other things when we meet. Nothing is settled with the Abbey,[3] but the Duke is confident and I have therefore called a meeting for Monday night at the Lion.[4]

BD

1 On the previous Friday (21 November), Lord Lyndhurst had taken the Great Seal in Wellington's provisional government.

2 Lyndhurst soon opened negotiations with Chandos to gain his support for the new administration. Chandos, in turn, sought a commitment to repeal the malt tax. Kitson Clark 205-6. D no doubt hoped that these two would overcome their mutual suspicion sufficiently to procure him a seat. See also app II.

---

1 Charles Buller (1806-1848), Radical MP for Liskeard 1832-48.

2 Presumably in payment for 'The Carrier-pigeon'. See **348**.

3 Lord Carrington (sometimes called 'The Abbot' by D) lived at Wycombe Abbey, and D was continuing his attempt to secure Carrington's neutrality if not his support for the forthcoming Wycombe campaign. See **358**n4.

4 The meeting at the Red Lion in High Wycombe was apparently arranged to mobilize local support, with an eye to the imminent election. Parliament was dissolved on 29 December. The result was that D stood for a third time as a candidate for High Wycombe.

356 TO [LORD LYNDHURST] 31a Park Street, Grosvenor Square, [London], Thursday [4 December 1834]

ORIGINAL: Primrose League, London 1

EDITORIAL COMMENT: *Dating*: D had been in Wycombe briefly between 30 November and 3 December. He had received Durham's non-committal letter on 24 November (**353**n4 and **354**) and, whether or not there was a second Durham letter, D's intention obviously was to use the alleged urgency of a need to respond as a spur to urge Lyndhurst to stronger action on his behalf. It seems to have had the desired effect if the reports in **357** and **358** are accurate. 4 December 1834 seems to be the only logical date for this letter in such a sequence. The testimony of Greville (**357**n5) provides additional evidence. *Sic*: expences, Melborne.

31*a* Park St Grosr Sq | Thursday

private

My dear Lord,

It is with real reluctance, I may even say with extreme pain, that I tease you any further respecting my affairs. I assure you, it is very difficult for me to express the deep sense of gratitude which I feel for all your kindness.

I have just received a communication from Lord Durham which imperatively commands my decision.[1] The circumstances of my | recent absence from town, and his quitting it this morning, allow me time which otherwise I co[ul]d not have well obtained. Lord D. has offered me a seat in the expected Parlt. for the mere legal expences, and, alarmed as I apprehended by some rumors which have reached him, entreats me in case I decline his proposal not to enter the house, but wait the result of the great experiment, as he is confident it will be all over in six months.[2] He assures me this | conduct will not affect his future good dispositions towards me and urges[?] anything in short but joining the Tories.

I have only to observe that altho' I am myself far from sanguine as to your success, I wd. sooner lose with the Duke and yourself than win with Melborne and Durham, but win *or* lose I must – I cannot afford to be neutral. How then, my dear Lord, am I to | act?

Believe me ever,
your obliged and very
grateful Ser[van]t
B. Disraeli

1 No such letter has been found. Durham's response to D's earlier request for help (**353**n4) suggests that such evidence of a change of heart would be difficult indeed to locate.

2 A Tory government, the life of which Durham predicted accurately.

TO SARAH DISRAELI [London], Monday [8 December 1834] 357

ORIGINAL: H A/I/B/83

COVER: Miss Disraeli | Bradenham House | High Wycombe

POSTMARK: (1) In circle: Z | DE-8 | 1834

PUBLICATION HISTORY: LBCS 29, dated 28 November 1834, prints an altered version of the last sentence of the first paragraph, and the third paragraph (with some omissions), conflated with extracts from **358** and **359** and with two sentences from an original not located, which reads: 'The Duke and the Chancellor are besetting old Carrington in my favour, that they say he must yield. I am not sanguine, but was recommended to issue the address.' RD has a footnote to 'the address': 'To the electors of High Wycombe'. Unlike D's other election manifestos, this one does not appear in the press, nor is there a copy of it in the Hughenden papers. For this campaign D seemed to rely on *The Crisis Examined*, a printed pamphlet of his Wycombe Speech of 16 December. See also **360** and **361**. M&B I 265, dated 28 November 1834, reprints extracts from the LBCS conflation.

EDITORIAL COMMENT: *Sic*: Frazers, insured.

Monday

My dearest,

Old Carry,[1] as they call him here, arrives in town today, and L[yndhurst] with whom I dined yesterday intended to see him at four o'ck: but I am sorry to say that the youngest Copley is at this moment so dangerously ill, that her life is in peril, and this may interfere terribly.[2] D'Orsay, proud of his previous | success is working Bob very hard, and is very sanguine.[3]

D'O says that his portrait in Frazers is like a Drum Major.[4]

The Duke wrote a strong letter to Granville S[omerset] – chairman of the Election comm[itt]ee say[in]g that if Wycombe was not insured something else must be found for D. as "a man of his acquirements | and reputation must not be thrown away." L. showed me the letter which he sealed and sent. It is impossible to say how things will go:[5] but at present I have not thought proper to write to Durham – in haste.

D

1 Lord Carrington. See also **203**n1.

2 Sophia Clarence Copley was the youngest daughter of Lord Lyndhurst. She recovered, but the middle daughter, Susan Penelope, died in Paris on 9 May 1837.

3 D'Orsay was indeed cultivating Robert Smith on D's behalf (H B/XXI/D/289), but Smith's letter to D on 16 December attests to the failure of D'Orsay's blandishments. Smith refused D's proposal 'to ask for second votes and to require plumpers', arguing that such activities would violate his neutrality. The political division between father and son in the Smith family meant that each was reluctant to exert himself on behalf of any general party loyalty. Smith closed with the warning that 'anyone connected with my Father and me who uses our name or expects our influence in soliciting second votes acts against my positive instructions'. D was the victim of this policy, but then so too was Charles Grey. See **359**. H B/I/A/40.

For additional information on 'plumpers' see **223**n2.

4 *Fraser's Magazine* X (Dec 1834), facing page 645. The portrait (by Daniel Maclise) accompanies an essay on D'Orsay by William Maginn in his 'Gallery of Literary Characters'.

5 Lord Granville Charles Henry Somerset (1792-1848), second son of the 6th Duke of Beaufort, was Tory MP for Monmouthshire 1828-48.

Greville had observed in his journal two days earlier: 'The Chancellor called on me yesterday about getting young d'Israeli [*sic*] into Parliament (through the means of G[eorge] B[entinck]) for Lynn. I had told him G. wanted a good man to assist in turning out Billy Lennox, and he suggested the above-named gentleman, whom he called a friend of Chandos's. [Ed notes: '*1 line*

358 TO SARAH DISRAELI [London], Thursday [11 December 1834]

ORIGINAL: PRIN Parrish Collection AM 17270

COVER: Miss Disraeli | Bradenham House | High Wycombe

POSTMARK: (1) In circle: F | DE 11 | 1834

PUBLICATION HISTORY: LBCS 29, dated 28 November 1834, prints the third paragraph, from 'Entre nous' to 'Chandos', conflated with extracts from **357**&ph and **359**.

EDITORIAL COMMENT: There is no signature. *Sic*: inclosed.

Thursday

Dearest,

Rumsey's[1] letter was forwarded to me by the coach yesterday. I gave it to the Chan[cello]r[2] who took it with him to dinner at the Duke's[3] where there was a grand banquet to all the heads of the party. The C[hancello]r sat on the Duke's right; Chandos on his left and after having drawn the conversation to me (taking advantage of the friendly group) L[yndhurst] produced the epistle and Wellington was in such a rage that he instantly inclosed it to Carring[ton] with | the follow[in]g verbatim epistle

"My dear Lord,

The Ld C[hancello]r has this moment shown me the enclosed: we both think your conduct incomprehensible. This is an affair in which I am most interested, and I must come to a definite understand[in]g. The Ld C[hancello]r will have the honor of calling on yr L[ordshi]p tomorrow at 4 o'ck hereon, if convenient."

W[ellingto]n

of MS. here expunged.'] His political principles must, however, be in abeyance, for he said that Durham was doing all he could to get him by the offer of a seat, and so forth; if, therefore, he is undecided and wavering between Chandos and Durham, he must be a mighty impartial personage. I don't think such a man will do, though just such as Lyndhurst would be connected with.' III 117.

Bentinck was a Tory member for the two-member constituency of Lynn Regis, and a number of comments were made by Greville during the month recording his difficulty in finding a suitable running mate in the constituency for the January general election. On 7 December Greville noted: 'George sent to Sturges Bourne to know if he would come in for Lynn, but he would not hear of it. G. d'Israeli [*sic*] he won't hear of.' III 118. By 11 December he said 'with regard to Lynn, I have handed George B[entinck] over to W[illiam] Peel and Gr[anville] Somerset, and so washed my hands of it.' III 121. Eventually Sir Stratford Canning was persuaded to run, and, with Bentinck, was elected. See also (vol II) **405**n2.

For the more general uncertainties of the campaign see Richard, 2nd Duke of Buckingham and Chandos *Memoirs of the Courts and Cabinets of William IV and Victoria* (1861) II 148-9.

1 John Rumsey, law partner of Robert Nash with offices in Credon Lane, High Wycombe. Rumsey was a Dissenter and a Whig (Ashford 264, 270). The letter has not been located, but clearly he and Carrington were seeking to discourage further political efforts by D at High Wycombe.

2 Lord Lyndhurst.

3 The Duke of Wellington gave a grand dinner at Apsley House on the evening of 10 December. *The Times* (11 Dec 1834).

In a few minutes the audience will take place, Lyndht swears that Carring[ton] shall swallow the leek.[4] | Entres nous, Parlt will not be dissolved as speedily as is imagined, which is all in my favor, both as regards Wyc[ombe] or any other place. It is imposs[ib]le for anyone to be warmer than the Duke or Lynd. and I ought to say the same of Chandos.

The answer of Stanley, on which everything depends at present is hourly expected. Peel wrote him an admirable letter, which will be published in case Ld. Stanley declines office.[5]

Everything looks prosperous and well, and altho' I am not myself sanguine about Wyc: I cannot help believ[in]g that with such zealous friends all will yet go right – | you must be friends with Sir W.[6] who has written to me an amicable epistle and offering his assistance at Wyc.

TO MARIA D'ISRAELI [London], Monday [22 December 1834] 359

ORIGINAL: H A/I/C/8

COVER: Mrs. Disraeli | Bradenham House | High Wycombe | Bucks.

POSTMARK: (1) In circle: X | DE22 | 1834

PUBLICATION HISTORY: Although this letter is not to Sarah, RD includes it in LBCS 29, dated 28 November 1834, and prints the first two sentences of the second paragraph of this letter, conflated with extracts from **357**&ph and **358**.

EDITORIAL COMMENT: *Sic*: Niele.

Monday

My dearest Mother,

Lady Sykes sends you every kind message in the world, and hopes that if she cannot visit you at present you will only consider the visit deferred[1] – but she has so much to do in London at this moment, that she cannot be spared. I am very sorry, as she is far from well; but it is important for me, that she shd not leave town until the Election is | over.

I had a long conversation with Chas. Grey to day. He is bitter against the Smiths[2] but says they can only command ten or twelve votes. He says Niele[3] and Ashton are working ag[ains]t him but he *defies* them.

In haste

Your affec Son

BD

4 On 27 November Wellington had written to Carrington in the following terms: ' ... we are considering of the Measures to be adopted in case of a general Election and some of our friends who have this subject under their consideration have desired me to write to Your Lordship respecting the Borough of High Wycombe. One of the Members is Col. Charles Grey and it is proposed to oppose to him Mr D'Israeli if Your Lordship should have no objection and will afford him the Countenance which may be in Your Power.' H B/I/A/32. Carrington obviously remained adamant, though Wellington's published correspondence does not include this exchange.

5 Peel wrote to Stanley on 9 December inviting him to join the cabinet. On 12 December Stanley refused. Gash *Peel* 86.

6 Sir William Young was elected Tory MP for Bucks in January 1835.

---

1 Lady Sykes had visited Bradenham in June 1833, but did not do so again until July 1835. Sir Francis was on the Continent at this time.

2 See **357**n3.

3 John Neale, of Saint Mary's Street, High Wycombe, was Lord Carrington's agent. Ashford 288.

360 TO BENJAMIN AUSTEN

31a Park Street, Grosvenor Square, [London], Tuesday [30? December 1834]

ORIGINAL: BL ADD MS 45908 ff102-3

PUBLICATION HISTORY: M&B I 273, undated extract; Jerman 241, dated 'a few days before Christmas' 1834

EDITORIAL COMMENT: *Dating*: on 23 December *The Crisis Examined* was advertised as 'now ready'. *MP* no 19,982 (23 Dec 1834). This letter cannot be earlier than that date and, as Austen was supposed to have a copy, the last Tuesday in the month seems probable.

31a. Park St. Gr Sq | Tuesday

My dear Austen,

I only arrived in town on Sunday night. I stand astonishingly well at Wycombe and may beat the Colonel yet.[1] Had I the money, | I might canter over the C[ount]y, for my popularity is irresistible.

Tell me, my dear friend, when the money shd be paid into yr. bankers. I need | not say that under the extr[aordinar]y and unexpected circ[umstanc]es of the times, the latest moment in the month[2] *consistent with your convenience*, is very desirable by | me.

I have published my Wycombe speech[3] at the Ministers desire – you probably have got one, but I will send ano[the]r.

Yours affect[ionatel]y
with love to all
BD

361 TO LORD DURHAM

31a Park Street, Grosvenor Square, [London], Tuesday [30? December 1834]

ORIGINAL: LAMB 2

PUBLICATION HISTORY: S. J. Reid *Life and Letters of the First Earl of Durham, 1792-1840* (1906) I 370-1; Chester W. New *Lord Durham* (1929) II 274-5; M&B I 273-4, undated extract from Reid transcription

EDITORIAL COMMENT: *Dating*: by comparison with **360** and with Durham's reply of 1 January 1835.

Tuesday | 31a. Park St. | Grosvr Sq

The Earl of Durham

My Lord,

On arriving in town, I find the accompanying[1] had not been forwarded to you as I wished immediately. I now | enclose it.

1 Col Charles Grey.

2 Presumably January 1835.

3 *The Crisis Examined* was a printed version of the speech at Wycombe on 16 December 1834. A letter to Sarah of 26 December, recorded in Tragaskis catalogue 758 (27 April 1914) item 795, contains the information that Wellington had sent for fifty copies of the pamphlet.

---

1 *The Crisis Examined.*

To save you the trouble of reading the pamphlet, I have scored the passage in question p.25.[2] | 361 | 441
30 Dec 1834

I shd. grieve if you cd. for a moment have imagined that I cd. have ever spoken of your L[ordshi]p in any other terms but those of high and deserved consideration. |

As for the opinions contained in these pages, they are those I have ever professed, and I shd. grieve if your L[ordshi]p's junction with the Whigs[3] and | my continued resistance to a party who have ever opposed me even with a degree of personal malignity, sho[ul]d ever | place me in opposition to a nobleman whose talents I respect, and who, I am confident, has only the same | object in view with myself, which is to maintain this great Empire on a broad democratic basis, | and which I am convinced is the only foundation on which it can now rest.

Bel[ieve] me, my Lord, with every sentiment of consideration and esteem,
your obed S[ervan]t
B. Disraeli

2 The passage is: 'Very soon after its [the Reform ministry's] formation, Lord Durham withdrew from the royal councils; the only man, it would appear, of any decision of character among its members. Still it was a most "united" cabinet. Lord Durham only withdrew on account of his ill health. The friends of this nobleman represent him as now ready to seize the helm [*end of* D's *marginal scoring*] | of the state'. Copy in Lambton Archives inscribed by D to Lord Durham.

3 Durham was lord privy seal for two and a half years in Grey's reform ministry. Durham replied on 1 January 1835 enclosing a copy of his 1833 letter of resignation. H B/XXI/D/449.

APPENDIX I

POLITICAL NOTES – 1831-2

These three pages of manuscript were used by D, together with the aide-memoire in app II, in the composition of his accounts of political events which are to be found in vol II apps IV and V.

On Ld. Grey's resign[ati]on, B[rougha]m personally called on him to tender him the Privy Seal.

Committee on the Reform Bill. Sir Jas Graham, Ld J. Russell, Lord Durham, Ld. Duncannon – divided on the ballot 3 to 1 in favor. The one was Duncannon. Not known – Graham always insinuating it was himself. Had Ld Durham | lived wd. have made a communic[ati]on in the House of Lords, he was so indignant.

On leave to bring in the Reform Bill, Peel was anxious to meet it at once with a direct negative – it wd. have been thrown out by a very considerable majority – and the question wd. have been finished – Ld. Granville Somerset was the person who dissuaded | Peel. The consequence of the delay was the agitation of the country etc.

Ld. Ducannon twice offered O'C[onne]ll office – once under the governmt. of Ld Grey, with the Premier's sanction – It was the Mastership of the Rolls.

H A/III/D/iib/1-3

APPENDIX II

AIDE-MEMOIRE – 11-15 NOVEMBER 1834

These are the notes which D kept at the end of the week of 11 November 1834, and from which he reconstructed the events of the period when he came to write his narrative of them in September 1836. See vol II apps IV and V.

Nov 11th. Tuesday - 1834

Conference with Chandos at Wootton when I suceeded [*sic*] in obtaining the definite terms of the Country party.

Novr. 12th.

Interview with Lyndhurst in the evening. Arrival of the D[uke] of W[ellington] in town.

Novr. 13th.

Despatch to Chandos appris[in]g him of the Interview betn. Lyndhurst and Wellington this evening etc. etc. Failure of L. in | his proposals. The D. quitted town for Strathy. next day.

Novr. 14th.

Long conference with L at the Exchequer. Despatch to Chandos. Ministry discussed at Brighton and a messenger sent to Strathfieldsay.

Novr. 15th.

Dismissal publicly announced. The Duke at Brighton. Letter from the Duke to Lyndhurst. Conference this evening betn. myself and L. |

Novr. 16th.

H A/III/D/iic/1-3

APPENDIX III

THE MUTILATED DIARY

From 1 September 1833 to 12 November 1837 D *kept a diary which noted, at infrequent intervals, his reactions to developments in his career. As a result of a number of heavy overscorings in certain passages, together with whole pages which have obviously been removed, this is generally known as 'the Mutilated Diary'. The text written in the appropriate years has been included as an appendix to each of the first two volumes of the letters. The division has been made on the basis of the date on which the entry was written rather than on the date of the subject matter.*

Sept. 1. 1833

MEMS

I left England in the Spring of 1830, and returned to Bradenham Decr. 1831-32, having travelled over the South of Spain visited Gibralter and Malta Albania, the Morea, Attica and the isles, and wintered in Constantinople. From thence I went to Palestine and dined in [*bottom quarter of the page missing*] | the temperature so mild[.] From Jerusalem to Egypt where I remained six months visiting Thebes. I had previously visited Italy summer and autumn of 1826, and the Rhine I think 1824 then only eighteen, but I determined when descending those magical waters that I [*would*] not be a lawyer [*bottom quarter of the page missing*] |

1833

I have passed the whole of this year (that is until this present month Septr) in uninterrupted lounging and pleasure (with the exc[ep]tion of offering myself for Marylebone and writing a pamphlet, but the expected vacancy thank God did not occur) and one incident has indeed made this year the happiest of my life. How long will these feelings last? They have stood a | great test, and now absence, perhaps the most fatal of all – [*two lines crossed out – illegible*]

My life has not been a happy one. Nature has given me an awful ambition and fiery passions. My life has been a struggle, with moments of rapture – a storm with dashes of moonlight. Love, Poetry, | [*page(s) missing?*] achieve the difficult undertaking. With fair health I have no doubt of success, but the result will probably be fatal to my life. My disposition is now *indolent.* I wish to be idle, and *enjoy* myself, muse over the stormy past, and smile at the placid present. My career will probably be more energetic than ever, | and the world will wonder at my ambition. Alas I struggle from Pride. Yes it is Pride that now prompts me, not Ambition. They shall not say I have failed. It is not Love that makes me say this. I remember expressing this feeling to Bulwer as we were return[in]g from Bath tog[ethe]r, a man who was at that moment, | an M.P. and an active one, editing a political journal, and writing at the same time a novel and a profound and admirable philosophical work. He turned around and pressed my arm and said in a tone, the sincerity of which co[ul]d not be doubted. "It is true my dear fellow, it is true. We are sacrificing our | youth, the time of pleasure, the bright season of enjoymt – but we are bound to go on, we are bound. How our enemies wo[ul]d triumph were we to retire from the stage. And yet" he continued in a solemn voice "I have more than once been tempted to throw it all up, and quit even my country for ever!" | All men of high imagination are *indolent.*

I have not gained much in conversation with men. Bulwer is one of the few with whom my intellect comes into collision with benefit. He is full of thought and views at once original and just. The material of his conversation and many a hint from our colloquies he has poured into his "England and the English" a | fine series of philosophic dissertations. Lockhart is good for tete á tetes [*sic*] if he like you, which he did me once. His mind is full of literature, but no great power of thought. He is an overrated man. But the man from whom I have gained most in conversation is Botta, the son of the Italian historian whom I knew in Egypt, travell[in]g | as a physician in the Syrian dress – the most philosophic mind that I ever came in contact with. Hour after hour has glided away, while chibouque in mouth we have disserted [*sic*] together upon our Divan, in a country where there are no journals and no books. My mind made a jump in these high discourses. Botta was wont to say | that they formed also an era in his intellectual life. If I add to these my father, the list comprises the few men from whose conversation I have gained wisdom. I make it a rule now never to throw myself open to men. I do not grudge them the knowledge I co[ul]d impart, but I am always exhausted by composition | when I enter society, and little inclined to talk, and as I never get anything in return, I do not think the exertion necessary.

In the conversation of society the most brilliant men I know are perhaps Spencer (now in Paris) and Tom Moore. As a lively companion of ceaseless entertainmt and fun, no one perhaps equals | Charles Matthews [*sic*], the son of the comedian, but far excelling his father, who is I understand jealous of him. James Smith, tho' gouty, will nevertheless not easily find a rival as a *diseur des bons mots.* I met him at Genl. Phipps this year and he divided mankind into those who | walked to get an appetite for their dinner, and those who walked to get a dinner for their appetite. *Jeemes* Smith as the good old general, (who by the bye gives as pleasant little dinners as anybody in Town) ever calls him.

"General" says Lady Cork "when am I to dine with you"

"Name the day and your party, | Lady Cork."

"Well then the 20th. and you may ask whom you

like – only not Jeemes Smith or Jekyll I am tired of them."

But I am not Lady Cork, and was very much amused with Jeemes. Jekyll has his faculties but is deaf, like Lady Aldboro'. I cannot bear deaf people. | I feel for them so much, and I never can repeat what I say, not even to Princes.

The world calls me "*conceited*". The world is in error. I trace all the blunders of my life to sacrificing my own opinion to that of others. When I was considered very conceited *indeed*, I was nervous, and had self confidence / only by fits. I intend in future to act entirely from my own impulse. I have an unerring instinct. I can read characters at a glance; few men can deceive me. My mind is a continental mind. It is a revolutionary mind. I am only truly great in action. | If ever I am placed in a truly eminent position I shall prove this. I co[ul]d rule the House of Commons, altho' there wo[ul]d be a great prejudice against me at first. It is the most jealous assembly in the world. The fixed character of our English society, the consequence of our aristocratic institutions | renders a *career* difficult. Poetry is the safety valve of my passions, but I wish to *act* what I *write*. My works are the embodification [*sic*] of my feelings. In Vivian Grey I have pourtrayed [*sic*] my active and real ambition. In Alroy, my ideal ambition. The P.R. is a developmt. of my poetic character. | This Trilogy is the secret history of my feelings. I shall write no more about myself.

Beckford was so enraptured when he read "the Psychological" that he sent Clarke, his confidential agent and publisher with whom alone he corresponds to call upon me on some pretence, or other, and give him a description | of the person, converse etc. of the author of what he was pleased to style "that transcendant work". Clarke called accordingly and wrote back to Beckford that Disraeli was the most conceited person he had ever met in the whole course of his life. B. answered and rated C. roundly for his opinion, telling | him that what "appeared conceit in D. was only the irrespressible consciousness of Superior power". Some time after this when Clarke knew me better, he very candidly told me the whole story and gave me a copy of B's letter.

I shall always consider "the Psych" as the perfection of English Prose, and a chef d'ouvre [*sic*]. It has not paid its expences [*sic*]. V.G. | with faults which even youth can scarcely excuse, in short the most unequal, imperfect, irregular thing that indiscretion ever published, has sold 1000s and eight years after its public[ati]on, a new Edit: is announced to day. So much for public taste! |

The Utilitarians in Politics are like the Unitarians in Religion. Both omit Imagination in their systems, and Imagination governs Mankind. |

Seven weeks and not a line in my book

Brad[enham] Augt. 4th 1834. returned.
And now nearly a year has elapsed. And what an eventful one Let me sketch it. The end of 33. and spring of 34. passed with Henrietta in Essex, writing the three first books of the Rev: Epick: Returned to Bradenham before Easter, then to town and remained there until this moment. | a season of unparalleled success and gaiety. What a vast number of extraordinary characters have passed before me or with whom I have become acquainted.

Interviews with

Beckford
Lord Durham
O'Connell

three men all making a great noise. Will they be remembered when this book turns up, if ever it do? Perhaps O'Connell.

How sorry I am that I did not keep some record of the last | four months. I revived my acquaintance with the Sheridans with whom I was so intimate last year, but shall I ever be forgiven – Methinks the fair Helen wd be merciful if – but never, never!

Mrs. Norton. an Aspasia
Helen Blackwood.
Lady Seymour. three matchless sisters. And the mother and Lady Graham. |

I have become this year very popular with the Dandies. D'Orsay took a fancy to me and they take their tone from him. Lady Blessington is their muse, and she declared violently in my favor. I am as popular with first rate men, as I am hated by the second rate.

D'Orsay
Massey Stanley
Talbot
Lord Albert Conyngham
Marq. of Worcester |

Revived my acquaintance with Angerstein who thought I meant to cut him – an error I am very blind.

What a happy or rather amusing society Henrietta and myself commanded this year. What Delicious little suppers after the Opera! Castlereagh ever gay a constant attendant, and Ossulston, the pet of all | the women with his beautiful voice. What a singular character is Ossulston. He requires "studying". Then we made it a point always to have some very pretty women. Chas. Matthews ever there[.] Inimitable mimic! His animal spirits are extraordinary. Landseer (Edwin)[,] Grantly Berkeley. Seymour de Constant.

This last hero reminds me | of that extraordinary woman, Lady Dudley Stuart[,] and she again of her family – most of whom I knew – Lucien the

Prince of Canino, Joseph Ct. of Survilliers – Lady Dudley's little son, like the Emperor – And Lord Dudley must not be forgotten with his handsome, melancholy face, and then Lady Tankerville and her lovers. How much | I cd. write of this singular coterie! But this is a mem: which will recal [*sic*] them perhaps to my memory.

That singular woman the Ctss MtAlembert and Geraldine Foley: strange stories

---

Old Lady Salisbury and old Lady Cork. Met the Duke of Wellington at Lady Corks in his blue ribbon the eve of the day | Lord Grey resigned.

"He always wears the blue ribbond [*sic*], when mischief is going on" whispered Oss: to me.

Rogers hates me. I can hardly believe, as he gives out, that *V.G.* is the cause. Considering his age I endeavoured to conciliate him, but it is impossible. I think I will give him cause to hate me. |

Lady William Powlett.

Lady Frederick Bentinck.

I can hardly believe that the Norburys (a rich parvenue Irish family) sent out cards "Lord and Lady N and the Ladies Toler at home", but so they said one morning.

Lord Melbourne and Lord Mulgrave.

The blues – Lady Stepney, Lady Charlotte Bury. |

Lord Wilton and his Italian. The story I thought too good; but I believe *true* –

Comés to Signor Rubini

Comés ta Signoria Grizi [*sic*]

Dined with him at Lady Bs.

Extraordinary fate of women.

Lady Bless.

and

Lady Manners Sutton.

The Speaker appeared to me a bete when I was introduced to him by his wife. |

Visit to Beckford at the Opera and convers[ati]on of three hours. Very bitter and malin [*sic*], but full of warm feelings for the worthy.

Convers[ati]on of 3 hours with O'Connell next whom I sat at dinner.

Long convers[ati]on with Durham at Lady Bless's.

Lady Combermere

and

Lady Aldboro'
and
Mrs. Fox Lane |
Mrs. Eliot
Mrs. Abell
Mrs. FGerald
Mrs. Blackwood
Mrs. Bolton.

Lady Combermere

Mrs. Wn. Lewis

Bolton and his wife, a decoy duck.

Long convers[ati]on with Lord Lyndhurst. He sd. that if he were to choose a career *now*, it wo[ul]d to be at once | editor and proprietor of a first rate newspaper.

When Shee was elected P.R.A.[,] Rogers (his friend) sd. it was the greatest compliment ever paid to *Literature*.

O'Connell very communicative. Sd. that from being the son of a gentleman farmer he had raised himself to be *une des puissances du monde*– (his very words)

Sd. that the Clare Election was the most nervous moment of | his life.

I think he sd. he did not sleep a wink for 3 days. Had he failed, he wo[ul]d have been ridiculous for life. Did not determine on the step until he had tried every country gent: favorable to the Catholics. Two days after the election a legal flaw was detected in the registration of his voters by which, had it been | discovered in time, his majority and much more [?], wd. have been cut off.

LADY BLESSINGTONS EPIGRAMS.

In Rogers' Human Life
But little with its name this work agrees;
For nought of human or of life, one sees!
or to that effect

Scarce with its title doth this work agree etc. |

H A/III/C/1-41

[*For the remainder of 'The Mutilated Diary' see vol II app III*]

INDEX TO VOLUME ONE

References are to letter numbers.

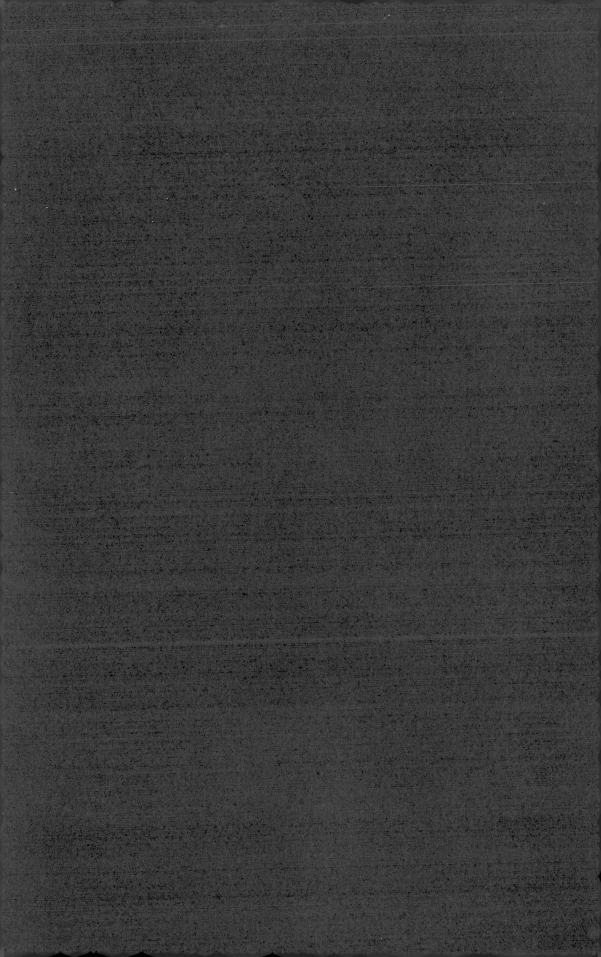